SECULAR JINNAH & PAKISTAN

What the Nation Doesn't Know

revised & enlarged

Libredux Publishing / UMT Press

This UK edition published December 2017 by Libredux Publishing, Nottingham, in association with the University of Management and Technology Press, Lahore

First edition published June 2010 by CheckPoint Press, Co. Mayo
Second printing published December 2010 by Paramount Books, Karachi

Book cover based on original design by Zafar E. Malik

British Library Cataloguing in Publication Data
A CIP catalogue record for this book is available from the British Library.

ISBN-13: 978-0-9571416-8-1

For the Nation

The Nation that doesn't know its Past
may forget its Future

Acknowledgements (first edition)

My sincere thanks to Dr Riaz Ahmad, Qutubuddin Aziz, Maqbool Mahmood Farhat, Dr Javid Iqbal, Hussain Kaisrani, Dr Safdar Mahmood, Prof. Sharif al Mujahid, Sharifuddin Pirzada, Prof. Muhammad Rafi and Lt. Col. Khan Adeeb Ahmed Umerzai (retd.) for all their help. I am grateful to Dr Sheila McDonough whose constructive feedback from the first edition of this book gave me much food for thought with regards to the second. I am indebted to Dr Waheed Ahmad for always taking the time to answer my questions, and for sending me some rare and useful literature.

Special thanks to Arif Rahman Chughtai for his valuable guidance at some crucial moments. Thanks kindly to Waqas Ahmed, a gentleman who took some trouble on a couple of occasions to obtain some obscure speeches. A heartfelt thank you to Zafar E. Malik, a dear family friend who has woven some magic on the book cover. Many thanks also to Dr Stephen Manning at CheckPoint Press for his patience and for his comments and advice at various stages.

I would like to acknowledge Iqbal Saleh Muhammad, Managing Director of Paramount Books for taking on my title and making its publication possible in Pakistan, and to express my appreciation to Muhammad Ali Khan, General Manager, Publishing and School Division, for being so helpful and doing everything to ensure the Pakistani edition was finalised in good time.

Finally, thanks to my mother, father and brother Shahid for their support and for putting up with me, especially on my bad days. To each of them goes my love.

Contents

Chapters

Appendices

Preface to the revised edition

Seven years after the first edition of this book, and twelve years after *Secular Jinnah*, the Munir quote persists in literature. Last year Muhummad Munir's book *From Jinnah to Zia* was released as an ebook, and it has again been reprinted this year in Pakistan, as a testament of its enduring popularity. This is not surprising, of course, nor is it among the reasons that I have written this revised edition.

Secular Jinnah & Pakistan has received a positive response from much of its readership and I have been heartened to find it being discussed and referred to among the general readership and the academia alike. The book has even been the central subject of a Master's thesis by a history student at Oslo University.

With the release of the first edition in 2010 in Pakistan, my previous publisher Paramount Books had planned to release a translation in Urdu but for technical reasons this never transpired and the project was abandoned. However, Mr Mahmood Alam Siddiqui, who had already done some work on the translation for Paramount, put me in touch with Professor Salim Mansur Khalid at the University of Management and Technology, Lahore, who expressed an interest in republishing the book and translating it in Urdu and Sindhi. The translations of this book will be released at a later date yet to be confirmed, and they will contain the material included in this revised edition.

Over the years I have also received a number of requests to put *Secular Jinnah* back in print. Those who made the request have indicated that its punchy style of narration and short length might appeal to a wider audience than does *Secular Jinnah & Pakistan*. While I appreciate the point, in my mind I have forsaken *Secular Jinnah* some years ago, not least because I am no longer the same indignant person who wrote that book. Despite the similarity of the titles, the first book of 2005 and the second of 2010 were completely different in their aims. The first was written solely to raise awareness of the Munir quote as a case of false attribution, while the second was the result of my deepened interest in the so-called 'ideological' aspect of the Pakistan story. Aside from the fact that it contained some factual errors, the first book *Secular Jinnah* was in many ways incomplete, and in any case its salient points have been preserved and expanded upon in *Secular Jinnah & Pakistan*.

My primary reason for revising this book was to add some material that I could not include either for lack of time or information the first time round. For example, I wished to discuss the important issue of how the ongoing ideological battle between the two broad intellectual groups – 'secularist' and 'religionist' – has adversely affected the education curriculum. This particular subject has been reviewed in Chapter 10, Myth no. 6. Other additions include further details on the role of Mountbatten in 1947 (Chapter 8), and a full review of the controversy over the drafting of the Delhi Resolution which called for a unitary Pakistan (Chapter 9). Further additions to the text, particularly in the extended footnotes, include details of how Chief Justice Munir and Governor-General Ghulam Mohammed worked together with Sir Ivor Jennings to justify the first dictatorship of Pakistan; notes on Scheduled Caste leader J.N. Mandal's political support of the Muslim League; commentary on the resistance of landlords to socialist economic reforms; and references to the work of Dr Andrew John Morrow, which provided invaluable historical evidence to support my review of the Quranic position on non-Muslims. These are the main additions but there are others scattered throughout this revised edition including (among others) biographical notes of other individuals, updates to account for recent scholarship, more notes on the Quran and Islam, minor personal details of Jinnah and his family, and extensive reviews of works only touched upon in the previous edition. This edition also contains an updated list of literature citing the Munir quote, including one or two examples from works published in the West, and also one instance in a PhD thesis, the author of which was evidently aware of the Munir quote even as he cited it (further details of this are provided in a footnote therein).

In revising this book I have also attempted to redress some criticisms that I received following the publication of the first edition. One criticism was the lack of commentary on provincial politics and in particular Bengal. Since my work has all along been focused on the Pakistan idea, I had not reviewed this in detail before, especially since it is known that Jinnah considered himself above what he called 'petty' local politics, but I have come to realise that this aspect of the Pakistan movement in itself provides an insight into how the various Muslim political leaders across India perceived the ideological dimension, as reflected in their political decisions. I have added brief information on provincial leaders and problems in scattered locations, while the issue of Bengal is reviewed Chapter 9. While I have not gone into nearly as much detail as many other commentators have done elsewhere, I hope that what I have written now at least partly fills the apparent gap.

Another criticism was that while I wrote much about what Jinnah said, I didn't show how his actions aligned with them (the critics insinuating that what he did and said were not always the same). I confess that I don't agree with this particular criticism, but nonetheless in Chapter 14 I have added a new subsection reviewing Jinnah's political powers as Governor-General of Pakistan. I have assessed some of his seemingly controversial decisions in light of the exceptionally difficult circumstances that existed in Pakistan's early days, and in so doing I have attempted to also show that he remained true to his reputed integrity throughout.

I would like to acknowledge again all of those who helped in various ways with the first edition, and to recall in tribute those who have since passed away. They are: Mr Maqbool Mahmood Farhat (April 2013), Dr Waheed Ahmad (July 2015), Dr Javid Iqbal (October 2015), Mr Qutubuddin Aziz (December 2015), and Mr Syed Sharifuddin Pirzada (June 2017). I remain forever grateful to them all.

With respect to this revised edition, I would like to express my profound gratitude to Professor Salim Mansur Khalid, for his kindness and immense patience while I took much longer to complete the revisions than originally intended; I am deeply thankful to Mr M. Alam Siddiqui for his part in bringing my book to print at UMT Press and for his tireless work on its upcoming Urdu translation; and offer my sincere thanks to Mr Mirza Muhammad Ilyas, Manager at UMT Press, for taking on the project. I must also acknowledge Mr Arsalan Sohail from Norway, for bringing up some useful points in our conversations. I am immensely grateful to Mr Tomasz Flasiński, a young Polish scholar, for his frank criticisms of the first edition and his generosity in sharing information. I am indebted to Mr Khurram Ali Shafique of Karachi, who took the time to answer my questions on Iqbal, and whose valuable feedback and insights on the Pakistan story have either validated or enriched my writing in this edition.

Finally, love to my parents, Fazal and Mukhtar Karim; to my brother and sister-in-law, Shahid and Irum Saba; and to my nephew and niece, Jinnah and Aminah. I couldn't have done this without them.

Saleena Karim
Nottingham, UK
15 December 2017

Preface to the first edition

This book is an entirely rewritten and updated sequel to *Secular Jinnah: Munir's Big Hoax Exposed* (2005). The original book was not so much about history, but rather the distortion of it. Likewise, the primary purpose of this sequel is to examine the inadvertent distortion of Pakistani history, but in addition it is a political biography of Mahomed Ali Jinnah, the founder of Pakistan.

All people interested in the history of India's partition invariably ask the same question: Why did Pakistan come into being? Or, what was the Pakistan idea? Historically, Pakistan was the outcome of a demand made by the Muslims of India to live in a country of their own, as they did not wish to be subjected to a perpetual minority status in a 'Hindu Raj' after the British transferred power. M.A. Jinnah and the Muslim League demanded a separate homeland, Pakistan, on the basis of the Two-Nation Theory – the idea that Hindus and Muslims were two heterogeneous 'nations' with completely different ways of life spiritually, socially, economically, culturally and politically. The ideological implications of this history however, are disputed; that is, historians and analysts have explored a number of possibilities but have not reached a consensus. After all, the Two-Nation Theory implied (and indeed Jinnah said) that Pakistan would be an 'Islamic state'. Yet the westernised, liberal image of the Muslim League leaders appears to contradict what we might expect to see in a *Muslim* political movement, i.e. one that has a supposedly religious or communal basis.

Focusing as we are on Jinnah's political career, this book addresses the issue of whether he had a secular or a religious vision for Pakistan, or perhaps something else. Historians and other commentators outside of Pakistan have traditionally placed Jinnah in the secularist category. Pakistani commentators meanwhile generally place him in one of three political categories: (i) The secularist (materialist), (ii) the religionist (orthodox Muslim), or (iii) the modernist (liberal Muslim). The problem of course is that most Pakistanis themselves fall into one or other of these categories, and so they tend to be motivated by a need to make Jinnah fit the category that corresponds with their own. The reason is obvious: Pakistan as a country has yet to find its place in the world, and Jinnah was its founder. Logically, we assume that if we can reach a consensus on Jinnah's thought, then we can also resolve the long-standing question of what kind of state Pakistan was meant to be, and thus how it should develop today. Pakistanis are tired of self-serving politicians, landlordism, nepotism, the rise of religious fundamentalism, corruption, economic instability, and the semi-predictable cycle between incompetent bureaucratic and military regimes. Hence for Pakistanis more than anyone else, the debate over Jinnah is a highly emotive subject, and at its heart is a battle of ideas. Pakistanis are really trying to work out something much bigger than just Jinnah's place in history. They are trying to find their own historical identity as well.

The 'secularist' and 'religionist' categories of thought (in the Pakistani context) have clear characteristics. Pure secularists believe in a complete divorce of religion and politics; that there must be absolute equality before the law and equal rights of responsibility; that there should be no restrictions based on either faith or gender for any post in the country, including the head of state; and that there should not be a state religion interfering with law and order. Pure religionists have essentially the opposite view, i.e. that religion and politics must go hand in hand; that equality before the law means that all minorities' rights of worship should be safeguarded; that a state religion is necessary for Muslims to be able to order their lives; and that even governmental posts should be restricted to Muslim males trained in the edicts of religion, in particular the head of state.

Hence we can clearly distinguish between these two categories of thought, but the modernist category – lying somewhere in the middle – is relatively misunderstood. There are actually two subcategories of what may be termed 'modernist': (a) One conceives the state in terms of a 'secular-Islam' synthesis, taking some values from traditional Islam and reconciling them with modern ideas on law, economics and the state; (b) The other rejects not only theocracy and secular materialism but 'synthesis' as well, since this idea is ultimately incompatible with the Islamic worldview as derived from the principle of *tauheed* (Unity of God). This group treats 'secular Islam' as a hybrid between conflicting ideas, and seeks an 'Islamic state' which is neither religious, nor materialist, nor secular-Muslim. Jinnah best fits the latter of these subcategories (b), but aside from the fact that this group is much smaller and thus not given much space in academic or other literature, analysts are prone to placing Jinnah in the secular-Muslim category (that is, when they are not categorising him as a pure secularist.) Similar is true of Iqbal, the Islamic philosopher and 'spiritual' founder of Pakistan, who is frequently treated either as a secular-Muslim or as an orthodox religious thinker. So from amongst the categories of political thought, the one that needs serious examination seems to have been overlooked. I aim to show that to understand Jinnah's so-called ideological leaning (and hence his intellectual link to Iqbal) requires a fresh and moreover objective evaluation of the categories of thought. In other words, we need to think outside the box.

In examining the Pakistan idea from an ideological standpoint, it is necessary to look at Iqbal's discussions on Islam as a 'moral and political ideal'. He taught that in Islam there is no such thing as a static state with rigid laws. No doubt Iqbal exerted much influence on Jinnah in the 1930s, and this influence stayed with Jinnah for the rest of his life. Yet in Pakistani scholarship, the intellectual links between Iqbal and Jinnah are not often described in detail. This was something I wished to draw attention to in this edition. Accordingly, the introductory chapter describes the point at which Iqbal and Jinnah became united in their thinking. I also introduce the essence of the Two-Nation Theory as being based not on religious communalism, but rather on idealism.

The second, third and fourth chapters are focused on the controversial Munir quote and how it has influenced the writings of those who argue for a 'secular Jinnah'. Chapter 2 is a retelling of my discovery of the quote, with updates accounting for my continued research since 2005, including for instance the documented fact that the Munir quote has its origins in the Munir Report of 1954. The third and fourth chapters look at the debates in the first Constituent Assembly of Pakistan, starting with the debates over the Objectives Resolution in 1949, and ending with the debates of 1954 over the first constitution of Pakistan as it was being finalised. The two sets of debates have one characteristic in common, namely the argument between the secularist and Muslim ministers over the ideology of Pakistan. But whereas in 1949 the Muslim ministers easily rebuffed the claims that Jinnah was a secularist who would have opposed the Islamic content of the Objectives Resolution, in 1954 the newly-published Munir Report gave secularist ministers the Munir quote, i.e. the line 'a modern democratic state with sovereignty resting in the people', which they used to devastating effect. These ministers were finally able to offer an effective challenge to the clause in the Objectives Resolution that 'sovereignty rests with Allah'. Before 1954, suggestions that Jinnah was a secularist had always been ignored as a minority opinion. The Munir Report gave non-Muslims and later secularists from amongst Muslims the confidence to allege that Jinnah too had a secular (materialist) vision for Pakistan.

The fifth chapter is a review of how today's commentators perceive and present a 'secular Jinnah', based on their common use of the Munir quote and the 'three piece argument', a pattern of argument having its origins in Chief Justice Muhammad Munir's *From Jinnah to Zia* (1979). Here I also provide an explanation of the main difference between the 'secular-Muslim' and the 'Muslim' category into which we might better place Jinnah and Iqbal. Following on from this, in Chapter 6 I have attempted to delineate the differences in the 'secular' versus Islamic worldviews. The former is dualist, the latter essentially monist. This is the psychological background that helps us differentiate between the 'secular-Muslim' (a) and the other 'modernist' Muslim (b). The two often appear to hold similar views on Islam and the state. Both are also liberal in their approaches, and this explains why so many analysts fail to differentiate between them.

In Chapters 7-8 we return to Jinnah's political life and begin with an in-depth analysis of the Lahore Resolution and its implications, followed by an outline of the 'Pakistan idea', both in its territorial and 'ideological' aspects and again uncovering the links between Jinnah and Iqbal. I have attempted to show that Jinnah's stated demand for partition (secession) was genuine, whilst emphasising that 'partition' did not mean 'balkanisation', i.e. the creation of two mutually hostile states. Chapter 9 is an overview of Jinnah's work in galvanising the Muslims as a 'nation'.

Chapter 10 is the longest section of the book, reviewing the 'myths of Jinnah'. I have aimed to show how misconceptions about Islam and the Two-Nation Theory have not only led to a misconstruction of Jinnah, but also to a misreading of history. Following the myths, in the eleventh chapter I review Jinnah's most controversial decision to accept the British Cabinet Mission Plan – which created a 'united India' – in 1946. I have aimed to show throughout that he made tough decisions in view of the peculiar circumstances with which he was faced.

In Chapter 12 I have explained why the inclusion of a Hindu in the first Constituent Assembly of Pakistan is not inconsistent with the idea of an Islamic polity. Here I have described the Quranic position on non-Muslims, and briefly reviewed subjects including citizenship and allegiance to the state, as well as what is meant by 'sovereignty in Allah'. Here I have also placed the most controversial line of Jinnah's 11 August 1947 speech in its proper context. Hopefully this also helps to clarify my approach with regards to the draft bill introduced by the late Pakistani politician Mr M.P. Bhandara, which sought to make the 11 August speech a substantive part of Pakistan's constitution (see Appendix VII).

Along with creating an image of a political 'secular Jinnah', many commentators have sought to show that he was 'secular' (meaning irreligious) in his private life as well. Unfortunately, in their enthusiasm to project Jinnah as an all round 'irreligious' personality, even a number of academics have failed to observe the rules of historic objectivity. The thirteenth chapter contains a review of these anecdotal myths and I have shown that virtually none of them have any basis in fact.

The final chapter provides an outline of how after partition Jinnah attempted to set in place the foundations for a Pakistan built upon Islamic ideals. Many people have complained that he did not do enough to start the process of constitution-building, but in fact (aside from the many other political problems distracting him) he did reiterate numerous principles in his speeches that are found in the Quran, and furthermore he acted upon them himself. When Muslims speak in terms of laying down a specific constitutional blueprint (in Pakistan or elsewhere) they are sorely missing the point. Building an Islamic polity is not about building a fixed structure. A bona fide 'Islamic state' must evolve to meet changing needs; but even as a dynamic political structure forever improving itself, it is nonetheless inspired by and rooted in Islamic idealism.

Saleena Karim,
Nottingham, UK
17 April 2010

Author's note

Miscellaneous and peculiar phrases

In this book the term 'pro-secularist' is used to refer to anyone who advocates a 'secular Jinnah'. This need not mean that a pro-secularist commentator is himself/herself a secularist. Similarly, not all advocates of a 'Muslim Jinnah' are necessarily themselves Muslim or supportive of an Islamic polity.

Muslim terms

For readers who are not familiar with Quranic or Muslim terms, a short glossary is included in the back.

Citations

Text within brackets [ ] that appear in citations denote comments or insertions that are mine. Text within parentheses ( ) that appear within citations are from the original sources.

Spellings in citations are generally left as they are in the original with exceptions only where it would be inconsistent with the text of this book – e.g. the letter *z* in some words (realize, emphasize) is substituted for the letter *s*.

Place names

Spellings and/or names of places in the main text are rendered as they were during the mid-twentieth century, e.g. Dhaka is spelt Dacca; Khyber Pakhtunkhwa is North-West Frontier Province; Sindh is Sind; Kolkata is Calcutta; Mumbai is Bombay.

Quran

In this book I have referred to several translations of the Quran rather than any particular one. My primary reference is Muhammad Asad's *Message of the Quran*, and my secondary reference is Abdullah Yusuf Ali's widely-known traditional translation. To a lesser extent I have also referred to two newer translations. One is Dr Shabbir Ahmed's

The Quran as it Explains itself (or *QXP*) which is the first translation completed in 'full public view' (online). The other is Laleh Bakhtiar's *The Sublime Quran*, the first English translation of the Quran by an American woman.

Websites

Secular Jinnah: **secularjinnah.co.uk**
Systems and other publications: **libredux.com**

Chapter 1
Jinnah's nationalism

Over the last six decades historians and analysts have discussed the mystery of Mahomed Ali Jinnah's political 'conversion' from Indian nationalism to Pakistani secessionism. It seems ironic that he was the supreme advocate of the Two-Nation Theory, the idea that Hindus and Muslims were two separate nations and could not live peacefully together. After all, at one time he was the 'ambassador of Hindu-Muslim unity', who wanted Indians to set aside their communal differences and stand united as one nation in the fight for Indian independence from the British. Yet this same man later demanded partition, and from the moment he made the demand he always maintained that Pakistan would be a state based on 'Islamic ideals'. The focus therefore has always been on Jinnah's so-called 'ideological' persuasion: Was he a secularist or was he a communalist? Was his outward 'conversion' to the Two-Nation Theory matched by a genuine internal, psychological change? If it was genuine, then what kind of Islam did he follow? If it was not genuine, then did he really aim for partition at all?

In this chapter I will attempt to show that it was Jinnah's innate sense of humanity, coupled with his experiences in the turbulent history of British India, which helped him discover his later faith in Islamic idealism. In fact, as I will also show through the course of this book, the question is less about Jinnah himself, and more about Islam and the Two-Nation Theory, both of which need to be examined from Jinnah's particular point of view versus that of his contemporaries.

Here we will review Jinnah's political career from the very beginning to the point of his abandonment of Indian nationalism. Two major events together altered Jinnah's ideological perspective. The first was the Round Table Conferences of 1930-31; the second was the Indian provincial elections of 1936-7. In short, his failure to secure freedom for India as a 'secular-Muslim' is the chief cause of his 'conversion'.

Inter-communal tension

The communal tension between Muslims and Hindus in British India has a long history dating back to the period of Muslim rule in India, which lasted almost a millennium and had come to a formal close less than twenty years before Jinnah's birth. (Bahadur Shah Zafar, the last Mughal Emperor, lost his throne to the British in the Mutiny of 1857 –

the last-ditch attempt of Muslims, aided by Hindus unwilling to submit to British rule or tolerate Christian missionaries, to hang onto their power). Many Pakistani historians have analysed the growth of the Hindu-Muslim divide starting from this period, from the beginning of the British Raj, which introduced secular education, bureaucracy and parliamentarianism, and then of course the growing mutual distrust between Hindus and Muslims, as it is considered the historical basis of the 'Two-Nation Theory' which led to the creation of Pakistan. Here however it should suffice to say that some Muslim rulers were better than others. It is hardly surprising that many ordinary Hindus in British India had an overall negative perception of the Muslim period. From their point of view, Muslims from Persia, Afghanistan and Central Asia had invaded and forced India to become part of the Muslim world. Some rulers had destroyed Hindu idols and temples, and had forced people to convert to Islam. Of course other rulers treated their citizens amicably regardless of their religion, at a time when civil equality was practically unheard of in other parts of the world. It has been even been suggested that the Mughal Empire was the world's 'first secular state', given that Hindus frequently had prominent positions in governance, in finance and in the military. [1] The Muslims also brought with them philosophy, art, architecture, and literature that enriched India, accounting for countless willing conversions to Islam (and indeed, the cultural enrichment went both ways). But this doesn't detract from the fact of Hindu resentment towards Muslim imperialism, a feeling that was perhaps made stronger by the fact that when it finally ended, it was only succeeded by British imperial rule.

Following the 1857 Mutiny and the end of Muslim rule, Muslims isolated themselves and shunned all things that were British, including education, at the cost of their own socio-economical advancement. Muslim religious leaders issued a *fatwa*, or Islamic decree, to declare learning the English language as *haraam* (prohibited). Subsequently very few Muslims were educated and even fewer worked in offices or had jobs in civil service. The Hindus meanwhile began attending universities, getting respectable jobs in offices and courts and becoming socio-economically advanced.

Nevertheless all Indians wanted self-rule, or *swaraj*, whether sooner or later. This was the reason for the formation of the All India National Congress in 1885. Although many Muslims joined the Congress in its early years, the question that was to frequently haunt them was what 'self-rule' meant, especially later when Hindutva (Hindu nationalist) movements began to rise and assert themselves. [2] Thus the All-India

---

1 Garth N. Jones, 'Pakistan: A Civil Service in an Obsolescing Imperial Tradition', in *Asian Journal of Public Administration*, December 1997, Vol. 19. No. 2 p.351

2 The Hindutva (still in existence today) is a movement for Hindu nationalism. It originated in British India when right-wing Hindus advocated a purely 'Hindu India'. They preceded

Muslim League was set up in 1906 in order to defend Muslim interests, and also, in view of the fact that Muslims were themselves partly to blame for their own problems, to 'promote among the Musalmans of India feelings of loyalty to the British Government'. [3] The Congress meanwhile was more openly committed to self-government, albeit within the British Empire.

Beginning of a career

Mahomed Ali Jinnah (born Mahomedalli Jinnahbhai [4]), the son of a merchant and eldest of seven children, was born in 1876 in Karachi. He was educated in both English and Gujurati in his hometown. In 1893 at the age of 16 he was sent by his father to London to begin a business apprenticeship, but within a few months he left it to study law at Lincoln's Inn. In 1896 at only nineteen years old Jinnah emerged as the youngest ever Indian to be called to the Bar. A degree certificate was issued to Mahomed Alli Jinnah (he had changed his surname by deed poll in 1894 [5]). Immediately after graduating he returned to India, and moved from Karachi to Bombay to establish his career, and to help support his family, who were struggling following the decline of his father's business. Jinnah was then Bombay's only Muslim barrister. [6]

After a difficult first couple of years, in 1900 Jinnah obtained a temporary six-month post as Presidency Magistrate in Bombay and made a strong impression on his British employers. [7] In 1901 he turned down the offer of a permanent position with a high salary in order to

---

Muslims in advocating a theory of 'two nations' but whereas Muslims made this the basis for self-determination, the Hindu version advocated a re-conversion of non-Hindus (especially Muslims). Its ideals were represented in groups such as Rashtriya Swayamsevak Sangh (RSS) and the Hindu Mahasabha. The latter in particular had a considerable influence on Hindu attitudes and even in politics.

3 As resolved at the first Session of the All India Muslim League, Dacca, 30 December 1906 (S.S. Pirzada (ed.) (1980 reprint) *Foundations of Pakistan: All-India Muslim League Documents: 1906-1947* (hereinafter '*Foundations*'). New Delhi: Metropolitan Book Co., Vol. I p.6); incorporated in the Aims and Objects of the League from 1907 onwards.

4 Name spelling as taken from a letter written in London by Mahomedalli Jinnahbhai to Lincoln's Inn, requesting that he be made exempt from an exam in the Latin language, dated 25 April 1893. (Saleem Qureshi (ed.) (1998) *Jinnah: The Founder of Pakistan (in the eyes of his contemporaries and his documentary records at Lincoln's Inn)* Karachi: Oxford University Press, p.59)

5 Hector Bolitho (1954) *Jinnah: Creator of Pakistan.* London: John Murray, p.9; Akbar S. Ahmed (1997) *Jinnah, Pakistan and Islamic Identity: the Search for Saladin* London: Routledge, p.4. In letter to the steward at Lincoln's Inn dated 30 March 1896 (S. Qureshi (ed.) 1998, p.71), Jinnah applied to have the record of his name as a student there changed before his call to the bar. He explained that he had dropped the suffix to his surname, 'bhai', because it meant 'Mr' in India and that at the time of admission he had 'happened to give the name after that fashion' (implying that 'Mr Jinnahbhai' contained an unnecessary repetition). He added that the 'name should be M. A. Jinnah and in full Mahomed Alli Jinnah.'

6 A. S. Ahmed 1997, p.4

7 Qutubuddin Aziz (1997) *Quaid-i-Azam Jinnah and the Battle for Pakistan* Karachi: Islamic Media Corporation, p.8

continue practising law, and established his own practice. Jinnah called his family to live with him in Bombay, and he was soon earning enough to help clear his father's debts, and also get two of his sisters married. [8] In addition Jinnah took on the responsibility of paying the education expenses of his siblings. [9] After his father's death in 1902, [10] Jinnah became responsible for his family's welfare. One of his sisters, Fatima Jinnah (1893-1967), would later become one of his chief allies during the Pakistan movement.

Seeking national unity

Like most of his compatriots in the early 1900s, Jinnah was a staunch Indian nationalist and an advocate of a united India for many years. Right from the very beginning of his career, even when he was practising law full time (and indeed before that [11]), he was exposed to and became increasingly interested in politics. He strongly associated himself with the All India National Congress party and quickly became one of its brightest young stars. His mentors were non-Muslim liberal politicians such as Hindu Gopal Krishna Gokhale [12] and Parsi Dadabhai Naoroji, [13] and this no doubt affected his attitude towards communal relations and separate electorates, which he opposed in principle, against majority Muslim opinion of the time. [14] Living though he was in British India, in which the social and intellectual divisions between Hindu and Muslim were manifest, he believed that India would not win its freedom unless the two communities worked together as equals. [15]

---

[8] Ibid.

[9] Fatima Jinnah (1987) *My Brother* Karachi: Quaid-i-Azam Academy, p.86. Jinnah's father had always believed in educating not only his sons but also his three daughters – teaching them English at home (ibid. p.48), at a time when educating women was generally discouraged.

[10] Jinnah's mother died giving birth while he was at Lincoln's Inn, not long after the death of Emi Bai, Jinnah's first wife. (For a brief overview of Jinnah's marriages see Chapter 13.)

[11] Jinnah had been an elected member of the British Committee of the Indian National Congress while still studying in England; Naoroji was also member of this committee. See also footnote 13 below.

[12] G.K. Gokhale (1866-1915), a prominent member of the Indian National Congress from the time it was founded in 1885. Considered one of the foremost Indian nationalist leaders of the early twentieth century, he exerted an early influence on both Jinnah and Gandhi. He was amongst the liberal politicians who believed in nationalism over communalism. He was the first to call Jinnah the 'ambassador of Hindu-Muslim unity'.

[13] D. Naoroji (1825-1917) a professor of Mathematics and Natural Philosophy, and the first Indian to become a professor in an academic institute of British India. He founded the British Indian Society in England, where he settled permanently and entered politics. Naoroji was the first Indian to be elected to the House of Commons, but he faced considerable racism. Jinnah met Naoroji whilst studying in England and no doubt this contact contributed to Jinnah's anti-imperialist and pro-self-government aspirations. See also F. Jinnah 1987, p.78-9.

[14] For the rest of his life, Jinnah would always hold both Gokhale and Naoroji in high esteem, describing Gokhale as 'a great Hindu', 'a tower of intellect', a man who 'championed the cause of the Mussalmans; and saying of Naoroji that he 'inspired us with some hope of a fair and equitable adjustment [in the early 1900s]'. See Presidential Address delivered at the

Muslims as equal

At the same time he actively demonstrated his concern for safeguarding the interests of his own community. From 1897, he was the member of the Executive Committee of the *Anjuman-i-Islamia* Bombay, an organisation concerned with the religious and social interests of the Muslim community. [16] In his very first speech in Congress in December 1906, in which a resolution was moved on the issue of Waqf-i-ala-aulad (Muslim law dealing with inheritance and trust) he expressed his appreciation that a question affecting solely the Muslim community was being raised by the Congress. It showed, he said, that Muslims could stand 'equally' on the Congress platform. [17] Jinnah voiced this sentiment again the next day at the same Session: 'The Mahomedan community should be treated in the same way as the Hindu community. The foundation upon which the Indian National Congress is based is that we are all equal'. [18] Later he also took on the Waqf issue himself, sponsoring the Musalman Waqf Validating Bill through the Viceroy's Legislature in 1913, which became the first ever private bill to become law. [19]

It was Jinnah's anti-imperial stance rather than an indifference to Muslim interests that explains why he refrained from joining the essentially pro-British Muslim League until 1913, some seven years after it was founded. When he did, it was because the League had brought its official rules more in line with a nationalistic programme, and that too under his personal guidance. [20] Thereafter it was through his

---

Muslim League Annual Session, Delhi, 24 April 1943. (K.A.K Yusufi (ed.) (1996) *Speeches, Statements & Messages of the Quaid-e-Azam* in 4 volumes (hereinafter 'Yusufi'). Lahore: Bazm-i-Iqbal, Vol. III, p.1693-4)

15 See Jinnah's letter to Syed Wazir Hasan, Secretary of the Muslim League, 21 May 1913, in which he expresses such thoughts clearly. (S.S. Pirzada (ed.) (1984-6) *The Collected Works of Quaid-i-Azam Mohammad Ali Jinnah* in 3 volumes Karachi: East-West Publishing, Vol. I p.94-6)

16 R. Ahmad (1990) *Quaid-i-Azam's Perception of Islam and Pakistan* Rawalpindi: Alvi Publishers, p.1-2.

17 Speech at Indian National Congress Annual Session, Calcutta, 27 December 1906. (R. Ahmad (ed.) (1996-2006) *The Works of Quaid-i-Azam Mohammad Ali Jinnah (1893-1924)* in 6 volumes (hereinafter '*Works*'). Islamabad: National Institute of Pakistan Studies, Quaid-i-Azam University, Vol. I p.79). Interestingly, the Muslim League was to come into being just three days later on 30 December.

18 Proceedings of the Indian National Congress Annual Session, Calcutta, 28 December 1906. (*Works* Vol. I, p.81). Emphasis in original.

19 S.M. Burke (ed.) (2002) *Jinnah: Speeches and Statements 1947-1948* Karachi: Oxford University Press, xxvii. The British Raj had been interfering with Muslim *waqf* laws since around 1873, denying Muslims the right to make settlements of their property by way of *waqf* to their children and extended families. (S. Mujahid (1981) *Quaid-i-Azam Jinnah: Studies in Interpretation* Karachi: Quaid-i-Azam Academy, p.5-6) The Validating Bill (5 March 1913) sought to reverse British policy and give the Muslims the right to make use of the *waqf*.

20 The Muslim League altered its official stance in 1912, once the British had reversed the partition of Bengal (partitioned in 1905, giving Muslims dominance in the East; it was annulled in 1911). Though he was still a Congressman, Jinnah was consulted by the League Secretary, Syed Wazir Hasan, on changing the League Rules. Jinnah attended a League meeting in Lucknow in December 1912 where a draft constitution was prepared and later

membership of both parties that he worked for a political union of Hindus and Muslims.

Jinnah cemented his reputation as the 'ambassador of Hindu-Muslim unity' in 1916, when as President of the Muslim League he was the chief actor in rallying the two major communities in a cooperative agreement which became known as the 'Lucknow Pact'. [21] Through the Pact the Congress formally recognised the right of Muslims to have 'special' electorates, and implicitly recognised them as being on an equal footing with Hindus. In return the League was to support the national aims of the Congress. Jinnah thus demonstrated his respect for Muslim opinion even if he did not fully agree with it personally. [22] From the very beginning, Jinnah made it clear that he did not think of his community as a 'minority', but an 'equal' part of the Indian body politic. This was the reason that he was not keen on separate electorates for Muslims. He did not have any particular alternative word to describe his view of the Muslim position, but in later years he would state that his Lucknow Pact was based on the principle that the Muslims were a separate 'entity', whilst the Congress had insisted on treating them as a 'minority' to be 'governed and ruled by the Hindu majority'. [23]

Gandhi's innovation

Before 1920, most of the old generation of Congress leaders had died, and Mahatma ('Great Soul') Mohandas Karamchand Gandhi (1869-1948) arrived on the scene. [24] He had returned from South Africa in 1915, where he had witnessed the worst racial discrimination against his countrymen and developed his form of non-violent protest, the

---

adopted in March 1913. The League now adopted a creed of seeking 'self-government through constitutional means … by promoting national unity… and by co-operating with other communities for the said purposes'. (See Syed Shamsul Hasan (1976) *Plain Mr Jinnah* Karachi: Royal Book Company, p.311-324).

21 The Lucknow Pact (properly called 'Congress-League Scheme of Reforms') represented a joint declaration from the Congress and League platforms that Indians expected to see a new constitution after the end of WWI, in which they would be granted self-government. In return for separate electorates the Muslim League was expected to support the Congress in its independence movement. This Pact served to bring together the two communities until the mid-1920s. Syed Wazir Hasan was the author of the original draft of the Pact; it was modified and finalised by Jinnah. (S.S. Hasan 1976, p.13)

22 See Jinnah's testimony at the Joint Parliamentary Committee, London, 13 August 1919, in which he affirmed that he contemplated the 'early disappearance' of separate electorates. When asked if he would like to 'do away in political life with any distinction between Mohammedans and Hindus' he answered: 'Yes. Nothing will please me more than when that day comes'. (*Works* Vol. V p.202)

23 Speech at Aligarh University Union, Aligarh, 6 March 1940. (Yusufi Vol. II, p.1157)

24 Jawaharlal Nehru (1889-1964) also entered the scene at around this time; he joined the Congress in 1920. A political disciple of Gandhi, he was amongst the new generation of Congressites pushing hard for total independence rather than just dominion status.

Satyagraha, [25] in response to what he saw as the evil outcome of modern materialism. Though he and Jinnah were equally ardent nationalists, were both London-educated barristers, and were both influenced by Gokhale, they had different approaches in dealing with the imperialist rulers. Jinnah believed in slow and steady constitutionalist methods, using 'British law skilfully against the British'. [26] Gandhi however was impatient for immediate results, and advocated civil disobedience and velvet revolution. He also wanted his people to return to their religious and cultural roots, and this was the basis of his approach to Indian nationalism. Unsurprisingly, Gandhi's more direct approach would prove most popular with ordinary Indians, Muslim and Hindu alike, for the time being. Gandhi had a natural flair for mass politics; his simple Hindu lifestyle and use of religious and cultural symbolism appealed to millions of Indians and also religious leaders. Yet this was to be the point that would divide Muslims and Hindus again, starting with Jinnah, within a few years.

Cooperation versus non-cooperation

In the years during and following World War I (1914-18), two issues occupied Indian minds. First, the British had been expected to bring in constitutional reforms that would give Indians self-government, in return for the service that native Indians had given to them in aiding the war effort. Secondly, the British and their allies pursued the dismemberment of the Ottoman Empire following their victory in the war, and Indian Muslims were strongly opposed to it. This was the start of the Khilafat movement, and we shall return to it shortly.

Jinnah had been following a policy of 'cooperation' with the British Government since 1917, to help bring about constitutional reforms that would be to the satisfaction of Indians. [27] His aim was not to support British interests, but to build up democratic methods to fight the bureaucracy. [28] He also understood the need for a 'gradual transfer of responsibility' to the Indians. [29] In order to hang onto its imperial control, the British Raj had deliberately adopted a tactic of giving little

---

[25] *Satyagraha* – coined by Gandhi, a Hindi word via Sanskrit meaning literally, 'holding onto truth'. He said this form of non-violent protest was different from 'passive resistance' as utilised in the West. See his statement on *Satyagraha*, in the 'Congress Report on the Punjab Disorders', 25 March 1920, in *The Collected Works of Mahatma Gandhi* (hereinafter 'CWMG'). New Delhi: Publications Division Government of India Vol. 20 p.39. (http://www.gandhiserve.org/cwmg/VOL020.PDF)

[26] A.S. Ahmed (1997) *Jinnah, Pakistan and Islamic Identity* London: Routledge, p.6

[27] For an overview of Jinnah's work on constitutional reforms from 1917-20, see Dr Riaz Ahmad's introduction in *Works* Vol. V, xxvi-xxxii.

[28] See Jinnah's speech at the All-India Home Rule League, Kandewadi, 24 January 1920. (*Works* Vol. V, p.336-354).

[29] Jinnah's evidence at the Joint Parliamentary Committee, 29 January 1919, as cited in R. Ahmad *Works* Vol. V, xxvii.

at the all-India level, and merely making concessions such as separate electorates for Muslims and landlords (*zamindars*) at the provincial level. This suited Muslims in provinces such as the Punjab, and tended to frustrate Jinnah's efforts to move towards a strong centre that would give Indians greater control. [30]

In March 1919, when Viceroy Lord Chelmsford permanently enforced the Rowlatt Act in an attempt to curb anti-British uprisings, [31] Gandhi and Jinnah were amongst the foremost leaders to attack it on the basis that it infringed civil liberties. Each expressed his disdain in his own manner. Jinnah resigned his Bombay seat on the Viceroy's legislative council. Gandhi started his *Satyagraha*, calling upon Indians to stage a nationwide non-cooperation movement against the government of British India, involving the boycott of British goods and civil services. Unfortunately, he did not anticipate that his programme would heighten communal passions in the way that it did. When Gandhi was subsequently banned entry into the Punjab, and two other Hindu leaders arrested for making seditious speeches, Amritsar became the scene of a bloody disaster. Fierce rioting ensued with the result that a number of Europeans were killed. In April 1919, after the British had imposed a ban on public meetings, protesters gathered in Jallianwala Bagh, an enclosed garden area with narrow entrances. They were unarmed. British troops sent to control the disturbances fired upon and killed 400 people and wounded 1200. [32] This act was seen as a point of no-return for Indians. They lost faith in British justice and with it their faith in constitutional cooperation also waned.

A humiliating form of martial law was next enforced in the Punjab, [33] and a horrified Gandhi called off the non-cooperation. The memory of the incident would stay with the Indian people. When at a Congress Session [34] it came to the question of accepting the reforms as embodied in the new constitution, the Government of India Act 1919, the Congressites with Amritsar still on their minds were determined to reject them. At this stage, Gandhi and Jinnah were in agreement that the

---

30 For a detailed discussion, see David Page, 'Mohammed Ali Jinnah and the System of Imperial Control in India 1909-30' in M.R. Kazimi (ed.) (2005) *M.A. Jinnah: Views and Reviews* Karachi: Oxford University Press, p.1-22

31 The British enlisted Indian soldiers for WWI, with the promise that they would give India dominon status (virtual sovereignty within the British Empire) in return. The Rowlatt Act consisted of 'martial law' measures taken during the war to control unruly public elements. Under the Act, anyone living in the British Raj who was suspected of terrorist activities could be detained indefinitely without trial. With the soldiers back home and Indians feeling agitated, the British extended the Act. Jinnah and Gandhi alike labelled it a 'black' Act. (M.R. Afzal (ed.) (1980) *Selected Speeches & Statements of Quaid-i-Azam Mohammad Ali Jinnah* Lahore: Research Society of Pakistan, Punjab University, p.112; S. Wolpert (2006) *Shameful Flight: The Last Years of the British Empire in India* New York: Oxford University Press, p.4).

32 S. Wolpert 2006, p.4

33 Ibid.

34 Congress Annual Session, Amritsar, 1-2 January 1920.

reforms should not be rejected out of hand, and that they should at least be accepted in the name of cooperation, whilst pushing the government to modify them.[35]

Meanwhile, the Khilafat issue was the main concern of Indian Muslims.[36] They wanted to prevent the dismemberment of the Ottoman Empire by Europeans including the British, and they wanted to save the Caliphate of Turkey in order to retain the Caliphate's control on Islam's holy places. They were also motivated by their anxiety to preserve the last symbol of the declining political power of the Muslim world. Jinnah had been the first Leaguer to bring up the Khilafat issue in the 'Lucknow Pact' Session in 1916, but otherwise Indian Muslims lacked organisation in expressing their grievances. In November 1919, Muslims held a conference presided by A.K. Fazlul Huq, where they formed a Khilafat Committee. Jinnah and Gandhi both attended, and both were also amongst the deputation of Indians led by Mohammad Ali Jouhar who presented the Khilafat Conference's grievances to the Viceroy on 19 January 1920. When the deputation failed, Gandhi (who just three weeks before had advocated cooperation) proposed a new civil disobedience movement, to force the British Government to address both the self-government issue and Khilafat issue simultaneously. He threw himself into the cause, chairing a committee charged with chalking out a programme for the civil disobedience, identifying the cause with Indian *swaraj*,[37] and aiming to bring about a Hindu-Muslim rapprochement.[38] Jinnah was uncomfortable, less with the idea of 'non-cooperation' itself, and more with Gandhi's execution of it. He was wary of inciting religious passions for a chiefly political cause, more so because of what had recently happened in the Punjab. He had kept a respectful distance before, and was about to do so again. 'He believed', as veteran Leaguer Shamsul Hasan writes, 'that resignations from services and boycott of Government institutions without making alternative arrangements would inevitably result in unendurable hardships for the Muslims. He felt that time [*sic*] was not ripe to subject the people to such a severe test'.[39] Ironically, Jinnah's cautious attitude would later prompt other Muslim leaders to unfairly complain that he was utterly disinterested in

---

35 See speeches of Gandhi and Jinnah at the Congress Annual Session, Amritsar, 1-2 January 1920. (*Works* Vol. V, p.271-3; 273-4 respectively)

36 For an in-depth review of the Khilafat issue, see M. Naeem Qureshi (1999) *Pan-Islamism in British India: The Politics of the Khilafat Movement 1918-1924* Leiden: Brill.

37 *Swaraj* – Hindi word (from Sanskrit) meaning 'own rule'.

38 This was the time that Hindu-Muslim solidarity reached its peak. As a token of goodwill, and a mark of appreciation of the Hindu support on the Khilafat issue, the Muslim League passed a resolution forbidding as far as possible the sacrifice of cows, an animal sacred to Hindus, during the Muslim 'Bakr Eid' festival (festival following the annual *Hajj* pilgrimage). Hindu leaders such as the Nehrus and Gandhi attended this session. (All India Muslim League Annual Session, Amritsar, 29 December 1919 – 1 January 1920; *Works* Vol. V, p.258)

39 S.S. Hasan 1976, p.18. See also M. N. Qureshi 1999, p.243.

the Khilafat cause. [40] Yet he was not the only one to demonstrate his misgivings. Particularly significant is the case of the Muslim idealist who started off as the secretary of the Khilafat Committee, but resigned because he felt that the movement and the 'object of some of its members' were 'dangerous' to Muslims. [41] He was the Islamic philosopher Dr Muhammad Iqbal (1877-1938).

In September 1920, both the Muslim League and the Indian National Congress held Special Sessions to consider Gandhi's resolution on non-cooperation. At the Congress Session in Calcutta (5-7 September 1920), the majority of the Congressites were opposed to Gandhi's resolution, but Gandhi's supporters from the Khilafat Committee including Shaukat Ali and Abul Kalam Azad saw to it that more delegates attended to vote in Gandhi's favour. [42] At the League Session meanwhile, Jinnah tactfully explained his own position. Whilst deploring the British policy of having used 'India's blood and India's gold' to 'break Turkey and buy the fetters of the Rowlatt legislation', [43] and warning that this might force Indians to take up non-cooperation, he added: '*though not necessarily the programme of Mr Gandhi*'. [44] Nevertheless, the resolution was adopted unanimously.

But it was Gandhi's next move that would effect the division between the two leaders. In October 1920 Gandhi had the constitution of the

---

[40] Dr Riaz Ahmad has cited from Jinnah's testimony at the Joint Parliamentary Committee, 29 January 1919, showing that he presented the Muslim grievance 'not as a matter of foreign policy' but as a chiefly religious one. Dr Ahmad suggests that Jinnah was aware that Turkey's fate was 'sealed', owing to Turkey's decision to ally with the Central Powers, and so the British would not and could not do anything to prevent it. Still, Jinnah did his duty by his community as a Muslim representative and voiced their grievances wherever he could both in England and in India. For further details, see introduction in *Works* Vol. V, xxxv–xxxvii.

[41] See Iqbal's letter to his friend (M. Niaz-ud-din Khan) dated 11 February 1920, in M. Iqbal (1954) *Makatib-i-Iqbal banam Niaz-u-din Khan* Lahore: Bazm-i-Iqbal, p.27. He also politely declined Gandhi's invitation to become Vice-Chancellor of the Jamia-Millia Islamia institute, which had been founded by the Khilafat Committee to educate Muslims during the non-cooperation movement (when Indians were boycotting British Indian colleges). Iqbal in this letter expressed his doubts about the 'religious aspect of the question of Education'. (See letter dated 29 November 1920; L.A. Sherwani (ed.) (2008 reprint) *Speeches, Writings & Statements of Iqbal* New Delhi: Adam Publishers, p.245-6). Though his ambivalence on the Khilafat issue puzzled his contemporaries at the time, his later writings offer some clues to suggest that he had looked at events in terms of the bigger picture. In 1928 he expressed his approval of the Turks' decision to dispose of the Caliphate, because to his mind, the imperialism long associated with it needed to go. He wrote: 'In its essence Islam is not Imperialism. In the abolition of the Caliphate which since the days of the Omayyads had practically become a kind of Empire it is only the spirit of Islam that has worked out through the Ataturk'. (Reply to Jawaharlal Nehru's criticism of Iqbal's statement on Qadianism and Orthodox Muslims, January 1936. Sherwani (ed.) 2008, p.234)

[42] S.S. Hasan 1976, p.19

[43] Presidential address at AIML Special Meeting, Calcutta, 6 September 1920. (*Works* Vol. V, p.432)

[44] Ibid. p.433-4. Emphasis mine.

Home Rule League (of which he had replaced Annie Besant [45] as chairman) changed so that it declared (implicitly but noncommittally) a severance from the 'British connection' and to make 'unconstitutional and illegal' methods permissible. [46] Jinnah and many of his colleagues were dismayed; he and eighteen others resigned. [47] Gandhi soon wrote to Jinnah asking him to reconsider. In his reply Jinnah explained why he could not do so:

> I thank you for your kind suggestion offering me 'to take my share in the new life that has opened up before the country'. If by 'new life', you mean your methods and your programme [of civil disobedience and demand for undefined *swaraj*], I'm afraid I cannot accept them; for I am fully convinced that it must lead to disaster. But the actual New Life that has opened up before the country is that we are faced with a Government that pays no heed to the grievances, feelings and sentiments of the people; that our own countrymen are divided; ... that methods have already caused split and division in almost every institution that you have approached hitherto ... and your extreme programme has for the moment struck the imagination mostly of the inexperienced youth and the ignorant and the illiterate. All this means complete disorganisation and chaos. ... I do not wish my countrymen to be dragged to the brink of a precipice in order to be shattered. [48]

His accusations were harsh, but they were only confirmed a few months later, when Gandhi repeated the performance by similarly altering the constitution of the Congress at the Nagpur Session of December 1920. Jinnah denounced the move, arguing that the correct course of action would be for Congress to pass a resolution issuing notice that the Government must address the reforms or face the possibility of severance. Changing the creed could hardly be 'considered as a notice' [49] (as Hindu leader Lala Rajpat Rai had claimed in his defence of the move). Respecting the democratic principle, Jinnah

---

45 Annie Besant (1847-1933), born in London, later moved to India and fought for Indian nationalism. She founded the Home Rule League in 1916 and was its president; but left because it had become 'intertwined' with religion. (H. Bolitho (1954) *Jinnah: Creator of Pakistan* London: John Murray, p.83)

46 Letter to Gandhi, 31 October 1920. (*Works* Vol. V, p.463-4). In fairness, Gandhi was telling the truth when he claimed that he was open on the question of whether *swaraj* was to be attained 'with or without the British connection' (see letter to Jinnah asking him to return to the Home Rule League, 25 October 1920; *Works* Vol. V, p.458), as is evidenced in his later politics. The change itself however was also unconstitutional because it had been passed with 109 votes to 42 (S. Mujahid 1981, p.525), falling four votes short of the three-quarter majority support usually required to validate a resolution, according to the rules and regulations of the Home Rule League. (*Works* Vol. V, p.463).

47 Resignation letter, 5 October 1920. (*Works* Vol. V, p.441-2)

48 Jinnah to Gandhi, 31 October 1920 (Op. cit. p.465)

49 Jinnah at Congress Annual Session, Nagpur, 28 December 1920. (*Works* Vol. V, p.507)

acknowledged that Congress was expressing the Indian will to make a declaration of independence, but stressed it did not have the means to carry it out.[50] He also warned that India would not be able to get 'independence without bloodshed', and that to assume otherwise was to make 'the greatest blunder'. His pleas were not only ignored, but utterly condemned by both Hindus and Muslims present.[51] This was the last Congress Session that Jinnah would attend. Thereafter he quit the Congress; but though he had received equally bad treatment from Muslims, Jinnah did not quit the Muslim League.

Deteriorating Hindu-Muslim relations

The loss of faith in the British Government and new zeal for revolutionary activism had initially brought the Muslims and Hindus together, but now it began to drive them apart. The Congress' support of Gandhi's revolutionary approach conflicted with Jinnah's methods and so the Lucknow Pact was effectively abandoned. Some Hindu groups were now increasingly promoting Hindutva, an exclusivist Hindu nationalism. The militant Hindu Mahasabha in particular opposed the Lucknow Pact and separate electorates. Meanwhile Congress antipathy towards Muslim political demands and a growing anti-Muslim religious movement at a social level would lead to Hindu-Muslim riots over the coming years.[52]

In addition, the foremost Muslim activists of the Khilafat movement were growing disillusioned with Gandhi.[53] They complained that non-Muslim Indians did not participate in the movement with the enthusiasm that the Muslims had expected from them.[54] The British also played their part in facilitating the estrangement between the two communities, in their differing treatment of Hindu and Muslim leaders.[55]

---

50 He referred to the Congress constitution of 1907 in which it was laid down that Congress had neither the 'will nor the means' to call for severance. (*Works* Vol. V, p.506)

51 Shaukat Ali was apparently enraged to the point that he even attempted to attack Jinnah. (S. Mujahid 1981, p.525-6; A.S. Ahmed 1997, p.62;)

52 From the early twentieth century, Hindu movements of *sangathan* (organisation) and *shuddi* (re-conversion) and reciprocal *tanzeem* and *tableegh* (organisation and proselytising) Muslim movements had also sprung up. In his letters to Jinnah in summer 1937, Iqbal would describe such developments including the riots as a 'civil war' – a term that would be deployed by Jinnah also in his presidential speech in the historic League Lahore Session of 1940.

53 The Ali brothers switched their allegiance to Jinnah and the League after losing faith in Gandhi. Mohammad Ali Jouhar (1878-1931) resigned from the Congress in 1924 and rejoined the League of which he remained a staunch supporter for the rest of his life. His elder brother Shaukat Ali (1873-1938) supported Jinnah in popularising the League's cause up until his death.

54 S.S. Hasan 1976, p.22.

55 In 1921 the British imprisoned more Muslims (including the Ali brothers for two years), whilst acquitting Hindu leaders (though of course they also imprisoned Gandhi in 1922 for two years). For a detailed discussion, see *Works* Vol. V, xxxv; and Vol. VI, xxxii-xxxiii; see

Of course Muslims were also to blame for their own misfortune. The extreme religious slogans employed by Khilafat activists [56] and the subsequent Moplah rebellion [57] served to drive a wedge between the two communities. Though the *Satyagraha* approach was supposed to be strictly non-violent, once again it had turned bloody. Gandhi called off the non-cooperation movement in February 1922, shortly after a mob set fire to a police station in Chauri Chaura, United Provinces, resulting in the deaths of 22 policemen (he was subsequently jailed for two years). The Muslims resented his decision as he made it without consulting them. The Indian Muslims were later left bewildered when in 1924, the Turks themselves decided to abolish the Caliphate.

The lone ambassador

Although communal tensions continued to rise over the next decade, Jinnah did not give up seeking a possible rapprochement between the two communities. He focused on building up the League (which had become sidelined with the dominance of the Khilafat Committee) and by the mid-1920s its standing was somewhat improved. In 1927, Motilal Nehru [58] suggested that if Muslims gave up demanding separate electorates he might convince the Congress to concede other Muslim demands. [59] The Delhi Muslim Proposals were the result. The essence of the proposals was that Muslims would be prepared to give up their demands for separate electorates if Sind (a Muslim majority area) was allowed to separate from Bombay, if representation was to be weighted on the basis of population in the Punjab and Bengal (the Muslim majority provinces), and a third of seats were allocated to Muslims in the Central Legislature. But soon after Congress showed a willingness to

---

also I.B. Wells (2005) *Ambassador of Hindu-Muslim Unity: Jinnah's Early Politics* Delhi: Permanent Black, p.125

56 There is no doubt that religious extremism tainted the Khilafat movement in India. Even its most prominent leaders sometimes made statements or raised religious slogans that were bound to incite fanaticism. It is for this reason that so many Hindus saw the Khilafat movement as representing a Muslim 'pan-Islamic' movement. See B.R. Ambedkar (1946a) *Pakistan or Partition of India.* Bombay: Thacker & Co. Ltd and S. Chavan (2007) *Mohammad Ali Jinnah: The Great Enigma* New Delhi: Authors Press for detailed critiques.

57 In Malabar, Bombay in 1921, the Moplah Muslims were particularly active, but in their religious fervour what had started out as an anti-British movement had turned anti-Hindu (as an uprising against the Hindu money-lenders and landlords), and so the Moplahs declared the setting up of an Islamic kingdom. They looted and killed as well forcibly converting Hindus to Islam. See Ambedkar 1946a, p.153-4 for a harrowing account. Again the British response was decisive, but deadly: over 2300 Moplahs were killed, and 25,000 convicted of rebellion. (A.S. Ahmed 1997, p.65)

58 Motilal Nehru (1861-1931) lawyer and politician, was father of Jawaharlal Nehru and a friend of Jinnah. Their fallout over the Nehru Report (1928; see below) and Jinnah's estrangement from Congress no doubt affected the political relationship between Jinnah and Jawaharlal Nehru.

59 Abdul Razzaq Shahid, 'All-India Muslim League: Split and Reunification (1927-30)' in *Pakistan Journal of History & Culture*, Vol. XXVIII, No.1, 2007; p.156

accept the proposals, the British conveniently stepped in with the appointment of the Simon Commission to produce a new constitution. There was uproar as not a single Indian was included in the Commission. Congress called for its boycott, as did most Leaguers, including Jinnah. But not all Leaguers agreed with the boycott; nor did they agree with the joint electorates outlined in the Delhi Muslim Proposals. The Muslim League soon split into two factions on these points, with Jinnah's faction supporting them, and Mian Muhammad Shafi's [60] opposing them. [61]

A year later, in response to the British Government's challenge that the Indians should try and draft a constitution on which they would all agree, the various parties of India met at the All Parties Conference at Calcutta, in February 1928. The Nehru Report (authored by Motilal Nehru) was written and published following the conference, demanding full independence (i.e. not just dominion status within the British Empire). It did not fully meet the demands in the Delhi Muslim Proposals, yet it rejected separate electorates. Muslims had demanded a third of seats at the centre; they were offered a quarter. Sind was to be given the right of separation, with the caveat that it must be financially self-sufficient. Unsurprisingly the Muslim League rejected the Nehru Report. To offer a compromise, Jinnah put together his famous 'fourteen points' (actually fifteen), summarising the bare minimum demands of Muslims including: A requirement that residuary powers be given to the provinces; that Muslims representation at the centre must be a third; Muslim religion, culture and education must be safeguarded; separate electorates and weightage must be granted; and that Sind must be separated from Bombay. The Congress would not concede to these demands, but at least Jinnah's efforts helped to repair the rift in the Muslim League. [62]

---

[60] Sir Mian Mohammad Shafi (1869-1932) was a Punjab leader and founding member of the Muslim League.

[61] Most Leaguers had originally supported the proposals. Shafi's later opposition (backed by Iqbal) has traditionally been put down to his pro-British stance. But evidence suggests that it was chiefly due to the fact that the Hindu Mahasabha had challenged the representative character of the Congress, considering itself the true authority to speak on behalf of Hindus. It opposed giving Muslims a majority in any province and wanted to impose joint electorates. In view of the Mahasabha position, Provincial Leaguers in Punjab, and later Muslim representatives across India, began to withdraw their earlier support. (A.R. Shahid 2007, p.157)

[62] The League reunited in February 1930. For details, see S. Mujahid 1981, p.392 fn

The Round Table Conferences

In November 1930, Jinnah left for England to attend the first of the Round Table Conferences, [63] and found himself in the middle of a deadlock. Muslims were now fully committed to separate electorates, and to strong provincial autonomy, [64] and the Congress was committed to the Nehru Report and so refused to attend. Congress leaders in India had felt they had complied with the demands of the Delhi Muslim Proposals, and so refused to concede separate electorates; and in fact they were not interested in further constitutional discussion unless the Nehru Report was fully implemented.

The British of course wanted to retain control at the centre, this being the substance of their imperial power, and they didn't want to hand it over to Indians, at least not immediately. [65] This motivated their decision to bring the Indian Princes (representing around 562 states, ruling almost two fifths of Indian territory between them) to the Conference. The Princes wanted to retain their despotic rule in their territories, which in turn was maintained by the imperial status quo. [66] Disinterested as the Princes were in a 'democratic' set up which might later adversely affect their interests, their inclusion in the talks could only serve to delay a constitutional settlement, and thus give the British more time in power. [67] Further, most of the Princes were either Hindus

---

63 The aim of the conferences was to resolve the constitutional crisis. Jinnah himself advanced the idea of holding the conferences in a letter to Prime Minister Ramsay MacDonald on 19 June 1929. (S.S. Pirzada (ed.) 1984-6 Vol. III, p.365-70)

64 At this point Jinnah differed with Iqbal, a strong proponent of the fullest provincial autonomy. Iqbal's famous address advocating a 'Muslim India within India' was soon to be delivered at the Allahabad Session of the League in December 1930. Iqbal's political stance of course was motivated by the need to preserve Islamic idealism. Keeping residual powers out of the centre and in control of the provinces would enable Muslims to have control wherever they were in majority, whereas in the centre these powers would always be in Hindu control by a majority of three to one. Only later did Jinnah comprehend this 'international' problem as the overwhelming factor.

65 They formally justified this by saying that they were worried about writing a new constitution when a 'large party' (i.e. the Congress) was missing from the proceedings and so it may wish to 'wreck' it by the principle of non-cooperation. Jinnah reminded the British Government that 70 million Muslims, the 'depressed classes', the Sikhs and Christians were no party to the non-cooperation movement; and besides which, he added: 'that party which you characterise as a large party – and I admit that it is an important party – it has not got the support of the bulk of Hindus'. (Plenary Session, First RTC, 28 November 1930; M.R. Afzal (ed.) 1980, p.313)

66 The Princely States had their origins in the end of the Mughal period. They had forged alliances with the East India Company when it began taking a political hold in India. The States were totally independent, and each was ruled by an Indian Prince, except that the British government controlled their relations with other states and internationally.

67 They didn't want to give up their sovereignty, and so were evasive when it came to discussing which subjects ought to be surrendered to the centre of the all-India federation. Jinnah understood the Princely States wished to retain their 'sovereign states' but stated – assuming an all-India federation was on the cards – that they would be expected to surrender certain powers to the centre. Instead of affirming their commitment, the Princes merely asked

or represented Princely States that had Hindu majorities. Their inclusion at the all-India centre (assuming they even sincerely agreed to it) would serve to simultaneously dilute Muslim representation and bolster Hindu representation. [68] Iqbal's statement at his Allahabad address in December 1930 summarises the problem succinctly. In his opinion:

> The best course, I think, would have been to start with a *British Indian Federation only*. A federal scheme born of an unholy union between democracy [i.e. all-India federation] and despotism [i.e. the Princes] cannot but keep British India in the same vicious circle of a unitary Central Government. [69]

Meanwhile, back in England, Jinnah (faced with the obstacles put up by the Princes) also said that he had 'serious doubts' about the 'all-India federation materialising', and so, like Iqbal, he pushed for British India at least to 'go ahead' and set up its own federation. [70] He also emphasised that a Hindu-Muslim settlement was in his opinion '*sine qua non*' [71] if there was to be any hope of a constitutional solution. [72] His sympathy for the Muslim view notwithstanding, at this point he still was still thinking like a traditional Indian nationalist and continued to fight for communal unity. So whilst he supported Muslims on certain questions, such as the separation of Sind from Bombay [73] and provincial autonomy, he believed that these were essentially matters of giving Muslims political 'safeguards', and that these, once conceded, would bridge the communal gap hindering the process of constitution-building. To Jinnah, getting power for Indians at the centre was his primary aim, and this could only be done if the communities were politically united as one nation. He thus told the British: 'India wants to be mistress in her own house', [74] and simultaneously stressed: 'you must give responsibility at the Centre – subject, of course, to my first condition', [75] by which he meant the communal factor: 'I maintain that *unless you provide safeguards* for the Mussalmans that will give them a complete sense of security and a feeling of confidence in the future constitution of the Government of India, and unless you secure their cooperation and

---

what the British Indian provinces were willing to surrender. (See Jinnah's remarks, First RTC, Federal Structure Committee, 5 December 1930; M.R. Afzal 1980, p.324-5)

68 See Iqbal's Allahabad address for his criticisms on this point. (Sherwani (ed.) 2008, p.16)

69 Ibid. p.17

70 Federal Structure Committee, 31 January 1931. (M.R. Afzal 1980, p.355)

71 *Sine qua non* – Latin; essential condition or prerequisite.

72 Op. cit. p.354

73 He advanced a strong case for the separation of Sind on 12 January 1931 at the Defence Committee (See his speech in M.R. Afzal 1980, p.380-5)

74 Plenary Session, First RTC, 28 November 1930 (M.R. Afzal 1980, p.314)

75 Federal Structure Committee, 13 January 1931 (M.R. Afzal 1980, p.355)

willing consent, no constitution that you frame for India will work for 24 hours.' [76]

Philosophical difference

Jinnah's was the voice of a 'secular-Muslim', for whom a communal problem could be resolved with political safeguards. [77] He did not yet appreciate Iqbal's tactful warning in Allahabad that national homogeneousness in India – a 'continent' – was extremely difficult to achieve; that 'Hindu India' would need a 'complete overhauling of her social structure' (meaning its caste system) if it was going to seriously demand the creation of a nation-state for all Indians; and that it needed to acquire the kind of political and ethical homogeneousness that Islam provided as a 'free gift'. [78] Iqbal had doubts that this could be resolved in the near future, and so he proposed the creation of a 'Muslim India within India'. [79] By this he did not mean (as he assured his audience) the introduction of 'religious rule'. [80] Nor was he necessarily making a 'demand' for a fully separate Muslim state at this time; he was merely making a 'guess' at what was coming in the future. [81] Nevertheless, Iqbal drove home the point that the problem was 'international and not national', that 'the Muslims of India are the only Indian people who can fitly be described as a nation in the modern sense of the word', and that this 'justified' the Muslim League's insistence on resolving the communal problem first and foremost. [82] He supported the Muslim demand for 'residuary powers in the provinces' (the technical phrase for 'sovereign states') [83] based on his acute awareness of the dichotomy between Muslim and Hindu idealism – a concept that would later be better known as the 'Two-Nation Theory'. He was already on the path of Muslim separatism. Jinnah however was clinging to the composite Indian nationalist ideal for the time being.

---

[76] Ibid. p.354

[77] Through the course of this book, I will explain the difference between the three liberal categories of thought in Pakistan: the pure 'secularist', the 'secular-Muslim', and the 'non-sectarian Muslim'. (See in particular Chapter 5 and Myth no. 10 (Chapter 10)

[78] Iqbal's Allahabad address (Sherwani (ed.) 2008, p.12, 26

[79],Op. cit. p.10

[80] Op. cit. p.12

[81] Iqbal's exact 'demand' in the address was worded as follows: 'I therefore demand the formation of a consolidated Muslim State in the best interests of India and Islam. ...[in order for India to have] an internal balance of power' (Op. cit. p.12). For Iqbal's clarification about the 'guess', see his letter to *The Times,* 12 October 1931, cited later in this book (Chapter 7).

[82] Iqbal's Allahabad address (Sherwani (ed.) 2008, p.25, 26)

[83] This technicality about 'residual powers' as 'sovereignty' – which I have taken from the text of one of Jinnah's speeches at the First RTC (1 December 1930; M.R. Afzal 1980, p.319) is important in interpreting the line ' ..."Independent States" in which the constituent units shall be autonomous and sovereign' in the Lahore Resolution of 1940.

A couple of days before Jinnah went back to London for the second Conference, [84] the Students' Union of Bombay organised a farewell party. Here he made a statement that would prove strangely portentous:

> *I am an Indian first and a Muslim afterwards*, and I agree that no Indian can ever serve his country if he neglects the interests of the Muslims, because it is by making Muslims strong, by bringing them together, by encouraging them and by making them useful citizens of the State that you will be able to serve your country. What is a State? What is representative government? *Does it mean that the 70 million Muslims should be tied hand and foot in a Constitution where a particular class of Hindus can possibly tyrannise over and deal with them as they like?* Is that representative government? Is that democratic government? Certainly not. … I have said this openly. I have no eye on any party. I have no mind for popularity. I can tell you honestly that the Hindus are foolish, utterly foolish in the attitude that they have adopted today. *Differences must be settled among ourselves.* [85]

He also highlighted the cause both of Muslims and the so-called 'Untouchables' (the lowest caste of Hindus), emphasising that if their collective interests were not looked after, India would not be 'a strong nation'. [86]

Political difference

Dr Muhammad Iqbal was one of the delegates at the second Conference (he had not attended the first). Already wary of British motives with regards to the centre, he felt it would be better to at least get some sort of responsible government established in the British Indian provinces whilst the issue of the all-India central government was still being hammered out.

Jinnah meanwhile maintained his line from the year before: 'I want you also to remember that no constitution you will frame will be acceptable to the Muhammadans unless their demands are complied with'. [87] Even when asked to offer an 'alternative' solution in case of an 'absence of a communal settlement by agreement', he insisted: 'you cannot possibly enact any constitution without a Hindu-Muslim

---

[84] Jinnah came back to India for just over a month and remained in England after the second RTC. He did not return until 1934.

[85] Speech at farewell party, Muslim Students Union, Bombay, 4 September 1931. (R. Ahmad (ed.) (1994) *Quaid-i-Azam Mohammad Ali Jinnah: Second Phase of his Freedom Struggle, 1924-1934* Islamabad: National Institute of Pakistan Studies, Quaid-i-Azam University, p.220-1)

[86] Ibid.

[87] Second RTC, Federal Structure Subcommittee, 26 November 1931. (M.R. Afzal 1980, p.409).

settlement.' [88] Yet in his anxiety to prove that the Muslims would 'not stand in the way of the constitutional progress of India', he also expressed his acceptance of the British view that provincial government could not be introduced immediately, and that therefore 'Provincial autonomy and responsibility at the Centre must take place simultaneously'. [89]

This in Iqbal's eyes was a 'very grave error',[90] since the issue of central responsibility could not be resolved until the all-India federation was set up; and that could not be set up until all parties agreed to participate – including the Princes. As for dealing with the prickly problem of provincial autonomy, this was last on the British Government's list of things to do. Hence to ask for provincial autonomy and central responsibility together was to ask for the impossible. As Iqbal later pointed out, this only deferred discussions on the Hindu-Muslim issue, and Muslim demands for provincial autonomy in Bengal and Punjab were not adequately addressed. [91]

Gandhi's condition

Meanwhile the British had also released Gandhi from prison so he could act as the representative of the Congress at the second RTC. [92] At the Minorities Committee set up to work through minority concerns, Gandhi provoked his compatriots by suggesting that the Congress was the only representative party of the Indian people, that the Indian minority delegates were unrepresentative as they were nominees of the Government (between them they actually represented around 46 per cent of the Indian population), [93] and that the Congress would address the minorities problem only after it had attained power.

The Muslim delegation expressed a willingness to cooperate with the Congress in return for concessions on their demands. Gandhi accepted this in his personal capacity but refused to wire the Muslim offer to the

---

88 Ibid. p.409-10

89 Ibid. p.407, 410

90 See Presidential address at the Annual Session of the All-India Muslim Conference, Lahore, 21 March 1932 (Sherwani (ed.) 2008, p.34). Iqbal was certainly referring directly to Jinnah's 26 November declaration, though he did not take Jinnah's name.

91 Ibid.

92 Congress had not attended the first conference because Gandhi was in jail for starting a civil disobedience movement (popularly called the Salt Satyagraha) over the British monopoly on salt. Though offered the chance to leave jail for the conferences, he had refused to attend unless other political prisoners were released. Gandhi attended the second conference as the lone Congress representative on condition that he must end the civil disobedience movement (the agreement was called the Irwin-Gandhi Pact). At the third conference, neither he nor Jinnah attended, but it is historically notable for the fact that it was at this time that the name 'Pakistan' was coined by Choudhary Rahmat Ali, a student in Cambridge, and his ideas were circulated amongst RTC delegates, though not treated seriously. For details, see Chapter 7.

93 This is what the minorities told the British Prime Minister when they handed him the Minorities Pact referred to above. (See B.R. Ambedkar (1946b) *What Congress and Gandhi have done to the Untouchables* Bombay: Thacker, p.67)

Congress Executive. In addition he expected Muslims not to support the Untouchables' (present-day Dalits) demand for separate electorates and even drafted an agreement for the purpose. [94] This minority group, some 60 million strong, was by far the worst off community in India. The 'Untouchables' were socio-economically disadvantaged and suffered terrible discrimination on account of their belonging to the lowest rank of the Hindu caste system. As such, according to the caste system theirs was not even technically recognised as a legitimate caste. Gandhi however was adamant that they were part of the Hindu community and thus they should not be treated as a political minority [95] (he would later use a similar argument against Muslims to the effect that they were mere Hindu converts to Islam and their religion was not a valid basis for their nationality). [96] The Muslims did not accept this condition.

Gandhi's own offer for a settlement on behalf of the Congress – a mere rehash of the Nehru Report – was summarily rejected by all minorities including Muslims. The minorities finally came together and issued joint demands in the form of an Indian Minorities Pact; these were in turn rejected by Gandhi. Nevertheless the minority delegates (except the Sikhs) signed and handed the Pact to the British Prime Minister at the final Minorities Committee meeting in November 1931.

Jinnah spurned

To make matters worse, not all in the Muslim ranks appreciated Jinnah's insistence on Hindu-Muslim unity, or his preference for joint electorates. For example Mian Fazl-i-Husain, a pro-British Punjabi leader and predecessor to Sikandar Hayat Khan, expressed his discomfort with Jinnah speaking on behalf of Muslims at the Conferences, given that Jinnah's views were not always acceptable to them. [97]

---

[94] See B.R. Ambedkar 1946b, p.72-4, 269. Ambedkar also said: 'It must be said to the credit of the Muslim delegates that they refused to be a party to such a black act' (p.324). Here he had deliberately employed Gandhi's phrase 'black act', which Gandhi used to condemn the Transvaal Asiatic Registration Act in South Africa. See also Iqbal's Presidential address at the Annual Session of the All-India Muslim Conference Lahore, 21 March 1932 (Sherwani (ed.) 2008, p.32)

[95] Dr Sheila McDonough has remarked that Gandhi actually had a 'paternalistic attitude' towards the Untouchables. He genuinely wanted to reform Hinduism and tackle the issue of untouchability, but naturally could not accept Untouchables separating themselves from Hinduism even politically. In this he was thinking in terms of an Indian nationalistic unity. For details, see S. McDonough (2002) *The Flame of Sinai: Hope and Vision in Iqbal* Lahore: Iqbal Academy, p.166-73)

[96] See for example Gandhi's article 'A Baffling Situation' on the Lahore Resolution, in *Harijan*, 6 April 1940. CWMG Vol. 78, p.110. (http://www.gandhiserve.org/cwmg/VOL078.PDF) The same thought process was behind the *shuddi* (re-conversion) religious movement advocated by right-wing Hindus.

[97] See letter of Fazl-i-Husain to the Governor of the UP (Sir Malcolm Hailey) cited in S. Mujahid 1981, p.393. Fazl-i-Husain also had ambitions that were Punjab (rather than Muslim India) orientated, whereas Jinnah always represented Muslims at the all-India level. He even

Jinnah now realised that he was alone at the RTC. Looking back five years later he was to remark:

> I displeased the Muslims. I displeased my Hindu friends because of the 'famous' 14 points. I displeased the Princes because I was deadly against their underhand activities and I displeased the British Parliament because I felt right from the beginning and I rebelled against it [*sic*] and said that it was all a fraud. Within a few weeks I did not have a friend there. [98]

The British realised this too, which is why they did not bother to invite him to the third conference (in fact it was not attended by Congress either). In later years Jinnah would describe these events and his own part in them in starkly self-depreciating terms:

> … Many efforts [to secure safeguards for all minorities] had been made since 1924 till the Round Table Conference. At that time, there was no pride in me and I used to beg from the Congress. I worked so incessantly to bring about a rapprochement that a newspaper remarked that Mr Jinnah is never tired of Hindu-Muslim unity. But I received the shock of my life at the meetings of the Round Table Conference. In the face of danger the Hindu sentiment, the Hindu mind, the Hindu attitude led me to the conclusion that there was *no hope of unity*. I felt very pessimistic about my country. The position was most unfortunate. The Mussalmans were like dwellers in No Man's Land; they were led by either the flunkeys of the British Government or the camp followers of the Congress. Whenever attempts were made to organise the Muslims, toadies and flunkeys on the one hand and traitors in the Congress camp on the other frustrated the efforts. I began to feel that neither could I help India, nor change the Hindu mentality, nor could I make the Mussalmans realise their precarious position. I felt so disappointed and so depressed that I decided to settle down in London. Not that I did not love India; but I felt utterly helpless. [99]

---

attempted to create alliances with like-minded leaders in Sind, NWFP and the UP (See S. Mujahid 1981, p.394-5 for details). In an attempt to gain support from the Punjab, Jinnah would later ask Fazl-i-Husain to preside at the Annual Session of the League in April 1936 where it would be decided to contest the provincial elections (see below), but as a supporter of the very reforms in the 1935 Act that the League officially denounced, the Punjab leader turned it down. Fazl-i-Husain died just three months after the Session, in July 1936.

98 Public speech at Lahore, March 1936 (W. Ahmad (ed.) (1992-2003) *Quaid-i-Azam Mohammad Ali Jinnah: The Nation's Voice* in 7 volumes (hereinafter 'NV'). Karachi: Quaid-i-Azam Academy, Vol. I, p.26)

99 Speech at meeting of the Aligarh Muslim University Union, 5 February 1938. (Yusufi Vol. II, p.723) Spellings retained from original.

Iqbal validated

In fact, it is Iqbal who emerges as the greater Muslim hero at the RTC. When Jawaharlal Nehru (who had not attended the RTC) accused the Muslims of being uncooperative and reactionary at the Conference, Iqbal released his own statement correcting this misconception: '[Nehru] has been led to believe that Mr Gandhi offered personally to accept all the Muslim demands on condition that Muslims assured him of their full support in the political struggle for freedom and that reactionaryism rather than communalism prevented Muslims from accepting this condition. This is a perfectly wrong statement of what happened in London.' He referred to the Aga Khan's statement that Muslims would have cooperated with the Congress at the RTC in return for concessions on their demands, and that Gandhi had refused to wire this Muslim offer to the Congress Executive. Iqbal also deplored Gandhi's 'most unrighteous condition' to stifle Muslim support for the Untouchables: 'It was pointed out to him [Gandhi] that it did not lie in the mouth of Muslims to oppose those very claims on the part of the Untouchables which they were advancing for themselves'. [100]

Furthermore, Iqbal correctly predicted that immediate provincial government was the only viable option for constitutional progress. He had suspected from the beginning that some Muslim delegates were 'badly advised by certain English politicians in rejecting the immediate introduction of responsible government in the provinces of British India'. [101] Since the Minorities Committee had also failed to reach an agreement, he dissociated himself from the delegation soon after handing in the Minorities Pact, and did not attend the Federal Structure Committee (as the Muslim delegates had formally made the decision not to attend). [102] Yet the delegation did later attend the Committee, where Jinnah indicated his support of the simultaneous introduction of provincial autonomy and central responsibility. Subsequent constitutional developments (as we shall see shortly) substantiated Iqbal's position on provincial government.

The neglected minority

Following the end of the second Conference and in view of the failure by the Indian leaders to come to an agreement, in August 1932 British Prime Minister Ramsay MacDonald granted some of the Muslim demands by way of a Communal Award, the most significant being that Sind was separated from Bombay. The other minority group of

---

[100] See Iqbal's statement explaining the attitude of Muslim delegates to the RTC, 6 December 1933. (Sherwani (ed.) 2008, p.287-8)

[101] Iqbal's Presidential address at the Annual Session of the All-India Muslim Conference, Lahore, 21 March 1932 (Sherwani (ed.) 2008, p.34)

[102] Ibid.

significance, the 'Untouchables', demanded that the same concessions of the Award be also granted to them. When the British also granted the Untouchables the Communal Award, Gandhi, who was back in prison for further civil disobedience activity, began a fast to the death in protest of what he viewed as a threat to national unity. The leader of the Untouchables, Dr B.R. Ambedkar (1891-1956), was forced to compromise, resulting in the 'Poona Pact' in September 1932. [103]

Jinnah for his part had also fought Gandhi on the issue of the Untouchables' demands at the Conference and pleaded with him to grant them separate electorates if they wished to have them. In 1935, Jinnah would express his appreciation of the Poona Pact in principle (though not the methods employed to achieve it), which he viewed as a 'protection and safeguard' for the Depressed Classes. [104] Jinnah believed that the Poona Pact had sufficiently safeguarded the Untouchables' rights and thus worked in the greater interests of securing national unity. [105] He would eventually realise that his view in this matter was misguided. [106] (Years after the event, he would often remark that he had always been more concerned for the plight of the Untouchables than he had for the Muslims.) [107]

---

103 Although the Pact reserved a higher number of seats (128 instead of the original 78 granted in the British Award) for the Untouchables at the provincial and central levels (whilst retaining joint electorates), Ambedkar wrote that the Communal Award had in fact given them far more power to the Untouchables by granting them a 'double vote, one to be used through separate electorates and the other to be used in the general electorates', while the Poona Pact 'took away' this 'priceless privilege'. (Ambedkar 1946b, p.90). He resented Gandhi's religiously-informed politics and later called him 'the greatest enemy the Untouchables have ever had in India'. (B. Nichols (1944) *Verdict on India* London: Jonathan Cape, 1944, p.38) Ambedkar also adopted a political line similar to that of the Muslims. He told Beverley Nichols: 'The key-note of my policy is that we are *not* a sub-section of the Hindus but a separate element in the national life.' (Op. cit. p.40; emphasis in original). After partition, Ambedkar became India's first Law Minister and a major contributor in drafting the constitution. It should be noted however that he probably would never have been able to join the Indian government at all, had it not been for Jogendra Nath Mandal's campaign to ensure Ambedkar was elected to the Indian Constituent Assembly in 1946, at a time when Ambedkar himself had failed to secure a provincial assembly seat in the elections that year, and, contrary to more widespread viewpoints, Congress was absolutely determined to 'ensure his exclusion' from the Constituent Assembly. See Dwaipayan Sen 2012, p.335-8. (Full reference provided in Chapter 8, footnote 22)

104 Speech at the Legislative Assembly, 4 February 1935. (W. Ahmad (1991) *Quaid-i-Azam Mohammad Ali Jinnah Speeches, Indian Legislative Assembly 1935-1947* Karachi: Quaid-i-Azam Academy, p.32)

105 Jinnah said that he had 'begged' of Gandhi to reconsider his stance about the Untouchables, and 'ultimately he [Gandhi] did realise … by recognising and giving this protection and safeguard to the Depressed Classes, won them over, and today he is still working for their amelioration'. (Ibid.)

106 Jinnah commented on the same incidence with reference to Ambedkar's writings at the League Session at Delhi in April 1943, and expressed his thorough disapproval of Gandhi's attempts to manipulate the Muslims and Untouchables at the RTC. (Yusufi Vol. III, p.1700)

107 See ibid; also Jinnah's address to the Eid Reunion Gathering, New Delhi, 5 November 1946 (Yusufi Vol. IV p.2447)

A new beginning

Jinnah remained in England following the end of the second RTC. He lived in Hampstead, where he resumed his legal practice. Back in India, the Muslim League was floundering. Muslim Leaguers unanimously elected Jinnah League President in his absence, and pleaded with him to come back.

The Indian nationalist in Jinnah was down, but not out. As he himself testified, [108] even after his return in April 1934 he looked for a way to bring about Hindu-Muslim unity, right up until the provincial elections of 1936. Perhaps he had held Gandhi as the sole culprit for wrecking communal unity at the RTC. [109] In February 1935, he and then Congress President Rajendra Prasad (1884-1963) [110] agreed upon a Jinnah-Prasad formula in which again separate electorates would be given up in return for concessions to safeguard Muslim interests. But the formula failed because of disapproval from the Hindu Mahasabha. [111]

By now, the Government of India Act 1935 had been formulated by the British following the failed Round Table Conferences, and it was enacted in August that year. It substituted the previous unitary system for a federal structure, and involved British Indian provinces alone. Rulers and leaders throughout the subcontinent were uncooperative for their individual reasons, and so only the provincial portion of the Act could be put into effect. This at least moved India forward, in line with Iqbal's views at the RTC.

The provincial elections began in 1936. Though Jinnah had always had an aversion to provincial politics, he led the League in contesting the elections. This was the first time that the League had contested elections at an all-India level. Jinnah's intent was to bolster support for the League as well as to look after Muslim interests. The League, which had always been considered by most as a body of upper-class Muslims with no mass following, adopted a mass contact policy for the first time in 1936, [112] with Jinnah stating his intent to put the League in 'a position so as to be able to speak with unchallenged authority for the 80 million Musalmans in India', even whilst expecting to 'cooperate' with progressive bodies including the All India National Congress. [113] 'Cooperation' in this case no doubt meant the formation of coalitions

---

108 See speech at meeting of the Muslim University Union, Aligarh, 5 February 1938 (Yusufi Vol. II, p.724)

109 See Jinnah's presidential speech, AIML Annual Session, Delhi, 24 April 1943. (Yusufi Vol. III, p.1689-1725)

110 Rajendra Prasad (1884-1963) later became the president of India when it became a republic in 1950.

111 Jinnah issued a statement on 7 July 1937 explaining the issue (NV Vol. I, p.151-2).

112 The League resolution dated 12 April 1936 declared that the League would contest the elections because it was essential that the Muslims 'organise themselves as one party'. (NV Vol. I, p.573).

113 Press statement, 24 July 1936. (NV Vol. I, p.61)

after the elections, in accordance with the new constitution. [114] Jinnah toured all over India, giving numerous talks in universities and colleges, and at public meetings, as well as leading the Muslim League. Now sixty years old, he began to establish his 'super star' [115] status in this campaign, raising the profile and popularity of the League almost single-handedly. [116] The Muslims of India soon began calling Jinnah 'Quaid-i-Azam', meaning 'Great Leader'.

Testing Iqbal's nationalism

In 1936, Jinnah had not completely given up on Indian nationalism, but he was beginning to show signs of change. He had met with Iqbal a number of times in England and they had long been colleagues. But 1936-8 was a period in which Iqbal became Jinnah's self-attested 'spiritual support'. [117] We know little of the ideas exchanged between them during this crucial period, except for what exists in Iqbal's letters to Jinnah, and Jinnah's own comments on them. Tragically, Jinnah's replies are missing, but he did later write that Iqbal had 'played a very conspicuous part' behind the scenes in uniting Muslims in minority and majority provinces. [118] As he also confessed, Iqbal's views (which were at any rate 'substantially in consonance' with his own) had 'finally' led Jinnah to the 'same conclusions' as Iqbal regarding the 'constitutional problems facing India'; and they were later given 'expression' in the 'united will of Muslim India as adumbrated in the Lahore resolution' (the League's most famous resolution which demanded Muslim independence). [119] At any rate Jinnah's political decisions, his speeches and statements provide ample evidence of the gradual but definite 'ideological' shift from 'secular-Muslim' to simply 'Muslim', in the Quranic sense of the term. By 1938, this shift would be complete; but it was not a 'religious' change. Jinnah had no theological discussions with

---

114 Under the 1935 Constitution, Muslims remained in a statutory minority in the legislatures even in provinces where they were a majority. 'Even if they scored 100 per cent success,' Jinnah explained in 1946, 'they could not form Ministries without entering into a coalition'. (NV Vol. IV, p.478)

115 See A.S. Ahmed 1997, p.91-92 for some remarkable examples of how much Indian Muslims hero-worshipped Jinnah.

116 From the late thirties onwards, the number of Muslims joining the League rose exponentially, as reflected in the numbers attending its Sessions. At the 1930 Allahabad Session where Iqbal gave his famous address, fewer than 75 delegates attended. In April 1936, the number of delegates at the League session numbered 200, with 5000 attendees; a year later in Lucknow, it rose to 2000 delegates and 15,000 attendees. By the time of the historic Lahore Session of 1940, the number of attendees was reportedly over 100,000 (S. Mujahid 1981, p.35-36). In the forties, the League's membership would number in the millions.

117 Speech at public meeting to mourn Iqbal's death, Calcutta, 21 April 1938. (Yusufi Vol. II, p.795)

118 See Jinnah's foreword in M. Iqbal (1974 reprint) *Letters of Iqbal to Jinnah* (hereinafter '*Letters of Iqbal*') Lahore: Sh. Muhammad Ashraf, p.5 (originally published 1942)

119 Ibid. p.6 (a spelling error has been corrected).

anyone, at least not on record. The letters of Iqbal, influential though they were, contain statements not on Islam as a 'religion', but on 'Islam as a moral and political force'. [120] In the end, Jinnah's 'conversion' would actually come as a result of his political experiences in this period.

Possibly the very first time that Jinnah used the term 'nation' instead of 'minority' was on 12 April 1936, when the League resolved to contest the elections. [121] He remarked that the Muslims needed to 'organise themselves', to 'compel the Congress to approach them for cooperation'. Then 'the Muslims could arrive at a settlement with the Hindus as *two nations*, if not as *partners*'. [122] That this occurs in 1936 is also significant, in that it is the earliest direct indication of Iqbal's influence. Both the words 'nation' and 'partner' appear here. 'Partner' is indicative of Jinnah's long-held belief in Indian nationalism, in which Hindus and Muslims were to be politically become one unit. 'Nation' however is a word Jinnah had never used before; and most importantly, he would almost never repeat it over the following three years. In view of the time gap, it is almost as if Jinnah in 1936 was about to test a theory. Were Hindus and Muslims capable of acting as two partners, as he vainly hoped, or was Iqbal's theory of two nations about to become an established fact?

A prophecy fulfilled

Though the Congress won the elections, Jinnah looked upon the results optimistically. The figures showed that the Congress won a majority in seven out of eleven provinces, whilst the League did not win a single one. The League candidates won barely five per cent of the Muslim votes. [123] However the League did secure almost half the number of seats it had contested (Jinnah himself claimed figures of between 60-70 per cent). [124] This was a remarkable achievement, given that the League had merely existed on paper in 1934 before Jinnah's return to the scene, that Congress had had a two year head start in organising its Parliamentary Board, and that the traditional provincial parties had maintained a

---

[120] Iqbal to Jinnah, 20 March 1937

[121] Waheed Ahmad has noted that this is the first appearance of the word 'nation' coming from Jinnah, to the best of his research. (NV Vol. I, p.368 fn)

[122] See Brief Minutes of the Proceedings of the AIML Annual Session, Bombay, 11 & 12 April 1936. (NV Vol. I, p.40)

[123] Bolitho 1954, p.113

[124] Jinnah claimed figures of between 60 and 70 per cent in success rates in the 'seats contested by the League candidates'. See his Lucknow Session speech, 15 October 1937 (NV Vol. I, p.177), and also his foreword to *Letters of Iqbal* (p.4). Z.H. Zaidi has suggested that this discrepancy might be explained by the fact that the League did not contest all Muslim seats available; for instance it did not put up any candidates in Bihar, Orissa, NWFP or Sind. (See Z.H. Zaidi, 'Aspects of the Development of Muslim League Policy', in C.H. Philips & M.D. Cartwright (eds.) 1970 *The Partition of India: Policies and Perspectives* Massachusetts: MIT Press, p.253)

strong hold on their respective provinces for many years. [125] This was enough to convince Jinnah that making the Muslim League the 'unchallenged authority' of Muslim India was a feasible goal. Reminding his colleagues that they'd had a mere six months in which to contest the elections, he thus assured them that there was 'no need for us to despair' about the results. [126]

The Congress meanwhile took its victory in the elections as indisputable proof that it alone was the authoritative representative of the Indian people. [127] Before the elections were even over, it had assumed a 'Muslim mass contact' policy to win Muslim support by promoting its socialist policy, [128] and thus to try and topple the League. In the provinces where it had secured a majority, the Congress now expected the League (and other parties) to effectively dissolve itself and sign the Congress pledge unconditionally. In the United Provinces (a Muslim minority province), where the League had won 29 (plus one special seat) out of 64 Muslim seats, it sought a coalition ministry with the Congress; but Congress was not obliged, on the strength of its position in the UP Legislature, to do so. [129]

Assured of its political domination, the Congress next got to work on the social system. The Wardha Scheme of education, the brainchild of Gandhi, was enforced in the Congress-ruled provinces in March 1938. Its commendable provision of free, self-sustaining and compulsory primary education notwithstanding, it had many facets that were deemed unacceptable to Muslims, including the inculcation of *Ahimsa* (Hindu/Buddhist/Jainist doctrine of non-violence) and the introduction of the Hindustani language [130] whilst simultaneously suppressing Urdu. (Muslims were already sensitive to the issue because the British had already replaced Persian with English as the official language of India in the previous century). In addition, the song *Bande Mataram*, an anti-Muslim song from a Hindu novel, [131] was to be sung in all schools,

---

[125] In Bengal the League secured a third of seats, but only one seat in the Punjab.

[126] Presidential address, AIML Annual Session, Lucknow, 15 October 1937. (NV Vol. I, p.177)

[127] J. Nehru declared even before the elections were over that there were only two parties in India – the British and the Congress. Jinnah retorted in a press statement that there was a third – the Muslims. (Public speech, Calcutta, 3 January 1937; NV Vol. I, p.108)

[128] Nehru introduced a socialist policy for the Congress to try and raise the living standards of the Indian people, but was met with some resistance by conservative and capitalist elements, most famously from Sardar V. Patel. While the policy aimed to combat poverty, it was also used to try and woo Muslims via mass contact.

[129] Ayesha Jalal (1994 reprint) *The Sole Spokesman: Jinnah, the Muslim League and the Demand for Pakistan* Cambridge: Cambridge University Press, p.32.

[130] Hindustani was neither pure Hindi nor Urdu, but a mixture of both. Hindi and Urdu have similarities in vocabulary and grammar, but use different scripts. In combining them, Muslim critics felt their language was being culturally undermined.

[131] *Bande Mataram*, meaning 'Hail to the Motherland', appeared in the novel *Anandamath* by Bankim Chandra Chatterjee, published in 1882. It was a political novel based on the Sanyasi

though it was denied that the song was being made a national song, and all children were expected to salute the picture of Gandhi, which Muslims considered idolatrous. Though Gandhi's scheme did not officially include religious education of any kind in its syllabus, Muslims and indeed other communities believed that this was nevertheless an institute for the imposition of Hindu culture. [132] This was what Jinnah was referring to when he accused the Congress of being 'absolutely determined to crush all other communities and cultures in this country and establish Hindu Raj'. [133] The League produced three reports cataloguing Muslim experiences and complaints, and the *Dawn* produced a series of 32 articles based on a six-week investigation in the U.P. and Bihar. [134]

Of course, Gandhi had made never made a secret of his intent to make Hindustani the *lingua franca* of India and his philosophy of *Ahimsa* and *Satyagraha* a part of the national consciousness. He had long believed that non-violence was a universal truth to be found in every religion, and practised by all sages and prophets from Buddha to Jesus to Muhammad [135], and as he had already developed it in South Africa, in his mind it could be made a cohesive force to unite all Indians in his homeland. Jinnah was not entirely unsympathetic to this sentiment and never had he objected to the idea of national integration in principle, but he couldn't accept any programme which imposed one culture and simultaneously suppressed another. He made this clear at a student union in early 1938, even as he was heckled by Hindu students. The *Hindustan Times* reported after the event:

> [Jinnah] would not grudge it, if they decided that Hindus all over India should have one common language. 'Let me have the same desire – that all Muslims should learn Urdu. It is through language that ideas spread. If you compel us to learn Hindi, our children will be saturated with Hindu culture. Language is a medium to acquire ideas'. [136]

---

rebellion that occurred against Muslim rule in Bengal. (See editorial note, NV Vol. I, p.545-7 for further details)

132 Conversely, Hindus resented the Muslims for what they perceived as a Muslim 'superiority complex' carried over from the time that they ruled the subcontinent.

133 See Presidential address at AIML Session, Patna, 25 December 1936. (NV Vol. I, p.329).

134 The League reports were known as the 'Pirpur Report', November 1938 (reporting grievances in all Congress Provinces), the 'Shareef Report', December 1939 (covering Bihar), and 'Muslim Sufferings under Congress Rule', December 1939 (a reprint of a press statement by A.K. Fazlul Huq on the situation in Bengal). (See short overview in NV Vol. I, p.548-551)

135 Article calling for civil disobedience against the Asiatic Registration Act of the Transvaal Colony (Apartheid legislation) in South Africa, titled 'Divine Law', in *Indian Opinion*, 27 July 1907. CWMG Vol. 7 p.88. http://www.gandhiserve.org/cwmg/VOL007.PDF

136 Speech at Students' Union, Anglo-Arabic College, Delhi, 3 February 1938, as reported in *Hindustan Times*, 4 February. (Yusufi Vol. II, p.718) A couple of students reportedly challenged Jinnah's claim that the Congress was a Hindu organisation. He counter challenged

The Light meanwhile reported his speech as follows:

> … the Hindus have sought to impose upon us *Bande Mataram* in the Assembly Halls and expect us to salute it. They have sought to impose Hindi upon the Mussalmans. Whilst I respect the philosophy and culture of others I love and adore my own, and can never agree to the coming generation thus being lost to Islam.[137]

The slow awakening

Jinnah before the mid-1930s is probably best described as a 'secular-Muslim'. [138] We already know that he always wanted Muslims to be treated as 'equal' rather than as a 'minority', and so he had stuck fast to the principle of Indian nationalism, ignoring all distinctions of caste and creed, to try and unite Indians against the British. But two major events – the Round Table Conferences, and the provincial elections of 1936-7 – together served to change Jinnah's perspective for ever. At the RTC he had learned that his noble ideals appealed to no one. If at that time he had blamed Gandhi alone for introducing religion into politics, then the provincial elections proved otherwise; Iqbal's warnings about the inextricable connection between the Hindu caste system and Congress politics were proven correct. That many of the biggest leaders of Congress (the Nehrus, C.R. Rajagopalachari, M.M. Malaviya) belonged to the Brahmin and other higher castes was no accident; it was by virtue of their castes that they had the socio-economic advantages to facilitate their entry into positions of power. A great many of them did not, in theory at least, allow their religion to dictate their politics, but their culture and societal structure – the essence of their nation – was too great a force; it was practically unstoppable. So whilst the agnostic socialist Pandit Jawaharlal Nehru [139] expressed surprise and concern at hearing that Muslims (and other communities) were complaining of communal tyranny, [140] he was in no position to do anything about it. His political constituents also happened to be the religious disciples of Gandhi, and then in Congress itself there were those conservative

---

them with the question of why colleges upheld a segregation practice in their dining halls. (Ibid. p.715)

137 Speech at meeting of the Muslim University Union, Aligarh, 5 February 1938, as text appears in *The Light*, February 1938. (Yusufi Vol. II, p.729)

138 For evidence of this in his speeches, see Myth no. 10 (Chapter 10)

139 Nehru famously wrote in his autobiography: 'The spectacle of what is called religion, or at any rate organized religion, in India and elsewhere has filled me with horror, and I have frequently condemned it and wished to make a clean sweep of it.' J. Nehru (1941) *Toward Freedom: The Autobiography of Jawaharlal Nehru* New York: The John Day Company, p.240.

140 In January 1939 Nehru offered to refer the complaints of the League against the Congress ministries to an impartial tribunal. Jinnah in turn requested that Nehru first read the Pirpur Report. See Jinnah's press statement, 5 January 1939 (NV Vol. I, p.342-3)

Hindus who believed in authoritarianism even whilst upholding Gandhian non-violence. This was certainly the case with prominent Congressman Sardar Vallabhbhai Patel (1875-1950), second-in-command after Nehru, known as the 'Iron Man', who also happened to be chairman of the Congress Parliamentary Board supervising the Congress-dominated ministries after the elections. This is why Dr Ambedkar candidly wrote:

> It is no use saying that the Congress is not a Hindu body. A body which is Hindu in its composition is bound to reflect the Hindu mind and support Hindu aspirations. The only difference between the Congress and the Hindu *Maha Sabha* is that the latter is crude in its utterances and brutal in its actions while the Congress is politic and polite. Apart from this difference of fact, there is no other difference between the Congress and the Hindu *Maha Sabha.* [141]

Jinnah and Iqbal also expressed similar opinions to the effect in 1937. Iqbal wrote privately to Jinnah in June:

> The Congress President has denied the political existence of Muslims in no unmistakeable terms. The other Hindu political body, i.e., the Mahasabha, whom I regard as the real representative of the masses of the Hindus, has declared more than once that a united Hindu-Muslim nation is impossible in India. [142]

Jinnah said publicly at Lucknow in October:

> On the very threshold of what little power and responsibility is given, the majority community have clearly shown their hand that [*sic*] Hindustan is for the Hindus; only the Congress masquerades under the name of nationalism, whereas the Hindu Mahasabha does not mince words. [143]

The commencement of World War II brought an unexpected end to the Congress-dominated government. On 3 September 1939, Viceroy Linlithgow declared that Britain was at war with Germany and that India was expected to assist in the war effort. Congress leaders were outraged that they had not been consulted before the announcement. Their response was to demand immediate independence. Linlithgow rejected the demand, and by November Congress ministers had resigned

---

141 B.R. Ambedkar 1946a, p.30

142 Iqbal to Jinnah, 21 June 1937. (*Letters of Iqbal*, p.22-23)

143 Presidential address at the League Session, Lucknow, 15 October 1937. (NV Vol. I, p.178)

from the provincial cabinets, automatically putting the British back in power. Many Congress leaders ended up in jail. The League meanwhile was more supportive of the war effort, a decision that would make the British somewhat more sympathetic to Muslim sentiments up until partition. The League marked a 'Day of Deliverance' from Congress rule on 22 December. These events left the League in a position develop a mass Muslim following relatively uninhibited by Congress interference until the end of the war in 1945.

The aftermath of the 1936-7 elections had no doubt proved an ominous sign for the future of Muslim India. Muslim provincialist leaders including Sikandar Hayat Khan of Punjab, Fazlul Huq of Bengal, and Saadullah of Assam saw the merit of joining the League to strengthen their own power, and they did so in October 1937 at Lucknow. The Muslim League for the first time became an all-India body for the Muslims in name and in spirit. At this session, the Muslim League unanimously passed a landmark resolution to change its creed. Its revised objective became 'the establishment in India of full independence in the form of a federation of free democratic States in which the rights and interests of the Mussalmans and other minorities are adequately and effectively safeguarded in the Constitution'. [144] Significantly, 'India' clearly meant the subcontinent, and the supporters of the resolution held that 'India did not comprise a single nation'. [145]

Jinnah is not on record having used the word 'nation' again until 1939 (barring only two exceptions we will cite shortly), not quite a year after Iqbal's death, when he addressed staff at the Aligarh University. Aligarh was the legacy of Sir Syed Ahmad Khan the educationist (1817-1898), who had encouraged Muslims to educate themselves in Western languages and in the sciences, at a time when such pursuits had been decreed *haraam* (prohibited). As all Pakistanis know, Sir Syed is also credited with having been the first to describe the Hindus and Muslims as two nations. Jinnah appealed to the Aligarh intelligentsia to stop thinking as 'careerists' seeking posts within the 'Bureaucratic' or the 'Congress camp', and to stop 'styling themselves as Nationalist Muslims' (the common term for Indian Muslims who worked in Congress). He wanted them to 'grasp one principle – self confidence and moral, cultural and political self-consciousness'. He also said: 'I make no secret of the fact that Muslims and Hindus are *two nations* and the Muslims cannot maintain their status as such unless they acquire national self-consciousness and *national self-determination.*' [146] From then on, Jinnah became the supreme advocate of the 'Two-Nation Theory'. It is not without significance that in his famous exposition of the theory in his

144 Resolution at Annual Session, Lucknow, 17 October 1937. (*Foundations* Vol. II, p.274)

145 Words of Zafar Ali Khan, seconding the resolution. (Ibid.)

146 Public speech, 12 April 1939. (NV Vol. I, p.368)

most important speech at Lahore in March 1940, he borrowed from the thought of the Aligarh professors.[147]

From 1939 onwards, the League increasingly adopted a hardliner policy and began contemplating alternative constitutions to the 1935 Act that would give Muslims the widest autonomy possible. Some Muslims would always remain unenthusiastic about such moves. Indeed, Khalid Shamsul Hasan has remarked, with direct reference to Jinnah's April 1936 speech, that 'the Quaid's idea of organising the Muslims as a nation was not acceptable to the Muslim leadership.'[148] Nevertheless on 23 March 1940, Jinnah and the League passed the historic 'Lahore Resolution' making a demand for (eventual) total independence. It soon became better known as the demand for 'Pakistan'. Though some people would always believe that the Lahore Resolution was a 'bargaining counter', and that the League's aim was simply parity in an all-India centre, Jinnah always maintained that it was a serious demand for partition. Over the next few years, the British, the Congress and other small parties came up with a number of schemes in an attempt to offer a constitutional solution that would be to the satisfaction of all and would facilitate the transfer of power from British to Indian hands. Most of these schemes invariably leaned in favour of a united India. Jinnah and the Muslim League never quite committed to any of these schemes (with perhaps one exception which at any rate was not quite as it seemed on the surface. We will review this later).[149]

In an interview in 1946, Jinnah stated: 'India is a state of nationalities including two major nations, and all we claim is a distinct sovereign state for our nation – Pakistan.' The man who had once described himself as an 'Indian first and a Muslim afterwards' now dismissed the idea of India as one united country: 'I don't regard myself as an Indian'.[150] Pakistan would emerge the following year.

Fathers of the nation

Iqbal undoubtedly had a strong influence on Jinnah. In the thirties, Jinnah had not been wholeheartedly supportive of Muslim separatist demands, viewing them as a mere political 'safeguard'. In fairness to Jinnah, provincial autonomy was purely a political pursuit even for many of the Muslim leaders who demanded it at the time. Iqbal's

---

147 See our discussion of Jinnah's presidential speech at the Lahore Session, in Chapter 7.

148 K.S. Hasan (1992) *Sindh's Fight for Pakistan* Karachi: Royal Book Company, v. (Khalid Hasan was the older brother of the Muslim Leaguer Syed Shamsul Hasan.)

149 The Cabinet Mission Plan of 1946 offered by the British in 1946 is viewed by some as proof that Jinnah was prepared to accept a place in a united India. In this book we will show that the League's acceptance was both reluctant and conditional, in view of both the implications of the Plan and Jinnah's negotiations with Viceroy Wavell. See our review in Chapter 11.

150 Interview to foreign editor, *News Chronicle* (London); Delhi, 12 April 1946. (NV Vol. IV, p.624)

support of these same demands however was based on his far-sighted philosophy, and so his peculiar position was somewhat misunderstood. In 1930 Iqbal had spoken of securing some form of independence in the Northwest of India, focusing on the Muslim-majority areas and particularly the Punjab. Jinnah by contrast had hitherto always been focused on the centre, which in theory would look after the interests of Muslims all over India.

From 1937 onwards, when Congress rule began in the provinces of British India and its effects became increasingly manifest, Iqbal made a number of comments and suggestions in his letters that would later be expressed in Jinnah's political actions. Iqbal also wrote that he considered Jinnah 'the only Muslim' capable of leading the Muslims through the 'storm' of the political crisis.[151]

His comments include:

- The whole future of Islam as a moral and political force in Asia rests very largely on a complete organisation of Indian Muslims. (20 March 1937)
- The League will have to finally decide whether it will remain a body representing the *upper classes of Indian Muslims or Muslim masses.* (28 May 1937)
- If Hinduism accepts social democracy it must necessarily cease to be Hinduism. For Islam the acceptance of social democracy in some suitable form and consistent with the legal principles of Islam is not a revolution but a return to the original purity of Islam. ... in order to make it possible for Muslim India to solve these problems it is necessary to redistribute the country and to provide one or more Muslim states with absolute majorities. *Don't you think that the time for such a demand has already arrived?* ... Muslim India hopes that at this serious juncture *your genius will discover some way out* of our present difficulties. (28 May 1937)
- The atheistic socialism of Jawaharlal is not likely to receive much response from the Muslims. The question therefore is how is it possible to solve the problem of Muslim poverty? And the *whole future of the League* depends on the League's activity to solve this question. (28 May 1937)
- I have come to the conclusion that if this system of [Islamic] Law is properly understood and applied, at least the right to subsistence is secured to everybody. But the enforcement and development of the Shariat of Islam is impossible in this country without a *free Muslim state or states.* (28 May 1937)

---

151 Letter dated 21 June 1937 (*Letters of Iqbal*, p.20-1)

- A separate federation of Muslim provinces ... is the only course by which we can secure a peaceful India and save Muslims from the domination of non-Muslims. Why should not the Muslims of North-West and Bengal be considered as nations entitled to *self-determination*, just as other nations in India and outside India are? (21 June 1937)
- The Muslims of North-West India and Bengal ought at present to *ignore Muslim minority provinces.* (21 June 1937)
- The League ought to concentrate all its activities on the North-West Indian Musalmans. (11 August 1937)

Until the end of his life, and as we shall see throughout this book, Jinnah frequently borrowed ideas directly from Iqbal – including his thoughts on Muslim unity, on Islamic ideals of liberty, justice and equality, on economics, and even on practices such as prayer. Jinnah's use of the term 'nation', again taken from Iqbal, is the most significant. The philosopher in turn had borrowed his concept of nationalism from both Ernest Renan [152] and Sir Syed Ahmad Khan, and discussed it in light of his knowledge of the Quran. Iqbal's concept of nationality was not based strictly on communalism, or religious affiliation. It was based on the Islamic worldview, which we will review in Chapter 6.

Jinnah was thus inspired by Iqbalian thought when he said:

> The ideology of the League is based on the fundamental principle that Muslim India is an independent nationality. ... We are determined, and let there be no mistake about it, to establish the status of an independent *nation* and an independent *State* in this subcontinent. [153]

Central to this concept of 'nationality' (and separate from the territorial demand) [154] was 'Muslim unity', a theme recurrent in most of Jinnah's speeches in the last few years of his life, both before and after partition. By the end of 1938, he had dropped the term 'Hindu-Muslim unity', and had become the advocate of 'Muslim unity' instead. To the best of my research, Jinnah's last references to Hindu-Muslim unity may have been in June 1938, when he said that Muslims were ready for 'communal unity' (i.e. between Hindus and Muslims), but that this unity could only be arrived at 'between two equal *parties*'. [155] At a post-election League Executive Council meeting in March 1937, Jinnah was

---

[152] Iqbal even mentioned Renan's characterisation of what constitutes a nation in his Allahabad Address.

[153] Presidential address, AIML Annual Session, Madras, 14 April 1941 (Yusufi Vol. III, p.1386)

[154] For reasons on why this separation of nation and state is important, see criticisms of the Muslim religious leaders against the Two-Nation Theory in Myth no. 8 (Chapter 10)

[155] Speech at public meeting, 5 June 1938 (NV Vol. I, p.258)

reported as having told his colleagues: 'Sink or swim; die or live; but live as a united *nation.*' [156] Similarly on 8 October 1938 he called for 'cooperation between the various communities in India', adding that 'India is a country of different *nationalities*'. [157] These latter examples of the word 'nation' are both before his address at Aligarh University cited earlier; they represent Jinnah's transition from advocating 'Hindu-Muslim unity' to communal 'cooperation'. It also reflects the growing enthusiasm for Muslim independence both in himself and in his contemporaries. In the speeches that followed, Jinnah increasingly focused on building Muslim unity alone, mainly in view of preparing them for the long-term goal of partition. [158] He did not speak of 'Hindu-Muslim unity' at all after the end of the 1930s. But since in Islam 'Muslim unity' is only a precursor to universal human unity, Jinnah always spoke of 'friendship' and 'cooperation' with other communities and even forming pacts, and always upheld these principles in his dealings with these communities. He was never a 'communalist' inducing a fear of the religious 'other'. Like Iqbal, he was neither seeking nor endorsing a theocracy for the Muslim state; this was why he wanted to set Muslims 'free from the reactionary elements of Muslims' including the 'undesirable elements' within 'Maulvis and Maulanas'. [159]

Jinnah's political decisions and his ideas on Islam as a polity also follow Iqbal's thinking almost perfectly after 1939. Throughout the rest of this book, I will attempt to show the links between the thoughts in Iqbal's letters above as well as his other statements, with those of Jinnah in the forties. The founder of Pakistan constantly reminded Muslims to unite on the basis of their 'nationality', right up to his death on 11 September 1948. He pulled it off within his own lifetime – just.

The problem was that few people in the Muslim leadership had ever learned the real meaning of the Two-Nation Theory. Within a few years, the fragile unity maintained by Jinnah began to falter. Personal jealousies and intrigues amongst the leaders resurfaced to the detriment of Pakistan at all levels: Socially, economically and politically. Worst still, academic, political and public opinion on the Pakistan idea and indeed Jinnah's ideological stance soon became sharply divided.

And this is where the story really begins.

---

156 Meeting at ML Executive Council, New Delhi, 21 March 1937. (NV Vol. I, p.136)

157 Address at the Karachi Municipal Corporation, Karachi, 8 October 1938 (NV Vol. I, p.291; emphasis mine.)

158 For example: when at a function in 1944 a Sikh religious leader in 1944 urged Jinnah to 'propagate the mission of unity and fuse the masses with the universal whole', Jinnah replied in his address that he endeavoured to obey the principles of his faith, and had before him 'the humble task of uniting the *Musalmans* and working for their social, educational and political uplift'. (See *Civil & Military Gazette* report of Jinnah's public address at a tea party, Lahore, 28 March 1944; NV Vol. III, p.443; emphasis mine)

159 Speech at meeting of the Muslim University Union, Aligarh, 5 February 1938 (Yusufi Vol. II, p.727). *Maulvis and Maulanas* are terms for Muslim clergy. Jinnah also indicated that he was not referring to *all* Muslim clergy, but to a 'section of them'.

Chapter 2
The Munir quote

The late Chief Justice Muhammad Munir's book, *From Jinnah to Zia* (1979) was one of the bestselling books in Pakistan's history. It could also be safely said that it is one of the most influential books in secularist circles, because Munir was probably amongst the first Pakistanis to openly claim that Jinnah was a secularist. The approximate order of his argument (to be described later in this chapter) has been copied faithfully time and again, to the extent that it has become a standard argument for a secular Jinnah. This was the conclusion I had reached by the time I finished writing the first edition of *Secular Jinnah* (2005). Though I have not changed my position, much has happened since that time and in this book we will continue the story.

Background

First, however, let us begin with a summary outlining the background of the 'Munir quote'. In 2004, I was double-checking some references for an English translation of my father's book *Quran aur Pakistan.* [1] One of the chapters was a rebuttal of Muhummad Munir's book, and I had obtained a copy in order to insert the extracts as they were taken from the original English text.

I happened to leaf through the book and came across a passage on page 29 which reads:

> The pattern of Government which the Quaid-i-Azam had in mind was a secular democratic government. This is apparent from his interview which he gave to Mr Doon Campbell, Reuter's Correspondent in New Delhi in 1946, in the course of which he had said:

[1] F. Karim (2003) *Quran aur Pakistan* Islamabad: Bazm-e-Ilmo-Fann International. The book was a compilation of the Muslim thinker G.A. Parwez's writings and also my father's poetry. The translation was not subsequently published for reasons relating to problems obtaining some original references.

> "*The new state would be a modern democratic state with sovereignty resting in the people and the members of the new nation having equal rights of citizenship regardless of religion, caste or creed*". [2]

Up until I read that passage, I had shared the view of those who argue that Jinnah's vision for Pakistan was Islamic (though not sectarian or religious); but for the next few minutes after reading that passage, Munir's quote had me reconsidering my position. The words 'a modern democratic state' used in conjunction with 'sovereignty resting in the people' implied an advocacy of a so-called 'secular' democracy as it is understood in the West, like the contemporary version in vogue. Yet this passage seemed to be in direct contrast to Jinnah's own clear statements that Pakistan would not simply emulate the Western democratic form of government, but would uphold Islamic ideals.

Looking again at the quote, I spotted a grammatical issue which compelled me to look for the full text of the interview cited by Munir. In short the problem was with the syntax: 'The new state *would* be a modern democratic state', which as such made no sense. Normally we would expect someone to say: 'The new state *will* be a modern democratic state'. The text as cited by Munir was written in the conditional clause, without giving the condition. Therefore my preliminary reason for trying to find the full text was to ascertain its context in grammatical terms. [3] At this point I had no reason to doubt the authenticity of the text itself.

After some hunting, [4] within a few weeks I had obtained the full text of the interview, and the following had emerged:

- The date of the Reuters interview of Jinnah with Doon Campbell as provided by Munir was simply the year: 1946. [5] No proper reference was provided anywhere in the book. [6] The actual date of this interview however is 21 May 1947. [7]
- The full transcript of the interview appears in the first volume of Z.H. Zaidi's *Jinnah Papers*. This in turn was obtained from an original typewritten document containing corrections in

---

2 M. Munir (1980 edition) *From Jinnah to Zia* Lahore: Vanguard Books, p.29. Emphasis in original.

3 Ironically, I later discovered that this was not a grammar mistake as such, but a style of journalistic quotation from the early 20th century that is now obsolete.

4 The detailed account of the search was given in the first edition of *Secular Jinnah* (2005).

5 Incidentally, Jinnah did also use the very same words ('popular representative', 'caste, colour or creed') in an interview to foreign press representatives on 14 November 1946. (NV Vol. V, p.384)

6 Munir, op. cit.

7 S. Karim, op. cit. p.7. Mr Ardeshir Cowasjee of *Dawn* kindly pointed out the correct year in his correspondence to me at the time.

Jinnah's own handwriting as well as his signature, [8] confirming the textual authenticity of this particular interview.

- The particular wording of the text as given by Munir does not appear in the interview. [9]

A careful scrutiny of the transcript reveals a counterpart of sorts to Munir's quote. Here is Munir's quote again:

> The new state would be a modern democratic state with sovereignty resting in the people and the members of the new nation having equal rights of citizenship regardless of religion, *caste or creed.* (Emphasis mine)

Here's the real version:

> But the Government of Pakistan can only be a popular representative and democratic form of Government. Its Parliament and Cabinet responsible to the Parliament will both be finally responsible to the electorate and the people in general without any distinction of *caste, creed* or sect, which will be the final deciding factor with regard to the policy and programme of the Government that may be adopted from time to time. [10]

These two passages are worded completely differently from each other. The only words the quotes literally have in common are 'caste' and 'creed'. The counterparts for Munir's 'modern democratic state' and 'sovereignty resting in the people' respectively are 'democratic form of government' and 'popular representative', and even these are technically in reverse order compared with Munir's version.

Before we look at what Mr Jinnah's answer means, we must note some other details that are never mentioned by other commentators as they do not consult the original transcript of the interview. Firstly, the above statement was given in answer to a specific question. Doon Campbell had asked of Jinnah: *On what basis will the central administration of Pakistan be set up?* [11] In other words, he wanted to know the thoughts of Jinnah regarding the nature of Pakistan. He wanted to know whether it would be a secular state or a religious state, and how this would affect its relationship with neighbouring

---

[8] See Z.H. Zaidi (ed.) (1993) *Jinnah Papers: Prelude to Pakistan*, Vol. I Part I. Lahore: Quaid-i-Azam Papers Project, p.845. (Hereinafter 'Jinnah Papers')

[9] S. Karim 2005, p.8-9

[10] Interview with Doon Campbell, Reuters' correspondent, New Delhi, 21 May 1947. (Jinnah Papers Vol. I, p843-4.; also Yusufi Vol. IV, p.2563). Emphasis mine.

[11] Ibid.

territories.[12] It was an opportunity for Jinnah to call Pakistan a secular state if he chose, and this would have surely suited the Western audience for whose benefit the interview was being conducted. Secondly, the questions were given to Jinnah in writing a day before the interview, giving him time to prepare his answers. Thirdly, Jinnah was trying to explain Pakistan's rationale to this audience in general terms, as this is what Doon Campbell expressly asked of him. [13] His answers to the questions in that interview were prepared with this in mind. Campbell's letter to Jinnah's private secretary, dated 20 May 1947, contains an enclosure of the questions he was going to ask:

> The questions are essentially those of the "man in the street" – the "man in the street" in Britain and Europe, in the Near and Middle East; in Canada and the Americas, in the countries of Asia. They are broad and general rather than technical. Some may have been answered many times before but in the context of the developing situation they have assumed fresh topicality and pertinence.
>
> I do hope Mr Jinnah will feel disposed to answer some, if not all of the questions. [14]

Now for a brief analysis of Jinnah's answer:

- Jinnah makes it clear that he does not have the authority to decide the basis of the 'central administration of Pakistan' single-handedly. He states that the Pakistan Constituent Assembly will be responsible for making this decision.
- Instead of calling the proposed Pakistan a 'modern democratic state', Jinnah says only that it will have a 'democratic form' of government. He was actually averse to imitating 'modern' (read: contemporary) democracy as a political system, [15] considering it a failure. [16]

---

[12] The order of the questions from the transcript make this quite clear: *Q*: Do you envisage the formation of a Pan-Islamic state stretching from the Far and Middle East to the Far East after the establishment of Pakistan? *Q*: On what basis will the central administration of Pakistan be set up? What will be the attitude of this Government to the Indian States? *Q*: In general terms what will be the foreign policy of Pakistan? Will it apply for membership of the United Nations? (Yusufi Vol. IV, p.2562-4)

[13] However Jinnah also spoke quite candidly to western audiences about the Muslim intent to build an Islamic polity on many occasions. See for example his speech to the American Broadcasting Corporation, 13 December 1946; his interview to Beverley Nichols, published 1944; his Broadcast talk to the people of Australia as Governor-General: 19 February, 1948; and his interview with the *Manchester Guardian*, 25 October 1939.

[14] Doon Campbell to Jinnah's private secretary, 20 May 1947 (Jinnah Papers Vol. I, p. 806; also reproduced in full in S. Karim 2005, p.32). Quotation marks in original.

[15] In the past century capitalism has invariably operated within Western democracy and so defines the 'modern' West itself. In his speech at the opening ceremony of the State Bank of Pakistan, Karachi, 1 July 1948, Jinnah blamed 'the economic system of the West' for creating

- The 'policy and programme of the Government that may be adopted from time to time' is, from the Quranic perspective, a clear reference to a change of policy in accordance with the principle of 'mutual consultation' (verse 42:38).

In short, the real words of Jinnah are characteristic of his level-headed pragmatism, rather than the romantic language of the Munir quote.

Having compared the two versions of the quote, at that time I concluded that Munir had simply not consulted the original English text of the interview, and therefore his quote was likely a paraphrase of an Urdu translation turned back into English. [17]

Popular sovereignty and the Quranic position

Munir's 'sovereignty resting in the people' is borrowed directly from the 'social contract' school of thought. The idea of popular sovereignty has ultimately come to mean separation of religion (and spirit) from the state based on a Christian dualist worldview. (We will discuss the Islamic worldview in Chapter 6). Yet even Jean Jacques Rousseau considered popular sovereignty to be a spiritual concept, based on the idea that the 'voice of the People is the voice of God'. [18] Of course there is no denying that the freedom to choose is a natural law and innate in humans. We possess the faculty of free will and are able to live any way we please. The term 'sovereignty in the people' may be considered a contemporary expression for the human right to exercise free will, which finds its sanction in the Quran:

> Whoever chooses to follow the right path, follows it but for his own good; and whoever goes astray goes but astray to his own hurt ... (17:15)[19]

> And had God willed, He could have made them one community ... (42:8)[20]

'almost insoluble problems for humanity', for failing to 'eradicate friction from the international field' and for being 'largely responsible for the two World Wars'. He advised Pakistan against adopting it. (Yusufi Vol. IV p.2787)

16 See Jinnah's Presidential Address at the Annual Session of the All-India Muslim League in April 1941, in which he describes democracy as having 'failed' as quoted in Myth no. 2 (Chapter 10).

17 S. Karim 2005, p.11-13

18 As cited from Rousseau's *Letters from the Mountain* in James Miller (1984) *Rousseau: Dreamer of Democracy* Indianapolis: Hacket Publishing Co., p.108. Miller comments in parentheses: 'Although in calling the voice of the people the voice of God, Rousseau was merely invoking something of a republican truism, *vox populi vox dei*, he seems to have taken the motto rather more seriously than some of his predecessors.'

19 Muhammad Asad's translation.

20 Laleh Bakhtiar's translation. What is implied here is that humanity could have been like the rest of nature, which does not have free will.

Let there be no compulsion in *deen*. (2:256) [21]

The Quran effectively states that free will is a natural law sanctioned by God. Taken from this perspective, the idea of popular sovereignty (as distinct from the absolute sovereignty of God[22]) is the mere assertion of a natural law and its 'morality' is not in question. However 'sovereignty in the people' as a feature of most modern democratic states is generally considered to be an exclusively 'secular' principle. This is because in European history the principle was introduced in opposition to the 'sovereignty of God', which in the West means a Church-State, or theocracy. In Pakistan the fact that the constitution contains a well-known clause declaring that sovereignty belongs to Allah makes this point all the more significant, and has caused much controversy (more on that later). [23]

In the first edition of *Secular Jinnah* (2005) I did not discuss the concept of either sovereignty in God or in the people. At that time I felt it was sufficient to emphasise that the Munir quote was misleading because of its peculiar syntax. My point was that the words 'modern democratic state' used *in conjunction* with 'sovereignty resting in the people' was what made the quote fallacious, [24] because all 'modern democratic' states are avowedly secular. [25] Besides which, it was (and remains) my view that Jinnah generally avoided using conceptually fuzzy terminology and 'sovereignty in the people' – with its secular connotations – is one such term. It has been the subject of debate amongst Europe's thinkers for centuries; but in short it means the right of self-determination and the right to choose the government. Of course in practice, once the government has been chosen the sovereignty of the people becomes limited. [26] This is true of all modern democratic states, because sovereignty is passed by consent (election) to the legislature.

---

21 Ali's translation. The original rendition uses the word 'religion' (and Bakhtiar uses the term 'way of life') but I have replaced it with the Arabic word *deen*. See Chapter 6 for full explanation.

22 In Islam humans cannot have absolute sovereignty over their entire existence, in the sense attributed exclusively to the Creator. The Quranic view is that the only means of unlocking human potential is to abide by His principles, and predicts that ultimately humanity will come to realise this for itself by the end of time. See for example Quran verses 3:26, 25:26. I make the same point clearly in my *Systems* (2012), albeit without mentioning 'sovereignty' explicitly.

23 For discussion on the controversial clause in the Objectives Resolution, see Chapters 3-4; for the Quranic position, see Chapter 12.

24 See S. Karim 2005, xi, 3

25 This attitude towards the 'modern' state can be seen for example in S.C. Chattopadhyaya's speeches in the first Constituent Assembly of Pakistan (see Chapter 4), and also in works such as Prakash Almeida's *Jinnah: Man of Destiny* (quoted in Chapter 13, subsection 'Iskander's question')

26 While the phrase also implies that the people have full control of the constitution and sociopolitical affairs, this is not so in practice. Regular elections, fixed terms of office, occasional referendums and multi-party systems are the only facets of a modern democratic state that give it the semblance of 'sovereignty in the people' (instead of 'one man, one vote, once' it is 'one man, one vote, once every four years').

The same is true in Islam. The only difference between the two is that in the former, the sovereign authority remains human, and so a group of humans will always rule over others and laws will always be framed as a matter of political expedience. In Islam, sovereignty is said to be effectively handed to God, but this does not carry the connotation that it does in the West. It does not mean a theocracy. As we will show in Chapters 2 and 3, this was also the view of the early leaders of Pakistan.

Jinnah said numerous times that the Muslims of India demanded their right to self-determination and to choose their government. The assumption was that they would choose to live by Islamic principles in their new state. The Munir quote however gives the impression of a purely secular state. For these reasons I became convinced that Jinnah would not generally use the term in his speeches, and that if he ever did, as a constitutionalist he would no doubt make the context clear. [27]

Jinnah on popular sovereignty and the modern state

Over the years, I have found only two other instances of 'sovereignty in the people' attributed to Jinnah. One is a personal note written in Jinnah's hand, and the other is a press interview of Jinnah dated 11 May 1947. The date is similar to that of the Reuters' interview (and of course Munir himself never gave the correct date), but in any case its content does not match the Munir quote. We will return to this latter quote shortly.

The note in Jinnah's hand was quoted in a well-known Indian newspaper in 2005, and was obtained from Dr Z.H. Zaidi's *The Jinnah Papers.* The newspaper article reads:

> With great feeling he wrote in May 1947 on a piece of paper meant for himself which Zaidi has reproduced. Jinnah wrote "Pakistan means not only a matter of power and security, of loaves and fishes; there are things *of the spirit* involved in it. It means *sovereignty of people* and it will be all that it stands for. Will not people say with those Arabs who said, 'What does it matter, how weak and poor our homelands are, if only we are masters in them'." [28]

Though the article provides a date of 'May 1947', the original note is in fact undated,[29] which leads us to assume that the date given above is simply borrowed from the corrected date of the Munir quote. Dr Zaidi believed that the note represented Jinnah's own thoughts on what

---

27 S. Karim 2005, p.14

28 Book review: 'Jinnah Papers: Documenting partition', in *The Tribune*, 16 August 1998. Emphasis mine. (http://www.tribuneindia.com/1998/98aug16/sunday/head3.htm) Last accessed 29 Dec 2009.

29 See Jinnah Papers Vol. I, p.974

Pakistan meant to him, [30] but having done my own research I have discovered that Jinnah had in fact copied a passage from an article written by the British civil servant Sir Frederick Puckle in 1946 and published in the journal *Foreign Affairs.* The article was titled *The Pakistan Doctrine: Its Origins and Power,* and it was a discussion on the Two-Nation Theory. [31] But the most interesting part of the passage above is that 'sovereignty of the people' is considered a 'thing of the spirit'. This is most likely what drew Jinnah to the passage. [32]

This leaves the aforementioned press interview. It is the only public statement of Jinnah I have ever encountered in which he refers explicitly to the 'sovereignty of the people':

> Last August, Mr Patel accused me of what he called an intransigent attitude on my part and in reply I pointed out that the demand for Pakistan was based on the right of *self-determination* which is the *birthright of Musalmans* and it is not and cannot be a justifiable issue. Any intelligent man would understand that the right of self-determination is an inalienable right of a nation and the recognition of the *sovereignty of the people of that nation* by a democratic process. [33]

Jinnah is arguing for the right of 'self-determination' as the 'birthright of Musalmans'. He explicitly speaks of the 'sovereignty of the people of that nation', again reiterating that the question is of self-determination. To repeat what I have already said, Jinnah's assumption was that the people – that is, the Muslim nation – would choose an Islamic and not a 'modern democratic' form of government. The point should become clearer as we proceed through this book.

Jinnah's peculiar statements on popular sovereignty and the 'modern democratic' state take the following form:

> It is now the voice of the League, the *voice of the people*, it is now *the authority of the Millat* that you have to bow to, though you may be the tallest poppy in the Muslim world. [34]

> The *modern democratic* form of Government is not suitable to the genius of the Indian People. … We want a true *democracy in*

---

[30] See Zaidi's description of the note in his contents pages, op. cit. cxx

[31] Frederick Puckle, 'The Pakistan Doctrine: Its Origins and Power' in *Foreign Affairs* (New York) Vol. 24, No. 3, April 1946, p.526-538.

[32] The importance of the word 'spirit' can be seen in Chapter 6.

[33] Interview with Associated Press of America, New Delhi, 11 May 1947. (NV Vol. VI, p.107-8)

[34] Presidential Address delivered at the ML Annual Session, Delhi, 24 April 1943. (Yusufi Vol. III, p.1691)

accordance with Islam and not a Parliamentary Government of the Western or Congress type.[35]

Jinnah has spoken of the people and the *millat* together. *Millat* is an Urdu word used exclusively for the Muslim community (and can also be used to refer to a 'nation').[36] He has also disavowed rather than advocated a 'modern democratic' state (and he did this more than once).[37] Throughout this book I will expand upon the full significance of these above statements, but for now they should suffice to maintain my original point that the Munir quote is false both in its syntax and in its connotations.

Actual origin of the Munir quote

Even after the publication of *Secular Jinnah* I continued to take an interest in knowing where the Munir quote had been cited. At the time of writing the first book I had been working with only a handful of examples, but since that time I have found scores of instances in books, journals, and newspapers. I have listed some of them in Appendix VIII. The quote has certainly been used hundreds of times over the decades and continues to appear in new literature up to the present.

As a result of the ongoing search, I have found what I believe is the original instance of the Munir quote. It appeared for the first time in another very famous publication, the full title of which is: *Report of the Court of Inquiry Constituted under Punjab Act II of 1954 to Enquire into the Punjab Disturbances of 1953.* It is better known as the 'Munir Report', having again been authored by Muhammad Munir (and M.R. Kayani), in his capacity as President of the Court of Inquiry. The quote appears on page 201, and we shall examine its appearance therein shortly.

In May 1953, a public inquiry was set up to investigate the circumstances leading to some riots that had occurred in the Punjab during March-April that same year. These riots had begun due to the refusal by the then Prime Minister of Pakistan, Khwaja Nazimuddin,[38] to submit to the demands of some ulema[39] that the main group of the Ahmadis be declared out of the fold of Islam[40] and that the members of

---

35 Address to the Hostel Parliament of Ismail Yusuf College, Jogeshwari (Bombay), 1 February 1943. M.A. Harris (ed.) (1976) *Quaid-i-Azam*. Karachi: Times Press, p.174

36 See Iqbal's New Year Broadcast from the Lahore Station of All-India Radio, 1 January 1938. (Sherwani (ed.) 2008, p.300)

37 See *Hindustan Times* report of Jinnah's press conference, 13 July 1947 as cited in Myth no. 7 (Chapter 10).

38 For biographical note, see Chapter 3, footnote 75.

39 Ulema / ulama – from an Arabic word meaning 'wise' or 'learned', the plural term for Muslim religious leaders or Islamic scholars (singular: *alim*).

40 Munir Report, p.185. The religious leaders' opposition to the Ahmadis was primarily due to claims made by its founder, Mirza Ghulam Ahmad, that he was a new prophet succeeding the

their faith, including most notably Muhammad Zafrullah Khan (1893-1985), be forcibly removed from key governmental posts. The situation had deteriorated to the point that Martial Law had been briefly put into force in Lahore. The report summarising the findings of the inquiry was submitted to the Government in April 1954.

The report made Munir a celebrated name in Pakistan for its frank discussion regarding the background of the religious-political issues leading up to the riots. However it also had ramifications that went far beyond its original subject matter and scope. Munir himself acknowledges this in the introduction to his *From Jinnah to Zia*, when he writes that following the submission of the Munir Report to the government, the 'demand for an Islamic State receded and the Ulama were thrown into the background'. [41] With time the Munir Report became one of the most oft-quoted and influential resources in secularist discourse. As we will see in later chapters, certain statements from the report have been used not only in historical and other academic literature, but they have even been used in the Constituent Assembly of Pakistan by certain members who wished to create a secular constitution for Pakistan.

Returning now to the present subject, the way the Munir quote is presented in the 1953 Report differs from Munir's later book in one important aspect. This is how it appeared in the Report:

> Before the partition, the first public picture of Pakistan that the Quaid-i-Azam gave to the world was in the course of an interview in New Delhi with Mr Doon Campbell, Reuter's Correspondent. The Quaid-i-Azam said that the new State would be a modern democratic State, with sovereignty resting in the people and the members of the new nation having equal rights of citizenship regardless of their religion, caste or creed. [42]

Other than the fact that the date of this interview is not provided anywhere in the Munir Report, the major difference here is that the quote is not appearing as a verbatim statement. There are no quotation marks. This immediately nullifies the grammar issue which led me to look for the origin of the quote in the first place. At this point at least, we can say that Munir was merely offering a reworded summary of

---

Prophet Muhammad, and that he was also the reincarnation of Jesus and Krishna. These claims violated the Islamic view that Muhammad is the final Prophet (the 'seal' of the prophets – Quran 33:40) and there will be none after him. A much smaller splinter group of Ahmadis, who identify themselves as the Lahore group, differ from the main Ahmadi community in that they hold M.G. Ahmad to be a reformer rather than a prophet. In Pakistan today all Ahmadis are treated as non-Muslim by law under Ordinance XX of 1984, on the basis that since M.G. Ahmad declared himself a prophet, to follow him is tantamount to accepting his prophethood.

[41] Munir 1980, xvi.

[42] Munir Report, p.201

what he understood to be the spirit of Jinnah's statement in the interview. He was not necessarily claiming outright that these were the very words of Jinnah. Therefore we cannot place the blame on him if other people misinterpreted this particular rendition of the quote as literally representing Jinnah's words.

Neither in the Munir Report nor in his later book did the late Chief Justice see fit to reference his sources. However Munir placed quotation marks around the Munir quote in *From Jinnah to Zia* (and not in the older Munir Report). This suggests that Munir was not directly quoting Jinnah, but rather he was quoting from the Munir Report. Yet he himself misread his own Report and gave the wholly misleading impression that he was quoting Jinnah's words verbatim. We should note that again there was a failure on the part of later commentators to spot the error.

The three-piece argument

The Munir quote is only one part of a three-piece argument originally submitted by Munir. It does not represent the whole of the argument for a 'secular Jinnah', but it does form the most significant portion of the firsthand evidence attributed to Jinnah. The three parts of the argument below are taken from *From Jinnah to Zia* in order of appearance:[43]

- The Munir quote (supposedly citing Jinnah's interview with a Reuters correspondent in 1946);[44] used to claim that the Objectives Resolution,[45] which declares that 'sovereignty rests with Allah' is at odds with the concept of sovereignty resting with the people[46] and by implication, against Jinnah's vision
- Jinnah's speech as President of the Constituent Assembly of Pakistan on 11 August 1947, described as the 'clearest exposition

---

43 The first two of these points originally appeared in the Munir Report also, with the difference that Jinnah was not explicitly described as a secularist. (Ibid.)

44 Munir 1980, p.29

45 The Objectives Resolution was first written contribution to the constitution of Pakistan (passed in 1949 by then Prime Minister Liaquat Ali Khan), and it eventually formed the preamble to the constitution. Though its original movers (i.e. the Muslim members of the first Constituent Assembly) stressed that Pakistan's constitution would not be a theocracy, the Resolution has remained a matter of controversy because of certain clauses which, its opponents allege, created a back door to a potential theocracy.

46 Munir op. cit. p.36, 77-8. See also Munir Report, p.203, 210. On page 203 of the Report it is written: 'The Quaid-i-Azam's conception of a modern national State, it is alleged, became obsolete with the passing of the Objectives Resolution on 12th March 1949.' In his later book however, Munir more explicitly makes the connection between the wording of the Objectives Resolution and the wording of the Munir quote: 'Liaquat Ali Khan knew that the Quaid-i-Azam would not agree to any such [Objectives] Resolution as it was directly opposed to the views he had publicly expressed more than once, and it was a complete contradiction of his idea of a *modern democratic secular state* [emphasis mine]. … The Quaid-i-Azam had said that in the new state sovereignty would rest with the people. The [Objectives] Resolution starts with the statement that sovereignty rests with Allah.' (Munir 1980, p.36)

of a secular state' [47] because (according to Munir) Jinnah believed that 'religion would be an affair of the individual and will [*sic*] have nothing to do with the administration of the State', [48] and also because a statement about equality regardless of 'caste and creed' appear both in the Munir quote and the 11 August speech
- Jinnah's statements that Pakistan would not be a theocracy [49]

Perhaps unsurprisingly, these three references to Jinnah also appear frequently in pro-secularist literature, as I will demonstrate later. This was certainly the case in three of the four examples which I originally examined in *Secular Jinnah*, [50] though at the time I discussed the issue primarily with emphasis on the first two points – i.e. the 11 August speech and the Munir quote together, since they had been emphasised as a pair on two separate occasions in Munir's book [51] and consequently tend to be paired in pro-secularist literature also (for a number of reasons that should become apparent as we continue). Suffice it to say that in this edition too we will focus on what we are calling the 'two-pronged argument': The use of the Munir quote alongside the 11 August 1947 speech. These two quotes are often, though not always, juxtaposed with the 'sovereignty of Allah' clause in Pakistan's first constitutional document, the Objectives Resolution. In Chapters 4 and 5, we will reveal the first instance of the two-pronged argument following the publication of the Munir Report, and will review the influence of this argument. Before that however, we should briefly review why Munir equates an 'Islamic state' with a religious, or theocratic, state.

What constitutes an Islamic state?

When Munir raises his third point about Jinnah's stance against theocracy, he also confounds his argument. Despite insisting in the beginning that Jinnah was an outright secularist, nevertheless he admits that in at least one of these statements against theocracy Jinnah had also referred to Islamic principles.[52] He also acknowledges that Jinnah had

---

[47] Ibid. The phrase: 'clearest exposition' has been copied directly or reproduced in phrases of a similar wording in other pro-secularist commentaries.

[48] Munir 1980, p.32. See also Munir Report, p.203

[49] Munir 1980, p.30

[50] These four examples are examined again in Chapter 5.

[51] Munir 1980. p.29, 75.

[52] See Jinnah's broadcast to the people of United States, 26 February 1948: 'I do not know what the ultimate shape of this constitution is going to be, but I am sure that it will be of a democratic type, embodying the essential principles of Islam. … Islam and its idealism have taught us democracy. It has taught equality of men, justice and fairplay to everybody.' (NV Vol. VII, p.216) Also cited in Munir 1980, p.30-1)

affirmed his commitment to Islamic idealism in numerous speeches.[53] Consequently, Munir's argument becomes somewhat noncommittal. In an attempt to get round the obvious contradiction, he suddenly moves to the thoughts of former judge Dr Javid Iqbal[54] to claim that 'secularism is an integral part of Islam'.[55] Based largely upon this statement, Munir concludes that Jinnah 'used the words Islamic socialism but they were used in their pragmatic sense, not in their doctrinaire sense.'[56] His thinking is only partly correct. Jinnah indeed spoke of a state that was Islamic in the ethical sense, and not in the ecclesiastical sense. But this is not quite what Munir means. By 'doctrinaire', he implies a determination to use a fixed, outdated version of an Islamic state. By 'pragmatic', he means a progressive state that is evolving with the needs of its time, and apparently he does not consider this a quality of an 'Islamic' state.[57] That Jinnah put the word 'Islamic' in front of the word 'socialism' is irrelevant to Munir, and this is where his mistake lies. In Islam no system or state can exist in a 'doctrinaire' sense (i.e. as a fixed institution), because to treat it as such means crystallising it, contrary to the principle of change in the Quran. Therefore Munir has his facts essentially back to front. What he calls 'pragmatic' is Quranic, and what he calls 'doctrinaire' is not.

Later in his book Munir also makes the paradoxical statement: 'The Quaid-i-Azam wanted a modern secular democratic state based no doubt on Islamic principles.'[58] The problem is that he is thinking in simple terms of a divorce between 'church and state', based on a dualist worldview, whereas some of the so-called 'modernists' are better aware of the essentially monist worldview of the Quran. These are freethinking Muslims who also happen to oppose a religious or theocratic state and yet make a point of never using the word 'secular' alongside Islam. They are sometimes called modernists as Munir does in his book. More often they are understood to be closet secularists (mostly by Western commentators), or sometimes they are even branded fundamentalists (by some Muslim secularists); but under objective scrutiny we find they do not fit into any of these categories. Nor do they think as 'secular-Muslims', the other modernist group who believe that it is possible to borrow from traditional Shariah law and reconcile it with modern ideas on the state. The main difference between these

---

53 Munir 1980, p.30-32. Munir quotes Jinnah speeches as they are cited in Javid Iqbal's book *Ideology of Pakistan.*

54 Dr Javid Iqbal (1924-2015), who during his career worked as a senator and as a judge of Pakistan's Supreme Court, was also the son of the Islamic philosopher and 'spiritual father' of Pakistan, Dr Muhammad Iqbal.

55 Munir 1980, p.32 (citing J. Iqbal)

56 Ibid. p.32-3

57 See also Munir Report, p.210.

58 Munir 1980, p.140. Note the insertion of 'secular' into 'modern democratic state' in his text, with the obvious psychological repercussions. See also p.34: 'so far as the Quaid-i-Azam is concerned he was strongly in favour of a *modern secular* constitution.' (Emphasis mine)

groups is their understanding of the word 'secularism'. This difference can be illustrated by looking at Javid Iqbal's statement cited above in its proper context, but this takes us into a philosophical discussion; we will do so in Chapter 6.

A secular-Muslim approach

It is difficult to ascertain precisely what Munir's position is with respect to Jinnah, Islam and the state. He does not summarise his views clearly anywhere in his book and so there is much room for confusion. The essence of his argument is that if even the ulema cannot define a Muslim or indeed Islam, then an Islamic state of perhaps any kind is untenable. What emerges from this is that Munir is thinking much like the present-day proponents of 'secular Islam': He seems to believe there is a possibility of reform in Muslim thought; he writes optimistically about modernist thinkers who have made innovative contributions in reforming Muslim countries as well as thought in the twentieth century.[59] Towards the last few pages of his book he also briefly outlines the views of Pakistani 'modernists' (as opposed to both secular-Muslims and pure secularists) who hold that 'the principles of Islam should be made the basis of the legal system', [60] before returning finally again to his advocacy of 'secularism in Islam'.[61] His brevity in dealing with the modernist view, as compared with his latter placement of secular Islam on these pages, suggests that although he personally acknowledges the dynamic capacity of Muslim thinking, he feels it is better to stick with secularism as a quick and decisive solution to the ideological and political problems in Pakistan.

Looking more carefully at Munir's book, we also discover that much of his objections to 'Islam' are actually based on his criticisms of the religious institute bearing the same name. He does not believe, for instance, that Islam and democracy are compatible. An entire chapter is dedicated to debunking the concept of 'Islamic democracy', on the basis that democracy as it is practised today – including its components of adult franchise, parliamentary legislature and multi-party election – was 'not a form of government during the life of the Holy Prophet and the four Caliphs that succeeded him' and therefore it is antithetical to it. [62] In other chapters he also discusses the problems concerning religious freedom and apostasy in the 'Islamic state' (meaning the theocratic state) [63] which run counter to the 'secular' principles of religious tolerance and freedom. Here in fact he is deriving his evidence from

59 Munir 1980, p.148-50
60 Op. cit. p.170
61 Ibid. p.171 et seq.
62 Op. cit. (Chapter XI), p.109 et seq.
63 Op. cit. (Chapter VI), p.41 et. seq.

interviews of ulema carried out during the Public Inquiry of 1953 and recorded in the Munir Report. He highlights two key points, namely that no two ulema could define a Muslim, and yet all the ulema were unanimous on the point that in an Islamic state apostasy is punishable with death [64] (A closer look at these interviews however reveals a problem which we will come to later [65]). Munir uses these points – having come from the custodians of contemporary Islam – as authoritative proof that an Islamic state will invariably discriminate against non-Muslims, and will also discriminate against Muslims from minority sects and potentially prescribe capital punishment for them on the basis that they are apostates. Later in his book however, when discussing punishment in Islam (and Pakistan), [66] he actually defends the Islamic position, partly by showing that some draconian Shariah laws (e.g. stoning to death for adultery) are opposed to the actual teachings of the Quran. Later still his tone changes again; here he quotes a Hadith (oral tradition) of the Prophet of Islam to try and show it is possible to be a Muslim whilst separating 'worldly' matters from the spiritual sphere. This tradition, says Munir, 'introduces secularism in Islam'.[67]

It could be said that Munir's arguments come across as very muddled and self-contradictory. [68] This is due in no small part to his two-pronged argument, one half of which comprises a false quote and the other half which comes from a genuine quote that has been misread. We also have another possible explanation from Dr Javid Iqbal, which was reported in *Dawn* in 2004. [69] Dr Iqbal originally wrote a rebuttal to the Munir Report in his work titled *Ideology of Pakistan.* [70] According to the *Dawn* report, Munir supposedly took these comments on board and 'corrected' his position on the Quaid-i-Azam in his *From Jinnah to Zia.* [71] This explains

---

64 Ibid. p.45-8. In traditional Islam – meaning the religious institution – apostasy is generally understood to be punishable with death. This concept however has no sanction in the Quran.

65 See Myth no. 1 (Chapter 10)

66 Munir 1980 (Chapter XII), p.119 et seq.

67 Munir refers to a well known Hadith of Prophet Muhammad in which he reportedly said: 'I am no more than a man but when I enjoin anything respecting religion receive it, and when I order anything about the affairs of the world, then I am nothing more than a man.' (as cited in op. cit., p.145-6)

68 See also S. Mujahid 1981, p267-8, in which Munir's contradictory arguments are described as 'fallacious'.

69 See article in *Dawn*, 'Javid Warns of National Disintegration: Changes in Curricula, 20 March 2004' which states: 'Mr Javid said that he had rebutted Mr Munir's contention in his book on the ideology of Pakistan that the Quaid was on record having said more than once that Islam was the basis of Pakistan. Mr Munir had later corrected himself ...' The newspaper reports that Dr Iqbal rebutted Munir's 1979 book; but this cannot be the case, since Javid Iqbal's *Ideology of Pakistan* was published as early as 1959, and in this book Dr Iqbal criticised the Munir Report. In *From Jinnah to Zia*, Munir quotes from Dr Iqbal's rebuttal from the 1971 reprint, (op. cit. p.69-73) but not once does he claim that he has changed his position on Jinnah.

70 J. Iqbal (1959) *The Ideology of Pakistan and its Implementation.* Lahore: Sh. Ghulam & Sons

71 *Dawn* states that Javid Iqbal himself claimed that Munir 'corrected' himself, but Dr Iqbal has indicated that this is not the case (personal correspondence to S. Karim, 2009).

Munir's references to Dr Iqbal's book, but we find no sign of any correction. [72] At best we find a few fleeting references to Jinnah's pro-Islam speeches and an explanation that this is 'secular Islam', in view of his three-piece argument. Munir has in fact misquoted Dr Iqbal to support his own ideas, rather than quote him to make a correction. [73]

Back to the beginning

Though *From Jinnah to Zia* is the more commonly used resource of pro-secularist commentators today, the argument in that book has its roots in the Report of 1954. This Report was originally written with a view to discover the circumstances behind the Punjab riots of 1953. The Committee investigating the riots obtained some testimonies from the ulema in order to show that the problems had occurred because religious extremists believed that the Objectives Resolution – which endorses Islam – effectively gave them the right to interfere in state policy.[74] The Committee concluded that had the perpetrators of the riots been treated as 'a pure question of law and order, without any political considerations', it would have taken just 'one District Magistrate and one Superintendent of Police' to thwart their activities before they got out of control. [75]

The authors of the Report stressed that their reason for collecting the evidence from the ulema was not 'to write a thesis against or in favour of [an Islamic] State.' [76] Yet when Munir later reproduced the same evidence in *From Jinnah to Zia*, he did so expressly to discredit the Objectives Resolution and to undermine the ideological basis of the state.[77] It is not that he was the first person to do so. In fact his book seems only to echo the view of Pakistani secularists who had used the Munir Report for their own political ends from as early as 1954, just months after its publication. As we shall see in the following two chapters, they had referred to the salient points of the Report with a view not merely to prevent the formation of a theocracy, but to prevent the formation of any state with an Islamic basis.

---

72 See Munir 1980, p.69-73, in which he writes some replies to Javid Iqbal's rebuttal.

73 See Chapter 6 for our review on Javid Iqbal's statement on secularism and Islam.

74 See Munir Report, p.186: 'Almost all the *ulama* whom we questioned on the subject have stated that the demands are a corollary from the Objectives Resolution passed by the Constituent Assembly of Pakistan on 12th March, 1949, and from that religio-political system which they call Islam.' Having pointed out that these were the very same religious parties that had opposed the creation of Pakistan and the irony (and hypocrisy) that they were the ones now calling for an 'Islamic state', the Committee suggested that the problems had escalated only because the religious parties were able to exploit the Objectives Resolution to justify their demands. (Ibid.)

75 Munir Report, p.387

76 Ibid. p.231

77 Munir 1980, p.25, et. seq.

Chapter 3
1949: Before the Munir quote

The Muslims of India understood the Pakistan idea as meaning a place where they would be given better opportunities to live as free people and to flourish at the socio-economic level. They also understood that these opportunities would be available not simply because they would be a numerical majority, but because the law of the land, being based on Islamic principles, would guarantee it. Whether or not anyone today believes that a political expression of Islam can actually make this guarantee, there can be no doubt that this is what the masses believed, and to a large extent still believe.

The leading personalities of the original Muslim League were liberal-minded and progressive Muslims, and most of them were also very vocal about their desire to see Islamic rule implemented in Pakistan, but they all understood that this would not entail the establishment of a theocracy. Speaking on behalf of the League, Jinnah had said: 'I have no doubt in my mind that a large body of us visualise Pakistan as a people's government', and 'the constitution of Pakistan can only be framed by the *millat* and the people'. [1]

With time almost the entire *millat* in India eventually backed the League in its call for independence. The only Muslims opposed to Pakistan happened to belong to religious parties with the self-appointed custodians of Islam as their leaders. They claimed that the Pakistan movement was being led by irreligious 'westernised' individuals who were Muslims in name only, and that Pakistan would undoubtedly become a secular state in practice, never mind the claims of its supporters to the contrary. Knowing as they did that the name 'Pakistan' meant 'land of the pure', the religious leaders came up with the insulting nickname 'Na-Pakistan' ('land of the impure') as a counterpart name to describe the rest of India. [2] This idea of 'Pak' versus 'Na-Pak' (implying hatred of India and Hindus) was falsely attributed to the League in an attempt to rouse the ire of non-Muslims as well as the

---

1 Jinnah's Presidential address at the ML Annual Session, Delhi 24 April 1943. (Yusufi Vol. III p.1720)

2 The name 'Pakistan' was an acronym based on the territories that were supposed to end up within its borders: Punjab, Afghanistan (N.W. Frontier), Kashmir, Sind and Baluchistan. Additionally, the word *Pak* means pure, and so *Pakistan* also means 'land of the pure' or 'holy land'.

nationalist (pro-Congress) Muslims throughout the subcontinent. [3] These religious leaders also called Jinnah the 'Ka'fir-i-Azam'. [4] They objected to the Two-Nation Theory on the grounds that it was nationalistic and against the pan-Islamic ideal. They would rather join the fight for secular India than (as they saw it) for pseudo-Islamic Pakistan. The question is: Why?

Hardly anyone has offered an answer to this question. At any rate the secularists of Pakistan are not concerned with finding one. It is quite enough for them that the officially recognised custodians of Islam opposed Pakistan. They focus more on the hypocrisy of those religious parties, which after partition suddenly decided to become politically active and try to claim Pakistan as their 'Islamic state'. The secularists lay much of the blame for this development on the first Constituent Assembly of Pakistan for introducing the Objectives Resolution – a document containing the 'Aims and Objects of the Constitution' [5] – as the first contribution to the constitution in 1949. The Objectives Resolution was to act as a short guide to the process of constitution-making, to ensure that the nation upheld the highest principles (amongst others) of democracy and social justice 'as enunciated by Islam'. In his opening speech presenting the Resolution to the Assembly, Liaquat Ali Khan [6] had described it as 'next in importance only to the achievement of independence.' [7] Secularists allege that the Islamic content in the Objectives Resolution created a backdoor to a potential theocracy and so its entire spirit goes against the wishes of Jinnah, who, as they are wont to point out, had passed away some six months before the Resolution was moved. [8]

The Objectives Resolution has always been the main target of criticism primarily because of a clause relating to sovereignty in its Preamble, which we shall examine shortly. In recent times, this intellectual criticism has been translated into action. In 2007, an attempt was made by a minister (now deceased) [9] to reduce the status of the Objectives Resolution by incorporating the speech of 11 August 1947 into the constitution, and furthermore to place it above the Objectives

---

[3] Indeed Abul Kalam Azad, the Congressite Muslim divine, once stated: 'I must confess that the very term Pakistan goes against my grain. It suggests that some portions of it are pure while others are impure.' (Azad's press statement on 15 April 1946; NV Vol. IV, p.634 fn)

[4] 'Quaid-i-Azam' means 'great leader'. 'Ka'fir-i-Azam' means 'great unbeliever'.

[5] This was the original title of the Objectives Resolution.

[6] Liaquat Ali Khan (1895-1951), one of the central figures of the Pakistan movement. Famously described by Jinnah as his 'right hand man', Khan was the first Prime Minister of Pakistan, and he drafted and moved the Objectives Resolution. He was assassinated in 1951 for reasons that have never been clearly established.

[7] Speech of Liaquat Ali Khan, 7 March 1949. (G.W. Choudhury 1967, p.24)

[8] See for instance Munir 1980, p.36, and Air Marshall Asghar Khan's address to the Jinnah Society, Karachi, 20 April 2009 (as quoted by A. Cowasjee, 'Wise Words from an Old Warrior' in *Dawn*, 26 April 2009).

[9] M.P. Bhandara, (1938-2008). For biographical details, see Appendix VII

Resolution in order of appearance. The intent of its advocate was to place what was deemed to be a 'secular' speech above the undoubtedly 'Islamic' resolution, and thereafter claim that the constitution had been 'secularised', having the stamp of Jinnah himself on it. It happens that I took a personal interest in this story at the time and contacted this minister, which led to some unexpected developments. I have included the details of what happened in Appendix VII.

It is important that we look at the original Constituent Assembly debates that took place on the subject of the Resolution, not only because of the Resolution's constitutional and historical importance, but also because of the controversy surrounding it, and in particular the arguments of the secularist ministers in and the evidence they used to try and prevent its adoption in the Assembly. Since our focus is on the much-disputed 'ideology of Pakistan', the following discussion is limited to the arguments raised and the answers given by various individuals on the subject of the Objectives Resolution. I will not pass any comments whilst quoting from the transcript for the time being; we are simply reproducing the views of those involved in the debates of the time.

The Objectives Resolution disputed in the Constituent Assembly

When the Objectives Resolution was submitted to the Assembly by Liaquat Ali Khan on 7 March 1949, it received much criticism, mainly from the non-Muslim members of the Assembly. Though a few Muslims (mostly outside of the Assembly) were also unhappy with the Resolution, we shall leave aside their criticisms here, since the nature of these criticisms differed from that of the non-Muslims.[10]

The main issue of contention, as we have already mentioned, was the issue of sovereignty of God versus that of the people. The first paragraph of the Objectives Resolution reads:

> Whereas sovereignty over the entire universe belongs to God[11] Almighty alone and the authority which He has delegated to the

---

[10] In short, the few Muslims who unequivocally criticised the Resolution were from amongst the ulema. They felt that the Resolution placed too great an emphasis on the rights of non-Muslims and they disagreed with the idea of delegation of the power of God to Pakistan's people regardless of religion or creed. (See G.W. Choudhury (1959) *Constitutional Development in Pakistan* Lahore: Longman, Green & Co Ltd., p.57-8)

[11] The word 'God', obviously included as a universal reference to the Creator, was later replaced with 'Allah' via an amendment introduced by East Bengal minister Mohammad Akram Khan, when the Objectives Resolution became the Preamble of Pakistan's constitution. See its discussion and adoption on 27 October 1953, in *Constituent Assembly of Pakistan Debates: Official Report (1947-54)* in 21 volumes (hereinafter 'CAP Debates') Karachi: Government of Pakistan, Vol. XV No. 15, p.480-85.

State of Pakistan through its people for being exercised within the limits prescribed by Him is a sacred trust. [12]

The response from the non-Muslims was that this particular clause 'ought to be deleted'. [13] Mr S.C. Chattopadhyaya, [14] leader of the opposition party (Pakistan Congress Party) and the chief dissenter, maintained that all powers ought to rest with the people, and that the inclusion of God in the Resolution negated this. He also questioned what was meant by 'limits', and who would decide these limits. He suggested that in the future a despotic Muslim could abuse the clause to establish the 'Divine Right of Kings afresh'. [15] In other words, he treated the idea of sovereignty of God as it is understood in the West. [16]

The non-Muslim members also criticised the fourth paragraph of the proposed Resolution which stated that 'the principles of democracy, freedom, equality, tolerance and social justice, *as enunciated by Islam*, shall be fully observed' (emphasis mine). The objection was that by bringing Islam into the clause, the aforementioned principles had different implications for Muslims and non-Muslims, and differentiated between them as a (religious) majority versus minority. [17] In addition, Mr Chattopadhyaya quoted from a Muslim religious book [18] to allege that non-Muslims cannot be the head of an Islamic state, that the status of the non-Muslims in such a state is generally lower than that of the Muslims, and that there was no such thing as democracy in Islam.[19]

---

[12] Speech of Liaquat Ali Khan on Objectives Resolution, 7 March 1949. (CAP Debates Vol. V No. 1, p.1)

[13] Speech of Shri Sris Chandra Chattopadhyaya, 12 March 1949 (CAP Debates, Vol. V No. 5, p.89)

[14] Shri Sris Chandra Chattopadhyaya (1873-1966) was a former Indian Congress member who had chosen to remain in his native East Bengal after partition. In Pakistan he was the leader of the Pakistan Congress Party.

[15] Speech of S.C. Chattopadhyaya, 12 March 1949 (CAP Debates Vol. V No. 5, p.89-90). Chattopadhyaya made this statement despite Liaquat Ali Khan explaining in his opening speech in the days before that the principle of sovereignty of God as mentioned in the Resolution 'is not a resuscitation of the dead theory of Divine Right of Kings or rulers, because, in accordance with the spirit of Islam, the Preamble fully recognises the truth that authority has been delegated to the people, and to none else, and that it is for the people to decide who will exercise that authority.' (7 March 1949; CAP Debates Vol. V No.1, p.2-3)

[16] L. Binder (1961) *Religion and Politics in Pakistan* California: University of California Press, p.144

[17] S.C. Chattopadhyaya, 12 March 1949 (CAP Debates Vol. V No. 5, p.92)

[18] He referred to a Jamaat-i-Islami publication (ibid p.91). He also referred to conversations he'd had with 'some Maulanas from the Punjab' (ibid. p.90). G.W. Choudhury wrote with regret that the non-Muslim members had 'found it convenient to borrow passages from the utterances and writings of some extremists among the ulema, which had found no favour with the Muslim public.' (G.W. Choudhury 1959, p.87)

[19] CAP Debates Vol. V No. 5, p.91. Mr Chattopadhyaya's contentions, especially those about Islam and democracy, read remarkably like Munir's arguments in *From Jinnah to Zia*, as we will show in Chapter 4.

Further, the non-Muslim members alleged that the Objectives Resolution went against the wishes of Jinnah who had 'unequivocally said that Pakistan will be a secular state',[20] and who had intended to 'separate politics from religion'[21] in Pakistan. They brought in Jinnah's speech of 11 August 1947 (and only this speech) to substantiate their claims.[22] It was on these grounds that the non-Muslim members opposed the Islamic connotations of the Resolution and any move to make Pakistan an 'Islamic state'.

Based on these concerns, another leading member of the Congress Party, Mr B.K Dutta, moved two amendments to the Resolution: One, to have its first paragraph removed in its entirely, and two, the fourth paragraph, which contained the words, *as enunciated by Islam* to be edited to include 'other religions'. Other suggestions for amendments included that the Resolution should contain a reference to the 'Fundamental Human Rights of the United Nations Organisation', and that the word 'democratic' should be inserted into the document.[23]

Defence of the Objectives Resolution

The members of the ruling Pakistan Muslim League defended the Objectives Resolution with certitude. Liaquat Ali Khan and Sardar Abdur Rab Khan Nishtar[24] in particular made a strong case in favour of the Resolution and they did their best to allay the fears of the non-Muslim members. The Muslims' arguments are important, as they give us a good idea of how they understood the implications of the Resolution and most importantly, how they viewed the essence of an 'Islamic state'.

On the day Liaquat Ali Khan initially moved the Resolution, he had already given a speech which provided a clear and unambiguous explanation of what the Resolution meant. Before any objections to the sovereignty question were even raised, he had said:

> ... it has been made clear in the Resolution that the State shall exercise all its powers and authority through the chosen representatives of the people. ... This naturally eliminates any danger of the establishment of a theocracy. It is true that in its literal sense, theocracy means a Government of God; in this sense, however, it is patent that the entire universe is a theocracy,

---

20 See Birat Chandra Mandal's speech, 9 March 1949 (CAP Debates Vol. V No. 3, p.48)

21 Chattopadhyaya's speech on 12 March 1949 (CAP Debates Vol. V No. 5, p.93)

22 Ibid. This was the only proof that they offered at this time.

23 See the proposed amendments as listed in CAP Debates Vol. V No. 5, p.98-100.

24 Sardar Abdur Rab Khan Nishtar (1899-1958) was another prominent member of the Muslim League, and in Pakistan, he became the first Governor of Punjab. Himself a religious moderate of deep convictions, he was, alongside Liaquat Ali Khan, one of the more vocal proponents of an Islamic Pakistan, and unequivocally opposed to religious extremism.

> for is there any corner in the entire creation where His authority does not exist? But in the technical sense, theocracy has come to mean a Government by ordained priests … who claim to derive their rights from their sacerdotal position. I cannot over-emphasise the fact that such an idea is absolutely foreign to Islam. Islam does not recognise either priesthood or any sacerdotal authority; and, therefore, the question of a theocracy simply does not arise in Islam. [25]

Similarly Mian Mohammad Iftikhar-ud-Din[26] said that contrary to concerns that the Objectives Resolution gave the constitution a 'theocratic approach', it was not 'any the more theocratic, any the more religious than the Resolution or the statement of fundamental principles of some of the modern countries of the world.' [27] He reminded the House that referring to God in a constitution was not without precedent, and gave the example of Ireland as having a constitution 'which starts with somewhat similar words about God'. He also referred to the British Empire nations, practically all of which derived their authority 'through the agency of the king from God'. [28]

All the Muslim Leaguers were also unanimous on the fact that there is no official priesthood or 'licensed ulema' in Islam and so 'the Muslims can appeal to no other authority on earth than the people.' [29] In response to the suggestion to insert the word 'democratic' (to supersede Islam) in the Resolution, Sardar Nishtar said:

> I do not think, Sir, there can be genuine doubt in the mind of any person about the fact that what is meant by the Mover of this Resolution is a democratic constitution in the real sense of the term. It might be said then: Why don't you accept the word 'democratic'? Let me tell my friends that it is I think very right on the part of the Mover of the Resolution that he has avoided this

---

25 Liaquat Ali Khan, 7 March 1949 (CAP Debates Vol. V No. 1, p.3)

26 Mian Mohammad Iftikhar-ud-Din (1907-1962) was a liberal Muslim and an advocate of socialism. Sometimes referred to as a communist, a charge he denied, his socialist tendencies were either inspired by or at least in consonance with Islamic idealism, and for him it was not simply enough to name a country Islamic; it had to be followed through with meaningful action. As Minister for Rehabilitation of Refugees after partition, he proposed radical land reforms as a way to ease the settlement of migrants coming in from India and attributed these reforms to Islamic socialism. His proposals were met with hostility from landlords in the Pakistan Muslim League, prompting him to resign from his position. He was expelled from the League in April 1950 and in the same year he formed the short-lived secular Azad Pakistan Party. He continued to have problems with the government – including its takeover of his newspaper *Pakistan Times* under press control laws – until his death at the age of 54.

27 Speech of Mian Iftikhar-ud-Din, 10 March 1949 (CAP Debates Vol. V No. 4, p.51)

28 Ibid.

29 Ibid. p.52

> word. ... The word 'democratic' has lost all its meaning in the present-day world ... [30]

This echoed a similar statement made by Jinnah in 1940. [31] Having listed the monarchy of England, the presidential system of America, and France, Holland and Communist Russia as vastly different examples of countries that all claim to be 'democratic', Sardar Nishtar continued:

> Now how to interpret this word 'democratic' in the present-day world? [*sic*] How to interpret it when kings and no kings, presidents and no presidents, parliamentary system of Government and non-parliamentary system of Government and even a State like Russia, which is accused by the so-called democracies to be a dictatorship – all claim to be democratic states. I think it was better to avoid the word 'democratic', to give the real features of the State and leave it to the people to judge for themselves whether ours is a good constitution or a bad constitution. ... The nature of the State has not been described but the features – the important features – have been given. If the word 'democratic' had been used it would have been interpreted in the light of the present-day multifarious interpretations of this word that exist in the world in different manners by different people. [32]

In a similar vein, he negated the allegation that the words *as enunciated by Islam* would create 'patrician' and 'plebeian' classes, by saying that the concept of higher and lower classes was 'anti-Islamic'. [33] These arguments supported Liaquat Ali Khan's contention in his opening speech of 7 March 1949:

> You would notice, Sir, that the Objectives Resolution lays emphasis on the principles of democracy, freedom, equality, tolerance and social justice, and further defines them by saying that these principles should be observed in the constitution *as they*

---

30 Sardar Abdur Rab Khan Nishtar 's speech, 10 March 1949; (CAP Debates Vol. V No. 4, p.58)

31 In 1940 Jinnah criticised the Congress' idea of democracy in India by explaining that democracy means different things in different countries: 'They have kept sixty millions of people [*sic*] as untouchables; they have set up a system which is nothing but a "Grand Fascist Council." Their dictator [Gandhi] is not even a four-anna member of the Congress. They set up dummy ministries which were not responsible to the legislatures or the electorate but to a caucus of Mr Gandhi's choosing. Then, generally speaking, democracy has different patterns even in different countries of the West.' (Yusufi Vol. II, p.1159)

32 Sardar Abdur Rab Khan Nishtar 's speech, 10 March 1949 (CAP Debates Vol. V No. 4, p.58)

33 Ibid. p.59

> *have been enunciated by Islam*. It has been necessary to qualify these terms because they are generally used in a loose sense. For instance, the Western Powers and Soviet Russia alike claim that their systems are based upon democracy, and, yet, it is common knowledge that their polities are inherently different. [34]

With regards to the suggestion that the Resolution should contain a reference to the United Nations Declaration on Human Rights, Sardar Nishtar pointed out that comparing the text of the whole UN document with a single clause of the Objectives Resolution revealed it already contained 'much more' than the UN document. [35] It was a fair claim. The guidelines of the UN document notwithstanding, this was a period when apartheid was coming into force in South Africa; when non-white citizens of the US had fewer rights than white citizens; and when many countries had still not offered suffrage to women. The constitution was looking to make better guarantees for its people than other countries offered their peoples at that time.

Responding to the allegation that the Muslim members were going against the wishes of Jinnah, Sardar Nishtar remarked that 'Pakistan was demanded with a particular ideology' and that the Resolution did not go 'against the declarations of Quaid-i-Azam'. [36] Again, this supported a statement of a similar sentiment in Liaquat Ali Khan's opening speech.[37]

On the last day of the debates over the Resolution, Liaquat Ali Khan tackled the contention of Mr Chattopadhyaya that no non-Muslim could be head of state. He described the claim as 'absolutely wrong' and explained why:

> Sir, my friend said that these people told him that in an Islamic State – that means a State which is established in accordance with this Resolution – no non-Muslim can be the head of the administration. This is absolutely wrong. A non-Muslim can be the head of the administration under a constitutional government with limited authority that is given under the constitution to a person or an institution in that particular State. [38]

---

[34] CAP Debates Vol. V No. 1, p.3. Emphasis mine.

[35] Sardar Nishtar's speech, 10 March 1949 (CAP Debates Vol. V No. 4, p.60). See also Dr I.H. Qureshi's speech of 9 March 1949 (CAP Debates Vol. V No. 3, p.42), which makes a similar argument.

[36] Sardar Nishtar's speech, 10 March 1949 (CAP Debates Vol. V No. 4, p.62)

[37] Liaquat Ali Khan: '… by achieving independence we won an opportunity of building up a country and its polity in accordance with our ideals. I would like to remind the House that the Father of the Nation, the Quaid-i-Azam, gave expression to his feelings on this matter on many an occasion, and his views were endorsed by the nation in unmistakable terms.' (7 March 1949; CAP Debates Vol. V No. 1, p.2)

[38] Liaquat Ali Khan, 12 March 1949 (CAP Debates Vol. V No. 5, p.95)

Liaquat Ali Khan informed Mr Chattopadhyaya that the material he had used to support his objections had been produced by 'so-called ulemas' who had 'misrepresented the ideology of Islam' and were 'out to disrupt and destroy Pakistan'.[39] He reminded Mr Chattopadhyaya that these views did not represent that of 'the vast majority of Mussalmans'.[40] Liaquat Ali Khan's sentiments stemmed from the fact these theocratic ideas came from the same religious parties that had opposed the creation of Pakistan and which therefore had no public support in the country.

On the whole, the Muslim members were adamant that the Objectives Resolution was not a prelude to a theocracy. It may appear that the non-Muslim members were refusing outright to listen to them, but this is not necessarily the case. Here are the remarks of K.K Datta, another non-Muslim member who expressed his opposition to the Resolution, but having heard Liaquat Ali Khan's opening speech, conceded:

> It is a constitution meant for the people of Pakistan – Muslims and non-Muslims. As has been said, I must say the expression is a happy one in the preamble of the resolution itself, that the Almighty *Allah* [41] has delegated authority to the State of Pakistan through its *people*. It has not been limited to any one faith but to anyone and everyone who claims to be a citizen of Pakistan. … I am not a Muslim but what I understand by this is that the system of Government is also intended to be democratic. Islam recognises no distinction based upon race, colour or birth. [42]

Similarly, we find that though the Muslim members generally supported the Resolution in principle, they were not quite unanimous with regards to the content. Mian Iftikhar-ud-Din for instance criticised its wording. Although he understood the spirit of the first paragraph, he felt that it lent itself to 'mischievous interpretations':

> The authority descends to the people and not to the State and to say that through the people it comes to the State is all right, but why mention the State separately? … We know that the final authority to decide about the limits, the final authority to interpret the rights of the people, is the people themselves. To bring in, therefore, the agency of the state is to confuse the issue. [43]

---

39 Ibid. p.94

40 Ibid. p.95

41 The original text of the Objectives Resolution draft contained the word 'God', not 'Allah' (though technically there is no difference in sentiment). See relevant text of the Objectives Resolution presented by Liaquat Ali Khan, as reproduced earlier in this chapter and in Appendix VI.

42 K.K. Datta, 9 March 1949 (CAP Debates Vol. V No. 3, p.21; emphasis in original)

43 Speech of Mian Iftikhar-ud-Din, 10 March 1949 (CAP Debates Vol. V No. 4, p.51-2)

His primary concern was that a government in power could misuse the Preamble to justify a dictatorship:

> An occasion may arise when the state may give the excuse or the party in power may say that the people have exceeded the limits prescribed by the Almighty, and it may refuse to obey the people. [44]

On that count he was only reiterating the feelings of non-Muslims such as B.C. Mandal who felt that whilst the present members may have been reassured and made to understand the true spirit of the Resolution, there was still a danger that the 'posterity may misinterpret it'. [45]

Mian Iftikhar-ud-Din was the only vocal critic from among the Muslims in the Assembly, [46] though unlike the non-Muslim members he was not objecting to the sovereignty clause. Rather, he supported it. He was in fact more concerned that the Assembly was failing to put into place the beginnings of 'a proper Islamic constitution, a fine ideology, *a new way of achieving real democracy*'. He said there was nothing in the Resolution to make it a 'real Islamic democracy and constitution which would have been for the people and of the people'. [47] He wanted the Constituent Assembly to:

> … *incorporate those principles which will make real democracy possible*. And if it fails to do so that, at this stage I do hope it will do so in the actual constitution and then the world will know what we really meant by the *Islamic conception* of democracy and social justice. [48]

Academic verdict

Mian Iftikhar-ud-Din's warning notwithstanding, in the end the Constituent Assembly voted in favour of the Resolution.[49] Unfortunately the best efforts of the Muslim members had done little to allay the fears of the non-Muslim members. The Muslims voted in favour, and the Hindus (being the only non-Muslim group present) voted against. [50] It is

---

[44] Ibid. p.52

[45] Sardar Nishtar's speech (citing B.C. Mandal), 10 March 1949 (CAP Debates Vol. V No. 4, p.61)

[46] As noted in Choudhury 1959, p.58.

[47] Mian Iftikhar-ud-Din, 10 March 1949 (CAP Debates Vol. V No. 4, p.55). Emphasis mine.

[48] Ibid. (Emphasis mine)

[49] Mian Iftikhar-ud-Din was not present the day the Resolution was put to the vote.

[50] The tally of the votes for/against the Objectives Resolution is not shown in the record of the CAP Debates for 12 March 1949. However there is a tally of names recorded for that day when Liaquat Ali Khan presented an amendment (as proposed by Bhupendra Kumar Datta on 8 March 1949) to have the 'sovereignty … belongs to God' paragraph removed. The votes are counted as 10:21 (10 'ayes' from Hindus vs. 21 'noes' from Muslims); thereby the

not clear whether this is because the non-Muslims remained in doubt about the implications of the Objectives Resolution, or whether it was because none of the amendments they had suggested were adopted. It could simply be that the Hindu members were following a direct order of their leader to vote against the Resolution. [51]

Historians writing shortly after 1949 have differing views about what the Resolution actually meant for Pakistan. Prof. G.W. Choudhury has written that it was 'widely welcomed' in the country, as it reflected 'the aspirations and ideals of the people.' [52] He has also observed that the Resolution 'did not give any special privilege to the ulema, much less be run by them,' and that the Constituent Assembly 'was quite explicit in resolving that if Pakistan was to become an Islamic State, it should do so by the choice of its citizenry'. [53] Prof. Leonard Binder's views have some parallels with Choudhury's but do not quite meet in agreement. To Binder as well as to Choudhury, the Resolution implied a constitution for Pakistan which would not be identical with traditionalist and static concepts of Shariah [54] law envisioned by the ulema; hence, suggests Binder, the absence of the word 'Shariah' in the Objectives Resolution. [55] He notes that the main difference in opinion between the Muslim and non-Muslim members was centred on how each side interpreted 'sovereignty in God'; the non-Muslims were treating it 'in the supposedly technical sense as a term of political science' (i.e. a theocracy), whereas the Muslims understood it either as a 'polite nod in the direction of the mosque', or as a 'moral force joined to politics'.[56] He states further that the Resolution was sufficiently vague so as to be appealing to most sections of Muslims. He draws particular attention to the haziness of the sovereignty clause, remarking that the Resolution makes 'God sovereign, the people sovereign, parliament sovereign, and the state sovereign in Pakistan,' adding, 'it would indeed be a narrow-minded person who was not satisfied with such a compromise.' [57] Thus

---

amendment was negated (CAP Debates Vol. V No. 5, p.98). At any rate we can assume that the majority of non-Muslims (if not all) voted against the Objectives Resolution.

51 On the last day, just before the votes were cast and counted Mr Chattopadhyaya had essentially suggested that nothing could change his mind about the Resolution: 'I cannot persuade myself to accept this Resolution and my instruction to my party would be to oppose this Resolution.' (CAP Debates Vol. V No. 5, p.89) It would seem that Mr Chattopadhyaya was so vehemently opposed to the Objectives Resolution that he had no intention of either casting a vote himself or allowing anyone from his party to vote for it.

52 G.W. Choudhury 1959, p.59

53 G.W. Choudhury 1959, p.51

54 Shariah: A word for Muslim law. From the fundamentalist viewpoint, establishing Shariah means the recreation of early Muslim civilisation to the letter. This is of course a static view of Islam that is in direct conflict with the ever-evolving needs of human society as well as the teachings of the Quran.

55 L. Binder 1961, p.147

56 Ibid. p.144, 145

57 Ibid. 1961, p.149

he implies, cynically, that the Objectives Resolution was created for the appeasement of everyone but it was satisfactory to no one.

Here we might add the views of the late Chief Justice of Pakistan, Alvin R. Cornelius. [58] A Christian, Cornelius was well-versed in Islamic law, and he had his doubts regarding the long-term success of a purely materialistic society. For this reason he was of the opinion that Islamic values should be incorporated into Pakistan's legislation. In a personal letter in 1965, he wrote:

> ... I have learnt that a non-Muslim can only be a full citizen of Pakistan if, *on the secular side*, [59] he conforms to the requirements of the Objectives Resolution ... So far as I can see, at present, this is entirely possible, and would be easy, if there were some *formulation of the basic principles contained in the Scriptures of Islam*, in regard to equality, tolerance, social justice etc. [60]

Cornelius is not disconcerted by the Islamic content of the Objectives Resolution. Like Mian Iftikhar-ud-Din, he has identified the key to resolving the whole issue: The need to isolate the core principles of the Quran [61] that guarantee civil equality, social justice, freedom of conscience, etc. and to incorporate them into the constitution, so as to prevent misuse and misinterpretation.

The 'third ideology'

The record of the debates in the Constituent Assembly in March 1949 shows us that the Muslim vision for Pakistan was generally for a state that was in line with Jinnah's repeated declarations that Pakistan would 'not be a theocratic state' but rather an 'Islamic democracy'. It was to be brought into conformity with other modern states insofar as its operational structure was concerned, but whilst other (i.e. secular) democratic states were based on materialist values, Pakistan was to be built up 'on morality and on higher values of life than what materialism can provide.' [62] Some members hoped (as was said) that Pakistan would not choose between the 'two ideologies' of capitalism and communism, but would offer a 'third ideology' [63] representing an 'alternative system

---

[58] For biographical information, see Appendix II

[59] Emphasis in original.

[60] Alvin R. Cornelius to Dr Ralph Braibanti, 3 July 1965, in Ralph Braibanti (ed.) (1999) *Chief Justice Cornelius of Pakistan: An Analysis with Letters and Speeches* Karachi: Oxford University Press, p.184). Emphasis mine, except on the words 'on the secular side'.

[61] For a list of the core principles of the Quran, see Appendix I

[62] See Liaquat Ali Khan's remarks winding up the debate on the Resolution, 12 March 1949 (CAP Debates Vol. V No. 5, p.98)

[63] Nazir Ahmad Khan's speech, 12 March 1949 (CAP Debates Vol. V No. 5, p.82)

of life'.[64] Pakistan was going to innovate, not imitate. It would represent neither secularism nor theocracy, but, in line with Iqbal's thought, Islam moving in 'its own original spirit and with the spirit of modern times'.[65]

As romantic and idealistic as they may seem, these were the promises made in the first Constituent Assembly of Pakistan in 1949. Here we should place the remarks in the context of the wider political picture in the aftermath of World War II. The horrors of the war and the scale of destruction had made the countries of the world determined never to allow a repeat of it. The United Nations had adopted the Universal Declaration of Human Rights in December 1948 and the Declaration was understood to be a precedent to an international bill of rights. The appearance of Pakistan at this time was historically significant, especially since the Caliphate had recently been abolished (an event comparable to the end of theocracy and monarchy in Europe), and the Muslim world had entered a period of political uncertainty. Pakistan was seen by many (including Jinnah [66]) as an opportunity for the Muslims of India to create a new Islamic society, one which perhaps would provide an example for others to follow, and to give the Muslim world an honourable place in the comity of nations.

Secularists amongst Muslims

Though the record of the debates seems to show that there were only two distinct groups – Muslim and non-Muslim – in dispute over the Objectives Resolution, the reality is a little more complicated. So far, we have accounted only for those who openly defended the idea of Pakistan as an 'Islamic state'. Many of them had a what may be called a 'liberal' understanding of Islam, like Jinnah, Iqbal and Sir Syed Ahmad Khan before them; others leaned more towards traditionalism, and in a few cases, fundamentalism. This explains some of the contention between the Muslim members regarding the content of the Resolution. There was however another group of Muslim politicians whose views differed from that of their peers. They were secularists who were interested in seeing Pakistan as a conventional secular state rather than any sort of Islamic state. Both G.W. Choudhury and Leonard Binder have mentioned that in early Pakistan, the secularists among the Muslims were 'few' in number but 'very powerful'.[67] Prof. Choudhury interviewed some of these individuals and summarised their view as follows:

---

[64] Sardar Nishtar's speech, 10 March 1949 (CAP Debates Vol. V No. 4, p.62)

[65] M. Iqbal's Presidential speech at ML Annual Session, Allahabad, 29 December 1930. (Sherwani (ed.) 2008, p.13)

[66] Examples of Jinnah's speeches containing such sentiments appear in this book. See for example his speech at the State Bank of Pakistan cited in Myth no. 3 (Chapter 10), and his speech at Chittagong in Myth no. 10.

[67] L. Binder 1961, p.8; G.W. Choudhury 1959 p.76

> Their model is a secular democratic westernised state; they would probably accept Turkey as an example. Their apprehension is that if Pakistan accepts an Islamic Constitution the *Mullah* will control the State; they hold *Shariat* cannot be adequate for a modern complex society. … They point out that religions express unchanging precepts while life goes ahead and needs change rapidly. … It may be added here that like the *ulema* they look upon *Shariat* as static and incapable of any further development. They do not agree with the liberal advocates of an Islamic State that *Shariat* may be given a dynamic interpretation. … They expect that religiosity, the emotion on which Pakistan was based, will soon disappear and wish for a Kamal Ataturk in Pakistan to found a secular State. [68]

Neither Prof. Choudhury nor Prof. Binder tells us who these individuals were, [69] but it can safely be said that it was probably due to their awareness of majority public opinion that most Muslim secularists preferred to remain anonymous. This is likely also the reason that they deliberately remained silent on the issue of the Objectives Resolution at the time. In any case, it could be said that the constitution that evolved in the hands of the First Constituent Assembly had enough in common structurally with a 'secular' state to satisfy them for the time being. [70] Only later, after the activities of the extremist religious parties created a crisis, and thereby played in their favour, did the Muslim secularists of Pakistan gradually become more vocal. The Lahore riots of 1953 and the subsequent Munir Report would later become the secularists' best proof of the folly of allowing religion to interfere in politics. The irony however is that while non-Muslims had worried about religious despots overthrowing the government, the first person to later flout the principle of democracy and dissolve the Constituent Assembly in October 1954 was an affirmed secularist. He was the second Governor-General [71] of Pakistan, Malik Ghulam Mohammed. [72]

---

[68] G.W. Choudhury 1959 p.76-7. Spellings and emphases of Muslim terms retained from original text.

[69] Binder does however point at them through their own statements and actions that indicate they support a secular state, or that they believe religion and politics ought to be kept separate (op. cit. p.303-4, 361, 364). They include (among others) Iskander Mirza and Ghulam Mohammed.

[70] As we will show in the next chapter, this was certainly true for the fiscal part of the constitution.

[71] Up until the implementation of the Pakistan constitution of 1956, the title of Pakistan's head of state was Governor-General.

[72] Ideologically Ghulam Mohammed (1895-1956) is a perplexing personality. He was the first Finance Minister of Pakistan (1947-51), and became Governor-General of Pakistan (1951-55) after Liaquat Ali Khan's assassination. He retained this position until illness forced him to resign. Scholarship tends to agree that Ghulam Mohammed was an able finance minister, as evidenced by his work on Pakistan's budget in the early years of Pakistan. In toeing the League party line he appeared to back a secular-Muslim synthesis, as indicated in the evolving

1949-1954

On the day that the Objectives Resolution was adopted in 1949, the Constituent Assembly set up a Basic Principles Committee to determine the basic principles of the future constitution which would have to be consistent with the aims set out in the Objectives Resolution. The Report produced by this Committee would provide the foundations of the constitution. As the Resolution was Islam-orientated, in April 1949 a subcommittee (Board of the Talimat-i-Islamia) representing scholarly opinion was set up to make its own recommendations on making the constitution Islamic. [73] This board was viewed with suspicion by many, especially non-Muslims, who felt that such steps were being taken to turn Pakistan into a theocratic state. In fact the Board existed strictly as an advisory body, and was not made up of 'fanatics'. [74] It also had very little impact until after 1951, when Khwaja Nazimuddin [75] had taken over as Prime Minister following the assassination of Liaquat Ali Khan. The first Interim Report of the BPC (1950) had contained almost nothing in terms of what the ulema (at least from the orthodox section) wanted to see in an Islamic constitution. [76] It appears that under Liaquat Ali

---

BPC Report (discussed above). He is also credited with organising the first International Islamic Economic Conference in 1949, although Liaquat Ali Khan initiated this conference via a tour of Muslim countries expressly undertaken to strengthen political ties (L. Binder p.188-9), and the idea was based on Jinnah's hopes for an Islamic economic system that might be an example for the world (see Jinnah's address at the Opening Ceremony of the State Bank of Pakistan as cited in Chapter 10, Myth no. 3). The conference was attended by delegates across the Muslim world, and in his opening speech Ghulam Mohammed advanced the idea of a Muslim bloc with what he called an 'Islamic politico-economical ideology' (See his opening speech, 25 March 1949; as reproduced in *The Islamic Review* Vol. XXXVIII, No. 2 (February 1950), p.34, 35). His speech at this conference makes a strong advocacy of Islam as 'ideology' and there is no allusion at all to secularism. Yet his actions as Governor-General, as detailed in the next chapter, signify (as historians including G.W. Choudhury and L. Binder maintain) that he was a secularist all along, especially in view of his close alliance with Munir. Understandably, his ideological inconsistency as well as his authoritarianism has invited distrust and condemnation from later commentators.

73 More specifically, the aim of the Board was to work on how to implement the 'enabling clause' of the Objectives Resolution in practice. (L. Binder 1961, p.156. For the full text of the Objectives Resolution and its enabling clause, see Appendix VI)

74 See A.H. Syed (1982) *Pakistan: Islam, Politics and National Solidarity* New York: Praeger Publishers, p.80. Syed adds that the ulema were willing 'gradualists and often ready to compromise.' (Ibid.)

75 Khwaja Nazimuddin (1894-1964) was originally Chief Minister of East Bengal. He became Governor-General of Pakistan after Jinnah, acting as a figurehead while Liaquat Ali Khan, then Prime Minister, commanded authority in practice. After Liaquat Ali Khan's death in 1951, Nazimuddin relinquished the post in order to take over as Prime Minister, while Ghulam Mohammed became Governor-General. Ghulam Mohammed was very ill (having suffered a stroke) and it was assumed that he too would be simply a figurehead, but subsequent events proved otherwise (see above).

76 The Directive Principles of State Policy in the 1950 Interim Report was the only section in which the 'Holy Quran and the Sunna' were mentioned explicitly. (G.W. Choudhury (1967) *Documents and Speeches on the Constitution of Pakistan* Dacca: Green Book House, p.34) There was no limitation on who could be Head of State (later the criterion for Head of State became

Khan's leadership, the views of the ulema had not been given precedence. Prime Minister Khwaja Nazimuddin however seemed more predisposed towards traditionalist Islam and to the opinion of the ulema. In 1952 he presented a new constitutional draft in which 'a board of ulema' (not his words) [77] would be authorised to help the president decide which legislation was repugnant to the Quran and Sunnah (traditional practices) under certain conditions. [78] However this was met with strong public disapproval, so the Constituent Assembly rejected the proposal. In the final BPC Report of 1954 – by which time Muhammad Ali of Bogra was Prime Minister – the power to decide what was repugnant to the Quran and Sunnah was given to the Supreme Court.

The 1952 draft also contained clauses explicitly demanding the abolition of *riba* (interest) 'as soon as may be possible to do so', without giving any timeframe, and the 'proper organisation of zakat, [79] Waqfs [80] and Mosques'. [81] Most significantly perhaps, his draft was the first to include the requirement that the head of state should be a Muslim. However, the draft was also self-contradictory, reflecting a secular-Muslim thought process. [82] Whilst *riba* (interest) was to be abolished in

---

that he/she must be a Muslim). The rest of the Interim Report reads like any other contemporary constitution. It contains almost nothing to distinguish it from a contemporary secular state – except of course the Objectives Resolution, which was to become incorporated into the Constitution 'as a Directive Principle of State Policy, subject to the provision that that this will not prejudice the incorporation of Fundamental Rights in the Constitution at the proper place'. (Part I, paragraph 1; G.W. Choudhury 1967, p.34)

77 These are the words of Choudhury in op. cit. 1959, p.79, possibly borrowing from the language utilised by the ulema themselves in their suggested amendments to the BPC Report 1952, with reference to the repugnancy clause. See end of next footnote.

78 See Chapter III, paragraph 5 (G.W. Choudhury 1967, p.72). The proposal was interpreted by later commentators to mean that a 'board of ulema' (meaning clerics) would have been given this jurisdiction (again see G.W. Choudhury 1959, p.79), but ulema were not explicitly mentioned either in the draft or in Mr Nazimuddin's opening speech in which he explained the purpose of the Board (22 December 1952; Choudhury 1967 p.63). Paragraph 5 of the Report actually stated that there should be 'a Board consisting of not more than five persons well versed in Islamic Laws'. No provisions were made about the qualifications required for being a Board member. Furthermore, the Board was to act merely as an advisory body to the Head of State. It would assess a given bill and make recommendations regarding a given bill if (and only if) a Muslim member raised a formal objection to the bill on the basis that it might be repugnant to the Quran or Sunnah. The final decision to accept, amend or reject the bill would at any rate remain with the Federal Legislature (though it also required that the majority of Muslim members be present and voting). Incidentally we find the term 'Board of ulema' in the text of the ulema's own suggested list of amendments to the BPC Report 1952 (see their list dated 11-18 January 1953; as reproduced in G.W. Choudhury 1967, p.987).

79 *Zakaat*: see Chapter 14

80 *Waqf* – in Muslim inheritance law, money or property bequeathed by a Muslim for religious, educational or charitable purposes.

81 BPC Report 1952, Chapter II, Paragraphs 2, a-e. (G.W. Choudhury 1967, p.70)

82 See Prime Minister Nazimuddin's opening statement as he presented the finished Report to the Constituent Assembly on 22 December 1952: 'We should also remember that the Objectives Resolution laid certain heavy responsibilities upon us in so far as the principles enunciated by Islam had to be interpreted in terms of democratic constitutional practice of the 20th century. Such a course needed careful thinking, discussion and deliberation so that

Chapter II, money bills were to be made exempt from the 'repugnancy' clause of Chapter III. [83] It could be that whoever was responsible for the wording implicitly understood *riba* to mean 'usury' (*excessive* interest) and not merely 'interest'; [84] but this does not change the fact of the contradiction insofar as numerous fiscal matters – crucial to the running of this otherwise Islamic state – were to be relegated to the 'secular' sphere. [85] One obvious consequence of this was to indefinitely postpone any serious discussion on landlordism, even though Liaquat Ali Khan (as well as others including Mian Iftikhar-ud-Din) had intended to abolish this contemptible practice as a part of government policy. [86] The draft thus both supported and obstructed Islamic economics, betraying the lack of intellectual cohesion among even the early leaders of Pakistan.

Most historians agree that Mr Nazimuddin was not a strong political leader. Prof. Choudhury observes that it was during Nazimuddin's tenure that political rivalries led to factions in the cabinet. [87] The final straw came when Mr Nazimuddin failed to nip the Ahmadi controversy

---

we could bring about a *synthesis* not only of the fundamental teachings of our faith and the requirements of progressive democracy but also of the requirements of the 20th century and best elements in our own tradition and history.' (CAP Debates Vol. XII No. 2, p.47; emphasis mine.) Since Nazimuddin was also inclined towards conservative traditionalism, his statement for synthesis suggests an attempt to account for the standpoint of both sides of the intellectual divide, including on the (secular side) former Finance Minister Ghulam Mohammed, who had been appointed as Governor-General in October 1952.

83 Chapter III, paragraph 7. (G.W. Choudhury 1967, p.73).

84 See dictionary definition of the word *riba* given in Chapter 14

85 Incidentally, the ulema also pointed out this contradiction in 1953, describing the exemption to money bills as 'a clear vote of no-confidence against Islam in one of the Sections of our Constitution' [*sic*]. But they accepted that since there might necessarily be an adjustment period and in view of the 'practical difficulties' involved, the exemption should only remain in force for a limit of five years. ('Ulema's Amendments to The Basic Principles Committee's Report', Jamaat-i-Islami, Karachi, 11-18 January 1953; as reproduced in G.W. Choudhury 1967, p.988)

86 Liaquat Ali Khan always had a reputation for defending the economic rights of underprivileged people. In 1943 Jinnah had described him as a 'thorough proletarian'. (Speech on the occasion of the election of Nawabzada Liaquat Ali Khan as the Honorary General Secretary of the AIML at the Karachi Session, 26 December 1943; NV Vol. III, p.356) As Finance Minister in pre-partition India's Interim Government (1946-7), Liaquat Ali Khan demonstrated his loyalty to the proletariat; in the budget he presented on 28 February 1947, he proposed a tax of 25 per cent tax on all business profits totalling over 100,000 rupees. V.P. Menon, the right-hand man of Sardar Patel, has described the Congress' reaction thus: 'This was interpreted in Congress circles as an attempt to penalize the Hindu capitalists (who largely financed the Congress) and to bring about dissension between the right wing and the socialist group within the Congress Party.' (V.P. Menon (1957) *The Transfer of Power in India* Princeton: Princeton University Press, p.348). The budget had later become known as the 'Poor Man's Budget'. Later as Pakistan's Prime Minister, Liaquat Ali Khan's objective of outlawing landlordism was met with strong resistance from capitalist landlords (*zamindars*), who had tried to obtain religious sanction for continuing their exploitive existence from some unscrupulous orthodox ulema. For a detailed albeit cynical discussion of Liaquat Ali Khan's policy, see L. Binder 1961, p.185-190; 211. For a brief review of Mian Iftikhar-ud-Din's advocacy of socialist policies, see footnote 26 above.

87 G.W. Choudhury 1959, p.43; also R. Ahmad 1981, p.58.

in the bud. [88] It is likely that the political embarrassment to Pakistan caused by Prime Minister Nazimuddin's poor handling of the Punjab disturbances ultimately gave Ghulam Mohammed an excuse to dismiss his ministry in April 1953, though this certainly wasn't the only reason; Ghulam Mohammed was also among those Punjabi politicians who had strongly opposed the federal provisions in the 1952 BPC Report, since they favoured East Bengal. [89] Whilst Nazimuddin's dismissal was certainly an undemocratic move, it raised little protest from the Constituent Assembly, [90] probably because Ghulam Mohammed had the support of some ministers in the Cabinet [91] (not to mention from the military; the new cabinet contained a number of army officers including Iskander Mirza and Muhammad Ayub Khan, both of whom respectively later headed authoritarian regimes as President of Pakistan). Thereafter Ghulam Mohammed appointed Muhammad Ali of Bogra as Prime Minister, and some of those who replaced Nazimuddin's ministry publicly indicated that Pakistan may now develop as a 'secular' (non-theocratic) state.[92]

Yet under the new 'secular' government, even while progress was made with regards to federal representation that would satisfy both wings of the country, [93] the evolving BPC Report and finalised constitution fared no better on the ideological front than it had under Nazimuddin's, receiving blunt criticism in the Constituent Assembly for

---

88 See Chapter 4.

89 Christophe Jaffrelot (2015) (translated by Cynthia Schoch) *The Pakistan Paradox: Instability and Resilience* New York: Oxford University Press, p.207-8. The earlier 1950 Interim Report had been criticised by East Bengal for under-representing their province in the upper house of the parliament (all the provinces were given parity of representation, even though East Bengal had a bigger population than the entire West wing of Pakistan). The 1952 BPC Report, by contrast, attempted to redress the parity issue in the upper house by turning the provinces of West Pakistan into nine units and allocating seats accordingly, but it came under fire from the Punjab (including Ghulam Mohammed), as this effectively gave East Bengal the same representative power as that of every other unit combined (notwithstanding East Bengal's peculiar geopolitical position as being simultaneously a wing of Pakistan as well as a single unit). (See also G.W. Choudhury 1959, p.107-112)

90 Nishtar however (who was amongst the dismissed ministry members) expressed his condemnation in Urdu verse:

نیرنگِ سیاستِ دوراں تو دیکھئے　　منزل انھیں ملی جو شریکِ سفر نہ تھے

'Look at the irony of contemporary politics / Those who shunned the Caravan have reached the Destination!' (as cited in S. Mujahid 'Sardar Abdur Rab Nishtar: an Appreciation' in *Dawn*, 30 December 2006)

91 G.W. Choudhury 1959, p.44.

92 See Binder 1961, p.303-4, for some quotations made by one or two such ministers to the press. One of them used the word 'secular' explicitly as a contrast to 'theocratic', and another said that the 'church' should be subordinated to the state, whilst also recognising that the state would be guided by the principles of Islam. Since even most mainstream Muslims would agree that there is no theocracy sanctioned in Islam, it is clear what is meant here by 'secular'.

93 Under the 'Bogra formula', as it was known, the 9 units of Pakistan became 4, thereby creating a better balance of representation.

its un-Islamic character; [94] and in any case, as will be discussed in the next chapter, it would never be implemented.

[94] The speeches of Mian Iftikhar-ud-Din from the West Punjab side and Abul Kasem Khan from the East Bengal side on 22 October 1953 are sufficient to illustrate the level of contempt shown (by Muslim ministers at least) towards the lack of Islamic provisions in the Report during this period. Iftikhar-ud-Din decried the fact that Liaquat Ali Khan's promise in 1949 to show the world a 'real' democracy had been reduced by the Constituent Assembly into a mere 'slogan', and that the new constitution, far from being 'Islamic', was 'derogatory to the ideology' and had 'betrayed' the 'interests of the Muslims' as well as the 'minorities' (CAP Debates Vol. XV No. 11, p.292, 294). Abul Kasem Khan warned that simply calling Pakistan an 'Islamic State' in name would not be enough to make it so; he was anxious to 'stress … very strongly' that the people '[would] not be satisfied if we fail in securing for them the substances of Islam, the substance of freedom, the substance of existence without which it would be futile for us to expect that we can offer them an ideology which is better than capitalism on the one hand and communism on the other.' (Ibid. p.283)

Chapter 4
1954: Debate to dissolution

In the previous chapter we saw that an ideological dichotomy existed among the early leaders of Pakistan. Throughout the ongoing process of constitutional wrangling, the non-Muslim members of the Constituent Assembly (who, as we have noted already, were the only vocal secularists in Pakistan at the time) had continually decried the Objectives Resolution for supposedly being against the wishes of the Quaid-i-Azam, but they had always been hard put to find any declarations in support of their claim, except for the speech of 11 August 1947. [1] The secularists amongst the Muslims had been generally silent, and as we shall see now, they remained so in 1954. The majority of their peers were still committed to an 'Islamic state' which would uphold Islamic principles without conforming to fundamentalist thought. However as we shall see, there was a lack of consensus as to what constituted the features of such a state. The result was a BPC Report of 'compromises', which only served to prove the lack of cohesion, whether political or religious, between the various Muslim leaders (not to mention the discord between these and non-Muslim leaders).

Overview

In this chapter, we shall take an in-depth look at the debates of 1954, in which the non-Muslim members of the first Constituent Assembly brought in new and improved evidence to argue against the proposed 'Islamic state', evidence which would also a direct effect on academic and public perceptions of Jinnah and the Pakistan idea in the coming years. From the Muslim ministers' counterarguments we will also see some of the attempts to imbue the constitution with Islamic principles.

Historians have often visited these debates to assess the reasons behind the forced dissolution of the first Constituent Assembly. Here we are focusing on the ideological dimension of these debates, which at any rate took up far more time of the Constituent Assembly in those few weeks than is perhaps appreciated. Nevertheless, the events leading up to the dissolution can be summed up as follows.

---

1 Interestingly Dr Khalid bin Sayeed, in his publication of 1960 (and apparently unaware of the Munir quote), describes the 11 August 1947 speech as a 'singularly secular note'. (Khalid bin Sayeed (1960) *Pakistan: The Formative Phase*, Karachi: Pakistan Publishing House, p.409)

As we have noted previously, Ghulam Mohammed had already shown his willingness to take a heavy-handed approach in sacking Nazimuddin's Cabinet in 1953.[2] Though no one had openly opposed his decision, the real feelings of certain members in the Constituent Assembly became manifest over the next year, through amendments to the present constitution [3] that were designed to gradually strip the Governor-General of most of his powers and transfer them to the central government. The ministers were clearly trying to insure themselves from similar acts of dismissal in the future. These actions were arguably questionable in ethical terms. On the one hand, the Governor-General's position had always been (after Jinnah's death) that of a constitutional head whilst the Prime Minister and the Cabinet wielded power; [4] and since the amendments only solidified the supremacy of the parliament, they could, as Prof. Choudhury holds, be viewed as a step towards the proper establishment of a parliamentary democracy. [5] On the other, as Prof. Binder points out, it was also (at least in part) a personal tactic against Ghulam Mohammed; transitional laws were also written such that he was the only one who was not assured of continuing in his present job when the constitution would go into effect. [6] Most significantly however, Ghulam Mohammed never formally expressed any concern about the development of the BPC Report until after 21 September 1954, when some final amendments were hastily rushed through the House, without due consideration to normal procedure.

All in the name

For the moment, let us go back a few weeks to 24 August 1954. On that day, the Assembly gathered to discuss the Report of the Committee on Fundamental Rights of Citizens of Pakistan and on Matters Relating to Minorities. There had been much contention on allowing separate electorates for minorities (the Hindus of East Bengal were against separate electorates), and so this was the issue raised in the early part of the meeting. It was essentially a political issue; soon however, the discussion took a more ideological slant. Again it was Mr Chattopadhyaya who shifted the focus of the conversation. He first

---

[2] Prof. Choudhury states that Ghulam Mohammed had the support of a 'group within the cabinet', without taking names. (G.W. Choudhury 1959, p.42, 44)

[3] The powers granted to the Governor-General at the time of partition are reviewed in Chapter 14, subsection 'Jinnah's power'

[4] See G.W. Choudhury 1959, p.39-43. However he also makes it clear that he does not condone their actions.

[5] G.W. Choudhury 1959, p.143

[6] L. Binder 1961, p.355-6. The position of 'Governor-General' was to be replaced with 'President', and during the transitional period before the next election, the serving Governor-General would not automatically become President, but rather a provisional President would be elected by the Constituent Assembly.

accused the present government of having become increasingly apathetic to minority concerns and leaning too much in favour of the ulema who were trying to exert their influence on state policy. He condemned Khwaja Nazimuddin for having 'succumbed' to the 'maulanas'. [7] His party felt that after Liaquat Ali Khan's death, the various constitutional and legislative drafts had changed to the extent that non-Muslims were effectively about to lose their rights of citizenship. Looking at the transcript, we find that the non-Muslims had three major grievances: First, the fact that only a Muslim could be head of state; second, the so-called 'repugnancy clause'; and thirdly, the fact of Pakistan being legally called an 'Islamic state'. If Pakistan became an Islamic state, they argued, non-Muslims would no longer be allowed to be members of the Legislature. Although the power to interpret whether a given law conformed to the 'repugnancy clause' had been given to the Supreme Court, the non-Muslim members feared that someone would soon challenge this and give this power back to the religious elite. [8] They believed that some mullahs would not accept legislative decisions made by the Supreme Court. They also expressed their anger at the provision for an 'Ecclesiastical Department to propagate Muslim religion', which they interpreted to mean that no non-Muslim would be allowed to propagate his/her faith on pain of 'death'. [9] As before, they raised the argument that in an Islamic state, the punishment for apostasy is death, this time bringing in the Ahmadi issue as their case in point. [10]

The non-Muslim members believed that the aforementioned features of the BPC Report would turn Pakistan into a 'theocratic state with Mullah raj [*sic*] at the helm of affairs'. [11] Therefore they demanded that the Constituent Assembly ought to 'revise and repeal the words 'Islamic Federation'' [12] and take every step necessary to make Pakistan a secular state. They went as far as to give Turkey and Indonesia as examples of Muslim-majority countries that were presently secular states, and that even other Middle-Eastern nations with close to 100 percent Muslim populations had not 'declared themselves as Islamic states' because they supposedly knew 'some difficulties will arise.' [13]

---

7 CAP Debates Vol. XVI No. 23, p.289

8 This claim was made despite the fact that all citizens were allowed to appeal to the court on contentious issues regardless of faith. Paragraph 7 of the BPC Report (1954) reads: 'Every citizen of Pakistan should have a right to challenge the validity of the legislation on the ground of such repugnancy'. (*Report of the Basic Principles Committee* (hereinafter 'BPC Report 1954') (adopted 21 September 1954) Karachi: Government of Pakistan, p.4. Emphasis mine).

9 See Mr Chattopadhyaya's speech, Debates Vol. XVI, p.292-3. The clause in question was Chapter III, paragraph 11 (p.5 of the BPC Report 1954).

10 CAP Debates Vol. XVI No. 23, p.289, 293

11 Ibid. p.289

12 Ibid. p.290. As such, the exact words 'Islamic Federation' did not appear in the BPC 1954 document.

13 Ibid. p.290

Déjà vu

As had happened before, the Muslim leaders, led by Sardar Nishtar, were quick to defend the BPC Report at the next Constituent Assembly meeting. [14] To summarise briefly, Sardar Nishtar reminded the House that whilst the head of state had to be a Muslim, all other positions, including that of the Prime Minister, were open to all citizens of Pakistan regardless of caste, creed or sect. [15] The religious prerequisite for the presidency was compared to the religious requirement for the monarchy of other nations; in fact the president would be a 'constitutional head' with fewer powers than the Queen of England. [16] Besides which, he argued, nothing barred non-Muslims from becoming a 'Minister or even Prime Minster of Pakistan,' which both involved an advisory role to the president and therefore wielded more authority. [17] They could also become Commander-in-Chief of the Army.

The accusation regarding the supposed inability of non-Muslims to participate in the legislature was refuted with the argument that the non-Muslims had been afforded the exact same rights as Muslims in suffrage and in joining the Legislature, and were equally entitled to become chief justice of the Supreme Court, with all the accompanying legislative powers. [18] In response to the allegation that non-Muslims would not be allowed to propagate their faiths, Sardar Nishtar reminded the House that the universal right to propagate one's faith had been incorporated into the Fundamental Rights document at article 10. [19] Furthermore, the actual purpose of setting up the so-called ecclesiastical department, as he would explain later, was not proselytisation but education. It was in the best interests of all citizens to be familiar with the principles of Islam in order that they would be equipped to protect their own rights using those same principles. [20]

Finally, with regards to the repugnancy clause, Sardar Nishtar said the Quran itself recognised that there was a 'sphere of life which has been left to the discretion of the people'. In traditional Islamic terminology, he maintained, matters falling into this category 'are known as *Mabahat*', [21] and cover '95 percent of affairs'. [22] His point was that Pakistan could adopt a contemporary type of legislature without

---

[14] See text of proceedings, 31 August 1954. (CAP Debates Vol. XVI No. 24, p.301 et seq.)

[15] Sardar Nishtar, CAP Debates, Vol. XVI No. 24, p.325

[16] Ibid.

[17] Ibid.

[18] Ibid.

[19] Text reads: 'Freedom of conscience and the right to profess, practice and propagate religion is guaranteed.' *Fundamental Rights of Citizens of Pakistan and on Matters Relating to Minorities* (adopted 7 September 1954) Karachi: Government of Pakistan, Part II paragraph 10.

[20] See speeches of Abdul Hamid and Sardar Nishtar, 21 September 1954. CAP Debates Vol. XVI No. 31, p.526-7, 560 respectively.

[21] *Mabahat* (or *mubah*), a word for permissible, allowed, proper, or lawful.

[22] Sardar Nishtar, 31 August 1954. (CAP Debates Vol. XVI No. 24, p.328)

infringing upon the principles of the Quran. Whilst the concept of adaptability in Islam is not necessarily wrong in itself, in view of what was being introduced in the BPC Report it was a weak argument. In no way could it justify the exemption of fiscal matters (essential in shaping the nature of the state) from the repugnancy clause and for delaying the 'abolition of *riba*' for at least 25 years. [23] Quite rightly (as we shall see later in this chapter), this discrepancy was seized upon by the non-Muslims in the opposition, and no explanation was offered on the Muslim side. [24] Later, Sardar Nishtar would offer the additional argument that the repugnancy clause had been stated in a negative form, [25] which is usually legally significant; but this too would be insufficient to convince the opposition.

Enter the Munir Report

So far we see that the debate followed a similar pattern in both 1949 and 1954. The non-Muslim members received the constitutional drafts with alarm, and the Muslim members tried to explain and counter where necessary (though at times, the arguments seemed to be between Mr Chattopadhyaya and Sardar Nishtar more than anyone else). However, there was one fundamental difference between the two sets of debates (aside from the intellectual gulf among various Muslim members), and that was the evidence.

In 1949, when relations between the Constituent Assembly members were relatively cordial, the opposition party opposed the Objectives Resolution on the grounds that it opened a backdoor to theocracy. In support of their contention, the non-Muslim members referred to the literature of fundamentalist parties to support their allegations. They in turn were rebuked for giving attention to the fanatical views of people who were at any rate 'traitors' and the former opponents of partition and Pakistan. Jinnah's name was of course brought into the argument, along with his speech of 11 August 1947, to remind the House that

---

23 BPC Report 1954, Chapter III article 10 (Compare with the 1952 draft mentioned in Chapter 3, where no time frame was given). It is far more likely, however, that materialism was the sole motivation behind the inclusion of these articles. Binder has observed that whilst the Governor of the State Bank (Zahid Hussain) had understood the term *riba* to mean 'interest' of any amount, some members of the Constituent Assembly felt that since *riba* was now to be eliminated 'as and when' rather than 'as soon as' it would be acceptable to also review the definition of the term *riba*. A.K. Brohi for example was of the opinion that 'we are entitled to adjust it [*riba*] to suit the given conditions and it has in fact been so adjusted down the ages.' (28 October 1953; CAP Debates Vol. XV No. 16, p.511; as cited in L. Binder 1961, p.329-30)

24 See Dr Raj Kumar Chakraverty's speech, 21 September 1954 (CAP Debates Vol. XVI No. 31, p.508) and Shri Kamini Kumar Datta's speech. (Ibid. p.520)

25 In other words, the statement did not read: 'Laws *must* conform to the Quran and Sunnah' (a positive statement) but rather: '*No* Legislature should enact any law which is repugnant …' See Nishtar's speech on 21 September 1954. CAP Debates Vol. XVI No. 31, p.558

Pakistan ought to be a secular state, but this attempt too was soon laid to rest with references to other speeches of Jinnah suggesting otherwise.

With the publication of the Munir Report in 1954 however, the secularists acquired what they saw as an authoritative critique of the Islamic state, highlighting the confused and at times extreme views of ulema from various schools of thought. Furthermore, it presented a new, hitherto unquoted speech of Jinnah, the words of which were conveniently at variance with the words of the Objectives Resolution, [26] and which at the same time had words in common with the speech of 11 August 1947, thereby supporting the contention that Jinnah was a secularist. What made the Report even more appealing to the secularists was that it was produced by two educated Muslims who also happened to be judges. (After the Court of Inquiry was concluded, Munir became Chief Justice of Pakistan (or Chief Justice of the Federal Court, as it was known before it became the Supreme Court).

The Chattopadhyaya quote?

We have already reviewed the ideological dimension of the debates on 24 August 1954, but we have yet to see how the opposition party used the Munir Report.

Again, Mr Chattopadhyaya took the lead:

> … latterly we found that they [Muslims] want to establish an Islamic State. My friend, Khwaja Nazimuddin, said one day 'Why are you afraid of [an] Islamic State?' We knew why we are afraid of [an] Islamic State! This has got a technical meaning. What are the rights of the non-Muslims in the Islamic State? I said late Mr Jinnah *told me* Pakistan would be *a modern democratic state.* [27]

The source of his quote is immediately obvious today, but it would not have been so at the time. Chattopadhyaya introduced the evidence:

> On this point, my friend, Sardar Nishtar, said he wanted evidence. Mr Jinnah was an old friend of mine. We were in the same party, the extremist party in the Congress. I had [a] long discussion with Mr Jinnah on the 21st of March, 1948. That was my last meeting with him in Dacca. … when I met him, he kept me there for 45 minutes. … some of the other visitors were furious that I had spoilt their chances of meeting him. … I shall quote what he said. I have not the book with me … but now I

---

[26] The Objectives Resolution declares that sovereignty belongs to Allah; in the Munir quote, it belongs to the people. See the 'three-piece argument' of Munir's *From Jinnah to Zia* as reviewed in Chapters 2 and 5.

[27] CAP Debates, Vol. XVI No. 23, p.288. Spellings are rendered as in the original here and throughout.

quote [from memory]. He said the new State would be a *modern* State. I shall give the evidence to Mr Nishtar, when I have got the book.[28]

The book in question is of course the Munir Report, as he soon confirmed. Note here that Chattopadhyaya is referring to the day that Mr Jinnah had met Hindu and Scheduled Caste deputations from the East Pakistan Assembly. The event was highly publicised, and in his address to these deputations Jinnah had assured them that minorities would be safeguarded and protected. As for matters relating to the constitution, he had explicitly stated that they would be dealt with by the Constituent Assembly (and hence he declined to answer their questions himself that day).[29] This is particularly important in light of Mr Chattopadhyaya's speech to the House, in which he remembered:

> ... Mr Jinnah *told me* the new State would be a modern democratic State, with sovereignty resting in the people.[30]

Mr Chattopadhyaya alleged that these were Jinnah's private words in 1948, as opposed to 1946, or 1947 (depending on whom you ask). The Munir Report itself provides no date whatsoever, but it does refer to Doon Campbell and Reuters.[31] Yet strangely, whilst Mr Chattopadhyaya implied that his meeting with Jinnah was memorable, he had never thought to bring up this immensely significant statement regarding the nature of the state before.

Origin of the two-pronged argument

His obvious error aside, next Mr Chattopadhyaya emphasised his point further, in case anyone had missed it:

> Remember the words, 'in the people'. The sovereignty will not rest with God, but sovereignty will rest with people.[32]

This exact argument has since been repeated by numerous secularists (starting of course with Munir in 1979)[33], long after Mr Chattopadhyaya's speech. The Munir Report at least did not directly take this line of argument, though it mentioned the supposed 'restriction

---

28 Ibid. Emphasis mine.

29 See end of press report (*Dawn* 22 March 1948) on Jinnah's address to the Hindu and Scheduled Caste Deputations of East Pakistan Assembly, Dacca, 21 March 1948. (NV Vol. VII, p.261-2).

30 CAP Debates, Vol. XVI No. 23, p.288.

31 Munir Report, p.201

32 CAP Debates, Vol. XVI No. 23, p.288.

33 See Munir 1980, p.36

on the sovereignty of the people' in an Islamic state.[34] It is only in 1979 that Munir directly compared the sovereignty of the people with that of God.[35] Also note that Chattopadhyaya is the first to go on record as having misread the Munir quote. He attributed the words literally to Jinnah; but as we have noted already, Munir himself did not do the same until 1979. Likewise, early commentators writing in the fifties and sixties did not make Mr Chattopadhyaya's error, even when they cited the Munir quote, until after the publication of *From Jinnah to Zia*.[36]

Returning to the transcript, next he referred to the speech of 11 August 1947:

> Mr Jinnah spoke only of one nation ... so he said that the members of the new nation will have equal rights of citizenship ...[37]

He went on to add:

> [Jinnah] never contemplated [an] Islamic state and never thought of [the] two nation theory after getting Pakistan. ... Religion is a different thing and should not be brought in the State. Afterwards, it was decided that Pakistan will be [called] 'Islamic Republic of Pakistan' ... This idea did not come when Mr Jinnah was alive; it did not come when Mr Liaquat Ali Khan was alive. The Interim report submitted by Mr Liaquat Ali Khan in 1950 does not speak of an Islamic State ...[38]

We can see here that the Munir quote has been used to support the speech of 11 August 1947, apparently proving beyond doubt that Jinnah and Liaquat Ali Khan were secularists, and thus the two pieces of evidence have appeared in tandem to launch an attack against any sort of Islamic polity. This is also perhaps the first time that this 'two-pronged' argument appears on record. Evidently therefore, either Mr Chattopadhyaya discussed the Munir Report with its author behind closed doors,[39] or Munir later copied Chattopadhyaya's argument

---

34 Munir Report, p.210

35 Munir 1980, p.36

36 See for instance Binder 1961, p.342, and Choudhury 1959, p.63. In both cases it is Munir and not Jinnah, to whom the quote is attributed. However Binder writes that 'Jinnah's *various* statements that Pakistan would be a *modern democratic state* were also recalled' in the Munir Report. (Ibid. Emphasis mine.)

37 CAP Debates, Vol. XVI No. 23, p.288-9

38 Ibid. p.289

39 This possibility is not as far-fetched as it may seem; earlier in the 1949 debates over the Objectives Resolution, Mr Chattopadhyaya mentioned that he had spoken at length to some 'maulanas' to gauge their opinion on the Islamic state. (See CAP Debates, Vol. V No. 5, p.90)

in toto from the transcript of the Constituent Assembly Debates and reproduced it in his 1979 book. [40]

Chief evidence

We come now to 21 September 1954, when the first Constituent Assembly of Pakistan opened the doors for what would turn out to be its very last day of business. It was also the day of a prolonged and heated debate that took up most of the day in four separate meetings, and produced some 73 pages (A4 size) of transcript. Much of what was said had been repeated before, but we should look at some of the remarks made by various members. This was the day the final BPC Report was due either to be adopted or rejected. We will skip the early morning session for the time being, and go straight to the bulk of the discussion of that day. We will return briefly to the early morning session at the end of the chapter.

Prof. Raj Kumar Chakraverty of the opposition began with the pronouncement that his party did not consent to the proposed constitution, calling it the 'doing of a communal party'. [41] Then he proceeded to list five 'discriminations' in the BPC Report: The name 'Islamic Republic'; the repugnancy clause; the religious restriction for the head of state; the provision for an 'Ecclesiastical Department' for the 'preaching' of Islam; and finally, the separate electorates issue. [42] Even as he listed these five grievances, he said:

> … if anybody wants to know the implications of the Islamic State *I would draw his attention to the Report of the Punjab Disturbances Enquiry Committee Report* where the finding has been given clearly and unequivocally that the non-Muslims can never have equal rights with the Moslems in an Islamic State. … it is not open to anyone to tell us, in view of the finding based upon good evidence, and the evidence of the leading Maulanas, [and] the finding of *no less a person than the present Chief Justice of the Federal Court*, that there is equality for all. [43]

He brought in part of the Report to support his contention that non-Muslims in Pakistan would be reduced to the status of '*zimmis*' [44] with

[40] See the two-pronged argument in Munir 1980, p.29-33

[41] CAP Debates Vol. XVI No. 31, p.505

[42] Ibid. p.505-6

[43] CAP Debates Vol. XVI No. 31, p.505-6. Emphasis mine.

[44] *Dhimmis / Zimmis* (NB: The following is the traditional Muslim explanation): non-Muslims who are protected by law within the Islamic state. They are free to practise their faith and retain their personal laws. They do not have to fight in war alongside the Muslim community or pay *zakaat* (Muslim 'tax' used primarily to tackle poverty); but in lieu of not fighting in war they are required to pay an 'exemption tax' (*jizya*), an amount that is at any rate supposed to

fewer rights than Muslim citizens, emphasising at the same time that he was reading the Chief Justice's 'finding' on the subject, and not just another (fundamentalist) mullah's interpretation. He also reminded the House of the recent Punjab disturbances and asked whether the other minorities of Pakistan should also expect to meet a similar fate in Islamic Pakistan. [45]

Throughout that day, the opposition members made reference to the Munir Report no fewer than eighteen times; Mr Chattopadhyaya alone quoted from it at least eight times. [46] The two-pronged argument was also stressed a couple of times by different members. [47] They wanted the constitution secularised and the name 'Islamic Republic' omitted from the country's formal designation.

Tough questions

However, we should not take this to mean that the non-Muslim members were being deliberately disruptive throughout or that their allegations against the proposed 'Islamic' character of the Republic were wholly without substance – far from it. To the contrary, they raised some legitimate criticisms and made some pertinent suggestions. Here are some relevant extracts:

> They have laid down in section 4 that nothing should be repugnant to the Holy Quran and Sunnah, but then in section 10 they have provided that for 25 years the money matters should be exempt from the operation of Quranic laws. Sir, the Quran prohibits the giving and taking of interest and many other things regarding money matters [*sic*], but they are not to be followed by the people and country for twenty-five years. There is no consistency or logic in the Constitution that we are going to adopt today. [48]

> … Then, Sir, take the election of the Head of the State. He should have been elected directly by the votes of the people; but he is going to be elected by the votes of the few members of the Central Legislature only. [49]

---

be lower than the rate of *zakaat* paid by the Muslim community. (Adapted from M. Asad, *Message of the Quran*, footnote on *jizya* at 9:29)

45 See CAP Debates Vol. XVI No. 31, p.507

46 For this reason Sardar Nishtar dryly remarked that Mr Chattopadhyaya was 'very enamoured' with the Munir Report. CAP Debates Vol. XVI No. 31, p.560

47 CAP Debates Vol. XVI No. 31, p.531, 547

48 Dr Raj Kumar Chakraverty, CAP Debates Vol. XVI No. 31, p.508

49 Ibid.

> … I have been going through the newly framed Constitutions of some of the countries of Europe – I mean newly framed after the devastation of the war. I submit that the latest conceptions about social security and economic matters ought to be included in the constitution …[50]

This would obviously mean the inclusion of socialist principles.[51] Hence the same speaker adds:

> … the expression "Islamic Republic" does not create any disquiet in my mind. … But I do claim one thing: there must be a clear exposition of what do you mean by Islamic Republic. [*sic*] … Is it an imitation of Russia, because they did adopt the socialist system as the framework of the Constitution? Is it on that idea? Certainly not. Because we find that there was an attempt in clause 4 [repugnancy clause] but it was abandoned in clause 10 [where money matters were made exempt]. … Really no ideology of Islam has been put down in the Constitution itself. … I can say definitely that this expression has no meaning and is without any intention.[52]
>
> Sir, I have not the speech of the Honourable Prime Minister before me, but I remember that he told [me] the other day that "if I had the power, I would have done away with all the provinces." But what have you done? Instead of doing away with the provinces, you have created provinces.[53] … if you like to do away with the provinces and economise the cost of administration, then do it today.[54]

In addition, the non-Muslim members took pains to point out:

> What is [an] Islamic constitution? The Head of State will the Khalifa; he would be the real Head of State and all powers will vest in him – practically absolute monarch … But what is the position of the President in Pakistan? You have given him no

---

[50] Shri Kamini Kumar Datta, CAP Debates Vol. XVI No. 31, p.516

[51] That said, not all non-Muslim members shared this view. Shri Bhupendra Dutta said he preferred 'quick capitalist development,' and that 'secular, sovereign, parliamentary democracy is pre-eminently the political system that history has evolved for such development.' (CAP Debates Vol. XVI No. 31, p.543) He had also said that creating an 'Islamic constitution' as a 'remedy against the spread of communism … is a quack remedy.' (Ibid. p.542-3)

[52] Shri Kamini Kumar Datta, CAP Debates Vol. XVI No. 31, p.519-20

[53] Mr Datta was referring to Part V of the BPC Report 1954 which declared that the states of Bahawalpur, Khairpur and Baluchistan were to be treated as provinces.

[54] Shri Dhirendra Nath Datta, CAP Debates Vol. XVI No. 31, p.537

power … Is it the position of the Head of the Islamic State, or is it the position of the Head of State in a *modern democratic State*? [55]

… attempts have been made to curtail the power of the Head of State, as is evident from our conduct today this morning.[56] … [Since] the Governor-General abused the power at a certain stage, the framers of the Constitution have taken care to see that the Head of State cannot abuse that power and so all the powers have been taken away from him but still we have given the name Islamic Republic of Pakistan. [57]

These latter two loaded remarks reveal that the amendments relating to political powers were based on political rivalries and that Islam was not really the issue.

As to the rest of the concerns raised by the opposition, let us see how the Muslim Leaguers responded. [58]

Whither unity, faith and discipline?

In the late morning session, Begum Jahan Ara Shah Nawaz [59] opened with an attempt to pacify the members of the opposition. She asked them all to be mindful of the fact that the constitution 'is only a quibbling of words', that it 'is not a rigid thing' and that 'it can always be changed'. [60] She mentioned her own quiet dissatisfaction with certain aspects of the BPC Report:

I for one would have been much happier if we had not incorporated the provision about the Head of State, but let me assure my Pakistani brethren on the Opposite Benches that it is only a translation of what is actually going to happen. … secondly I would have been much happier if the word "Sunnah" were not there, because I believe the word Quran [*sic*] would have been sufficient. [61]

---

55 S.C. Chattopadhyaya, CAP Debates Vol. XVI No. 31, p.533

56 In the early morning session, a number of last-minute amendments were rushed through the House to finally put all powers in the hands of the central government, as described later in this chapter.

57 Shri Dhirendra Nath Datta, CAP Debates Vol. XVI No. 31, p.536

58 Some of these responses have been cited out of order to illustrate the point more clearly.

59 Begum Jahan Ara Shah Nawaz (1896-1979) was one of only two women in the first Pakistan Constituent Assembly, best remembered for her tireless efforts in working for the recognition of women as equals throughout her career. She was the first woman Muslim Leaguer, and daughter of League founder Mian Mohammad Shafi.

60 CAP Debates Vol. XVI No. 31, p. 511

61 Ibid. p. 512. Begum Shah Nawaz had in 1952 also added a note of dissent against the religious requirement for the head of state. (Binder 1961, p.226)

She also reminded the opposition that in 'the Western democracy which we have introduced', the minority must at times be prepared to 'merge their opinion' with that of the majority in order for the system to function effectively, because doing otherwise would be 'killing this democracy from the very beginning'. [62] However her words fell on deaf ears; the non-Muslim members used similar words to recommend that the separate electorates for minorities be abolished to allow these communities to be 'merged' with the majority. [63]

Most of the Muslim members (barring a few) [64] were either unable or unwilling to answer the concerns, legitimate or otherwise, of the non-Muslim members. At any rate, a number of them were more interested in discussing provincial autonomy than anything else. [65] The ones who did answer these questions found themselves covering the same ground that they had in 1949. A weary Sardar Nishtar commented that the 'nature of the criticism levelled against the Objectives Resolution was also exactly on similar lines'. [66] In trying to deal with the introduction of the new evidence, namely the Munir Report, he could only argue that it contained 'not the finding of the Court' on what constitutes an Islamic state, but rather, the views of certain individuals. [67] A.K Brohi did only marginally better when he quoted a section from the same Report in which Munir had written:

> We have dealt at some length on the subject of an Islamic State not because we intended to write a thesis against or in favour of such a State, but merely with a view to presenting a clear picture of the numerous possibilities that may in future arise if [the] true causes of the ideological confusion which contributed to the spread and intensity of the disturbances are not precisely located. [68]

Mr Brohi produced this excerpt in order to show 'the whole thing in its proper perspective', [69] i.e. that the Munir Report was not itself passing comment on the 'Islamic state'. Brohi's argument was not without merit, but in hindsight we can see that those learned judges, the authors of the Report, had written a mere disclaimer to forestall

---

62 CAP Debates Vol. XVI No. 31, p. 512

63 See Shri Kamini Kumar Datta, CAP Debates Vol. XVI No. 31, p. 518, and Shri Dhirendra Nath Datta, ibid. p.537

64 Nurul Amin, Abdul Hamid, A.K. Brohi and Sardar Nishtar all made relevant contributions.

65 Ahmad E. Jaffer, for example, said he would leave it to 'Sardar Nishtar and other leaders' to reply to these questions. (CAP Debates Vol. XVI No. 31, p.522), and then he repeated the request given by Nawab Mohammad Khan of Jogezai only moments earlier that the Constituent Assembly should grant Baluchistan provincial autonomy. (p.522 et seq.)

66 CAP Debates Vol. XVI No. 31, p. 557

67 Sardar Nishtar, CAP Debates Vol. XVI No. 31, p. 561

68 Munir Report p.231, as quoted in CAP Debates Vol. XVI No. 31, p.568

69 CAP Debates Vol. XVI No. 31, p.568

criticism; [70] and it lost all meaning in 1979, the moment Munir used the same 'findings' to the very end he was denying in the above passage.

A well-intentioned Sardar Nishtar deployed his skills as a constitutional lawyer to argue his best, but his and others' efforts were marred in advance by their collective actions to try and remove the Governor-General, as well as their making practically the whole economy exempt from the repugnancy clause. No attempt whatsoever had been made in the final BPC Report to socialise monetary matters or introduce land reforms, [71] and so even the best-intentioned Muslim members could not (and did not) answer the challenge posed by the non-Muslim ministers. They could not define the ideology of the Islamic Republic because it contained nothing to suggest that it was living up to the promises made in 1949 to introduce 'Islamic socialism'. [72] Little wonder then, that today's secularist commentators do not take the old Leaguers' talk of Islam seriously; and under these circumstances we can hardly fault them for taking a dim view of the Objectives Resolution.

The brief remarks of Mr P.D. Bhandara [73] are noteworthy in this regard. He was the only non-Muslim member who did not oppose the Islamic content of the BPC Report outright. He had also recognised the merits of the Objectives Resolution in 1949, and had not opposed separate electorates, [74] to the disgruntlement of his peers. He supported

---

[70] See also A.H. Syed, (1982), p.78: 'In the introduction to their report, Justices Munir and Kayani stated that their encounter with the ulema during the enquiry had been a "novel" but an "exceedingly pleasant" experience. At another point, they noted that it had not been their intention to argue for or against the Islamic state. But a careful reading of their report leaves little doubt that they regarded the ulema as unprogressive, and that they viewed the ulema's advocacy of an Islamic state as fraught with serious complications and difficulties, which would divide and disrupt the country, instead of uniting and strengthening it. The judges undertook a lengthy analysis of the statements of Iqbal and Jinnah, including the latter's August 11 address, to show that neither Iqbal nor Jinnah had envisaged Pakistan as an Islamic state.' It is not clear from this however, whether Prof. Syed means that the judges were simply opposed to a theocracy, or whether he thinks they were quietly advocating a 'secular' state.

[71] This was irrespective of the recommendations of the Pakistan Planning Committee's 'Five Year Plan'. See footnote 53 on Zahid Hussain in Myth no. 3 (Chapter 10).

[72] The term 'Islamic socialism' was used most famously by Jinnah, as well as the early leaders of Pakistan. Liaquat Ali Khan considered the abolition of landlordism a necessary step towards establishing this Islamic socialism. Ironically, Sardar Nishtar did reiterate the supposed intent to 'run our country on the basis of Islamic socialism' on the day of the debate we are presently reviewing, (CAP Debates Vol. XVI No. 31, p.558), but the argument does not hold water in light of the discrepancies inherent in the BPC Report of 1954.

[73] Little biographical information is available on Peshotan Dhanjibhoy Bhandara, except that he was a Parsi businessman and the only non-Hindu member of the first Constituent Assembly. In 1952, he was the only non-Muslim member who supported separate electorates and weightage for the 'Scheduled Caste' Hindus of Pakistan – he even acted as their representative. (See his speech on 19 April 1952; CAP Debates Vol. XI No. 8, p.215-6) His son, Minocher Peshotan Bhandara (1938-2008), was the Pakistan National Assembly Minister who famously moved a Bill incorporating the substance of Jinnah's 11 August speech into the constitution in 2007.

[74] For an academic review of the Muslim viewpoint on separate electorates, see G.W. Choudhury 1959, p.44-6, 95-6. Whilst recognising that separate electorates may normally

Begum Shah Nawaz's statement that no constitution was ever perfect, and said that the defects inherent in this one would hopefully be 'removed' as they were 'discovered and proved.'[75] Yet he was also gravely concerned that the proposed legislation was inconsistent, cumbersome and bureaucratic. Using eloquent language, he said:

> The Constitution as at present framed, is far from Islamic. *The very essence of an Islamic Constitution which is brevity and simplicity is conspicuous by its absence.* It has a tendency of making our top-heavy administration still heavier at the top. ... The sooner our leaders discover this grievous error the better as our economy which is strained to the utmost ... will not be able to bear the strain of a further burden ... In the process of evolution gained by experience, I trust our Constitution will be remodelled to *conform more to the tenets of Islam* and will be so designed as to rid our present administration of the vast amounts of red-tape, inefficiency, corruption and nepotism. *So long as these evils persist and corrupt our administrative system we will not be justified in labelling our Constitution as Islamic.*[76]

This insightful individual added further:

> Another conspicuous delinquency is the *absence of that cohesion* that will unite the country. The tendency on the part of our present administrators is to encourage provincialism, which is a menace which will cut to the very roots of our existence. Here again, *an important precept of Islam is ignored.*[77]

When the BPC Report was finally put to the vote that evening, again all who voted in favour were Muslims, and all who voted against were non-Muslims.[78] Unsurprisingly, there was much ill-feeling when the BPC Report was adopted. As the President of the House declared that 'the *Ayes* have it', the members of the opposition party cried out in

---

'prevent the development of a united national feeling', he argues that Jinnah himself had supported separate electorates for caste Hindus and scheduled-caste Hindus in pre-partition India. The higher caste Hindus were fewer in number but when treated as a combined group with scheduled caste Hindus, they tended to win more seats. In Hindu society, these two groups were divided socially and so their collective representation by caste Hindus was inequitable from a political point of view. A separate electorate had been sought to redress the balance, but this had been thwarted following Gandhi's interference with the threat of a fast 'until death'. In Pakistan, Caste Hindu ministers naturally opposed the same proposal because they saw it as a 'threat to their hold over the scheduled-caste Hindus', while the Scheduled Caste Hindus publicly demanded a separate electorate for themselves. (Op. cit.)

75 CAP Debates Vol. XVI No. 31, p. 515

76 Ibid.

77 CAP Debates Vol. XVI No. 31, p. 516

78 Names not appearing on the list of voters include P.D. Bhandara and Sardar Nishtar.

protest: '*Noes* have it.' [79] It was an ominous sign of what was to come the following month.

The limits of compromise

From the record of the debates in August and September 1954 (leaving aside the political problems) we can see that the Muslim members genuinely did not believe the BPC Report outlined the characteristics of an outmoded 'Islamic state'. In fairness, and contrary to the fears of non-Muslim Pakistanis or the claims of later secularist commentators, there were in fact no fundamentalist views incorporated into the BPC Report. Nevertheless, it certainly was an inconsistent document, representing traditionalist and modernist views of Islam, as well as secularist views. Attempts had been made to create a document that compromised between various shades of thought – Muslim and otherwise – and tried to placate all members of the Muslim population, which was of course a sheer impossibility. Whilst compromise may be considered necessary in politics, here it came at the cost of undermining the Islamic idealism for which Pakistan originally stood. The persisting problem therefore, as we have noted already, was a lack of intellectual unity amongst the members of the Constituent Assembly. They had failed to learn an important lesson from Jinnah (not to mention the Quran[80]) on the limits of compromise:

> ... I remember John Morley's book *On Compromise*. ... There is a good chapter in it on the limits of compromise, and the lesson it teaches regarding the pursuit of truth and the limitations on our actions in practice are worth pondering over. In the pursuit of truth and cultivation of beliefs *we should be guided by our rational interpretation of the Quran* and if our devotion to truth is *single-minded* we shall, in our own measure, achieve our goal. In the translation of this truth into practice however, we shall be content with so much, so much only, as we can achieve without encroaching upon the rights of others, whilst at the same time *not ceasing our efforts always to achieve more.* [81]

Aside from this, we also have seen the immediate impact of the Munir quote and the two-pronged argument on the secularists' arguments in the first Constituent Assembly in 1954. Its long-term impact on the pro-secularist argument in general cannot be understated. Binder

---

[79] CAP Debates Vol. XVI No. 31, p.571

[80] See Quran verse 6:116: 'Now if you pay heed to the majority of those (who live) on earth, they will but lead you astray from the path of God: they follow but (other people's) conjectures, and they themselves do nothing but guess.' (Asad modernised; parentheses in original).

[81] Eid Day Broadcast, 13 November, 1939. NV, Vol. I p. 414

acknowledged as early as 1961 that the Munir Report had become 'a classic of sorts, though not an unbiased one'. [82] Choudhury stated that the argument for a secular Jinnah and a 'modern national state' had 'received added importance in view of its acceptance in the Report'. [83] But none of the early historians could have foreseen the extent to which this 'acceptance' would inspire Pakistani secularists over the coming years. This something we will look at in detail in the next chapter. [84]

A taste of things to come

We end this chapter with a final reference to the debates of 21 September 1954. Prior to the closing discussion of the BPC Report, the existing text of the temporary constitution [85] was amended so as to completely deprive the Governor-General of his ability to dismiss his ministers. This was, as we have mentioned already, the final part of a series of amendments [86] that had gradually restricted the powers of the Governor-General and put them in the hands of the central government. Up until this point the Governor-General had not formally expressed any objection to these changes, but the last minute amendments were moved in haste, with virtually no discussion. [87] To make matters worse, the Constituent Assembly also chose to finalise the BPC Report on a day when the Governor-General was away on tour, making it seem more obvious that this was a personal attack. [88]

The Assembly decided they would reconvene and put the new constitution into effect on 28 October 1954; [89] but with only four days to go, on 24 October 1954, Ghulam Mohammed dissolved the Constituent Assembly via proclamation (without explicitly saying that he had done so) and declared a state of emergency. Significantly, his proclamation also defied protocol by failing to mention which Section of either the temporary constitution or the Indian Independence Act 1947 [90] was being used to dissolve the Assembly. [91] Given that the Governor-General did not actually possess the constitutional power to dissolve the

---

82 Binder 1961, p.238

83 Choudhury 1959, p.63. Prof. Choudhury's words 'modern national state' are evidently borrowed from the Munir Report (p.203).

84 See also M.P. Bhandara's constitutional bill as reviewed in Appendix VII.

85 The temporary constitution was an adapted version of the Government of India Act 1935.

86 See G.W. Choudhury 1959, p.142-3 for details of the specific changes.

87 The 'discussion' of these amendments that day – if it can be called that – covers a mere four pages of transcript. Comparatively, the transcript dedicated to the last-minute arguments – almost exclusively of an 'ideological' nature – takes up around 68 pages. See CAP Debates Vol. XVI No. 31, p.499-502, 503-571 respectively.

88 Choudhury 1959, p. 43

89 See Editor's Note in CAP Debates Vol. XVI No. 31, p.572

90 The Indian Independence Act 1947, by which independent India and Pakistan officially came into being, contained some provisions for the running of the countries' respective governments, including their powers to frame laws. Further details are given in Chapter 14.

91 See Ghulam Mohammed's formal proclamation (referenced in next footnote).

Assembly, this is not surprising. His only stated reason for issuing the proclamation was that he had 'come to the conclusion that constitutional machinery has broken down' and that the Constituent Assembly had 'lost the confidence of the people and can no longer function'. He also added that as 'the ultimate authority vests in the people', elections will be held 'as early as possible'. [92] It's an ironic statement, given his own undemocratic and illegal action against the Constituent Assembly, not to mention that he also immediately set up a new Cabinet of ministers whose ethos was to introduce a 'controlled democracy'.[93] They thought that the people of Pakistan were not sufficiently mature as a nation to take on a democratic system of the type seen in developed countries. [94] It's no secret that Ghulam Mohammed also aimed for the 'suppression of Islamic provisions' [95], but his new regime soon had to bow to public pressure to create a constitution with Islamic features. [96] This part of the story however, takes us beyond the scope of this book. We need only note that after the dissolution of the first Constituent Assembly, it took another two years before the first constitution of Pakistan was finally promulgated on 23 March 1956, and unbeknown to its framers it was a portent of Pakistan's historical identity crisis; for by virtue of the tug of war between secularists and religionists of all shades, it was, in effect, a document of secular-Islam synthesis.

We will leave our historical review here, except to mention that when Tamizuddin Khan [97] challenged Ghulam Mohammed's action against the first Constituent Assembly in the Sind Chief Court in November 1954, its judges ruled unanimously that Ghulam Mohammed had acted beyond his jurisdiction, and restored the Constituent Assembly. When the Government appealed this decision to the Federal Court (then the highest court in the land) in March 1955, Chief Justice Muhammad Munir claimed that he did not know whether or not the

---

[92] The Gazette of Pakistan (Extraordinary) Karachi, p.1919; as reproduced in R. Ahmad (1981) *Constitutional and Political Developments in Pakistan 1951-54* Rawalpindi: Pak-American Commercial Ltd., p.97; also reproduced in CAP Vol. XVI, p.572

[93] Choudhury 1959, p.147 and Binder 1961, p.361, both citing Major General Iskander Mirza's infamous statement in *Dawn*, 31 October 1954.

[94] Choudhury 1959, p.147. (Ironically this had been the attitude of British rulers in India also, and they had used it to justify their imperial autocracy. See Jinnah's speech at the Lucknow Session of the Muslim League in 1916, quoted in Myth no. 10 (Chapter 10))

[95] Binder 1961, p.364

[96] Choudhury 1959, p.174-5. See also op. cit. p.70-71, in which Choudhury describes the views of the intelligentsia of the period. They too advocated an 'Islamic state', but not of the type envisioned by the ulema. In addition he explains why the Pakistani people in general also 'emphatically refuse to identify' the Islamic State with theocracy, and do not believe in 'giving privilege or exclusive power to the *ulema*'. (Ibid. p.71)

[97] Tamizuddin Khan (1889-1963) hailed from Bengal. He was President of the Pakistan Constituent Assembly after Jinnah's death in 1948, and President of the 1949 Basic Principles Committee. He was also Speaker of the Pakistan National Assembly until his death in 1963.

Governor-General had acted legally, [98] and 'purposely' did not want to go into it. [99] But nevertheless he rendered the ruling of the Sind Chief Court invalid on technical grounds – namely, that the Sind Chief Court did not have the power to rule in favour of Tamizuddin, as the law granting it this power had never received the assent of the Governor-General (who exercised assent on behalf of the British Crown). [100] Consequently, every single law that the Assembly had passed via its own procedures [101] instead of receiving the Governor-General's assent now fell 'outside the limits' of the working constitution, rendering them invalid. [102] Munir also held that since Pakistan was a Dominion of Great Britain, [103] the Constituent Assembly was not a truly sovereign body [104] – a shocking position with which the Federal Court judges on the bench all agreed, [105] with the exception of Justice A.R. Cornelius,

---

98 This was a statement made some time after the ruling, reported in *Dawn*, 14 April 1955 (cited in Choudhury 1959, p.151).

99 Cited in Choudhury 1959, p.149

100 Ibid.

101 According to a procedural rule (Rule 62) of the Constituent Assembly, any bill passed by the Assembly became law once it was published in the official gazette of Pakistan under the authority of the President of the Assembly. This rule had been introduced in the Constituent Assembly on 24 February 1948, with Jinnah himself present as President, and adopted on 22 May 1948. Significantly, before the events of 1954 none of the Governors-General of Pakistan, Jinnah and Ghulam Mohammed included – had ever brought the validity of the laws into question (ibid. p.149, 150).

102 *All-Pakistan Legal Decisions* 1955, Federal Court no. 240, p.298. Up to 46 laws were rendered invalid as a result of the Federal Court's ruling (G.W. Choudhury 1959, p.150).

103 In his written judgement on the case, Munir stuck to using the word 'Dominion' even though it had fallen out of use soon after 1947 (replaced with 'Commonwealth'), as the term incorrectly implied sovereign subordination. He also overlooked the fact that the role of the British monarch in Commonwealth nations had recently changed form. Following the constitutional establishment of India as a full 'republic' in 1949 (creating a technical difficulty for the British monarch who was supposed to be the head of every Commonwealth nation), the Commonwealth Prime Ministers' Conference of the same year issued the London Declaration, which allowed India to retain its Commonwealth membership while changing the British monarch's role in the new republic from a constitutional to a symbolic head. This change applied by extension to all Commonwealth nations.

104 Both Chief Justice Munir and Ghulam Mohammed colluded with world-class British constitutional scholar Sir Ivor Jennings (who, it seems, was responsible for much unscrupulous meddling in the constitutional affairs of post-colonial nations) to undermine the sovereign status of the Constituent Assembly and by implication, render all laws passed by its procedure invalid; and declare the Governor-General the only legitimate authority in the land, based on his power of assent on behalf of the British Crown. For details of Jennings' role in formally advising Ghulam Mohammed (as well as Munir in private), see H. Kumarasingham, 'A Transnational Actor on a Dramatic Stage – Sir Ivor Jennings and the Manipulation of Westminster Style Democracy: The Case of Pakistan' in *UC Irvine Journal of International, Transnational and Comparative Law* Vol. 2 (Spring 2017), p.33-56; also A. G. Noorani, 'Court Martial: The Great Betrayal', in *Dawn*, 27 October and 1 November 2008; and Allen McGrath (1996) *The Destruction of Pakistan's Democracy* Karachi: Oxford University Press.

105 Contrary to Munir and the Federal Court's take on Pakistan's sovereignty, Jinnah himself had remarked that the Constituent Assemblies of India and Pakistan had 'supreme power … to change anything they like' after partition. (Press conference, New Delhi, 13 July 1947; NV Vol. VI, p.285) He took pains to clarify that the Governors-General of the two countries

who wrote a note of dissent 53 pages long in defence of Pakistan's independence and the sovereignty of its Constituent Assembly. [106]

Hence, whilst Munir did not directly rule in favour of Ghulam Mohammed, his decision against the Sind Chief Court effectively gave the Governor-General a victory by default. [107] The same man who just the year before had waxed lyrical about 'sovereignty resting in the people' via a misquote, now cast doubt on the sovereignty and independence of the nation itself, thereby creating a further state of emergency in Pakistan.

Not to mention that in upholding the 'doctrine of necessity', [108] Chief Justice Muhammad Munir paved the way for every despotic leader of the future – irrespective of ideological inclination – to dissolve the government whenever he found it expedient. [109]

---

were 'chosen of the people and not, as it is ordinarily understood, appointed by the King as was the practice in India in the past' – and dismissed the idea that the Governor-General held office at 'His Majesty's pleasure', calling it 'nothing but a form' (ibid. p.278). On 11 August 1947 he again sought to 'emphasise' that Pakistan's Constituent Assembly was a 'sovereign legislative body' with 'all the powers' (CAP Debates Vol. I No. 2, p.18) And Jinnah held fast to this position. While Section 6 of the Independence Act expected the Governor-General to assent to new bills 'in his Majesty's name', Jinnah reportedly 'disliked' the rule (Khalid bin Sayeed (1968 revised) *Pakistan: The Formative Phase 1857-1948*, London: Oxford University Press, p.253-4). Jinnah may well have disliked the concept of assent generally, since it originated in medieval England where laws required 'royal assent' (formal approval) of the monarch before they could be enacted. (Royal Assent is legally retained by the British monarch up to the present). This probably explains why the Constituent Assembly introduced Rule 62 (described in footnote 101 above) into its procedures as an alternative means of passing laws. It is also probable that since Jinnah was growing ever more frail (he died only a few months after the rule was introduced), Rule 62 was a means of avoiding having to give his formal assent to every single bill. In 1950, after Jinnah's death, Section 6 was even amended to delete the references to 'His Majesty'.

[106] A brief note on Cornelius' life and his thoughts in favour of Islam as a polity is included in Appendix II.

[107] Binder 1961, p.368.

[108] In the Pakistani context the 'doctrine of necessity' has come to mean the extra-constitutional power to dissolve the government and declare a state of emergency. In justifying his decision on Ghulam Mohammed's case Munir took his precedent from the maxim of medieval cleric and jurist Henry de Bracton: 'that which is otherwise not lawful is made lawful by necessity,' and the statement of 18th century jurist Lord Mansfield (William Murray): 'an act which would otherwise be illegal becomes legal if it is done bona fide under the stress of necessity'. See *All-Pakistan Legal Decisions*, 1955, Federal Court, no. 435 (Reference by HE the Governor-General; Special Reference No. 1 of 1955)

[109] Damning accounts of Munir's role in the decline of Pakistan into autocracy can be found in C. Jaffrelot 2015, Chapter 7; also Asad Ali Khan, 'Landmark Judgment: Tamizuddin Khan versus Federation of Pakistan', at *Pakistan Institute of International Affairs* blog, 4 November 2014. https://pakistanhorizon.wordpress.com/2014/11/04/landmark-judgment-tamizuddin-khan-versus-federation-of-pakistan/ (Last accessed 3 July 2016). See also Jaffrelot op. cit. Chapter 5 for a detailed account of Ghulam Mohammed's 'bureaucratic-authoritarian ethos' and his 'reservations toward a democratic regime' (ibid. p.207-8).

Chapter 5
Munir's legacy: The butterfly effect

So far we have looked at the origin of the Munir quote and how it helped to create the two-pronged argument (and subsequently the three-piece argument). It appeared for the first time in the Munir Report of 1954, but Mr Chattopadhyaya was the first who wrongly cited it as a verbatim statement of Jinnah. Not only was this error repeated in front of the first Constituent Assembly, but no one recognised it as such and so it was not corrected. Thereafter the Munir quote remained largely forgotten until after 1979, with the publication of Chief Justice Munir's *From Jinnah to Zia*. Again the error was not spotted or corrected until as recently as 2004.

When I first released *Secular Jinnah* in 2005, one or two people suggested that perhaps I was making too much of a fuss over what was essentially just one false quote. However, it is not simply that the quote is false. It has been used time and again to try and prove that the speech of 11 August 1947 is strictly 'secular' in tone. It was necessary for pro-secularist commentators to do this because on its own the 11 August speech does not do much to convince the advocates of a 'Muslim Jinnah', with the exception of some fundamentalist or otherwise naïve religionists. It also creates the illusion that Jinnah made more than just one 'openly secular' statement in the 1940s (as if just one more is supposed to counter hundreds to the contrary). Here we might also note the difference in the treatment of the 11 August 1947 speech and the Munir quote by the two broad groups of commentators. Advocates of both sides will readily make reference to the former, but only pro-secularists tend to bring up the latter. In fact I have rarely come across direct references to the Munir quote made by the pro-Muslim Jinnah group, which only confirms that almost everyone implicitly accepts it as a strictly secular statement. [1] Two such rare instances include Prof. Choudhury's *Constitutional Development in Pakistan* and Prof. Sharif al Mujahid's *Quaid-i-Azam: Studies in Interpretation.* [2] In both these

---

[1] The words 'modern' and 'democratic' have been used together by another of Jinnah's contemporaries, whose political orientation has never been in doubt: the Indian National Congress leader Jawaharlal Nehru (1889-1964). He described the secular state as the 'cardinal doctrine of modern democratic practice, that is, the separation of the state from religion.' (Jawaharlal Nehru in *The Hindu* 17 July 1951 and 11 April 1950; as cited in Donald E. Smith (1963) *India as a Secular State* Princeton: Princeton University Press, p.155).

[2] See G.W. Choudhury 1959, p.63; S. Mujahid 1981, p.254.

examples, the authors were citing from the Munir Report and so both understood that the words were not Jinnah's but Munir's.

Then there is the literary dissection of the quote, which we have not yet discussed in detail. The words 'sovereignty in the people' have been taken and juxtaposed with the words 'sovereignty of Allah' which appear in the Objectives Resolution, with the obvious intent of undermining it. Yet aside from the fact that the Munir quote is a false quote to begin with, this is also a deceptive argument, taking advantage of a flawed understanding of the 'sovereignty of Allah' as the basis of a theocratic state. From the historical analytic viewpoint, individuals who take this line of argument have also blithely ignored the views of the authors of the Objectives Resolution on the subject, which still exist on record, and which we have already seen in Chapter 3. We know from their statements that they understood 'sovereignty in Allah' not as it is in the West, but in Muslim terms. The old Leaguers felt that they were simply reiterating what Muslims all believe about the absolute authority of God in the universe, and that their inclusion of God in the constitution was hardly without precedent. They were adamant that the statement 'sovereignty of God' would not lead to a theocracy, for theocracy puts power into the hands of a few individuals and so goes against Islam. In an act of prudence nonetheless, to try and completely eliminate the possibility of 'mischievous interpretations', they included the line: 'the authority which He has delegated to the State of Pakistan *through its people ...*'

Here, there and everywhere

We noted at the beginning of Chapter 2 that Munir's argument (whether in the two-pronged or three-piece format) has been copied time and again, to the extent that it has become the standard for the pro-secularist position. In the first edition of *Secular Jinnah* I listed four examples from various commentators to illustrate this point:

- Ishtiaq Ahmed, university professor, in his journal article *Pakistan Democracy, Islam and Secularism: A Phantasmagoria of Conflicting Muslim Aspirations* [3]
- Ardeshir Cowasjee, senior columnist, in his article *Back to Jinnah* [4]
- Abdus Sattar Ghazali, journalist, in his book *Islamic Pakistan: Illusions and Reality* [5]

---

[3] I. Ahmed, 'Pakistan Democracy, Islam and Secularism: A Phantasmagoria of Conflicting Muslim Aspirations' in *Oriente Moderno*, Vol. XXIII (LXXXIV). No.1. 2004, p.13-28

[4] A. Cowasjee, 'Back to Jinnah' in *Dawn*, 3 February 2002.

[5] A.S. Ghazali, (1996) *Islamic Pakistan: Illusions and Reality* Islamabad: National Book Club

- Pervez Amirali Hoodbhoy and Abdul Hameed Nayyar, university professors, in their co-authored article *Rewriting the History of Pakistan* [6]

There are however many more we could choose from. It would be impossible for us to go through each of these other cases in any detail but in order to demonstrate the extent of Munir's influence, in Appendix VIII I have listed a selection of books and articles in which the Munir quote and the two-pronged argument appears. For the purposes of this chapter we will stick with the above examples, and will merely outline the arguments and comment on them.

We'll start by looking at the commonalities with these sources. Comparing the precise wording, the date, and the references in each case, we find that with the exception of the late Mr Cowasjee, all of these writers:

- listed Munir's book as their reference
- gave the date as 1946 instead of 1947 (since their common source was Munir)
- used the same wording: 'The new state *would* be a modern democratic state ...'

Ardeshir Cowasjee is the exception. He did not reference the source of his quote, though of course there is insufficient room to do so in a newspaper column. He corrected the grammar: 'The new state *will* be a modern democratic state' (emphasis mine). Finally, from the text of his article it is clear that he knew the correct year was 1947 (see extract from his article below). It seems probable that he obtained the correct year from Prof. Sharif al Mujahid's *Studies in Interpretation.* [7]

Three chestnuts

Now we'll examine how these commentators have argued for a secular Jinnah, bearing Munir's three-piece prototype in mind. Once again for a lack of space I will avoid passing comments or going into the full contents of the articles; I will merely present the evidence as it has been produced in them.

---

[6] P.A. Hoodbhoy & A.H. Nayyar, 'Rewriting the History of Pakistan', in M. Asghar Khan (ed.) (1985) *Islam, Politics and the State: The Pakistan Experience*, London: Zed Books, p.164-177

[7] See S. Mujahid 1981, p.254. Prof. Mujahid in turn had ascertained the correct date for himself, having originally obtained it from the *Deccan Times*, 25 May 1947 (Ibid.), which he had quoted from in a separate publication some years previously (namely S. Mujahid, 'India - Pakistan Relations: An Analysis', in Dept. of International Relations/Karachi University (1964) *Foreign Policy of Pakistan: An Analysis* Karachi: The Allied Book Corporation, p. 32)

P. A. Hoodbhoy and A. H. Nayyar

First, here is part of the article by Prof. P.A. Hoodbhoy and Prof. A.H. Nayyar, both of whom are physicists, educationists and political activists. They share a deep concern prevalent amongst liberal Pakistanis that their homeland's education system is corrupt. They discuss this problem in their report, which was published as a chapter in a book edited by the late Air Marshal M. Asghar Khan. The focus of their article was the historical bias in modern Pakistani textbooks. They explain that current Pakistani textbooks portray Jinnah as man of 'orthodox religious views who sought the creation of a theocratic state'. Later in the article they present two major pieces of evidence to show that Jinnah was a secularist. The first is as follows:

> ... [Jinnah's] famous 11 August 1947 speech before the nation *is the clearest possible exposition* of a secular state in which religion and state are separate from each other:
>
> We are starting with the fundamental principle that we are all citizens and equal citizens of one State. . . Now I think that we should keep that in front of us as our ideal, and you will find that in due course of time Hindus would cease to be Hindus and Muslims would cease to be Muslims, not in the religious sense, because that is the personal faith of each individual but in the political sense as citizens of the state. You may belong to any religion or caste or creed - that has nothing to do with the business of the State. [8]

The second piece of evidence follows immediately after the first:

> In an interview to Doon Campbell, Reuter's correspondent in New Delhi in 1946, Jinnah made it perfectly clear that it was Western-style democracy that he wanted for Pakistan:
>
> The new state would be a modern democratic state with sovereignty resting in the people and the members of the new nation having equal rights of citizenship regardless of their religion, caste or creed. [9]

Here we see the reproduction of the two-pronged argument which pairs the 11 August 1947 speech with the Munir quote. Finally they introduce one of Jinnah's statements against theocracy:

---

[8] Hoodbhoy & Nayyar, op. cit. p.170. Emphasis mine, to illustrate the parallel in Munir's text: '[Jinnah's] speech as President of the Constituent Assembly on 11th August 1947 is one of the *clearest expositions of a secular state*.' (Munir 1980, p.29)

[9] Ibid.

> Note the highly significant phrase 'sovereignty resting in the people'. In contrast, in Maulana Maudoodi's Islamic state, 'sovereignty rests with Allah'. *Thus, Jinnah rejects the basis for a theocratic state.* This is stated even more explicitly in his 1946 speech before the Muslim League convention in Delhi: 'What are we fighting for? What are we aiming at? *It is not theocracy, nor a theocratic state.*'[10]

And this completes the three-piece argument.

Abdus Sattar Ghazali

The journalist Abdus Sattar Ghazali is presently the executive editor of the online magazine *American Muslim Perspective* and also chief editor of the *Journal of America.* In the past he has worked for various news channels in Kuwait and also for the Pakistani newspaper the *Dawn.* His book *Islamic Pakistan: Illusions and Reality* is practically entirely composed of passages from other sources. In the opening line of his first chapter, he quotes one of Jinnah's speeches from 1948:

> In any case Pakistan is not going to be a *theocratic* state to be ruled by priests with a divine mission. We have many non-Muslims – Hindus, Christians and Parsis -- but they are all Pakistanis. They will enjoy the same rights and privileges as any other citizens and will play their rightful part in the affairs of Pakistan.[11]

He uses the above quote as a prelude to outlining his beliefs regarding Jinnah. He provides two pieces of evidence from Jinnah's speeches:

> Before the establishment of Pakistan, the first public picture of Pakistan that Jinnah gave to the world was in the course of an interview in New Delhi (1946) with the correspondent of Reuter's news agency: the new state would be a modern democratic state, with sovereignty resting in the people and the members of the new nation having equal rights of citizenship, regardless of their religion, caste or creed.
>
> ...[Jinnah's] speech as President of the Constituent Assembly on 11th August 1947 is one of the clearest expositions of a secular state.[12]

---

[10] Ibid. p.170-1 (Emphasis mine)

[11] Jinnah's broadcast talk on Pakistan to the people of United States of America, Karachi, 26 February 1948; as cited in A.S. Ghazali (1996) *Islamic Pakistan: illusions & Reality* Islamabad: National Book Club, p.6

[12] Ibid. Here Ghazali copies Munir's words verbatim without providing a reference. See Munir 1980 p.29 for comparison.

This passage has been reproduced straight out of the Munir Report, which we cited earlier. [13] The three-piece argument appears in a slightly different order, but again the Munir quote and 11 August 1947 speech have been paired just as they are in Munir's *From Jinnah to Zia*.

Finally, Mr Ghazali adds (quoting an article from *Dawn*):

> Even after his unambiguous proclamation of August 11, 1947, Jinnah did not leave anything to interpretation and took every opportunity to drive home his commitment to a secular Pakistan. One could go on quoting *ad infinitum from his speeches and observations.* [14]

Yet like so many others, he has confined his firsthand evidence of Jinnah to the three-piece argument.

Duplicating the two-pronged argument

Prof. Ishtiaq Ahmed and Ardeshir Cowasjee have also presented their arguments in a similar fashion, but as such they both make only an indirect reference to Jinnah's anti-theocracy speeches, whilst directly reproducing the two-pronged argument. In the following short extracts, I have added emphasis wherever the relevant evidence appears. Note that neither of these commentators has produced any other speeches of Jinnah as supporting evidence. We can see this from the extracts below.

Ardeshir Cowasjee

Mr Ardeshir Cowasjee (1926-2012) is the only non-Muslim example in our review. He was a veteran columnist of *Dawn*, known for his outspoken and leftist views. In his article, *Back to Jinnah*, he suggests that he is supporting then President Musharraf's 'vision of what Pakistan's founder had in mind for his country, a vision he intended to bring to material form'. Soon he refers to two of Jinnah speeches as firsthand proof of his being a secularist:

> Three months before the partition of the subcontinent, in an interview with Doon Campbell of Reuters, Jinnah firmly stated: "The new state will be a modern democratic state with sovereignty resting in the people and the members of the new nation having equal rights of citizenship regardless of religion, caste or creed." He repeated this on August 11, 1947, whilst addressing the

---

[13] See Munir Report, p.201

[14] Op. cit. p.7, quoting M.H. Askari, 'Not a Theocratic State', *Dawn* 19 August 1992

> members of his Constituent Assembly, making it doubly clear to them that religion is not the business of the state.[15]

Whilst he does not bring in the anti-theocracy speeches of Jinnah in this particular article, he condemns the Objectives Resolution for containing 'a mish-mash of the general principles of an "Islamic" state and the accepted concepts of a modern "democratic" state'. [16] He views it as a document that mixes religion and politics, and which contravenes the essence of the 11 August 1947 speech and the Munir quote.

Ishtiaq Ahmed

Prof. Ishtiaq Ahmed is Professor Emeritus of Political Science at Stockholm University and Honorary Senior Fellow at the Institute of South Asian Studies, National University of Singapore. Presently he is Visiting Professor at Government College University, Lahore. A renowned political scientist, he seems fully cognisant of the significance of Munir's views in relation to the 'ideological' debate. He refers to the writings of the late Chief Justice frequently in his own work, [17] and considers Munir's *From Jinnah to Zia* to be 'the most powerful secularist challenge in intellectual terms'. [18]

In the journal article that we are reviewing, Prof. Ahmed suggests that 'modernists' and 'fundamentalists' have each had their turn in trying to shape the structure of the state, and that so far secularists have been marginalised. Prof. Ahmed reviews the fundamentalist, modernist, and secularist viewpoints of the Pakistan idea. He finds that the fundamentalist and modernist views respectively are not faithful to that of Jinnah, who 'actually preferred a secular state.' [19] As proof of this, he looks to the following evidence:

> When asked to elaborate on what sort of state Pakistan would be, Jinnah dismissed allegations *that it would be a theocracy*. This theme was consistently emphasized in interviews to foreign newspapers and broadcasting companies. [20]

Immediately after this, Prof. Ahmed also cites the Munir quote. Later he also mentions the 11 August 1947 speech, about which he comments:

15 A. Cowasjee, 'Back to Jinnah' in *Dawn*, 3 February 2002

16 Ibid. Quotation marks around the words 'Islamic' and 'democratic' are retained from the original.

17 See for example I. Ahmed (1987) *The Concept of an Islamic State: an Analysis of the Ideological Controversy in Pakistan* London: Frances Pinter (based on his doctoral thesis of 1985).

18 I. Ahmed, 'Secularists and Jinnah's 11th August Covenant', in *Daily Times,* 11 January 2005.

19 I. Ahmed 2004, p.14

20 Op. cit. p.16

> This speech has been the subject of great controversy in Pakistani politics. It seems that Jinnah wanted to supplant the notion of 'Muslim nationalism' with 'Pakistani nationalism'. The change was most significant but it was not consistent with the main argument upon which the separatist demand had been justified: that Muslims were a nation in their own right. [21]

In short he sees the speech as a formal renunciation of the Two-Nation Theory. The speech has indeed raised controversy, mainly from those with a strictly religious view of Islam and those who do not understand the full implications of the Two-Nation Theory. We will return to the 11 August 1947 speech as well as the Two-Nation Theory later in this book.

Denial

We have observed from the above review that there is very little, if any, evidence within Jinnah's speeches to back the pro-secularist argument. Aside from this, the main criticism levelled against pro-secularist commentators is that though they know Jinnah never used the word 'secular' for Pakistan, they deny the Islamic content of hundreds of his speeches. But it is not that they are ignoring the existence of such speeches. In fact pro-secular commentators do acknowledge them, but they also see a paradox between these speeches and Munir's three-piece argument for a 'secular Jinnah', and so they have come up with a number of theories to explain the apparent paradox. Here we will briefly review the three main types found in our examples:

Islam as a propaganda tool

This is the most common argument, and it is found in the article by Hoodbhoy and Nayyar (as well as A.S. Ghazali and I. Ahmed). Whilst they acknowledge that Jinnah made references to Islam, Hoodbhoy and Nayyar note that these speeches seem to contradict the 'outright secular declarations' [22] that they had quoted earlier in their article. By way of an explanation, they write that it was because the Muslim League had received some support from some 'influential ulama' in the mid-forties, which by coincidence (they allege) is when we see the most Islamic content in Jinnah's speeches. [23] They are open-minded enough however to also concede the possibility that Jinnah may have understood 'Islam

---

[21] Op. cit. p.19

[22] Hoodbhoy & Nayyar 1985, p.171

[23] Ibid.

in such liberal terms that he saw no essential conflict between it and his desire for a modern, democratic state along Western lines.'[24]

The ambiguity theory

Ishtiaq Ahmed also believes that Islam was a propaganda tool, but he also thinks the situation is a little more complicated. The basic premise of his article is to prove that Jinnah was deliberately ambiguous in his speeches. Ahmed writes that this was because Jinnah 'preferred a secular state', but that his speeches contained Islamic overtones because 'his public campaign for Pakistan was heavily dependent upon the invocation of Islam and Muslim 'ulama.'[25] He concludes that both modernists and fundamentalists were brought into the Muslim League's fold under the assumption that their respective ideas would be implemented in Pakistan. This to him explains why 'religion and politics were intimately connected' in the Muslim League, and also explains the mental background behind the Objectives Resolution:

> The modernistic and fundamentalist experiments that we have examined above were therefore no accident or deviation from what the idea of Pakistan represented at both the leadership and mass level.[26]

Ahmed laments that whilst Jinnah 'tried to supplant Muslim nationalism with Pakistani nationalism by declaring religion a private affair of the individual', his was a lone secularist voice amongst the majority of Indian Muslims representing one shade of Islam or another.

The above theories are harmful to Jinnah since they imply that he was thinking like a self-serving politician, manipulating the masses to gain support by deceptive means. If we accept them as true, then the sheer number of Islamic statements in his speeches would indicate that he was a pathological liar, regardless of the fact that to date all the biographical literature available on Jinnah has always indicated that friends, critics and adversaries alike have recognised his integrity and honesty.[27]

---

[24] Ibid.

[25] I. Ahmed 2004, p.14

[26] Op. cit. p.26

[27] Biographers Larry Collins and Dominique Lapierre for example, who hold the most negative views of Jinnah, nevertheless acknowledge him as 'a man of unassailable personal honesty and financial integrity', whose 'canons were sound law and sound procedure'. (L. Collins and D. Lapierre (1975) *Freedom at Midnight*. New York: Simon & Schuster p.116). Nehru, despite his strong opposition to Jinnah's politics, conceded in his book written while imprisoned at Ahmadnagar Fort prison during the Quit India Movement: 'Jinnah was able, tenacious and not open to the lure of office, which had been such a failing of so many others' (J. Nehru (1946) *The Discovery of India* New York: The John Day Company, p.395). Former Viceroy of India Lord A.P. Wavell, upon hearing of Jinnah's death in 1948, admitted in his memoirs that he 'never liked Jinnah, but had a certain reluctant admiration for him and his

Secular Islam – the synthesis theory

When it comes to Jinnah's anti-theocracy statements, many commentators choose to overlook their full context. Take a look at the following speech of Jinnah in which he mentions theocracy:

> The great majority of us are Muslims. We follow the teachings of the Prophet Muhammad (peace be on him). We are members of the brotherhood of Islam in which all are equal in rights, dignity and self-respect. Consequently, we have a special and a very deep sense of unity. But make no mistake: Pakistan is not a *theocracy* or anything like it. *Islam demands from us the tolerance of other creeds* and we welcome in closest association with us all those who, of whatever creed, are themselves willing and ready to play their part as true and loyal citizens of Pakistan. [28]

It is important to note here that Jinnah has expressly mentioned Islam as a counterforce to theocracy in this speech. He has described Islam as a 'brotherhood' in which 'all are equal in rights, dignity and self-respect'. In his broadcast speech to the people of America a week later, Jinnah also calls Pakistan 'the premier Islamic state', [29] even as he adds that 'in any case Pakistan is not going to be a theocratic state', [30] demonstrating that in his view the former term is by no means a synonym for the latter. Most pro-secularist commentators who refer to the above speech are only interested in the line: 'in any case Pakistan is not going to be a theocratic state'. They omit the references to 'Islam' and the 'premier Islamic state' in the same speech.

Secular-Muslim commentators meanwhile believe that Jinnah was part of a 'synthesis' movement, and that this explains the appearance of both secular and Islamic content in his speeches. Therefore they lay claim to be the only group who are not afraid to quote certain passages in full. [31] Abdus Sattar Ghazali is one such commentator. He believes that Jinnah was a 'secular liberal' [32] but that he took some of his ideals from Islam.

---

uncompromising attitude.' (Archibald Percival Wavell (Earl of) & Penderel Moon (ed.) (1973) *Wavell: The Viceroy's Journal* London: Oxford University Press, p.442). Dr Ambedkar, who was at times fiercely critical of Jinnah and also Muslims, but nevertheless a supporter of the Pakistan demand, has remarked about Jinnah in his *Pakistan or Partition of India*: 'it is doubtful if there is a politician in India to whom the adjective incorruptible can be more fittingly applied' (1946a, p.323). For Muslim testimonies on Jinnah's character, see for example A.S. Ahmed 1997, xx, 89-91.

[28] Broadcast talk to the people of Australia as Governor-General, 19 February, 1948. (NV Vol. VII, p.190)

[29] Jinnah's broadcast talk on Pakistan to the people of United States of America, Karachi, 26 February 1948. (NV Vol. VII, p.213)

[30] Ibid. p.216

[31] See for example M.R. Kazimi, 'Pakistan: The Founder's View' in *Journal of Management and Social Sciences* Vol. 4, No. 1, (Spring 2008), p.47

[32] Ghazali 1996, p.7

He writes:

> *Jinnah's speeches are abound with references to the Islamic principles of social justice and fairplay*, but he made it clear, on more than one occasion, that he was against theocracy. He had *consistently opposed theocratic ideas and influences and never minced his words about his commitment to a secular state.* [33] "Make no mistake: Pakistan is not a theocracy or anything like it. Islam demands from us the tolerance of other creeds and we welcome in closest association with us all those who of whatever creed are themselves willing to play their part as true and loyal citizens of Pakistan."
>
> On another occasion Jinnah said: "The great majority of us are Muslims. We follow the teachings of the Prophet Muhammad (PBUH). We are members of the brotherhood of Islam in which all are equal in rights, dignity and self-respect. Consequently, we have a special and a very deep sense of unity. But make no mistake: Pakistan is not a theocracy or anything like it." [34]

Unlike the advocates of secularism proper, Mr Ghazali has no issue with quoting both the directly Islamic and the anti-theocratic statements of Jinnah. But since to him 'anti-theocracy' automatically means 'pro-secularism', in the same chapter he also writes:

> Jinnah was basically a secular liberal who had studied British political history and practiced common law. For such a man the Muslim cause, which inescapably bound up with Islam, embraced nationalism and patriotism as well as the strict meaning of religion. He wanted to see Pakistan as an embodiment of dynamic and forward-looking Islam. Jinnah believed that Islam fosters, upholds and extols values such as freedom, equality, solidarity and social justice which may also be termed secular or humanistic; these, he repeatedly emphasized, constitute the bases of Pakistan's polity. [35]

(Note that the last part of the passage is borrowed from another academic, ironically one who happens to argue for a 'Muslim Jinnah'.) [36]

---

[33] This particular sentence of Ghazali's text (emphasised) is evidently taken from H. Alavi, 'Ethnicity, Muslim Society, and the Pakistan Ideology' in Anita M. Weiss (ed.) (1986) *Islamic Reassertion in Pakistan: The Application of Islamic Laws in an Islamic State* New York: Syracuse University Press, p.41.

[34] Ghazali 1996, p.12-13

[35] Op. cit. p.7-8 (Emphasis mine)

[36] This time, see S. Mujahid 1981, p.266-7 for the original. Whilst Ghazali confuses the issue and takes it to a pro-secularist conclusion, the original text in Prof. Mujahid's book reads: 'Jinnah believed that Islam fosters, upholds and extols values such as freedom, equality, solidarity and social justice which may also be termed secular or humanistic; these, he

Later Mr Ghazali also writes:

> A firm believer in Islam and democracy, he [Jinnah] was confident that Pakistan would work towards a democratic order since Islam is inherently democratic in its content, tenor, and spirit. "Islam and its ideals have taught us democracy. It has taught equality of man, justice and fair play to everybody." [37]

To the untrained eye, these views may seem virtually identical to what I myself wrote in *Secular Jinnah* (2005). However there are some clear-cut differences between what I tried to present and the secular-Muslim view, and these will be outlined shortly. First, here is what Mr Ghazali concluded about the 'ideological' position of Jinnah:

> In any case, Jinnah put all controversies about the role of religion in politics at rest by declaring that religion was a private matter between man and his Creator, that it had nothing to do with business of the state ... [38]

Here, Ghazali has interpreted the 11 August 1947 speech as meaning that religion will have no place in politics – though this is not quite in fact what Jinnah said (more on that later). [39] Hence he is either Jinnah a pure secularist, or a secular-Muslim – though with the hotchpotch of sources from which he plagiarises to make his case, it is sometimes difficult to tell which one he is really advocating.

Confusion in the modernist category

It is impossible to categorise secular-Muslim commentators either as purely pro-Islam or pro-secularism. They advocate (in the words of Ishtiaq Ahmed) a 'synthesis between classical Islamic teachings on law and political theory with modern Western ideas'. They thus acknowledge Jinnah both as a secularist and as a Muslim.

This brings us to a problem that I was not aware of until after the publication of the original *Secular Jinnah*. Of the three main types of commentator we have in the debate over Jinnah, the 'modernist' is a category which needs re-examination. Generally speaking, we can divide the two furthest poles of thought as follows:

---

repeatedly emphasized, constitute the bases of Pakistan's polity. *Thus, Jinnah's conception was essentially Islamic.*' (Emphasis mine)

[37] Ghazali 1996, p.13

[38] Op. cit. p.20

[39] See Myth no. 5 (Chapter 10) and Chapter 12

- The fundamentalist religionist group – i.e. those with a strictly religious view of Islam, who wish to recreate a past medieval version of an 'Islamic state'
- The fundamentalist secularist group – i.e. those who seek a materialist state and are thus opposed to any form of religious or even spiritual influence over politics

Most ordinary Pakistanis – at least those in the socioeconomic middle classes – do not fall into either category. They know in simple terms that 'Islam is a way of life', but as they do not have a sophisticated understanding of the point, it is practically a rhetorical statement. Therefore they are effectively open to all ideas including those of fundamentalists and secularists, both of which again have usually misunderstood the Islamic worldview. In short, much of the Pakistani nation is as yet ill-informed about the Islamic worldview one way or another, and this is half of the 'ideological' problem in Pakistan.

As for those who do give the matter serious thought, some either become religionists or eventually reject what is considered a religious-cum-political concept and become secularists. Many more however find that they are satisfied by neither extreme viewpoint, and so they end up somewhere in the middle, usually thinking along the lines of 'synthesis' between 'classical (or historical) Islam' and 'modern West'. They view this as a reconciliation of matter and spirit, since it does not apparently conflict with their personal religious beliefs (whether traditionalist or liberal), and they erroneously attribute the synthesis idea to Iqbal and Jinnah. The remarks of the humanist historian Hamza Alavi are worth noting in this regard:

> Today's true heirs of Pakistan's founding ideology are the Secularists, many of them believing Muslims, who reject and repudiate the idea of exploitation of Islamic ideology in pursuit of political ends. If Islamic Modernism was the initial ideology of the emerging Muslim salariat, it has long ceased to be a live intellectual movement and has been marginalised. It exists in small and peripheral groupings such as the Tulu-e-Islam group led by Ghulam Ahmed Pervaiz. Many of the basic ideas of Islamic Modernism *have passed into conventional wisdom.* Insofar as they still have currency, *they are accommodated within secular political attitudes.* [40]

Dr Alavi has practically described the growth of 'secular Islam'; it is increasingly becoming the popular Muslim view; its followers borrow notions from 'Islamic Modernism' in underdeveloped form and acquire

[40] H. Alavi, 'Ethnicity, Muslim Society, and the Pakistan Ideology' in Anita M. Weiss (ed.) (1986) *Islamic Reassertion in Pakistan: The Application of Islamic Laws in an Islamic State* New York: Syracuse University Press, p.42

an essentially 'secular political attitude' separated from a private religious faith; and we can safely assume it also accounts for the viewpoint of many Muslim Leaguers in early Pakistan. Alternatively, some are 'secular-Muslim' in their personal viewpoint of the state but also believe that Jinnah himself was a pure secularist, [41] and this attitude of course is largely down to the Munir quote. Then there is another much smaller subcategory that fully comprehends the real implications of the 'matter / spirit' question in Islam, and which is therefore distinct from the 'secular-Muslim' group. Alavi has referred properly to this group as 'Islamic modernist'.

However other academics place the entire mass of Muslims with a 'middle-ground' view, secular-Muslim or not, into one fuzzy category of 'modernism', and this results in a problem of another kind. Here is Ishtiaq Ahmed's description of modernist thought:

> … Among the modern-educated Muslim gentry, consisting of constitutional lawyers, writers, academics and others who constituted a majority of the higher and middle-rank leadership of the Muslim League an idealized version of a progressive Islam had been cultivated since at least the time of Sir Syed Ahmed Khan who laid the foundations of the Muslim modernist movement in the second half of the 19th century. In fact he assumed a radically unorthodox position that virtually rendered the old type of *shari'a*-oriented Islam obsolete by insisting that Islam was completely compatible with modern scientific discoveries and knowledge. His followers did not follow up consistently with such a disposition and instead began to *seek a synthesis* between classical Islamic teachings on law and political theory with modern Western ideas. Nobody represented this tradition more forcefully than Allama Iqbal whose six lectures … are a classic example in such formulations. Although stimulating to read, the lectures are an exercise in speculative thought rather than a sustained argument for any particular philosophical or political standpoint. *One can even assert that it has been the source of considerable confusion.* Typically it has inspired people to believe in things like 'reformed *shari'a*' 'Islamic democracy' and so on. [42]

To Prof. Ahmed, all 'modernists' are the confused intellectual followers of Sir Syed Ahmad Khan; they have missed the point of his uniquely 'radically unorthodox' position altogether. Ahmed's argument is partly correct, in that the synthesis inherent in 'secular Islam' is not in line with Sir Syed's thought; but his claim that Iqbal is the foremost advocate of synthesis – and the source of 'considerable confusion' – is

[41] See for example A.S Ghazali 1996 and M.R. Kazimi 2008

[42] I. Ahmed 2004, p.20 (Emphasis mine except on Islamic terms)

absolutely without foundation.[43] It is astonishing that he makes such a statement when on the other hand he also believes that Iqbal's lectures 'are an exercise in speculative thought rather than a sustained argument for any particular philosophical or political standpoint'.

In fact the 'confusion' of which Prof. Ahmed complains is not applicable to all modernists, but all modernists are being tarnished with the same brush because of it. After a number of years thinking about the problem (and having had my own work misconstrued by a secular-Muslim commentator) [44] I have come to realise that there has never been a broad consensus on Jinnah's 'ideological' stance for the simple reason that the category of thought under which he falls has not been adequately characterised and appraised, if at all. Scholarship appears unaware of the difference between the secular-Muslim and 'other' subcategory. Yet whilst the two may have surface-level similarities in their respective arguments, they differ in fundamental aspects.

Although Prof. Ahmed has acknowledged the 'unorthodox' modernist position of Sir Syed, he has wrongly suggested that all who came after him are following the muddled notion of synthesis. A much smaller modernist subgroup does indeed exist, in which we find the name of Dr M. Iqbal, and, as I hope to demonstrate through this book, Jinnah. Each individual is as unique as Sir Syed in his/her ways and means, and so can appear scattered, but certain characteristics unite them all intellectually, whilst separating them from the proponents of secular Islam. Dr Javid Iqbal has said that the difference between the two subcategories comes down to a 'conventional' versus 'reconstructive' interpretation of Islam as *deen*. [45] I will introduce my own term for this other group shortly (though I am in agreement with him in principle), but first we should note the two characteristics that allow us to discern between it and the secular-Islam group:

- The proponents of secular Islam believe that Islam ought to be formally relegated to the status of a religion, i.e. a 'personal relationship between individual and God'. The other group asserts that Islam is not merely a religion i.e. it is not about personal salvation, and so relegation is meaningless in this case.
- Since the proponents of secular Islam view Islam strictly as a religion, they believe that a political expression of Islam means a theocracy that discriminates not only against other faiths but

[43] For a detailed discussion of Iqbal's particular viewpoint, see Chapter 6.

[44] See my correspondence with Dr Kazimi described shortly in this chapter.

[45] Personal correspondence to S. Karim, October 2009. Dr J. Iqbal has always maintained that the Pakistan movement was not about 'conventional' (sectarian/religious) Islam. See for example his article 'Reminiscences', in (L.H. Merchant & S. Mujahid (eds.) (2009) *The Jinnah Anthology* Karachi: Oxford University Press, p.96, where he mentions that he presented the same argument in articles published in *Dawn* (circa 1946) in the days when Jinnah was still alive.

also minority Muslim sects. The other group maintains that if a community divides (and thus discriminates) on sectarian or even political lines, it cannot legitimately call itself Muslim, and so there is no question of a sectarian problem in a bona fide 'systemic expression', or *deen*, of Islam.

(I acknowledge that the implication of the second characteristic I have just mentioned is unpalatable to many Muslims who follow various 'schools of thought', but it must be mentioned for the purposes of clarification. Dr J. Iqbal has also said that secular-Muslim modernists find these differences 'difficult to digest'. [46])

As the differences revolve around sectarianism (and division in general), hereinafter I will refer to the 'other' group as 'non-sectarian' modernist. As such when it comes to the political sphere the secularists as well as both the modernist groups are looking to put an end to sectarian discrimination. This is the reason why we find surface-level similarities in some of their arguments. But whereas all other modernists and secularists are concerned with the preservation of sectarianism in the personal sphere (albeit for the reason of respecting pluralist sensibility), the proponents of 'non-sectarian Islam' [47] maintain that an intellectual unity on the basis of Islamic ethics automatically closes such divisions, without detriment to the cultural, ethnic or linguistic diversity of human society. In short, they endorse cultural pluralism but are moral absolutists. They are motivated, whether implicitly or explicitly, by the Islamic worldview, which teaches that the supposed dichotomy between matter and spirit is not real, but down to human perception; and it is only once people realise this that they will 1) *comprehend* what unity really means and therefore 2) will come to *embody* this precept.

The advocates of this worldview take different routes in attempting to promote and realise this ideal, but their aim is identical nonetheless. Hence in the philosophical field they actively call for a complete overhaul of the present approach to Islam, in order to finally reject sectarianism in all its forms. This is what Dr M. Iqbal – the 'spiritual founder of Pakistan' – did in his aptly titled lectures *Reconstruction of Religious Thought in Islam*, and (in fact) in all of his work and in his poetry. At the practical level, they find ways of bringing communities together in social or political unity. This is what M. A. Jinnah did as the founder of Pakistan.

---

46 Personal correspondence to S. Karim (October 2009)

47 I am aware that the term 'non-sectarian Islam' is a tautology, but again I have used it purely for the purposes of clarification between the subgroups.

A case in point

Unsurprisingly, every single reference to the Munir quote I have encountered to date can be traced to either *From Jinnah to Zia* or the Munir Report, but I did come across one exception. Hence before we move to the next chapter, here I will mention my personal experience with an advocate of the 'secular-Muslim' view, who incidentally took exception to my original *Secular Jinnah.* Dr Muhammad Reza Kazimi is a former editorial consultant at Oxford University Press in Pakistan, as well as a historian and literary critic, and is best known for his work on Liaquat Ali Khan. He gave my book a negative review in Dawn in 2006, accusing me (without any evidence) of advocating an 'oligarchy' on the one hand, and claiming that there was 'no difference' between my argument and Munir's on the other. [48] I was puzzled that he had misconstrued my actual position, but I never issued a rejoinder.

I was surprised however, when I discovered that some two years after reviewing my book, Dr Kazimi had written an article titled *Pakistan: The Founder's View* in which he had used the Munir quote, and had even got the date wrong. [49] Interestingly, and unlike every other commentator to date, his stated source of the quote was one of the well-known *Transfer of Power* volumes, rather than either of Munir's publications. I checked the source in question, and when I couldn't find the Munir quote in it, I contacted him. He double-checked his sources and it eventually emerged that he had in fact given an erroneous reference. Furthermore he could not recover the actual source that he used. He made it clear (and I believe him) that this was a genuine mistake on his part. During the course of our correspondence he also explained what it was about my book that he had found untenable. He believed that I had denounced the concept of sovereignty in the people, and therefore was pro-theocracy. In reality I had wilfully ignored the subject of sovereignty in the first book because the sovereignty issue is really connected to the 1949 debates on the Objectives Resolution, which occurred after Jinnah's death, whereas I was focused on the statements he made during his life. In reply I explained to Dr Kazimi that I did not object to the concept in principle, insofar as it is merely a contemporary expression for the right of humans to choose their own destiny, as sanctioned in the Quran. [50] But insofar as it is a term of political science, derived from Western

---

[48] See Dr Kazimi's review of *Secular Jinnah*, 'Ideological or Secular?' in *Dawn*, 14 August 2006.

[49] M.R. Kazimi, 'Pakistan: The Founder's View' in *Journal of Management and Social Sciences* Vol. 4, No. 1, (Spring 2008), p.47-8

[50] I was thinking in particular of verse 2:256: 'Let there be no compulsion in religion (*deen*): Truth stands out clear from Error.' (A. Yusuf Ali's translation). It goes without saying nevertheless that the Quran demands from its adherents, to borrow Iqbal's words, 'loyalty to God, not thrones'. See Quran verse 20:114: (Know,) then, (that) God is Sublimely Exalted, the Ultimate Sovereign, the Ultimate Truth.' (Asad) This concept is further explored in Chapter 12.

historical experience of the Church-State, [51] and most importantly, used to refer to a transfer of authority to a (human) body that holds all the power, with no requirement for 'spiritual' checks and balances, [52] this is where anyone who argues for a 'Muslim Jinnah' may have cause to object. I also explained that my actual objection in *Secular Jinnah* was to the use of false evidence, which goes against the historical method. [53]

I have mentioned this incident because my argument in *Secular Jinnah* was treated simultaneously as either representing a fundamentalist view or that of a closet secularist. [54] Following the publication of the book I found that my having described Islamic principles in practical terms on the one hand and refusing to countenance Jinnah as a secularist on the other was welcomed by most ordinary Muslim readers as well as academics, but incurred the wrath of both the secularist and the secular-Muslim readership. This experience proved to be most useful as it was this that led me to rethink the general categories of thought in the ideological debate.

---

[51] Medieval western experience of the Church State of course also includes the monarch with absolute power.

[52] 'Spiritual checks and balances' here mean laws of accountability included within a constitution to prevent corruption and despotic behaviour. This would be the opposite of realpolitik – where legislative and political decisions are made upon expediency, irrespective of any ethical or moral considerations. The usual language employed by modernists for such spiritual checks and balances – and which was also employed in the much misunderstood Objectives Resolution – is that we should introduce 'limits' to human 'sovereignty'.

[53] Personal correspondence to Dr M. R. Kazimi (March 2009). The relevant portion of my reply reads: 'At no point did I object to sovereignty in the people in principle. From a Quranic point of view this concept only affirms the God-given right to exercise free will. My focus was on what Jinnah's words actually were; and so what I actually objected to was the putting of words in people's mouths, which goes against the basic rules of the historical method. The phraseology as it appears in Munir's version implies a 'secular modern' state as it is generally understood in Western usage. But the actual version stated only 'popular representative' and 'democratic form'. My point was that, thanks to his experiences with the British and Congress in trying to work out constitutional solutions that claimed to be democratic, Jinnah was not interested in simply mimicking a 'modern' (or contemporary) type of democracy. He was interested in creating a progressive constitution which suited the genius of Pakistan's people. It is true Jinnah never advocated a theocratic state, as he had an Iqbalian understanding of Quranic principles. It is equally true that he did not advocate a 'secular' state as it is generally understood, because the word 'secular' has at its root a Christian concept regarding spirit and matter which is not in line with the Muslim view.'

[54] Similarly, Javid Iqbal's *Ideology of Pakistan* has been understood by some reviewers as taking an 'extreme modernist' position, and as concealing 'danger' (religious) by others. See reviews printed in J. Iqbal 2005 edition, p.194 and p.199 respectively.

Chapter 6
Iqbal on non-sectarian Islam

In this chapter, we will look at how Chief Justice Munir misunderstood a statement in Dr Javid Iqbal's book, thereby illustrating the difference between the 'secular-Muslim' and non-sectarian viewpoint. The following discussion should also help illustrate why we can safely place Dr Muhammad Iqbal into the 'non-sectarian' category of philosophers, based on his criticism of 'secularism' as a dualist concept.

Dr Javid Iqbal's view

In Chapter 2 we noted that Muhammad Munir had misconstrued Javid Iqbal's statement on secular principles and Islam. Here is the text as it is cited in Munir's book:

> Islam does not recognise the distinction between the 'spiritual' and the 'profane'. According to Islam the spiritual and temporal obligations are not only connected with each other but it is incumbent on every Muslim to constantly endeavour to realise the spiritual values while performing the temporal obligations. Hence secularism is an integral part of Islam and it is for this reason that the Islamic State assimilates the qualities of an ideal secular state. [1]

This text however has not been cited accurately, nor has Munir understood it in its proper context. I cite the latter portion of the text again, this time from the original book (Javid Iqbal's *Ideology of Pakistan*, 1971 edition):

> Hence 'Secularism' is an integral part of Islam and it is for this reason that the Islamic State assimilates the qualities of an ideal 'Secular State'. [2]

In the original book we see that Javid Iqbal has placed quotation marks around the terms 'secularism' and 'secular state'. He has done this to emphasise that he is aware of the controversy involved in using

[1] Munir 1980, p.32. Munir cites from the 1971 reprint edition of J. Iqbal's *Ideology of Pakistan*.
[2] J. Iqbal (1971 edition) p.4. (The 2005 edition (p.15) renders the same line a little differently)

these terms, as well as his understanding of the fact that the Islamic worldview does not recognise a dichotomy between the 'secular' (material) and spirit. This fact becomes clear when we see the full passage in which this sentence appears:

> Islam does not recognise the distinction between the 'spiritual' and the 'profane'. According to Islam the spiritual and temporal obligations are not only connected with each other but it is incumbent on every Muslim to constantly endeavour to realise the spiritual values while performing the temporal obligations. Hence 'Secularism' is an integral part of Islam and it is for this reason that the Islamic State assimilates the qualities of an ideal 'Secular State'.
>
> In the positive sense a 'Secular State' means a State which guarantees religious freedom to every citizen and which, without distinction of religion or race, endeavours to promote the material advancement and welfare of all its citizens. The Islamic State of Pakistan, as envisaged by Quaid-i-Azam, embraces the qualities of an ideal 'Secular State'. [3]

Note that in the last sentence, Javid Iqbal is referring to an 'Islamic State ... envisaged by the Quaid-i-Azam'. He acknowledges that it 'embraces the qualities' of an ideal secular state, but not that it *is* a secular state, nor that it is a fusion or synthesis of secularism and Islam.

He continues:

> In this State every citizen is granted the right of religious freedom. Sunnis, Shias, Wahabis and other sects of Islam, Hindus, Christians, Parsis, Buddhists and their numerous sects are free to profess their respective personal faiths and be governed by their respective personal codes of law. Islamic theology recognises a distinction of meanings in the words 'Mazhab' and 'Din'. 'Mazhab' means personal faith, viewpoint or path; whereas 'Din' means a body of those universal principles of Islam which are applicable to the entire humanity. Therefore, in this sense, the state of Pakistan does not have any specific 'Mazhab', because it is *neither founded on nor projects the personal viewpoint of any particular Islamic sect*, but like an ideal 'Secular State', to promote the material advancement and welfare of all its citizens without distinction of religion or race, is one of its numerous duties. Thus, in the political sense, irrespective of their religion or race, all Pakistanis are citizens of the State of Pakistan on equal terms. This very important aspect of the State of Pakistan was clarified by Quaid-i-

---

[3] Ibid.

Azam in his famous presidential address to the Constituent Assembly on 11th August, 1947 … [4]

Dr J. Iqbal shows that the speech of 11 August 1947 is not out of line with the principles of Islam, because neither it nor an ideal secular state can discriminate on the basis of faith (or sect). To explain, he has pointed to the difference between *mazhab* (the Arabic word for religion) and *din* (*deen*). The latter is also usually translated as 'religion', but in fact there is no real equivalent in English. It is often translated as a 'way of life', [5] but this too does little to convey its full meaning. Dr J. Iqbal has made a good attempt at a short description when he says that (Quranic) *deen* refers to a body of the universal principles of Islam, which are applicable to the whole of humanity. To him as well as other Pakistani modernists, it is practically a synonym for the 'ideology' of Pakistan. In fact the word *deen* (as a root word) has a number of meanings, among which the primary ones are obedience, submission and habit, [6] and which together mean the collective behaviour (i.e. established practices, and not merely the proclaimed ideal principles) of any culture or civilisation at a given time. The principles governing this behaviour come from every sphere of the civilisation, including its religion, its societal experiences, its philosophy and its political setup. This 'behaviour' of the collective can prove either to be beneficial or destructive to humanity and the world at large. *Deen* therefore is essentially an anthropological term. It is not a word for culture per se, but it certainly influences the shape of cultures. [7] An example from the Quran is the ancient Egyptian society, the *deen* of which may be

---

[4] Ibid. Emphasis mine.

[5] See for example Laleh Bakhtiar's translation of Quran verse 2:256.

[6] E.W. Lane's Lexicon (hereinafter 'Lane'), Book I (Part 3), p.942-5 (under entry دين). 'Obedience' and 'submission' are the two primary meanings of *deen* (verb); a third primary meaning (noun) is 'custom', or 'habit'. Other listed derivative meanings include: to borrow upon credit, or become indebted; to rule, govern or manage; to possess or own; to become habituated; to hold, confirm or pronounce; to exercise authority over; a way, course of manner or conduct; state or condition; subjection, sovereign or ruling power; rain; judge, ruler or governor. None of these meanings points explicitly to religion. Lane demonstrates that the word 'religion' usually used as a translation for *deen* is derived only by implication of the fact that in the Quran, 'obedience' (primary meaning of *deen*) is to God. So the verse 2:256 usually rendered 'there is no compulsion in religion (*deen*)' in fact literally reads: 'There shall be no compulsion in obedience'. (p.944) Lane explains further via a translation of verse 3:19 (he incorrectly points to 3:17). He writes: 'It is said … "Verily the only true religion [*ad-deena*] in the sight of God is El-Islam." *Ad-deen*a is a name for "That whereby one serves God". It is applied to Religion, in the widest sense of this term, *practical and doctrinal*.' (Ibid. Emphasis mine) Further, it is not without significance that the first Islamic state was founded by the Rasool in *Medina* – which was 'so-called because it had, or held, in possession, or under authority'. (p.945)

[7] For a thought-provoking discussion on why 'Muslim culture' exists less in reality than as a symbolic idea, see A.H. Syed 1982, p.98-111.

summed up as despotism, capitalism and theocracy. [8] A contemporary example of a *deen* is that of the civilisation of the 'West', broadly comprising countries including the European nations, America, Canada and Australia (and others), which generally follow a political philosophy of secular nationalism (ignoring its ethnic and economic strains). Contemporary Western *deen* is based partly (amongst other things) on Europe's bitter experiences with theocracy and monarchy, the work of various scientists and philosophers during (in particular) the Enlightenment period, and, just as importantly, the contribution of Christian thought which historically binds nearly all Western countries together. In his classic book *The Meaning of Pakistan*, F. K. Khan Durrani has used the German word 'Weltanschauung' [9] to describe Islam's 'philosophy of life', [10] which could thus be used as the nearest European equivalent word for *deen*.

We should add that the word Arabic *mazhab* – containing the idea of a 'personal' or individual faith [11] – does not appear at all in the Quran. This highlights that the Quran is focused on the mental background of cultures and nations, and the ethics of political and religious systems. It is a discourse on the problems of various '*deens*' (understood holistically as modes of human existence), rather than a mere text prescribing religious values and doctrines, which at any rate tend to ignore the mundane political and sociological dimensions of human life.

In Islam, since *deen* is holistic, with universal values that transcend notions of creed as well as race, it naturally takes no limited sectarian views into consideration. Therefore, to borrow the words of Javid Iqbal, Pakistan 'is neither founded on nor projects the personal viewpoint of any particular Islamic sect'. With this brilliant point Javid Iqbal obliterates the sectarian problem posed in theocracy, and simultaneously justifies the idea of Pakistan as an 'Islamic state', as distinct from both a religious, or theocratic state and a materialist, or secular state. He is implying that we can afford to set aside the *mazhab* of all Muslim sects in the political sphere, along with their respective discriminative doctrines; [12] after all, to do otherwise would be to contravene the true character of Islam as a non-sectarian *deen*. [13] Thus guided by the *deen* of Islam, Pakistan is meant to be a state that is true to the Quran's

---

8 See Quran 29:39, 40:23-26

9 *Weltanschauung:* lit. 'worldview'.

10 F. Durrani (1944) *The Meaning of Pakistan* Lahore: Sh. Muhammad Ashraf, p.156

11 Lane, Book I (Part 3), p.982 (under entry ذهب). Root meanings include (amongst others): to go, to pass; to waste or whither away; to banish or expel; to carry away; to become lost, or disappear; to pursue a way, course or mode; to have a particular opinion, persuasion or belief; to regard in one's own way, interpret.

12 All religious sects tend to define themselves with doctrines that serve, among other things, to discriminate against other sects. This goes against the Quranic principle of unity (30:31-2). See also 42:15 for how the Rasool was instructed to deal with sectarianism peacefully.

13 Hence he has also said unequivocally that 'there is no room for sectarianism in Islam'. (J. Iqbal 2005 edition, p.15)

'spiritual' (or universal) principles of justice, liberty and solidarity. But it cannot call itself *Islamic* until it actively practises what it preaches. Realising this is so important that Dr Muhammad Iqbal alludes to it in the very first sentence of the preface to his lectures on *The Reconstruction of Religious Thought in Islam:*

> The Quran is a book that emphasizes 'deed' rather than 'idea'.[14]

This point should become clearer as we continue.

The ontological background

When Dr Javid Iqbal stated that 'secularism is an integral part of Islam',[15] he was actually reiterating his father's discussion on the ontological [16] worldview in Islam. The following is an extract of Dr Muhammad Iqbal's explanation, from a lecture in which he reviewed the secular nationalism of Turkey:

> In Islam the spiritual and the temporal are not two distinct domains, and the nature of an act, however secular in its import, is determined by the attitude of mind with which the agent does it. ... It is *not true* to say that the Church and the State are two sides or facets of the same thing. *Islam is a single unanalyasble reality which is one or the other as your point of view varies.* ... The spirit finds its opportunities in the natural, the material, the secular. All that is secular is therefore sacred in the roots of its being. ... There is no such thing as a profane world. ... The State according to Islam is only an effort to realize the spiritual in a human organization. [17]

The philosopher makes the point that in Islam the perceived dichotomy between matter and spirit is something of an illusion. He takes the view that ultimately matter has an unquantifiable phenomenon at its root, for which he uses the word 'spirit' [18] (we could also refer to it as Creative thought). [19] Hence, says Dr M. Iqbal, in Islam

---

14 M. Iqbal (1971 reprint) *The Reconstruction of Religious Thought in Islam* (hereinafter '*Reconstruction*'). Lahore: Sh. Muhammad Ashraf, v.

15 J. Iqbal 1971, p.4

16 Ontology – a branch of metaphysics concerned with the study of existence.

17 *Reconstruction*, p.154-5. Emphasis mine.

18 'Matter is spirit in space-time reference ... the merely material has no substance until we discover it rooted in the spiritual' (Ibid.)

19 See *Reconstruction* p.31: 'It is, however, possible to take thought not as a principle which organizes and integrates its material from the outside, but as a potency which is formative of the very being of its material. Thus regarded thought or idea is not alien to the original nature of things; it is in their ultimate ground and constitutes the very essence of their being .... thought and being are ultimately one'.

'all that is secular is sacred in the roots of its being', and 'there is no such thing as a profane world'. Placed against this background, Dr M. Iqbal's use of the word 'secular' above is very clear. He uses it as a synonym for every material thing as well as every mundane human act. Whereas the principle behind dualism is that 'being' and 'non-being' (matter and idea/spirit) are separate, in Islam the two are inextricably linked. They are one and the same; they are neither separate, nor are they merely two facets of the same thing. The apparent dichotomy is down purely to human perception. In the Quranic view, an idea is expressed in the physical world through human action, and its worth as a 'spiritual' value is either confirmed or falsified from the consequences of the act (Quran: 2:256). Hence it is only in the Quran that the phrase 'an atom's weight of good' makes literal sense (99:7-8). The philosopher says further that it is the 'attitude of mind' behind an act that determines whether it is 'spiritual' (i.e. in harmony with the Natural Order) or not, and not strictly the act itself. Hence a religious or ritual act may have less value than a practical act, depending on the mindset behind it. We can better understand this by means of an analogy: In light of the Quran, a landlord who prays religiously yet whose income is derived solely from the exploitation of underprivileged people is less spiritual than an ordinary working man who, despite his best intentions, does not pray regularly but actively dedicates his life to alleviating poverty. The former man is neither psychologically nor (therefore) actively spiritual; the latter man is. [20] In the collective (or political) context, a society or state can only be described as 'Islamic' or spiritual if it *actively* works to bring about socio-economic equity, to guarantee freedom of religion and thought, and to uphold equality before the law.

It is with this in mind that Javid Iqbal remarks: 'the Islamic State assimilates the qualities of an ideal 'Secular State'.' It does not matter what its name is, as long as it functions with a view to upholding the principle of *tauheed* [21] in practice. As a 'God-conscious' state, [22] possessing the quality of united allegiance amongst its people, it must be just and free. Since it is also inspired by the workings of the ever-

---

[20] The Muslim scholar Dr Fazlur Rehman was thinking along similar lines when he wrote: 'a person who does not actively cooperate in the welfare of humanity is devoid of *din* or faith'. (F. Rehman (1967) *Some Reflections on the Reconstruction of Muslim Society in Pakistan*; as cited in S. Mujahid (2001) *Ideology of Pakistan* Islamabad: International University, p.134. Likewise Jinnah once said that 'Islam really means action. … And action implies society of man'. See also Quranic verses 9:19, 107:1-7, which makes this point clear.

[21] *Tauheed*: A word referring to a united belief in one and the same Creator. The word does not appear directly in the Quran but is derived from certain verses on His Oneness such as 112:1 and 12:39 containing the words *aahadun* (oneness of being, indivisible, unique) and *wahidun* (oneness of attributes, unity, original source) respectively. In the political context this also means a united allegiance to a set of universal principles (based on the Quranic axiom that the Creator is the Primary Cause and thus Owner of earthly resources) and hence can be described as Civil Unity. See also Asad's commentary notes on verse 112:1)

[22] Here I have borrowed Asad's phrase from his translation of the Quran.

changing natural universe, it is inherently progressive and dynamic.[23]

However it seems that Munir has failed to grasp the profound and wide-ranging implications of the Islamic worldview, which explains his later claim that Jinnah 'wanted a modern secular democratic state based no doubt on Islamic principles'.[24] A dichotomy between material and spirit remains firmly in Munir's mind, and so he seems to infer that Jinnah stood for 'secular Islam', i.e. that secularism can be used to temper the religion and prevent it from interfering in politics. To many Muslims this idea is absurd as they already understand that the principles of religious tolerance and freedom of conscience are in tune with the Quran. Ironically, and in contradiction of himself, even Munir has acknowledged this to be the case.[25]

The dualist problem

However it should also be noted, with respect, that Javid Iqbal's choice of wording has probably contributed somewhat to the misunderstanding on the part of Munir. Dr J. Iqbal has written that '...'secularism' is an integral part of Islam'[26] (emphasis mine). Despite the fact that he has taken care to put quotes around the terms 'secularism' and 'secular state', the statement still inadvertently gives the impression that an entire body of thought, including its dualistic background, is integral to Islam. The primary principle of secularism today is to dissociate its subject (usually the state) from both religious and spiritual affairs, and this is in conflict with the Islamic viewpoint outlined above. Dr M. Iqbal has also mentioned that the secular nationalists of Turkey borrowed from the history of European ideas, and that therefore their theory of state is 'misleading inasmuch as it suggests a dualism which does not exist in Islam.'[27] Historically, modern secularism has evolved from what began as an intellectual response to the religious elitism of the Church and in particular the persecution of Christian movements that were not in line with the Roman Catholic Church. The motive for advocating the separation of church and state at this time therefore, was a desire to introduce the principle of universal religious tolerance and freedom. In short, the secularists of the time were looking merely to put an end to

---

23 Dr M. Iqbal has described the workings of the total natural universe as 'the habit of Allah' (*Reconstruction* p.56), taking from the Quranic phrase *sunnatallah* (lit. 'God's way': 33:62, 35:43 and 48:23) which is often understood as referring to natural law. Iqbal writes: 'Thus the view that we have given gives a fresh spiritual meaning to physical science. The knowledge of nature is the knowledge of God's behaviour'. (p.57) Later he subconsciously borrows from the language of natural science again when he asks whether the 'Law of Islam' (jurisprudence) is 'capable of evolution', and suggests that the question 'is sure to be answered in the affirmative'. (p. 162)

24 Munir 1980, p140

25 Op. cit. p.134

26 J. Iqbal 1971, p.4

27 *Reconstruction*, p.155-6

sectarian discrimination. The growth of the deist movement in particular contributed to the secession between state and church (i.e. the institute supposedly built upon Revealed religion).[28] But since the psychological background of this movement was rooted in dualism, secularism has come to mean a disavowal not only of the church state (or religious state), but also any state claiming to be based upon spiritual principles. The wider, humanist definition of 'secular' has also entered the dictionary,[29] and this is how it was understood even by the Muslim members of the first Constituent Assembly of Pakistan, which is why they wished to create an Islamic polity that avoided the shortcomings of both theocracy and secularism. Therefore Dr Javid Iqbal might have spared his work from misinterpretation had he avoided referring to the ism, though he could have safely said that certain humanist principles correspond with Islamic principles.

On sectarianism

We have already seen that Dr Javid Iqbal has offered a clear-cut description of Pakistan as a non-sectarian 'Islamic state'. I have also attributed the logic of his argument to the Islamic worldview as described by his father, Dr Muhammad Iqbal. In order to corroborate the link between them, we should also look briefly at what the philosopher had to say on Islam and sectarianism. He was inspired to a degree by Sufi 'mysticism'[30], but he identified himself with no particular branch of theology. He himself said that he wilfully avoided 'the use of expressions current in popular Revelation Theology' and that he considered himself a 'critical student' with a preference for the scientific

---

[28] Deism – a rationalist view of God based on reason instead of Revelation, most popular in the 17th and 18th centuries. It is derived from the ideas of the ancient Greek philosopher Epicurus (341-270 BC) who believed that whilst deities might exist, they did not interfere with the lives of human beings. Deism followed a similar philosophy, teaching that God created humans with thinking minds and then left it to them to make use of their intellect to find Him and moral principles. Deists advanced the view that such principles are self-evident, that Revealed religion cannot claim to own or dictate them, and that therefore Scripture, the supposed source of religion, is unnecessary. Hence they advocated the criticism of Scripture, which in the beginning was meant to challenge the supremacy of the Orthodox Church, though not necessarily the existence of a Creator. However, due in part to the accompanying growth of scepticism, later thinkers became more openly either agnostic or atheistic.

[29] The primary definition of 'secular' offered in one dictionary for example is: 'not religious, sacred, or *spiritual*' (*Compact Oxford English Dictionary of Current English*; third edition, Oxford University Press, 2008). This wider definition is behind disputes on whether some countries like the UK are true examples of secular states. See for example S. Karim, response to letter titled 'Ataturk's Legacy', in *Dawn*, 15 June 2007.

[30] Iqbal preferred to look at mysticism as 'metaphysics hidden under the veil of religious phraseology'; he was however critical of what he called 'Hellenic-Persian Mysticism' which is strictly religious and essentially monastic. He also considered 'freeing humanity from superstition' as the 'ultimate ideal' of Islam, again underlining how little he identified it with religion as it is commonly understood. See Sherwani, (ed.) 2008, p.154, 78 and 117 respectively.

approach.[31] Hence he was equally comfortable in objectively discussing the approaches of Sunni and Shia denominations, as well as the essentially non-denominational Mutazilla [32] and Sufi approaches. His broad outlook has led some academics such as Ishtiaq Ahmed to say he does not represent a 'particular philosophical or political standpoint'. [33] Of course it is precisely this broad outlook that enables us to place him in the 'non-sectarian' category of thought. Let us review again the two characteristics from Chapter 5 that separate the proponents of secular-Islam synthesis from the proponents of non-sectarian *deen*:

- The proponents of secular Islam believe that Islam ought to be formally relegated to the status of a religion, i.e. a 'personal relationship between individual and God'. The other group asserts that Islam is not merely a religion, i.e. it is not about personal salvation, and so relegation is meaningless in this case.

The following citations from Iqbal's works should help us identify which of the categories of thought applies to him:

> ... the structure of Islam as a society is almost entirely due to the working of Islam as *a culture inspired by a specific ethical ideal.* [34]

> Islam is more than a creed; it is also a community, a nation. [35]

> The inner cohesion of such a nation would consist not in ethnic or geographic unity, not in the unity of language or social tradition, but in the *unity* of the *religious and political ideal* ... [36]

> Is religion a private affair? Would you like to see Islam, as a *moral and political ideal*, meeting the same fate in the world of Islam [*sic*] as Christianity has already met in Europe? ... the construction of a policy on national lines, if it means a displacement of the Islamic principles of solidarity, is simply unthinkable to a Muslim.[37]

---

31 See Iqbal's paper 'Islam as a Moral and Political Ideal', 1909. (Sherwani (ed.) 2008, p.98-9)

32 *Mutazilla* was the name used to describe a rationalist group of scholars in early Islam (9th Century AD) who all believed in applying both reason and revelation, but because of their respective individual differences, they did not represent a sect as such.

33 See I. Ahmed 2004, p.20

34 Iqbal's Allahabad address, 29 December 1930. (Sherwani (ed.) 2008, p.4.

35 'Islam as a Moral and Political Ideal' (Sherwani (ed.) 2008, p.114)

36 Article, 'Political Thought in Islam', 1911; Sherwani (ed.) 2008, p.141

37 Allahabad address. (Sherwani (ed.) 2008, p.7-8)

The conclusion to which Europe is consequently driven is that religion is a private affair of the individual and has nothing to do with what is called man's temporal life. Islam does not bifurcate the unity of man into an irreconcilable duality of spirit and matter. In Islam God and the universe, spirit and matter, Church and State, are organic to each other. [38]

Politics have their roots in the spiritual life of man. Islam is not a matter of *private opinion.* [39] It is a society, or, if you like, a civic church. ... I am opposed to nationalism as it is understood in Europe ... because I see in it the germs of *atheistic materialism* which I look upon as the greatest danger to modern humanity. [40]

The essential difference between the Muslim Community and other Communities of the world consists in our peculiar concept of nationality. ... we all believe in a *certain view of the universe* ... [41]

[Nationalism] comes into conflict with Islam only when it begins to play the role of a political concept and claims to be a principle of human solidarity demanding that Islam should recede into the background of a mere private opinion and cease to be a living factor in the national life. [*sic*] [42]

... according to the law of Islam there is no distinction between the Church and the State. The State with us is *not a combination* of religious and secular authority, but is a unity in *which no such distinction* exists. [43]

A careful reading of history shows that the Reformation was essentially a political movement, and the net result of it in Europe was a gradual displacement of the *universal ethics of Christianity* by systems of *national ethics*. The result of this tendency we have seen with our own eyes in the Great European War which, far from bringing any workable *synthesis* of the two opposing system of ethics, has made the European situation still more intolerable. [44]

---

38 Allahabad address. (Sherwani (ed.) 2008, p.5)

39 Compare this statement with the meaning of *mazhab* as a 'personal opinion'. See footnote 11 above.

40 Presidential address, Annual Session of the All-India Muslim Conference, Lahore, 21 March 1932 (Sherwani (ed.) 2008, p.31)

41 Lecture, 'The Muslim Community – A Sociological Study' M. A. O. College, Aligarh, 1910 (Sherwani (ed.) 2008, p.121)

42 Article, 'Islam and Ahmadism' (replying to questions raised by Jawaharlal Nehru). (Sherwani (ed.) 2008, p.238)

43 'Political Thought in Islam' (Sherwani (ed.) 2008, p.141-2)

44 *Reconstruction*, p.163

> Nor is the idea of separation of Church and State alien to Islam. The doctrine of the Major Occultation of the Imam in a sense effected this separation long ago in Shi'a Persia. *The Islamic idea of the division of the religious and political functions of the State must not be confounded with the European idea of the separation of Church and State.* The former is only a division of functions as is clear from the gradual creation in the Muslim State of the offices of *Shaikh-ul-Islam* and Ministers; *the latter is based on metaphysical dualism of spirit and matter.* Christianity began as an order of monks having nothing to do with the affairs of the world; Islam was, from the very beginning, a civil society with laws civil in their nature though believed to be revelational in origin.[45]

The discerning reader will have seen that Iqbal has comprehended Islam as a 'unity of the political and religious ideal', with no synthesis and no distinction, and that in fact to him the idea of 'synthesis' is a distinctly European (and dualist) view. These few quotes alone are sufficient to counter Ishtiaq Ahmed's baseless charge that Iqbal was a leading voice of synthesis.[46] From these passages we can also see more than a hint of the Two-Nation Theory which was practically the mantra of the Muslim League in the 1940s.

Moving on, again from Chapter 5:

- Since the proponents of secular Islam view Islam strictly as a religion, they believe that a political expression of Islam means a theocracy that discriminates not only against other faiths but also minority Muslim sects. The other group maintains that if a community divides (and thus discriminates) on sectarian or even political lines, it cannot legitimately call itself Muslim, and so there is no question of a sectarian problem in a bona fide 'systemic expression' or *deen* of Islam.

Again we can cite a few instances of Iqbal's statements to verify which of the two categories represents his view:

> Nor should the Hindus fear that the creation of autonomous Muslim states will mean the introduction of a kind of *religious* rule in such states. *I have already indicated to you the meaning of the word religion, as applied to Islam.*[47]

> Is it possible for you to achieve the organic wholeness of a united will? Yes, it is. Rise above your *sectional interests and private*

---

45 'Islam and Ahmadism' (Sherwani (ed.) 2008, p.235

46 See Chapter 5

47 Allahabad address (Sherwani (ed.) 2008, p.12)

> *ambitions*, and learn to determine the value of your individual and collective action, however directed on material ends, in the light of the ideal which you are supposed to represent. Pass from matter to spirit. *Matter is diversity; spirit is light, life and unity.* [48]

> There is no aristocracy in Islam. … There is no privileged class, no priesthood, no caste system. … But are we Indian Mussalmans true to this principle in our social economy? Is the organic unity of Islam intact in this land? Religious adventurers set up different sects and fraternities, ever quarrelling with one another; and then there are castes and sub-castes like the Hindus'. … we are suffering from a *double caste system* – the religious caste system, sectarianism, and the social caste system, which we have either learned or inherited from the Hindus. … I condemn this accursed *religious and social sectarianism* … Islam is one and indivisible; it brooks no distinctions in it. There are no Wahabies, Sh'ias, Mirzais or Sunnies in Islam. Fight not for the *interpretations* of the truth, when the truth itself is in danger. … Let the idols of *class distinctions and sectarianism* be smashed for ever …[49]

The last of these passages gives us the surest evidence that Iqbal denounced sectarianism and class division whether religious, social or economic; and most importantly, he actively called upon Muslims to abolish all divisions and return to the 'spiritual' unity that Islam demands of them.

It is also worth seeing what Jinnah had to say about Iqbal. The following excerpt is taken from a tribute on Iqbal's death anniversary, and it reveals not only how well Jinnah understood Iqbal's legacy, but also the intellectual connection between the two men.

> Iqbal was not a merely a preacher and a philosopher. He stood for courage and action, perseverance and self-reliance, and, above all, faith in God and devotion to Islam. In his person were combined the idealism of the poet and the realism of the man who takes a practical view of things. *Faith in God and unceasing and untiring action is the essence of his message.* And in this he emerges *truly Islamic.* He had an unflinching faith in Islamic principles and success in life meant to him the realisation of one's self, and to achieve this end the only means was to follow the teachings of Islam. *His message to humanity is action and the realisation of one's self.*

---

48 Allahabad address (Sherwani (ed.) 2008, p.29). The latter line to which I have added emphasis is a reference to political (nationalistic) as well as religious division, versus the 'spiritual' position of unity. It also implies the difference between materialist dualism and spiritual monism.

49 'Islam as a Moral and Political Ideal' in Sherwani (ed.) 2008, p.116-7. Spellings retained from original.

Although a great poet and philosopher, he was no less a practical politician. With his firm conviction and faith in the ideals of Islam, he was one of the few who originally thought over the feasibility of carving out of India an *Islamic state* in the north-west and north-east zones which are the historical homeland of the Muslims. ... [I] pray that we may live up to the ideals preached by our national poet so that we may be able to *give shape to these ideals in our sovereign state of Pakistan* when established.[50]

That Jinnah understood the Islamic worldview as Iqbal did is also evident from his speeches and letters. Aside from others that appear throughout this book, here is just one example:

All social regeneration and political freedom must finally depend on something that has a deeper meaning in life. And that, if you will allow me to say so, is Islam and *Islamic spirit*.[51]

Conclusion

From this discussion I have tried to show why the word *deen* presently has no European language equivalent. We have also seen the subtle yet significant difference between 'non-sectarian modernist' and secular-Muslim thought, and how in this case, a misunderstanding from an advocate of the secular-Muslim view has led to the misappropriation of the non-sectarian view.

It is easy to see why non-sectarian modernists avoid using the word 'secularism', and why similarly secularists avoid the word 'Islam'. The reason is the same: Both are concerned about mischievous interpretations or misuse of their respective ideas. The various groups of secularists are still convinced that Islam is ultimately just a religion, and this goes some way to explaining why most of them will not even contemplate Pakistan as a state based on Quranic principles or *deen*. Similarly, the wider definition of secularism leads most modernists (and many other Muslims) to treat it as an advocacy of 'political atheism' or nihilism, which is why they anxiously seek a state in which spiritual principles are recognised and acted upon. Investigating ways to get past the communication problem is a task not only for secularist and Muslim thinkers, but also linguistic analysts.

---

[50] Tribute to Iqbal, Lahore, 9 December 1944. (NV Vol. IV, p.24-5. Emphasis mine)

[51] Eid Day broadcast, Bombay, 13 November 1939 NV Vol. I, p.413. Emphasis mine. For other examples, see Public address, Chittagong, 26 March 1948 as cited in Myth no. 10 (Chapter 10); and Jinnah's interview with Beverley Nichols, as cited in Myth no. 6.

Chapter 7
1940: Deferred secession

> The only solution for the Muslims of India, which will stand the test of trial and time, is that India should be partitioned so that both the communities can develop freely and fully according to their own genius economically, socially, culturally and politically. The struggle is for the fullest opportunities and for the expression of the Muslim national will. *The vital contest in which we are engaged is not only for the material gain but also for the very existence of the soul of the Muslim nation.* … I have said often that it is a matter of life and death to the Mussalmans and is not a counter for bargaining. [1]

From the moment that the Muslim League passed the Lahore Resolution on 23 March 1940, rumours began that the implied partition demand it contained could not be anything more than a ruse, a political bargaining counter. Both the British and the Congress took up this attitude, less out of political expedience and more because it was based on an erroneous assumption about Jinnah, whose reputation as an Indian nationalist and ambassador of Hindu-Muslim unity had long preceded him. As we have already seen, the beginnings of a separatist attitude already existed among some Muslims, but as we will see throughout this book, it was only with Jinnah at the helm that the movement took off in earnest.[2]

1 Presidential address at the Special Pakistan Session of the Punjab Muslim Students' Federation, Lahore, 2 March 1941. (Yusufi Vol. II, p.1339). Emphasis mine.

2 According to the late Dr Waheed Ahmad, who has done a staggering amount of work collecting and publishing compilations of Jinnah's speeches, Liaquat Ali Khan was the first important member of the League to openly suggest 'dividing the country … on a religious and cultural basis', almost a year to the day before the Lahore Resolution (see his public speech, 25 March 1939, in NV Vol. I, p.357). Jinnah publicly acknowledged a fortnight later that the Working Committee was examining a number of schemes including those that advocated a division into Hindu and Muslim India. (*Civil & Military Gazette* report, 11 April 1939; NV Vol. I, p.364-7)

Strains of Muslim separatism

Although charges of 'separatism' were levelled at the League practically from the moment of its establishment, [3] up until the end of the 1930s most Muslim leaders and particularly those from Muslim-majority provinces viewed separatism in strictly in all-India terms, and not in secessionist terms. They remained stuck in the mentality of pushing for strong provinces, a weak federal centre, and separate electorates. It is also true however that Muslims sought to be treated as more than a mere minority long before the 1940s. Even the Lucknow Pact of 1916, Jinnah's major contribution to Hindu-Muslim unity, had been drafted with this in mind. [4] Before the third Round Table Conference, Muslims had gone as far as calling for 'completely autonomous Federal States of *equal status*', [5] based on the general consensus among them that they were not a community but a 'nation'.[6]

Embittered by the experiences of living under a domineering Congress Government at the end of the 1930s, Muslim leadership developed a more hardliner separatist attitude than before, but only gradually. Provincial leaders joined the League but many did so out of political expediency, and even into the 1940s some were willing to cooperate with the Congress when it suited their personal interests.

Two distinct strains of separatism began to emerge by the beginning of the 1930s. Here we will refer to 'separatism' as meaning a demand for provincial autonomy, separate electorates and a weak centre. 'Secession' will mean partition where the Muslim state(s) and Hindu states(s) would both be fully autonomous and independent and the only relationship between them would be in the form of international treaties and pacts, i.e. there would be no centre. ('Balkanisation' – the creation of two mutually hostile states – was never on the agenda.)

Arguably the two earliest Muslim voices for secession were Muhammad Iqbal (1877-1938) and Choudhary Rahmat Ali (1897-1951). In 1930, whilst the Muslims of India fought for provincial autonomy at the Round Table Conferences, Iqbal declared at Allahabad that he would

---

[3] See for example Jinnah's discussion of and response to such charges in his Lucknow Pact speech of December 1916. (Mohammad Umar (ed.) (1973) *Quaid-i-Azam Mohammad Ali Jinnah: Rare Speeches 1910-1918* Karachi-Sukkur: Al-Mahfooz Research Academy, p.148-50)

[4] This was what Jinnah himself claimed in 1940. See his speech at the Aligarh University Union, Aligarh, 6 March 1940. (Yusufi Vol. II, p.1157), in which he said that the Pact was signed in the spirit that 'two separate distinct entities were entering into a mutual settlement'. Of course it is true that Jinnah had always viewed Muslims and Hindus as equal members of the body politic and it was for this reason that he personally disagreed with separate electorates in his early career.

[5] Resolution of the Executive Board of the Muslim Conference, Delhi, 21 August 1932 (chaired by Dr M. Iqbal). Cited in W. Ahmad, 'Choudhary Rahmat Ali and the Concept of Pakistan' in *Journal of the Research Society of Pakistan*, January 1970, p.19. (Emphasis mine)

[6] Aga Khan, Presidential speech at the All-Parties Muslim Conference, Delhi, 31 December 1928 (Ibid.)

prefer to 'go farther than the demands' being made by his contemporaries. [7] He wanted to see the Punjab, NWFP, Sind and Baluchistan 'amalgamated into a single State'. In his view this was likely to be the 'final destiny' of Muslims at least in North-West India. [8] We will come back to Iqbal's scheme later in this chapter. [9] Here we will review the thought of Choudhary Rahmat Ali, usually credited as the first activist for a separate nation-state, and whose anxiety for preserving the unity of Muslims is particularly pertinent in light of events since Pakistan's creation.

Founder of the name

Choudhary Rahmat Ali was a Cambridge-based student originally from the Punjab. Though he lived in England until his death, he was arguably the earliest Muslim activist for partition. Rahmat Ali is best known for coining the name PAKSTAN (minus the 'i'): an acronym of the provinces Punjab (P), NWFP (Afghan – A), Kashmir (K), Sind plus the last few letters of Baluchistan (-STAN). It also happens to mean 'pure/sacred land'. Rahmat Ali called for the creation of a 'Pakstan' (sometimes also calling it 'Pakistan' with an 'i' in the same text) in his pamphlet of January 1933, titled *Now or Never: Are we to Live or Perish for Ever?* in which he referred to himself on the title page as 'Founder, Pakistan National Movement'. He described Hindus and Muslims as heterogeneous societies and demanded their immediate separation to prevent the destruction of Muslims 'for ever'. [10] At the time of publication it was widely ignored or dismissed by most Muslim leaders including those in the League, and received more attention from the British media. Later he developed upon the idea and suggested a scheme for a 'Pak Commonwealth of Nations', to include Muslims not only in zones of North-East India but also Afghanistan, Sri Lanka and Bengal (the latter states had not been included in his original Pakistan scheme; Bengal was to be another Muslim state called Bangistan). [11] These nations would have no political ties with the Hindu-majority areas of the subcontinent.

---

[7] On 21 January 1929 the All Parties Muslim Conference had passed a resolution laying down Muslim demands, calling for the creation of a federal system for India with residual powers in the provinces, separate electorates and weightage of representation in Hindu-majority provinces. Jinnah had presented his 'Fourteen Points' embodying these demands at the League's Council meeting on 28 March 1929.

[8] Iqbal's Presidential address at the Annual Session of the Muslim League, Allahabad, 29 December 1930 (Sherwani (ed.) 2008, p.11)

[9] For more on Iqbal's Allahabad address and what it entailed see also Chapter 1.

[10] Choudhary Rahmat Ali (1933) *Now or Never: Are we to Live or Perish for Ever?* Cambridge: The Pakistan National Movement, paragraph 17 line 9. (Pages are not numbered).

[11] Even after partition Rahmat continued to view the two wings of Pakistan as 'two countries' – Pakistan and Bangistan. (Choudhary Rahmat Ali (1947) *Pakistan: The Fatherland of the Pak Nation* Cambridge: The Pakistan National Liberation Movement, p.339)

Rahmat Ali made it clear from the beginning that his scheme was 'basically different' from Iqbal's relatively modest idea outlined at Allahabad in 1930. Whereas Iqbal had suggested the 'amalgamation' of just the north-western and eastern Muslim-majority provinces into a 'single state forming a unit of the All-India Federation', Rahmat Ali wanted these provinces to form 'a separate Federation of their own outside India', [12] in which his 'Pakistan' and the 'Commonwealth', aside from being candidly secessionist, also covered much wider territory. Indeed, in the long term he anticipated that the 'Commonwealth' would form a pan-Islamic continent, which he dubbed the 'Pak Plan'. As serious territorial adjustments were proposed in order to make this happen, and since in any case circumstances had not quite reached the point at which any Indian Muslim was ready to seriously contemplate secession (notwithstanding Iqbal's tentative prediction[13]), most of his contemporaries viewed Rahmat Ali's scheme as unrealistic. [14]

Rahmat Ali would never be happy with the Pakistan that eventually came into being, on either territorial or ideological grounds. He called it 'Pastan' ('shadow of Pakistan') [15] as it did not include Jammu and Kashmir, Delhi Division or undivided Punjab and Bengal and Assam. To Rahmat Ali, the acceptance of this much smaller 'shadow' was tantamount to having destroyed the unity of the *millat* and wrecked the 'Pak Plan and Pak ideology' [16] that he had envisioned. He also expressed fears that the various parties entering politics in the new country were 'neglecting the supremacy of religion in the Pak ideology' and warned that this would lead to the revival of 'provincialism' that historically had already 'weakened the solidarity of our *Millat*' in British India. [17] Though Rahmat Ali moved to Pakistan briefly in April 1948 intending to live there permanently, his bitter condemnation of the country's founders (particularly Jinnah) was probably seen as borderline seditious at the time, and in turn Rahmat Ali soon felt he was not welcome in Pakistan. He left the country by October 1948, shortly after Jinnah's death, [18] and returned to Cambridge, where he would remain until his death in 1951.

---

[12] Op. cit. paragraph 11, lines 15-20.

[13] See Chapter 1, subsection 'Philosophical difference'.

[14] Details on reactions to Rahmat Ali's pamphlet and his 'Pak Commonwealth' originally obtained from W. Ahmad 1970, p.11-28. Supplementary primary sources cited in this edition.

[15] Choudhary Rahmat Ali (1947 third edition) *Pakistan: The Fatherland of the Pak Nation* Cambridge: The Pakistan Liberation Movement, p.341, 360

[16] Ibid. p.339.

[17] Ibid. p.345. Rahmat Ali's 'Pak ideology' was based on the idea that the unifying religious bond of the *millat* was far superior to anything that bound a *qaum*, or nation. (Ibid.)

[18] It is unclear whether Rahmat Ali left Pakistan of his own volition, or he was asked to leave. The latter version of events is given for instance in K.K. Aziz (1987) *Rahmat Ali: A Biography* Stuttgart: Steiner Verlag Wiesbaden, p.435. The former version is given by a friend of Rahmat Ali (S.M. Jamil Wasti (1982) *My Reminiscences of Choudhary Rahmat Ali* Karachi: Royal Book

Background to the Lahore Resolution

Whilst the Muslim minority provinces came round to the idea of partition sooner, [19] a number of leaders from the biggest and most important Muslim majority areas were less enthusiastic about the same idea, for the obvious reason that they felt more safe and comfortable where they lived and had fewer grievances regarding the political status quo. As these provinces also had narrow Muslim majorities, their leaders faced pressure to prove their loyalties to their provinces on cultural, tribal, and linguistic grounds over religion. No doubt they also had to listen to non-Muslim fears about the dangers of a 'Muslim Raj', and perhaps felt obliged to prove themselves by denying all talk of Muslim separatism. This may also explain the claims made by some Muslim Leaguers that Jinnah did not really want partition. Likewise, some provincial leaders were so focused on getting provincial autonomy that they were unwilling to surrender it at all, whether within India or in Pakistan. In addition, as we will see in the next chapter, there was no proper consensus on what 'Muslim culture' meant, and this caused confusion over what this meant for 'Muslim nationalism' and the Pakistan idea. These are the factors we must bear in mind in reviewing the Lahore Resolution. [20]

The territorial demand in Lahore Resolution is often described as 'vague'. [21] Indeed the Lahore Resolution was an open-ended document. However it should not be read in terms of what Jinnah may have personally wanted at the time, but in terms of the lack of consensus in Muslim opinion on the Indian constitutional crisis.

In 1939, the League began considering alternative schemes to the Government of India Act 1935. A committee headed by Jinnah was set up to examine those schemes that were already in existence as well as new ones that came in over the next year. [22] The day before the committee was set up, Liaquat Ali Khan had remarked that 'if the Hindus and Muslims cannot live amicably in any other way, they might

---

Company, p.14), who also mentions that by 1950 Rahmat Ali's friends had convinced him to return to Pakistan again, but he died before he could do so (ibid. p.15-16).

19 This is notwithstanding the fact that the earliest voices of secession – Iqbal and Rahmat Ali – were both from the Punjab.

20 See Appendix IV for Lahore Resolution text.

21 See for the best-known instance, A. Jalal 1994; see also S. Mujahid 1981, p.397, who mentions that Jinnah removed 'ambiguity in the Lahore Resolution' in his correspondence with Gandhi in 1944.

22 See resolution at Muslim League Committee meeting, Meerut, 26 March 1939 (NV Vol. I, p.639). It seems that the committee never officially convened until February 1940 (see above), though individual Leaguers from this committee were busy developing their own schemes or supporting those that they favoured. Abdullah Haroon for instance took interest in one by Dr Syed Abdul Latif of Hyderabad, which, despite recommending a loose federation, was viewed by Haroon as a first step to Muslim independence. Sikandar Hayat meanwhile developed his own scheme independently.

be allowed to do so by dividing the country in a suitable manner on a religious and cultural basis'. [23] The schemes ranged from secessionist to separatist (provincial autonomy in an all-India context). The most significant schemes and their impact (or lack thereof) on the Lahore Resolution are discussed in detail in Appendix III.

Nine schemes [24] were finally placed in front of the League in February 1940, at which point the Working Committee resolved to consider the 'Muslim demands and the future constitution of India', in view of the following 'broad outlines':

- Muslims are not a minority but a nation
- The British system of democratic parliamentary system of government is not suited to the genius and people of India
- Muslim majority zones in India should be constituted into Independent Dominions in relationship with Britain
- Muslims in Hindu majority zones must have their rights safeguarded and vice versa
- Units in each zone shall form component parts of the Federation of their respective zones as autonomous units [25]

Of the nine schemes placed in front of the League in February 1940 Rahmat Ali's Pakistan scheme (1933 onwards) and the Aligarh scheme of Dr S.Z. Hasan and Dr M. Afzal Husain Qadri (1939) came closest to being secessionist in tone. Next in terms of secessionist leanings was the confederacy scheme (1939) written by Major Kifait Ali. Two other notable schemes – by Dr Sayyed Abdul Latif of Hyderabad and Sikandar Hayat Khan of the Punjab – openly advocated all-India federations as a matter of necessity. Sikandar Hayat's British-backed 'zonal scheme' (1938-9) was the least popular, as it leaned the most in favour of federalism (loose though it was) and indicated a clear preference for Indian unity. This is not surprising, given that he was chiefly a

---

23 Liaquat Ali Khan's presidential address at the Meerut Divisional Muslim League Conference, Meerut, 25 March 1939. (NV Vol. I, p.357)

24 The nine schemes included those: 'prepared by the Nawab of Mamdot [Sir Shah Nawaz Khan of Mamdot; his name is actually a reference to Major Kifait Ali's confederacy scheme, which the Nawab of Mamdot financed and published], Dr Abdul Latif [Hyderabad], Mr Rizwan Ullah [S.M. Rizwanullah, United Provinces], Dr Afzal Hussain Kadri [M.A.H. Qadri, Aligarh], Khan Bahadur Kifayat Ullah [identity undetermined but probably the same 'Mr Kifayatullah' – possibly from East Bengal – who is mentioned in Khaliquzzaman 1961, p.341], Mr Asadulla of Calcutta [Asadullah, Dacca – see his letter to Jinnah dated 12 August 1945 in Jinnah Papers Vol. XII, p.25] and also the Pakistan scheme [Ch. Rahmat Ali, Cambridge] and the Khilafat scheme of the Muslim Students' Federation [Punjab]'. (See Jinnah's press interview, *Civil & Military Gazette*, 3 February 1940; NV Vol. I, p.449-50. The ninth, oddly absent from this list as printed in the press, is Punjab Premier Sikander Hayat Khan's zonal scheme.)

25 For complete text, see resolution no. 14 at Working Committee meeting, Delhi, 3-6 February 1940, presided by Jinnah. (NV Vol. I, p.651)

provincial autonomist. Dr Latif's 'cultural zones' scheme (1938 onwards) would also later be criticised for its interpretation of the Lahore Resolution, [26] as well as its references to an all-India centre.

The Lahore Resolution was drafted a few weeks later, and the above principles as well as elements of some of the nine schemes were incorporated into it. In particular, as we show in detail in Appendix III, it derived its content from both Major Ali's Confederacy scheme and the Aligarh scheme, which both also shared a common ideological element. Most significantly, the League wrote off both the all-India schemes of Hayat and Dr Latif. [27]

The Lahore Session

Jinnah declared in February 1940 that when he was 'convinced of the Muslims' readiness for a struggle', he would 'give them marching orders'. [28] By implication he knew that they were not ready yet. Therefore the Lahore Session (which took place just a few weeks later) was obviously not a 'marching order', but it was certainly an historical 'landmark' in which the League 'defined their goal'. [29] Every aspect of the Session, from its location, to Jinnah's presidential speech, as well as the Resolution itself, marked the trend of Muslim politics. The Session was held in Lahore, capital of the Punjab, and the Resolution was thereafter always referred to by the name of the city. [30] Over 100,000

---

26 See Qadri's criticism in Appendix III, footnote 41

27 Interestingly, Sikandar Hayat Khan of the Punjab, Sir Abdullah Haroon of Sind, and A.K. Fazlul Huq of Bengal all later claimed to have been the authors of the original draft. See *Foundations* Vol. II, xxii-xxiii. Some commentators have claimed that Zafrullah Khan also wrote a 'scheme' that became the basis of the Lahore Resolution. But unlike the other self-confessed schemes on the table, it was actually a memorandum that discussed how future constitutional negotiations might be conducted, in light of the prevailing Muslim stance. Ayesha Jalal has reviewed the memorandum and finds that the final Lahore Resolution 'bears some marks of this note' (op. cit. 1994, p.56), based on Zafrullah Khan's preference for an all-India federation over both the 'Pakistan scheme' of Rahmat Ali and the 'separation scheme' (Iqbal's Allahabad address). While according to Jalal he was also sceptical about the latter's practicality (ibid. p.55-6), we find Khan merely acknowledging that in the prevailing political climate Muslims would likely 'rally round' the 'separation scheme' (see p.131 of the memorandum). He implied that if the various Indian communities were to 'readjust their attitude towards each other' (ibid. p.150), fruitful discussions leading to an all-India federation might be possible. His was thus a typically separatist rather than secessionist view that was shared by most provincial leaders at the time. Khan's mention of a weak centre (p.131 of the memorandum) is similarly in line with the separatist view. (See the undated (but circa February 1940) memorandum; India Office Records, IOR MSS EUR F125/135).

28 Speech given at the unveiling of the portrait of the late scholar Shaukat Ali, Anglo-Arabic College, Delhi, 22 February 1940. (NV Vol. I, p.462)

29 See concluding remarks at the Lahore Session, 24 March 1940. (*Foundations* Vol. II, p.349). Also Jinnah's press interview, 26 March 1940. (NV Vol. I, p.496)

30 For a more detailed discussion, see S. Mujahid 1981, 396-7 fn. Furthermore, Iqbal had in his time suggested holding the 1937 Session of the League in Lahore for the following reasons: 'The enthusiasm for the League is rapidly increasing in the Punjab, and I have no doubt that the holding of the session *in Lahore will be a turning point in the history of the League* and

spectators were reported to have gathered at Minto Park to see Jinnah and the other Muslim leaders arrive. [31] Over the course of the Session, lasting three days, stirring speeches were given by provincial leaders from across India including the North-West Frontier Province, Baluchistan, Bengal, Punjab, Sind, Bihar, the Central Provinces and Hyderabad. Minority province leaders declared their support of the Lahore Resolution and indicated their willingness to help their co-religionists in Muslim-majority provinces achieve freedom, even at the price of their staying behind. [32]

The Resolution was moved by A.K. Fazlul Huq, then Premier of Bengal. In his speech Haq explained that though the Muslim population in India was 80 million strong, its distribution across the subcontinent put it at a disadvantage. He raised a point that would prove to be a constant thorn in the side for the League:

> Our friends will remember that even in the Punjab and Bengal our position is not very safe. In the legislatures we are not in such a large majority; *we have to seek the help of other interests and minorities to form coalition governments* which are the weakest form of governments known to constitutionalists. [33]

Loyalty to the League was always going to be an issue for Muslim leaders in the main Muslim-majority provinces. Non-Muslims in Bengal and Punjab would constantly put pressure on Muslim leaders in these provinces to put local allegiances above their loyalty to the League. [34] Nevertheless the Lahore Resolution was passed unanimously.

Jinnah's presidential speech

Other clues about Jinnah's thinking and his position on the separatist-secessionist scale are revealed in his speech at the historic Lahore Session, which was delivered the night before the Lahore Resolution was moved. The historian Prof. Robin Moore [35] has shown that the content of

---

an important step towards *mass contact.*' (Iqbal to Jinnah, 11 August 1937; *Letters of Iqbal to Jinnah*, p.25-6)

31 Figure reported by Associated Press of India, 25 March 1940. (*Foundations* Vol. II, p.326)

32 See proceedings of the third day at the Lahore Session, 24 March 1940 (*Foundations* Vol. II, p.344-5)

33 Fazlul Huq's speech at the Lahore Session, 23 March 1940. (*Foundations* Vol. II, p.342)

34 Fazlul Huq for example sympathised with Muslim sentiments in principle but in practice his loyalties were divided between the Muslim nation and his co-regionalists. He was expelled from the League in 1941 for a period of five years, after trying to form coalitions between his own Krishak Proja party and parties that were known to be anti-League. He rejoined the League once his compulsory term of expulsion was complete in 1946. He would eventually become the Governor of East Pakistan.

35 R. J. Moore, 'Jinnah and the Pakistan Demand', as reprinted in M.R. Kazimi (ed.) 2005, p.41-79

the speech, though given extempore, was partly adapted from both a letter written to him in 1939 [36] from Majlis-i-Kabir Pakistan's [37] secretary Ahmad Bashir of Lahore (not to be mixed up with Muslim Leaguer Mian Bashir Ahmad), and a criticism of Gandhi by the Aligarh professors Hasan and Qadri, in 1939. [38] Both of these individuals had a preference for secession.

Five months before the Lahore Session Bashir had written that the Hindu-Muslim problem was not 'intercommunal' but 'international'. He had contemplated a division of India into 'autonomous homogeneous states' for the 'two nationalities' with an 'international pact of goodwill' between them, thus making them as 'united and harmonious today as are France and Great Britain'. This was Bashir's particular definition of 'Indian Unity'. [39]

In his presidential speech, Jinnah made an almost identical statement borrowed from Bashir's political thought:

> The problem in India is not of an *intercommunal* character but manifestly of an *international* one ... to secure peace and happiness of the people of this *subcontinent*, the only course open to us all is to allow the *major nations* separate homelands by dividing India into 'autonomous national states'. There is no reason why these states should be antagonistic to each other. [40] ... It will lead more towards natural goodwill by *international pacts* between them, and they can live in complete harmony with their neighbours. [41]

Jinnah however omitted two crucial words. The first was 'Pakistan', and of course it was not used in the Lahore Resolution either. [42] The simple reason for this was that Choudhary Rahmat Ali's 'Pakistan' had

---

36 In this letter dated 21 October 1939, Bashir (a journalist by profession) had decried a statement of Viceroy Linlithgow (made on 18 October 1939) appealing for Indian unity.

37 Majlis-i-Kabir Pakistan, Lahore (literally 'Great Pakistan Association') was a group which upheld both Choudhary Rahmat Ali's Pakistan scheme and the realism of Iqbal in focusing on the North-West of India rather than integrating these regions into an all-India setup to their detriment. The Majlis had been promoting Rahmat Ali's Pakistan Scheme in Indian Muslim papers and journals, and though the League was never to formally acknowledge Rahmat Ali's contribution publicly, nevertheless the Pakistan scheme was amongst the nine proposals that were in front of the League by February 1940.

38 An article by Gandhi titled 'Opinions differ' had appeared in *Harijan*, 11 November 1939, written in criticism of a letter to him from Aligarh on the subject of Muslim nationhood. CWMG Vol. 77, p.80-83. (http://www.gandhiserve.org/cwmg/VOL077.PDF) Professor Syed Zafarul Hasan, Dr Burhan Ahmad and Ubaid Ullah petitioned Jinnah in counter to Gandhi's article on 15 November. (Typescript document in Quaid-i-Azam Papers, file no. 96 as cited in R.J. Moore, op. cit.)

39 See detailed citation by R.J. Moore, op. cit. p.55-6.

40 Quotation marks in original.

41 Presidential address at Lahore Session, 22 March 1940 (NV Vol. I, p.493)

42 Strictly speaking the word 'Pakistan' does not appear in Ahmad Bashir's letter either but this is a moot point; Bashir was the secretary of the Majlis-i-Kabir *Pakistan* and so supported the idea of a 'Pakistan' by virtue of his membership.

been named after specific provinces, but Jinnah did not wish to make specific territorial demands for the proposed state at this point, especially when Muslims were not unanimous on their exact aims. In addition Bengal was made part of a pan-Islamic union in Rahmat Ali's 'Pakistan' scheme (see earlier part of our review). But as we will see later in this chapter, Jinnah wanted to concentrate on just the two major zones in British India, and in line with Iqbal's thought he wanted them consolidated into one state. [43] At any rate the omission of the word 'Pakistan' in Jinnah's speech and the Lahore Resolution does not signify, as Moore contends, that Jinnah was opposed to partition in 1940.

The second word that Jinnah omitted was 'unity' (he used the word 'harmony', and criticised the 'artificial unity' of present British India). It was a word he had once used to refer to Hindu-Muslim unity, and with it the unity of India, but by this point he had stopped doing so. [44]

For the academic content of his speech, Jinnah could do no better than to look to Aligarh University, which as the brainchild of Sir Syed Ahmad Khan, was the intellectual base of the Two-Nation Theory. The Aligarh professors had described both Islam and Hinduism as not simply 'religions in the stricter sense of the word', but rather 'distinct social orders'. [45] They explained that Muslims and Hindus belonged to two different civilisations, had different religious philosophies, social customs, law, history, and literature. This made it impossible for them to evolve a common nationality. [46] Jinnah's better known version of their statement is again virtually identical. [47] The only solution was to divide India, enabling Muslims to develop everything from their spiritual to their political life in accordance with their ideals and genius. [48] In what appears to contradict the text of the Lahore Resolution that was to be moved the very next day, Jinnah also hinted that he ultimately sought one consolidated state:

---

[43] In his Allahabad address Iqbal had focused on just the Punjab and surrounding areas as a 'consolidated North-West Indian Muslim State', though he had also mentioned the right of Bengal's Muslims (alongside Punjabi Muslims) to demand statutory majority status in India. In a letter to Jinnah a few years later he wrote of the right of both the Punjab and Bengal to seek 'self-determination' as 'nations' (21 June 1937), but significantly, he ultimately believed that 'the life of Islam as a cultural force' in India depended on its 'centralisation in a specified territory' (Allahabad address). Dr Naeem Qureshi aptly summarises Iqbal's position thus: 'His contribution [to the Pakistan idea] lies in the fact that he brought the two contradictory forces of Islamic universalism and territorial nationalism closer together' (M. N. Qureshi 1999, p.67). With the advent of Pakistan movement in the 1940s, Jinnah, himself a life-long centralist, would take Iqbal's thinking further and aim to weld Punjab and Bengal into either a federal or confederal state.

[44] See Chapter 1, subsection 'Fathers of the nation' for details.

[45] The Aligarh professors were essentially describing Hinduism and Islam in terms of the Arabic word *deen*, but using contemporary language.

[46] R. J. Moore, op. cit. p.57-8

[47] Presidential speech at Lahore Session, 22 March 1940 (NV Vol. I, p.493-4)

[48] Ibid. p.495

> Mussalmans are a nation according to any definition of a nation, and they must have their own homeland, their territory, *and their state.* [49]

This was in line with Iqbal's call at Allahabad for a 'consolidated' state as the 'final destiny' of Muslims in at least northwest India.

Substance of the Lahore Resolution

The Lahore Resolution was a short document, calling for the creation of 'Independent States' (presumably two) out of the 'North-Western and Eastern zones' of India (it did not cover either the Muslim-minority provinces or even the Princely States). The provinces ('constituent units') inside each of these 'States' were to be 'autonomous and sovereign' (i.e. they would have residual powers). [50] This line was evidently included for the benefit of provincialist leaders who wanted to remain 'separate' whether within or outside India. One of Jinnah's earliest statements explaining the Resolution even suggests that it was included to attract minorities such as the Sikhs in the Punjab. Promising them provincial autonomy would perhaps make them feel safe in their homelands and be less fearful of joining a federation of Muslim states. [51]

It was not explicitly stated what relationship the two 'Independent States' [52] would have with each other, but a reference to the 'constitution' (singular) [53] for the Muslim 'regions' implied that they were expected to co-exist either in federation or confederation. [54] This open-ended line thus appears to take from Major Ali's Confederacy scheme. The provinces to be included were not mentioned by name at this point. Provincial borders would presumably remain as they

---

[49] Ibid.

[50] 'Sovereignty' in 'constituent units' is consistent with provinces having residual powers in a federal system. See Chapter 1, footnote 83.

[51] See statement on the Lahore Resolution, New Delhi, 31 March 1940, in which Jinnah assured Sikhs that Punjab would be an 'autonomous sovereign unit'. (NV Vol. II, p.2-3)

[52] The 'states' definitely meant the two general zones in the north-west and north-east respectively that were to eventually become East and West Pakistan, and not the provinces within them. See Jinnah's letter to Gandhi dated 17 September 1944, referred to in Chapter 8.

[53] The Pakistani historian Ayesha Jalal treats the same word (constitution) as implying an all-India centre (op. cit. p.59). But the word appears twice, once with reference to the non-Muslims in the proposed Muslim 'States', and again with reference to Muslims in Hindustan. It is thus referring to two constitutions. (See text of the resolution in Appendix IV) This point is further made clear in the League Annual Session in Madras, 1941 at which the League's Rules were altered to incorporate the Lahore Resolution. The paragraph outlining reciprocal safeguards was split into two and turned into two paragraphs, one relating to the Muslim regions (Pakistan) and their constitution, and the second relating to the Hindu regions (Hindustan) and their constitution respectively. The context of the word 'constitution' is irrefutable. See proceedings of the Annual League Session at Madras, April 1941. (*Foundations* Vol. II, p.371-2, 376).

[54] The meanings of 'federation' and 'confederation' are discussed in Chapter 11.

presently stood on the whole (including those of Bengal and Punjab); the 'adjustment' of borders was to be restricted to wherever it was practicable; small pockets of Muslim-populated areas lying in Hindu-majority zones could be separated and allowed to join adjacent larger Muslim zones (for example, Sylhet could be separated from Assam and joined to Bengal).

Nothing was said about the relation of these new 'States' with the rest of India, but the resolution demanded reciprocal safeguards for Muslims left behind in India in its constitution, and likewise for non-Muslims inside the proposed Muslim 'States' respectively. Like the Aligarh scheme, there was no reference whatsoever to a 'centre'. Sikandar Hayat Khan, then Premier of the Punjab and a staunch provincialist, later complained that he had drafted the original version of the Lahore Resolution but that the references to the centre had later been taken out. [55] This offers the first clue as to Jinnah's thinking. [56] At any rate, the League would later take the official stance that the 'Pakistan scheme does not visualize any kind of Central Government'. [57]

Partition as the final goal was implied in the final paragraph, in which the Working Committee of the Muslim League was authorised to frame a 'scheme of constitution providing for the assumption finally, by the respective regions of all the powers, such as defence, external affairs, communications, customs and such other matters as may be necessary.' The word 'finally' of course implied a transitional period in which to get on with constitution-making whilst the British gradually handed over power, and by the same token secession was implied to follow. [58] The form of government for this transitional period again was not outlined, as it was a matter for negotiation. [59]

The go-slow method

Therefore the Resolution was neither making an immediate secessionist demand, nor was it a bargaining counter. It was a deferred secessionist

[55] See Appendix III for Sikandar Hayat's remarks on the Lahore Resolution.

[56] In his statement on the Lahore Resolution, on 31 March 1940 Jinnah also added: 'As regards other zone or zones that may be constituted in the rest of India our relationship will be of an *international* character.' (NV Vol. II, p.4)

[57] See letter of Liaquat Ali Khan to Sikh leader Sir Jogendra Singh, 14 January 1942; as reproduced in full in NV Vol. II, p.4 fn); see also Dr M.A.H Qadri's letter to Abdullah Haroon referenced in Appendix III, footnote 41.

[58] Jinnah confirmed this himself. See his statement on the Lahore Resolution, New Delhi, 31 March 1940, in which he points directly to the final clause of the Resolution when asked about the Muslim states' relationship with Britain (NV Vol. II, p.4). See also record of interview between Jinnah and the Cabinet Delegation, 16 April 1946. (NV Vol. IV, p.647)

[59] Jinnah confirmed this in his letter to Gandhi, 17 September 1944 when he wrote that the Resolution 'does give basic principles and when they are accepted then the details will have to be worked out by the contracting parties'. (C. Rajagopalachari (ed.) (1944) *Gandhi-Jinnah Talks* New Delhi: Hindustan Times, p.17)

demand, since the Muslims of India were not as yet single-minded in their purpose. [60] They were not ready to follow Jinnah's 'marching orders'. Nevertheless the main focus of the Resolution was on the two large Muslim zones in India, and this was Jinnah's main reason for demanding its recognition as a prerequisite to further negotiations. Once it was conceded by the British and Congress, it would be easier to bring indecisive Muslims across the subcontinent round to the idea. [61] This 'go-slow' approach is consistent with Jinnah's methodology throughout his life, [62] as well as that of his spiritual mentor, Dr Iqbal (as we will see shortly).

Robin Moore writes that other Muslims such as the Sindhi leader Abdullah Haroon were more openly enthusiastic about partition than was Jinnah at the end of the 1930s, and that Jinnah only became fully committed to partition much later. [63] For supporting evidence he points to two events. First is a resolution passed in February 1940 by the Foreign Working Committee of the League which was presided by Haroon. This resolution explicitly called for the formation of a separate national home in the shape of an autonomous state', [64] whilst the Lahore Resolution, passed just four weeks later, was not as forthright. Secondly Moore refers to an incident in October 1938, when Haroon drafted a resolution recommending a division of India into two federations, one of 'Muslim states' and one of 'non-Muslim States', in the best interests of

---

60 Some historians have made observations that support our review. Dr Moore writes on the Resolution: 'The variety of its analogues goes far to explain the vagueness of the resolution over the delineation of the contiguous Muslim regions of north-western and eastern India and the contemplated relations between them. The notoriously obscure provision for 'territorial readjustments' was clearly a hold-all for additions to, as well as reductions of, existing provinces.' (op. cit. p.54) Prof. S.R. Mehrotra meanwhile writes that the Muslim League's opinion at this time was 'divided on three main questions: what areas should form part of "Muslim India"? Should "Muslim India" be completely separate and independent? Should there be a transfer of population between "Muslim India" and "Hindu India"?' He concludes that a lack of consensus in Muslim opinion accounts for the 'vagueness and imprecision' of the Lahore Resolution.' He adds: 'Whatever the views of the other League leaders, Jinnah had now crossed the Rubicon … With him at least the demand for Pakistan was neither a bluff nor a bargaining counter, but a solemn and irrevocable decision.' (S.R. Mehrotra 'The Congress and the Partition of India' in C.H. Philips & M.D. Cartwright (eds.) 1970, p.207, 208)

61 See record of interview between the Cabinet Delegation and Jinnah on 16 April 1946: 'Mr Jinnah said that once the principle of Pakistan was conceded the question of the territory of Pakistan could be discussed. His claim was for the six provinces but he was willing to discuss the area.' (NV Vol. IV, p.642) See also Jinnah's interview with the *Daily Herald*, 5 April 1946: 'The new nation must include all the six provinces with their present boundaries subject to any necessary territorial adjustments on both sides'. (NV Vol. IV, p.592)

62 See Chapter 1, subsections 'Gandhi's innovation' and 'Cooperation versus non-cooperation'

63 He writes that the British decision in 1945 for an 'early and complete withdrawal' rather than a 'gradual demission' of power forced Jinnah to fight for an immediate Pakistan. (R.J. Moore op. cit. p.66)

64 R. Moore op. cit. p.54, citing from the resolution. For its full text see *Civil & Military Gazette* report, 3 February 1940 (NV Vol. I, p.449-50)

the 'two nations'. [65] Jinnah reportedly encouraged a modification of the draft by reminding the Leaguers: 'the Government is still in the hands of the British. Let us not forget it. You must see ahead and work for that ideal which you think will arise 25 years hence.' [66] The final resolution recommended that the Muslim League 'review and revise the entire conception of what should be the suitable constitution for India which will secure honourable and legitimate status to them.' The text as Moore cites it does give the erroneous impression that there was no room for a secessionist leaning. Thus he considers this proof that in 1940 Jinnah was still thinking in terms of a united India. But in the first place, Moore has not cited the full text (taking it as he has from a partial quote in the introduction to S.S. Pirzada's *Foundations of Pakistan*). [67] The final resolution actually continues: 'and that this Conference, therefore, recommends to the All-India Muslim League to devise a scheme of Constitution under which *Muslims may attain full independence*.' [68] This on its own puts Jinnah's words into context and is perfectly in tune with his go-slow approach towards secession. [69] Incidentally it was in these days that Jinnah had begun speaking of India as containing 'different nationalities'. [70]

Iqbal's prediction

There is additional evidence to consider. In advising his colleagues to look ahead '25 years', Jinnah likely had fresh in his mind one of Iqbal's letters written to him a year before:

---

65 R. Moore op. cit. p.49

66 Ibid. (Moore takes his information from *The Statesman*, 14 October 1938; as cited in S.R. Mehrotra op. cit. p.207)

67 See *Foundations* Vol. II, xix

68 Jamil-ud-Din Ahmad (ed.) (1970) *Historic Documents of the Muslim Freedom Movement* Lahore: Publishers United, p.257; also K.K. Aziz (1979) *Muslims Under Congress Rule, 1937-1939: a Documentary Record* Islamabad: National Commission on Historical and Cultural Research, Vol. II, p.105. (Emphasis mine)

69 Jinnah similarly quoted the following well-known speech of British orator John Bright on several occasions: 'How long does England propose to govern India? Nobody can answer that question. But be it 50 or 100 or 500 years, does any man with the smallest glimmering of common sense believe that so great a country, with its 20 different nationalities and its 20 different languages, can ever be bound up and consolidated into one compact and enduring empire confine? I believe such a thing to be utterly impossible. (John Bright, 4 June 1858; as cited during Jinnah's interview in B. Nichols 1944, p.192; See also Jinnah's presidential address at ML Annual Session, Karachi, 24 December 1943; NV Vol. III, p.349)

70 Address at the Karachi Municipal Corporation, Karachi, 8 October 1938 (NV Vol. I, p.291). Emphasis mine. This was practically the only time that Jinnah had openly used the word 'nation' other than twice before (once in 1936 and again in 1937), before he made it a permanent part of his vocabulary from 1939 onwards. See Chapter 1, subsection 'Testing Iqbal's nationalism' for full details.

> I remember Lord Lothian told me before I left England that my scheme [71] was the only possible solution of the troubles of India, but that it would take *25 years to come*. Some Muslims in the Punjab are already suggesting the holding of a North-West Indian Muslim Conference, and the idea is rapidly spreading. I agree with you, however, that our community *is not yet sufficiently organised* and disciplined and perhaps the time for holding such a conference is not yet ripe. [72]

Some historians believe that at the time of his Allahabad address, Iqbal had been thinking in terms of an all-India solution and that he never contemplated anything along the lines of partition. In fact Iqbal maintained that he had not made any specific 'demand' one way or another, but that he could see the possibility of a separation movement in the future. When a British intellectual condemned the Allahabad address, implying that it advocated pan-Islamism, Iqbal refuted the claim in his letter to *The Times* in 1931 as follows:

> ... in this passage [73] I do not put forward a "demand" [74] for a Moslem state outside the British Empire, but only a guess at the possible outcome in the dim future of the mighty forces now shaping the destiny of the Indian sub-continent. No Indian Moslem with any pretence to sanity contemplates a Moslem state or series of states in North-West India outside the British Commonwealth of Nations as a plan of practical politics. [75]

Despite suggesting that separation was beyond the pale of 'practical politics' for the time being, Iqbal had also said that Muslims might one day seek 'self-government within the British Empire, or without the British Empire'. [76] At any rate he had envisioned 'the formation of a consolidated North-West Indian Muslim State' as their 'final destiny'. [77] He had also warned of the consequences should the Muslim demands of that time [78] not be met: 'a question of a very great and far-reaching

---

71 Namely the scheme of separation outlined in Iqbal's Allahabad address of 1930.

72 Iqbal to Jinnah, 21 June 1937. *Letters of Iqbal*, p.23. Emphasis mine.

73 Dr Edward Thompson's letter to *The Times*, 3 October 1931, pointed to the following passage of the Allahabad address: 'I would like to see the Punjab, North-West Frontier Province, Sind, and Baluchistan amalgamated into a single State. Self-government within the British Empire or without the British Empire, the formation of a consolidated North-West Indian Moslem State appears to me to be the final destiny of the Moslems, at least of North-West India.'

74 Quotation marks in original.

75 Letter to *The Times*, in reply to Dr Thompson, 12 October 1931. Bashir Ahmed Dar (ed.) (1967) *Letters and Writings of Iqbal* Karachi: Iqbal Academy, p.119–120

76 Sherwani (ed.) 2008, p.11.

77 Ibid.

78 See footnote 7 above for the demands.

importance will arise for the community. Then will arrive the moment for an *independent and concerted political action* by the Muslims of India. If you are at all serious about your ideals and aspirations, you must be ready for such an action.' [79] Iqbal had meant that whether or not he himself made a demand was of little consequence; the Muslim community itself was moving in this direction. (In any case he was hardly the first to make such a prediction, doing so as he was upon his observation of contemporary politics.[80]) This is confirmed in what he wrote to Jinnah in 1937 above, when he suggested that his prediction of separation may be realised within a quarter of a century. Iqbal also considered Jinnah the best candidate for guiding the Muslims through the coming 'storm'. [81]

The 'mighty forces' Iqbal refers to in his letter of 1931 are the Hindu-Muslim riots as a symptom of a much bigger problem between the two 'nations', including the weak political and economic position of Indian Muslims, as well as the dichotomy between 'atheistic socialism' and 'Brahminism', [82] neither of which was compatible with Islamic idealism. As we shall now see, towards the end of his life Iqbal became convinced that the time was drawing near to making the 'demand'. Hence he wrote to Jinnah:

> The problem of bread is becoming more and more acute. The Muslim has begun to feel that he has been going down and down during the last 200 years. Ordinarily he believes that his poverty is

---

[79] Sherwani (ed.) 2008, p.27. Very similar statements were later made by Jinnah in the League Sessions of 1937-8. In his Presidential address at the Lucknow Session in October 1937 he said: 'Eighty millions of Musalmans have nothing to fear. They have their destiny in their hands … Take your vital decisions – they may be grave and momentous and far-reaching in their consequences'. (NV Vol. I, p.182) In his Presidential speech at the Sind Muslim League Conference, Karachi, 8 October 1938, he emphasised that Congress had tried to 'liquidate' the League instead of cooperating after the 1936-7 elections, and had been 'forcing radical changes in the educational system' amounting to an imposition of Hindu culture upon Muslims. At the end, he warned: 'if reasons and arguments fail our *ultimate resort* must depend upon our own inherent strength and power'. (NV Vol. I, p.282-4, 287).

[80] Other individuals of the period who had commented on the improbability of establishing Hindu-Muslim unity include Abdul Halim Sharar (1890) Bepin Chandra Pal (1916), Bhai Parmanand (1923), Hasrat Mohani (1924), Lala Rajpat Rai (1924), Mohammad Ali Jouhar (1925), William Archbold (1925), the Aga Khan (1928), Sir Ross Masood (1929), Zulfiqar Ali Khan (1929), and more. Papers such as *The Times*, *The Economist* and *Empire Review* also predicted a possible partition of India in the future, and the possibility was discussed even in England in the House of Commons (1931). (See *Foundations* Vol. II, xiv-xvii).

[81] '…you are the only Muslim in India today to whom the community has a right to look up for safe guidance through the storm which is coming to North-West India, and perhaps to the whole of India.' (21 June 1937; *Letters of Iqbal*, p.20-21) See also his letter dated 28 May 1937: 'Muslim India hopes that at this serious juncture your genius will discover some way out of our present difficulties' (op. cit. p.20)

[82] Brahmin – the highest Hindu caste. Jinnah said that the Congress did not represent all Hindus, but only a certain section, namely the Caste Hindus – including the high-caste Brahmins.

due to Hindu money-lending or capitalism. The perception that it is equally due to foreign rule has not yet fully come to him. But it is bound to come. The atheistic socialism of Jawaharlal is not likely to receive much response from the Muslims. The question therefore is: how is it possible to solve the problem of Muslim poverty? And the whole future of the League depends on the League's activity to solve this question. If the League can give no such promises I am sure the Muslim masses will remain indifferent to it as before. Happily there is a solution in the enforcement of the Law of Islam and its further development in the light of modern ideas.

The issue between social democracy and Brahminism is not dissimilar to the one between Brahminism and Buddhism. Whether the fate of socialism will be the same as the fate of Buddhism in India, I cannot say. But it is clear to my mind that if Hinduism accepts social democracy it must necessarily cease to be Hinduism. For Islam the acceptance of social democracy in some suitable form and consistent with the legal principles of Islam is not a revolution but a return to the original purity of Islam. The modern problems therefore are far more easy to solve for the Muslims than for the Hindus. But as I have said above in order to make it possible for Muslim India to solve these problems it is necessary to redistribute the country and to provide one or more Muslim states with absolute majorities. Don't you think that the time for such a demand has already arrived? [83]

Hence Iqbal was predicting total separation in the long term based on the prevailing contemporary circumstances. According to the farsighted philosopher, Hindu-Muslim differences were irreconcilable; civil war was already looming, and only British presence was preventing its full breakout. [84] For 'many years' he had believed that Muslim self-determination was the only way to 'secure a peaceful India', whether this meant the creation of 'a free Muslim state or states'. [85] Jinnah and Iqbal were agreed that

---

[83] Iqbal to Jinnah, 28 May 1937. (*Letters of Iqbal*, p.17-19). I must acknowledge here that I have borrowed the last part of my argument – i.e. the citation of Iqbal's push for a 'demand' to be made – from a PhD thesis written by Muhammad Arshad. See M. Arshad (2001, unpublished PhD thesis) *Muslim Politics and Political Movements in the Punjab 1932-1942* Bahawalpur: Islamia University, p.362-3

[84] 'I tell you that we are actually living in a state of civil war which, but for the police and military, would become universal in no time. … The Congress President has denied the political existence of Muslims in no unmistakable terms. The other Hindu political body, i.e., the. Mahasabha, whom I regard as the real representative of the masses of the Hindus, has declared more then once that a united Hindu-Muslim nation is impossible in India. (Ibid. p.21, 22-23)

[85] 28 May 1937 (Ibid. p.18). By 'states' Iqbal evidently meant Bengal and Punjab together (see letter of 21 June 1937; Ibid. p.24); by 'state' he meant the 'amalgamated single state'

though separation was inevitable, it had to be organised properly and the overwhelming majority of Muslims in India had to become consolidated to give it sanction. Jinnah's famous motto 'unity, faith and discipline' probably has its origins in this thought-process.

comprising the provinces in the North-Western zone including Punjab, Sind and NWFP, as this had been his point of focus in his Allahabad address.

Chapter 8
The Pakistan idea

Earlier in this book we noted some of the parallels and the differences between Jinnah and Iqbal's political viewpoints in the 1930s, and the convergence of their opinions before Iqbal's death in 1938. Here we will outline Jinnah's position on the Pakistan idea, in terms of both the territorial and the 'ideological' aspects. The links to Iqbal are shown in the corresponding footnotes. We will also address the following key issues concerning the implications of the Pakistan demand: Jinnah's opposition to the partition of Bengal and Punjab; Jinnah's willingness to leave minority-province Muslims in India; and Jinnah's preference for a single consolidated state.

Territorial aspect:

It is true that the territorial borders of Pakistan (but not the demand for a separate state itself) were always up for negotiation. Not only the Muslim League and the Congress but all Indian parties as well as the British had to take part. Then there were several factors complicating the issue, including Congress intransigence on accepting the principle of Muslim separatism (motivated in part by economic and defence interests), the population distribution problem, the provincialist Muslim leaders who couldn't see past their own self-serving interests, and non-Muslims in Muslim-majority provinces, especially the Punjab and Bengal, who feared the introduction of a 'Muslim raj' or medieval 'Islamic state'. Had it not been for these factors, Jinnah and the League would perhaps have been more specific from the beginning. Nevertheless both the Lahore Resolution and Jinnah's statements do provide ample evidence of his thoughts regarding the general territorial aspect of the demand:

- Pakistan was to be confined to British India [1] in the North-Western (Punjab/Sind/NWFP) and Eastern zones

---

[1] Jinnah's interview to foreign press representatives, New Delhi, 14 November 1946. (NV Vol. V, p.385). He also said that the Pakistan scheme had 'nothing to do with the [Princely] States' (Interview with Mysore Officials, Bangalore, 19 May 1941 (NV Vol. II, p.249); again with regards to the States see interview to Reuters' correspondent Doon Campbell, New Delhi, 21 May 1947 (Yusufi Vol. IV, p.2563-4); Statement on the Lahore Resolution, New Delhi, 1 April 1940. (Yusufi Vol. II, p.1192)

(Bengal/Assam) of India where Muslims were in the majority. This is also reflected in the Lahore Resolution, and confirmed definitively in the Delhi Resolution of 1946. [2] (see Appendices)

- Jinnah was always open to the two regions either being a 'state or states', [3] i.e. becoming two separate states (countries) in a confederation (Pakistan union), or a single state (country) comprising the two regions as provinces (Pakistan federation). This again is reflected in the Lahore Resolution. Iqbal was also open to the two possibilities. [4] Furthermore, both men expressed a personal preference for a consolidated single state, [5] and this preference was again definitively stated in the Delhi Resolution. Jinnah also demanded a corridor between the two 'states' for the obvious reason of maintaining ease of access and thus closer relations between them.
- In effecting partition, Jinnah expected provincial borders to remain as they presently stood. The 'adjustment' of borders was to be restricted to wherever minor Muslim-majority districts happened to be geographically contiguous with larger Muslim-majority areas – e.g. Assam's Sylhet could be separated and joined to Bengal, leaving the rest of Assam free to enter Hindustan. [6] In Jinnah's mind this was no different to Sind's separation from Bombay in 1932. Jinnah thus wanted a 'nucleus Muslim territory surrounded by sufficient additional territory to make it economically viable.' He would not agree to anything which would 'derogate from the sovereignty of Pakistan'. [7]
- 'Pakistan' and 'Hindustan' would be fully sovereign nation-states, maintaining international relations in the form of treaties and agreements.[8]
- Jinnah realised that the distribution problem across India was such that he could only afford to concentrate on a clearly demarcated Muslim bloc. This meant that Muslims living in minority provinces would stay behind in Hindustan; but on the other hand, the situation for these Muslims would essentially

---

2 Iqbal's equivalent can be found in his letters to Jinnah dated 21 June and 11 August 1937, which are cited in Chapter 1, subsection 'Fathers of the nation'.

3 This is discussed later in this chapter.

4 See Iqbal's letters to Jinnah dated 28 May 1937 and 21 June 1937. (*Letters of Iqbal*, p.18, 24)

5 Jinnah's Presidential speech at Lahore Session, 22 March 1940 (extempore) (NV Vol. I, p.495); Iqbal's Allahabad address (Sherwani (ed.) 2008, p.11

6 See Lahore Resolution (reviewed in Chapter 7; full text is in Appendix IV)

7 Official record of Jinnah's interview with the Cabinet Delegation and Viceroy Wavell, New Delhi, 4 April 1946. (NV Vol. IV, p.588, 586 respectively)

8 Presidential address at Lahore Session, 22 March 1940 (NV Vol. I, p.493); Statement on the Lahore Resolution, New Delhi, 1 April 1940. (Yusufi Vol. II, p.1192-3)

remain unchanged whether Pakistan came into being or not. [9] Pakistan would at least secure the freedom of around three quarters of the Muslims of British India, as well as millions of Scheduled Castes or 'Untouchables', Sikhs, Christians and Parsis. Hence Jinnah sought reciprocal safeguards for minorities in Pakistan and Hindustan; this was outlined in the Lahore Resolution and reaffirmed in the Delhi Resolution.

- Jinnah envisioned that during the transitional period (the transfer of power, i.e. as the British gradually pulled out of India) a representative of the Crown would remain in temporary control of foreign affairs and defence; control of these subjects would be 'handed over in the future as and when this became possible'. [10]

Ideological aspect

- The Pakistan idea was based on the Two-Nation Theory; the Muslim nation wanted to live in a territory in which they would live in accordance with Islamic ideals rather than the ideals of 'Brahminism'. [11]
- All aspects of the new state – political, social, and economic – were to be built on Islamic ideals; [12] thus the state was to be centred on the concept of *tauheed* as described by Iqbal. [13]
- In accordance with Islamic ideals, Pakistan would have a democratic form of government, guaranteeing freedom of speech and conscience, and full equality to all regardless of caste, creed or colour. These ideals would be embodied in the constitution. [14]
- As an Islamic polity Pakistan would be a non-sectarian state; it would neither be religious (theocracy), nor secular (atheistic nationalism), nor a product of 'synthesis' (secular Islam). Its

---

[9] Statement on the Lahore Resolution, New Delhi, 31 March 1940. (NV Vol. II, p.1-2); Address to the Muslim Progress Society and Muslim Youth Majlis, Bombay, 3 January 1941. (NV Vol. II, p.125-6); Iqbal's letter to Jinnah dated 21 June 1937 (*Letters of Iqbal*, p.24)

[10] Jinnah's interview with H.V. Hodson, as recorded in Hodson's diary, 5 November 1941. (NV Vol. IV, p.835)

[11] Examples of Jinnah's explanation of the Two-Nation Theory are scattered throughout this book. For examples of Iqbal, see his 1930 Allahabad address (Sherwani (ed.) 2008, p.9-10, 25-26) and his letter to Jinnah dated 28 May1937 (Sherwani (ed.) 2008, p.18-19).

[12] Again, examples are scattered throughout this book.

[13] Iqbal's *Reconstruction*, p.154; Jinnah's address to the Bar Association on the occasion of the Holy Prophet's birthday, Karachi, 25 January 1948 (Yusufi Vol. IV p.2670)

[14] See Jinnah's numerous speeches to the effect, including his interview with Doon Campbell, Reuters' Correspondent, New Delhi, 21 May 1947 (Yusufi Vol. IV, p.2565) from which the Munir quote was contrived; also the 1949 Constituent Assembly Debates of Pakistan as covered in Chapter 3.

exact political shape would not matter as long as it was ethically or spiritually (and thus actively) Islamic. [15]

- Pakistan's economy would be neither capitalist nor socialist (nor would it be founded exclusively on any particular 'ism') but something containing the merits of both, whilst aiming at the Islamic ideal. [16]

Now let us examine the following few key issues, whilst keeping the whole 'Pakistan idea' in mind.

Jinnah was opposed to the partition of Bengal and Punjab

Both the largest Muslim areas of India – containing around two thirds of the whole Muslim population of the subcontinent – also happened to have narrow majorities. Bengal had a 55% Muslim population. Punjab had a 57% Muslim population. Consequently, the Congress in 1944 [17] and the British in 1946 [18] advocated the partition of these two provinces to allow the non-Muslim populations to reside in Hindustan. That Jinnah opposed the partition of these provinces is viewed by some as proof that ultimately he wanted provincial autonomy in a united India rather than a separate nation-state (i.e. that his pre-1936 political position had never changed). This of course is based on the erroneous assumption that the Two-Nation Theory was based on mere 'communalism', and that therefore Jinnah should logically have supported the idea of partitioning these zones.

In fact Jinnah's arguments opposing it were perfectly justified and had no bearing on the actual argument for the partition of India, which was supposed to work around existing provinces, and so create as little administrative and civil upheaval as possible. We have seen in Chapter 7 how the territorial demand was loosely outlined in the Lahore Resolution. To begin with, partitioning the two main Muslim provinces safely was hardly practicable owing to the distribution of the various communal populations. This was particularly true of the Punjab, where the Sikh community was almost evenly distributed across the province. Partition in both zones would split all communities and not just Muslims (and of course this is what eventually happened). Population transfer

---

[15] See Jinnah's statements in Myth nos. 3 and 12 (Chapter 10); also Iqbal's statement in his Allahabad address that Muslim states would not introduce 'religious rule'. (Sherwani (ed.) 2008, p.12)

[16] See Jinnah's address to the Members of the League Planning Committee, New Delhi, 5 November 1944. (Yusufi Vol. III p.1961); Speech on the occasion of the Opening Ceremony of the State Bank of Pakistan, Karachi, 1 July 1948. (NV Vol. VII, p.428-9); the Constituent Assembly Debates of 1949 (Chapter 3); Iqbal's criticism of Nehru's 'atheistic socialism' in his letter to Jinnah, 28 May 1937. (*Letters of Iqbal*, p.17-19).

[17] Rajogopalchari's formula: see Chapter 11, footnote 9

[18] See Chapter 11 on the Cabinet Mission Plan

would then become inevitable, and whilst Jinnah had prepared himself for such an eventuality, nevertheless he wanted to avoid needlessly uprooting countless numbers from every community, by preventing the partition of these major provinces in the first place.[19]

Another practical reason for keeping the two provinces united was to keep the two territories closer together. Bengal and Punjab were not geographically contiguous, but were around 700 miles apart.[20] With partition that gap would grow to 1000 miles.[21] Jinnah's demand for a corridor to link the two halves of Pakistan was already considered problematic, without a partitioning of the key provinces making it worse.

Jinnah was also strongly of the view that a misleading numbers game was being played in Bengal. Only the 'Caste Hindu vocal section' – barely a quarter of the total population of West Bengal – was actually in favour of partition, rather than the whole of the non-Muslim population.[22] His accusations were not unfounded. The Bengal Hindu

---

19 See Jinnah's meeting with Mountbatten, 8 April 1947 (NV Vol. VI, p.36-7). Mountbatten records that Jinnah gave cultural reasons for leaving the two provinces intact, and that 'Hindus have stronger feelings as Bengalis or Punjabis than they have as members of Congress' (Muslims were not mentioned). Jinnah's point was that no one but Congress was demanding the partitioning the provinces, and that even this was a 'bluff' to 'frighten him off Pakistan'. (Ibid.) There is no doubt that Jinnah was trying to prevent the foreseeable administrative and civil chaos that would come with a provincial partition.

20 See HMG's Statement on the Cabinet Mission Plan, 16 May 1946 (NV Vol. V, p.756)

21 See Jinnah's broadcast talk to the people of Australia, 19 February, 1948. (NV Vol. VII, p.189)

22 The Scheduled Caste Hindus were opposed because they feared a division would subject the major part of their population to a Hindu raj, and the rest to a Muslim raj. See Jinnah's note giving the League's position on the Viceroy's draft announcement, 17 May 1947 (NV Vol. VI, p.118. Caste Hindus population figure is obtained from the same interview (Hindu population of W. Bengal = 66%; Caste Hindus = 37% of this figure). Jinnah had made the same argument and used the same figures at a meeting with Mountbatten a few weeks earlier. (23 April 1947; NV Vol. VI, p.59). Note that it is generally accepted in scholarship that the Scheduled Caste Hindus changed their minds about partitioning Bengal after the successive Calcutta and Noakhali riots, explaining the eventual vote by a majority (25 of 30) of Scheduled Caste representatives in favour of Bengal's partition at the Bengal Legislative Assembly on 18 June 1947, as well as the overwhelming success of Congress against the Scheduled Castes Federation in the 1946 elections. (See for example Bidyut Chakrabarty (2004) *The Partition of Bengal and Assam, 1932-1947: Contour of Freedom* London: Routledge, p.111-113, which includes a reference to a memorandum from some Scheduled Caste groups favouring the partition of Bengal (ibid. p.138)). However, more recent scholarship has challenged this view of history with evidence of powerful propaganda, alleged bribery, intimidation and even vote rigging, as well as pointing to the electoral system that had put Scheduled Caste voters at a disadvantage thanks to the Poona Pact (see Chapter 1, footnote 103), and the political ostracising of SC Federation leader Jogendra Nath Mandal by the Congress and Mahasabha. These issues together offer a better explanation of why the Scheduled Castes Federation (founded by Ambedkar in 1942), which had been previously shown itself to be the real all-India representative organisation of the Scheduled Caste Hindus in the 1940s, suddenly lost the elections in 1946 and strengthened the Congress and Mahasabha's claim for the partition of Bengal. See Dwaipayan Sen, 'No matter how, Jogendranath had to be defeated: The Scheduled Castes Federation and the making of

leader Syama Prasad Mookerjee for example, who was also Mahasabha President, was demanding a Hindu homeland in Bengal and refused to contemplate letting West Bengal (or even Calcutta) go to Pakistan. As such he represented a minority opinion amongst Hindus, but he was too powerful to be either challenged or ignored. [23] This brings us to the economic factor, namely the port city of Calcutta (present-day Kolkata). Eastern Bengal had a greater (and poorer) Muslim population, whilst Calcutta was in the Western half. If Bengal was partitioned, East Bengal would naturally end up in Pakistan without the port. Dismissing the argument that Calcutta was largely a Hindu city, [24] Jinnah insisted on having Calcutta as Pakistan needed to have 'a port for each Muslim bloc'. In his opinion, Hindustan did not need Calcutta; it would already be getting 'Bombay, Madras and outlets through Ceylon'. [25] Calcutta had been the 'heart of Bengal'; [26] it had built itself up on the port as a trade centre and was its economic capital. Without Calcutta, East Bengal would be like 'asking a man to live without his heart'. [27] It would become a rural slum.

Jinnah was likely also aware that since neither Eastern nor Western Bengal would be prepared to give up the port, a partition of Bengal would actually result in its reunification with India later on. Hence he also maintained that if partition of the province was insisted upon, then Calcutta should become a free port [28] (as was suggested by the Cabinet Mission of 1946). [29] Even Louis Mountbatten (1900-1979), the last Viceroy of India, concluded that Nehru's strategy was to leave East Bengal in such a poor position that it would be 'bound sooner or later to

---

partition in Bengal, 1945 -1947' in *Indian Economic & Social History Review* 2012, Vol. 49 No.3, p.321–64. The article also provides evidence of 'substantial' opposition to partition amongst the Scheduled Castes even after the 1946 elections. (ibid. p.351-5).

23 S. Wolpert 2006, p.141; also Harun-or-Rashid (2003 revised) *The Foreshadowing of Bangladesh: Bengal Muslim League and Muslim League and Muslim Politics, 1936-1947* Dhaka: The University Press, p.283-4, 301-3. Opinion between members of the Bengal Provincial Congress Committee was also split, with some, including its leader K.S. Roy, in favour of a united Bengal, and others in favour of its partition. (B. Chakrabarty 2004, p.139-40)

24 Jinnah maintained that the Hindus in Calcutta, comprised mainly of Scheduled Caste Hindus who numbered a mere 600,000 at most, were imported labourers and were at any rate pro-Pakistan. See record of Cabinet Mission Delegation's meeting with Jinnah, 16 April 1946 (NV Vol. IV, p.642)

25 Jinnah's interview to *Western Mail* correspondent, 9 April 1946. (NV Vol. IV, p.621)

26 Jinnah's note on behalf of the ML on the draft declaration of the British Government's transfer of power, 17 May 1947 (NV Vol. VI, p.118)

27 Official record of Jinnah's interview with the Cabinet Delegation and Viceroy Wavell, New Delhi, 4 April 1946 (NV Vol. IV, p.588)

28 Jinnah's letter to Sir Eric Mieville (private secretary of Viceroy Mountbatten), 22 May 1947. (Sher M. Garewal (ed.) (1998) *Jinnah-Mountbatten Correspondence: 22 March-9 August 1947* Lahore: Research Society of Pakistan/University of the Punjab, p.69)

29 See Chapter 11.

rejoin India'.[30] Not only Jinnah and the Muslims, but also Gandhi, much of the Congress, and the Scheduled Caste Hindus, not to mention many British officials including the Governor of Punjab, Sir Evan Jenkins, and the Governor of Bengal, Sir Frederick Burrows, were all categorically against partition at the provincial level. Sikhs in the Punjab[31] and Caste Hindus in Western Bengal were the only ones who wanted it.[32] But Mountbatten heeded the advice of Nehru and V.P. Menon,[33] who convinced him that a division on communal lines was the best way to avert the possibility of civil war; and in addition Mountbatten and Nehru were both keen to move the transfer of power date forward (it was originally set for June 1948).[34] The three men worked together to draft the 3rd June Plan for the transfer of power.[35] All of this was done

---

30 Viceroy's Staff Meeting on 31 May 1947 (N. Mansergh et al. (eds.) (1970-1983) *Constitutional Relations Between Britain and India: The Transfer of Power* in 12 volumes (hereinafter '*Transfer of Power*'). London: Her Majesty's Stationery Office, Vol. XI, p.3)

31 The Sikhs (the Akali Dal party) were originally undecided on the notion of Punjab's partition, being aware that their evenly distributed population in the province would be practically sliced in two. The Punjab was both their national and spiritual home, being the birthplace of their religion. Some Sikhs including Master Tara Singh and Baldev Singh were distrustful of Muslims and demanded their own homeland, and others led by Giani Kartar Singh wanted to negotiate the possibility of a 'Khalistan' (lit. 'land of the pure' in Punjabi) in East Punjab being included as a unit of Pakistan. Unfortunately the inability of the League to convince Sikhs of their proper place in Pakistan, coupled with the intrigues of Punjab politics leading to distrust and even rioting between the two communities, eventually sealed Punjab's fate. Today the movement for 'Khalistan' still exists in India, and ironically it even looks to Pakistan for diplomatic support.

32 See footnotes 19 and 22 above.

33 V.P. Menon, the right-hand man of Patel, who was serving as Reforms Commissioner and was an advisor of Mountbatten, was also the author of the partition plan which was devised behind closed doors. See his own account of how he changed the British original plan in his *Transfer of Power in India* (1957), p.354-370. In his *Report on the Last Viceroy* Mountbatten also credits Menon with being the man who took a 'leading part' in redrafting what was to become known as the 3rd June Plan for transfer of power. (Lionel Carter (ed.) (2003) *Mountbatten's Report on the Last Viceroyalty, 22 March - 15 August 1947* New Delhi: Manohar, p.141). See also footnote 35 below.

34 In May 1947 Nehru proposed that the transfer of power date be brought forward to June 1947 (A. Jalal 1994, p.269), having already told Mountbatten that a lack of time for setting up Pakistan might 'frighten Jinnah into cooperation' on the interim government. (Meeting of Mountbatten and Nehru, 24 March 1947, in Carter (ed.) 2003, p.68) See also A.S. Ahmed 1997, p.141-2 and S. Wolpert 2006, p.143-4, 147-52 for Mountbatten's 'need for speed'.

35 Mountbatten confessed that on 10 May 1947 he showed Nehru an early draft for the transfer of power, based on a 'hunch' that he could trust his 'new-found friendship with Pandit Nehru to ask his personal opinion', despite unanimous opposition from his staff that it was 'a departure from the intended procedure that all the leaders should be shown the final version of the plan at the same time.' As the draft plainly stated that the transfer of power would be to 'more than one authority, if that should be the desire of the people of India' (implying that these authorities would be created by partition), Nehru objected that this created 'fragmentation and conflict' and 'complete balkanisation of India'. (Carter (ed.) 2003, p.132, 140-1) He wanted a plan that was in line with the long-term aims of the Cabinet Mission, which, as we will show in Chapter 11, was to tighten the federation and keep India united. Mountbatten altered the draft with the help of V.P. Menon to better accommodate Nehru's views (ibid. p.141-142). These changes included limiting the choice of the Punjab and

without Jinnah's knowledge, and in fact the Viceroy held off telling Jinnah anything in case he made a move to stop it. It was Mountbatten, Nehru and Patel who made a mockery of the partition principle by insisting on paring down divisions to the provincial and district level, and claiming that this idea was embodied in the Lahore Resolution. [36] Partition became balkanisation in their hands, and it was a move calculated to first force East Bengal and then the weakened West half of Pakistan back into a united India.

Furthermore, Mountbatten did not formally reveal the Radcliffe Award, which defined the borders of India and Pakistan, to Indian leaders until 16 August 1947, a day after India's independence. (He had received the award on 12 August and likely knew its salient details as early as the 9th. [37]) Mountbatten's stated reason was to prevent diplomatic fallout over the boundaries, [38] but it may really have been connected to last-minute interference on his part; and consequently countless people suddenly found themselves in the wrong country, prompting a mass exodus. History has recorded the catastrophic consequences of these manoeuvres. [39]

Bengal to either joining the Constituent Assembly as it presently stood or creating a new all-India one (in the original draft the provinces had the option to 'stand out independently' (ibid. p.132)); not expressly stating that there could be more than one 'authority'; and bringing the transfer of power forward to 'much earlier than 1948', so that no party (i.e. the League) would have enough time to introduce 'new Constitutions', thereby opening the possibility of a longer-lasting interim setup that might become 'permanent' (ibid. p.143). The draft received the sanction of Nehru and Patel, and became the basis of a partition of India in which even some *tahsils* (subdistricts) in districts such as Ferozepur and Gurdaspur, which in the original plan were supposed to come to Pakistan, were given to India (although India was unhappy that the Chittagong Hill Tracts with a largely Buddhist tribal population went to Pakistan). Mountbatten always denied claims of his personal interference in defining boundaries, and in his Report he wrote he had 'nothing whatsoever' to do with the work of the two (Punjab and Bengal) Boundary Commissions or Sir Cyril Radcliffe, their Chairman (Carter (ed.) 2003, p.220; also p.272). Yet a map today held in Pakistan shows that Radcliffe's original boundary lines had included these areas in Pakistan, and there is also evidence that implicates Mountbatten in having intervened to change them. See Carter's introduction in op.cit. p.11-12; S. Wolpert 2006, p.167-8.

36 See V.P. Menon 1957, p.355-6. The Congress had twisted the meaning of 'territorial adjustments' in the Lahore Resolution.

37 See Minutes of Viceroy's Staff Meeting, 9 August, *Transfer of Power* Vol. XII, p.611. Radcliffe had said the Punjab part of the award was ready for publication by the evening of the 9th. Mountbatten thought it might not 'be desirable to publish it straight away' as 'the earlier it was published, the more the British would have to bear the responsibility for the disturbances which would undoubtedly result'. Significantly, this meeting is not mentioned at all in Mountbatten's *Report on the Last Viceroyalty*.

38 Carter (ed.) 2003, p.273-4 Part F, paragraphs 158-161.

39 The partition of the two provinces and the subsequent exodus – possibly the biggest in recorded history at around 10 million people – in the summer of 1947 led to horrific bloodshed, especially in the Punjab. Conservative estimates of the numbers who were killed are around 100,000. However many consider this to be a low estimate and suggest figures of anywhere between 1-2 million, with up to 15 million people displaced. (A.S. Ahmed 1997, p.166). See also Yasmin Khan (2007) *The Great Partition: The Making of India and Pakistan* New Haven/London: Yale University Press, a sobering book detailing the horrors including

Ultimately a pragmatist, in 1947 Jinnah was even prepared, if all else failed, to let Bengal go as an independent state. From the beginning (taking the lead from Iqbal) [40] he had referred to Pakistan both in terms of a 'state' (federal, made up of the two blocs) and two independent 'states' (confederation); [41] hence he claimed 'one-fourth' of India's territory for 'one-fourth' of its population.[42] As such, his speeches indicate that he personally preferred Pakistan to be a single state, [43] and the Delhi Resolution of April 1946 – an update to the original Lahore Resolution – faithfully reflected this preference. We will come to this later. But with the situation being as precarious as it was, he was willing to let Bengal go its own way as a separate state so that it could remain united. [44] This is why, when Viceroy Mountbatten asked Jinnah in April 1947 what he thought of Bengal Prime Minister Huseyn Shaheed Suhrawardy's [45] proposal for the creation of a separate united

---

looting, killing, abduction and rape experienced by people on all sides – Hindu, Muslim and Sikh – as well as telling humanitarian stories of people who risked their own safety to save individuals and groups belonging to the communal 'other' amidst the carnage. Many historians in and out of the subcontinent condemn the British for their recklessness in handling the transfer of power; and Mountbatten's recommendation for the hasty withdrawal of British armed forces during the critical phase, which allowed civil violence to escalate virtually out of control. (The forces were to have 'no operational functions' and would 'not be available' for 'internal security purposes' after 15 August 1947 (Carter (ed.) 2003, p.191))

40 See Iqbal's letters as cited in Chapter 1, subsection 'Fathers of the nation'.

41 See Jinnah's interview to the International News Service of America, Bombay, 21 May 1942. (Yusufi Vol. III p.1571). A week later he also expressed his approval that the British had begun to recognise the Pakistan/Hindustan problem in terms of 'dominions instead of dominion' and '*unions* instead of federation' (emphasis mine). That he referred to unions clarifies that Pakistan could potentially be a union of two states, whether federal or confederal, in view of the geographical problem. (See Jinnah's appeal to the youth to join the Muslim National Guards Organisation, Bombay, 28 May 1942 (Yusufi Vol. III, p.1573)

42 Again see Jinnah's interview to the International News Service of America, Bombay, 21 May 1942. (Yusufi Vol. III, p.1571).

43 Examples are scattered throughout this book, beginning with Jinnah's Presidential speech at the ML Annual Session, 22 March 1940. See also subsection 'Jinnah wanted Pakistan to be a consolidated state' in this chapter (below).

44 Bidyut Chakrabarty has suggested that Suhrawardy's efforts for a separate united Bengal may have accidentally had the adverse effect of spurring on moves by the other parties towards the partition of the province, and that Jinnah might have realised this, which is why his arguments focused on keeping Calcutta within East Bengal. (Chakrabarty 2004, p.137-9).

45 Huseyn Shaheed Suhrawardy (1892-1963) was from Midnapore in West Bengal. In 1936 he became the General Secretary of the Bengal Provincial Muslim League. In the 1940s he served as the last Prime Minster of Bengal before partition, and along with Abul Hashim he played a central role in winning the overwhelming support of Bengali Muslims in the 1946 elections, following which he formed the only Muslim League government in India and became Bengal's Prime Minister. In 1947 he also advocated the united Bengal scheme, for which he is best known. Following partition he stayed on in Calcutta to assist Gandhi in his mission to quell Hindu-Muslim tensions in West Bengal. In 1949 he returned to Pakistan and joined the government despite attempts made to block him. Immediately after his return Suhrawardy left the Muslim League and joined the newly-formed Awami League that he had co-founded. In 1956 he became Prime Minister of Pakistan. He aimed to achieve economic equity between the two wings of Pakistan, though political pressure compelled him to resign a year later. In 1962 Suhrawardy was jailed for his activism against Ayub Khan's regime, and

Bengal that would join 'neither Pakistan nor Hindustan', he found that Jinnah was not at all perturbed. 'I should be delighted,' was Jinnah's now famous reply. 'What is the use of Bengal without Calcutta; they had much better remain united and independent; I am sure that they would be on friendly terms with us.' [46] Thus, despite his preference for a single state, Jinnah would have been content as long as the existing province was not partitioned, [47] and Bengal's Muslims (as well as other communities including Scheduled Caste Hindus) were spared from entering the Indian Union.

Note however that while Jinnah maintained his resistance to the partition of Bengal, he eventually ended his support for the United Bengal Plan. As Bangladeshi political scientist Harun-or-Rashid has shown, the main reason was that Suhrawardy was prioritising his provincialist loyalties. He was attempting (albeit in a sincere bid to win the confidence of the local Hindu populace) [48] to form a League-Congress coalition soon after the 1946 elections. This conflicted with the League's stance that it had not contested the elections in order to form ministries but to get a verdict on Pakistan. Prof. Rashid summarises the issue behind Jinnah's change of heart as follows:

> [Jinnah] had earlier expected that an independent Bengal would be a subsidiary Pakistan, i.e. a Muslim state, if it had to stay outside as a separate entity in order to retain its integrity. He now seems to have been convinced that, under a system of joint electorates and in view of the socialist leanings of some Bengali leaders it would not be what he had envisaged. It was most likely that Bengal would have been a secular state. With the preponderance of the Hindus and the total unreliability of Suhrawardy and Hashim, he might have feared that Bengal would not remain a potential ally of (West) Pakistan, which he had practically hoped for while endorsing Suhrawardy's scheme. [49]

Jinnah was prepared to leave some Muslims behind in India

Many advocates of a 'secular Jinnah' take the essentially apologist position that Jinnah would not have been prepared to leave so many of

---

was released after 7 months. In 1963 he went to Europe to undertake treatment for ongoing heart problems, and died later that year in Beirut, where he had been recuperating.

46 Record of Mountbatten's interview with Jinnah, 26 April 1947. (*Transfer of Power* Vol. X, p.452; NV Vol. VI, p.69-70).

47 For a detailed review of Jinnah's attitude on a separate Bengal, which corroborates our view above, see Harun-or-Rashid (2003 revised) *The Foreshadowing of Bangladesh: Bengal Muslim League and Muslim League and Muslim Politics, 1936-1947* Dhaka: The University Press, p.270-77.

48 Rashid 2003 (revised), p.224. Suhrawardy had also practically repudiated the Two-Nation Theory by referring to the Bengali Hindus and Muslims as 'one race' and offering joint electorates, which for League loyalists was going too far. (Op.cit. p.313)

49 Ibid. p.313

his co-religionists 'high and dry' [50] and so he could not have sought the partition of India. But they have fallen into the old Congress propagandist trap of taking 'partition' to mean 'balkanisation', i.e. the creation of two 'mutually hostile' states similar to the Balkan states. [51] This was the same alarmist language originally used by the opponents of the Pakistan demand and it was a subtle threat that Pakistan was being created expressly to be an enemy of India, and that it intended to revive Muslim imperialism. It was inflammatory, designed to stir up fear and mistrust, and most importantly, it was pure nonsense.

Since in their minds 'partition' is synonymous with 'balkanisation' (and especially in hindsight of the holocaust of summer 1947), some pro-secularist commentators endeavour to show that Jinnah never wanted partition. [52] Indeed 'balkanisation' was not what he wanted; after all he opposed the partition of the Punjab and Bengal – which truly entailed a 'balkanisation'. But Jinnah had clarified the real meaning of 'partition' at a mixed Hindu-Muslim gathering. He gave an analogy of 'two lions in one den' to explain the impossibility of a 'joint raj', and thus that 'the only solution is partition'. However this did not mean that they could not part as 'friends.' He assured those non-Muslims who would likely end up inside Pakistan's borders that they would be treated 'generously', based on the 'highest authority of our book in Islam'. [53]

Nevertheless partition did mean a severance of ties with the rest of India insofar as Muslims did not wish to be subjected to a political setup that would place them in perpetual minority status; and they wanted their own constitution and their own constituent assembly. This necessitated not the revision, but the annulment of the centre. [54] There is no doubt that Indian Muslims sought a nation-state, not provincial autonomy. Naturally even nation-states have international relations with other countries, and the most important international relationships are those between neighbouring states. But such treaties and agreements do not impair the sovereignty of the individual states. Thus Pakistan's sovereignty would be unaffected by any treaty relations with India, since, as Jinnah pointed out, a treaty is a 'voluntary exercise of sovereignty' which 'could be terminated' at any time. [55] Jinnah wanted

---

50 A. Jalal 1994, p.3

51 'Mutually hostile' is the dictionary definition of 'balkanisation', based on the historical break-up of the Balkan states and the Balkan Wars that led to the serious deterioration of European interrelations, and eventually to WWI.

52 The best known example is Ayesha Jalal. See Myth no. 11 (Chapter 10).

53 Speech at mixed Hindu-Muslim meeting, Ootacamund, 3 June 1941 (NV Vol. II p.259-60)

54 In response to the claim that the Pakistan areas were economically weak, Jinnah argued that with partition there would be 'no centre for India' and that the Pakistan areas would 'get for themselves the revenue' that would normally go to the centre, thereby improving their economic position. (See his Presidential address at the Muslim Students Federation, Lahore, 2 March 1941; Yusufi Vol. II, p.1335)

55 See official record of Jinnah's interview with the Cabinet Delegation and Viceroy Wavell, New Delhi, 4 April 1946 (NV Vol. IV, p.585)

cordial international relations between Pakistan and India. In particular he wanted pacts for defence and for securing the rights of minorities in both India and Pakistan. This would ensure that Muslims left behind in India would not be left 'high and dry'. But they would nevertheless have to accept the realities of the situation:

> … the Muslim minorities are wrongly made to believe that they would be worse off and be left in the lurch in any scheme of partition or division of India. I may explain that the Muslims wherever they are in a minority *cannot improve their position* under a united India or under one central government. Whatever happens, they would remain a minority … by coming in the way of the division of India *they do not and cannot improve their own position.*
>
> On the other hand they can, by their attitude of obstruction, bring the Muslim homeland and six crores [56] of the Muslims under one government where they would remain no more than a minority in perpetuity.
>
> It was because of the realisation of this fact that the Mussalman minorities in Hindu India readily supported the Lahore Resolution. The question for the Muslim minorities in Hindu India is whether the entire Muslim India of nine crore Muslims should be subjected to a Hindu majority *raj*, or whether at least the six crore of the Muslims residing in the areas where they form a majority should have their own homeland and thereby have an opportunity to develop their spiritual, cultural, economic and political life in accordance with their own genius and shape their own future destiny, at the same time allowing Hindus and others to do likewise. [57]

Partition would make no difference to the position of Muslims living in minority provinces – they already lived in these provinces as a 'sub-national group' [58] – but obstructing the demand would harm the interests of Muslim India as a whole. Jinnah assured Muslims in minority provinces that the creation of Pakistan as a separate state would in fact improve their position, because thereafter tensions would ease and the majority community in each respective zone would work to 'create a real sense of security amongst the minorities and win their complete trust and confidence.' [59] And if worst came to worst, they would at least 'have a homeland in Pakistan which will give you a

---

[56] *Crore*: Hindi word for 10 million.
[57] Statement on the Lahore Resolution, New Delhi, 31 March 1940. (NV Vol. II, p.1-2)
[58] See Jinnah's address at the Muslim Students' Conference, Jullundur, 14 November 1942 (NV Vol. III, p.98).
[59] Statement on the Lahore Resolution, New Delhi, 31 March 1940. (Op. cit. p.2).

shelter whenever you need it'.[60] At the same time, Jinnah stressed that they must be loyal to the country in which they resided: 'Just as I want every Hindu to be loyal to Pakistan, so do I want every Muslim in India to be loyal to India. There is no other alternative.'[61]

Indian Muslims in minority provinces heeded Jinnah's call, and they supported the League wholeheartedly. As Prof. Mujahid has observed, just as India's Muslims had supported the Khilafat movement for no material gain, similarly Muslims in minority provinces willingly supported the League's aim to free those in the majority provinces. They were not 'actuated by a desire to secure any material benefits for themselves', but by 'an altruistic spirit to see Islam triumph in a certain territory or region, though it might not be their own'.[62]

Jinnah wanted Pakistan to be a consolidated state

Jinnah said that he wanted a 'quarter of India' for its Muslim population, which happened to constitute a quarter (90 million) of the subcontinent's total population (400 million; 250 million of which was Hindu). In north-western and eastern India as a whole, around three quarters of the population was Muslim. The territory comprising Muslim India could take the form of either a 'state or states'.[63] Yet in his speeches even before 1946, he was far more likely to be heard speaking of Pakistan as a 'state' than as 'states', as an indication of his personal preference. Even at his presidential address at the Lahore session in 1940, where the Lahore Resolution would be passed the next day, Jinnah had said that the Muslims must have their own 'state'.[64]

Advocates of a 'Muslim Jinnah' implicitly follow the logic that speaking of one united state is in conformity with the pan-Islamic ideal of unity transcending time and space, and that this is the reason that Jinnah spoke of one state, but there is also another reason to consider. Speaking in comprehensive terms of a single 'state' (and calling for 'territorial adjustments')[65] was obviously more practical in order to

60 Interview with the deputation leader of the Coorg Muslims, New Delhi, 25 July 1947 (NV Vol. VI, p.321)

61 Ibid. p.319.

62 S. Mujahid 1981, p.397 fn

63 See Jinnah's interview to the correspondent of the International News Service of America, Bombay, 21 May 1942 (Yusufi Vol. III, p.1571). Here Jinnah mentioned both 'states' and 'state or states'. See also his interview to the *Daily Herald*, Bombay, 13 August 1942, *Tribune*, 16 August 1942, in which he says: 'Our aim is that those areas, where the Muslims vastly outnumber Hindus shall become a separate dominion or even dominions.' (NV Vol. III, p.39)

64 Presidential address at the ML Annual Session, Lahore, 22 March 1940. (NV Vol. I, p.495).

65 See text of Lahore Resolution, Appendix IV. Jinnah emphasises this point in his interview to Reuters' Duncan Hooper (7 December 1945; Yusufi Vol. III, p.2133): 'It is possible that there will have to be exchange of populations, if it can be done on a purely voluntary basis. There will also doubtless have to be frontier adjustments where primarily Hindu and Moslem lands are contiguous to the Hindustan or Pakistan States, as the case may be ... but first it is

justify the inclusion of territories that had marginal majorities (Punjab and Bengal) or even marginal minorities (e.g. Assam). Jinnah aimed to include as much of the Muslim population from the north-west and east of India as possible in Pakistan, and at the same time he needed to ensure Pakistan's economic stability. Jinnah therefore rejected what he called a 'mutilated' or 'moth-eaten' [66] Pakistan, i.e. one that satisfied neither the population nor the economic criteria. Of course it was in view of both these considerations that he later argued against the partition of Punjab and Bengal, which necessitated dividing the Muslim populations in these respective provinces as well as the economic assets. On the other hand, the League had made room for a Muslim confederation in the Lahore Resolution in case it became absolutely necessary to give problem provinces with narrow majorities more autonomy. This was something that Jinnah himself implied in an early statement on the implications of the Lahore Resolution, whilst addressing the apprehensions of the Sikhs in the Punjab. [67] Nevertheless, he confirmed his position on 'states' in 1944, in his correspondence with Gandhi. When Gandhi wrote to ask whether the constituent provinces in the two major zones would form 'independent states' (trying to get a clarification on the text of the Lahore Resolution), Jinnah wrote in reply that it meant they would be 'units of Pakistan', thereby clarifying that Pakistan as a whole was to be a single albeit federal state. [68] In 1945, he stated again:

> Our Pakistan government will probably be a federal government, modelled on the lines of autonomous provinces with the key power in matters of defence and foreign affairs etc. at the centre. But that will be for the constitution-making body, *our* constitution-making body, to decide. [69]

---

necessary to take the *present provincial borders* as the boundaries of the future Pakistan.' (Emphasis mine)

[66] See speech at the meeting of the Council of the All-India Muslim League, Lahore, 30 July 1944 (Yusufi Vol. III, p.1926).

[67] Jinnah said: 'I am sure they [the Sikhs] would be much better off in the North-West Muslim zone than they can ever possibly be in a united India or under one central government. ... It is obvious that whereas in a united India they would be mere nobodies, in the Muslim homeland, constituted of the western zone of the federated autonomous states including the autonomous sovereign state of the Punjab, the Sikhs would always occupy an honoured place and would play an effective and influential role.' (Statement on the Lahore Resolution, New Delhi, 31 March 1940; NV Vol. II, p.2)

[68] Jinnah to Gandhi, 17 September 1944 (C. Rajagopalachari (ed.) 1944, p.13, 17). This is made clearer still when on 21 September 1944, Jinnah also writes to Gandhi that 'Pakistan and Hindustan will be two separate sovereign states.' (Op. cit. p.21) For more about the 'states' versus 'state' controversy, see the end of Chapter 9.

[69] Interview to Duncan Hooper, Reuter's Special Correspondent, Bombay, 7 December 1945 (Yusufi Vol. III, p.2133). Emphasis mine.

Yet it is also true that there was a divided opinion regarding the geopolitical status of Pakistan even among Muslims who joined the movement for its establishment. Bengali Muslims expected it to exist in two parts, probably in confederation, even while sharing the same name. While this difference of opinion was political, it had an essentially ideological basis. We will review this in the next chapter.

Chapter 9
Lahore to Delhi

> Did we say anywhere that we should have Pakistan here and now?
> – *Jinnah at Madras, 1941* [1]

In the previous chapter, we provided evidence from within the Lahore resolution and the various speeches of Jinnah to demonstrate that the Lahore Resolution was a deferred demand for secession but it was a serious demand nonetheless. Here we will provide a rundown of Jinnah's strategy in forging the Muslims as a nation before he gave them 'marching orders' and led them to independence in the shape of Pakistan.

Organisation of Muslim India

> The work of the Muslim League has grown beyond the physical capacity of any single man. If you were to know what I have to attend to all alone, you will be astonished. [2]

From 1937 onwards, [3] Jinnah gave his all in uniting the Muslims of India. He continually raised funds, though to the end League never had the kind of financial backing the Congress took for granted. Nor did the League have nearly as much propaganda power, especially in the English language. As Leaguer Mirza Abol Hasan Ispahani writes: 'The English press was preponderatingly owned by Hindus ... Muslim news and views on important issues often went unrepresented or inadequately projected and insufficiently explained in English.' [4] To address this issue, Jinnah founded the weekly English newspaper *Dawn* in 1941, turning it into a daily a year later. He was the sole proprietor of

---

[1] Presidential address, Annual ML Session, Madras, 14 April 1941 (NV Vol. II, p.220).

[2] Presidential address (extempore), Annual ML Session, Karachi, 24 December 1943 (NV Vol. III, p.340)

[3] In 1941 Jinnah however stated that the League had laid down 'the first foundation of the revival' and the organisation of Muslims in April 1936. See his Presidential address at the Madras Session, April 1941 (NV Vol. II, p.211).

[4] M.A.H. Ispahani 1966, p.73. Likewise Jinnah told Beverley Nichols in 1943: 'The Hindus have organised a powerful Press and Congress-Mahasabha [*sic*] are backed up by Hindu capitalists and industrialists with finance which we [Muslim League] have not got.' (B. Nichols 1944, p.193)

both *Dawn* and the Urdu weekly (later daily) *Manshoor*, and he assigned Liaquat Ali Khan to supervise both papers on his behalf. [5]

Jinnah also became practically a one-man propaganda machine of the Muslim League. He personally toured up and down the subcontinent mustering mass support through countless speeches and statements, press interviews, and via his attendance at scores of civic functions, social and economic organisations, colleges and universities, and meetings with members of minority groups and tribal leaders. In around 1941 Jinnah introduced the motto: Unity, faith and discipline. [6] He also frequently spoke of 'justice and fairplay'. His emphasis throughout in fact was on the singular straightforward concept of Muslim unity. Here are some examples:

> Come to the platform of the League. If Muslims are united the settlement will come sooner than you think. [7]

> The Muslim League is not going to tolerate or allow anyone to create disruption among the Mussalmans by asking them to organise themselves separately into castes or tribes. We recognise no one as a Jat or a Pathan or even as a Shia or a Sunni. We can't tolerate any such caste being created and encouraged because it will not be possible to retain Pakistan if those distinctions were allowed. These castes are responsible for the slavery of India. [8]

> Give up the idea of Shia, Sunni, Wahabi. Unity should be our watchword. ... Some say we are Punjabis and others say that they are Bengalis or Delhiwallas. Such [an] attitude is baneful to Muslims. We are but servants of Islam. [9]

It is quite clear that these were more than mere slogans. They were an attempt to instil the idea of Muslim unity – that is, solidarity based on the concept of *tauheed*, which is opposed to division in all forms,

---

[5] See Jinnah's correspondence with Liaquat Ali Khan discussing *Dawn* and *Manshoor*, 2 August 1944 (NV Vol. II, p.791-2).

[6] This is around the time he introduced the motto to the best of my research, with possibly the earliest instance being 20 September 1941, where the words were in the order now usually used in Pakistan: 'Let our motto be faith, unity and discipline' (Message to Bengal students, Pakistan Conference, Calcutta, 19 September 1941; NV Vol. II, p.301-2). Jinnah did not always repeat the motto in the same order of words. Sometimes it was 'unity, discipline, faith' (NV Vol. VII, p.67; Afzal (ed.) 1980, p.418); at others it was 'faith, unity, and discipline' NV Vol. II p.301-2, 304, 305, 353; Yusufi Vol. III p.1870). Once he even used 'unity, faith discipline' and 'faith, unity, discipline' in the same speech. (NV Vol. VII, p.131).

[7] Speech delivered at the meeting of the Muslim University Union, Aligarh, 5 February 1938 (Yusufi Vol. II, p.727)

[8] Speech at the concluding Session of the Punjab Muslim Students' Federation Conference, Lahore, 19 March 1944. (Yusufi Vol. III, p.1863)

[9] Address at a meeting of Muslim girl students and ladies, New Delhi, 3 November 1946. (Yusufi Vol. IV, p.2444)

whether sectarian (Shia, Sunni), caste-based (Jat, Pathan), or provincial (Bengalis, Delhiwallas). When the Government collected data for its census records, Jinnah received enquiries from Muslims as to how they should fill in the census forms. Jinnah issued the following statement:

> I wish to emphasise particularly the following questions:
>
> **Question no. 3:** Race Tribe or Caste
> The answer by every Muslim should be that he is a Muslim.
>
> **Question no. 43:** Religion
> The answer should be Islam. [10]

Jinnah himself practised as he preached; he belonged to no sect. [11] The equality of human beings is based on the fact of their having a common origin (4:1). Thus equality is contained within the Islamic concept of unity. As Jinnah said before and after partition:

> It is the Great Book, [the] Quran, that is the sheet-anchor of Muslim India. I am sure that as we go on and on there will be more and more of *oneness* – one God, one Book, one Qibla, [12] one Prophet and one Nation. [13]
>
> *One God and the equality of manhood* is one of the fundamental principles of Islam. In Islam there is no difference between man and man. The qualities of equality, liberty and fraternity are the fundamental principles of Islam. [14]

He was equally adamant that religious minorities in Pakistan would be full citizens and there would be no attempts to make them change their faith. [15] This again is based on the Quranic teaching of oneness.

> Hindus and other communities following different faiths and belonging to different creeds will be treated in the first instance on the *basis of equality of manhood*. Islam enjoins us to treat our

---

10 Statement sent by mail at Bombay, 18 January 1941. The ML Secretary also sent these instructions in detail to all branches of the Muslim League. (NV Vol. II, p.130-1)

11 See Chapter 13, subsection 'Jinnah's sect'.

12 *Qibla* – a reference to the direction Muslims all face in union (towards the Kaaba in Mecca) when praying.

13 Concluding address, ML Annual Session, Karachi, 26 December 1943. (Yusufi Vol. III, p.1821)

14 Address to the Bar Association, Karachi, on the occasion of the Holy Prophet's birthday, 25 January 1948 (Yusufi Vol. IV p.2670)

15 See Jinnah's telegram to the Shia Conference organisers, Quetta, 1 October 1945: 'The Muslim League will never interfere with [the] faith and belief of any sect amongst Musalmans or non-Muslims and minorities.' (NV Vol. IV, p.240)

> fellowmen as equals. The Hindus and other communities in Pakistan will be treated with justice and fair play – nay, with generosity. That is the view of every responsible Musalman and, what is more, it is enjoined upon us by the highest authority – the Quran and the Prophet. [16]

Wherever he went he also emphasised the need for education, social uplift and the build-up of economic and industrial activity. He was directly involved in the establishment of the Muslim Chambers of Commerce and Industry in India (1944); he encouraged the establishment of the Muslim Commercial Bank (1947) and other banks, Orient Airways (1946),[17] Muhammadi Steamship Company (1947), etc. [18] He also inspired Indian Muslim students to organise themselves in the All-India Muslim Students' Federation (set up 1937). These bodies were independent of the League but were nevertheless inspired by its programme and policy. [19]

Aside from this, Jinnah organised the League's administrative activities. At his recommendation in 1941, the League appointed a committee to chalk out a 'five year plan' for the 'educational, economic, social, and political advancement of the Muslims'.[20] Due to some complications (mainly a lack of funds) the committee could not put the report together. [21] In December 1943, again at Jinnah's recommendation, the League set up 1) a Committee of Action to organise, coordinate and unify Muslims in India and also examine demands, proposals and suggestions that came in from the public; [22] 2) a Parliamentary Board as the supreme body for parliamentary activities including giving the League ticket to candidates and election organisation; 3) a Planning Committee for a 'five year programme' to implement social and economic uplift, state industrialisation in Pakistan zones, introduction of

---

16 See Jinnah's press statement in answer to Gandhi, 11 March 1942. (NV Vol. II, p.400); also his interview with *Daily Herald*, 5 April 1946 (NV Vol. IV, p.593)

17 Jinnah personally invested in Orient Airways, buying shares worth Rs 25,000. (Z.H. Zaidi, 'Economic Vision of the Quaid-i-Azam', in *The Pakistan Development Review* Vol. 40 No. 4 Part II (Winter 2001) p. 1149).

18 Ibid.

19 S. Mujahid 1981, p.441

20 See resolution passed at the League Annual Session, Madras, April 1941. (*Foundations* Vol. II, p.373-4)

21 For full details of the Planning Committee's work and the problems it faced, see Khalid Shamsul Hasan (ed.) (1991) *Quaid-i-Azam's Unrealised Dream* Karachi: Royal Book Company.

22 The Committee of Action itself later appointed a subcommittee to address the question of 'infusing true Islamic spirit amongst the Musalmans of India' and 'removing un-Islamic customs and ideas that have crept into the Muslim society of India', a Women's Subcommittee to build up political consciousness among women, and the Writers' Committee for the production of pro-League literature, amongst other activities. See proceedings of the ML Committee of Action from 1944-46, reproduced in NV Vol. IV, p.701-772.

free primary basic education, land reforms, improvements in labour and agriculture conditions, money-lending control, etc. [23]

Jinnah was authorised to appoint the members of these committees. He was particularly anxious about getting the very best people for the Planning Committee, which was supposed to carry out research in order to assess the economic potential of Pakistan. Whereas he appointed the members of the Parliamentary and Action Committees immediately, for the Planning Committee he took his time and some four months later (April 1944) he had selected a shortlist of around forty professionals including engineers, economists and scientists, some of whom were not even members of the Muslim League. Twenty-three of these ended up in the final list in August. [24] Jinnah donated towards the funding of the committee himself. [25]

The Committee held its first meeting in September 1944, and at its second meeting in November Jinnah was present. He addressed the Committee and stressed the importance of the research they were to carry out, since at that time there was much speculation as to the viability of Pakistan and insufficient actual data. In his layman's opinion, Pakistan would not be 'bankrupt', and it would be a 'powerful state', though obviously 'not as rich as Hindustan'. This prediction would later be proven correct. [26] He expected the Committee to examine the issues carefully and come to an 'authoritative' conclusion. He also emphasised:

> … in whatever problem you tackle there is one point which I must request you to keep in mind – and it is this. It is not our purpose to make the rich richer and to accelerate the process of the accumulation of wealth in the hands of a few individuals. We should aim at levelling up the general standard of living amongst the masses … *Our ideal should not be capitalistic but Islamic*, and the interests and welfare of the people as a whole should be kept constantly in mind. [27]

Later the Planning Committee stated in a memorandum that owing to a lack of available data, the report would have to be submitted in two parts. The first was to provide a general picture for the conditions across

---

23 See resolutions at ML Annual Session, Karachi, December 1943. (*Foundations* Vol. II, p.463-70; for appointment of the first two Committees, see op. cit. p.487-8)

24 K.S. Hasan (ed.) 1991, p.22-3

25 Op. cit. p.26

26 The first budget of Pakistan in 1948 confirmed that it was financially and economically sound. For details, see Chapter 14, footnote 46. For Jinnah's comments, see his speech at the presentation of Pakistan's new coins at Karachi, 1 April 1948 denouncing the 'false prophets' who had predicted the Pakistan would not be economically feasible (NV Vol. VII, p.309-12); and also Jinnah's Independence Day speech, 14 August 1948 (NV Vol. VII, p.441)

27 Address to the members of the League Planning Committee, New Delhi, 5 November 1944. (Yusufi Vol. III p.1961)

India, whilst the second half would deal more fully with the Pakistan areas. [28] The first part of the report was submitted along with the memorandum in July 1945. [29] The second part was never completed due to the dramatic turn of events starting with the provincial elections, the Cabinet Mission Plan, and then of course partition in 1947. [30]

The League was also hard at work reorganising itself to meet the change in direction of its policy. In 1938 at Patna, it authorised Jinnah (as President) to 'adopt such a course as may be necessary with a view to exploring the possibility of a suitable alternative' to the Government of India Act 1935, 'which would safeguard he interests of the Musalmans and other minorities in India'. [31] At this session it also resolved to set up a Muslim Women's Subcommittee of the League. [32] In 1941 the Lahore Resolution was incorporated into the Muslim League's constitution. [33] Liaquat Ali Khan explained that the implications of this amendment were that it would be 'an effective reply to those who had alleged that it was merely a counter for bargaining,' and that 'every Muslim who was to join the League from now onwards would have to take an oath of allegiance to Pakistan'. [34]

At the Annual Sessions of the League in 1938, 1940, 1941, 1942, and April 1943 the League's constitution was amended to give the Working Committee increasing control over the activities of the Provincial Leagues including the power to dissolve them, as well as the power to discipline Council Leaguers, and to authorise the president to take steps in furtherance of the objects of the League (as an emergency power). These changes were evidently introduced in order to keep unruly Leaguers in line. [35]

Jinnah reiterated throughout that the League was fighting for a separate nation-state of Pakistan, and continually denied that Pakistan was a 'bargaining counter'. The League's massive undertaking paid off. From 1938-1944, it won every provincial and central by-election in Muslim constituencies (barring just one). [36] By 1944, 28 out of 30 Muslim seats were held by Muslim Leaguers in the Central Legislature. [37]

Jinnah and his colleagues thus succeeded in building up a more

---

[28] K.S. Hasan (ed.) 1991, p.57

[29] It is included in full in op. cit. p.50-96

[30] Jinnah said in 1946 that Pakistan would be economically 'powerful', and happily reported that 'even the Congress party experts had a shock when they investigated the matter'. (Interview to BBC correspondent, New Delhi, 2 April 1946; NV IV p.574)

[31] Resolution at League Annual Session, Patna, December 1938. (*Foundations* Vol. II, p.321)

[32] Ibid. p.318

[33] Resolution at League Annual Session, Madras, April 1941. (*Foundations* Vol. II, p.371-2)

[34] Ibid. p.376

[35] Jinnah exercised this increased authority in expelling Leaguers such as Fazlul Huq and Begum Shah Nawaz for five years when they failed to toe the party line.

[36] By the end of 1943, the League had won 49 out of 50 by-elections it had contested. (See proceedings of the League Session at Karachi, December 1943; *Foundations* Vol. II, p.478)

[37] B. Nichols 1944, p.197

efficient and disciplined League and in rallying the masses for the League's stated goal of Pakistan. Leaving aside the untiring efforts of his friends and colleagues, the sheer amount of energy and dedication that Jinnah alone put into galvanising the Muslims as a nation is extraordinary. This would have been a feat for a fit young man; Jinnah was well into his sixties and his health was deteriorating quite rapidly. In view of our (frankly brief) account of the history, it is impossible to believe under these circumstances that Jinnah gave his all and united millions of Muslims across the subcontinent for a Pakistan that was no more than a 'bargaining counter'.

The 1946 elections

In June 1945, within a month of V-E Day, [38] the Viceroy announced the British intention to 'advance India towards her goal of self-government', [39] and that autumn, the British also announced fresh provincial elections (there had been none since 1936-7, owing to the War). Jinnah had fought the last provincial elections partly with a view to finding out 1) how much support the League already had 2) the feasibility of making the League the sole authoritative representative of Muslims in India. Since then, as we have already observed, he had dedicated himself to organising the Muslims as a united people.

He was confident now that barring the pro-Congressites, otherwise anti-League Muslims and some self-serving provincial leaders, the vast majority of Muslims were behind him. They had long been calling him the 'Quaid-i-Azam' – the Great Leader – and the time had finally come to give his people their 'marching orders'. Hence he declared that the Muslim League's intention was to contest the elections not in order 'to form ministries', but to 'get a verdict from Muslims on the Pakistan issue'. [40] In fact the League had been waiting for this opportunity since at least 1943.[41] Once again he began a tour all over India, repeating the same message:

---

[38] V-E Day – Victory of Europe following German surrender towards the end of WWII (8 May 1945).

[39] Viceroy Wavell's broadcast, New Delhi, 14 June 1945 (NV Vol. IV, p.866-71)

[40] See Jinnah's public address (Urdu), Peshawar, 24 November 1945. (NV Vol. IV, p.325)

[41] In the League Session at Karachi in December 1943 the League passed a resolution calling for a review of the British 'policy of staying elections of the Provincial and Central Legislature during the pendency of the war'. The purpose of demanding fresh elections was clear. Mohammad Isa moved the resolution and said that its purpose was to enable the 'Pakistan-minded' Muslim to have 'his due'. Yahya Bakhtiar of Baluchistan, in seconding the resolution, said that the government 'should run as the voter wants it'. Raja Ghazanfar Ali said he wanted a fresh election to 'correctly reflect the opinion of Muslim India, which stands solidly on Pakistan'. (*Foundations* Vol. II, p.478-9)

> ... we want the verdict of the electorate such as it is constituted of Muslims, whether they want Pakistan or whether they accept the Congress demand of *Akhand* Hindustan ... [42]
>
> I appeal to the Musalmans ... to solidly support the Muslim League candidate, no matter who he is. He may be a lamppost. ... every vote is *not for him but for Pakistan.* [43]
>
> It is not a question of winning a few seats or forming a Ministry. The issue is more complicated and vital. The entire world is looking to you for [your] verdict about Pakistan. [44]

He was confident enough to challenge the Congress to put up a Muslim candidate from their side if they wished; then if the Muslim verdict was against Pakistan, he would 'stand down'. [45] He was sure however that the Muslims were practically unanimous in their support of the League.

Sure enough, the 'verdict' of the voters was overwhelmingly in favour of Pakistan. The Muslim League won 439 out of 494 Muslim seats – an overall victory of almost 90 percent. In Punjab, the figure was 90 percent; in Bengal around 95 percent. It did not matter at all to the League that the Congress had won the general constituencies. The League had obtained the sanction of its own people to push for partition.

A unanimous declaration

On 7 April 1946, just a few days after Bengal's results had come through, the Muslim League broke from the norm and instead of its annual session it held the AIML Legislators' Convention, 'the first of its kind in the political history of the Muslim nation of India'. [46] Over 450 elected members of the Provincial Assemblies and 3500 delegates from across India attended. [47] On 8 April the Convention unanimously passed the Delhi Resolution (moved by Bengal Leaguer H.S. Suhrawardy) containing the unequivocal demand for Pakistan. The preamble to this resolution referred to the Congress rule in the late 1930s as proof that that the Hindus and Muslims remained 'two distinct nations'; and that the Muslims 'whose code is not confined merely to spiritual doctrines'

---

[42] Address, Baluchistan Muslim Students' Federation, Quetta, 18 October 1945. (NV Vol. IV, p.255. (*Akhand* Hindustan means: 'united Hindustan')

[43] Election message to Muslims in Bombay province, 23 March 1946. (NV Vol. IV, p.556)

[44] Public address, Mardan, 25 November 1945. (NV Vol. IV, p.330)

[45] Speech at a public meeting held under the auspices of the Baluchistan Muslim League, Quetta, 16 October 1945 (Yusufi Vol. III, p.2072)

[46] See proceedings of the ML Legislatures' Convention, Delhi, 7-9 April 1946 (*Foundations* Vol. II, p.505)

[47] *Eastern Times* editorial, 12 April 1946 (A. Saeed (ed.) (1983) *The Eastern Times on Quaid-i-Azam*. Islamabad: National Institute of Historical and Cultural Research, p.254)

stood in 'sharp contrast' to the 'exclusive nature of Hindu Dharma[48] and philosophy which has fostered and maintained for thousands of years a rigid caste system'. This was a definitive explanation of the Two-Nation Theory and it was set out in distinctly Quranic terms.[49] The resolution demanded partition on this basis and it included the following features:

- Pakistan was mentioned by name
- The six zones were named: Bengal and Assam in the north-east; NWFP, Punjab, Sind and Baluchistan in the north-west
- The six zones were to comprise a 'sovereign independent state' (not states)
- The minorities in Pakistan and Hindustan were to be provided with safeguards on the lines of the Lahore Resolution
- The acceptance of the 'demand of Pakistan and its implementation *without delay*' were the *sine qua non* for Muslim League cooperation in any interim government at the centre

One of the most outstanding features of the Resolution however is also its most controversial. We will return to it shortly.

This Resolution was thus the update to (though not a replacement of [50]) the Lahore Resolution. It represented not a majority of Muslim opinion, but its unanimous opinion; and so the League was in a position to make an unequivocal demand for immediate partition – notwithstanding the inevitable transitional period. At the end of the Conference Jinnah made the following remarks in his closing speech:

> What are we fighting for? What are we aiming at? It is not theocracy … now no question of minority or majority is left on the issue of Pakistan, it is now *unanimity* … I also belong to a minority province, [51] but let 70 millions of our brethren establish their 'Raj'. But it is not only that. If there is any safeguard known in the world for minority provinces, the more effective safeguard is the establishment of Pakistan. [52]

This was his reassurance to non-Muslims living in the 'Pakistan zones' that the so-called 'Muslim raj' would not be a theocracy, as well as a reminder that the Muslims in the 'Hindustan zones' were fully aware of the implications of the Pakistan demand.

---

[48] *Dharma* – Sanskrit term for the religious and social code that all Hindus are expected to abide by.

[49] The Quranic basis of the Two-Nation Theory is described in Chapter 12.

[50] The creed of the League contained the text of the Lahore Resolution from 1941 right up until partition.

[51] Jinnah lived in Bombay province.

[52] Concluding address at the Muslim League Legislators' Convention, 9 April 1946. (*Foundations* Vol. II, p.523)

We have just observed that the Delhi Resolution represented the 'unanimous' demand of Indian Muslims who supported the Muslim League. Before we end this chapter, we must also discuss the line of the resolution that has raised the most controversy after partition – that the six zones would comprise a single 'state' rather than 'states'.

One Pakistan or two?

As we have noted in the previous chapter, the Lahore Resolution was openly worded to include the possibility of a confederation of Muslims states as well as a federation, reflecting the lack of consensus among Muslims in the subcontinent. Unlike Jinnah and his supporters, who treated all the Muslims of India as a single 'nation' with one unifying 'Muslim culture', many other Muslims in Bengal (and outside of it, the foremost example being A.K. Azad) differentiated between the *millat* (community bound by Muslim faith), and the *qaum* (community bound by ethnicity, culture and geography). The former was a religious concept and not open to question. The latter was, in the minds of these Muslims, more correctly attributed to the English word 'nation' and its primary territorial definition.

By the early twentieth century (and indeed even today), ordinary Muslims across India and across the world placed their local cultures and tribal affiliations above their common faith as a basis of nationality. Outside of India, this was already leading to the creation of the many modern Arab and other Muslim nation-states in existence today. Within the subcontinent, a similar thought process was behind 'provincialism', i.e. the resistance shown by various provinces against any central structure, first in India, and later in Pakistan, that would infringe upon their socioeconomic autonomy and perceived cultural independence.

Nowhere in India did the consequences of this issue manifest themselves more clearly than Bengal, the larger of the two major Muslim-majority provinces. Ironically, many Bengali Muslims were possibly more supportive of the Pakistan idea than even their would-be compatriots in the Punjab. The Muslim and Scheduled Caste populace of East Bengal had suffered badly under feudalism, and both these communities saw Pakistan as an opportunity to see genuine and lasting change, as well as to escape from both the British rulers and the landlords, most of whom were Caste Hindus. For the Muslims of Bengal, the creation of Pakistan would usher in an Islamic form of socialism. Yet some among them – or their representatives – also conceived of a confederation, that is, 'two Pakistans'. We will return to this shortly.

Broadly speaking, among the Bengali leadership representing the Muslim League there were two ideological factions: one 'conservative', consisting of those who supported Jinnah's single state, including the Khwaja Nazimuddin, M.A.H. Ispahani and the Islamic scholar Mohammad Akram Khan; and the other 'progressive' faction consisting of the politically secular Huseyn Shaheed Suhrawardy and Muslim modernist scholar Abul Hashim.[53]

The conservative faction was loyal to Jinnah and the single state idea almost unquestioningly, so we need not review it here. The progressive faction held fast to the interpretation that the Lahore Resolution outlined a confederation of two Pakistans, even while it was principally loyal to the aspirations of the Muslim League.

Huseyn Shaheed Suhrawardy and Abul Hashim[54] were both in favour of a separate and united Bengal. Suhrawardy seemed to waver between his loyalty to the League and his province; and since he also advocated the 'United Bengal' proposal for an independent Bengal in 1947, attempted to form a League-Congress coalition in Bengal after the 1946 elections, and also chose to stay in India for some time after partition, Pakistani commentators on Suhrawardy have often viewed his motives with suspicion.

Abul Hashim is credited with having rallied the masses in Bengal to back the Pakistan demand, and like Suhrawardy, he was also a central figure in the United Bengal movement. Hashim was a brilliant Muslim thinker who strongly advocated the socialist ideals of Islam, leading to accusations that he was a clandestine communist, though he did not consider himself as such.[55] His decision to enter politics was motivated by his hopes for an Islamic state, but he did not believe in what he called 'Mr Jinnah's Two-Nation Theory', since it was based on the *millat*,

---

53 The views of A.K. Fazlul Huq, who like the progressive faction favoured a united separate Bengal, are not included here owing to his expulsion from the Muslim League from 1941-6. His Krishak-Proja Party stood against the League in the 1946 elections, and it was only after his defeat in that election that he applied to return to the League in September 1946.

54 Abul Hashim (1905-1974), the son of the Indian nationalist politician Abul Kasem, was born in a village in the district of Burdwan, West Bengal. As well as being a politician Hashim was a brilliant Muslim thinker. An ardent believer in Islamic socialism (he did not consider himself a communist), Hashim was at first involved in local Bengali politics and later joined the Muslim League with a view to getting rid of capitalist leadership in Bengal. But he did not believe in the Two-Nation theory and envisioned Bengal as an undivided, separate state, albeit one with ideological ties to Pakistan. In the 1940s as General Secretary of the Bengal Provincial Muslim League he worked alongside H.S. Suhrawardy, to whom he was related but didn't see eye to eye ideologically, to obtain the support of the Muslim masses for the Pakistan movement. Though he initially stayed in West Bengal after partition as leader of the opposition, he moved to East Pakistan in 1950. Having left the Muslim League, he co-founded the short-lived Khilafat-i-Rabbani Party (Caliphate of Divine Sustenance), but he became disillusioned when it didn't go in the direction he had hoped, and rejoined the League in 1956. Hashim, now totally blind, also continued with his academic pursuits, becoming the first Director of the Islamic Academy, Dacca, in 1960. He died in 1974.

55 Abul Hashim wrote in his autobiography: 'Islam did not come to the sub-continent directly from the caliphate [*sic*] of Medina but it came to us from Baghdad, the capital of Arab imperialism, through Persia. The Arabs conquered Persia and the Persians in turn conquered Arabia culturally. The result was a mixture of pure Islam with pre-Islamic culture of Persia. Orthodox Schools of Islam in India preached and practised the perverted Islam of Baghdad received through Persia. To them Islam of Medina is communism. This is why Khwaja Nazimuddin believed that I preached communism under the cover of Islam.' (A. Hashim (1974) *In Retrospection* Dacca: Subarna Publishers, p.79)

(which he saw as pan-Islamism) rather than the *qaum*. Instead he 'preached the multi-nation theory', [56] i.e. India was a subcontinent of nations (meaning *qaum*), and Bengali Muslims were a distinct nation or *qaum* even from Muslims elsewhere in India. In this respect his views were aligned with those of the Indian nationalist and pro-Congress ulema in the subcontinent. Unlike the Indian nationalists however he envisioned Bengal as an undivided, separate state, albeit one with ideological ties to Pakistan. In the 1940s as General Secretary of the Bengal Provincial Muslim League he worked alongside H.S. Suhrawardy, to whom he was related but didn't see eye to eye ideologically, to obtain the support of the Muslim masses for the Pakistan movement. He also drafted an election manifesto for the Muslim League in 1945 which contained his socioeconomic and ideological views on Pakistan; but since it aimed to abolish capitalist and landlord interests, the conservative faction condemned it using the 'communism' slur, and the manifesto was ultimately abandoned. It didn't help that the manifesto had referred to 'East Pakistan' and 'West Pakistan' in terms that more or less outlined their mutual independence.

However, Hashim is probably best known for being the only person to protest against the Delhi Resolution, which unequivocally defined Pakistan as a single sovereign state. Although the incident is not on record anywhere in the proceedings of the Convention, anecdotal accounts appear in M.A.H. Ispahani's *Qaid-e-Azam Jinnah as I Knew Him* and Choudhry Khaliquzzaman's *Pathway to Pakistan.* [57]

Hashim writes that when the resolution was put up for discussion at the Subjects Committee meeting, he objected to the singular word 'state', which replaced the word plural word 'states' from the Lahore Resolution. Jinnah is quoted as having replied: 'I see, the Maulana Saheb[58] [meaning Hashim] is banking upon the plural 's' which is an obvious printing mistake'. This was presumably a remark of dry humour, though Hashim would not have seen it that way. Once Jinnah was shown the original copy of the Lahore Resolution containing the word 'states' as signed in his own hand, Liaquat Ali Khan quipped that 'we lost our own case'. Jinnah then explained that ultimately he was less concerned about having 'one Pakistan' and more concerned about having 'one Constituent Assembly for the Muslims of India'. [59]

This latter remark at least makes sense in light of our analysis of Jinnah's views in Chapter 8. Bangladeshi political scientist Harun-or-Rashid, who has examined the story in detail, has criticised the remark, for arguably 'Jinnah could have claimed a single Constituent

---

56 A. Hashim op. cit. p.23

57 See M.A.H. Ispahani (1966) *Qaid-e-Azam Jinnah as I Knew Him* Karachi: Forward Publications Trust, p.144-5; and C. Khaliquzzaman (1961) *Pathway to Pakistan* Lahore: Longmans, p.341-5

58 *Maulana* – lit. 'master' – a term of address used to refer to Islamic scholars.

59 A. Hashim op. cit. p.109

Assembly ... without substituting the word 'state' for 'states' in the Convention resolution'. [60] While it is agreed that Jinnah much preferred a single federal state over a dual confederate state, we have also seen in this chapter that irrespective of the final wording, Jinnah remained open – albeit reluctantly – to either possibility, right up until partition. And by the same token, being the mover of the resolution that called for a unitary Pakistan did not stop Suhrawardy from pushing for the United Bengal plan, and from obtaining Jinnah's cooperation in the matter, if only for a while.

Numerous commentators have seized upon the 'printing mistake' line to make out that Jinnah had plotted all along to deprive Bengalis of their own right to independence. Their indignation is fuelled further by M.A.H. Ispahani's version of the story. His recollection is similar to Hashim's, but with an addition: After Jinnah was shown that the published records of the Central Office of the League also contained the word 'states', Jinnah allegedly 'directed that the records be rectified'. [61] As we will show shortly, the chief problem with Ispahani's claim is that there is absolutely no evidence to show that this supposed instruction was ever carried out.

Hashim next writes that he suggested edits to the draft which would have remained in line with the Lahore Resolution. Jinnah appeared to agree to the edits but in the end the League passed 'a modified form' of the original draft to which Hashim had objected. Hashim expresses his disappointment that Suhrawardy was the one who finally moved it. [62] Scholarship agrees that this was probably Jinnah's way of putting the controversy to rest before it went any further, though strangely, Suhrawardy was silent on the matter; and it remains open to question why Hashim was apparently the only person who voiced his opposition that day, even though other members of his faction including Suhrawardy were present. [63] That said, this is not the only instance of silence from the progressive faction during this crucial period. Prof. Rashid finds that neither Suhrawardy nor Hashim pushed the idea of a separate Bengal to voters 'in concrete terms' during the 1946 elections, an anomaly he calls 'incredible'. Subsequently, he writes, the 'people at large [in Bengal] came to be acquainted with Pakistan minus the ideal of a separate state ... which mainly remained the preserve of the top leaders, leading party workers and a group of intelligentsia.' [64] Perhaps they had deemed it unnecessary to push for a separate Bengal during the elections as their political views were already well known; or it could be that they focused on getting the masses behind the 'Pakistan'

---

60 H. Rashid 2003 (revised), p.237

61 M.A.H. Ispahani 1966, p144-5

62 A. Hashim op. cit. p.110

63 H. Rashid 2003 (revised), p.236

64 Ibid.

demand in principle, bearing in mind that its details could be worked out later, just as Jinnah wanted all parties to accept the principle of partition first, before discussing territorial and other details. [65]

Finally we come to Khaliquzzaman's account, which is interesting for different reasons. He contradicts both Hashim and Ispahani, in that he denies that any objection was raised at the meeting. He also claims to have written the original draft, and that he wrote 'state' instead of 'states' only incidentally, in 'subconscious' view of the fact that 'the word Pakistan denoted one state, federal and confederal'. [66] Prof. Rashid rightly questions the legitimacy of Khaliquzzaman's claim to having written the singular 'state', having found the typed copy of an early draft that contains the plural word 'states'. [67] However, since Prof. Rashid also acknowledges that almost 'no primary documents of the subjects committee debates are available', [68] it is impossible to either verify or dismiss Khaliquzzaman's claim entirely.

As a corroborating witness, Khaliquzzaman quotes Muhammad Ismail Khan, who was the Chairman of the Subjects Committee that drafted the Delhi Resolution. In the first of two letters written to Khaliquzzaman in 1953, Ismail Khan affirms that Khaliquzzaman was responsible for preparing the draft. [69] He writes further:

> ... no one to the best of my knowledge objected to the substitution of "State" instead of "States". Neither in the Subjects Committee nor in the open session of the Convention, not a word was uttered to protest against this fundamental change. The Lahore Resolution having become the basic creed of the League could not possibly be amended by a subsidiary body [such as the Subjects Committee]. ... If an objection had been taken at the time undoubtedly this change could not have been effected except at an open session of the League which was never called. [70]

In his analysis of the same issue, Prof. Rashid raises a similar point, writing that since the Delhi Resolution was passed at a Legislator's Convention rather than at an open session of the All-India Muslim League, it may be argued that said resolution was 'not an amendment' of the Lahore Resolution but rather a document designed to 'serve a particular purpose'. [71]

---

65 For Jinnah's statements, see for example record of interview between the Cabinet Delegation and Jinnah on 16 April 1946 as cited in Chapter 7, footnote 61; and Jinnah's interview with Beverly Nichols as cited in Myth no. 11 (Chapter 10).

66 C. Khaliquzzaman 1961, p.341.

67 H. Rashid op. cit. p.234 (Rashid refers to the draft as reproduced in '*Muslim League Legislators' Convention*, vol. 74-77').

68 Ibid. 233, 233fn

69 Khan to Khaliquzzaman, 12 Oct 1953 (Khaliquzzaman 1961, p.343)

70 Ibid.

71 H. Rashid op. cit. p.237

In his second letter, Ismail Khan addresses Hashim's claims about the 'printing mistake', and denies that the alleged incident ever took place: 'If the word had been a misprint, as is contended, how was it that it was not rectified when this [Lahore] resolution was converted into the creed of the League' [*sic*].[72] Ismail Khan remarks that even the last edition of the League's creed dated shortly before partition retained the original word 'states' from the Lahore Resolution.[73] This on its own counters Ispahani's claim about the order to have the records rectified, but there is more. An Indian academic likewise observes that the Lahore Resolution was incorporated unedited into the League's constitution in April 1941 at Madras, and further adds: 'When Gandhi sought enlightenment on the term 'independent states', Jinnah did not elaborate it. Nor did he point out that these words included in the Lahore resolution [were] due to a printing mistake.'[74] (We might recall that Jinnah's actual reply to Gandhi, cited earlier in this chapter, was that the word 'states' in the Lahore Resolution meant 'units of [a federal] Pakistan'). Then we might note the frequency with which Jinnah used the word 'states' in his public addresses, which were recorded in the press and elsewhere. How would the League have 'rectified' those countless instances? Not to mention that for Jinnah to ask for this retroactive rectification – or falsification – of the entire record is hardly consistent with his reputed integrity.

Our review of this controversy has shown that there is not much consistency between the various accounts, or sufficient evidence to verify what actually happened, or did not happen. We have visited it here only to show the political disagreement over the territorial aspect of the Pakistan idea as envisioned by Jinnah. We have also noted in Chapter 6 that in the Islamic worldview *deen* shapes cultures but is not a culture in itself. We can see how the conflicting Indian Muslims' views of 'Muslim culture' – that is, whether it is localised in the *qaum* or has pan-Islamic connotations for the world's *millat* – affected how they viewed the Two-Nation Theory, which in turn determined their political choices. This nuanced but important difference of opinion lies at the centre of what started as a communications failure between Muslims of Punjab and Bengal before the provinces became the two wings of Pakistan, and ended in their constitutional separation in 1971.

---

72 Khaliquzzaman op. cit. p.343-4. While in his letter Ismail Khan appeared to give Hashim the benefit of the doubt, at least with regards to the objection having been raised ('It is possible that I was out of the room'), he did not accept the claim about the misprint, which 'astounded' him. (Ibid. p.344)

73 Ibid.

74 Nair, M.B. (1990) *Politics in Bangladesh: A Study of Awami League: (1949-58)* New Delhi: Northern Book Centre, p.45.

Chapter 10
The myths of Jinnah

> Corruption is a curse in India and amongst Muslims, especially the so-called educated and intelligentsia. Unfortunately, it is this class that is selfish and morally and intellectually corrupt. No doubt this disease is common, but amongst this particular class of Muslims it is rampant.
>
> – *Jinnah to M.A.H. Ispahani, 6 May 1945* [1]

The following list of myths is taken from the original *Secular Jinnah*, with adjustments and additional evidence. Over the years many distorted ideas about Jinnah have sprung up from all manner of sources, and the most well-known ones appear here. They are found in literature written by educated people from all fields, including writers, lawyers, historians, and scientists. On the whole my primary source of evidence is Jinnah's speeches, but other external evidence is also included.

Many commentators have claimed that the Islamic content of Jinnah's speeches was only a device to win support, and that he was acting like a typical politician. But neither was the founder of Pakistan a 'typical' politician, nor can his speeches be treated as reflecting a typical politician's mindset. We do not make such crass comments about other great leaders of the world past and present such as George Washington or Nelson Mandela. If we were to follow this line of logic, could we not throw out Jinnah's speech of 11 August 1947 as mere rhetoric designed to meet the needs of a particular audience on a particular day? Instead of selectively highlighting certain evidence and ignoring the rest to support an argument, should the seeker of Jinnah's ideological leanings not be looking for a consistent factor that makes sense of all his speeches and actions?

---

1 M.A.H. Ispahani (1976) *M.A. Jinnah-Ispahani Correspondence, 1936-1948* Karachi: Forward Publications Trust, p.69

Myth no. 1: In recent years the 'establishment' has transformed Jinnah's image from that of a secularist to that of a deep-thinking Islamic scholar (P.A. Hoodbhoy 2007) [2]

In 2007, Prof. Hoodbhoy delivered a lecture in Karachi, and later turned parts of that lecture into at least two essays. In one of these essays, titled 'Jinnah and the Islamic State: Setting the Record Straight', [3] he cited two speeches of Jinnah to show he was a secularist, though on this occasion the Munir quote was not one of them.

Prof. Hoodbhoy suggested that during the Zia ul-Haq administration of the 1980s, the government made conscious efforts to present Jinnah as 'a deep-thinking Islamic scholar'. I have to admit I have never personally seen a Pakistani history textbook, which is where I assume such ideas may have been presented; but then I have also never come across any book of any kind which presents Jinnah as a scholar or a theologian. Even Prof. Sharif al Mujahid's *Studies in Interpretation* (1981), which was published in the same period, does not make such a claim.

Hoodbhoy's underlying point – sold somewhat like a conspiracy theory [4] – is that any argument for a 'Muslim Jinnah' ought either to be discounted or at least be treated with suspicion. But even the implication that Jinnah was widely considered a 'secularist' amongst his own people from the beginning is misleading. Any academic book of history from the fifties and sixties will testify that it was the 'secular Jinnah' argument that was given little credence in the beginning. [5] Thousands of letters sent to Jinnah from members of the public, academics, politicians and even religious scholars in and out of India, as well as countless articles and editorials written in Jinnah's time confirm that for most people, Jinnah was neither a theocrat nor a secularist. He was seen simply as a great Muslim leader.

What then, is a 'good' or a 'great' Muslim (correctly called *momin* [6] in the Quran)? Prof. Hoodbhoy characterises a 'good' Muslim as a religious, 'practising Muslim' (more on that in Chapter 13); and by 'scholar' he means someone who has an extensive knowledge of Muslim history and theories of sharia law as well as the Quran.

---

2 P.A. Hoodbhoy, 'Jinnah and the Islamic State: Setting the Record Straight' in *Economic and Political Weekly*, (Mumbai) Vol. 42 No. 32, 11-17 August 2007, p.3300-3303.

3 The second essay derived from the same lecture appears in L. H. Merchant & S. Mujahid (eds.) 2009, p.98-102.

4 See excerpt of Hoodbhoy's lecture cited in Chapter 13, in subsection 'Jinnah as a practising Muslim'.

5 See for instance G.W. Choudhury 1959, p.65. Even L. Binder, who differs in his attitudes towards Jinnah and Liaquat Ali Khan, nevertheless readily admits that the secularist element in early Pakistan was in the minority, albeit a politically influential one, and that the rest of the Muslim Leaguers of early Pakistan were more or less committed to some form of Islam.

6 A *momin* is beyond a Muslim in terms of his/her depth of personality. A Muslim has (at most) 'faith' in Islam; a *momin* has a sense of 'conviction' demonstrated in his/her entire lifestyle and behaviour. See Chapter 12 for further discussion.

Before answering the question on what characterises a good Muslim, here we should also mention the position taken in the Munir Report. One of the most famous points in the Report is that during the investigations into the Punjab riots of 1953, a number of ulema representing a variety of sects were asked what a Muslim is and that they all gave different answers. 'Keeping in view the several definitions given by the ulama,' concluded its authors, 'need we make any comment except that no two learned divines are agreed on this fundamental.' [7] However, we find that whilst there is truth to the statement, it is somewhat exaggerated, and the evidence used to support the statement is misleading. A closer look at the answers of the ulema shows that whilst indeed they show some variance, they nevertheless do show some agreement as well. Of the ten sets of answers that were reproduced in the Report, all of them mentioned the Prophet or Finality of the Prophethood, most of them mentioned belief in either God or the Unity of God, and just over half referred to the 'Day of Judgement'. [8] (Of these, the latter two happen to align with the three minimal conditions listed in the Quran as the means to 'salvation', to borrow Muhammad Asad's language). [9]

There is also a second and bigger problem with the Q&A text. Before reproducing the answers of the ulema, the Report explicitly states:

> This definition was asked after it had been clearly explained to each witness that he was required to give the irreducible minimum conditions which a person must satisfy to be entitled to be called a Muslim and that the definition was to be on the principle on which a term in grammar is defined. [10]

But if indeed this was done, and all that was required was a dictionary definition of what 'muslim' means, then all the ulema had misunderstood the question, for none of them actually answered it. There was in any case also some inconsistency with the questioning itself, as the questioners did not always ask for a 'definition'. In at least three cases, they simply asked: 'Who is a Muslim?', and in one case they even asked 'Who is a Muslim *according to you*?' [11] Consequently there is not one single dictionary definition of the word offered by these ulema, all of whom were concerned only with explaining what, in either their personal or sectarian opinions, *characterises* a Muslim.

The dictionary meaning of 'muslim' in Arabic is 'one who has (freely)

---

[7] Munir Report p.218

[8] Munir Report p.215-8

[9] See Asad's footnote for Quran verse 2:62, quoted in Chapter 12.

[10] Munir Report p.215

[11] Ibid. p.215-8. Emphasis mine.

submitted'.[12] In the Quran, a person who 'submits' is a member of a community actively committed to upholding the universal principles of solidarity, liberty and justice, since these principles have been laid down in the Quran and were exemplified in the life and career of the Prophet. Hence in the Quranic context, to follow the *deen* of Islam means that a person or community is 'willingly submitting to God'.[13] To put it another way, according to Dr M. Iqbal, whose intellectual influence on Jinnah is shown in this book, a Muslim is not identified by his or her theological knowledge, or even religious piety, but his understanding of the 'ethical ideal' of Islam, and more importantly, his ability to prove it in his deeds and actions. As the philosopher once said:

> Remember that Islam was born in the broad daylight of history. ... There is absolutely nothing esoteric in his [the Prophet's] teachings. Every word of the Quran is brimful of light and joy of existence. Far from justifying any gloomy, pessimistic Mysticism, it is an open assault on those religious teachings which have for centuries mystified mankind. ... Do not listen to him who says there is a secret doctrine in Islam which cannot be revealed to the uninitiated.[14]

Dr Iqbal is telling us that the principles of Islam are plain and easy to understand, and that they are profound precisely because all people are capable of comprehending them. There is no mysterious, esoteric or otherwise complicated teaching in Islam. To suggest otherwise would be to deny that the Quran contains a universal message addressed to all of humanity. Iqbal therefore refers to Islamic principles simply as 'equality, solidarity, and freedom'.[15] As he has also said, the Quran emphasises deed rather than idea[16] – i.e. the observance of such principles through positive action, whether at an individual or collective/state level. What made Jinnah an example of a great Muslim leader therefore was not his technical knowledge of theology, but rather his ability to translate what

---

12 See entry سلم in Lane Book I (Part 4), p.1412-14; the primary meanings of the root سلم are to become 'safe', 'secure', or 'free', and 'make peace', or 'reconcile'. The word 'Islam' shares the same root.

13 See Quran 2:112: 'Nay,-whoever *submits His whole self to Allah* and is a doer of good' (Ali's translation). This verse makes it clear that the word 'submit' has been given a qualifier, which in this case is Allah. The correct meaning of the verbal noun 'Islam' is 'willing submission' taking into account verse 2:256 ('no compulsion in *deen*') and the root سلم above.

14 Article, 'Islam and Mysticism' in *The New Era*, Lucknow, 28 July 1917. (Sherwani (ed.) 2008, p.156)

15 *Reconstruction*, p.154. Javid Iqbal has made a similar point in his *Ideology of Pakistan* and has dedicated a section to describing the ideals of equality, solidarity and freedom in turn, as well as the duty of the individual to the state. (See 2005 reprint, p.50-56)

16 *Reconstruction*, v.

he understood into his political actions. He not only said that Islam means action, [17] but he also led by example.

Myth no. 2: Jinnah sought a 'modern democratic state' or 'Western-style democracy'. (Munir Report p.201 & M. Munir 1980, p.29)

Munir's quote of the Reuters interview in which Jinnah allegedly used the terms 'modern democratic state' together with 'sovereignty resting in the people' is, as I have demonstrated already, a complete fabrication. Jinnah was in fact critical of the British form of democracy:

> … Muslim India will never submit to an all-India constitution and one central government. The British statesmen know that the *so-called democracy and the parliamentary system of government is nothing but a farce in the country*. It is not, as some people mix it up, a question of Muslims objecting to a government based on the brotherhood of man, as is often alleged by people who really do not understand what they are talking about when they talk of either democracy or Islam. Democracy means, to begin with, majority rule. Majority rule in a single nation, in a single society, is understandable, although *even there it has failed.* [18]

> Hindus and Muslims brought together under a democratic system forced upon the minorities can only mean [*sic*] Hindu raj. *Democracy of the kind* with which the Congress High Command is enamoured *would mean the complete destruction of what is most precious in Islam. … Mussalmans are a nation* according to any definition of a nation, and they must have *their own homelands*, their territory, *and their state.* … We wish our people to develop to the fullest our spiritual, cultural, economic, social and political life in a way that we think best and *in consonance with our own ideal* and according to the genius of our people. [19]

> Yes you [the Congress] may be the largest number; you may be more advanced; you may be stronger economically, and you may think that *the counting of heads* is the final judgment. But let me tell you – and I tell both of you [20] – that you alone or this organisation alone or both combined will never succeed in destroying our souls. You will never be able to destroy that

---

17 See Jinnah's broadcast from the All-India Radio, Bombay, Eid Day, 13 November 1939 (Yusufi Vol. II, p.1060)

18 Presidential address at the ML Annual Session, Madras, 14 April 1941. (Yusufi Vol. III, p.1384-5)

19 Presidential address at the ML Annual Session, Lahore, 22 March 1940 (NV Vol. I, p.494-5). It was at this Session that the historical Lahore Resolution was passed.

20 'Both of you' – Jinnah is referring to the British Raj and the Congress.

> culture which we have inherited, the Islamic Culture, and that spirit will live, is going to live and has lived.[21]

> Two years ago at Simla I said that the democratic parliamentary system of government was unsuited to India. I was condemned everywhere in the Congress press. I was told I was guilty of disservice to Islam because Islam believes in democracy. ... We cannot accept a system of government in which the non-Muslims merely by numerical majority would rule and dominate us. ... I have reached the conclusion that in India where the conditions are entirely different from those of the Western countries, the British party system of government and the so-called democracy are absolutely unsuitable.[22]

The democracy he criticised in all of the above passages is the contemporary British parliamentary form of democracy – i.e. 'modern' democracy. He stressed that Muslims and Hindus in India did not represent merely two communities, but two nations, and therefore the type of democracy which is usually applied to one homogeneous nation could not be applied in a subcontinent containing two. This was not an original idea, but one that had been borrowed from Sayyed Hussain Bilgrami of the Aligarh school of thought.[23] Hence Jinnah wanted Muslims to have their own state where they could design a constitution that reflected their own 'ideal'.

Jinnah's objection to Western-style democracy was documented at the time, as we can see from press reports of the period. For example, the *Civil & Military Gazette* reported in August 1939:

> The view that democracy is unsuited to the genius of India was expressed by Mr M.A. Jinnah speaking on the present political situation.
>
> The cultures of the two communities, Muslims and Hindus, were so different that the one having power naturally tried to run the other down. In such a country, comprising different nationalities, a democratic system of parliamentary government was, in his view, an impossibility.

---

[21] Speech of Mr Jinnah in the Imperial Council during the budget session 1939-40, Delhi, 22 March 1939. (G.H. Zulfiqar (ed. 1997) *Pakistan as Visualised by Iqbal and Jinnah*. Lahore: Bazm-i-Iqbal, p.52)

[22] Speech at the Muslim University Union, Aligarh, 6 March 1940 (Yusufi Vol. II, p.1158-9)

[23] Bilgrami was a contemporary of Sir Syed Ahmad Khan who argued that Western-style democracy was unsuitable as it overlooked the many races, castes and classes in India. (A.S. Ahmed 1997, p.56)

> What the future constitution should be was a matter to be yet decided. [24]

In another *Gazette* report a few months later he was quoted as follows:

> Mr Jinnah next refuted the cry that the Muslim League had denounced democracy. Democracy in the abstract was quite different from the democracy as practised. Democracy was like the Chameleon [*sic*] changing its complexion according to the environment. Democracy was not the same in England as it was in France or America. Islam believed in equality, liberty and fraternity but not the democracy of the western type – the democratic parliamentary system in which party government was the basic principle of the constitution. [25]

Jinnah is also on record as having said:

> The *modern democratic* form of Government is not suitable to the genius of the Indian People. [26]

This is the nearest we get to seeing any part of the Munir quote, and even here Jinnah is disavowing it, not supporting it. Only moments later, he explicitly describes what he expects to see in Pakistan's polity, and also what he does not expect to see:

> We want a true democracy in accordance with Islam and not a Parliamentary Government of the Western or Congress type. [27]

Jinnah's disavowal of the 'Western' form of democracy however should not be taken to mean that he was opposed to universal equality, or even that he was necessarily opposed to democratic system types altogether. On the contrary, his complaint was that 'modern' democracy – that is, democracy *as it stands today* – offers no real equality. It imposes majority rule by virtue of numbers, without consideration of whether the majority is right or wrong. [28] He explained on numerous

---

[24] Statement on democracy and present political situation in India, Bombay, 5 August 1939, as reported in *Civil & Military Gazette*, 6 August 1939. (Yusufi Vol. II, p.1020)

[25] Speech at a meeting in Bombay, 7 November 1939, as reported in *Civil & Military Gazette*, 11 November 1939. (Yusufi Vol. II, p.1057)

[26] Address to the Hostel Parliament of Ismail Yusuf College, Jogeshwari (Bombay), 1 February 1943. (M.A. Harris (ed.) 1976, p.174)

[27] Ibid.

[28] Many thinkers of the sociological field have been aware of the pitfalls of 'modern' democracy for at least a century. The 20th century economist Arthur Twining Hadley for example wrote: 'The extent to which democracy can be carried depends more upon *national education* than upon constitutional law. Few of the founders of modern democracy saw this at all clearly. The thing which seemed important to them was that the government should

occasions that the Congress was interested in exploiting this form of government solely to secure its permanent brute majority which would crush Muslims as a numerical minority. [29] However Jinnah made it absolutely clear that the 'Islamic democracy' of Pakistan (as he often termed it) would not discriminate against non-Muslims based on rule of numbers. We refer again to the same speech cited above:

> In Pakistan we shall have a state which will be run according to the principles of Islam. It will have its cultural, political and economic structure based on the principles of Islam. The non-Muslims need not fear because of this, for fullest justice will be done to them, they will have their full cultural, religious, political and economic rights safeguarded. As a matter of fact they will be more safeguarded than in the present day so-called democratic parliamentary form of Government. [30]

We can see from the above passage that Jinnah envisioned a state that would not merely emulate a 'modern democratic' or contemporary secular state, but would be run 'according to the principles of Islam', and so would also guarantee the 'fullest justice' to non-Muslims (as well as Muslims) in Pakistan. The fact that secularist and religionist commentators alike have failed to comprehend what Jinnah was actually saying is revealed in their selective use of evidence, betraying their discomfort with regards to the man who fits neither of their moulds.

---

carefully represent and conscientiously carry out the popular will. They did not see *how often the majority which was supposed to express that popular will was improperly educated regarding the facts at issue, and therefore at once shortsighted and selfish in its demands*.' (A.T. Hadley (1972 reprint), *Economic Problems of Democracy* New York: Books for Libraries Press, p.19-20; emphasis mine). This observation is in line with the Quranic verse 6:116: 'Now if you pay heed unto the majority of those (who live) on earth, they will but lead you astray from the path of God: they follow but (other people's) conjectures, and they themselves do nothing but guess.' (Asad modernised). On this verse Asad comments: 'Apart from leading man astray from spiritual truths, *such guesswork gives rise to the arbitrary rules of conduct* and self-imposed inhibitions to which the Qur'an alludes'. (Emphasis mine)

[29] See for example Interview to the *Manchester Guardian*, New Delhi, 25 October 1939 (Yusufi Vol. II, p. 1049-51); Speech at a Muslim meeting, Bombay, 7 November 1939 (Yusufi Vol. II p.1056-8); Article, 'The Constitutional Maladies of India' in *Time and Tide* (London), 19 January 1940 (Jamil-ud-din Ahmad 1942, p.111-9).

[30] Address at the Hostel Parliament of Ismail Yusuf College, Jogeshwari (Bombay), 1 February 1943. (M.A. Harris (ed.) 1976, p.173)

Myth no. 3: Islam was just a propaganda tool to win the support of the masses (I. Talbot 1984;[31] A. Jalal 1994, p.5; Hoodbhoy & Nayyar 1985, p.171; I. Ahmed, 2002[32])

If indeed Jinnah had used Islamic slogans[33] simply to win the support of Muslims until the time was right for him to reveal his objective for a secular state, then we could have accused him of being a dictator imposing his personal whims upon his people, not to mention a manipulative and dishonest leader. To the contrary however, he said time and again that the issue of forming the constitution would be left to the people:

> In a gathering of high European and American officials he was asked as to who was the author of Pakistan. Mr Jinnah's reply was 'Every Mussalman.'
>
> Now the question is how to get Pakistan? Raising his eyebrows and speaking in grim tones, Mr Jinnah said, 'not by asking, not by begging, not even by mere prayers, but by working with trust in God. *Inshallah!* Pakistan is now in your hands.'[34]

> The constitution of Pakistan can only be framed by *the Millat and the people.*[35]

Jinnah voiced the demand of Indian Muslims, no more, and no less. He was merely returning the right of self-determination to them, not fulfilling a personal ambition. This is why he had never offered his own programme for a specific political system:

> What is it that you want? All this talk of socialism, communism, national-socialism and every other *ism*[36] is out of place. Do you think you can do anything just now? How and when can you decide as to what form of government you are going to have in Pakistan? We are told by one party or another that we must have a democratic or a socialistic or a

---

[31] I. Talbot, 'Jinnah and the Making of Pakistan' in *History Today*, Vol. 34 Issue 2, 1984 p.5-10

[32] I. Ahmed, 'The Fundamentalist Dimension in the Pakistan movement' in *Friday Times*, 22-28 November 2002.

[33] The claim made in both of the articles by I. Ahmed (2004, p.22) and Hoodbhoy & Nayyar (1985, p.171) is that the religious leaders who joined the Muslim League in the later phase of the Pakistan movement (specifically, during the 1945 provincial elections) made use of Islamic slogans to win the support of the masses. See also I. Ahmed (2002) for a direct reference to the Muslim League's use of 'Islamic sentiments, slogans and heroic themes'.

[34] Report in *Dawn*, 10 March 1944. (Yusufi Vol. III p.1841)

[35] Presidential address at the ML Annual Session, Delhi, 24 April 1943 (Yusufi Vol. III, p.1720). On the subject of the *millat*, see also Myth no. 4.

[36] Italicised in original.

> "nationalistic"[37] form of government in Pakistan. These questions are raised to hoodwink you. At present you should just stand by Pakistan. It means that first of all you have to take possession of a territory. Pakistan cannot exist in the air. When you have once taken possession of your homelands the question will then arise as to what form of government you are going to establish. Therefore, do not allow your mind to be diverted by these extraneous ideas.[38]

Note he is saying *you*, not *I*.

In July 1947 in the weeks before partition Jinnah issued a statement for the protection of minorities in Pakistan at a press conference. The *Dawn* later reproduced some of the journalists' questions in an article. Of course one of these questions related to the issue of the structure of the government:

> Mr Jinnah refused to discuss the structure of the Government of Pakistan as that was a matter for the Constituent Assembly to decide.
>
> Q: What is your personal opinion?
>
> Mr Jinnah: No responsible man expresses his personal opinion in anticipation of the decision of a supreme body like the Constituent Assembly, whose function it is to frame the constitution.[39]

Nevertheless, whatever political system the people would choose, Jinnah constantly reiterated that he expected the constitution to reflect their aspirations and ideals:

> We have to fight a double-edged battle, one against the Hindu Congress and the other against [the] British Imperialist, both of whom are capitalist. The Muslims demand Pakistan, where they could live according to their own code of life, their own cultural growth, traditions and Islamic Laws.[40]

Just before partition he also explained to the Memon Chamber of Commerce in Bombay:

> In your Government you will be making the greatest contribution to what is known as social justice or in what I might

---

[37] Quotation marks included in original.

[38] Speech at the Muslim University Union, Aligarh, 9 March 1944 (Yusufi Vol. III, p.1847)

[39] Press conference, New Delhi, 13 July 1947. (Yusufi Vol. IV, p.2592)

[40] Speech at Frontier Muslim League Conference at Peshawar, 20 November 1945. (K.A.K. Yusufi (1988) *Quaid-i-Azam Muhammad Ali Jinnah: Some Rare Speeches and Statements, 1944-1947* Lahore: Punjab University, p.93)

> call a Socialistic Government. *Social justice is one of the fundamentals of Islam.* That is the duty of any state and it must show to the world that it believes in economic and social justice. [41]

Likewise he expected the economic system of the country to reflect Islamic ideals. Hence when he set up the Planning Committee in 1944 to look into the economic potential of the future Pakistan, he addressed its personnel as follows:

> It is not our purpose to make the rich richer and to accelerate the process of the accumulation of wealth in the hands of [a] few individuals. We should aim at levelling up the general standard of living amongst the masses … *Our ideal should not be capitalistic but Islamic*, and the interests and welfare of the people as a whole should be kept constantly in mind. [42]

If Jinnah (and the League) indeed used Islamic slogans as a propaganda tool, then after Pakistan was won Jinnah should have stopped using them. However, not only did Jinnah's use of these 'slogans' continue in the new state of Pakistan, but they continued even after the speech of 11 August 1947, the speech that is considered 'one of the clearest expositions of a secular state'. [43]

The following examples are dated after partition. The first is addressed to an American audience:

> The constitution of Pakistan has yet to be framed by the Pakistan Constituent Assembly. I do not know what the ultimate shape of this constitution is going to be, but I am sure that it will be of a democratic type, embodying the essential principles of Islam. [44]

The next one is addressed to foreign journalists:

> The constitution of Pakistan will be based on Islamic principles and tenets. [45]

Jinnah said that politically Pakistan would be democratic, and that its economy would be socialistic. [46] He even told the army after partition

---

41 Speech at a reception given by the Memon Chamber of Commerce, Bombay, 27 March 1947. (Yusufi Vol. IV, p.2534)

42 Address to the members of the League Planning Committee, New Delhi, 5 November 1944. (Yusufi Vol. III, p.1961)

43 Munir 1980, p.29

44 Jinnah's broadcast talk on Pakistan to the people of United States of America, Karachi, 26 February 1948. (NV Vol. VII, p.215-6)

45 Interview to Egyptian journalists, Lahore, 25 November 1947 (NV Vol. VII, p.109)

that it must 'stand guard over the development and maintenance of Islamic democracy, Islamic social justice and the equality of manhood' on its 'native soil'. [47] Hence he used both phrases, 'Islamic democracy' and 'Islamic socialism', to describe Pakistan in socio-political terms. As he told the Muslim League Council in December 1947 during a discussion on the future of the Muslim League following partition, including its name:

> Let it be clear that Pakistan is going to be a *Muslim State based on Islamic Ideals.* It was not going to be an ecclesiastical state. [*sic*] In Islam there is no discrimination as far as citizenship is concerned. The whole world, even [the] UNO has characterised Pakistan as a Muslim State. [48]

It goes without saying that none of the above statements fall under the category of electioneering slogans, being all dated after partition.

Just a few months before he passed away, a frail and dying [49] Jinnah made a special effort to attend the opening ceremony of the State Bank of Pakistan. [50] The State Bank Governor, Zahid Hussain, gave his address in which he thanked the guests and in particular Jinnah for attending. During his speech Mr Hussain explained the importance of having a central bank and the decision of the fledgling state to have one despite the difficulties involved and its lack of trained personnel. [51] He mentioned that the 'people of Pakistan' were demanding 'a clarification of the policy of government regarding the ideology which is to guide and inspire us in regulating our political, social and economic life'. Referring to the Islamic 'provision' for 'preventing concentrations of wealth without killing the essential incentive to individual initiative and enterprise', he said that it was 'this ideology which must inspire us in regulating our economic life'. [52] In other words, he envisioned an

---

[46] See for example Jinnah's interview to a representative of the Associated press of America, Bombay, 8 November 1945. (Yusufi Vol. III, p.2097)

[47] Address to Officers and men of the 5th Heavy Ack Ack Regiment, Malir (Karachi), 21 February 1948 (NV Vol. VII, p.199)

[48] Speech at the Meeting of the All-India Muslim League Council, Karachi, December 14-45 1947, 16 December 1947. (Yusufi Vol. IV, p.2656). For the context in which this statement was made, which is significant in its own right, see Myth no. 6.

[49] Jinnah suffered from tuberculosis for a number of years but downplayed its seriousness in public. He died on 11 September 1948 of pneumonia, a complication resulting from the pre-existing disease.

[50] That Jinnah made a special effort and was willing to cut short other engagements in order to attend was mentioned in Zahid Hussain's address (referenced in next footnote). Fatima Jinnah also mentioned that her brother went out of his way to attend the ceremony because he had a point to prove to those in India who had wrongly predicted that Pakistan would be bankrupt. (F. Jinnah 1987, p.21)

[51] Zahid Hussain's address at the Opening Ceremony of the State Bank of Pakistan, Karachi, 1 July 1948. (NV Vol. VII, p.423-4 fn)

[52] Ibid. p.425 fn

economic system that took the extreme of neither socialism nor capitalism – similar to what the Leaguers later promised in the Constituent Assembly. (We might add that Hussain later became the chairman of the Pakistan Planning Committee.)[53] He then announced the intention of the State Bank to establish an economic research organisation to 'devote special and unremitting attention to this most important aspect of our ideological problem'.[54]

Next Jinnah delivered his address. He echoed Zahid Hussain's sentiments, in thought-provoking language, that the State Bank 'symbolises the sovereignty of our state in the financial sphere'.[55] He also expressed his appreciation of the newly-announced research organisation:

> I shall watch with keenness the work of your Research Organisation in evolving banking practices compatible with Islamic ideals of social and economic life. The economic system of the West has created almost insoluble problems for humanity, and to many of us it appears that only a miracle can save it from [the] disaster that is now facing the world. It has failed to do justice between man and man and to eradicate friction from the international field. On the contrary, it was largely responsible for the two world wars in the last half century. The Western world, in spite of its advantages of mechanisation and industrial efficiency, is today in a worse mess than ever before in history. The adoption of western economic theory and practice will not help us in achieving our goal of creating a happy and contented people. We must work our destiny in *our own way*, and *present to the world* [an] economic system based on [the] true Islamic concept of equality of manhood and social justice. We will thereby be fulfilling our mission as Muslims and giving to humanity the message of peace,

---

53 Zahid Hussain (1893-1957) was something of a radical thinker. A Vice-Chancellor of Aligarh University and ally of Jinnah, he believed that interest should be completely abolished and that Arabic should become the national language of Pakistan. Under Hussain's chairmanship from 1953, the Pakistan Planning Committee put together the first 'Five-Year Plan' (for implementation from 1955-60) for Pakistan. It took into account the Islamic recommendations of the BPC Report of 1952, including that of abolishing *riba* as soon as possible. It has become best known for its firm recommendations for land reforms that aimed to put an end to feudalism. Quite conveniently for the feudal class, this plan was never implemented after the first Constituent Assembly's dissolution by Ghulam Mohammed and the subsequent political instability. A new Planning Commission was later established in October 1958 under Iskander Mirza's regime (less than a week before Ayub Khan took over), but Zahid Hussain did not live to see it. He died in 1957. Sadly his contribution to Pakistan has been largely forgotten today and he has not been given due recognition.

54 Ibid. p.425 fn

55 Speech on the occasion of the Opening Ceremony of the State Bank of Pakistan, Karachi, 1 July 1948. (Ibid. p.426)

> which alone can save it and secure the welfare, happiness and *prosperity of mankind.*[56]

The State Bank's Research Organisation was supposed to work towards the development of an economic system – an indisputably crucial part of the country's overall political setup – based on Islamic principles. Moreover, this economic system was supposed to become an example for the rest of the world. It had Jinnah's full support and reflected all that he had said in his pre-partition speeches.

Myth no. 4: On the rare occasion that a Muslim Leaguer tried to pass a resolution to call Pakistan an 'Islamic state', the rest of the Muslim League vetoed it. Jinnah and the educated elite of the Muslim League were not interested in an Islamic state. (A. Jalal 1994, p.96; H. Alavi 1986, p.41-2 [57])

Here we shall look specifically at the example given in Prof. Ayesha Jalal's book, *The Sole Spokesman* (1994 reprint). She contends that Dr Abdul Hameed Kazi drafted a resolution for an Islamic state but the Muslim League rejected it, at 'Jinnah's insistence'.[58] In fact two people – Dr Kazi and Sheikh Abdul Majid Sindhi had intended make a call to define Pakistan concretely as an 'Islamic state'. Kazi had gone as far as drafting a resolution to the effect. In a footnote Jalal writes that Kazi's proposal was rejected because, so she quotes, Jinnah thought this amounted to a 'vote of censure'[59] on every Muslim Leaguer. However the words she has quoted have been taken completely out of context. Ayesha Jalal has taken them from Jinnah's presidential address at the annual All-India Muslim League session in April 1943. In this speech, Jinnah sought to make it clear who actually had the right to decide the constitution of Pakistan. Here we will closely examine the speech that she cited from to reveal the true context of these words.

It is important to note that at the time that Jinnah gave this particular speech, most of the wealthy peasantries in the Muslim majority provinces of India did not cooperate with the Muslim League. They were still caught up in tribal and other local concerns, and wanted to retain their own power rather than have to share it with others. However there were a small number of landlords in the Muslim-minority United Provinces who had joined the League (this number grew across India

---

56 Ibid. p.428

57 In a revised version of his 1986 article, Hamza Alavi also added a reference to Ayesha Jalal to add support to his contention: 'Ayesha Jalal, in her excellent study of Jinnah's political role, records at least two occasions on which Jinnah successfully resisted attempts to commit the Muslim League to an 'Islamic Ideology'. (See H. Alavi in F. Halliday and H. Alavi (eds.) (1988) *State and Ideology in the Middle East and Pakistan* London: Macmillan, p.104).

58 Jalal (1994 reprint), p.96 (originally published in 1985)

59 Ibid. p.96 fn

later). Many historians believe that they had done so because local governmental policy changes in their respective regions were threatening their livelihood, and they hoped that they would fare better if they sided with the Muslim League in its call for independence and then reasserted themselves in the future independent state. There is no doubt some truth to this, but as we will show, Jinnah made it perfectly clear in his speech that the Muslim League was not so desperate for support from the landlords that it would be willing to part with its fundamental principles in exchange. In order to illustrate the actual context of Prof. Jalal's quote, it is necessary to give an overview of the contents of the whole speech.

Jinnah began with the prevailing issue of the day, which was getting the full support of the Muslim majority provinces. First he denounced the Bengal's Chief Minister Fazlul Huq [60] who had tried to divide Muslims to take power for himself (against the Muslim League's insistence on maintaining Muslim unity):

> Bengal has therefore shown us that there is no room for duplicity. ... It is now the voice of the League, the voice of the people, it is now *the authority of the Millat* that you have to bow to, though you may be the tallest poppy in the Muslim world. [61]

Then he appealed to the Punjab to join the Muslim call for independence:

> ... I particularly appeal to the delegates from the Punjab – people are all right in the Punjab ... please substitute love for Islam and your nation, in place of sectional interests, jealousies, tribal notions and selfishness. For these evils have over-powered you and you are being ground down for the last 200 years. [62]

Next Jinnah went back in time, giving an extensive overview of India's independence movement over the previous decades. He described the 'Hindu Nationalism' [63] that had become increasingly prevalent in the

---

[60] Abul Kasem Fazlul Huq (1873-1962) had manoeuvred against the League in Bengal in an effort to retain his provincial power (see also Chapter 7, footnote 34). He eventually resigned as Bengal Chief Minister in March 1943, at the request of the Governor of Bengal. (NV Vol. III p.179 fn)

[61] Presidential address (extempore), ML Annual Session, New Delhi, 24 April 1943 (NV Vol. III, p.179-80)

[62] Ibid. p.180

[63] 'Hindu Nationalism' – nationalism based on Hindu religious ideals; a movement for 'Hindu Raj'. Jinnah stated that the two-nation theory was thus not an idea that originated with the League, but which had been admitted by Hindus also (see footnote 167 in Myth no. 8). But whereas the 'Hindu nation' either wished for the 'Muslim nation' to be reabsorbed into Hinduism or at any rate to remain in India, Jinnah and the League advocated separation.

Congress, before reiterating the reasons why a democratic government under a united India could never work:

> When you [the Congress] talk of democracy, you are thoroughly dishonest. When you talk of democracy you mean Hindu raj, to dominate over the Muslims, a totally different nation, different in culture, different in everything. You yourself are working for Hindu nationalism and Hindu raj.
>
> Ladies and Gentlemen, *we learned democracy 1,300 years ago.* It is in our blood and it is as far away from the Hindu society as are the Arctic regions. You tell us that we are not democratic. It is we, who have learned the lesson of equality and brotherhood of man. Among you one caste will not take a cup of water from another. Is this democracy? Is this honesty? *We are for democracy. But not the democracy of your conception* which will turn the whole of India into a Gandhi *Ashram*; [64] or one society and nation will by this permanent majority destroy another nation or society in permanent minority and all that is dear to the minority. [65]

Note that Jinnah was alluding to the democratic principle of Islam, which occasionally he termed 'Islamic democracy'. To briefly look at a different speech:

> You have fought many a battle on the far-flung battlefields of the globe to rid the world of the Fascist menace and make it safe for democracy. Now you have to stand guard over the development and maintenance of Islamic democracy, Islamic social justice and the equality of manhood in your own native soil.[66]

(It is significant that Jinnah has separated 'Islamic democracy' from the democracy upheld by the rest of the world.)

To summarise the main points so far: Jinnah stated that in a typical democracy, the majority ultimately influences the form of the constitution. Since the majority in India's case was Hindu, the majority of the votes would naturally always go to Hindu representatives. This on its own was not necessarily a problem, but recent experience under Congress rule had already suggested that a united India would undoubtedly be permanently dominated by traditional Hindu religious ideals, as manifested sociologically within the caste system. [67]

---

[64] *Ashram* – word for a Hindu religious training institution. Italicised in original.

[65] Ibid. p.190

[66] Address to Officers and men of the 5th Heavy Ack Ack, Malir (Karachi), 21 February 1948. (NV Vol. VII, p.199)

[67] The caste system is the societal outcome of a belief in the recurring life cycle and in karma. According to this doctrine, being born into a lower caste implies that an individual has earned

Jinnah continued his assault on what he called a 'farce', [68] and then addressed Muslims with the following words:

> You will elect your representatives to the constitution-making body. You may not know your power, you may not know how to use it. This would be your fault. But I am sure that democracy is in our blood. It is in our marrows. Only centuries of adverse circumstances have made the circulation of that blood cold. It has got frozen and your arteries have not been functioning. But, thank God, the blood is circulating again, thanks to the Muslim League's efforts. It will be a people's government.[69]

At this point he gave a warning to a certain section of wealthy Muslims who assumed they would continue their exploitative living in the future state:

> Here I should like to give a warning to the landlords and capitalists who have flourished at our expense by a system which is so vicious, which is wicked and which makes them so selfish that it is difficult to reason with them. The exploitation of the masses has gone into their blood. *They have forgotten the lesson of Islam.* Greed and selfishness have made these people subordinate to the interests of others in order to fatten themselves. It is true we are not in power today. You go anywhere to the countryside. I have visited some villages. There are millions and millions of our people who hardly get one meal a day. Is this civilisation? Is this the aim of Pakistan? Do you visualise that millions have been exploited and cannot get one meal a day! [*sic*] If that is the idea of Pakistan, I would not have it. If they [the landlords] are wise they will have to adjust themselves to the new modern conditions of life. If they don't, God help them; we shall not help them. Therefore let us have faith in ourselves. Let us not falter or hesitate. That is our goal. We are going to achieve it. The constitution of Pakistan can only be framed by *the Millat and the people.* Prepare yourself and see that you frame a constitution which is to your heart's desire. There is a lot of misunderstanding. A lot of mischief is created. *Is it going to be an Islamic government?* Is it not begging the question? Is it not a question of passing a *vote of*

---

it from bad deeds in a former life and this justifies social restrictions such as the type of work he/she is allowed to do. Though today the caste system is on the decline in India, in the1940s it was still going strong, and so lower castes (and in particular the 'Untouchables') were in a severely disadvantaged position socially, economically and educationally. Jinnah was criticising this aspect of the Hindu social ideal when he said that in Hindu society, 'men are born unequal and should live as unequals'. (Statement in reply to Gandhi's appeal regarding an article published in *Dawn*; New Delhi, 11 March 1942; Yusufi Vol. III, p.1536)

68 NV Vol. III, p.200

69 Ibid. p.200-1

> *censure* on yourself? The constitution and the government will be what the people will decide. [70] The only question is that of minorities. [71]

Looking at this passage more closely, we see that Jinnah addressed the landlords, denouncing their 'exploitation of the masses', contrary to 'the lesson of Islam'. This was a criticism of the old system of 'feudalism' (as Pakistanis still call it) or landlordism. Referring to the extreme poverty prevalent in their regions, Jinnah challenged anyone to assert that this would be the state of affairs in Pakistan. Next, he referred to some 'misunderstanding' and 'mischief', alluding to a ruse revolving around the issue of the constitution (he didn't take any names). Taking the available information into account, we know that he is referring to Dr Kazi's resolution. [72] But Jinnah is not suggesting that Kazi was wilfully making mischief. [73] It seems from Jinnah's speech that Kazi (supported by other Leaguers) [74] had drafted the resolution in order to make it clear to the landlords in Punjab that they could not expect to continue the feudal system in Pakistan. The point in Jinnah's address was therefore two-fold. First, he asserted (in support of Kazi and other anti-capitalists) that feudalism would not be allowed to continue in Pakistan. Second, Jinnah suggested that rushing ahead and defining a constitution for a state that had not yet come into existence was liable to lead to 'mischief' and 'misunderstanding'. M.S. Toosy, a contemporary of Jinnah, has given the following version of events which makes the point plainly:

> Dr Abdul Hamid Kazi of Bombay had sent a notice to the Muslim League Working Committee that he wanted to move a resolution to define Pakistan which in his opinion meant the establishment of a Muslim State on the lines set by the first four Caliphs of Islam. Before this resolution could be moved, the Quaid-i-Azam received a telegram from Anjuman-i-Isna-Ashriya,

---

[70] 'The constitution and the government will be what the people will decide' – Jalal has quoted this line in her book (A. Jalal 1994, p.95-6) but has ignored the previous references to the *millat*.

[71] NV Vol. III p.201

[72] See *Foundations* Vol. II, p.440 fn, which is reproduced in footnote 74 below.

[73] In the original edition of *Secular Jinnah* I wrongly concluded that Kazi was the unnamed mischief maker. At the time I had scant information regarding contemporary reactions to the Session's proceedings which I have since found in sources such as those detailed in the main text above. Having taken this additional evidence into account, and finding it consistent, I hereby correct my error.

[74] The explanatory footnote in *Foundations* Vol. II, p.440 reads: 'Before the opening of the Thirtieth Session, a section of the Muslim Leaguers had proposed that … the future Constitution of Pakistan would be based on the Quran. And Dr Abdul Hameed Kazi of Bombay actually circulated a draft resolution, which he intended to move at the Session, to the effect that the Constitution of Pakistan would be based on the concept of *Hakoomat-i-Ilahiya* (i.e. the principles evolved by the first four Caliphs). However, in view of the Quaid-i-Azam's Presidential Address, Dr Kazi did not move his resolution.'

> Lucknow, to the effect that "if Pakistan meant the setting up of a government on the pattern of the first three Caliphs, the Shias will fight tooth and nail against such a conception". I was keenly interested to know how the Quaid-i-Azam would solve this riddle and define a Pakistan to the satisfaction of all Muslim schools of thought. In the meeting of the Muslim League Working Committee held in Delhi in March, 1943, the Quaid-i-Azam clarified the whole position thus: "Before I permit the mover to speak in support of his resolution, let me clarify the whole position. So far as I understand, and this will be the opinion of every sane-minded Muslim, Pakistan at this stage means the transfer of political power from the British Government to Muslim hands. … Once this political power is transferred to us, *then it will be the appropriate time* for us to … decide what form of government will suit us according to our special circumstances and conditions as a Muslim nation … We want a Muslim homeland wherein the Muslims will be free to choose their own government and conduct their affairs according to their tradition and genius, deriving inspiration from the fundamental principles of Islam …" [75]

Toosy of course is quoting Jinnah from memory, but how he has understood the import of Jinnah's message is important. Any talk about creating an 'Islamic state' was liable to cause controversy amongst the sectarian-minded religious elements, not to mention the landed class (see below). Kazi's intent to recreate the *Hakoomat-i-Ilahiya* (a state based on the Caliphate evolved during the classical period), however well intentioned, was as good as calling for a religious state. [76] An editorial from *The Eastern Times* makes exactly the same point (see the excerpts cited shortly).

Returning to Jinnah's speech, he was assuring the impatient Leaguers including Kazi that Pakistan would surely not allow feudalism to continue, since it was opposed to the spirit of Islam, and besides which, the constitution would be dealt with *after* Pakistan was won. If some landlords were presently calling for Pakistan to be an 'Islamic state', then it was likely an act of 'mischief'. Landlords had traditionally worked with local ulema to maintain their hold on their constituencies.[77]

---

[75] M.S. Toosy (1976) *My Reminisces of Quaid-i-Azam: A Collection of Interviews and Talks with Quaid-i-Azam during November 1942 to May 1943* Islamabad: Ministry of Education, Government of Pakistan, p.48

[76] Jinnah's idea of an 'Islamic state' would be not to literally recreate any past Islamic polity, but to establish a state that was Islamic by virtue of the democratic and socialistic principles in its constitution. See Chapter 12, subsection 'Jinnah's Pakistan' for a detailed discussion.

[77] See *Eastern Times* editorial, 28 April 1943 (Saeed (ed.) 1983, p.58). Unfortunately this same political tactic continued in Punjab after partition, with landlords utilising the influence of religious groups to defend their right of private property rights according to Islam, as well as by appealing provincialist sentiments. See Ilyas Chattha 'The impact of the redistribution of

They were aware that the Muslim masses expected to see socio-economic equity in Pakistan, and that this would be detrimental to their own vested interests. [78] They thought that by getting there first and showing themselves to be the champions of an 'Islamic state' (and thus also claiming the right to formulate its constitution) they would obtain 'Islamic' sanction from the ulema to continue their exploitive form of living once Pakistan was achieved. [79] Jinnah effectively said that it did not matter what the landlord and the capitalist thought because the constitution would be decided by the *millat* and the people. The *millat* were the ones who knew the lesson of Islam, of justice and fairplay. That was the form of constitution they would be voting for. Obviously they would not support an 'Islamic state' of the type conceived by the landlords and their allies from among the ulema. Therefore in calling for an 'Islamic state' these landlords were effectively passing a 'vote of censure' on themselves.

Jinnah is thus repudiating the theory that the landlords who joined the Muslim League would have benefited economically. Whilst scholars may be correct about the landlords' motives, they are certainly mistaken in contending that the entire Muslim League 'did not pose a threat to such interests'. [80] Jinnah had previously made the plain declaration that Pakistan would have its 'cultural, political *and economic* structure based on the principles of Islam'. [81] Later that same year, in December 1943, he would also back his words with action. [82]

An editorial from *The Eastern Times* gives us an idea of contemporary Muslim reaction to this session of the Muslim League. On the attempts to move the resolution for an 'Islamic state', the editor remarks:

Pakistan's evacuee property on the patterns of land ownership and power in Pakistani Punjab in the 1950s', in Roger D. Long et al. (eds.) (2016) *State and Nation-Building in Pakistan: Beyond Islam and Security (Routledge Contemporary South Asia Series)* Abingdon: Routledge, p.24, 29.

78 All had all heard Jinnah's oft-repeated declarations that Pakistan would stand for Islamic social justice and Islamic democracy – hardly the ideal environment for hard-nosed capitalists and landlords.

79 Indeed this is what some landlords tried to do in Pakistan, some time after Jinnah's death. See footnote 86 on Liaquat Ali Khan in Chapter 3.

80 I. Ahmed, 2002. In fact some Muslim Leaguers posed a definite threat to capitalist and right-wing interests. There were stark differences of economic opinion among the League members, some of whom had socialist leanings and took the 'Islamic socialism' concept to heart, and others comprising successful landlords and capitalists who evidently did not take the 'socialist' element seriously, despite what any of their peers (including Jinnah), let alone the public, might have said on the matter. The latter group later proved unwilling to make the sacrifices required to create a level economical playing field in Pakistan, and this led to serious disputes when it came to policymaking. For an example of such a dispute, see the biographical footnote on Mian Iftikhar-ud-Din in Chapter 3 (footnote 26). For an in-depth review of events during this period, see Ilyas Chattha op.cit. p.13-35; and also Khalid bin Sayeed (1956, PhD thesis) *The Central Government of Pakistan 1947-1951* Montreal: McGill University, p.90-108.

81 See Address to the students of Ismail College, Bombay, 1 February 1943. M.A. Harris (ed.) 1976, p.173

82 See Jinnah's work in setting up the AIML Planning Committee in Chapter 9.

> It is very satisfactory to note that the motions of both Dr Abdul Hameed Qazi of Bombay and Sheikh Abdul Majid Sindhi, asking for a definition of the economic and political constitution of the Pakistan State, *were shelved for the time.* [*sic*] … neither the economic character nor the political constitution of the Pakistan State can be determined or brought into line with that of the ideal Islamic State by a simple resolution of the All India Muslim League. … Also to expect that vested interests, landlords and capitalists, will immediately surrender all their privileges on hearing the word "Islam" is to put too high a premium on human nature and shows a woeful lack of political sense. Such an economic revolution as the Islamic State implies calls for a process of *revolution in the thoughts of men.* … Those who now press for such revolutions must work for such a *mental revolution.* [*sic*] [83]

Other educated Muslims in India agreed with the gradual approach, i.e. that education had to precede reformation. Bahadur Yar Jung stated at the Muslim League Annual Session later the same year:

> The purpose of this Planning Committee is to work upon a socio-educational, economic and political system for Pakistan from a purely Islamic point of view, in order to enable Indian Muslims in general, and Pakistani Muslims in particular, to lead their lives.
>
> The whole world knows that no revolution can be accomplished without a complete mental revolution; in fact world history testifies that before a revolution can even begin, people must first undergo a mental revolution. [84]

Likewise in 1944, in his preface to *Speeches, Writings & Statements of Iqbal*, Latif Ahmad Sherwani wrote the following on Iqbal's suggestion for educating Muslims:

> The nation will be safe only when the common mass of the people become sufficiently enlightened and organised to take their destiny in their own hands, and the most effective way of bringing about such an enlightenment is the establishment of what the Allamah [Iqbal] called cultural institutes.
>
> … neither power nor material gain had any attraction for Iqbal. He demanded the establishment of a separate sovereign Muslim State in north-west India, not as an

83 *The Eastern Times*, 4 May 1943. (A. Saeed (ed.) 1983, p.68-9) Spellings of names retained from original; emphasis mine.

84 Bahadur Yar Jung's speech, ML Karachi Session, 26 December 1943. (B.Y. Jung 2000 (reprint), p.20) Translated from Urdu. For a detailed look at Bahadur Yar Jung's speech, see Myth no. 12.

> escape from Hindu domination, but in order that Muslims might be able to live a truly Islamic life and establish an ideal society. … The Allamah lays down an ideal and points out the ultimate purposes which the sovereign State of Pakistan will seek to serve while the Muslim League's objective is the establishment of the State without which those ultimate purposes cannot possibly be attained. Given the State, it will be up to the Muslims, if they believe in Islam and its purposes, to utilise the State for the realisation of those purposes. [85]

In another *Eastern Times* editorial, the following comment appears with regards to Jinnah's speech:

> This was not mere theatrical flourish on Mr Jinnah's part nor what is called the "vote-catching stunt". Those who have had occasion to see Mr Jinnah from closer range know that it was no attempt to seek cheap popularity among the masses. He has never sought popularity by surrender of principles for he is too proud for that. His sympathy for the poor is genuine, and if it ever came to a choice between the rich and the poor, we believe that Mr Jinnah would stand by the latter. [86]

The editorial confirms that the 'pronouncement was needed' to counter the propaganda of anti-League elements that had been calling it a 'body of landlords and capitalists'. [87] The editor states further that 'best way to reform it and rescue it from the hands of the landlords is to get into it and not merely to stand aloof from it.' [88]

Finally, the editorial also confirms that no Muslim had interpreted Jinnah's reference to a 'vote of censure' as a 'no vote' to Islam itself:

> Mr Jinnah's warning may have been sounded [*sic*] unpleasant to vested interests, but what he said was a plain economic truth, and it is just as well that he has said it. The Muslims have dreamed the dream of Pakistan with a view to having a better and more equitable economic system. They want to create a society in which all shall work and nobody shall be without work, in which there may be no multi millionaires, but none shall be hungry and everyone shall have opportunities of progress and advancement that his talents deserve, apart from whether he is rich or poor by birth. *It will be an ideal Islamic state*, whereas the existence of abject

---

85 Sherwani (ed.) 2008, vii-viii (from reprinted preface to first edition)

86 *The Eastern Times*, 28 April 1943. (A. Saeed (ed.) 1983, p.57)

87 Ibid.

88 Ibid.

poverty side by side with accumulated hoards of wealth and luxury is a negation of that state. [89]

Thus there can be no doubt regarding the true context of what Jinnah was saying, especially since he used the word *millat* – an Urdu word usually reserved for the Muslim community [90] – more than once during the course of this speech. He included 'the people' in his statement too, along with the *millat*. The *millat* means of course Muslims, and 'the people' means the rest of the people, i.e. the religious minorities.

Of course some might interpret this to mean that since the majority would have the deciding vote on the constitution (and since in this case the majority would be Muslim), the minorities' rights would be in danger of being compromised. Incidentally, having made clear that Pakistan was not being sought for the interests of landlords, Jinnah was equally anxious to assure the minorities that they had nothing to fear in a territory which, it was assumed, would be under the rule of Islam. Hence he continued:

> The only question is that of minorities. The minorities are entitled to get a definite assurance and ask: "*Where do we stand in the Pakistan that you visualise?*" [91] That is an issue of giving a definite and clear assurance to the minorities. We have done it. We have passed a resolution [i.e. Lahore Resolution] that the minorities must be protected and safeguarded to the fullest extent and as I said before any civilised government will do it and ought to do it. So far as we are concerned our own history, *our Prophet has given the clearest proof* that non-Muslims have been treated not only justly and fairly *but generously.* [92]

This statement is consistent with another that he had made a couple of months earlier, and which is worth repeating:

> In Pakistan we shall have a state which will be run according to the principles of Islam. It will have its cultural, political and economic structure based on the principles of Islam. The non-Muslims need not fear because of this, for fullest justice will be done to them, they will have their full cultural, religious, political and economic rights safeguarded. As a matter of fact they will be

---

89 Ibid. p.59

90 Jinnah mentioned the '*millat* and the people' together to ensure that everyone understood that the non-Muslim minorities were included as having a voice alongside the Muslims. He evidently wanted to prevent confusion amongst those who use the term *millat* or *ummah* to refer exclusively to Muslims.

91 Quotation marks in original. Emphasis mine.

92 Presidential Address at the ML Annual Session, Delhi, 24 April 1943. (NV Vol. III, p.201)

> more safeguarded than in the present day so-called democratic parliamentary form of Government. [93]

We also have an example from just a few months before partition:

> We assure the Hindus that in Pakistan the minorities will be treated justly, fairly, and generously. ... You may rest assured that you will be safer under our system of government than you will under a Government which is based on one man rule. If it is good it is Islam and if it is bad it is not Islam. Islam is Justice. [94]

Whenever Jinnah spoke of Pakistan's Islamic character, we find that he always laid any notions of religious discrimination to rest immediately, by reminding those present that Muslim society was duty-bound, taking its lesson from the Prophet of Islam no less, to treat its minorities 'not only justly and fairly *but generously*'.

Myth no. 5: Jinnah's speech of 11 August 1947 was the 'clearest exposition of a secular state', since Jinnah advocates the protection of the minorities. (M. Munir 1980, p.29)

We have seen in the previous myth that Jinnah stressed the importance of minority rights as a matter of Muslim duty. The speech of 11 August is famous for the fact that it was made extempore, without notes. Writers from all camps have noted that Jinnah words were spontaneous and spoken from the heart. [95] Pro-secularist commentators have stated that in this speech he revealed his preference for a 'secular' Pakistan. They quote the 11 August speech primarily because of the following statements (the following passage is taken from Munir's book):

> You may belong to any religion or caste or creed – that has nothing to do with the business of the State (Hear, hear). ...We are starting in the days when there is no discrimination, no distinction between one community and another, no discrimination between one caste or creed or another. We are starting with this fundamental principle that we are all citizens and equal citizens of one State (Loud Applause).

---

93 Address at the Hostel Parliament of Ismail Yusuf College, Jogeshwari (Bombay), 1 February 1943. (M.A. Harris (ed.) 1976, p.173)

94 Speech at a reception given by the Memon Chamber of Commerce, Bombay, 27 March 1947. (Yusufi Vol. IV, p. 2538)

95 Bolitho contradicts this by claiming that Jinnah worked 'for many hours' on the speech (Bolitho 1954, p.197). Jinnah's speech itself however is self-evidently delivered extempore ('I cannot make any well-considered pronouncement at this moment, but I shall say a few things as they occur to me'; NV Vol. VI p.360), and so Bolitho's information is incorrect here.

> ... Now I think you should keep that in front of us as our ideal, and you will find that in [the] course of time Hindus would cease to be Hindus and Muslims would cease to be Muslims, not in the religious sense, because that is the personal faith of each individual but in the political sense as citizens of the State. [96]

In fact Jinnah made this statement because in the past history of many countries the religious majority has discriminated against other religions and minorities. The same is true of some countries even today:

> As you know, history shows that in England conditions, some time ago, were much worse than those prevailing in India today. The Roman Catholics and Protestants persecuted each other. Even now there are some States in existence where there are discriminations made and bars imposed against a particular class.
>
> ... Today, you might say with justice that Roman Catholics and Protestants do not exist; what exists now is that every man is a citizen, an equal citizen of Great Britain and they are all members of the Nation. [97]

He spoke of the dangers of sectarian discrimination, and this of course is the known history behind the development of the secular state which is designed primarily to prevent sectarian tyranny. However, whilst today's secular states may or may not enforce the principle of universal civil rights, in a systemic expression of Islam the enforcement of this principle is mandatory, since it is a core principle of the Quran. A bona fide 'Islamic state' is duty bound to protect the rights of all human beings, whatever their colour, caste or creed:

> We have conferred dignity [98] on the children of Adam[99] (17:70) [100]

Obviously, if it fails to uphold universal human rights, then the state is not Islamic, no matter what it calls itself.

As an aside, one Pakistani historian has recently reviewed the reference to English history in more detail, and concluded that there may be more to Jinnah's words here than anyone from any camp has ever noticed before. Iqbal scholar Khurram Ali Shafique writes:

---

96 Presidential Address to the Constituent Assembly of Pakistan, Karachi, 11 August 1947 (as quoted by Munir 1980, p.30). Quotation marks in the original text have been omitted here.

97 Same address, CAP Debates Vol. I No. 2, p.20

98 'Conferred dignity', i.e. they are worthy of respect by virtue of being human.

99 The 'children of Adam' means obviously 'humankind' and therefore means all human beings regardless of religious persuasion.

100 Muhammad Asad's translation.

> … both the liberals and the conservatives in Pakistan have been missing the main point of the Quaid's famous speech … It is usually overlooked that the speech of the Quaid emphasizes a vision for the future that is to be achieved *gradually*: 'in course of time Hindus would cease to be Hindus and Muslims would cease to be Muslims,' etc. [101]

Shafique makes an intriguing observation: The secularisation of England necessarily began with the implementation of laws expressly designed to prevent certain communities – namely Catholics (and also Jews and atheists) – from entering government service. Jinnah's speech, Shafique shows, was referring to the fact that:

> (a) the Roman Catholics and the Protestants used to persecute each other; (b) then they began to discharge the duties imposed on them by the government of their country and 'went through that fire'; (c) now, they are equal citizens of Great Britain. [102]

These laws, he notes, were not fully repealed until more than 200 years later, when circumstances had changed and there was greater affinity between the two Christian denominations. Shafique argues that such *seemingly* discriminatory measures were part of a gradual process:

> Hence, it seems wrong to presume that the Quaid was promising on August 11 that discriminatory laws would never be passed in Pakistan because the example he chose from history was of a people who obeyed their government even when its commands appeared to be discriminatory. The Quaid was actually promising that *if* the citizens of Pakistan do this, as the citizens did in Britain, they too would become a nation of equal citizens 'in course of time'. The British, according to the Quaid, faced these 'realities of the situation' and succeeded in transcending them only because they 'had to discharge the responsibilities and burdens placed upon them by the government of their country and they went through that fire step by step.' … [103]

(In the context of Pakistan, 'discriminatory' laws might have included, in Jinnah's time, the decision to retain the Muslim League's policy of

---

[101] K.A. Shafique, 'What the Quaid said on August 11, 1947, and how it has been distorted' at *Marghdeen* blog, 9 August 2016. http://marghdeen.com/what-the-quaid-said-on-august-11-1947-and-how-it-has-been-distorted/ (Last accessed 11 August 2016). Emphasis mine.

[102] Ibid.

[103] Ibid. Emphasis in original.

only allowing Muslims in its membership, which was denounced by its critics as communal.[104])

Shafique finally remarks that the two poles of thought in Pakistan have evidently 'pushed us back' to the point similar to when the Roman Catholics and Protestants persecuted each other, and asks when Pakistanis will come to 'respect the law, irrespective of one's political views or religious beliefs.'[105]

Exactly what then, in Jinnah's mind, was to come in the 'course of time'? He may have referred to the history of Europe, but this does not automatically mean that he was inspired by dualist secularism. Looking at his speeches in toto, we can safely say that it was the Quranic principle that inspired his call for toleration and equality. Even in his pre-partition speeches he had linked so-called secular or humanist principles e.g. 'fairplay' and 'justice' with Islam on numerous occasions:

> The acid test of success of any government of a representative character is that the minorities must feel that they will have *fairplay and justice*. ... I am confident that when the time comes, the minorities in our homelands will find that with our traditions, and our heritage and *the teachings of Islam, not only shall we be fair and just to them but generous*. ... We believe in action, we believe in statesmanship and in practical politics.[106]

The words 'justice' and 'fairplay' are in fact the English equivalents of the Quranic words *adl* (justice) and *ihsan* (indemnification):

---

104 On 14 and 15 December 1947 the All-India Muslim League held a Council Session in which it was resolved that the party would now be split into two, with one being renamed as the Pakistan Muslim League, while the other of the original name remained in India. While most Council members supported it, Suhrawardy objected to the split for the reason that he thought not enough had yet been done to protect minorities on both sides of the divide. He also wanted the League to now admit non-Muslim members 'on a national basis' rather than a communal one. Another Leaguer wanted to remove the word 'Muslim' from the resolution on the grounds that Pakistan was not Islamic enough to merit being called a 'Muslim state'. Some have claimed that Jinnah too was open to the idea of a non-communal League, but if this is true, it seems he made no attempt to convince his colleagues as such. Instead he responded to both objections – one secular, the other religious – by reminding the Council on 15 December that Pakistan was to be a 'Muslim state based on Islamic ideals' and not an 'ecclesiastical state' since in Islam there is 'no discrimination as far as citizenship is concerned'. He also expressed his hope that the All-India Muslim League would not dissolve but continue its vital work of protecting Muslim rights in India (which it did; the Indian Union Muslim League exists even today and it serves Muslim and non-Muslim minorities alike). In the end the Council voted overwhelmingly in favour of the resolution to create a separate 'Pakistan Muslim League'. (Details obtained from the proceedings of the AIML Council meeting at Karachi, 14-15 December 1947; as reproduced in NV Vol. VII, p.495-504).

105 Ibid.

106 Presidential address at the ML Annual Session, Madras, 14 April 1941. (Yusufi Vol. III, p.1386) For another example, see Presidential address delivered at the ML Annual Session, Delhi, 24 April 1943 as reviewed in Myth no. 4.

> Allah enjoins justice and kindness, and giving [107] to kinsfolk (16:90) [108]

Here again Jinnah refers to Islamic teachings as his inspiration for the treatment of non-Muslim citizens:

> The great majority of us are Muslims. We follow the teachings of the Prophet Muhammad (peace be upon him). We are members of the brotherhood of Islam in which all are equal in rights, dignity and self-respect. *Consequently, we have a special and a very deep sense of unity.* But make no mistake: Pakistan is not a theocracy or anything like it. *Islam demands from us the tolerance of other creeds* and we welcome in closest association with us all those who, of whatever creed, are themselves willing and ready to play their part as true and loyal citizens of Pakistan. [109]

Jinnah has spoken out against theocracy and reminded his audience that equality and tolerance are part and parcel of Islam. This passage is particularly significant since it is taken from a speech made well after partition, and well after 11 August 1947. Here is yet another example that Jinnah claimed to be inspired by Quranic rather than secular idealism. In 1943, the *Morning News* reported:

> 'As far as we are concerned,' Mr Jinnah said, 'we make this solemn declaration and give this solemn assurance that we will treat your minorities not only in a manner that a civilised government should treat them *but better because it is an injunction in the Quran to treat the minorities so.*' [110]

It seems rather inconceivable that someone who had taken his beliefs on human rights from Islam and the Rasool [111] would suddenly announce that he was a secularist. Furthermore, it is significant that neither the word 'secular' nor the phrase 'modern democratic state'

---

[107] See Chapter 14, subsection 'Socio-economic justice' for further information on *adl* and *ihsan*.

[108] Pickthall modernised.

[109] Broadcast talk to the people of Australia as Governor-General, 19 February, 1948. (NV Vol. VII, p.190)

[110] Address to the students of Ismail College, Bombay, 1st February 1943; as reported by *The Morning News*, 2 February 1943. (Ibid. Vol. III p.1674). Another version of the same speech reported in *Times of India* on 2 February 1943 reads: 'He was prepared to give a solemn assurance that the Muslims would treat the minorities even better than any other civilised Government treated their minorities, because that was the injunction of their highest religious authority – the QORAN.' See M.A. Harris (ed.) 1976, p.175. (Spellings and capitalisation retained from original)

[111] Rasool – word for Messenger of God; can be used for any prophet but is generally used to denote the final Prophet of Islam.

appears even once in any of his speeches on Pakistan. The speech of 11 August 1947 is no exception. It is only due to a confused understanding of secularism and Islam that so many have misconstrued it. The most controversial line in the whole speech is the one in which Jinnah said:

> … Hindus would cease to be Hindus, and Muslims would cease to be Muslims, not in the religious sense, because that is the personal faith of each individual, but in the political sense as citizens of the State. [112]

Some commentators believe that this is a secular statement because of an implied separation of religion from politics. However this is entirely untrue. For one thing, read the sentence properly and we find that Jinnah has not separated 'religion' from politics (i.e. in the sense of separating spiritual or Quranic law from politics). He has simply said that people would be equal irrespective of faith, [113] and indeed a *Dawn* editorial on the subject of the speech published shortly afterwards confirms this. [114]

It seems that Jinnah was also answering a statement made that day by Mr Kiran Sankar Roy, leader of the newly established Pakistan Congress Party. The *Pakistan Times* reported Mr Roy's speech as follows:

> Speaking about the minorities, Mr Roy said that if Pakistan meant a secular democratic state, a state which would make no difference between citizen and citizen irrespective of caste, creed or community, he would assure him that he (Mr Jinnah) would have their utmost cooperation. [115]

Roy also admitted that he and his Congress colleagues were 'not very happy' about either the 'division of India' or the 'partition of the Punjab and Bengal', but they would 'accept the citizenship of Pakistan with all its implications'. [116] He was evidently seeking an assurance from Jinnah that Pakistan would be a state in which there would be no discrimination based on religion. It could also be that he was pushing for Jinnah to explicitly confirm that Pakistan would be a 'secular state'.

---

112 Presidential Address to the Constituent Assembly of Pakistan, Karachi, 11 August 1947. (CAP Debates Vol. I No. 2, p.20)

113 Prof. S.M. Burke, a Pakistani Christian commentator, has written: '[When the 11 August speech] is read with the Quaid's other pronouncements it becomes quite clear that he was recommending generous treatment to non-Muslims not as a commendable secular principle, but as a mandatory Islamic injunction' (S.M. Burke (ed.) 2002, lxi). See also our brief discussion of the *Misaq-i-Medina* in Chapter 12.

114 *Dawn* editorial, 'Perverse Propaganda', 26 August 1947, as cited in K. Sayeed 1968 (revised), p.255.

115 As reported in *Pakistan Times*, 13 August 1947 (NV Vol. VI, p.358-9 fn)

116 Ibid. p.359 fn. Roy (along with Suhrawardy, Abul Hashim and Sarat Chandra Bose) had been among those who had advocated a united and independent Bengal in the spring of 1947.

Jinnah did indeed assure all minorities of equality before the law, and this was enough to satisfy Roy and other non-Muslims. But Jinnah nevertheless did not say that Pakistan would be a 'secular democratic state'. He had always said that it would be an 'Islamic democracy', and he never moved from this position. To further understand this point requires a deeper understanding of a number of Quranic principles. There is insufficient room to discuss these in detail here, but in Chapter 12 we will review the principles of the Quran that help make sense of Jinnah's supposedly controversial words. In the meantime, it is worth noting how one biographer of the Quaid-i-Azam has interpreted the speech. In his *Jinnah: Creator of Pakistan*, Hector Bolitho produced Jinnah's passage above and commented:

> The words were Jinnah's: the thought and belief were an inheritance from the Prophet who had said, thirteen centuries before, 'All men are equal in the eyes of God. And your lives and your properties are all sacred: in no case should you attack each other's life and property. Today I trample under my feet all distinctions of caste, colour and nationality.' [117]

Bolitho here has quoted from the well-known final *khutba* (sermon) of the Rasool shortly before his death. Either this means we should accept the Prophet of Islam as a secularist, or this means we need to rethink what the Quran teaches about the treatment of fellow human beings socially, economically and politically.

Myth no. 6: Jinnah never used the words 'ideology of Pakistan'. In fact no one used the words until at least 1962. (M. Munir 1980, p.28; Nayyar & Salim (eds.) 2003, p.16-17[118])

Munir has played a semantics game to make a claim that is patently untrue. Jinnah may or may not have used the exact words 'ideology of Pakistan' in that precise order, but nevertheless he linked 'ideology' and Pakistan on a number of occasions, as we shall see shortly.

Munir also claims that for the first 'fifteen years after the establishment of Pakistan, the Ideology of Pakistan was not known to *anybody* until 1962 when a solitary member of the Jamaat-i-Islami for the first time used the words'. [119] The obvious implication here is that the phrase has been introduced by the religious element in Pakistan and should thus be treated with suspicion. However, once again the evidence belies the claims. Munir himself makes references to the book titled *Ideology of Pakistan* by Javid Iqbal, which, he does not seem to realise,

---

[117] H. Bolitho (1954) *Jinnah: Creator of Pakistan*. London: John Murray, p.197

[118] A.H. Nayyar & Ahmad Salim (eds.) (2003) *The Subtle Subversion: The State of Curricula and Textbooks in Pakistan* Islamabad: Sustainable Development Policy Institute

[119] Munir 1980, p.28. Emphasis mine.

was originally published in 1959.[120] Furthermore, in the introduction to his book Dr Iqbal has explained that in the 1950s President Muhammad Ayub Khan 'distributed a questionnaire among the intellectuals of the country so they could provide him with an answer as to what is the *Ideology of Pakistan*.'[121] Dr Iqbal's book therefore was written as a response to the questionnaire and its title was inspired by it.

For the sake of argument, we can also provide ample proof that references to the ideology of Pakistan appear on record not only before 1962 but also before partition:

> Of course there is no conflict between the policy of the League and Iqbal's ideal so far as *Pakistan ideology* [*sic*] is concerned.[122]

This line appears in the preface of the very first edition of the well-known book *Speeches and Statements of Iqbal*. The preface was written by the compiler, Latif Ahmad Sherwani, and dated May 1944.

Another instance, appearing in a diary entry by Colonel S. Shahid Hamid – the private secretary of Field Marshal Auchinleck[123] – dated 3 August 1947, describes a party at his house in New Delhi just two weeks before partition, which Jinnah and British guests attended. It reads:

> He [the Quaid] paid great tribute to the late Sir Syed Ahmed Khan who, he said, was the founder of the two nations theory. He said that the *ideology of Pakistan* must be preserved ...[124]

The Colonel's recollection of Jinnah's words is not in question here. It is sufficient for our purposes to note that he has used the words 'ideology of Pakistan' in his diary as early as 1947.[125]

For a third, we find the term 'Pakistan ideology' in F.K. Khan Durrani's *The Meaning of Pakistan*, and as with Sherwani above,

---

120 Munir makes it quite clear that he believes the book appeared for the first time in 1971 (op. cit. p.69).

121 Javid Iqbal (2005 reprint) *Ideology of Pakistan* Lahore: Sang-e-Meel Publications, p.7. Emphasis mine.

122 Sherwani (ed.) 2008, viii. Emphasis mine. Text has been corrected to conform to the original edition printed in 1944 (Lahore: Al-Manār Academy).

123 Field Marshal Claude John Eyre Auchinleck (1884-1981) was the last Commander-in-Chief in British India up to 1947.

124 Colonel S. Shahid Hamid's diary entry dated 3 August 1947 (Major-General S. Shahid Hamid (1993 reprint) *Disastrous Twilight: A Personal Record of the Partition of India*. London: Leo Cooper, p.219)

125 Still, for argument's sake we note that Jinnah did once say publicly: 'Pakistan not only means freedom and independence but the *Muslim ideology, which has to be preserved*, ...' (Message to the Frontier Muslim Students' Federation Conference, Peshawar, 15 June 1945; Yusufi Vol. III, p.2010). The style certainly matches that of the statement in the Colonel's diary.

'Pakistan ideology' to Durrani meant Iqbal's ideal as outlined in his Allahabad address. This book was also printed in 1944. [126]

In 1945, Raghib Ahsan, a Bihar-born Bengali Muslim Leaguer, wrote to Jinnah about preparations for the election campaign of 1945-6. He was particularly keen to stress the necessity of adopting, as he mentioned several times, the following two issues:

> ... (1) [the] Goal of Pakistan and (2) the Ideology of *Fikr-i-Islami* as the two planks of our appeal to the electorate. [127]

Ahsan added that he wanted the League to adopt *Fikr-i-Islami* or (as he also wrote) 'Islamic Ideology' as part of the membership pledge of the Bengal Muslim League to 'defeat the Communist threat to our Islamic solidarity and integrity'. [128] Jinnah, in his reply, acknowledged that these matters were 'very important', [129] and, as we have already seen, these two issues were indeed placed at the heart of the election. [130]

Fatima Jinnah, sister of the Quaid, has not only mentioned the 'ideology of Pakistan' as early as March 1954, [131] but in 1961 she has also spoken of 'Islamic ideology', and has even offered a definition:

> If you muster courage and go forward as quickly as you can, you can *build up the country on true Islamic ideology.*
>
> Now let us understand what Islamic ideology means. It means democracy, brotherhood, truthfulness and justice. These are the pillars of Islam. [132]

In May 1950, Columbia University awarded Liaquat Ali Khan an honorary doctorate in Law. After the award ceremony, Khan attended a dinner function at New York's Town Hall and made a speech, the following excerpts of which are relevant to our discussion:

> To us the 15th of August, 1947, was a great day. On that day we, the Muslims, had a double sense of freedom foreign rule had come to an end and *we had a country of our own where,* without fear of a dominating majority, we could hold our own opinions, worship God in our own way, speak our own language, follow our own customs and *pursue our own ideology* towards a fuller and richer life.

---

126 F. Durrani (1944) *The Meaning of Pakistan.* Lahore: Sh. Muhammad Ashraf, p.147

127 S.S. Pirzada (ed.) 1977, p.317-8.

128 Ibid.

129 Jinnah to Ahsan, 2 June 1945 (op. cit. p.318).

130 See Chapter 9, subsections 'The 1945 elections' and 'A unanimous declaration'.

131 Fatima Jinnah's speech at a public meeting, Dacca, March 1954 (Salahuddin Khan (ed.) (1976) *Speeches, Messages and Statements of Madr-i-Millat Mohtarama Fatima Jinnah (1948-1967)* Lahore: Research Society of Pakistan, p.70)

132 Speech at a function of Memon Jamaat, B.M.B School ground, Karachi, December 1961 (S. Khan (ed.) 1976, p.300)

> ... A question I am sometimes asked is what is the *ideology of Pakistan as a State*? I will try and tell you this in a few very simple but very clear words. We Muslims believe in God and His supreme sovereignty. ... We believe in democracy, that is, in fundamental human rights including the right of private ownership and the right of the people to be governed by their own freely chosen representatives. We believe in equal citizenship for all whether Muslims or non-Muslims, equality of opportunity, equality before law. We believe that each individual, man or woman, has the right to the fruit of his own labours. Lastly we believe that the fortunate amongst us whether in wealth or knowledge or physical fitness, have a moral responsibility towards those who have been unfortunate. These principles we call the Islamic way of life. You can call them by any name you like. [133]

Munir, by contrast, claims that the word 'ideology' is never used in connection with a country. [134] However an ordinary dictionary offers the following definition: 'Ideology – body of ideas and beliefs of a group, nation, etc'. [135]

Now see the context in which Jinnah used the word 'ideology' with reference to the Lahore Resolution in the following passage:

> In order that there should be no room left for misunderstanding and that no doubt should be left in the mind of any intelligent or sensible Indian – it does not matter to which class or community he belongs – let me clarify our position with regard to our goal. What is the goal of the All-India Muslim League? *What is its ideology and what its policy?* Let me tell you as clearly as I can possibly define it, that the goal of the All-India Muslim League is this: *We want the establishment of completely independent States* ... We do not want in any circumstances a constitution of an all-India character with one government at the centre. We will never agree to that. If we once agree to that, let me tell you, the Muslims will be absolutely wiped out of existence. ... It is not, as some people mix it up, a question of Muslims objecting to a government based on the brotherhood of man, as is often alleged by people who really do not understand what they are talking about when they talk of either democracy or Islam. [136]

---

133 Liaquat Ali Khan (1950) *Pakistan: The Heart of Asia (Speeches in the United States and Canada May and June 1950 by the Prime Minister of Pakistan)* Massachusetts: Harvard University Press, p.28, 32-33

134 Munir 1980, p.25

135 Collins Gem English Dictionary, HarperCollins (1992)

136 Presidential address at ML Annual Session, Madras, 14 April 1941. (Yusufi Vol. III, p.1384-5)

In the same speech, he repeated his point even more clearly:

> The ideology of the League is based on the fundamental principle that Muslim India is an independent nationality. … We are determined, and let there be no mistake about it, to establish the status of an *independent nation and an independent State* in this subcontinent.[137]

Jinnah clearly connected the word 'ideology' with the idea that the Muslims of India constituted a separate nation, i.e. the Two-Nation Theory. We find this acknowledged in a book written by a notable non-Muslim personality. The Untouchables' leader Dr B.R. Ambedkar wrote that 'the name Pakistan' expresses 'the ideology underlying the two-nation theory'.[138] Similarly, Hyderabad academic Dr Sayyed Abdul Latif, best known for his proposal for a constitutional scheme for India, sent a circular letter in May 1941 to certain Congress and Muslim League leaders, in which he wrote: 'there are two obstacles which we shall have to get over at all costs. One is the ideology which the Muslim League has developed aiming at the partition of the country; the other is the opposition to that ideology.'[139] All of these statements come some forty years before Munir claimed that the word is never connected with a country.

And on the subject of the Two-Nation Theory, what is the 'Muslim nation'? British writer Mr Beverley Nichols asked Jinnah this exact question before writing his famous book *Verdict on India.* The question and Jinnah's answer is worth keeping in mind:

> **SELF** When you say the Muslims are a Nation, are you thinking in terms of religion?
>
> **JINNAH** Partly, but by no means exclusively. *You must remember that Islam is not merely a religious doctrine but a realistic and practical Code of Conduct.*[140] I am thinking in terms of *life*,[141] of everything important in life.[142]

Jinnah has described Islam not as a religion but as a 'practical Code of Conduct'. This fits precisely with the description of the 'non-sectarian Muslim' (ignoring the fact of the tautology) who sees Islam as being not

---

137 Ibid. p.1386

138 B.R. Ambedkar (1946 edition) *Pakistan or Partition of India.* Bombay: Thacker & Co. Ltd., p.6.

139 Circular letter dated 15 May 1941, reproduced in S.A. Latif (1943) *The Pakistan Issue* Lahore: Sh. Muhammad Ashraf, p.104.

140 Emphasis mine.

141 Emphasis on the word 'life' is in original.

142 B. Nichols 1944, p.189-90.

a religion but an all-encompassing *deen*. Jinnah's answer thus echoes Iqbal's concept of the 'nation':

> Islam is more than a creed; it is also a community, a nation. [143]

To those who may be tempted to call Jinnah's statement mere rhetoric, we must note that Mr Nichols had not actually recorded it in the original interview. Before he printed his book, he sent Jinnah a typed draft of the interview for his approval. [144] The sentence in the quote above appearing in italics was not in the original draft. Jinnah inserted it himself in his own handwriting, and subsequently the amended draft was printed with the sentence included. This incident demonstrates the importance Jinnah gave to the point that Islam was more than a mere 'religious doctrine'.

Hopefully we can now also see why it was possible for Jinnah's peers to also say without any fear of self-contradiction that the Pakistan demand (and its 'ideology') was not about religion, but about Islam. Liaquat Ali Khan made such a statement in 1949, during the Objectives Resolution debate:

> You would remember, sir, that the Quaid-i-Azam and other leaders of the Muslim League always made unequivocal declarations that the Muslim demand for Pakistan was based upon the fact that the Muslims had a *way of life and a code of conduct*. They also reiterated the fact that *Islam is not merely a relationship between the individual and his God* ... It expects its followers to build up a society for the purpose of good life – as the Greeks would have called it, with this difference, that Islamic "good life" is essentially based upon *spiritual values*. [145]

(We have already seen how frequently Liaquat Ali Khan, amongst others, referred to the 'ideology' of Pakistan during the debates of 1949. [146] The word 'ideology' also appears in the BPC Report of 1954. [147])

Unfortunately, the attempts of religionists and despots [148] alike to 'Islamise' Pakistan within the confines of their limited vision have

---

143 'Islam as a Moral and Political Ideal' (Sherwani (ed.) 2008, p.114)

144 This draft with amendments and Mr Nichol's letter to Jinnah is reproduced in NV Vol. III, p.370

145 Liaquat Ali Khan, 7 March 1949. CAP Debates Vol. V No. 5, p.4. We have already shown the difference between a 'spiritual' (Islamic) personality and a non-spiritual personality in Chapter 6.

146 See Chapter 3, with reference to Liaquat Ali Khan, Sardar Nishtar and Mian Iftikhar-ud-Din.

147 BPC Report 1954, Chapter II (Directive Principles of State Policy), paragraph 8.

148 Binder has commented that whilst the ulema are frequently attacked for their conservatism and backwardness, they are nevertheless sought by those who wish to obtain the votes of the public. (Binder 1961, p.26)

caused immeasurable harm to the original Pakistan idea. The proof of this can be seen in Hoodbhoy and Nayyar's article reviewed earlier in this book. They have written that the phrase 'ideology of Pakistan' only became popular after 1977, with the commencement of Zia ul-Haq's 'Islamisation' programme which saw educational reforms designed to make the citizens of Pakistan more consciously religious, to integrate it with their national identity, and to therefore create a religious state. This necessitated a 'revised history'[149] of partition:

> The recasting of Pakistani history is an attempt to fundamentally redefine Pakistan and Pakistani society and to endow the nation with a historic destiny. Islam is the integrative ideology, its enforcement a divine duty. Viewed from this angle, it becomes essential to project the movement for Pakistan as the movement for an Islamic state, the creation of which became a historic inevitability with the first Muslim invasion of the subcontinent. The revised history of Pakistan uses much the same idiom, and the same concepts of Islamic state and of politics in Islam, as the *Jamaat-i-Islami*. Its wholesale dissemination through educational institutions demonstrates both the influence of the *Jamaat* on education as well as the confluence of interests and philosophy of military rulers and the *Jamaat*. [150]

We can see that the authors are mixing up religious sectarian thought with Islamic idealism and so they condemn the 'ideology of Pakistan' on erroneous grounds. Nevertheless it is fair to ask, as they did, whether the term or the sentiment 'ideology of Pakistan' was ever a popular idea before partition, and indeed whether Jinnah used the term. We have already provided evidence that it was a popular idea in the public imagination, but what about Jinnah?

We will return to this question, but first we must take a look at another well-known report edited by Prof. Nayyar, this time in collaboration with Ahmad Salim, an archivist and writer. Titled *The Subtle Subversion: A Report on Curricula and Textbooks in Pakistan,* [151] the report was produced in 2003 by the non-governmental organisation the Sustainable Development Policy Institute (SDPI), as part of a project calling for educational reform in Pakistan. This body has received international recognition as one of the top think tanks in South East Asia. [152] A number of educationists contributed to the SDPI report, highlighting the biases, inaccuracies, and cultural and religious

---

[149] P.A. Hoodbhoy & A.H. Nayyar 1985, p.176

[150] Ibid. (Emphases on *Jamaat* and *Jamaat-i-Islami* retained from original)

[151] For full reference, see footnote 118.

[152] The SDPI ranked 15th in the list of top think tanks in South East Asia and the Pacific, and 104th overall worldwide. See James G. McGann, (2016) '2015 Global Go To Think Tank Index Report'. Philadelphia: TTCSP Global Go To Think Tank Index Reports, Paper 10.

insensitivity of material in Pakistani textbooks. The report, along with other similar works produced by others at around that time, received much media and academic attention, which either directly or indirectly contributed towards significant changes to Pakistan's education syllabus in 2006. [153]

But however legitimate their criticisms of the 'falsehoods, distortions and omissions concerning [Pakistan's] national history'[154] in textbooks may have been, this does not detract from the fact that their report contains one or two significant inaccuracies of its own, owing in part to an uncritical dependency on Chief Justice Munir's writings. One example, which is pertinent to this myth, appears at the beginning of the report in a section summarising its contents:

> The curriculum as well as textbooks excessively emphasize the "Ideology of Pakistan" which is a post-independence construction devised to sanctify their politics of those political forces which were initially inimical to the creation of Pakistan.[155]

In the first chapter Prof. Nayyar offers the following proof:

> Many scholars have forcefully argued, with the help of historical record that the term Ideology of Pakistan is a construction that did not exist when Pakistan was created. Justice Munir has very clearly identified the first time when the phrase was coined. In his monograph *From Jinnah to Zia* he writes: ... [156]

---

153 Changes include the wholesale deletion of all communal references. The words 'Hindu' and 'non-Muslim' no longer appear, perhaps in an attempt to promote communal neutrality in a syllabus that still aims at the outset to 'promote an understanding of the ideology of Pakistan, the Muslim struggle for independence and endeavours for establishing a modern welfare Islamic state' (Ministry of Education (2006) National Curriculum for Pakistan Studies IX-X, 2006. Islamabad: Government of Pakistan, p.1). There is also a new emphasis on the 'economic deprivation' of Indian Muslims alongside the 'values of Islam' as the basis for 'ideology of Pakistan', while strangely, socioeconomic factors alone are to be considered for the evolution of the Two-Nation Theory (ibid. p.2). Another change, which received press attention at the time (see e.g. *Daily Times*, 7 December 2006 and *Dawn* editorial 9 December 2006), is a learning objective to 'trace the role of minorities in Pakistan with specific reference to Quaid-i-Azam's speech of 11 August 1947, defining their status' (op. cit. p.13). Prof. Nayyar would later complain that with these words the syllabus 'misses out completely on requiring children to understand Jinnah's statement in support of separating religion and state' (A.H. Nayyar, 'Stop Distorting Jinnah's Words' in *The Express Tribune*, 13 August 2013). Earlier, in October 2004, M.P. Bhandara had moved a resolution in Pakistan's National Assembly to have Jinnah's 11 August 1947 speech included in the country's curricula at all levels (see also a more detailed review of his political work in Appendix VII). On 23 March 2015, this was enacted in practice when the Sindh government announced its intention to include the speech in its provincial secondary education syllabus (Classes 8-10). See press coverage in *Dawn* and *The Express Tribune*, both 24 March 2015.

154 Op. cit. x

155 Nayyar & Salim (eds.) 2003, vi

156 Ibid. p.16

Having cited the passage from Munir's *From Jinnah to Zia* that is the subject of our myth, Prof. Nayyar adds:

> Thus the phrase Ideology of Pakistan had no historical basis in the Pakistan movement. ... Although – as Justice Munir has noted, with which any authority on the Quaid-i-Azam would agree – the Quaid never uttered the words Ideology of Pakistan, yet the curriculum documents insist that the students be taught that the Ideology of Pakistan was enunciated by the Quaid. ... Needless to say no textbook has ever been able to cite a single reference to Mr Jinnah using the term Ideology of Pakistan. [157]

In fact an honest authority on Jinnah would only agree that this is semantics. The real question is whether a single textbook has shown that Jinnah linked 'Islam' and 'Pakistan' to refer directly to the concept, regardless of the precise wording. We will return to this shortly.

At the end of Chapter 2 Nayyar explains what he sees as the fundamental issue with linking 'ideology' and 'Pakistan':

> The problem with stating that the Ideology of Pakistan was inherent in the founding premise of Pakistan is not just that it is historically untrue. An emphasis on it gives a message to non-Muslim Pakistanis that Pakistan is only for Muslims and that they do not have a place in it. [158]

This statement reveals a genuine fear of a state run by religious fundamentalists on the one side, and either a complete lack of knowledge of, or dismissal of, the actual position of Islam on theocracy and non-Muslim citizens on the other.

It also happens that the statement denying the historicity of Pakistan's 'ideology' is effectively contradicted by Ahmad Salim in Chapter 3 of the same report, where he acknowledges that in 1947 (when Jinnah was still alive) the first All-Pakistan Educational Conference recommended 'Islamic ideology as the basis of education'. [159] What Salim does not mention is Jinnah's message to this inaugural conference, which is important to note, and the main part of which we are quoting in full:

> You know that the importance of education and the right type of education, cannot be over-emphasised. Under foreign rule for over a century, sufficient attention has not been paid to the education of our people and if we are to make real, speedy and substantial progress, we must earnestly tackle this question and

---

[157] Ibid. p.16-17

[158] Ibid. p.19

[159] Ibid. p.66

> bring our educational policy and programme on the lines suited to the genius of our people, consonant with our history and culture, and having regard to the modern conditions and vast developments that have taken place all over the world.
>
> There is no doubt that the future of our State will and must greatly depend upon the type of education we give to our children, and the way in which we bring them up as future citizens of Pakistan. Education docs not merely mean academic education. There is [an] immediate and urgent need for giving scientific and technical education to our people in order to build up our future economic life and to see that our people take to science, commerce, trade and particularly well-planned industries. We should not forget that we have to compete with the world which is moving very fast in this direction.
>
> At the same time we have to build up the character of our future generation. We should try, by sound education, to instil into them the highest sense of honour, integrity, responsibility and self-less Service [*sic*] to the nation. We have to see that they are fully qualified and equipped to play their part in the various branches of national life in a manner which will do honour to Pakistan. [160]

We already know that by 'the genius of our people', and 'our history and culture', Jinnah can only mean that of Muslims. His language use here echoes that of his presidential speech at the Lahore Session in March 1940. There he had also asked Muslim intelligentsia to 'come forward as servants of Islam' and 'organise the people economically, socially, educationally and politically'. [161] The resolution of the All-Pakistan Educational Conference does not conflict with his message.

The SDPI report emphasises that Jinnah envisioned a 'secular Pakistan' reflecting 'his highly liberal, democratic and tolerant worldview'. [162] Unfortunately, since the authors are focused entirely on criticising the 'exclusionary and sectarian worldview' of fundamentalist schooling, [163] this prevents them from even mooting the possibility of a 'Muslim Jinnah'. Indeed, the word 'modernist' appears just once in the whole report, and neither is it explained what this word means, nor whom it represents. [164] Subsequently, instead of seeking out moderate

---

[160] Quaid-i-Azam's Message to the Pakistan Educational Conference, 27 November 1947. (Ministry of the Interior/Education Division (1983 reprint) *Proceedings of the Pakistan Educational Conference, Held at Karachi, from 27th November to 1st December 1947*. Islamabad: Government of Pakistan, p.5)

[161] NV Vol. I, p.495 (Emphasis mine). See Presidential address at the ML Annual Session, Lahore, 22 March 1940, (Ibid. p.494-5 as cited in Myth no. 2.)

[162] Op.cit. p.76

[163] Ibid. p.1

[164] The word appears in Chapter 3 by Ahmad Salim: 'The textbooks during Ayub era, however, were a balance between traditionalists and modernists.' (Op.cit. p.66.)

and modernist educationists for transparent dialogue, the authors of the report merely push in the other fundamentalist direction, with the predictable outcome (to borrow Syed Ahmad Jaffar's words, again from the same report) that educational reforms continue to '[oscillate] between liberal and conservative approaches' and produce 'conflicting themes' in the 'same syllabus'.[165] Note that a decade after the publication of the report, the same authors are now lamenting the reintroduction of education material that counters the 2006 reforms they had championed.[166] In short, the education syllabus suffers from the same conflicts that appeared in the BPC Report of 'compromises' in 1954, and it should hardly surprise us to find that the human causes of these conflicts are also the very same.

Returning now to the question at hand, it is true that Jinnah made relatively few references to ideology, probably for the reason that the word 'ideology' had become negatively associated with fascism by the 1940s.[167] At any rate the Quaid-i-Azam preferred to use other terms for what he was describing, and 'ideal' in particular (as did Iqbal). As he once said of the philosopher's aims:

> Although a great poet and philosopher, he was no less a practical politician. With his firm conviction and faith in the ideals of Islam, he was one of the few who originally thought over the feasibility of carving out of India an *Islamic state* in the north-west and north-east zones which are the historical homeland of the Muslims. ... [I] pray that we may live up to the ideals preached by our national poet so that we may be able to give shape to these ideals in our sovereign state of Pakistan when established.[168]

Moreover, it could also be said that 'ideology' is not a wholly appropriate term, as more often than not it represents a crystallisation of ideas, whereas Islam emphasises adaptability to changing conditions. This would probably explain why Iqbal never used the word, to the best of my knowledge.[169] Simply by flicking through Jinnah's speeches, we

---

165 Ibid. p.111.

166 See Azhar Hussain, Ahmad Salim et al. (2011) *Connecting the Dots: Education and Religious Discrimination in Pakistan. A Study of Public Schools and Madrassas* Washington: United States Commission on International Religious Freedom, p.49; and A. H. Nayyar (2013) *A Missed Opportunity: Continuing Flaws in the New Curriculum and Textbooks After Reforms* Islamabad: Jinnah Institute, p.43.

167 See for example Jinnah's statement in reply to Gandhi's appeal regarding an article published in *Dawn*, New Delhi, 11 March 1942 (Yusufi Vol. III, p.1537-8). Here he quoted a statement made by Dr Ambedkar on 25 February 1942: 'The Congress chooses to forget that Hinduism is a political ideology of the same character as the Fascist or Nazi ideology and is thoroughly anti-democratic.'

168 Tribute to Iqbal, Lahore, 9 December 1944. (NV Vol. IV, p.24-5)

169 Dr Sheila McDonough has commented on the same point: 'It has not generally been understood that Iqbal never used the words *ideology*, or *identity*. He did not use these words,

can find numerous instances of the word 'ideal' in connection with Pakistan:

> 'We want to live and let live according to *our own ideals*, aspirations and mode of life,' said Mr Jinnah adding, '*that is our Pakistan*.' [170]

> You have asked me to give you a message. What message can I give you? *We have got the greatest message in the Quran for our guidance and enlightenment. … Let us work up to that great ideal. …* Let us forego our personal interests and convenience for the collective good of our people and for a *higher and nobler cause. Pakistan aims at it* and if we stand united, organised and faithful to our cause, the time is not far off when we shall achieve our goal and prove ourselves worthy of our wonderful and glorious past. [171]

This is an unambiguous description of the 'great ideal' that 'Pakistan aims at'. It is an ideal taken from the Quran.

> Mussalmans must assert themselves in this country and outside and although our enemies with the help of a few selfish Muslims are carrying on enormous false propaganda against us, yet, I am sure, that no power on earth can resist the onward rush of 90 millions who [are] determined to materialise their *ideal of Pakistan* and to stand united on a soil which they can call and claim as their own homelands. [172]

> … may God Almighty grant us and all those who have undertaken to serve it, strength to construct and build Pakistan and make it a great country and [*sic*] realise *our ideal* that we shall make it one of the greatest nations of the world. [173]

---

nor did he think in this way. Poets are the most precise of all humans in their use of words. They mean what they say, and they choose their words carefully.' (S. McDonough 2002, p.210. Emphasis in original.). Even in a recent study that is devoted in part to exploring Iqbal's view of Islam as 'ideology', we find not one quote of Iqbal in which he uses this word; and indeed its author implicitly acknowledges this when he remarks that Iqbal described 'Islam as a social *nizam* (order)'. (See Iqbal Singh Sevea (2012) *The Political Philosophy of Muhammad Iqbal: Islam and Nationalism in Late Colonial India* New York: Cambridge University Press, p.113)

[170] Interview to Fraser Wighton, Reuters' Special Correspondent, New Delhi, 30 March 1946. (Yusufi Vol. IV p.2261)

[171] Message to NWFP Muslim Students Federation, 4 April 1943. (Yusufi Vol. III p.1687)

[172] Message to the Bohra Students of Karachi, Bombay, 14 January 1941 (Yusufi Vol. II, p.1312)

[173] Message to *Dawn*, Karachi, 12 August 1947 (Yusufi Vol. IV p.2606)

> All I require of you now is that every one of us to whom this message reaches must vow to himself and be prepared to sacrifice his all, if necessary, in building up *Pakistan as a bulwark of Islam* and as one of the greatest nations whose *ideal is peace* within and peace without.[174]

> Let it be clear that Pakistan is going to be a Muslim State based on *Islamic Ideals.*[175]

And finally, we do also have a few direct references to 'ideology' and Pakistan from Jinnah. The first, incidentally, is addressed to Western audiences in the United Kingdom and America:

> Our scheme of division of India gives Hindus three-fourths of the country and the Muslims the remaining one quarter of India, thereby giving the two nations scope and opportunity to develop in accordance with *their own culture and ideology*, so as to contribute to the peace and advancement of the world as a whole.[176]

Let it never be said that Jinnah tuned his speeches to suit different audiences. In all our examples, including the above as well as those below, Jinnah also reveals the ethical source of this 'ideology', whilst also linking it directly to Pakistan:

> … you must work and work hard [*sic*] and make the Muslim League still stronger. By doing so you will contribute substantially not only to the honour of the crores[177] of Muslims but to the crystallisation of a free Muslim state of Pakistan where Muslims will be able to offer the *ideology of Islamic rule.*[178]

> Pakistan *not only* means freedom and independence but the *Muslim ideology*, which has to be preserved, which has come to us as a precious gift and treasure and which, we hope, others will share with us.[179]

---

174 Public address at University Stadium, Lahore, 30 October 1947. NV Vol. VII p.96. Emphasis mine.

175 Speech at the Meeting of the All-India Muslim League Council, Karachi, December 14-15 1947; as reported by *The Daily Gazette*, 16th December 1947. (Ibid. p.2656)

176 Jinnah's tape-recorded interview to the BBC, London, 13 December 1946 (NV Vol. V, p.476). The same message was broadcast to the American people through the American Broadcasting Corporation (ABC) on the same day. (See Yusufi Vol. IV, p.2475-6)

177 *Crore* – Hindi word for 10 million.

178 Speech at a public meeting, Mardan, 24 November 1945 (Yusufi Vol. III p.2118)

179 Message to the Frontier Muslim Students' Federation Conference, Peshawar, 15 June 1945 (Yusufi Vol. III, p.2010)

Myth no. 7: Jinnah's stance against theocracy proves that he was a secularist. (M. Munir 1980, p.32)

This is based upon a misconception regarding a state run on Islamic principles versus a theocracy as it is generally understood. Theocracy is not actually possible in Islam because it negates the Quranic principle of human equality (or civil equity) (17:70, 49:13). The Quran states:

> It is not (possible) for *any human being* to whom Allah had given the Scripture and wisdom and the prophethood that he should afterwards have said to mankind: Be slaves of me instead of Allah. (3:79) [180] (emphasis mine)

To clarify the meaning of this verse: The verse is referring specifically to Jesus within the context of this particular surah. A 'man to whom is given the Book, and Wisdom' of course refers to Jesus' position of having been given the divine law and the responsibility to judge in the affairs of people in light of this law (hence 'wisdom' [181]). However, in today's context, the same principle can apply to anyone in a government committed to Islam. 'The prophethood' of course refers to a man decreed a Messenger. [182] In context of this verse, 'Be slaves of me' is actually a reference to service, or obedience, and not worship. In Arabic usage, although the word *ibadat* does mean 'worship' as well as 'service' and 'obedience', *ibadat* in the sense of 'worship' is restricted to deities and the devil, i.e. supernatural entities. [183] In grammatical terms it never means 'worship' with reference to human beings. Thus in the above verse, in which a human authority is explicitly mentioned, *ibadat* obviously translates not as 'worship' but as 'service' in the sense of 'obedience'. The verse can thus be accurately translated as 'Be servants of me', as Dr Shabbir Ahmed has done. [184] The Quran asserts that no human being, whether a civilian, a government official, or even a Messenger (3:161), has the right to mix and enforce his or her own concepts of legislation that are contrary in spirit to its teachings. This

---

[180] Pickthall modernised.

[181] Asad translates the Arabic word *hukm* as 'sound judgment', which is a literal translation, rather than Ali's word 'Wisdom' (which is actually a translation of *hikmah*; see also Asad's commentary for verse 3:79). This makes it clearer that the word is a reference to having decision-making authority, e.g. as a governmental official or in a court of law. Likewise Bakhtiar has translated the word as 'critical judgment'.

[182] A. Yusuf Ali uses the term 'prophetic office'.

[183] Lane, Book I (Part 5) p.1934: 'the verb is used in these senses [religious service or worship] only when the object is God, or a false god, or the Devil.'

[184] See Dr Shabbir Ahmed's translation of verse 3:79. Likewise Bakhtiar has also used the word 'servants'. While Asad and Ali use the word 'worshippers', in light of the rest of the verse referring to the power of judgement as well as the Book and the prophethood, this is obviously not the best word, as it implies ritual service. 'Servant' is more in line with the essentially juristic tone of the verse.

principle, together with the declaration of human equality in verse 17:70, removes any possibility of discrimination against anyone living in a bona fide 'Islamic state'. Furthermore, when all the citizens – Muslim and non-Muslim alike– become law-abiding citizens [185] of a Quranic constitution, the age-old concept of rulers and subjects is eliminated. This is why Jinnah said:

> Islam is not only a set of rituals, traditions and spiritual doctrines. Islam is also a code for every Muslim which regulates his life and his conduct in even politics and economics and the like. It is based on the highest principles of honour, integrity, fairplay and justice for all. *One God* and the *equality of manhood* is one of the fundamental principles of Islam. [186]

Now consider the following analysis. Answer the following questions truthfully and we can only draw one conclusion:

- Is this a secular statement? No: Jinnah spoke of Islam as a 'code' regulating politics and economics.
- Is this a theocratic statement? No: in theocracy not all people are equal before the law.
- Is it an Islamic statement? Yes: Jinnah took his inspiration from the Quran (3:79, 17:70). Also note that the latter sentence I have emphasised contains a clear reference to *tauheed.*

Now let us analyse the following passage, bearing in mind the same three questions. Note that this is taken from a press conference in July 1947, barely a month before Jinnah's famous so-called 'secular' speech of 11 August. The questions and answers read as follows:

> **Question:** Will Pakistan be a secular or theocratic state?
>
> **Mr Jinnah:** You are asking me a question that is absurd. I do not know what a theocratic state means.
>
> A correspondent suggested that a theocratic state meant a state where only a people of a particular religion, for example, Muslims, could be full citizens and non-Muslims would not be full citizens.
>
> **Mr Jinnah:** Then it seems to me that what I have already stated is like throwing water on a duck's back (Laughter). For goodness sake, get out of your head the nonsense that is being talked about. What this theocratic state means I do not understand.

---

185 For a detailed explanation see Chapter 12.

186 Address to the Bar Association, Karachi, on the Holy Prophet's birthday, Karachi, 25 January 1948 (Yusufi Vol. IV p.2670).

> Another correspondent suggested that the questioner meant a state run by Maulanas.[187]
>
> **Mr Jinnah:** What about the Government run by pandits[188] in Hindustan? (Laughter) 'When you talk of democracy', Mr Jinnah went on, 'I'm afraid *you have not studied Islam.* We learnt democracy thirteen centuries years ago.'[189]

(In mentioning 'pandits', Jinnah was evidently taking a jab at Pandit Nehru.)

Some pro-secularist commentators claim that Jinnah did not technically either confirm or deny that Pakistan would be secular in the above interview – that he avoided answering the question.[190] But according to a report in the *Hindustan Times* printed the next day, this is not the case at all:

> Mr Jinnah evaded many important questions by describing them as either 'foolish' or 'unnecessary'. … A barrage of questions was however shot at Mr Jinnah by correspondents keen to know what the state of Pakistan was going to be like. The Governor-General-designate of Pakistan got up from his chair and telling the correspondents that they had no more useful questions to ask walked out of the room. But before he left a correspondent asked him: 'I presume from what you have said, Mr Jinnah, that Pakistan will be a *modern democratic state.*' Mr Jinnah quickly replied: 'When did I ever say that? *I never said anything to that effect.*'[191]

It is true that the *Hindustan Times* was a pro-Congress paper and thus liable to contain biased coverage of Jinnah's activities, but it is equally true that Jinnah never used the words 'modern democratic state' to describe Pakistan. The report is thus at least partly accurate.

Similarly Jinnah never tried to enforce his own ideas about the constitution on his people. He left it to them to make their decisions, in line with a certain Quranic directive:

---

187 The version of this press conference that I have cited differs slightly in different compilations. In another book of speeches in my possession, Jinnah's comment implying that India was being run by the Hindu equivalent of 'maulanas' has been edited out (see M.A. Jinnah (2000) *Jinnah: Speeches and Statements 1947-1948*. Karachi: Oxford University Press, p.15). In this case, the text ends up reading: 'Then it seems to me that what I have already stated is like throwing water on a duck's back. When you talk of democracy, I'm afraid you have not studied Islam. We learnt democracy 1300 years ago.' The answers to two different questions have been combined into one.

188 Pandit – a religious scholar, usually a Brahmin.

189 Press conference, New Delhi, 13 July 1947 (NV Vol. VI, p.283-4)

190 See for example P.A. Hoodbhoy 2007, p.3301

191 *Hindustan Times*, 14 July 1947 (NV Vol. VI, p.276 fn)

> ... I have had one underlying principle in mind, the principle of *Muslim democracy*. It is my belief that our salvation lies in following the golden rules of conduct set for us by our great law-giver, the Prophet of Islam. Let us lay the foundation of our democracy on the basis of truly Islamic ideals and principles. *Our Almighty has taught us that "our decisions in the affairs of the State shall be guided by discussions and consultations".* [192]

Myth no. 8: All religious parties resisted the Pakistan movement because they held that the Muslim League sought a secular state. (Munir Report, p.201 [193] & M. Munir 1980, p.33; Hoodbhoy & Nayyar 1985, p.171; Nayyar & Salim (eds.) 2003, p.17)

The point raised here is that the religious parties were hypocritical in their political affiliations before and after partition. Pro-secularist commentators have often presented it as a challenge to anyone arguing for a 'religious' state. However it is erroneous to suggest that the religious parties opposed Pakistan simply because they held it would be secular. They were after all supporting a secular India. Many of them actually took a political stand and joined forces with the Congress in the name of Indian nationalism. This contradictory behaviour has not escaped the notice of all in the pro-secularist camp. Hoodbhoy & Nayyar have written:

> Since the movement for Pakistan was rooted in the social, cultural, and religious distinctions between Muslims and Hindus, one might logically expect that Muslim religious parties would have played a major, if not a leading, role in mobilising the Muslim masses. Paradoxically, aside from exceptions of no great importance, these parties had bitterly opposed Jinnah and the demand for Pakistan. [194]

The authors have noted further that the ulema opposed Pakistan on the grounds that 'nationalism was antithetical to Islam', yet at the same time some of these parties were 'aligned with the Congress' and fought for united India as Indian nationalists. However Hoodbhoy and Nayyar have not provided any explanation for the contradiction. One possibility

---

192 Speech at Sibi Durbar, Sibi, 14 February 1948. (Yusufi Vol. IV p.2682) Quotation marks in original. Jinnah here has made a reference to Quran verse 42:38.

193 Munir Report p.201: '...the parties who are now clamouring for the enforcement of the three demands [against the Ahmadis] on religious grounds were all against the idea of an Islamic State. Even Maulana Abul Ala Maudoodi of Jama'at-i-Islami was of the view that the form of Government in the new Muslim State, if it ever came into existence, could only be secular.'

194 Hoodbhoy & Nayyar (1985).

comes from the Muslim Leaguers themselves, who complained that during the provincial elections of 1936, ulema from the Jamiat-ul-Ulema-i-Hind (Ulema Party of India) and the Ahrars initially supported the League. It was only when it emerged that the League had scant funds that these ulema suddenly switched over to support Congress. [195]

Still, this isolated case does not explain the conduct of all the ulema, so now we are presented with the real crux of the matter. Either the ulema were all hypocrites or the reality was a little more complicated than first seems. It is true that their objection was to the Two-Nation Theory, because in their view the idea was mixing up Western notions of statehood and nationalism with Islamic brotherhood which is meant to transcend time and space. It is clear that most ulema actually objected to what they saw as synthesis and which was therefore harmful to the purity and integrity of Islam. (Other sectarian-minded Muslims of course were simply unable to comprehend the idea of a 'non-sectarian' Islamic state. They were convinced that Pakistan would inevitably have to follow the Shariah of one sect or other, and this was their reason for opposing the Pakistan demand. [196]) Whilst the universalistic ideal that the ulema were defending is not wrong in itself, they too had misunderstood the essence of the Two-Nation Theory. It was not simply about territorial nationalism or even simple communalism, but an idealism affecting every aspect of human existence. This is why we find that not only Muslims, but some Hindus also described India's problem as being about two nations – where 'nationality' meant a particular idealism. [197] Some militant Hindus in fact had been advocating Hindutva

---

195 See Jinnah's press statement in which he merely calls the switch in allegiance 'a mystery' (18 August 1938; NV Vol. I, p.266; also C. Khaliquzzaman 1961, p.156-8; and also K.S. Hasan 1992, v)

196 We see this reflected for example in the attitude of some Shia leaders. In July 1944 the President of the Shia Political Conference (Syed Ali Zaheer) wrote a lengthy letter to Jinnah asking him to 'elucidate and define the status of the Shias in the scheme of Pakistan'. Zaheer feared that Pakistan, if established as an Islamic state, would put the Shias' religious and political rights in danger. Jinnah gave a short reply to reiterate his stance that there was 'no need for the Shias to think that they will not be justly treated' and that it was a 'great disservice to the Muslim cause to create any kind of division between the Musalmans of India'. A few months later the Shia Political Conference spent two days deliberating over this correspondence, only to pass a resolution on 22 October stating that they found Jinnah's reply 'highly unsatisfactory'. (For correspondence and full text of this resolution see NV Vol. III, p.666-9). Similarly, on 25 December 1945 the All Parties Shia Conference passed a resolution opposing the Pakistan demand. The Conference believed that 'the establishment of Pakistan would ostensibly result in the establishment of the Hanafi Shariat [i.e. Sunni Islam] in that area, a Shariat which was fundamentally different from the Shariat Jaffri or Imamia law which was followed by the Shias'. (*Indian Annual Register*, Vol. II (1945), p.162)

197 In the Annual Session of the League in April 1943 Jinnah explained that even at the turn of the century when he was still a Congressite there was a 'section dreaming in terms if Hindu raj.' (NV Vol. III, p.182). He quoted from a book written in 1916 by the well-known Hindu leader, Bepin Chandra Pal, to demonstrate that Hindu nationalism had existed conceptually for a long time. The quote reads: 'National differentiation among us, therefore, have not been based upon territorial demarcations only or upon political or economic competitions and

based on a theory of two nations long before the Muslims demanded separation on the same basis. Hence the League claimed that Muslims could not even expect social, let alone political justice in a united India because the notion was inimical to the Hindu ideal. Hence Jinnah said as early as 1938:

> The Congress … want to impose Hindu Raj, culture and philosophy. It is against that mad *idealism* that I have rebelled since April 1936. [198]

Muslims were not the only ones making this claim. In his study of India, Mr Beverley Nichols observed:

> Hinduism in its most extreme and aggressive form is a living and turbulent force. Its voice rises above the roar of the factories and the workshops, it dominates the assemblies of politicians and students. … [In Hinduism, the] only thing which you *must* believe, with all your heart and soul, is the law of caste. You must believe that sixty million of your fellow men are 'untouchable'. You must believe that you are polluted if you eat certain foods and damned if you drink with certain people. Caste is the sheet anchor of the Hindu ship, which might otherwise have dashed itself to pieces on the rocks of sterner and more solid faiths. It seems hardly necessary to observe that it is the precise negation of democracy, for which the Hindus clamour so loudly. [199]

The League complained that a society steeped in a caste system could not sincerely implement a democracy which is supposed to operate on the principle of equality. Of course the Indian Muslims were hardly the paragons of unity, liberty and justice either; they too were (and continue to be) divided into tribal as well as sectarian classes, but this is another subject and so we will not go into it here. For now we should note that Jinnah did not have any issues with the Hindu community in general, but rather with an increasingly religious and influential

---

conflicts, but upon *differences of culture*. Under the Muslims we had, whether Hindus or Musalmans, one common government but that *did not destroy the integrity of Hindu culture*. … And that special character and culture is the very soul and essence of what we now understand as *nationalism*. This is by no means a political idea or ideal. It is something that touches every department of our collective life and activity.' (Ibid. Emphasis mine.)

198 Concluding address to the Muslim League Conference, Karachi, 12 October 1938. (Yusufi Vol. II, p.877). It is interesting that Jinnah has said that he has fought this idealism since April 1936. It was on 12 April 1936, the day that the League declared its intention to contest the provincial elections, that Jinnah used the word 'nation' for the first time: 'Muslims could arrive at a settlement with the Hindus as *two nations*, if not as *partners*'. See Chapter 1, subsection 'Testing Iqbal's nationalism' for details.

199 B. Nichols 1944, p.66, 68. Emphasis in original.

leadership within Congress. [200] He was strongly of the opinion that 'Congress does not represent not only the Mussalmans of India but even a large body of the Hindus, the Depressed Classes, the non-Brahmins and other minorities.' [201]

Iqbal had taken a similar view. As an intellectual, he had made the case for Islamic idealism even more clear. In discussing the need of 'Hindu India' to assert itself as a nation, he explained:

> We [Muslims] are 70 millions and far more homogeneous than any other people in India. Indeed the Muslims of India are the only Indian people who can fitly be described as a nation in the modern sense of the word. The Hindus, though ahead of us in almost all respects, have not yet been able to achieve the kind of homogeneity which is necessary for a nation, and which Islam has given you as a free gift. No doubt they are anxious to become a nation, but the process of becoming a nation is a kind of travail, and in the case of Hindu India, involves a complete overhauling of her social structure. [202]

His point was that the Hindu caste system had already put up 'social barriers' not only between Hindus and non-Hindus, but between Hindus and Hindus. Insofar as a nation demands homogeneousness, Iqbal further stressed that 'India is a continent of human groups belonging to different races ... even the Hindus do not form a homogeneous group'; [203] hence 'Hindu India' needed a 'complete overhauling of her social structure' to reach the status of nationhood. More importantly, he also made it clear that Islam creates 'no social barriers' between Muslims and non-Muslims. [204] Iqbal here provided yet another clue as to what constitutes 'Muslim nationalism'.

Returning to our original discussion, Jinnah also reached out to other minorities in India, including Parsis, Sikhs, Christians and the so-called 'Untouchable' and depressed Hindu classes, promising them full equality in Pakistan because the idea of class distinction or division is absolutely contrary to the spirit of Islam. The Quran itself recognises only two types of 'party' (or thought): One that 'allies with God and his Rasool' (i.e. follows the teachings of the Almighty as sent through His Prophet),

---

200 See for instance Jinnah's Presidential address at the Sind ML Conference, Karachi, 8 October 1939 (Yusufi Vol. II, p.865-6); Speech at a tea-party, Journalists' Association, Allahabad, 5 April 1942 (Yusufi Vol. III p.1559)

201 Press conference, New Delhi, 13 April 1942 (Yusufi Vol. III p.1561)

202 Iqbal's Allahabad address, December 1930 (Sherwani (ed.) 2008, p.26

203 Ibid. p.10

204 Ibid. p.26. Iqbal uses the term 'people of the Book' for non-Muslims. It may be added here that Muslim thinkers throughout history have usually concluded that most faiths carrying a Scripture – from Christianity, Judaism and Zoroastrianism, as well as Hinduism, have a root in Truth and so all have a claim to being amongst 'people of the book'.

and the other that does not. [205]

Munir has cited the Muslim scholar Abul A'la Maududi [206] as having written in 1946 that if Pakistan was established, then by virtue of its significant non-Muslim population it could only become a secular state. [207] Later, after a large portion of these non-Muslims migrated out of Pakistan, Maududi reportedly changed his position and said: 'now the conditions are different and we can have a purely Islamic State'. [208] Of course this does not alter the fact of the religious parties' early alignment with the All-India National Congress, the party representative of an even bigger Hindu population. However, once we consider every facet of the issue, we can begin to make sense of it. Here is a passage from the Munir Report that helps us put the matter into perspective:

> It has been repeatedly said before us that implicit in the demand for Pakistan was the demand for an Islamic State. Some speeches of important leaders who were striving for Pakistan undoubtedly lend themselves to this construction. These leaders while referring to an Islamic State or to a State governed by Islamic laws perhaps had in their minds the pattern of a legal structure based on or mixed up with Islamic dogma, personal law, ethics and institutions. No one who has given serious thought to the introduction of a religious State in Pakistan has failed to notice the tremendous difficulties with which any such scheme must be confronted. Even Dr Muhammad Iqbal, who must be considered to be the first thinker who conceived of the possibility of a consolidated North Western Indian Muslim State, in the course of his presidential address to the Muslim League in 1930 said:
>
> "Nor should the Hindus fear that the creation of autonomous Muslim States will mean the introduction of a kind of religious rule in such States. The principle that each group is entitled to free development on its own lines is not inspired by any feeling of narrow communalism".

---

205 See Quran 5:56 and 5:80. We will review this point and its implications for minorities in Chapter 12.

206 Abul A'la Maududi (1903-1979) was a Sunni theologian and founder of the party Jamaat-i-Islami (founded 1941). He opposed the League's version of the Pakistan demand (though not a separate Muslim state in itself), for reasons outlined shortly below. After partition he moved to the new country while the Jamaat-i-Islami decided to split in two, with one half remaining in India to continue its religious activities, and the other headed by Maududi in Pakistan. Today the Jamaat-i-Islami is a Pakistani political party and seeks to create an Islamic state.

207 Munir 1980 p.33, citing Maududi's article in *Tarjuman-ul-Quran*, February 1946.

208 Interview of Maududi during the Punjab Disturbances Inquiry, as cited in Munir 1980, p.33-4. The interview is from the record of proceedings; however the full text of this interview, though cited in Munir's *From Jinnah to Zia*, does not appear in the Munir Report.

> When we come to deal with the question of responsibility we shall have the occasion to point out that the most important of the parties who are now clamouring for the enforcement of the three demands on religious grounds were all against the idea of an Islamic State. Even Maulana Abul Ala Maudoodi of Jama'at-i-Islami was of the view that the form of Government in the new Muslim State, if it ever came into existence, could only be secular.[209]

In this passage the authors of the Report have acknowledged that 'implicit in the demand for Pakistan was the demand for an Islamic State', but they also imply that the only people presently demanding such a state are the ulema. They tentatively suggest that Pakistan as an 'Islamic state' was likely originally conceived as a 'legal structure based on or mixed up with Islamic dogma', i.e. a secular-Islam synthesis. They then quote Iqbal's Allahabad address of 1930 to show that at any rate the state was never meant to be 'religious'. (In light of our earlier discussion of *deen* as understood by Iqbal and Jinnah, comment is hardly necessary.) Finally, we have Maududi's singled-out statement on behalf of the religious elite saying that Pakistan was expected to become a secular state.

Now we can take the rest of the evidence into consideration. The Muslim Leaguers, as we have already seen, themselves claimed to be committed to an 'Islamic state' – i.e. one that was to be actively run on the principles of justice, fairplay, and solidarity (mark: *actively*). Not only Jinnah but other Leaguers spoke of Islamic democracy and Islamic social justice. We have also already noted the objection of the ulema to the 'territorial nationalism' of the Two-Nation Theory. This means that the ulema were in fact aware of the League's stated Islamic objectives, but simply didn't agree with them. In short, since the League was not a religious party, the ulema did not consider its views on Islam to be valid. At the same time, the ulema had long been considered the official custodians of Islam. They had the ability to sway much of Muslim public opinion. Knowing what the Muslim League was claiming to offer, namely an 'irreligious' Islamic state with a non-sectarian policy, the ulema almost certainly saw the idea as a threat to their own power.

Maududi's view is of significance here, given both his religious and political prominence later in Pakistan. Like most ulema he also treated the Pakistan idea of the League as being representative of a secular-Muslim synthesis view, which was practically the same as calling it simply a secular state; hence his argument that pro-Pakistan 'Muslim nationalists' could hardly be expected to create an 'Islamic' state. He viewed Jinnah and the League as secularists exploiting Islam in the

[209] Munir Report, p.201

pursuit of material ends. [210] Maududi believed it was futile for Indian Muslims to fight for separation if ultimately under the Muslim League's leadership the new state would be as 'irreligious' as a united India. For this reason he never formally joined or supported the Muslim League. At the same time however, he was equally disdainful of Husain Ahmad Madani and Abul Kalam Azad's [211] 'composite' Indian nationalism. [212] To borrow the words of political scientist Prof. Vali Nasr: 'Contrary to popular assertion, he was not opposed to Pakistan, but he objected to Jinnah and the Muslim League's conception of it.' [213] In this respect Maududi represents a minority view among the ulema, the majority of whom supported composite nationalism and objected to a separate Muslim state altogether.

Faced therefore, with a choice between a League that had proclaimed from every platform that it would give not an inch to theocracy, and a secular, 'composite nationalist' Congress which would not interfere with their religious leadership in India, it is perhaps not so surprising that we should find the greater number of ulema opting for the latter. (It should be added nonetheless that a smaller number of traditionalist ulema – most famously Shabbir Ahmad Usmani [214] – did actively lend their support to the Muslim League.)

In order to challenge the credibility of the League, the main line of attack the ulema adopted was to question the religiosity of its members. It is well known that most of the religious elite deemed anything 'Western', including education and language (i.e. English) as *haraam* (prohibited), and thus 'un-Islamic'. Anyone who actively pursued these

---

210 See A.A. Maududi (1939) *Musalman aur Maujuda Siyasi Kashmakash* (The Muslim and the Present Political Conflict) Pathankot: Tarujuman al-Quran, Vol. III p.25

211 Husain Ahmad Madani (1879–1957) was the head of the pro-Congress Jamiat Ulema-i-Hind. He was a staunch advocate of composite nationalism (meaning Hindu and Muslims as being part of a composite but politically united nation), and for this he received bitter religious criticism from Maududi. Abul Kalam Azad (1888-1958) was a leading Muslim member of the Congress and he vehemently opposed the Muslim League's claim to being the sole representative of the majority of Muslims. Like Madani he is best known for his advocacy of composite nationalism.

212 Later in Pakistan Maududi and his party the Jamaat-i-Islami modified their view and became 'gradualist', meaning that whereas before they considered themselves obliged to avoid participation in Pakistan's 'un-Islamic' political system, and advocate *jihad* as a revolutionary movement, after 1948 they aligned with some traditionalist politicians to introduce Islamic reforms more gradually. (See Aziz Ahmad (1967) *Islamic Modernism in India and Pakistan 1857-1964* Oxford: Oxford University Press, p.215-8)

213 V. Nasr (2000) *International Relations of an Islamist Movement: The Case of the Jama'at-i Islami of Pakistan* New York: Council on Foreign Relations, p.9.

214 Shabbir Ahmad Usmani (1887-1949), A Deoband scholar, founded the Jamiat Ulema-i-Islam in 1945 to campaign for Pakistan as well as to counter the pro-Congress Jamiat Ulema-i-Hind. Other pro-League ulema include Mufti Muhammad Shafi, Pir Jamaat Ali Shah, Zafar Ahmad Uthmani and Amin ul-Hasanat (also known as the Pir of Manki Sharif). For more examples, see K. M. Chaudhary and N. Irshad, 'The Role of Ulema and Mashaikh in the Pakistan Movement' in *Pakistan Journal of Life and Social Sciences* (2005), Vol. 3 (Nos. 1-2), p.33-36.

things was deemed a heretic.[215] The fact that many of the central members of the League were well educated, wrote and spoke good English, and were not 'practising Muslims',[216] was ample proof that they were not religious enough, and they were too 'westernised'. Scholars of every camp[217] have documented the anti-Western feeling amongst the religious elite. Jinnah himself remarked during a speech in which he criticised the 'undesirable elements' amongst the ulema, that if people took issue with the League members then they ought to join the League and make improvements rather than just complaining about it or joining forces with the Congress:

> The personnel of the League is far from being perfect. It is no use making allegations; it is no use telling me this man is bad or that man is undesirable. If you are really in earnest your only course is to join the League and make improvements.[218]

Yet the majority of the ulema rejected the invitation. After the establishment of Pakistan, they waited until Jinnah and his closest allies were out of the way before they entered the political arena to try and claim the country for themselves.

As we have already seen, pro-secularist commentators have been quick to point out the contradictory behaviour of the ulema. Looking again at Hoodbhoy and Nayyar's example, we can see that they mainly sought to emphasise that no 'devout' Muslim backed the Pakistan movement, and thus it had a lack of 'Islamic' representation. Yet they have ignored some powerful Muslim personalities of the Muslim League, such as the brothers Shaukat Muhammad Ali and Muhammad Ali Jouhar (known as the 'Ali brothers'), the underrated Islamic scholar Bahadur Yar Jung, and, of course, Muhammad Iqbal. These are just a few of the better known names, but there are many others, men and women, from before and during the Pakistan movement's formal existence. Some of them were qualified Islamic scholars, they all understood the essence of the Two-Nation Theory, and they all advocated the unity of Indian Muslims. Those who tried to interfere with this unity were naturally denounced by Jinnah and the League as traitors and fifth-columnists.

---

215 One such 'heretic' was Sir Syed Ahmad Khan (1817-1898), who incidentally also coined the term 'Two-Nation Theory'. He built Aligarh University – the first Muslim university in India – and ardently campaigned to ensure that more Muslims became educated, at a time when their educational standard lagged far behind that of other communities.

216 See A.S. Ahmed 1997, p.77, 196, 201-2; I. Ahmed, 2004, p.17

217 See for example A.S. Ahmed 1997, p.198-9; I. Ahmed 2004, p.17. For a detailed look at Maududi's religious criticisms of Jinnah and the League, see A.H. Syed 1982, p.27-38; A. Ahmad 1967, p.213-4

218 Speech at the meeting of the Muslim University Union, Aligarh, 5 February 1938 (Yusufi Vol. II p.727)

Myth no. 9: Jinnah merely wanted a homeland for the Muslims, not an Islamic state. (M. Munir 1980, p.140; Hoodbhoy & Nayyar 1985, p.168; H. Alavi 2001;[219] Nayyar & Salim 2003, p.76)

We need not reiterate the difference between an 'Islamic state' of the type that pro-secularists refer to, and the type described in this book. Suffice it to say that in light of the available evidence, the Pakistan idea was not merely about giving Muslims a homeland, but about giving Islam a space in which to revive them. Some of Jinnah's statements to the effect (that have caused discomfort for some secularists) include:

> There will be no Islam without the establishment of Pakistan.[220]

> ... if a Hindu Empire is achieved it will mean the end of Islam in India, and even in other Muslim countries.[221]

> Pakistan is not only a practicable goal but the only goal if you want to save Islam from complete annihilation in this country.[222]

> The only solution for the Muslims of India, which will stand the test of trial and time, is that India should be partitioned so that both the communities can develop freely and according to their own genius economically, socially, culturally and politically. The struggle is for the fullest opportunities and for the expression of the Muslim national will. *The vital contest in which we are engaged is not only for the material gain but also for the very existence of the soul of the Muslim nation.*[223]

In all of these examples Jinnah speaks of saving *Islam*, not merely the Muslims of India. Pro-secularist commentators rarely acknowledge these statements of Jinnah for the obvious reason that to them saving Islam suggests a communalist movement and a religious state. Dr Kazimi has this problem in mind when he writes:

> If we insist that Pakistan was created on an ideological basis, it implies that no matter how fair and accommodative Hindu leaders had been, no matter how evenly the British had held the scales, Muslims would have still divided the country. On the other side, an empirical basis means that Islam is a complete code of life

---

219 H. Alavi (2001) *The Rise of Religious Fundamentalism in Pakistan.* Paper given at the South Asian Conference on Fundamentalism: Role of Civil Society. Dhaka, Bangladesh, 1-2 June.

220 K.A.K. Yusufi 1988, p.114

221 Speech at a tea party, Cairo, 19 December 1946 (Yusufi 1988, p.198)

222 Speech at the Muslim University Union, Aligarh, 10 March 1941. (Yusufi Vol. II p.1350)

223 Presidential address at the Special Pakistan Session of the Punjab Muslim Students Federation, Lahore, 2 March 1941. (Yusufi Vol. II, p.1339). Emphasis mine.

> providing for both a majority and minority status of Muslims. It was bitter political experience which led Muslims to opt for partition. A decision which not only divided India, but according to our foreign critics, also divided the Muslim community. Let us not over stress the ideological aspect.[224]

Dr Kazimi is not wrong in saying that 'bitter experience' led Muslims to fight for partition. This of course was the historical cause of the Pakistan movement. On the other hand, the underlying cause of that 'bitter experience' was the Hindu religious ideal. The Muslims' political grievances were thus not merely 'empirical' but 'ideological' also. The Pakistan movement was likewise 'ideological' for this reason, and this was the deeper meaning of the Two-Nation Theory. Therefore Kazimi's other point – that the 'ideological' aspect implies the Muslims would have divided the country no matter what – is based on a minor flaw in his logic. Iqbal had warned in 1930 that the caste system went against the democratic principle and so 'Hindu India' required a 'complete overhauling' of its 'social structure'[225] if it was to successfully accommodate other communities in a consolidated Indian nation. When the Congress came into power in 1937, its aggressive politics and imposition of Hindu culture at the expense of others (not only Muslims) created much civil unrest and proved Iqbal's point; and this brought about Jinnah's 'conversion' to the Two-Nation Theory. It is true that liberal Hindu thinkers had called for social reforms for decades, but at that time they were in the minority. Had Muslims stayed on in India, it is likely that these reforms would have not been deemed as urgent as they subsequently became with the rude awakening that occurred in 1947. There is little doubt that it took partition for India to finally realise the extent of the communal problem, which after all had not been confined to Hindu-Muslim relations, but also affected Hindu relations with other communal groups, and even internal relations between its own castes. Only then did its leaders finally recognise their mistakes, and so they drew up a constitution which aimed at abolishing the caste system, and began the process of political and social reform, in an endeavour that continues to this day.[226]

---

224 M.R. Kazimi 2008, p.47

225 See Iqbal's Allahabad address.

226 The enormous inter-communal tensions in India – which after all were not confined to Hindu-Muslim relations – were the impetus of this crucial intellectual change, and led to the first important steps to towards the 'complete overhauling of her social structure' that Iqbal, amongst others, had advocated for Indian society. Gandhi was one other such voice; he had concluded that the present caste system was 'very antithesis of the *varnashrama*' – the ancient social division of Hindu society, into four *varna* or classes: Priests (Brahmin), warriors, merchants, and peasants. These classes were thought to be natural and not manmade, i.e. people were naturally born in the class best suited to their inherent individual skills and abilities. It was on the basis of *jati* (from the Sanskrit root *jan* meaning 'to beget') that a more rigid social construct developed later to become the contemporary caste system. *Jati* number

Muslims were theoretically in a better position to throw off the shackles they had worn in India and to build a state based on Islamic idealism. Unfortunately the early leaders were themselves inadequately equipped to deal firmly with the cacophony of voices making conflicting ideological demands, to the detriment of the Pakistan idea. As we have already observed, they failed when they forgot the limits of compromise, and put petty personal rivalries above the service of their nation.

Myth no. 10: Jinnah was a secularist all his life and evidence can be found in his speeches (Hoodbhoy & Nayyar 1985, p.170; A.S. Ghazali 1996, p.6-7; A. Cowasjee 2002; I. Ahmed 2004, p.14-19)

We have already seen in Chapter 1 that Jinnah was a 'secular-Muslim' in his earlier life. He truly believed in the secular principle of leaving religion out of the political sphere, but even from an early phase he also defended Muslim values in the realm of politics, most famously with the Wakf bill. Even when he was in Congress, Jinnah actively demonstrated his concern for the interests of his own community. We have mentioned in Chapter 1 that from 1897, he was a member of the Executive Committee of the Anjuman-i-Islamia Bombay (and *Anjuman-i-Islamia* School was later a beneficiary of Jinnah's will [227]). He left the Congress

---

thousands of divisions instead of four, fix people's livelihoods and social status at birth, and determine rules on everything from marriage to diet. Gandhi taught that the ancient caste system (*varnashrama*) did not advocate social inequality or set up social barriers; and that untouchability had no sanction in Hindu scripture and should be eradicated (see his article 'Caste has to Go' in *Harijan*, 16 November 1935; CWMG Vol. 68, p.151-3. (http://www.gandhiserve.org/cwmg/VOL068.PDF) Dr Ambedkar, leader of the so-called Untouchables (now Dalits), was another important figure in effecting the change; he was the major contributor in drawing up India's post-independence constitution which aims at abolishing the caste system as a religio-political force. Features of the constitution include the outlawing of untouchability and the formal legalisation of inter-caste marriage. Social reforms involving 'positive discrimination' – usually involving quotas for places in public service, educational and political institutes – have had mixed results and caused controversy. All these changes notwithstanding, at the social level – where the caste system has exerted the most influence – changes have been slower to come about, especially in rural areas. Inter-communal tensions do also persist, helped along by those far-right Hindu elements that still adhere to Hindutva ideals. Dalits also continue to struggle against social discrimination. Nevertheless there is no doubt that India has made some genuine attempts to tackle the problems inherent in the caste system.

[227] In his will made in 1939 and never changed after that date, Jinnah bequeathed, in the following order: Rs.25,000 to the *Anjuman-i-Islam* School Bombay, Rs.50,000 to the University of Bombay, and Rs.25,000 to the Arabic College, Delhi. His residuary estate including corpus was to be split equally between three more educational institutes, namely Aligarh University, Islamia College in Peshawar, and Sind Madressa in Karachi (where he had received most of his primary education). These are princely sums, worth almost quarter of a million British pounds in today's money, just for the first three institutes listed above. According to Prof. Sharif al Mujahid in his introduction to *In Quest of Jinnah*, the total worth of these charitable gifts including the residuary estate and corpus is the equivalent of around half a million British pounds today (for details of the actual payout see S. Mujahid (ed.) 2007, xx, xxxi).

as early as 1920 but did not begin to revise his views on politics and religion until the 1930s.

We also know that pro-secularist commentators rely most heavily on the three-piece argument (Munir quote / 11 August 1947 / anti-theocracy) for Jinnah's 'secular' speeches post-partition. But we have already reviewed these speeches, so we need not bring them in here. There is no doubt that Jinnah's earliest speeches do contain references to the secular ideal of keeping religion out of politics; in fact when we place his earlier and later speeches in juxtaposition we can soon see the gradual change from a 'secular-Muslim' to a 'non-sectarian Muslim'.

Instead of handpicking select speeches to demonstrate this (which could be justly construed as subjectivity on my part), we will review some speeches as cited by someone with a pro-secularist viewpoint. Here are some examples as cited by the well-known Indian Muslim writer and lawyer, A.G. Noorani:

> [Jinnah] said in the Central Legislative Assembly in 1925: "For God's sake do not import the discussion of communal matters into this House." In the same forum he said on February 7, 1935: "Religion should not be allowed to come into politics. Religion is merely a matter between man and God." Safeguards for the minorities "is a political issue". Differences between Hindus and Muslims were "a national problem and not a communal dispute", he wrote to Chagla on August 5, 1929. On February 1, 1943, the advocate of Pakistan repeated: "religion ... is strictly a matter between God and man".[228]

Of the five quotes cited in succession above, four are perhaps not surprising at all, as they are all dated pre-1936. We will come to the fifth one, dated 1943, shortly.

Early phase – secular-Muslim

Moving in chronological order, the first two dated 1925 and 1929 are typical of the secular-Muslim Jinnah. These were the days when he considered the Hindu-Muslim dispute as being 'communal', when in his view Muslims were a 'minority' that demanded 'safeguards'. But Jinnah was never a pure 'secularist' – i.e. what could be termed a 'political atheist'. Evidence of this can be found in his presidential address at the League Session in 1916 where the historical Lucknow Pact was adopted. Here he spoke on the constitutional problems of India, and responded to arguments put forward by the British bureaucracy against the Indian demand for self-government. One of these arguments was that

[228] A.G. Noorani, 'Jinnah in India's History' in *Frontline* magazine, Vol. 22 Issue 16, Jul-Aug 2005.

'democratic institutions cannot thrive in the environment of the East'.[229] Jinnah's response was:

> Why? Were democratic institutions unknown to the Hindus and Mohammedans in the past? What was the village *panchayat*?[230] What are the history, the traditions, the literature and the *precepts of Islam*? There are no people in the world *who are more democratic, even in their religion*, than the Mussalmans.[231]

At this point he was, like most of his Muslim liberal colleagues, the product of secular-Islam synthesis.

Transitional phase – intellectual reconstruction

In February 1935, Jinnah had been back in India for less than a year. The question for many historians has been whether Jinnah was already a changed man, or whether his transition to Islam came later. The speech that Noorani has cited from provides evidence that neither proposition is true, and that Jinnah was actually in the middle of an intellectual transformation. Noorani has only cited a short portion of the speech. We need to see more of it to ascertain its context. Jinnah was referring to a speech by the leader of the opposition in the Legislative Assembly (Bhulabhai Desai). Jinnah said:

> I entirely reciprocate every sentiment which the Honourable Leader of the Opposition expressed, and I agree with him, that religion should not be allowed to come into politics, that race should not be allowed to come into politics. Language does not matter so much, I agree with him, if taken singly one by one, religion is merely a matter between man and God, I agree with him there entirely;[232]

But Jinnah did not stop there. He continued:

> I agree with him there entirely; but I ask him to consider this – is this a question of religion purely? Is this a question of language purely? No, Sir, this is a question of minorities and it is a political issue. (*Some Muslim Honourable Members:* "Civilisation and culture.")

---

229 Here we note the parallel between this statement and Ghulam Mohammed's attitude in introducing a 'controlled democracy' in 1954.

230 *Panchayat*: Tribal council.

231 Presidential address at the ML Annual Session, Lucknow, 30 December 1916. (M. Umar (ed.) 1973, p.144)

232 Speech in the Central Legislative Assembly on the motion to consider the Report of the Joint Committee on Indian Constitutional Reform, New Delhi, 4 February 1935. (W. Ahmad 1991, p.31)

> ... Now, what are the minorities? Minorities mean a combination of things. It may be that a minority has a different religion from the citizens of a country. Their language may be different, their race may be different, their culture may be different, and the *combination of all these various elements ... makes the minority a separate entity* in the State, and that separate entity as an entity wants safeguards.[233]

Whilst Jinnah did not stop using the term 'community' for Muslims, his use of the word 'entity' is significant. Bear in mind that this speech was given a year before Jinnah used the word 'nation' for the first time. It is clear that by 1935 he was rethinking the Hindu-Muslim problem. Muslims were more than a minority; they were an entity. They differed not 'singly' on religion, or language, or culture, etc., but on a 'combination' which made them an 'entity'. Further, as an 'entity' they were naturally seeking more than mere 'safeguards'. In fact they had been seeking something closer to political parity since the 1920s.[234] Jinnah stuck to using the word 'safeguards' for the time being, but only for a lack of a better one. Thus he is in a transitional phase. By the end of the 1930s, he would fully realise that the problem was not about 'communities', and so he would begin to talk about 'nations' with the right of self-determination. The important technical difference between these two terms is explained in Durrani's *The Meaning of Pakistan*:

> Political philosophers make a distinction between a Community and a Nation. The distinction is of a fundamental nature as it makes a serious difference between the political right respectively to a Community and to a Nation. According to them, a Community has the right of insurrection only, whereas a Nation has the right of *secession as well.*[235]

Durrani also points to Dr Ambedkar's statement that 'a community has a right to safeguards, a nation has a right to demand separation'.[236] This reveals the significance of Jinnah's 1936 statement (the day the League resolved to contest the provincial elections) that 'Muslims could arrive at a settlement with the Hindus as *two nations*, if not as *partners*'.[237] The constitutionalist in him was open as to whether he

---

233 Ibid. Emphasis mine.

234 They had been demanding a third of seats at the centre as well as provincial autonomy, though the population of Muslims in India was around a quarter.

235 F. Durrani 1944, p.19. Emphasis mine.

236 Ibid. p.20. Durrani has quoted from Ambedkar 1946a, p.322, which is dedicated to discussing the difference between community and nation, safeguards and separation.

237 See Brief Minutes of the Proceedings of the ML Annual Session, Bombay, 11-12 April 1936. (NV Vol. I, p.40; the corresponding footnote explaining that this was probably the first record of Jinnah having used the word 'nation' is on p.368 fn)

would continue to work for a united India in which the Muslims were a community, or whether he would finally accept Iqbal's claim that they were a nation. By 1940, his final decision became public knowledge. Two years of Congress rule had revealed that constitutional safeguards were not enough; [238] Jinnah would say within a few years, following Iqbal's line, that the problem was not 'intercommunal' but 'international'. [239] Secession therefore was to prove the only option. Aside from the technical significance of his change in language use, we already know that Jinnah's take on the word 'nation' was Iqbalian. [240]

Final phase – Muslim Jinnah

The fifth of Jinnah's statements cited by Noorani is taken from his speech at Ismail College, Bombay in February 1943. As we have already shown in Chapter 6, the separation of sectarian religion (*mazhab*, as opposed to *deen*) from the state is hardly un-Islamic. Rather it helps to restore the Quran's inviolable anti-sectarian principle (4:48). [241] But the statement nevertheless needs closer inspection.

This version of the statement was printed in an article in the *Morning News*. Note that this paper reproduced only a few lines from the speech and summarised the gist of the rest, though on that day Jinnah had spoken for around an hour. [242] Since so little of the actual speech is presented in the article, we can see that this has created a problem:

> Earlier in his speech Mr Jinnah denied that the Muslim League was fighting for religious rights or that it was a communal organisation in the same sense in which the Hindus understood it. The religious rights of the Mussalmans were embedded in their souls and none could take them away.
>
> 'Which government,' he asked, 'claiming to be a civilised government can demolish our mosque or which government is going to interfere with religion which is strictly a matter between God and man? The question is that the Mussalmans are a nation, distinct from the Hindus.
>
> "The Muslims ruled over this country for nearly 800 years and for the past two centuries both the Hindus and Muslims were ruled by the British. During the last half of a century [*sic*] people

---

238 Ambedkar raised the same point and referred to the example of Europe, where 'experience showed that safeguards did not save the minorities'. (Op. cit 1946a, p.102)

239 Presidential address at ML Annual Session, Lahore, 22 March 1940 (NV Vol. I, p.493). Iqbal had said at his Allahabad address that the Indian problem is 'international and not national'. (Sherwani (ed.) 2008, p.25)

240 See Jinnah's interview with Beverley Nichols, cited in Myth no. 6.

241 See Chapter 12.

242 See M.S. Toosy 1976, p.33

> have begun to think and strive [*sic*] that any government must be responsible ultimately to the people". [243]

We can see that the excerpts from Jinnah's speech are presented in a haphazard fashion. Conceptually it is inconsistent. The journalist responsible for writing the article does not understand the real meaning of the Two-Nation Theory and so presents Jinnah's speech illogically. In fact it does not even read in his usual style.

Now let's look at another version – longer and almost completely verbatim – as printed by the Orient Press Agency, which was the first press agency established by and for Indian Muslims. First, here is the Orient Press' version of the line quoted in the *Morning News* as 'religion ... a matter between God and man':

> Islam is not only a mere *religion* but a *complete code of life.* Islam means peace with *God* and peace with *man.* [244]

There is barely even a passing resemblance between the two versions. Here Jinnah is describing Islam as something beyond religion, and relevant in every sphere of human life. The Orient Press version of the speech continues:

> The entire life of [the] Muslim nation whether it may be social, cultural, political or economic is governed by Islam. In Pakistan we shall have a state which will be run according to the principles of Islam. It will have its cultural, political and economic structure based on the principles of Islam. The non-Muslims need not fear because of this ... As a matter of fact they will be more safeguarded than in the present day so-called democratic parliamentary form of Government.
>
> ... [The] Muslim League and Muslim India is not fighting for any religious issue. Religion is embedded in our very soul and not only in our body. ... The *modern democratic* form of Government is not suited to the genius of the Indian People. People have begun to realise this and now they want a coalition Government. They have begun to realise that [a] hundred million Musalmans can ever be treated as a minority. [245]

Note the clear differences between the latter part of the above excerpt, and the last sentence of *Morning News* version, which has evidently taken either a secular or secular-Muslim interpretation of Jinnah's

---

243 Address to students at Ismail College, Bombay, 1 February 1943. (Yusufi Vol. III, p.1673-4)

244 Same address, as recorded by Orient Press Agency, 1 February 1943. (M.A. Harris (ed.) 1976, p.173). Emphasis mine.

245 Ibid. p.174

speech. Towards the end, Jinnah also reiterates his point that:

> … We want a true *democracy in accordance with Islam* and not a Parliamentary Government of the Western or Congress type. [246]

The Orient Press Agency's version of the speech is unquestionably more accurate. It is consistent within itself, it is more orderly, and it reads much more like the countless other speeches that Jinnah gave as a Muslim leader:

> Today in this huge gathering you have honoured me by entrusting the duty to unfurl the flag of the Muslim League, the flag of Islam, for you cannot separate the Muslim League from Islam. Many people misunderstand us when we talk of Islam particularly our Hindu friends. When we say "This flag is the flag of Islam" they think we are *introducing religion into politics* – a fact of which we are proud. *Islam gives us a complete code. It is not only religion but it contains laws, philosophy and politics.* In fact, it contains everything that matters to a man from morning to night. *When we talk of Islam we take it as an all-embracing word.* We do not mean any ill will. The foundation of our Islamic code is that we stand for liberty, equality and fraternity. [247]

And here is a profound statement in one of Jinnah's most outstanding speeches on the Pakistan idea, delivered at Chittagong in March 1948:

> You are only voicing my sentiments and the sentiments of millions of Musalmans when you say that Pakistan should be based on [the] sure foundations of social justice and Islamic socialism – no other 'ism' – which emphasise equality and brotherhood of man. …
>
> This biggest Muslim State came into being on 15th August, 1947. It was a great day in our history. But on this great day, it was not merely a Government which came into existence. I can understand the limitations of those amongst us whose minds have moved fast enough to realise that 15th of August ushered in such a State and such a Nation. It is natural for some to think only in terms of Government, but the sooner we realise and adjust ourselves to new forces, the sooner our mind's eye is capable of piercing through the horizons to see the limitless possibilities of our State and our Nation, the better for Pakistan. Then and then alone it would be possible for each one of us to realise the great

---

246 Ibid.

247 Speech in reply to the address presented by the Muslims of Gaya, 1 January 1938. (Yusufi Vol. II p.692)

ideals of human progress, of social justice, of equality and of fraternity, which, on the one hand, constitute the basic causes of the birth of Pakistan and also the limitless possibilities of evolving an ideal social structure of our State.

I reiterate most emphatically that Pakistan was made possible because of the danger of complete annihilation of the human soul in a society based on caste. Now that the soul is free to exist and to aspire, it must assert itself, galvanizing not only the State but also the Nation. [248]

Myth no. 11: Jinnah did not really want partition. He knew a partition demand would be acceptable to majority-province Muslims but not to either the Congress or the British. The Lahore Resolution was thus used as bargaining counter in his efforts for getting better constitutional rights for the Muslims in united India. (A. Jalal 1994, p.57 [249])

Though numerous commentators have treated the Lahore Resolution as a 'bargaining counter', today it is most commonly associated with the historian Prof. Ayesha Jalal, whose thesis and subsequent book *The Sole Spokesman* (1985) focuses on the idea. Yet surprisingly, in recent years she has strongly condemned what she describes as a 'gross distortion' of her original argument by her would-be supporters as well as her critics. In 2005, her article titled 'Between Myth and History' was published in a book edited by M.R. Kazimi. [250] In the article she has stated:

> My book *The Sole Spokesman: Jinnah, the Muslim League and the Demand of Pakistan* (Cambridge, 1985) delineated the uneasy fit between the claim of Muslim "nationhood" and the uncertainties and indeterminacies of politics in the late colonial era that led to the attainment of sovereign "statehood". Instead of grasping the salience of the argument, some historians and publicists on both sides of the 1947 divide have interpreted this as implying that the demand for a Pakistan was a mere "bargaining counter". In so far as politics is the art of the possible, bargaining is an intrinsic part of that art. To suggest, as some have glibly done, that Mohammed Ali Jinnah used Pakistan as a mere

---

[248] Public address, Chittagong, 26 March 1948. (NV Vol. VII, p.289, 290-291)

[249] Jalal is certainly not the first to describe the Pakistan demand as a 'bargaining counter' (see footnote 256 below for other examples), but she is most commonly associated with the theory, as her thesis was built upon it.

[250] A. Jalal, 'Between Myth and History' in M.R. Kazimi (ed.) (2005) *M.A. Jinnah — Views & Reviews* Karachi: Oxford University Press. It was also reprinted in *Dawn* twice, on two commemorative dates in the Pakistani national calendar: 23 March 2005 and 25 December 2005 (Lahore Resolution day and Jinnah's birthday respectively).

> ruse against the Congress is a gross distortion of not only my argument but of the actual history.[251]

Although Jalal's article was written before the publication of my first book, and though I had read it, I readily acknowledge that I too chose to review her argument in terms of the 'bargaining counter', because I was more interested in discussing the myth that has, by her own admission, taken precedence. But whilst she claims in her article above that people have 'interpreted' her argument as 'implying' Pakistan was a bargaining counter, this is hardly a fair statement. With respect, it was she who used the term 'bargaining counter' for the Pakistan demand, and then no fewer than three times.[252] Here is the best known example:

> By apparently repudiating the need for any centre, and keeping quiet about its shape, Jinnah calculated that when eventually the time came to discuss an all-India federation, British and Congress alike would be forced to negotiate with organised Muslim opinion, and would be ready to make substantial concessions to create or retain that centre. *The Lahore resolution should therefore be seen as a bargaining counter*, which had the merit of being acceptable (on the face of it) to the majority-province Muslims, and of being totally unacceptable to the Congress and in the last resort to the British also. This in turn provided the best insurance that the League would not be given what it now apparently was asking for, but which Jinnah in fact did not really want.[253]

The term appears clearly in the passage. Most readers have interpreted it in the same way – that is, a fully separate Pakistan was presented as an untenable demand, with the hope that it would make the Congress more agreeable to a lesser demand, i.e. parity in an all-India setup. Pakistan as a country born of partition was thus a mere threat; parity (or near enough)[254] at the centre was the real aim. This interpretation is not so far removed from Jalal's actual argument, which is that the Pakistan that came into being in 1947 was not the one he wanted, i.e. he did not aim for 'secession'. We will return to this shortly.

Aside from this, the term 'bargaining counter' was originally deployed by the Congress propaganda machinery in the 1940s. It was obvious sensationalism, designed to rouse ire and suspicion on the Muslim side. Both the British and the Congress took up this attitude, partly out of political expedience but also from an erroneous assumption about Jinnah, whose reputation as an Indian nationalist and 'ambassador of

[251] Kazimi (ed.) 2005, p.120

[252] See A. Jalal 1994, pp. 57, 61, 187.

[253] A. Jalal 1994, p.57. Emphasis mine.

[254] Op. cit. p.201 (Even the parity demand here is described as a 'bargaining counter')

Hindu-Muslim unity' had long preceded him. It is also true that some Muslim leaders such as the Punjab's Sikandar Hayat Khan did not faithfully toe the League's line; they did not want partition and publicly disavowed the idea. [255] Their apologetic stance evidently contributed somewhat to the myth about Pakistan as a bargaining counter.[256] At any rate the claim was strongly refuted by Jinnah and his genuine supporters in the League. [257]

Conversely, not all Hindus dismissed the Pakistan demand. Dr Ambedkar for example was of the opinion that the Congress was 'merely indulging in wishful thinking' by choosing to treat it as a bargaining counter. He raised a valid point: If the Muslims did not really want partition, then what did they want? Ambedkar answered: '*No one knows.*' He acknowledged that no one amongst the Muslim Leaguers (let alone Jinnah) had ever 'disclosed it'. [258] He believed that the undisclosed 'alternative to Pakistan' would surely be 'many degrees worse' for Congress; in his view, Muslims would likely demand nothing short of parity in any future constitution.[259] In this he is in agreement with Jalal. But whereas Jalal attributes this 'alternative' demand to a Jinnah who never voiced it, Ambedkar points to non-League Muslim schemes, including the Hyderabad [260] scheme of reform (1939, 1946), a scheme advanced by a Muslim leader of the Nationalist Party (again in Hyderabad, 1940) and the resolutions passed at the Azad Muslim Conference held in April 1940 (comprising of anti-League non-Congressite Muslims). All three of these schemes pushed for political parity. [261] From the League's side, we could also add Iqbal's two alternatives from his Allahabad address of 1930: He said that the Muslims should either demand a 'redistribution of British India', or stick to the demands set out by the 'Muslim League and the All-India Muslim Conference' including 'separate electorates' and '33 per cent representation in any Central Legislature'. [262]

---

255 See Hayat's speech in 1941, as cited in Appendix III

256 This would explain why Congressman V.P. Menon has suggested that it was some *Muslims* who called Jinnah's demand for Pakistan a 'bargaining weapon'. (V.P. Menon 1957, p.83, 106) See also Ayesha Jalal's interview of Punjab Leaguer Mian Mumtaz Daultana in 1980, in which Daultana claims Jinnah never wanted partition and that this was why he accepted the Cabinet Mission Plan. (A. Jalal 1994, p.202 fn)

257 For Jinnah's statements, see Chapter 11. For Liaquat Ali Khan's position, see his speech at the Madras Session, April 1941, cited in Chapter 9.

258 B.R. Ambedkar 1946a, p.187 (Emphasis mine)

259 Ibid.

260 Hyderabad was one of the Princely States with a Muslim ruler. The All-India Muslim League was technically a body representing the Muslims of British India only; but in 1940 Bahadur Yar Jung, himself from Hyderabad, set up the All-India States Muslim League.

261 B.R. Ambedkar 1946a, p.189-194

262 Allahabad address (Sherwani (ed.) 2008, p.21)

Ambedkar left out the Congressite Muslims in his review, but their case is no less intriguing. During the ill-fated first Simla Conference [263] of 1945, Abul Kalam Azad (then Congress President) came up with a scheme 'in his personal capacity' to give Muslims parity in the central cabinet and central legislature (at least in the short term), weightage in accordance with the Lucknow Pact, fully autonomous units with the right to secession, and the possibility of alternating the union premiership between Hindu and Muslim in successive terms. [264] Though Azad also included joint rather than separate electorates at the centre, his scheme did not differ far from Ambedkar's hypothesis. [265] Unsurprisingly Gandhi forbade Azad from making the scheme public, and it never formally came up at Simla, though evidently the British were quietly aware of it. [266] V.P. Menon later told H.V. Hodson in an interview, in referring to Azad's scheme, that the nationalist Muslims in the Congress were 'only a very whit behind' the Muslim League in their thinking. In fact Congress felt that compared to Azad, Jinnah was being 'kinder to us' in demanding only the Muslim-majority areas. [267] Partition therefore (in Ambedkar's mind at least) seemed to be the better alternative for the Congress, if they indeed sought to be the chief arbiters of political power in an independent India. [268]

Nevertheless, some Indian and British commentary has continued to hold onto the 'bargaining counter' theory up to the present day, [269] and in recent years the far-right Indian political party, the BJP, [270] has promoted the idea with the obvious and absurd aim of opening the door to an eventual re-absorption of Pakistan. [271] Little wonder then, that

---

263 The first Simla Conference was an attempt by Lord Wavell to bring about an agreement to 'advance India towards her goal of self-government' (Wavell's broadcast announcement, 15 June 1945; NV Vol. IV, p.867). It aimed at the creation of a new Executive Council made up entirely of Indian representatives, including an equal number of caste Hindus and Muslims, with only the posts of Viceroy and Commander-in-Chief reserved for the British.

264 See secret telegram from Sir Evan Jenkins to George Abell on 25 August 1945, with respect to an intercepted letter of Azad to Gandhi dated 2 August 1945 detailing Azad's scheme (original letter is now lost). (*Transfer of Power*, Vol. VI, p.156)

265 See Ambedkar's list of features comprising his 'guess' of the 'Muslim alternative' in op. cit. p.188

266 See footnote 264 above.

267 See Menon's tape-recorded interview to Hodson, Bangalore, 7 September 1964. (NV Vol. IV, p.941 fn)

268 Ambedkar 1946a, p.195

269 See for instance M.C. Chagla (1973) *Roses in December* Bombay: Bharatiya Vidya Bhavan, p.80; Ajeet Jawed (1998) *Secular and Nationalist Jinnah* New Delhi: Kitab Publishing House, p.272; I. Talbot 1984

270 Bharatiya Janata Party (Indian People's Party)

271 The furore in 2005 over BJP leader L.K. Advani's calling Jinnah's 11 August speech the 'classical espousal of a secular state' (an obvious reiteration of Munir's statement in *From Jinnah to Zia*), and another BJP leader Jaswant Singh's (2009) recent book which merely reproduced Jalal's central argument (*Jinnah, Partition and Independence* New Delhi: Rupa & Co) are two high-profile examples of such an attempt to plant the seed for an eventual reunion of India. The well-known Indian Muslim historian Asghar Ali Engineer meanwhile has

Jalal's book received much praise from Indian and British historians, and was met with equal hostility from Pakistani historians.[272]

Of course, raising the possibility of reunion today was not Jalal's intent as an academic, but she did nevertheless remark on the last page of her book that 'Jinnah never quite abandoned his strategy of bringing about an eventual union of India on the basis of Pakistan and Hindustan'.[273] Most people reading that sentence register only the first half referring to a union. In fact she has implied a confederation between sovereign states – Hindustan and Pakistan – rather than a federation between federal states. It suggests a relationship governed by international law.[274] But this is where things get confusing.

Jalal has written that in 1946 Jinnah was open to either a 'confederation with non-Muslim provinces on the basis of parity at the centre' or 'as a *sovereign state*, it would make treaty arrangements with the rest of India about matters of common concern'.[275] She has clearly called the first of Jinnah's choices a confederation, but what the second choice is supposed to be, is anybody's guess. What is a 'sovereign state' to Prof. Jalal? Does she mean a fully independent nation-state, or does she mean an autonomous province that possesses residual powers? Both can technically be described as 'sovereign' states. Looking at her phraseology, 'a sovereign state' with 'treaty arrangements' certainly reads like a relationship between nation-states. Yet paradoxically she also maintains elsewhere that Pakistan 'did not translate into a *secessionist demand* for a Muslim nation-state, but was intended as the building block for a confederal arrangement with the Hindu majority provinces, or Hindustan, at the subcontinental level.'[276] This is a long-winded way of saying that she does not endorse the 'partition' theory, which she equates with communalist 'balkanisation'.[277] For thirty years she never clarified her statement on the Hindustan-Pakistan relationship, which reappeared in her later works virtually word for word.[278] Her noncommittal stance led one puzzled academic to remark:

---

suggested that there could be conciliatory moves towards a subcontinental confederation involving not only India and Pakistan but also Sri Lanka and Nepal (See A.A. Engineer, 'Some thoughts on Confederation in the Sub-Continent', in *Secular Perspective*, 16-30 September, 2009). Unsurprisingly, many Pakistanis are suspicious of all such suggestions.

272 Conversely, some Indians view the book as a form of apologetic, whilst some Pakistanis – invariably secularist commentators – sympathise with Jalal's view.

273 A. Jalal 1994, p.293

274 Op. cit. p.187

275 Op. cit. p.241. Emphasis mine.

276 See 'Exploding Communalism: The Politics of Muslim Identity in South Asia' in S. Bose & A. Jalal (eds.) (1997) *Nationalism, Democracy and Development: State and Politics in India* Delhi: Oxford University Press, p.93

277 See A. Jalal 1994, p.54. She also equates the word 'partition' with a 'clarion call of Islam' and 'pitting Muslim India against Hindustan', as against a 'union' with 'real political choice and safeguards'. (op. cit. p.122)

278 A. Jalal, *Pakistan: a Dialogue Between History and Politics*, lecture delivered at the fifth Manzur Qadir Memorial Lecture, Lahore, December 1989

'It is not clear whether Jalal is arguing that Jinnah did not want an independent Pakistan, that he wished to fight for the security of the Muslims of India but within an Indian frame.'[279]

It is only as recently as 2013 that an explanatory adverb [280] added to her original statement from the *Sole Spokesman* has given a clearer idea of her position:

> Once the British and the Congress agreed to the principle of "Pakistan," Jinnah was prepared to discuss whether the proposed Muslim state would forge a confederal relationship with the rest of India or enter into treaty arrangements on matters of common interest between two essentially sovereign states – Pakistan (representing the Muslim-majority provinces) and Hindustan (representing the Hindu-majority provinces). In either case, Jinnah wanted something close to parity with the Congress at the all-India level since Muslims as a nation had a right to an equal share of power with the Hindus. If it was to cover the interests of Muslims in both the majority and the minority provinces, "Pakistan" had to remain part of an all-India whole. [281]

Thus it seems Jalal's phrase 'essentially sovereign' does mean autonomous provinces with residual powers.

A year later in her next book, she repeats the above lines virtually verbatim, and then stresses that in 'keeping with that aim, Jinnah made it a point to always speak of Pakistan and Hindustan and not Pakistan and India'. [282] As an example of evidence she refers to the following statement of Jinnah:

> "We are not enemies of the Congress," he told a group of Punjabi Muslim and Hindu students in August 1944, "though we disagree on certain issues. If we must have a separate State," he continued, "that will not mean we shall have nothing to do with each other." He had no doubt that "both Hindus and Muslims will be happy when Pakistan is established" as it was in their best

---

http://www.tufts.edu/~ajalal01/Articles/mqmlecture.pdf (Last accessed 23 May 2010); A. Jalal 2005, p.122; see also Prof. Jalal's interview to *Tehelka* magazine, Vol. 6 Issue 34, 29 August 2009

279 A.S. Ahmed 1997, p.30

280 While Jalal attached the new word 'essentially' to 'sovereign' as early as 1995 (See A. Jalal (1995) *Democracy and Authoritarianism in South Asia: A Comparative and Historical Perspective* Cambridge: Cambridge University Press, p.14), it was not until 2013 (referenced in next footnote) that she expressly differentiated between the 'essentially sovereign' federal state as one option, and confederation as the other.

281 A. Jalal (2013) *The Pity of Partition: Manto's Life, Times, and Work Across the India-Pakistan Divide* Princeton: Princeton University Press, p.8-9

282 A. Jalal (2014) *The Struggle for Pakistan: A Muslim Homeland and Global Politics* Cambridge: Belknap Press/Harvard University Press, p.29.

> interest. They would never "allow anybody, whether he is Afghan or Pathan, to dominate us" because "India is for Indians." It would be "foolish of the Hindus, and vice versa," not to come to the defense of Pakistan if it were invaded by any outside power.[283]

We have already discussed the issue of Muslims in minority provinces in Chapter 8 (subsection 'Jinnah was prepared to leave some Muslims behind in India') so we need not repeat it here. As for the latter part of Jalal's statement above, it is true that Jinnah often referred to 'Pakistan' and 'Hindustan', but this carries no significance whatsoever. We already know that Jinnah treated India correctly as a 'subcontinent' and not a country. In fact he made a very similar statement to the one she cites above just a couple of months later, in which he said:

> I have said so several times. We will say, 'Hands off India' to all outsiders. Pakistan will not tolerate any outside design or aggression on this *subcontinent*. We will observe something like the Monroe Doctrine. [284]

But for the benefit of those who did see it as a country, in 1946 Jinnah even went as far as to say that he was not an Indian. [285] That same year he spoke of a partition to create 'two Indias', and he had used the same words much earlier in 1940. [286]

Notwithstanding the issues we have just noted, Jalal does at least offer one compelling description (based on Jinnah's conversation with a British Major in February 1946) of a technical 'all-India' that may have been acceptable to Jinnah and indeed his Muslim supporters, in which Pakistan and Hindustan would, for all intents and purposes, be divided into nation-states on the basis that the centre would have 'an executive but no legislature'. Of course, as she herself confirms, even this setup would only have lasted 'for the time being', i.e. as long as the British remained in India during the transitional period. [287]

Even if we can see a partial agreement between her view of the politics and that of any commentator who believes Jinnah ultimately sought partition, Jalal's entire argument relies on an assumed 'immaculate silence' [288] on the part of Jinnah. She believes that Jinnah 'deliberately' kept the 'demand' for Pakistan 'vague'. [289] This perhaps

---

283 Ibid., citing Jinnah's interview to representatives of Punjab Students' Federation, Lahore, 5 August 1944 as reported in *Dawn*, 6 August 1944 (see also Yusufi Vol. III, p.1938).

284 Interview to *Daily Worker* of London correspondent, Bombay, 14 October 1944, as reported in *Dawn*, 16 October 1944 (Yusufi Vol. III, p.1954). Emphasis mine.

285 For details, see Chapter 13, subsection 'Jinnah's confession that he is still an Indian'.

286 For full references, see Myth no. 12, footnotes 297 and 298 below.

287 See A. Jalal 1994, p.174-5, citing from Major Wyatt's notes.

288 Op. cit. p.186

289 Op. cit. p.242

explains why she too has not been more specific with her argument, at least until recently. Of course, there is no doubt that the territorial demand was complicated by several factors, as we have already noted in Chapter 8. These factors naturally hindered all discussions on defining borders and thus served to stall the creation of Pakistan. Indeed Jinnah often said that India's constitutional problem was 'most complex' and had 'no parallel in any part of the world'. [290] But the fact of the complexity should not be equated with 'deliberate' ambiguity.

Jinnah was not deliberately vague about Pakistan. He had become one of the most successful and highest paid lawyers in Bombay [291] because of his ability to present a case with precise, cogent arguments. His advocacy of the Two-Nation Theory was clear and definitive. His repeated demand for an independent state was unequivocal – even if some people including Muslim Leaguers were uncomfortable with it. This same complexity of the issue also contributed to Jinnah's most controversial political decision in 1946. We will discuss this in more detail in Chapter 11.

We will end our review of this myth with the brief testimony of a British historian who seemed to have no trouble understanding the Pakistan demand. Sir Reginald Coupland, whose field of expertise was colonial history, also had an academic interest in India. He travelled there in 1941 sponsored by Nuffield College to 'study its constitutional problem'. [292] In carrying out his research he interviewed most major leaders and politicians, both British and Indian. He was on the verge of returning to Britain to write up his findings when he was appointed to the Cripps' Mission. Soon afterwards he wrote a monograph about his observations there. In his preface he writes that Sir Stafford Cripps gave him permission to publish it on the understanding that it was 'a personal and wholly unofficial record' and that Coupland was 'solely' responsible for the statements and opinions it contained. [293]

Prof. Coupland interviewed Jinnah twice in January 1942 [294] and from these interviews he ascertained the territorial aspect of the Pakistan demand as follows:

> There is more than one conception of what Pakistan means, but the official definition – Mr Jinnah himself explained it very lucidly to me – is a Moslem State or States comprising the North-West Frontier Province, the Punjab, and Sind on the one side of India and Bengal on the other. Those Moslem States, with

---

[290] See speech at Edwardes College, Peshawar, 27 November 1945 (Yusufi Vol. III, p.2124)

[291] Bolitho 1954, p.17. Jinnah was in his time the youngest Indian barrister to qualify from Lincoln's Inn in London (at just 19 years old); and when he began his legal practice in 1896 he was the only Muslim barrister in Bombay. (A.S. Ahmed 1997, p.4)

[292] R. Coupland (1942) *The Cripps Mission* London: Oxford University Press, p.4

[293] Ibid.

[294] See editor's note, NV Vol. II p.787 fn; information taken from Coupland's diary.

> modified boundaries, would share on an equal footing with 'Hindustan' in the coming enfranchisement of India. They would constitute a distinct dominion or dominions. There would be no all-India government at all.[295]

This 'lucid' explanation from a logician to an academic neatly encapsulates all that we have shown in Chapter 8 regarding the territorial aspect of the Pakistan demand, as outlined in the Lahore Resolution.

Myth no. 12: No one in the Muslim League knew what Pakistan meant. Jinnah's statements on the subject were vague and ambiguous – deliberately so. (A. Jalal 1994, p.242; I. Talbot 1998, p.94;[296] I. Ahmed 2004, p.13)

Leaving aside the other Leaguers for the moment, there are two parts to this myth. One is that Jinnah was vague about the territorial shape of Pakistan (and in particular about whether the Lahore Resolution meant partition or union). We have already discussed this part in Myth no. 11 and Chapter 8 (and will come to it again in Chapter 11), so we need not repeat it here. The other part of the myth is that Jinnah was deliberately vague about Pakistan's constitutional shape and that he used Islamic 'slogans' merely to muster Muslim support. I have already outlined the 'ambiguity theory' that has been used to explain away Jinnah's references to Islam in his speeches. But merely saying that Jinnah was deliberately vague about the constitution fails to convince anyone who is familiar with his statements on the subject, especially in light of the Two-Nation Theory.

In this book we have already explained in detail what the Two-Nation Theory means (and meant for the Pakistan demand). There is also no doubt about the failure of many of Jinnah's contemporaries – whether Muslim or non-Muslim – to understand it. Here is one example. In April 1946, Jinnah met with the British Cabinet Delegation to present the League's case for their consideration before they outlined the Cabinet Mission Plan. One of the delegates, A.V. Alexander, wanted to know the background to the Pakistan demand. He asked whether the difference between Hindus and Muslims was 'essentially racial or religious'. In reply Jinnah explained that after the arrival of Islam in India, any section of the Hindu community that converted to Islam was 'thrown out of every department of social life', and that thus they had developed essentially separately from the rest of the Hindu community for centuries, with the result that there were now 'two different civilisations

---

295 Ibid. p.16

296 I. Talbot (1998) *Pakistan: A Modern History* London: C. Hurst & Co.

with deep roots side by side'. [297] He also explained that the Muslims believed in different principles from the Hindus, namely 'one God' and the 'equality of men'. This justified the Muslim demand for the establishment of 'two Indias with nothing more than treaties and agreements between them'. [298] In light of everything we have observed of Jinnah in this book, his explanation of the Two-Nation Theory is perfectly clear. He did not consider the issue to be about mere race or even religion. His phraseology 'civilisations with deep roots', was clearly the nearest he could get to explaining that the issue was about *deen*, but his point failed to register with Alexander, whose own dualistic worldview unconsciously prejudiced his view of Jinnah's reply. Hence he concluded, as he wrote in his diary, that Jinnah 'never really gave a definite answer'. [299]

For most pro-secularist commentators, the 'Muslim nation' was and remains a purely political term. [300] For Ayesha Jalal it is also a practical synonym for parity at an all-India centre. She has written at the very beginning of her *Sole Spokesman* that 'Jinnah's appeal to religion was always ambiguous ... his use of the communal factor was a political tactic, not an ideological commitment.' [301] Of course she is obliged to take this line as follow-through to her argument about the 'vagueness' of Jinnah's demand for a separate state. [302] In fact every time – without exception – that she addresses the so-called 'communal' factor and Jinnah's reactions to certain questions about the nature of the state, she gives quotes out of context and interprets events through the prism of secular Islam. [303]

For example, with reference to Iqbal's letter to Jinnah describing the economic principles of Islam as the only solution of Muslim poverty, [304] she complains that Iqbal offers no real solutions; but adds that Jinnah was at any rate 'too shrewd and too secular to chase this particular hare'. [305] She has missed the obvious point that neither Jinnah nor Iqbal ever offered specifics for an economic system since this would be a matter for Muslims to work upon together when the time came to do so. At any rate both men were agreed that a contemporary political

---

297 Official record of Jinnah's interview with the Cabinet Delegation and Viceroy Wavell, New Delhi, 4 April 1946. (NV Vol. IV p.581-2)

298 Ibid. p.581. He had likewise stated his intent to meet Gandhi 'to discuss the details of two Indias' one week after the Lahore Resolution was passed. See press interview, *Manchester Guardian*, 30 March 1940. (NV Vol. I p.509)

299 Alexander's diary entry, 4 April 1946 (NV Vol. IV, p.582 fn)

300 See for example R.J. Moore, 'Jinnah and the Pakistan Demand' in M.R. Kazimi (ed.) 2005, p.60

301 A. Jalal 1994, p.5

302 See Myth no. 11.

303 She has reportedly described herself as a 'secular Muslim' (See her interview in the *New York Times*, 26 December 1998), but at any rate she presents Jinnah as a pure secularist.

304 Iqbal to Jinnah, 28 May 1937 (*Letters of Iqbal*, p.17)

305 A. Jalal 1994, p.42

expression of Islam would be a 'social democracy'. Iqbal stated as much in his letter to Jinnah dated 28 May 1937.[306] Jinnah likewise said numerous times that he expected the economic system of Pakistan to be socialistic; and hence he advised the State Bank in 1948 to evolve an economic system based on 'Islamic ideals'.[307]

Similarly, Jalal has claimed that at the League Session in December 1943, Jinnah 'carefully' avoided answering Bahadur Yar Jung's[308] challenge that if Pakistan's polity was not to be built on Quranic principles, then he did not want it.[309] In fact, aside from not putting the incident in context, Jalal has not consulted the original record and so she has missed an important part of Jung's speech.[310]

The original record of the proceedings (in Urdu) show that Jung said: 'Sir Quaid-i-Azam! This is how I have understood Pakistan, and if your Pakistan is not like this, we do not want it.' To this Jinnah replied with a smile: 'Why are you challenging me *ahead of time*?'[311] This is consistent with Jinnah's remarks at the Annual Session of the League in April 1943, in which he explained that Pakistan's constitution would be dealt with only after Pakistan was won.[312] Jung responded: 'No Quaid-i-Azam, I am not presenting a challenge. Through this "challenge" I want to make it clear to your people that you want the type of Pakistan that has just been discussed in brief.'[313]

To put this incident in context, Jung was appraising the League's newly appointed Committee of Action and the Planning Committee and had just explained that the purpose of these bodies was to lay the foundations for an eventual 'Quranic system of Government'[314] in Pakistan. Bahadur Yar Jung delivered his Urdu speech towards the end

---

306 See letter as cited in Chapter 7.

307 See Myth no. 3.

308 Bahadur Yar Jung (Muhammad Bahadur Khan, 1905-1944) was from Hyderabad, Deccan and famed for his stirring Urdu orations. A close ally of Jinnah, he often translated Jinnah's speeches into Urdu. A one-time *jagirdar* (feudatory), he renounced his titles when the Ruler of Hyderabad prohibited *jagirdars* from participating in politics. He joined the Khaksar movement in 1938 but resigned in protest after the assassination attempt on Jinnah in 1943 allegedly by a Khaksar member. He was the founder-President of the All-India States Muslim League. He died suddenly in June 1944, of suspected poisoning. (Biographical information adapted from S. Mujahid 1981, p.670). Jinnah in his tribute to Jung said that 'his passing away has deprived us of one of the greatest advocates of Muslim welfare and progress'. (Statement, Srinigar, 26 June 1944; NV Vol. III, p.515)

309 A. Jalal 1994, p.120

310 In her thesis Jalal cited from the translation of this incident as it appears in *Foundations* Vol. II, p.486. Here we are referring to the original Urdu transcript.

311 Emphasis mine.

312 See Myth no. 4 for full review of Jinnah's speech in April 1943.

313 The rendition above is my own translation, taken from the original Urdu as printed in Bahadur Yar Jung (2000 reprint) *Manshoor-i-Pakistan: Quaid-i-Millat Nawab Bahadur Yar Jung ki Tareekhi Taqreer* Karachi: Bahadur Yar Jung Academy, p.24. Bahadur Yar Jung's speech was delivered on 26 December 1943, and this booklet is a reprint of the original Urdu transcript.

314 B.Y. Jung 2000 (reprint), p.19

of this Session and, taking the lead from Jinnah, [315] he sought to drive home the point that the appointment of these committees was an 'appropriate step' to that end. [316] He said: 'Your Quaid-i-Azam has said more than once that Muslims have no right to frame the constitution and law in any one of their states.' The meaning of this statement is made clearer in the next sentence: 'Their constitution is *already laid down and it is in their hands* – and that is the Holy Quran.' [317] This was his way of saying that Muslims already had all the guidelines they needed in the Book with which to build up the functioning state. [318] Jung thus added: 'That which is not based on the Book of Allah and the ways of the Prophet, is a satanic polity and we seek God's shelter from it.' [319]

In response – and this is the part that Jalal has missed – according to the transcript, Jinnah hit his hand on the table enthusiastically and said: 'What you say is absolutely correct.' Jung in turn asked the audience to 'witness that Quaid-i-Azam has stamped his approval of my speech.' [320] He had already emphasised that no 'revolution' would be realised without a 'mental' revolution preceding it. [321] The English translation of the transcript that Jalal referred to happens to omit the part in which Jinnah emphatically indicated his agreement. This goes some way to explaining why she has wrongly assumed that Jinnah 'avoided' giving his support to Jung. When read in full however, it is clear that the speech explicitly supported all that Jinnah had said in his own address in the days before. Jinnah had even said in his concluding remarks (given before Bahadur Yar Jung's speech) that the 'Great Book, the Quran' was the 'sheet anchor' of the Muslims. [322] Bahadur Yar Jung only echoed this sentiment. His speech was hardly 'in sharp contrast' [323] to Jinnah's thought.

We should note however that *The Sole Spokesman* is over thirty years old and is not necessarily a total reflection of Prof. Jalal's present position. Her more recent assessment of Iqbal's legacy and its implications for Pakistan reveals a notable degree of perceptiveness, and

---

315 In his speech at this Session Jinnah had referred to the growing demands from the public that the League ought to establish bodies to deal with matters such as 'national industries' and 'a national system of Muslim education'. He expressed his appreciation of 'these proposals, suggestions and demands', and explained that whilst these demands could not be met immediately, the League was to set up the Committee of Action to organise and coordinate activities towards meeting them. (Presidential speech at the Annual ML Session, 24 December 1943; NV Vol. III, p.341).

316 B.Y. Jung 2000 (reprint), p.19

317 Ibid.

318 In this he was making a point similar to that which Jinnah had made in his presidential speech at the April 1943 Session.

319 Op. cit. p.20.

320 Ibid. p.19-20.

321 Ibid. p.20. This part of the speech is quoted in full in Myth no. 4, along with similar sentiments from other thinking Muslims.

322 Concluding remarks, 26 December 1943. See full citation given in Chapter 9.

323 A. Jalal 1994, p.120 fn

is in places exceptional.[324] Yet she has also said that 'the meaning of secularism has been distorted', and so she does not see 'Islam and secularism as opposites necessarily'.[325] If by this she means that the word 'secular' is unfairly maligned by some, then this is a legitimate point. But 'secular*ism*' of course is an entirely different matter. At any rate it remains to be seen whether or not Prof. Jalal will ever come to reassess her view of Jinnah as a 'secularist'.

Hopefully our review of Jinnah's speeches (especially in Myth nos. 2 and 3) has already demonstrated that the 'ambiguity theory' has no real justification. Nevertheless we can again take a look at some examples of Jinnah's speeches and statements to see what exactly his position was with regards to the constitution of the future country.

First, to revisit a speech we have quoted once already:

> What is it that you want? All this talk of socialism, communism, national-socialism and every other *ism*[326] is out of place. Do you think you can do anything just now? *How and when can you decide as to what form of government you are going to have in Pakistan?* We are told by one party or another that we must have a democratic or a socialistic or a "nationalistic"[327] form of government in Pakistan. These questions are raised to hoodwink you. At present you should just stand by Pakistan. It means that first of all you have to take possession of a territory. Pakistan cannot exist in the air. When you have once taken possession of your homelands *the question will then arise as to what form of government you are going to establish.* Therefore, do not allow your mind to be diverted by these extraneous ideas.[328]

Here Jinnah has asked his people to focus on obtaining independence first; the constitution would come later. This is the reason why he did not actively encourage or promote proposals for *any* constitution – Islamic or otherwise – during the 1940s.

Furthermore, as a testament of his integrity, he never advanced any personal suggestions either. For example in July 1947, when partition had already been announced,[329] Jinnah issued a statement assuring the protection of minorities in Pakistan at a press conference. The *Dawn* later reproduced some of the journalists' questions in an article.

324 See A. Jalal, 'Ideology and the Struggle for Democratic Institutions' in Victoria Schofield (ed.) (1997) *Old Roads, New Highways: Fifty Years of Pakistan*. Karachi: Oxford University Press; also A. Jalal (2000) *Self and Sovereignty: Individual and Community in South Asian Islam since 1850* London: Routledge

325 Ayesha Jalal interview, *Dawn*, 14 July 2005

326 Italicised in original.

327 Quotation marks included in original.

328 Speech at a Meeting of the Aligarh Muslim University Union, Aligarh, 9 March 1944 (Yusufi Vol. III p.1847)

329 Partition was announced in June 1946.

Naturally, one of these questions was on the structure of the government. As the *Dawn* reported:

> Mr Jinnah refused to discuss the structure of the Government of Pakistan as that was a matter for the Constituent Assembly to decide.
>
> Q: What is your personal opinion?
>
> Mr Jinnah: No responsible man expresses his personal opinion in anticipation of the decision of a supreme body like the Constituent Assembly, whose function it is to frame the constitution.[330]

We can see that though Jinnah commanded much respect and authority, he was no dictator, and he had no intention of simply forcing his own ideas upon his people. He made it perfectly clear that he would not work alone in framing the constitution. That was a job for the entire Constituent Assembly. But he made it equally clear, as we have seen, that he naturally expected to see the Muslims create a constitution that reflected their ideal and not merely continue with the British system that had been imposed on them for the past 150 years.

The critics however were seeking something much more substantial; they wanted specific details on borders, and they wanted to see a political and economic blueprint for Pakistan. In his interview to Beverley Nichols, Jinnah answered them as follows:

> **SELF** The most common accusation of your critics is that you have not defined Pakistan with sufficient precision – that there are many details of defence, economics, minorities, etc., which you have left deliberately vague. Do you think that is a just criticism?
>
> **JINNAH** It is neither just nor intelligent, particularly if it is made by an Englishman with any knowledge of his own history. When Ireland was separated from Britain, the document embodying the terms of separation was approximately *ten lines*. Ten lines of print to settle a dispute of incredible complexity which has poisoned British politics for centuries! All the details were left to the Future – and the Future is often an admirable arbitrator. Well, I've already given the world a good deal more than ten lines to indicate the principles and practice of Pakistan, but it is beyond the power of any man to provide, in advance, a blue-print in which every detail is settled. Besides, Indian history proves that such a blue-print is totally unnecessary. Where was the blue-print when the question of Burmah's separation was decided at the Round Table Conference? Where was the blue-

330 Press conference, New Delhi, 13 July 1947. (Yusufi Vol. IV, p.2592)

> print when Sind was separated from Bombay? The answer, of course, is 'nowhere'. It didn't exist. It didn't need to exist. The vital point was that the principle of separation was accepted; the rest followed automatically.[331]

Bearing in mind what we have seen of Jinnah's stance on the constitution of Pakistan, we can now examine a piece of evidence that is regularly presented by one or two pro-secularist commentators in backing the 'ambiguity' theory. We will cite from Prof. Ishtiaq Ahmed:

> As late as February 1947 at least the top leaders of the Muslim League (ML) did not have any clear idea about what sort of state Pakistan would be. A few months later on 14 August it had come into being as an independent and sovereign state in the Indian subcontinent. This fact comes out patently in what the Governor of Punjab Sir Evan Jenkins wrote in his confidential fortnightly report to the Viceroy Field Marshall Sir Archibald Percival Wavell about his meeting with the Muslim League leader Khwaja Nazim-ud-Din on 18-19 February 1947:
>
> In our first meeting (18 February, author's note) Khwaja Nazim-ud-Din admitted candidly *that he did not know what Pakistan means, and that nobody in the ML knew*, so it was difficult for the League to carry on long term negotiations with the minorities.[332]

This evidence is used to suggest that the Muslim Leaguers were allowed to believe what they liked about the constitution of future Pakistan but that no one actually knew what it was meant to be.[333] Ayesha Jalal, in referring to the same incident, has called it an 'astonishing revelation'.[334] Indeed it is; for according to Sir Jenkins' report, Nazimuddin is supposedly speaking as a proxy on behalf not only of himself but also the entire Muslim League, including, we presume, Mr Jinnah himself.

To provide a little background, these alleged remarks appear in Evan M. Jenkins' confidential fortnightly report to Viceroy A.P. Wavell. As the Muslims were numerically in majority in the Punjab, non-Muslims (in particular the Sikhs) had been concerned about the implications of Muslim-majority rule in the province should Pakistan come into being, especially as the failing interim government at the all-India level was making partition increasingly likely. In January 1947, when communal

---

331 B. Nichols 1944, p.189. Spellings and emphasis retained from original.

332 I. Ahmed 2004, p.13 (Spellings retained from original; emphasis mine). See also I. Ahmed 2002, where he has produced the same evidence.

333 A. Jalal 1994, p.4: 'But from first to last, Jinnah avoided giving the demand a precise definition, leaving the League's followers to make of it what they wished.'

334 Op. cit. p.238

tensions were rising exponentially across India, [335] the coalition ministry [336] of the Punjab banned the Muslim League National Guard, [337] accusing it of raising a private army, and so declaring it unlawful. [338] Some of the National Guard members were also arrested. The Muslim League denied the charge levelled at the National Guard, describing the ban and arrests as an infringement of the civil liberties and political rights of Muslims in the Punjab. [339] At the ground level, demonstrations were held in Lahore. Jenkins wrote to Wavell regarding the agitation:

> The Muslim League leaders did their best to avoid incidents but their demonstrations were extraordinarily provocative, e.g. non-Muslims did not relish boasts about the coming Muslim rule ... The widespread belief of the Muslim demonstrators that Muslim Raj was round the corner has had a deplorable effect on communal feeling. [340]

Mr Nazimuddin was brought in to try and find a means of settling the dispute between the coalition government and the Punjab Muslim League. The Premier of the Punjab (Malik Khizar Hayat Khan Tiwana) thought it 'inadvisable' to meet Nazimuddin in person, [341] in case his non-Muslim Indian peers in the coalition construed this as an act of disloyalty. Therefore Nazimuddin met with Jenkins, the Governor of the Punjab.

With the whole background in mind, we have a good idea of how to interpret Mr Jenkin's report:

> At our first discussion Khwaja Nazim-ud-Din admitted candidly that he did not know what Pakistan means, and that nobody in the ML knew, so it was difficult for the League to carry on long term negotiations with the minorities. [342]

---

335 This was at the time of a failing interim all-India government, when communal tensions were rising all across India.

336 The coalition (comprising Unionist, Congress and Akali Dal representatives) represented Muslim, Hindu and Sikh communal interests respectively. (S. Mujahid 1981, p.724)

337 ML National Guard: A volunteer group of the League, originally set up to help Punjab soldiers returning from war. Jinnah urged Muslim youth to join the Guard in 1942 (mid-WWII, when there was a danger of Japanese invasion) and so protect themselves against 'enemy action' from outside as well as 'internal troubles'. (Appeal to the Muslim youth to join the Muslim National Guards Organisation, Bombay, 28 May 1942; Yusufi Vol. III, p.1572-3)

338 A Hindu militia wing of the Hindu Mahasabha was also banned at this time on the same grounds. (NV Vol. V, p.534 fn)

339 See Jinnah's press statement, Karachi, 26 January 1947. NV Vol. V, p.525-9. Also: ML Working Committee Resolution No. 2, Karachi, 29 January – 2 February 1947. (NV Vol. V, p.586-9)

340 Jenkins to Wavell, 28 February 1947. (Lionel Carter (ed.) (2006) *Punjab Politics: 1 January 1944 – 3 March 1947* New Delhi: Manohar, p.368)

341 Jenkins to Wavell, 28 February 1947. (Ibid. p.366)

342 Ibid. p.366-7

We already know the following to be true: first, Jinnah had asked the Leaguers not to begin debating the particulars of the constitution when Pakistan had not yet come into existence territorially; second, Jinnah had said that whatever the form of the constitution, it would reflect the idealism of its people; and third, as outlined in the Lahore Resolution, he had told Hindus and Muslims alike that Pakistan would treat all minorities fairly and justly as a mark of a commitment to this idealism. But in Jenkins' statement above it is not clear under what context Nazimuddin made his alleged admission. Was it entirely unprompted, or had Jenkins asked him a question about the communal problem to which he had given the above answer? Jenkins does not specify either way, so we may never know. But knowing what we do about Jinnah's clear stance on Pakistan's constitution and on minorities, it should hardly come as a surprise if Nazimuddin said that 'no one knew' the exact shape of the future constitution, or indeed its geographical shape, which would affect the distribution of the populace. Pakistan did not yet exist on the map. This is more likely the meaning of Nazimuddin's so-called admission. Still, it is possible that he literally meant to say no one knew what Pakistan meant politically or ideologically, and whether non-Muslims would be full citizens and have full political representation – and that this affected the League's ability to negotiate with the minorities. If this is so, and his statement has been accurately recorded, then Mr Nazimuddin has only confirmed what we already know about the lack of intellectual unity amongst the Muslim League leaders. It betrays the extent of Muslim ignorance on Islam and its position on non-Muslims in the state. It also suggests that Mr Nazimuddin had not paid any attention to Jinnah's oft-repeated statements about Pakistan and minorities. But are we so sure that these were Nazimuddin's exact words? Or did Jenkins, a sincere Briton attached to the idea of a united India, whose sympathies naturally extended to the mixed-communal coalition, and who had expressed his low opinion of the separatist Muslim League and indeed Jinnah in writing,[343] simply hear what he wanted to hear?

---

343 Jenkins believed that Muslims had an 'extreme communal attitude' and were not offering a fair deal to non-Muslims. (Jenkins' note, 18 February 1947; ibid. p.364). He told Nazimuddin that the League must treat the 'non-Muslim minorities as partners and not as inferiors and subordinates'. (Jenkins draft note, 18 February 1947; ibid. p.360) These comments could suggest that the Punjab Leaguers' had failed to allay the fears of their non-Muslim peers. However Jenkins himself acknowledged that the problem went both ways, since 'the all-India political parties were controlled by their respective High Commands, [and so] … Congress Ministers were undoubtedly influenced by all-India Congress policy and Muslim League leaders could act only under instructions from the Muslim League High Command'. (Ibid. p.364). A few days after the announcement by the British to leave India by June 1948 (HMG Statement of 20 February 1947), Jenkins wrote a telegram to Pethick-Lawrence updating him about the situation in the Punjab. At the end he wrote: 'Unless Muslim League change their tone completely which seems most improbable there may be an abandonment of present constitution and attempts to establish Muslim or Sikh rule by force. I intend to avoid a

Whatever an individual commentator may decide about the accuracy of Jenkins' record, this particular evidence is certainly not sufficiently persuasive to support the hypothesis of 'ambiguity'.

Section 93 situation [emergency Governor's rule] if I possibly can but prospect of independence in 16 months' time is not conducive to moderation and Muslim League will act under instructions from Jinnah who knows little and cares less about the real interests of the Punjab.' (Telegram dated 25 February 1947. (*Transfer of Power* Vol. IX, p.816)) Evidently then, Jenkins harboured some resentment towards the League 'High Command' because it sought partition and he believed that it was apathetic to Punjab's local interests.

Chapter 11
Cabinet Mission: Word games

Whilst the Congress and the British Government always thought Jinnah was playing a high-stakes game of poker, [1] he himself preferred the analogy of chess. [2] In Chapter 9 we outlined the Pakistan movement from 1937-1946. Here we will look at one of Jinnah's most controversial political decisions in light of this history and ask whether he did indeed renege on his stated commitment to partition. This chapter is essentially a continuation of our review of Myth no. 11 – that the Pakistan demand was a 'bargaining counter'.

Poker or chess?

Despite the erosion of relations between the League and the Congress in the twenties, despite Jinnah's permanent resignation from the Congress in protest of the rise of Hindu communalism and growing indifference to Muslim demands of their political rights, despite the fallout over the Nehru Report, despite the failure of the Round Table Conferences, and despite the widespread condemnation of Congress rule from 1937-9, [3] Britons and Hindus had difficulty accepting that Jinnah was serious in making a demand for secession. For example, Viceroy Linlithgow considered 'Jinnah's partition scheme' (as he called it) as being 'very largely in the nature of bargaining'. He felt that Jinnah had:

> put forward this scheme … partly to dispose of reproach that Moslems had no constructive scheme of their own; partly to offset the extreme Congress claim to independence, &c. ; and Congress contention that Congress is the mouthpiece of India; and that a Constituent Assembly on the basis of adult suffrage is the only machinery for deciding future progress … [4]

---

[1] Commentators of the time often described the 'game' in terms of poker. Ayesha Jalal borrowed the same language in her *Sole Spokesman.*

[2] See Jinnah's Presidential speech ML Annual Session, Patna, 26 December 1938 (Yusufi Vol. II, p.915); Brief minutes at ML Annual Session, Bombay, 12 April 1936 (NV Vol. I, p.38)

[3] For details of Jinnah's career and his conversion to 'Muslim nationalism', see Chapter 1.

[4] Secret Telegram from Governor-General Linlithgow to Secretary of State for India, dated New Delhi, April 6, 1940. (National Archives UK, War Cabinet: Memoranda (WP(G) Series), CAB 67/5/46) Spellings retained from original.

Chakravarti Rajagopalachari, a disciple of Gandhi, summed up the Congress' reaction to the resolution in one sentence: 'Most Congress men in India remember a time when Mr Jinnah did not differ from themselves either spiritually, economically, culturally, socially or politically'.[5] He added that in his opinion Jinnah was only after a weak centre and strong provinces. [6]

The Hindu press 'fathered' the word 'Pakistan' – borrowed from Ch. Rahmat Ali's much-aligned scheme for immediate partition – to describe the partition demand, and though the intent was to cause dissention amongst certain sections of Muslims and incite fear amongst non-Muslims, the League accepted it and began using it as a synonym for the Lahore Resolution. [7]

Many politicians in British and Congress circles believed that Jinnah's real aims were 'separatist' and not 'secessionist', and that what he said was not what he meant. This explains the attitude of the British and Congress in making proposals that either put Pakistan just out of reach [8]

---

5 Rajagopalachari's interview to the *Hindustan Times*, New Delhi, 27 March 1940, appearing in *Leader*, 30 March 1940 (NV Vol. II, p.5 fn)

6 Ibid. p.6 fn. Rajagopalachari would later propose a formula that recognised the right of self-determination for Muslims, but which (largely due to Gandhi's input) was riddled with impossible caveats. See footnote 9 below.

7 Jinnah said in 1940: 'As a matter of fact the Lahore Resolution embodies a principle which is popularly known as Pakistan and therefore there is no difference between the two.' (Public speech, Rambaugh recreation ground, Karachi, 23 December 1940, under the auspices of the City Muslim League. (NV Vol. II, p.101). See also Jinnah's Presidential address at the ML Annual Session, April 1943 (NV Vol. III, p.202). Here Jinnah explained that the word 'Pakistan' was being misused to create the notion that there would be 'Pak' (pure) and 'Na-Pak' (impure) zones in India. This was part of the attempt to imply that 'partition' meant 'balkanisation', and in addition that it meant Muslim imperialism. Having dismissed the propaganda, Jinnah thanked the Hindu propagandists for 'giving us one word' to use in place of the 'long phrase' (i.e. 'Lahore Resolution').

8 The 'Draft Declaration' dated 30 March 1942 (better known as the Cripps offer) proposed a new union of India (Dominion status), to be established after WWII. It contained a provision whereby any province or Princely State had the right (after the constitution was written up) to refuse to accede to the union, in which event it would retain its present constitutional position. This implied that any free provinces could then come together and form a dominion of Pakistan. An initially interested Jinnah explicitly asked for clarification that this would be the case (see Cripps' note of his interview with Jinnah, 25 March 1942; *Transfer of Power* Vol. I, p.481). As to how a province would exercise the right of non-accession, Cripps suggested that the Legislative Assembly of a given province could vote on the matter, and a plebiscite could be taken if that vote came too close to count as definitive. (Ibid.) The problem was that under the present system (1935 Act), even clear Muslim-majority provinces (e.g. Sind) had relatively small Muslim representation in the Legislative; and in Punjab and Bengal, the bare-majority Muslim provinces, the problem was even worse. The plebiscite principle would be based on the whole adult population and not the majority community, which was again the most problematic for the bare-majority Muslim provinces. The League viewed this as a denial of their 'inherent right to self-determination'. Since Cripps' draft had failed to recognise the Muslims as a nation, had showed a preference for a single union (instead of 'two or more independent Unions in India'), and had made the creation of Pakistan a 'remote possibility', the League resolved not to accept the draft. (Working Committee resolution, New Delhi and Allahabad, 27 March-11 April 1942; NV Vol. II, p.529-33) The Congress also rejected the

or made it so unattractive so as to guarantee that Jinnah would reject it.[9] The latter was the approach of the Cabinet Mission of 1946.

Cabinet Mission Plan overview

Before we begin, it is necessary that we take a brief look at the main differences between a federation and a confederation. Understanding these is the key to understanding not only why Jinnah 'controversially' accepted the Cabinet Mission Plan, but also what the British were actually offering.

In short, a federation has a strong centre, and the sovereignty of the states or provinces is subordinate to the centre. Finances for the centre are usually raised by compulsory taxation of the participating states/provinces. A federation tends to be legally recognised as a single country, and secession for any province/state is very difficult if not impossible. A confederation by contrast has a weak centre, and participating states have either near total or total sovereignty. Subjects at the centre are usually confined to defence, foreign affairs and communications. The centre is financially supported by voluntary payments rather than by taxation. Participation is entirely voluntary and the states always have the right to secede. A confederation is more likely to form between two or more countries (nation-states). [10] An obvious example of a federation is today's Pakistan, and an example of a confederation (notwithstanding some academic arguments over its status) is the European Union.

Jinnah had maintained since 1940 that whilst he was open to 'compromise and an honourable settlement', the Muslim League would not accept any proposals for a Hindu-Muslim organisation 'representing

---

draft on the grounds that the right of non-accession went against the principle of a united India. (29 April-2 May 1942; NV Vol. II, p.543-4, 592-4)

[9] Chakravarti Rajagopalachari's formula (or CR formula, 1944) was sanctioned by Gandhi for a Hindu-Muslim settlement. Gandhi later held his famous talks (in his personal capacity) with Jinnah with this formula on the table. The Congress would offer the League a 'Pakistan' after the war, and after India had been granted independence as a 'single national unit.' This national government of India would have (and retain) a federal centre containing subjects including not only foreign affairs, communications and defence, but also customs, commerce etc. It would have an overwhelming Hindu majority. A commission would be set up to demarcate Pakistan's territory on the basis of 'absolute majority' Rajagopalachari said 'absolute' was meant in the legal sense; Gandhi said it was meant to apply to areas with 75% or higher Muslim population. This automatically implied that Punjab and Bengal having bare Muslim majorities would be partitioned. Jinnah rejected the formula on the basis that it did not give 'independence' to Pakistan, but a 'form of provincial autonomy' within an 'overwhelmingly Hindu federal authority'. (Interview to a foreign correspondent, Bombay, 6 October 1944; Yusufi Vol. III, p.1951)

[10] See European Commission for Democracy through Law (1994), *The Modern Concept of Confederation* (Collection, Science & Technique of Democracy, No. 11) Strasbourg: Council of Europe, p.52-4; Kimmo Kiljunen (2004) *The European Constitution in the Making* Brussels: Centre for European Policy Studies, p.5-6; J.F. Zimmerman (2008) *Contemporary American Federalism: the Growth of National Power* Albany: State University of New York, p.3-4

all India'.[11] On the subject of the Lahore Resolution he had said:

> And no man can lay down a scheduled programme because it will depend upon so many factors that may develop and the nature of obstacles that may be created. We will have to deal with the situation from time to time as it may develop. But I know that Muslim India will not shirk any sacrifice as we have definitely made up our minds for the realisation of the goal that we have set in front of us. This is not a passing phase and it is a mistake to think that the methods of a constituent assembly will make any change in the solid opinion of the Mussalmans.[12]

In another interview on the Lahore Resolution, when Jinnah was asked about the expected relations of this separate Muslim homeland with Britain, he referred directly to the final clause of the Resolution, and added: 'As regards other zone or zones [*sic*] that may be constituted in the rest of India our relationship will be of an international character.'[13] Jinnah did his best to convince the doubters and those who did 'not want to understand'.[14] He bluntly told a London journalist that the British Government, the Parliament and the British public were making 'the greatest mistake' if they thought that the Pakistan demand was merely 'a counter for bargaining, or for treating it as the uncompromising attitude of the Muslim League'.[15]

True to Jinnah's statements, the Muslim League did eventually 'compromise' and (briefly) accepted the historically famous British Cabinet Mission Plan in June 1946. Some commentators refer to the Mission Plan as proof of their claim that Jinnah did not really want partition, because he persuaded the League to accept it despite the fact that technically the Plan had 'rejected Pakistan'.[16] But then, certainly in the minds of the British, it was only a technicality.[17] To begin with, in

---

[11] Interview to the Press explaining the significance of the League's decision at the Lahore Session, Lahore, 25 March 1940. (Yusufi Vol. II, p.1186)

[12] Ibid. p.1187

[13] Statement on the Lahore Resolution, New Delhi, 1 April 1940. (Yusufi Vol. II, p.1192-3) Note he has referred even to the rest of India (not just Muslim India) in terms of a 'zone or zones'. His references to 'state or states' for Muslim India therefore is not about ambiguity on his part, but the simple fact that he could predict no more or less about India's shape in the foreseeable future than anyone else.

[14] Presidential Address at the ML Annual Session, Madras, 14 April 1941. (Yusufi Vol. III, p.1384)

[15] Interview to a London newspaper, Bombay, 3 January 1941 (Yusufi Vol. II, p.1306)

[16] See for example A. Jalal 1994, p.202

[17] Jalal has made a similar observation, and has quoted a letter between two British officials stating that the Mission aimed to produce something 'which Jinnah can regard as conceding Pakistan and Congress can regard as not conceding it'. (Croft to Monteath, 3 May 1946 (*Transfer of Power*, Vol. VII, p.410); cited in A. Jalal 1994, p.192)

April 1946 [18] the British drafted two alternative schemes to be presented to the various Indian parties:

- **Scheme A:** the formation of a 'Union of all-India'. [19] India would be reorganised into three groups: One consisting of Hindu-majority provinces, the second consisting of Muslim-majorities provinces, and the third of the Princely States. This technically rejected Pakistan as a fully sovereign state but gave it more territory. All the provinces including Sind, Baluchistan, NWFP, Punjab (minus Gurdaspur district) and Bengal (plus perhaps Sylhet district of Assam) would be part of the Muslim group and would remain united, while the Princely States might enter the union as a separate 'federation'. [20] The groups would have equal representation, and be allowed to draw up their own separate constitutions, placing a minimal number of subjects at the centre which were necessary to maintain the 'union'. [21] To boot, this union would run for fifteen (later ten) years, [22] after which point any group of provinces unhappy with the setup would be free to secede from the union.
- **Scheme B:** the partition of India. The subcontinent was to be divided into two fully sovereign states of Hindustan and Pakistan, and the Princely States could either federate to whichever of the two they wished, or remain independent. [23] The catch was that owing to the communal factor a sovereign Pakistan would not be given the whole of Punjab and Bengal. The provinces would have to be partitioned, [24] though Calcutta might become a free port. [25] Jinnah would end up with a 'moth-eaten' Pakistan, one that he had already rejected in 1944. [26]

It hardly takes a constitutional expert to see that the British had deliberately made the union as attractive as possible and simultaneously

[18] Memorandum by Stafford Cripps, undated (April 1946), outlines the earliest draft (NV Vol. V, p.715-23)

[19] Ibid. p.717

[20] Brief prepared by Wavell, undated (11-12 April 1946) (NV Vol. V, p.733)

[21] Ibid. The subjects were defence, foreign affairs and communications – the same minimal subjects which are characteristic of confederation.

[22] The original period was 15 years as suggested by both Sir Stafford Cripps and Wavell (See Note by Stafford Cripps, undated (but cir. 11-12 April 1946); and Brief prepared by Wavell, undated (cir. 11-12 April 1946), in *Transfer of Power* Vol. VII, p.234, 251 respectively). Likewise 15 years was suggested to Jinnah by the Cabinet Delegation in their meeting 16 April 1946 (NV Vol. IV, p.639)

[23] Memorandum by Stafford Cripps, undated (NV Vol. V, p.718)

[24] Ibid. p.718-21.

[25] Ibid, 721. The reason for the offer was that 'Calcutta is predominantly a Hindu area and yet without it, it hardly seems possible to contemplate an Eastern Pakistan.' (Ibid.)

[26] The CR formula: see footnote 9.

made partition untenable. They preferred Scheme A on account of difficulties including the division of assets and the army. They knew that the defence problem could technically be resolved with an international treaty and by giving both countries Dominion status, but they also feared that a partitioned Pakistan and Hindustan might follow 'divergent foreign policies', with Hindustan leaning towards Russia and China (since Congress was turning socialist) and Pakistan leaning towards the Muslim States of the Middle East. [27]

On 8 April, in light of its recent overwhelming victory in the Indian elections, the League had passed its famous Delhi Resolution, updating the Lahore Resolution and making a definitive demand for Pakistan. The very next day, Wavell and the Cabinet Delegation held the first of a series of meetings in which they discussed how they would present the case to Jinnah in a manner as to gently force his hand. First they decided to make it clear that the Muslims would not be allowed to have Calcutta on any basis except in Scheme A. [28] If Jinnah insisted on a separate Pakistan, they intended to make it clear that 'the area referred to in plan B was all he would get'; he would not be able to 'justify his claim to Pakistan on the basis that it would be a sovereign state'. [29] They also added the secession clause (based on an idea originally advanced in the Cripps' Mission of 1942) [30] which technically made for a 'tripartite *confederation*', though they consciously decided amongst themselves not to publicly refer to it as such. [31]

When the delegation met with Jinnah on 16 April, they pressed upon these points. Jinnah asked how Pakistan fitted into the proposed scheme, and the delegates – who up until that point had wilfully avoided using the word 'Pakistan' in their description of said 'union' – replied that the 'larger Pakistan' within this Scheme would 'come together with Hindustan on terms of equality' with a minimal centre, where it would be '*states* that counted and not the *number of*

---

[27] Record of meeting, 10 April 1946 (NV Vol. V, p.725).

[28] Brief prepared by Wavell, undated but cir. 11-12 April 1946. (NV Vol. V, p.735)

[29] Record of meeting, Cabinet Delegation and Viceroy Wavell, 10 April 1946 (NV Vol. V, p.725-6)

[30] See footnote 8.

[31] See record of meeting, Cabinet Delegation and Wavell on 13 April 1946. The relevant portion reads: 'It was agreed that the proposal for an all-India Union on a minimum list of subjects should not be put to Jinnah on the basis that it would be a tripartite confederation of Hindustan, Pakistan, and the [Princely] States.' (NV Vol. V, p.735). In recent years a retired Indian bureaucrat who has reviewed the features of the British Cabinet Plan has concluded: 'It would be clear beyond doubt that what the Cabinet Mission Plan proposed was a Confederation ... Undoubtedly, the Cabinet Mission Plan intended partition of India into Pakistan and Hindustan, which simultaneously would join in a Confederation. This, we suggest, was misleadingly described as "all-India Union"; it is misleading because "Union" implies "political ties that bind". The appellation "Union" or "Federation" was a subterfuge.' (Yuvraj Krishan (2002) *Understanding Partition: India Sundered, Muslims Fragmented* Mumbai: Bharatiya Vidya Bhavan, p.52-3)

individuals in them'.[32] This established, as Jalal has succinctly put it, 'an equality underwritten by the law of nations'.[33] As far as the British were concerned, it was a matter of individual perspective as to whether this (unspoken) confederation meant a united India or a partition in all but name.

The constitutionalist in Jinnah soon realised that whilst there was technically to be a union for ten years,[34] the three Groups would be separate in every way that mattered. There was scant difference between this setup and Jinnah's own demand for 'two Indias with nothing but [international] treaties between them'.[35] International relations – especially between neighbouring countries – always involve treaties on subjects such as foreign affairs and defence. These same subjects – communications, defence and foreign affairs – were being relegated to the centre in the Mission Plan's proposed union, and secession was part of the deal. A full Pakistan complete with undivided Bengal and Punjab was thus possible after ten years, and it would even be free to develop itself as it wished in the meantime. It is not without significance that Jinnah used the term 'confederation' as well as the terms '*Hindustan* Group' and '*Pakistan* Group' (as opposed to the British terminology Groups 'A' and 'B') when discussing the Mission Plan in public.[36] Nation-states had been merely rendered in the form of Groups, and the 'centre' was practically just the medium in which to execute international treaties. Word games however, did not take away from the substance. Hence Jinnah wanted Congress to accept the Groups, and in return he would accept the central 'constitution-making machinery' – working on the assumption that it would be 'sovereign' in practice but not by law, and that there would be two constituent assemblies to allow the Groups to draw up their own constitutions.[37]

---

32 Record of interview between Cabinet Delegation and Jinnah, New Delhi, 16 April 1946 (NV Vol. IV, p.640-1)

33 A. Jalal 1994, p.187. Emphasis mine.

34 See footnote 22.

35 Interview with Cabinet Delegation and Viceroy Wavell, New Delhi, 4 April 1946 (NV Vol. IV, p.583). I have inserted the clarifying term 'international' partly because so many commentators take any reference to 'treaties' as being automatically indicative of federation in an Indian Union. Jinnah had used the word 'international' in criticising Cripps's offer in 1942: 'the Musalmans feel deeply disappointed that the entity and integrity of the Muslim nation has not been expressly recognised. … India was never a country or nation. India's problem is *international* in this *subcontinent*'. (Presidential address at the ML Annual Session, Allahabad, 4 April 1942; NV Vol. II, p.428-9. Emphasis mine.)

36 Press statement, Simla, 22 May 1946 (NV Vol. V, p.16). The British steadfastly stuck to using the terms 'Muslim-majority' and 'Hindu-majority' Groups, and 'Union'.

37 See delegate A.V. Alexander's diary entry dated 6 May 1946: 'Mr Jinnah said that the only way to prevent complete partition was for the provinces to group themselves together by choice and that we should set up a constitution-making machinery which *de facto* would be sovereign though not *de jure*. He rejected the suggestion that there should be one constitution-making body and suggested that the representatives of Groups … *meet separately for all matters* except those concerning the Union constitution.' (NV Vol. V, lxvi; emphasis mine except on Latin terms.)

Unsurprisingly, Congress was unhappy with the concept of Groups. At the second Simla Conference held to fine-tune the Plan before it was to be issued publicly, objections on both sides led to a stalemate, and the British decided to issue their own statement on 16 May. [38] As expected they formally recommended Scheme A, the 'union', but now the scheme had been changed:

- The original 'B' or 'Pakistan Group' was split into two (Punjab and Bengal now became Groups 'B' and 'C' respectively) [39]
- There was to be one constituent assembly instead of two, with an overwhelming Hindu majority at the centre [40]
- The secession clause was altered so that all a Group could do after ten years was 'call for a reconsideration of the terms of the constitution'
- The union centre was to deal with foreign affairs, defence, and communications; and the centre was to be given 'powers necessary to raise the finances' for all of these subjects

This made the confederation closer to a federation. Its sole saving grace was the compulsory Grouping, which in principle remained intact. Jinnah was dismayed that the plan allowed only for a single constituent assembly in the short-term, and that the noose had been tightened in the long-term with the alteration of the escape clause. He also denounced the fact that the central subjects were being manipulated:

> There is no indication at all that the communications would be restricted to what is necessary for defence, nor is there any indication as to how this Union will be empowered to raise finances required for these three subjects, while our view was that finances should be raised only by contributions and not by taxation. [41]

The British were in a hurry to get the 'short-term' plan (constitution-making process) underway so they could leave India and save face as having left it technically united. This meant the formation of an Interim Government to remain in effect in the transitional period, until the long-term constitution for the independent union of India could be drawn up. On 3 June Jinnah sought Wavell's assurance that in the event that the

38 See NV Vol. V, p.746-765 for full Mission statement of 16 May 1946.

39 The Princely States were not allocated to any of these Groups.

40 The Hindus had a three-to-one majority in British India alone; the addition of the Princely states to British India in this scheme meant that the centre diluted Muslim representation significantly further. This had also been one of the major issues at the Round Table Conferences of the 1930s.

41 See Jinnah's statement on the Mission's 16 May announcement, Simla, 22 May 1946. (NV Vol. V, p.19)

League accepted the Interim Government and the Congress refused, the British would go ahead with forming said Government and would give the League the right to join it. [42] Then there was the matter of seats representation in the Interim Government. Wavell was at this point proposing an Interim Government formula of 5:5:2 (Congress: League: minorities), but it was not yet finally decided. Jinnah warned that it would be 'very difficult' [43] for the League to accept anything short of parity in the Interim Government. Wavell implicitly assured Jinnah that the Interim Government would adhere to the parity principle, by allowing Jinnah to show the formula to his colleagues in the League. Wavell later denied having given this exact assurance. [44]

Jinnah did his utmost to get all parties to accept the redeeming features of the original Mission Plan as a confederation. He tried to get the opting-out clause time reduced from ten to five years, only to be shouted down by Sardar Patel who accused him of laying bare 'the reality behind the grouping proposal'. [45] Jinnah disavowed the alteration of the secession clause, maintaining that 'the revision of the constitution provided for after 10 years *implied* a right of secession'. [46] (We might add that the Secretary of State acknowledged the League's right to push for this interpretation and to get it accepted by the constitution-making body.) [47] Jinnah also opposed the raising of finances by state taxation, he tried to keep the central subjects confined to those consistent with a confederation, and even aimed to restrict communications to what was 'necessary for defence' only. [48] This and his insistence on parity in both the short-term and long-term plans, regardless of the fact that Muslims were outnumbered three to one in India, together speak volumes about his determination to retain the 'foundation and the basis' [49] of Pakistan in the Plan.

---

42 In Jinnah's interview with Wavell, 3 June 1946 (NV Vol. V, p.26-8), Wavell gave a verbal assurance and Jinnah asked for it to be put down in writing. The Prime Minister (Clement Attlee) later did not permit Wavell to put it formally in writing, but he did authorise Wavell to give a 'personal assurance' (see draft notes for Jinnah, 3 June 1946; NV Vol. V, p.28 fn). Wavell offered this 'personal assurance' in writing on 4 June 1946. (NV Vol. V, p.786)

43 Jinnah's interview with Wavell, 3 June 1946 (NV Vol. V, p.27)

44 Jinnah to Wavell, 19 June 1946; also Jinnah's press statement, 29 June 1946. (NV Vol. V, p.82, 96-7 respectively).

45 See record of fourth meeting at Second Simla Conference, 6 May 1946 (*Transfer of Power* Vol. VII, p.442)

46 Jinnah's interview with Cabinet Delegation and Viceroy Wavell, 25 June 1946 (*Transfer of Power* Vol. VII, p.1045). See also press statement at Simla, 22 May 1946 (NV Vol. V, p.15, 20-21).

47 Op. cit. *Transfer of Power* Vol. VII, p.1045

48 Jinnah's statement on the Mission's 16 May announcement, Simla, 22 May 1946. (NV Vol. V, p.16)

49 Jinnah's address at the Muslim League Council meeting, 5 June 1946. (NV Vol. V, p.29)

Conditional acceptance

Jinnah's efforts are also reflected in the resolution of the Muslim League's Council meeting on 6 June 1946. At this meeting, held in secret, Jinnah recommended that the League accept the Mission Plan. He assured them that the 'foundation and the basis of Pakistan' were as yet contained in the Mission scheme. The League took into account the above assurances about the Interim Government, as well as the 5:5:2 formula still on the table, before reluctantly opting to accept. [50] In their resolution accepting the Plan, the Council put it on record that their decision was being taken in light of:

> ... [the League's] earnest desire for a peaceful solution, if possible, of the Indian constitutional problem, and inasmuch as the basis and the foundation of Pakistan are inherent in the Mission's Plan, by virtue of the compulsory Grouping of the six Muslim provinces in Sections B and C, is willing to cooperate with the constitution-making machinery proposed in the scheme outlined by the Mission in the hope that it would ultimately result in the establishment of complete sovereign Pakistan ...
>
> ... and it will keep in view the opportunity and the right of secession of provinces or Groups from the Union which have been provided in the Mission's Plan, by implication. [51]

Nevertheless, forty years of experience of dealing with the Congress had taught the League to be wary, and so the Council included an escape clause of its own:

> The ultimate attitude of the Muslim League will depend on the final outcome of the labours of the constitution-making body, and on the final shape of the constitutions which may emerge from the deliberations of that body jointly and separately in its three Sections.
>
> The Muslim League also reserves the right to modify and revise the policy and attitude set forth in this resolution at any time during the progress of deliberations of the constitution-making body, or the Constituent Assembly ... [52]

The League's acceptance of both the short-term and long-term plans was conditional. It reserved the right to pull out at any time.

The ordinary Muslims of India were initially outraged (though some with better political acumen had more accurately gauged the

[50] See Jinnah's letters to Wavell, 8 and 19 June 1946. (NV Vol. V, p.94-5, 82 respectively)

[51] Muslim League Council resolution, New Delhi, 5-6 June 1946. (NV Vol. V, p.560)

[52] Ibid. p.560-1

situation).[53] They had voted for the League in the last election on the basis that it would fight for partition. Hindus and Muslims alike mistakenly thought that the League's acceptance of the Plan meant that 'Pakistan had been buried once and for all and that India's unity had been preserved.' But Muslims across India would soon come to appreciate the 'constructive and statesmanlike attitude' of Jinnah in thinking ahead and avoiding 'the snare laid for him'.[54]

A week after the League's formal acceptance, Wavell informed Jinnah of his intent to change the formula to 5:5:3 (totalling 13 seats) owing to opposition from Congress on the original. The extra seat was to be allotted to a Scheduled Caste Hindu who would be a nominee of Congress. Yet even this wasn't deemed satisfactory by Congress, who wanted 15 seats, could not accept a Scheduled Caste seat because it implied that the Scheduled Castes were a minority outside of the Hindu body politic, and 'could not accept anything in the nature of "parity" even as a temporary expedient'.[55] At the same time, they wanted to include a 'nationalist Muslim' within their own quota,[56] to which Jinnah strongly objected.

Three days later, in its statement of 16 June, the Mission announced a compromise formula of 5:5:4, to include one Parsi. Amongst those whom Wavell invited to join the Interim Government, he did not include a Congress Muslim but he gave the Scheduled Caste Hindu seat to a Congressman, effectively giving the Congress six seats instead of five. Not only was the parity principle between the Congress and the League violated, but the overall League representation came down to just over a third owing to the new total of 14 instead of the original of 12 seats. This also affected the distribution of portfolios in the Interim Government. However, paragraph 8 of the statement also contained a variant of Wavell's earlier assurances to Jinnah to the effect that if one or both of the 'two major parties' (i.e. the Congress and the League) did not accept the long-term union plan as outlined on 16 May, the British would go ahead and set up an Interim Government which would be 'as representative as possible' of all parties that had accepted it.[57]

The Congress deliberately stalled in giving its decision on the short-term Interim Government. It had not even been willing to give its 'final opinion' on the Mission's 16 May announcement of the long-term

---

53 See for example following letters addressed to Jinnah after the 6 June meeting: letter of Begum Shah Nawaz, 8 June 1946; also Major Mian Kifait Ali, 7 June 1946. Major Ali (pen name 'A Punjabi) is best known for his constitutional scheme for India titled *A Confederacy for India.* (Letters obtained from: W. Ahmad (2009) *The Punjab Story: 1940-1947* Islamabad: Government of Pakistan, p.199, p.411 respectively. Other congratulatory letters from the public appear on op. cit. p.197-200)

54 *Eastern Times*, 16 June 1946. (Saeed (ed.) 1983, p.264)

55 Azad to Wavell (letter drafted by Nehru), 25 June 1946. (NV Vol. V, p.957). Quotation marks around 'parity' appear as in original.

56 Ibid. p.958

57 Cabinet Mission statement, 16 June 1946 (NV Vol. V, p.790)

Plan.[58] On 25 June Congress President Abul Kalam Azad sent his letter to Wavell containing the Congress decision (this decision was supposed to have been given by 23 June).[59] It had been formally agreed earlier that the League should give its decision after the Congress leaders had given theirs.[60] Azad's letter was again ambivalent on the issue of the long-term plan, and appeared to accept the 16 June statement regarding the Interim Government with reservations. Congress stuck to its guns regarding what it wanted in terms of the number of seats, on parity, on grouping, and on its right to include a Muslim within its quota. Having received a copy of this letter that evening from the Viceroy, the League took the precaution of withholding comment on Azad's letter 'for the present' and resolved to nevertheless accept the 16 June statement.[61]

The next day on 26 June, the Congress Working Committee resolved that it was 'unable to accept the proposals for the formation of an Interim Government as contained in the statement of June 16', and simultaneously declared its intent to 'join the proposed Constituent Assembly with a view to framing the constitution of a free, united and democratic India'.[62] The Congress did not technically reject the idea of an Interim Government outright, but rather sought an alternative 'representative and responsible provisional government' to its liking, 'at the earliest possible date'.[63]

This decision was good for the League. Not only did it confirm its suspicions about the Congress' strategy, but it also meant that paragraph 8 could be implemented and the League could join the Interim Government without Congress. However, the British put a different interpretation on paragraph 8. The same day that the Congress rejected the Interim Government, the Mission 'adjourned' negotiations, called for elections to the new Constituent Assembly, and created a 'temporary caretaker' government instead of setting up the Interim. The Mission Delegation also announced their intention to return to England by 29 June.[64] Jinnah deplored the British for having gone back on their 'pledged word' and urged that the Constituent Assembly elections be postponed in light of the Mission's decision to delay the formation of the Interim Government, but to no avail.[65]

---

58 See Congress Working Committee resolution on 16 May Mission Statement, 24 May 1946. (NV Vol. V, p.630)

59 NV Vol. V, p.956. Azad did however write to Wavell on 24 June 1946 to confirm that the preliminary decision had been 'taken yesterday' to reject the Interim Government, but that Congress wanted to meet again on the subject and so details of the reasons for the rejection would follow later. (Ibid.)

60 See Jinnah's press statement, New Delhi, 27 June 1946. (NV Vol. V, p.73)

61 ML Working Committee resolution, New Delhi, 25 June 1946 (NV Vol. V, p.570)

62 Congress Working Committee resolution, Delhi, 26 June 1946 (NV Vol. V, p.632-3)

63 Ibid. p.633

64 Cabinet Mission statement, 26 June 1946. (NV Vol. V, p.791-2)

65 Jinnah to Wavell, 28 June 1946. (NV Vol. V, p.105). Wavell denied any foul play at the time, but upon his return to London in December 1946 he admitted his mistake in his note to

Nehru's disclosure

About a week later, Nehru replaced Azad as President. [66] In his first public speech as Congress President on 7 July, he boldly confirmed the real position of the Congress:

> There is a good deal of talk of the Cabinet Mission's long-term plan and short-term plan. So far as I can see, it is not a question of our accepting any plan – long or short. It is only a question of our agreeing to go into the Constituent Assembly. That is all, and there is nothing more to it than that. We will remain in the Assembly so long as we think it is good for India …
>
> ... What will be the outcome of this Assembly? It may be that it does not function for long … it may be we may get something out of it … But it seems to me rather fantastic for the Cabinet Mission to tell us that, after ten years, we are going to do this or that. … I cannot imagine anybody laying down any rule for India ten years hence. When India is free, India will do just what it likes.[67]

His remarks were quite self-explanatory, and his act of supposed 'sabotage' sent shockwaves across India (we'll come to that shortly). In a press interview three days later, he was even more explicit. When asked to expand upon his comments that the Congress had committed itself only on entering the Constituent Assembly, he replied:

> As a matter of fact if you read the correspondence that has passed between the Congress President and the Cabinet Mission

---

the Prime Minister and other Ministers. He also confirmed that both the League and the Congress had been open and upfront about their intentions: 'The Cabinet Mission Plan was as good as could have been framed in the circumstances … but neither Mission nor HMG adhered to their original intention with sufficient directness of purpose. In particular the Mission gave Jinnah pledges on May 16, which they had not honoured. Congress has been reasonably honest that they never meant to carry out the Plan as the Mission intended, unless they were forced to, and said so. League have also been reasonably honest and would have attempted to carry out the Mission's Plan had HMG stuck to it firmly.' (Wavell's note dated 2 December 1946; *Transfer of Power* Vol. IX, p.240-1)

66 Jinnah always viewed the Muslim cleric A.K. Azad (1888-1958) as a quisling Muslim; he famously refused to shake Azad's hand, and called him a 'puppet President' (Interview to International News Service of America, Bombay, 21 May 1942; Yusufi Vol. III, p.1571) during his tenure as Congress President (1940-1946). Azad was made President when much of the Congress leadership ended up in jail during WWII for refusing to cooperate in the war effort. Azad's Presidency was also a show of Congress' representative status, to try and prove that the Muslim League was not the sole representative of Indian Muslims, and also an attempt to regain Muslim mass support following the widely condemned Congress-dominated government between 1937 and 1939. Much of Azad's correspondence and resolutions were drafted by J. Nehru (NV Vol. V, lxxxvi). He resigned his tenure on 6 July 1946, only a week after the Mission Delegation left India, and Nehru took his place.

67 Nehru's Presidential speech, Congress session, Bombay, 7 July 1946. (NV Vol. V, p.855-6)

> and the Viceroy, you will see in what conditions and circumstances we agreed to go into this Constituent Assembly. [68]

(On the point of correspondence, Jinnah had already noticed a hint in Azad's 25 June letter that the British were offering concessions to Congress.[69] Viceroy Wavell himself later admitted his own dubious part in the affair to the Prime Minister in London. [70])

People both in India and Pakistan have blamed Nehru almost exclusively for supposedly sabotaging the Mission Plan, suggesting that he was determined not to share power with the League in a united India,[71] but this is neither fair nor backed by the evidence. If Nehru's views did not reflect those of the Congress, why did his colleagues not go up in arms, calling for his resignation? Why had they voted in favour of the ambivalent resolution of acceptance on 26 June? Congress had always sought a united India with a strong centre in which Hindus had the biggest share of the power. This was why it had aimed to get rid of the Grouping and the parity principle in the Plan, and had formally rejected the Interim Government. [72] Nehru had merely brought the full significance of the Congress' strategy out into the open. He was only being frank.

Jinnah responded by reiterating the League's long-running suspicions. He made special reference to Azad's letter of 25 June, about which (as we have seen) the League had wilfully withheld its comments up until this point:

> It has been clear from the outset to those who understood from the letter of the President of the Congress of June 25, addressed to the Viceroy and the resolution of the Congress Working Committee that followed it [the] next day, rejecting the Interim Government proposals contained in the statement of the Cabinet Delegation and Viceroy, dated June 16, that the so-called acceptance by the Congress only of [the] long-term plan of May 16, was never intended to honour its terms and obligations with the desire to carry out the scheme in the spirit of constructive and friendly co-operation. …

---

68 Nehru's press interview, Bombay, 10 July 1946 (NV Vol. V, p.859)

69 Jinnah had publicly expressed on 27 June that though he did not have 'the correspondence that passed between them', he nevertheless suspected from Azad's letter of 25 June that the Viceroy had been assuring the Congress of there being 'no parity' between the League and Congress in his formula, whilst simultaneously writing to Jinnah (20 June) that 'the proportion of members by communities will not be change without the consent of the two major parties'. (See press statement, New Delhi, 27 June 1946; NV Vol. V, p.78-9)

70 See footnote 65 above.

71 See for example A.K. Azad (1959) *India Wins Freedom: an Autobiographical Narrative* Bombay: Orient Longman, p.155-60; A.S. Ahmed 1997, p.114

72 For evidence of Patel and Gandhi's roles, see A.G. Noorani, 'Jinnah and Partition' in *Frontline* magazine, Vol. 22 Issue 18, 27 August – 9 September 2005

> ... They are going into the Constituent Assembly as has now been so frankly and clearly defined by Pandit Jawaharlal Nehru, on his assumption of office as the President of the Congress, 'to achieve their objective'. He has also made it quite clear that they are not going to honour any of the terms of the long-term plan ... This is simply because they have secured a brute majority of 292 against 79 Muslims in the Constituent Assembly. [73]

On 29 July, just three weeks after Nehru's statements, the League withdrew its acceptance of the Mission Plan and called for 'Direct Action', which, despite Jinnah's clear declarations that it was to be a peaceful protest, [74] turned violent and brought the country to the brink of civil war. [75] On 'Direct Action Day' itself (16 August 1946), terrible rioting occurred in Calcutta and surrounding areas, and became known as the Great Calcutta Killings. Muslims and Hindus fought in various parts of India over the following months. [76] Jinnah unreservedly condemned all Muslims who had taken part in the rioting against his express orders.[77]

On 10 August 1946, Congress passed a resolution claiming that it had from the beginning accepted the scheme in its entirety, whilst maintaining that its resolution of 26 June must stand. It also accepted the Viceroy's invitation to form a new Interim Government. [78] On 24 August the Viceroy announced the new formula: An Executive with 14

---

73 Interview to the Associated Press of India on the statement made by Pandit Jawaharlal Nehru, Hyderabad, 13 July 1946. (Yusufi Vol. IV, p.2331; NV Vol. V, p.188-120)

74 Address at press conference, Bombay, 31 July 1946 (Yusufi Vol. IV, p.2353-60); Press interview, Bombay, 5 August 1946 (NV Vol. V, p.180-181).

75 It might be mentioned that at around the same time (15 August 1946) the Scheduled Castes Federation had arranged an 'anti-Poona Pact Day' to raise their voices for political autonomy for their community. During that same day and throughout the month there were marches in rural towns of Bengal, and these were supported by the Muslim League. Protests held in other parts of India also indicate the size of the support the Federation had among the community it represented. For further details, including discussion of the under-appreciated strength of the League-Federation collaboration during this period, see Dwaipayan Sen 2012, p.325-7.

76 A.S. Ahmed 1997, p.114. Although the Great Calcutta Killings were instigated by Direct Action Day, both communities were equally culpable, although in this case the greater number of casualties were Muslims (B. Chakrabarty 2004, p.101, citing a report on the riots written by Bengal's Inspector General of Police in 1946). A couple of months later in October 1946, Noakhali became the scene of riots directed at Hindus of all castes. Bihar was next to be hit by a massacre in December 1946, this time directed at Muslims, while in the NWFP that same month Sikhs and Hindus were massacred. And in Punjab March 1947 onwards, mutual violence ensued between Muslims and Sikhs. Scholarship has shown that these conflicts, despite being attributed primarily to communal tensions at an all-India level, often had localised and opportunistic causes as well; and so incidents in one part of India were not always 'retributive', or a direct consequence of, incidents in another. See Paul Brass, 'The Partition of India and Retributive Genocide in the Punjab, 1946–47: Means, Methods, and Purposes' in *Journal of Genocide Studies*, Vol. 5, No. 1 (2003), p.70-101.

77 Press interview, Bombay, 17 August 1946; NV Vol. V, p.214-5

78 Congress Working Committee resolution, Wardha, 10 August 1946. (NV Vol. V, p.636-50; exact date of resolution obtained from NV Vol. V, p.194)

seats, of which 6 would be given to Congress, 5 to the Muslim League (should it decide to join), and the remaining 3 to other minorities. [79]

The League was against the proposal, but with the ongoing riots as a symptom of a looming civil war, in October 1946 it joined the Interim Government. Jinnah informed the Viceroy that 'in the interests of Musalmans and other communities' they knew it would be 'fatal to leave the entire field of administration of the Central Government in the hands of Congress', and so they were joining under duress. [80] In light of the need to protect Muslim and non-Muslim interests alike, the League gave one of the seats in its quota to the leader of the Scheduled Castes Federation in Bengal, Jogendra Nath Mandal. [81] Part of the reason may have been to counter Congress' insistence on having a Muslim in its quota, [82] but Mandal's inclusion also served to highlight that the Scheduled Caste Hindus would 'rather live as free and honourable men in the Muslim fold or any other fold' than in the 'Hindu fold'. [83]

Over the next couple of weeks Jinnah also made several public statements to reiterate the League's actual position. Here we need cite only one example:[84]

> Of the Interim Government, Mr Jinnah said in response to questions that the Muslim League Ministers were there 'as sentinels who would watch Muslim interests in the day to day administration of Government.' ...
>
> Asked if he favoured abandoning the Interim Government, Mr Jinnah replied: 'I have said this: It was forced upon us. The present arrangement I do not approve of.' [85]

It was only natural that in this 'forced' coalition, irrevocable disagreements on the long-term Plan would lead to a political deadlock.

---

79 Viceroy's broadcast, New Delhi, 24 August 1946. (NV Vol. V, p.939-43)

80 See Jinnah's letter to Wavell dated 13 October 1946, (part of the Jinnah-Wavell correspondence released to the press) in *Dawn*, 29 October 1946. (Yusufi Vol. IV, p.2437)

81 See Jinnah's letter to Wavell containing list of nominees, 14 October 1946 (NV Vol. V, p.339-40)

82 Dwaipayan Sen however holds that this is a cynical view of why Mandal was given the seat. The move was likely made in a genuine spirit, given that Jinnah had fought for the Scheduled Caste Hindus at the Round Table Conferences in the early 1930s (D. Sen 2012, p.341-2).

83 See Mandal's comments at the Eid gathering, New Delhi, 5 November 1946 as reported in *Dawn*, 7 November 1946 (NV Vol. V, p.357-8); See also the *Dawn* report of 5 November 1946 on the Scheduled Castes Conference quoted as declaring its condemnation of British dishonesty 'which sacrificed the rights of seven crores of Scheduled Castes by leaving them entirely at the mercy of caste Hindus' (Ibid. p.358 fn). For biographical note on Mandal, see Appendix II.

84 For more examples, see Jinnah's press conference, Karachi, 25 November 1946 (Yusufi Vol. IV, p.2467-8); Interview to Miss Cummings of the Christian Science Monitor, New Delhi, 9 November 1946 (Ibid. p.2453)

85 Statement at a press conference attended by foreign correspondents, New Delhi, 14 November 1946; as reported by *Dawn*, 15 November 1946. (Ibid. p.2457)

Indeed Jinnah had warned beforehand: 'every proposal will be looked upon by me from the point of view of its value towards the achievement of the Pakistan demand, while the Congress will look at it from the point of view of avoiding Pakistan and establishing Akhand Hindustan and Hindu raj over the entire sub-continent of India'. [86] The situation became critical. In December 1946, British Prime Minister Clement Attlee attempted to resume negotiations, inviting M.A. Jinnah, Liaquat Ali Khan, Jawaharlal Nehru, and Baldev Singh for talks in London, but with tensions between Hindu and Muslim communities having reached a peak, and leaders on all sides refusing to budge from their respective positions, it was clear that the Cabinet Mission had failed.

Gandhi's last try

On 20 February 1947 the British Government announced its intent to transfer power to India by June 1948, and in March 1947, Mountbatten took over from Wavell as Viceroy. The question remained as to whether there would an interim all-India setup, or immediate partition to create India and Pakistan.

In one last attempt to broker a peacemaking deal and prevent immediate partition, in April 1947 Gandhi drafted a scheme in which Jinnah was to be offered the premiership of a united India during the interim period, the power to form a cabinet of his choosing, and the right to present 'a scheme of Pakistan even before the transfer of power.' [87] Nehru was willing to go along the scheme, if only in order to strengthen the centre during the transfer of power, but in the end Congress leaders decided it would likely not succeed, [88] and so it was never shown to Jinnah. [89]

In the end, partition became inevitable. Unfortunately, instead of a 'surgical operation',[90] it would entail the 'balkanisation' that almost nobody wanted.

---

[86] See Jinnah's interview to the press warning that India stands at the brink of civil war, Bombay, 10 September 1946 (Yusufi Vol. IV, p.2414).

[87] See Gandhi's 'Outline of Draft Agreement' dictated to Lord Hastings Ismay, Chief of Staff, 4 April 1947. CWMG Vol. 94, p.228-9.(http://www.gandhiserve.org/cwmg/VOL094.PDF)

[88] Jinnah had summarily dismissed a similar offer in the past. See his speech in the Central Legislative Assembly on the Indian Finance (No. 2) Bill, New Delhi, November 19, 1940. (Yusufi Vol. II, p.1274)

[89] See record of interview between Rear-Admiral Viscount Mountbatten of Burma and Pandit Nehru in *Transfer of Power* Vol. X, p.154-5; Ibid p.208. Mountbatten for his part had in early April 1947 'tried out on Mr Jinnah, without divulging the source, the main essentials of Mahatma Gandhi's scheme', and had found Jinnah to be 'utterly horrified' by the suggestion. (Carter (ed.) 2003, p.65)

[90] Mountbatten's record of his first interview with Jinnah, New Delhi, 5-6 April 1947 (NV Vol. VI, p.29)

Chapter 12
Non-Muslims in an Islamic polity

The Quran does not recognise the concept of majorities and minorities. It teaches that all humans are born equal on the basis of their having a common origin (4:1). It teaches that a true democracy rests not on the principle of simple majority rule (6:116) but rather on the principle of consensus (aiming for unanimity) by 'mutual consultation' (42:38). It also teaches that humans only differ by the type of *deen* that they follow; and that strictly speaking there are only two types of human society: One that lives by the universal spiritual principles of liberty, justice and solidarity, and the other that does not (5:56-7). This is the Quranic basis of the Two-Nation Theory. It has nothing to do with communalism, and everything to do with the active behaviour of a society that claims to be 'good'. (2:148)

Jinnah's appointment of a Hindu in the first Constituent Assembly of Pakistan (the Scheduled Castes leader Mr J.N. Mandal) is considered by some to be proof that he was building Pakistan as a 'secular' state. It is our thirteenth myth. In order to reassess this claim, we must first become familiar with the Quran's position on the civil rights of non-Muslims. In this book we will not review the concept of non-Muslims as *dhimmi* ('protected ones') or *jizya* (traditional term for 'poll tax' paid by the *dhimmi*), as these are not presently applied in any contemporary Muslim country, and in any case, these two interlinked concepts have an historical basis, whereas we are more interested in the Quran's timeless principles as they apply to us today. [1]

---

[1] See Chapter 4, footnote 44 for a short traditional explanation of the terms *dhimmi* and *jizya*. It should suffice to say however that the word *jizya* appears only once in the Quran, and the word *dhimma* ('covenant' or 'contract'- Lane Book I (Part 3), p.976) appears only twice – but the word *dhimmi* does not appear at all. This means that the idea of *dhimmi* is an historical development in Islam and is subject to review in light of present-day conditions. The word *jizya* is derived from the root ج ز ي with the meaning of 'repay' or 'compensate' (see Lane Book I (Part 2), p.422)). The Quran does not explicitly state that *jizya* is to be paid as a *tax* by the *dhimmi*, but rather as a *penalty* (or fine) by those who had committed crimes of treason – that is, they had violated the terms of existing treaties between the 'believing' and 'non-believing' (or dissenting – see discussion in this chapter) tribes in Medina at that time (Surah 9, especially verses 9:2, 6-11, 29). Abdullah Yusuf Ali in his commentary for verse 9:29 acknowledges that the root meaning of *jizya* is 'compensation' and 'poll tax' is a 'derived meaning'. He adds that *jizya* always was 'partly symbolic and partly a commutation for military service, but as the amount was insignificant and the exemptions numerous, its symbolic character predominated'. (Ali, fn 1281-2). Dr Shabbir Ahmed meanwhile describes *jizya* as 'War Reparations to be paid by the aggressors, and not any kind of tribute or tax as generally

In this chapter we will also put the speech of 11 August 1947 in context of the Quranic position on non-Muslims.

Myth no. 13: Jinnah appointed a Hindu in the first Constituent Assembly of Pakistan, consistent with his intent to create a secular state. (M. Munir 1980, p.35; A.S. Ghazali 1996, p.7)

This argument is based on a prevailing belief that in an Islamic polity, non-Muslims must necessarily have limited civil rights, i.e. only Muslims can take governmental posts. This belief however is based on some grave misconceptions about the nature of a bona fide Islamic state, i.e. one that is actively Islamic.

As such, an 'Islamic state' can take any form. It does not have a fixed or institutionalised structure which would limit it in a specific time and/or space; rather, its structure at any given time is always founded upon Quranic (i.e. universal) principles. These principles are simply justice, liberty and solidarity. They are the very essence of *tauheed* [2] put into practice, or, as Iqbal has eloquently described it:

> The essence of 'Tauhid' as a working idea is equality, solidarity, and freedom. The state, from the Islamic standpoint, is an endeavour to transform these ideal principles into space-time forces, an aspiration to realise them in a definite human organisation. [3]

Bearing the above in mind, the characteristics of the 'Islamic state' that I am about to describe happen to represent (structurally) a constitutional form of government. But it is my personal view that since Islam as a polity is about spirit in action, in the future it is possible for the government to dissolve completely, once its role as an administration becomes entirely obsolete (this is hard to imagine without having understood the big picture, as it were, of Islam's legacy, but there is insufficient room to go into that here).

I also strongly advise having a copy of the Quran to hand (almost any well-known translation will do) whilst reading this section. Most of the verses relevant to this discussion have been quoted in full but I have also referenced many simply by their numbers.

---

but erroneously translated.' He cites Raghib Isfahani's Quran dictionary *Al-Mufraadat fi Gharib al-Quran* in pointing out that the correct Arabic word for 'tribute' is not *jizya* but *kharaj*, as seen at Quran 18:94. (Shabbir Ahmed, commentary on verse 9:29). Taken together, all this is indicative of *jizya* being a one-time penalty and not an ongoing tax or tribute.

2 *Tauheed* (oneness and unity of God): see also Chapter 6, footnote 21.

3 *Reconstruction*, p.154

What is an 'Islamic' state?

Most people including many Muslims believe that the only possible political expression of Islam is theocracy, that is, a government run by clergy. In a theocracy a non-Muslim has no rights in government, but then again believers considered 'not pious enough' or 'in the wrong sect' are also deemed unfit for the job. It is this aspect of theocracy that causes its downfall. Placing humans in social hierarchy, according to the Quran, inevitably leads to tyranny; and of course tyranny can never endure. The Quran describes the characteristics of tyranny in its own unique way. First it refers to the three symbols of tyranny – Pharaoh, Qaroon and Haman, who represent political, economic and religious tyranny respectively (29:39) – and then it provides an analogy for the weakness of tyrannical institutes:

> The parable of those who take protectors other than Allah is that of the spider, who builds (to itself) a house; [4] but truly the flimsiest of houses is the spider's house; – if they but knew. (29:41) [5]

The Quran does not advocate a theocratic system. It clearly states that everyone – Muslim or not – is recognised for his/her worth on an individual basis. There is no difference between Muslim and non-Muslim in this regard:

> *Whoever* rallies to a good cause shall have a share in its blessings; and *whoever* rallies to an evil cause shall be answerable for his part in it: for, indeed, God watches over everything. (4:85)[6]

Scholars such as Dr Muhammad Hamidullah and Prof. Sharif al Mujahid have referred to historical documents in order to prove that the early Islamic civilisation not only treated non-Muslims as equal citizens,[7] but also gave them positions of responsibility in the Government; [8] and Dr John Andrew Morrow's work on the Prophet's covenants reveals this in much more detail. [9] This is perfectly in tune with the Quran. It does not teach a certain class of Muslims to act as

---

4 The spider's web is an analogy for a system that easily traps people but cannot withstand any pressure. See Dr Shabbir Ahmed's commentary for this verse.

5 Ali's translation.

6 Asad's translation. Emphasis mine.

7 See also discussion of *Misaq-i-Medina* later in this chapter.

8 M. Hamidullah (2003 reprint) Chapter 12 ('Status of non-Muslims in Islam') in *Introduction to Islam*. New Delhi: Kitab Bhavan; S. Mujahid, 'Jinnah's Vision: An Indivisible Pakistani Nationhood' in *Journal of Management and Social Sciences* Vol. 5, No. 1, Spring 2009

9 J.A. Morrow (2013) *The Covenants of the Prophet Muhammad with the Christians of the World* Washington/New York: Angelico Press/Sophia Perennis.

rulers over the rest of the people. Instead it declares that all humans have equal civil rights [10] in the eyes of the law; and to successfully create a stable society simply requires all citizens to fulfil their civil obligations regardless of race or personal faith, as we will see later in this chapter. No human rules over another, since it is the law (the 'Word of God') that acts as the final authority:

> ... with Allah [11] rests the End and Decision of (all) affairs. (31:22) [12]

Nor can any human alter the law once it is put into effect:

> Say: It is not possible for me to substitute it [Quranic law] of my own accord. I follow nothing but what is revealed to me. (10:15) [13]

The Quran therefore offers a principle similar to that of constitutional democracy in which no human can rule over another, since the constitution itself is the authority. The people who work directly in government are not rulers, but administrators. This includes the head of state, who in light of the above verse possesses no power to appease any vested interests. This is all that is meant in the term 'sovereignty of Allah', and likewise this is the sole 'limit' placed upon the 'sovereignty of the people' (and perhaps this also explains the language of the sovereignty clause in Pakistan's Objectives Resolution).

It follows that the core principles of the constitution are designed chiefly to bring people to socio-economic equity. Economically it is socialistic rather than capitalistic (and in this respect it differs from a Western 'modern democratic state'. This was Jinnah's point in his speech at the State Bank of Pakistan in 1948). [14] As is the case with any constitutional democracy, an Islamic polity demands full compliance with its core laws, all of which are socio-political in nature. I have included a list of these 'core principles' in Appendix I. They form the foundation (3:7) of an Islamic polity. They represent the bare minimum requirement for setting up such a state. Implementation of and compliance with these core laws is essential; otherwise the government

---

[10] In short, socio-economic equity of all members of society regardless of race, caste, creed or sect (Quran 17:70; 16:90).

[11] Since no one can communicate with God directly, His Book provides authoritative guidance. Hence to 'follow Allah' is to follow the principles in His Book. See for example the words 'book', 'revelation', 'decision', and/or 'guidance' as they appear in the following verses (using Ali's translation): 2:2, 2:38, 2:120, 4:105, 5:43-5, 6:71, 6:114, 6:155, 7:52, 14:1, 16:102, 22:41, 31:22, 39:1-2, 39:23, 39:41, 42:10, and 87:3.

[12] Ali.

[13] Bakhtiar.

[14] This speech is cited in Myth no. 3 (Chapter 10)

can potentially take any form whether presidential, parliamentary or anything else.

Jinnah's Pakistan

As we will see in the final chapter, it was this type of political setup that Jinnah hoped to see implemented, and in the ten years before partition right up until the day he passed away he took relevant steps towards achieving this goal. However, most people look to today's 'Islam', which has grown largely out of some very detrimental religious ideas and traditions, and they see a contradiction between what normally passes for a pious Muslim and the so-called 'westernised' Jinnah. It is this line of thinking that ultimately leads some people to the 'secular Jinnah' hypothesis. Indeed Jinnah was not thinking of a religious state based on the sectarian teachings of conventional Islam, but as Prof. Sharif al Mujahid [15] has correctly noted, there is no point in trying to link Jinnah's thought with conventional or traditional Islam, since he was actually following the example of classical Islam, [16] which ironically, whilst much older, was a far more progressive model. Here it's worth mentioning the thoughts of Canadian scholar Dr John Andrew Morrow, who has compiled a book of immense importance containing the various covenants that the Rasool made with contemporary Christian communities. He has observed: 'The ideas enshrined in the covenants are so advanced that they represent a radical departure from the conventions of the time.' [17]

Yet even this does not mean a literal reinstatement of the Islamic state as it existed in the classical period. Rather, it means reviving the *spirit* of that Islamic state. An Islamic polity reinvents an existing political system in light of its own idealism and principles. As Iqbal puts it in his Allahabad address, Islam has in the past 'assimilated and transformed many ideas expressive of a different spirit'. [18] For example, during the time of the Prophet, the political system in vogue was monarchy. The outstanding features of traditional monarchy are that it is nepotistic, despotic and frequently sanctioned and supported by a theocratic element. In the classical period the Caliphate was the Muslim parallel to the monarchical systems prevalent across the world at that time. [19] But

---

15 '... we have failed to establish linkages between Jinnah's and classical (not traditional) Islam's view-points.' (S. Mujahid, referring to Dr Fazlur Rehman, in 'The Islamic Dimension' in *Dawn*, 25 December 2001)

16 'Classical Islam' meaning the decades in which the four 'rightly-guided' Caliphs – Abu Bakr, Umar, Ali and Uthman – presided.

17 J.A. Morrow 2013, p.361. For full bibliographical reference, see footnote 9.

18 Sherwani (ed.) 2008, p.6.

19 Dr Morrow likewise remarks that if the Prophet's contemporaries 'viewed him as a king or a war-lord with imperial ambitions' it was only 'because this [monarchy] was the *only conceivable political system at the time*.' (J.A. Morrow 2013, p.356). Emphasis mine.

it took monarchy and reinvented it within the dictates of Islamic idealism. The Caliph was elected by a democratic process; he was neither nominated by his predecessor, [20] nor did he merely inherit his position from his ancestors, as is the norm in traditional monarchy. [21] Non-Muslim citizens were treated not as political or religious 'minorities', but as equal members of the state with equal responsibilities. [22] It was the spirit, not the form, which made the early Muslim civilisation 'Islamic'.[23]

Pro-secularist commentators argue that Jinnah revealed his preference for a secular state on 11 August 1947. However Jinnah himself always claimed to be taking his political inspiration from the Quran and the final Messenger:

> … our Prophet (Peace be upon him) not only by words but by deeds treated the Jews and Christians, after he had conquered them, [24] with the utmost tolerance and regard and respect for their faith and beliefs. The whole history of Muslims, wherever

---

[20] The Prophet himself did not personally choose a successor. Morrow writes: 'Although divinely-appointed, [*sic*] even the Prophet requested yearly pledges of allegiance from his followers, as did many of the early Caliphs. This was not an imposition, an obligation, or something simply ceremonial in nature … It was an opportunity for the people to express their support, or lack thereof, of their current ruler.' (J.A. Morrow 2013, p.358)

[21] Later the Caliphate did change into a nepotistic monarchy and arguably this (along with the onset of materialist-motivated Muslim imperialism) marks the beginning of the moral decline of the Muslim world. This decline occurred over the course of a millennium; it gradually eroded the political stature of Muslim civilisation and led to its formal annihilation in the early twentieth century. The ineffectual Ottoman Empire self-destructed when the Turks decided to abolish the Caliphate in 1924.

[22] It might be added that even during the successive centuries in which it gradually showed a moral decline, the Muslim civilisation remained the most progressive in the world in terms of its treatment of non-Muslims.

[23] This justifies Durrani's statement that the 'The State headed by the Holy Prophet and his immediate four successors was a democracy and not a theocracy.' (F. Durrani 1944, p.159). Interestingly, Chief Justice A.R. Cornelius may have been subconsciously connecting the old Caliphate and an ideal monarchy when he suggested: 'I incline to the view that benevolent or constitutional monarchy is most in line with WAHDAT [integral unity].' (Letter to Dr Braibanti, 1 March 1978, in R. Braibanti (ed.) 1999, p.198). Of course some Muslims today advocate a presidential rather than a parliamentary system on the very same basis. Dr Morrow meanwhile remarks that leadership 'need not be vested in a single person', describing the Islamic state as 'a kind of democratic theocracy which is fundamentally different from both modern western democracies and the sort of archaic theocracy represented by Pharaonic Egypt'. (J.A. Morrow 2013, p.358) He adds: 'while there are democratic elements in Islam, the Islamic state is not a "liberal democracy" in the Western sense of the term. Democracy, for Muslims, must operate within the framework of Islam.' (Ibid. p.358-9)

[24] Jinnah was referring to events in early Islamic history, which include the implementation of the *Misaq-i-Medina* (Compact of Medina) described briefly in this chapter. It was after the Prophet conquered the Jews and Christians in Yatrib (later renamed Medina) that the *Misaq-i-Medina* was drafted.

they ruled, is replete with those humane and great principles *which should be followed and practised.* [25]

> *We have got the greatest message in the Quran for our guidance and enlightenment.* ... Let us work up to that great ideal. Let us utilise our great potentialities in the right direction. Let us forego our personal interests and convenience for the collective good of our people and for a higher and nobler cause. [26]

> Man has indeed been called God's Caliph in the Quran and if that description of man is to be of any significance it imposes upon us *a duty to follow the Quran*, to *behave towards others as God behaves towards His mankind.* [27]

> The Prophet was a great teacher. He was a great lawgiver. He was a great statesman and he was a great Sovereign who ruled. No doubt, there are many people who do not quite appreciate [*sic*] when we talk of Islam. ... Thirteen hundred years ago he [the Prophet] laid the foundations of democracy. [28]

Note that in the latter speech cited above, Jinnah actually denied the rumours that Pakistan's constitution would not be Islamic. [29] Elsewhere he made it absolutely clear that:

> The constitution of Pakistan will be based on Islamic principles and tenets. [30]

In other words he wanted to prove the veracity of Islamic teachings by putting them into action in Pakistan. Quoting the Quran, he explained:

> ... I have had one underlying principle in mind, the principle of *Muslim democracy*. It is my belief that our salvation lies in following the golden rules of conduct set for us by our great law-giver, the Prophet of Islam. Let us lay the foundation of our democracy on the basis of truly Islamic ideals and principles. Our

---

[25] Speech on the inauguration of the Pakistan Constituent Assembly, 14 August 1947. (Yusufi Vol. IV p.2610)

[26] Message to NWFP Muslim Students Federation, 4 April 1943. (Yusufi Vol. III, p.1687)

[27] Eid day broadcast from All-India Radio, Bombay, 13 November 1939 (Yusufi Vol. II, p.1061). The Quran verse in question is 10:14: 'We made you vicegerents (*khalaifa*) on the earth'. The word *khalifa* – (in singular) means successor, from which the idea of the Caliphate originates. Jinnah seems to have borrowed his understanding of the Caliphate from Iqbal, who believed that a Caliphate need not be 'vested in a single person' but could also be consistent with an 'elected assembly'. (*Reconstruction* p.157)

[28] Address to the Bar Association, Karachi, on the occasion of the Holy Prophet's birthday, Karachi, 25 January 1948 (Yusufi Vol. IV, p.2670)

[29] Ibid. p.2669

[30] Interview to Egyptian journalists, Lahore, 25 November 1947. (NV Vol. VII, p. 109)

> Almighty has taught us that [31] "our decisions in the affairs of the State shall be guided by discussions and consultations". [32]

It goes without saying that the purpose of 'discussions and consultations' is to tend to the affairs of the state. This means all practical matters – economy, education, healthcare, crime, etc. – all the things that any state has to deal with on a daily basis. These issues affect every member of society, regardless of religion or race. Common sense dictates that for any country to run efficiently all the communities within the state must take part in the political process. How can the concerns and issues of any community be addressed unless they or their representatives have a platform from which they can voice them?

As expected of anyone in his position, Jinnah was a pragmatist. He rightly took 'mutual consultation' as taken directly from the Quran (3:159, 42:38) to mean consultation with all citizens of the state, regardless of caste, creed or sect. [33] Since he took his inspiration from the Quran, he called it 'Islamic Democracy' and 'Islamic Social Justice'. He combined contemporary terms with those of the Quran, but in doing so he did not deviate from their Islamic connotations.

But is this in line with Islamic teachings or not? To answer this question is to confront the crux of the issue.

The Quran on non-Muslims

Before we begin, a note: Throughout this section, we are looking closely at some Quranic verses which explicitly address a society of *momineen* (literally, 'believers'), [34] i.e. the people who formed the first Islamic society under the leadership of the Rasool. Muslims today treat the word *momineen* as synonymous with 'believing Muslims'. But whilst in contemporary Islam, the difference between a 'Muslim' and a 'believer' (*momin*) is merely treated as a difference in piety, in strictly Quranic terms there is in fact a significant technical difference between the two terms. A discussion of this difference is beyond the scope of this book;

---

[31] Quotation marks in original.

[32] Speech at Sibi Durbar, Sibi, 14 February 1948. (Yusufi Vol. IV, p.2682). Jinnah has quoted verse 42:38.

[33] Some scholars would argue that 'mutual consultation' refers only to *momineen* (i.e. pious believers, not even mere 'Muslims') amongst themselves. Acknowledged though it is that in theory only *momineen* can be fully trusted to adhere absolutely with the core principles of the Quran, this is not possible to achieve at the present time (nor is it likely to be the case in the foreseeable future), for the simple reason that *momineen* are few and far between and there is no process currently in place to positively identify them. In any case, wherever the constitution is the authority, it should be sufficient to include the constitutional safeguard that all people can participate in government as long as they do not tamper with the core of the constitution, in line with Quran verse 10:15 cited above. This at least aims at the Islamic ideal.

[34] *Momineen*: plural of *momin*, one who has full conviction (*eiman*) in the divine origin of Quranic or universal laws.

but in view of the fact that the Quran claims to contain a universal code of ethics relevant for all time, I have made use of more contemporary and political language so that today's reader can better relate to the spirit of the Quranic message. Hence here we will treat the term *momineen* as synonymous with the word 'nation' as we have used it in this book, since both the terms *momineen* and 'nation' imply a society that adheres to a common idealism. Wherever the Quran addresses the society of *momineen*, we will treat it as addressing us today, in context of a hypothetical Muslim state with a multicultural population. [35] *Ka'fireen* (usually translated as 'unbelievers') and *munafiqeen* (usually translated as 'hypocrites') will likewise be treated in contemporary terms to which the reader can better relate.

Those who contend that Muslims cannot trust non-Muslims to play a sincere part in the Islamic Government derive their argument from certain passages in the Quran. These include, amongst others:

> O you who believe! Take not for friends unbelievers rather than believers: Do you wish to offer Allah an open proof against yourselves? (4:144) [36]

> O you who have attained to faith! Do not take the Jews and the Christians for your allies: they are but allies of one another – and whoever of you allies himself with them becomes, verily, one of them; behold, God does not guide such evildoers. (5:51) [37]

> O you who believe! Take not into your intimacy those outside your ranks: They will not fail to corrupt you. They only desire your ruin: Rank hatred has already appeared from their mouths: What their hearts conceal is far worse. (3:118) [38]

(What immediately stands out about these verses is the fact that none of them is saying outright: 'Don't involve non-Muslims in the government'.)

The first two verses cited above are taken by some naive people to mean that Muslims should not befriend non-Muslims. They usually come to this conclusion from a superficial reading of Abdullah Yusuf Ali's translation, in which he uses the word 'friend'. Of course the notion that this is about personal friendship is preposterous. Many

---

[35] As Morrow correctly notes, Medina, the first Islamic state was 'composed primarily of Jews and polytheists, with only several hundred Muslims. … [and it was] not an Islamic State aimed only at Muslims.' See Morrow's interview to *Patheos*, 2 December 2013. http://www.patheos.com/blogs/takeandread/2013/12/muhammads-word-to-christians-of-the-world-a-qa-with-john-andrew-morrow/ (Last accessed 21 June 2016)

[36] Ali modernised.

[37] Asad.

[38] Ali modernised.

scholars rightly use the word 'ally' (e.g. M. Asad, S. Ahmed) – which is more accurate, since the verse is political in tone – but as I will show, to say that it simply means 'political ally' is not wholly correct either.

Now we will look at these verses more closely.

4:144

> O you who believe! Take not for friends unbelievers rather than believers: Do you wish to offer Allah an open proof against yourselves? (4:144) [39]

The first verse above is in fact a warning against hypocrisy. 'Hypocrites' (*munafiqeen*) according to the Quran are those who claim to be loyal to the law (and by extension, the state), but are not loyal in practice. They prefer to follow their own selfish whims, and thus are guilty of state treason. In the verses preceding 4:144, we are warned not to inadvertently begin behaving as 'hypocrites' do (4:135-8). We are then advised not to engage in discussion with those who ridicule God's law (4:140, 6:68) and treat it as an inane, idealistic religion rather than a workable code of life, in case we feel obliged to compromise with such people just to gain their acceptance or approval ('be honoured by them' (4:139 Asad)). These people represent an internal source of rebellion against the state. They are, in short, dissidents (*ka'fir*) in disguise. [40] They hide behind a façade of loyalty to cause disputes amongst the rest of the body politic and to bring some of them under their influence. We are warned not to allow such elements to divide us and lead us astray from the law which keeps us united (4:88-9).

Hence when the Quran states (to paraphrase), 'don't ally yourselves with *ka'fireen*', it effectively means, 'don't be misled by the ideas of dissidents, no matter how persuasive or impressive they may seem (2:204, 63:4), since their ideas are misguided and contrary to Quranic ideals'. (Our analysis is in agreement with Asad's commentaries on verse 4:139 and at various points in the fifth surah of the Quran, as well as Dr Morrow's analysis of the early historical evidence). Note that the word 'unbeliever' is the common translation for the Arabic word *ka'fir*, but doesn't convey the complete meaning of the word. *Ka'fir* is actually a word for a person who is fully conversant with Quranic teachings, but chooses not abide by them (45:6, 47:32) – invariably for selfish reasons (2:86, 7:169, 27:14, 29:49, 29:66, 30:7). [41] Such a person has 'rejected' the

---

[39] Ali modernised.

[40] Morrow's analysis concurs with the Quranic definition: 'the *munafiqin* were unbelievers who pretended to be Muslims and who sided with their enemies.' (Op. cit. p.372)

[41] See also Asad's footnote at 74:10 for a fuller description of the etymology of *ka'fir*.

law; he/she is a dissident, or 'unbeliever', as Ali translates it. [42] The Quran has not outlawed 'allying' with those who simply don't believe in its divine origin (i.e. followers of other faiths as a whole). Rather, it warns against allying with those who reject outright that its core laws have any practical value [43] and hence are bent on violating them for their own interests. This also includes the quisling 'hypocrites', who are not really interested in noble ideals such as universal civil rights, and only want to secure power for themselves. However all citizens who believe in the practical worth of the constitution are expected to take part in administrative 'consultations', as long as they understand that no one – whether Muslim or non-Muslim – can introduce legislation that is in conflict with the core laws of the constitution (10:15 as cited earlier).[44] This fact should become more obvious once we have taken a look at the other relevant verses from the Quran.

5:51

> O you who have attained to faith! Do not take the Jews and the Christians for your allies: they are but allies of one another – and whoever of you allies himself with them becomes, verily, one of them; behold, God does not guide such evildoers. (5:51) [45]

To understand the meaning of the second verse it is necessary to keep in mind that during the time in which the Quran was revealed Jews and Christians had not yet decided to separate religion from politics. Their religions still dominated their whole lives, politically and socially as well as morally. The verses prior to 5:51 describe the Jews and Christians who had been sincere followers of the principles of Biblical Revelation (5:44) before later generations strayed from it. [46]

Therefore verse 5:51 is actually warning against (in this case) a section of Jews and Christians who might want to introduce political-religious ideals that contradict the core of the constitution. It is not excluding all

---

42 Asad's translation for *ka'fireen* (plural of *ka'fir*), 'deniers of the truth' is lengthier but nevertheless more accurate. It is the exact opposite of a *momin*, a person who has full conviction not only in the practical worth of the constitution but also in its divine origin.

43 See verses 60:8-9, in which it is written that God does not forbid equitable treatment of non-Muslims who do not fight against us on account of Islam (60:8) – i.e. those who live peacefully alongside the rest of society. He only forbids us from forging political allegiances with those who actively oppose the principles embedded in the Quran (60:9).

44 Verses such as 4:123 and 4:135 also make it clear that even 'believers' cannot implement policies based on their own self-serving 'desires', or ideas that are contrary to the universal principles of the Quran.

45 Asad.

46 This includes their failure to follow many of the laws still enshrined in the Biblical texts today. They had chosen to ignore certain Biblical principles to suit their own interests (5:66). The Quran states: But why do they come to you for decision, when they have (their own) Torah before them? – Therein is the (plain) command of Allah; yet even after that, they would turn away. For they are not (really) People of Faith. (5:43) (Ali modernised)

Jews and Christians, or even the adherents of any particular faith. [47] Hence the Quran also states:

> And if (others) come to believe in the way you believe, [48] they will indeed find themselves on the right path; and if they turn away, it is but they who will be deeply in the wrong … (2:137) [49]

Later in the same surah it is stated that people who are law-abiding citizens – whether they call themselves 'Muslim' or not – are treated exactly alike:

> Those who believe (in the Quran), those who follow the Jewish (scriptures), and the Sabians [50] and the Christians – *any* who believe in [the law of] Allah and the Last Day, [51] and work righteousness – on them shall be no fear, nor shall they grieve. (5:69) [52] (Emphasis mine)

(We will return to this point shortly). [53]

Hence verse 5:51 helps to clarify that 'don't ally yourself with the unbelievers' is not simply about political alliance; as Asad has astutely observed, it is about a 'moral alliance'. [54] In other words, forging an alliance with *ka'fireen* (rejecters) is to adopt their way of thinking in systemic terms. [55] And Abdullah Yusuf Ali, who (as we noted earlier) uses the word 'friends', makes it clear in his commentary that this means we cannot look to such parties or 'help and comfort'. [56]

---

[47] Not all Jews and Christians or other non-Muslims are treated with suspicion according to the Quran (2:62, 5:69). Going by the name 'Jew' 'Christian', etc. has no bearing on being a law-abiding citizen in a Quranic society.

[48] 'You (who) believe' means 'you who acknowledge the Quran' (S. Ahmed, commentary on 2:62). See also translations of verses 2:62 and 5:69 by both Ali and Asad.

[49] Asad.

[50] The Sabians (also known as Mandaeans) are a small Gnostic monotheist group whose religion contains elements of Christianity, Judaism and Magianism (Zoroastrianism).

[51] Belief in the 'Last Day' not only refers to the Day of Judgement but also the concept that whatever we do, right or wrong, has a consequence which will catch up with us eventually, one way or another. See whole of Surah 99 – only eight verses long – which describes the Last Day, especially verses 99:7-8: 'Then shall anyone who has done an atom's weight of good, see it! / And anyone who has done an atom's weight of evil, shall see it.' (Ali)

[52] Ali.

[53] See subsection 'Citizenship and allegiance to the state' below.

[54] See Asad's commentary throughout the fifth surah. See also discussion of the Arabic word *hizb* (party, partisan) in Chapter 14, footnote 50 for linguistic evidence that the principle concerns a moral alliance.

[55] See also verses 2:120, 2:145, 3:85, 4:123, 5:48-9, 5:77, 6:56, 6:150, 13:37, 42:15, 45:18, and 53:29.

[56] Ali, commentary on verse 5:51.

3:118

> O you who believe! Take not into your intimacy those outside your ranks: They will not fail to corrupt you. They only desire your ruin: Rank hatred has already appeared from their mouths: What their hearts conceal is far worse. (3:118) [57]

The third verse is worded slightly differently to the first two in terms of its Arabic. Instead of the word 'ally', it uses 'confidant'. As Asad has noted in his commentary, many scholars take this verse to mean that no non-Muslims can be trusted as political confidants, i.e. entrusted with responsibility in matters involving national security. However Asad disagrees with their view, citing verses 60:8-9 [58] to make his point. Having considered the evidence from the other relevant verses we have seen already, it is clear that Asad is correct. We need only to examine the context in which verse 3:118 appears to see that it is consistent with the others we have looked at already.

Once again it is warning us to guard against both internal and external sources of rebellion against the state – in other words, against both duplicitous and dissident elements. Preceding verses exhort us to 'hold fast' (3:103) by the law and warn us not to 'fall into disputations' (3:105) and become divided, since this would be a direct violation of Quranic teachings and would thus be tantamount to committing *shirk*.

Shirk is the antonym of *tauheed*. It means 'to make someone a partner' and implies dividing or sharing, whether of property or authority. In the Quran it means a partner sharing in the authority that belongs to God, and so it is also a reference to polytheism. [59] Indulging in *shirk* is the only unpardonable offence according to the Quran (4:48). It represents treason not only against the state but also humanity. [60]

Hence the Quran warns us not to pay heed to the advocates of anti-Quranic ideas, as this would amount to state treason ('[they] would render you apostates after you have believed' (3:100)). [61] At the same time however, verses 3:113-4 describe and commend the 'People of the Book' who are true to the laws of Revelation (3:114) and promises that their loyalty will not be in vain, and that they will reap the benefits of being law-abiding citizens (3:115). They are described as being 'among

---

57 Ali modernised.

58 See footnote 43.

59 See Lane Book I (Part 4), p.1541

60 This is because a division of authority confuses people, and out of a misguided sense of loyalty to their religious sect or political party (30:31-2) they become distrustful of the 'other'. Distrust can easily turn to hatred, and eventually violence, murder, and even genocide will follow. These crimes irreversibly damage humanity by depriving it of the people who can affect the course of history for the better.

61 Ali modernised. 'People of the Book' refers to members of faiths that claim to follow Revelation (i.e. the monotheistic and in particular the Abrahamic faiths)

the righteous' (3:114) [62] (Ali uses the phrase 'ranks of the righteous'). These verses are referring to the People of the Book, but also apply to anyone who wholeheartedly believes in the concept of one God and in the universal law of consequence (2:62; 5:69 as above). Hence it becomes clear that verse 3:118 is only warning us to be wary of whom we choose as our political allies and representatives (2:204, 3:100). Our choice is not between faiths (i.e. Muslim versus non-Muslim) but between people who uphold 'spiritual' ideals of justice, solidarity and liberty versus those who uphold 'non-spiritual' self-serving ideals in line with the law of the jungle. We are warned not to trust those whose selfish traits are common knowledge (3:118: 'Rank hatred has already appeared from their mouths' [63]); if given the opportunity to fulfil their ambitions, they may cause much unforeseen destruction (3:118: 'What their hearts conceal is far worse').

Citizenship and allegiance to the state

Now let us look carefully at verse 2:62, which closely resembles 5:69 quoted earlier:

> Those who believe (in the Quran), and those who follow the Jewish (scriptures), and the Christians and the Sabians, – any who believe in [the law of] Allah and the Last Day, and work righteousness, shall have their reward with their Lord; [64] on them shall be no fear, nor shall they grieve. (2:62) [65]

Dr Shabbir Ahmed is one of only a few scholars to fully appreciate the significance of the verses 2:62 and 5:69. In his translation of the Quran he has suggested that others may have failed to compare other relevant verses to them and thus overlooked their importance. He writes:

> Reflecting on the above verses makes it clear that the belief in Allah and the Last Day must be in accordance and conformity with the Qur'an. Verses 2:62 and 5:69 emphasize that [the] mere giving of a name to one's religion or creed carries no importance.[66]

---

62 Asad.

63 See also verse 47:30 – 'you will know them by the tone of their speech' (Ali modernised).

64 'Lord' is not an accurate translation for the Arabic word *Rabb*, which actually refers to God's attribute of nourishing and nurturing everything in the universe via physical natural laws. A more accurate word would be 'Nourisher'.

65 Ali.

66 S. Ahmed, commentaries on verses 2:62 and 5:69. Asad has also made similar comments in his preamble to the fifth surah.

Asad agrees with this sentiment:

> The above passage – which recurs in the Qur'an several times - lays down a fundamental doctrine of Islam. With a breadth of vision unparalleled in any other religious faith, the idea of "salvation" is here made conditional upon three elements only: belief in God, belief in the Day of Judgment, and righteous action in life. [67]

Abdullah Yusuf Ali too concurs:

> Here, as in Sura Al-Baqarah (ii:62), [*sic*] the Qur-ān underscores the importance of true and genuine faith, which is to be judged by a sincere belief in Allah and man's accountability to Him *backed by a righteous conduct rather than by mere forms or labels.* … the People of the Book are being reminded that it is through sincere belief and righteous conduct rather than pretentious claims that man can win his Lord's pleasure and achieve ultimate success. [68]

In other words, abiding by the law is more important than formally professing a particular faith. The benefits of the state are thus available to all faithful citizens. To quote 5:69 again:

> Those who believe (in the Quran), those who follow the Jewish (scriptures), and the Sabians and the Christians – *any* who believe in [the law of] Allah and the Last Day, and work righteousness – on them shall be no fear, nor shall they grieve. (5:69) [69] (Emphasis mine)

Shortly before this verse the Quran also states:

> For, *all* who ally themselves with God and His apostle and those who have attained to faith – behold, it is these partisans of God who shall be victorious! (5:56) [70]

In the above verse, forging an alliance with God as well as His Messenger and 'those who have attained to faith' (i.e. 'believers') is presented as the opposite of forging an alliance with 'unbelievers' (see 5:57). (Incidentally, this is where the Quranic basis of the Two-Nation Theory lies.) Of course the phrase 'ally with God' cannot be taken

---

[67] Asad, commentary on verse 2:62.

[68] Ali, commentary on verse 5:69. Emphasis mine.

[69] Ali.

[70] Asad (Emphasis mine).

literally; it is clearly figurative and refers to adopting His law (*deen*), consistent with its use in verses relating to dissidents (*ka'fireen*) and quislings (*munafiqeen*). It is also significant that the above verse addresses humanity as a whole; it is not simply addressing 'believers' but also to *all* who join them. This means that non-Muslims who are loyal to the state are automatically considered 'allies' of the believers:

> ... so long as they [non-Muslims] remain true to you, be true to them: for, verily, God loves those who are conscious of Him. (9:7) [71]

This is confirmed again in verses 2:111-2:

> And they say: "None shall enter Paradise unless he is a Jew or a Christian." Those are their (vain) desires. Say: "Produce your proof if you are truthful." / Nay, – *whoever* submits His whole self to Allah and is a doer of good, – He will get his reward with his Lord; on such shall be no fear, nor shall they grieve. (2.111-2) [72]

Again it is made clear that it is not belonging to a particular faith, but being a loyal citizen that is important. As long as all citizens 'submit' to the law of the land, they are entitled to the 'reward', or privileges, from the state. They are full citizens of one and the same nation or *ummah*, [73] regardless of caste or creed. The latter sentence of verse 2:112 above, 'on such shall be no fear, nor shall they grieve', links this particular verse directly to verses 2:62 and 5:69, both of which use the same words and address people of varying faiths. Hence Asad writes in his commentary for verse 2:112:

---

[71] Asad.

[72] Ali modernised. Emphasis mine.

[73] *Ummah*: An Arabic word for community, or citizens of the state, including Muslims and non-Muslims. There is a debate on whether the word *ummah* refers exclusively to Muslims or all citizens of an Islamic polity irrespective of religion. Many traditionalist scholars insist that it is a word solely for 'Muslims'; they are probably inadvertently influenced by theocratic ideas. However, as others point out, historical documents, including the *Misaq-i-Medina* (as discussed above) from the early Islamic period suggest otherwise. As such the overall etymology of the word does not reveal anything to imply that it means anything more than the word 'nation', 'community', or 'collective' (see Lane Book I (Part 1), p.90). Therefore it can be safely said that the word *ummah* refers to all the citizens of an Islamic state – irrespective of personal faith, since being 'law-abiding' does not necessitate being a believing 'Muslim' (see also Quran 49:14). Possible corroborating historical evidence has emerged in Morrow's work on the covenants of the Rasool, in which he shows that the current Muslim definitions of terms such as '*momin*', '*muslim*' '*mushrik*', '*ka'fir*' and '*munafiq*' represent an etymological evolution somewhat removed from their meanings at the time of the Prophet. (J.A. Morrow 2013, p.370-1). He observes: 'As for the Jews and Christians, there seems to have been some confusion among them as to the term *muslim* or submitter. Some communities appeared to have the impression that Islam or submission was *political submission* to the Prophet Muhammad and not necessarily submission to the religion he preached'. (Op. cit. p.372) Emphasis mine.

> Thus, according to the Qur'an, salvation is not reserved for any particular "denomination", but is open to everyone who consciously realises the oneness of God, surrenders himself to his will and, by living righteously, gives practical effect to this spiritual attitude. [74]

If God does not even discriminate among faiths for entry into the Garden, how can there be discrimination in a state which is supposed to be sanctioned by Him?

The Quran makes it clear that everyone who is a loyal citizen of the state and believes in the practical worth of its constitution – irrespective of personal faith (2:62, 5:69) – has a right to participate in its political processes as long as they do not attempt to alter the constitution to suit their own limited human vision, beyond what is acceptable. [75] In contemporary terms this is 'owing allegiance' to the state.

Jinnah expressed these sentiments in several of his speeches to the people of Pakistan:

> Minority communities must not by mere words but *by actions show this, that they are truly loyal* and that they must make [the] majority community feel that they are true citizens of Pakistan. [76]

> [The minorities] will have their rights and privileges and no doubt, along with it goes the *obligation of citizenship*. Therefore, *the minorities have their responsibilities also and they will play their part* in the affairs of this State. As long as the minorities are *loyal to the State and owe true allegiance* and as long as I have any power, they need have *no apprehension* of any kind. [77]

The last sentence in that second quote is almost perfect paraphrase of the verse quoted earlier from the Quran:

---

[74] Asad, commentary on verse 2:112.

[75] In order for any state to remain effective at all times there is a level of flexibility in the legislation in order that its society can keep up with the times as they change and as new situations arise. Likewise an Islamic polity must always be dynamic (i.e. by constantly settling its 'affairs' (3:159, 42:38) in accordance with the circumstances of a given time; and it is done by 'mutual consultation' (42:38). Constitutional alterations however cannot contradict or abrogate the core principles of the Quran. No citizen, whether Muslim or non-Muslim, or even the head of state, has the right to change the core laws which ultimately protect the rights of all human beings. Doing so is tantamount to usurping God's authority. All citizens including the head of state must remain equal in all respects as human beings under the authority of God, i.e. His constitution.

[76] Speech in reply to the address presented by a deputation of members of the Quetta Parsi Community, Quetta, 13 June 1948. (Yusufi Vol. IV p.2780)

[77] Statement on protection for minorities in Pakistan, New Delhi, 13 July 1947 (Yusufi Vol. IV, p.2587)

> … *any* who believe in Allah and the Last Day, and work righteousness – *on them shall be no fear, nor shall they grieve.* (5:69) [78]

Whether or not Jinnah paraphrased the Quran consciously we may never know, but there is no doubt that his words were in line with Quranic teachings. After all, the above verse is not about individual 'good deeds' or scoring points for personal salvation; it is about creating a stable society of law-abiding citizens who in turn live at peace with fellow human beings. Muslims and non-Muslims alike can be acknowledged as good citizens; they all have a responsibility to take part in the political process, as long as they don't stray from the core of the constitution. The Quran has not explicitly stated that certain key positions in government should be allotted only to 'believers', [79] but rather that all affairs of the state should be handled through mutual consultation (42:38), whilst its administrators remain mindful not to forge false moral alliances.

The speech of 11 August 1947 in context

It follows that none are forced to believe in the sanctity of the law in accordance with the Quranic injunction:

> Let there be no compulsion in *deen.* (2:256) [80]

This guarantees universal civil equality and leaves personal faith (*mazhab*) out of the political sphere, [81] which is what Jinnah really meant by his immortal words:

> You may belong to any religion or caste or creed – that has nothing to do with the business of the State. …

---

[78] Ali.

[79] In the first edition of *Secular Jinnah* I suggested that the only possible 'exception to this rule is the Head of State' (S. Karim 2005, p.95 fn). The reasoning behind this was based on the idea that the *momineen* (those with *eiman* – conviction – in the divine origin of the Quran) would be likely the most committed or patriotic members of a state founded upon its laws. To my mind it was also in tune with the classical Caliphate (though arguably a Caliph is head of the Muslim world rather than head of just a particular state). It is not dissimilar to the prevailing law in many modern states, such as the USA, where only a natural-born citizen can become head of state, based on the criterion of nationality. However I added that there would have to be a process for identifying suitable candidates, for example through academic and psychological testing and from thorough checks on their personal background for their contributions to society. On the other hand, if the constitution is made the authority and no one can tamper with it, then obviously there is room to allow a non-Muslim head of state. As we have seen, this seems to have been the view of the founders of Pakistan also. Since the head of state also has a symbolic value, it would ultimately be down to the framers of the constitution to decide upon this issue.

[80] Ali.

[81] See Chapter 6 for discussion on *mazhab* versus *deen* and the implications for the state.

> ... Hindus would cease to be Hindus, and Muslims would cease to be Muslims, not in the religious sense, because that is the personal faith of each individual, but in the political sense as citizens of the State. [82]

Whilst this principle is undoubtedly one of an ideal secular state, in an Islamic state the same principle is founded on an entirely different worldview. For this reason alone the above is more accurately described as an Islamic statement.

Furthermore, Jinnah's speech is no different in content or spirit to early Muslim historical rule. [83] The very first Muslim political document the *Misaq-i-Medina* – the Compact of Medina, said to have been penned by the Prophet of Islam in around 622 AD, and arguably the first constitution in the world – laid down the rules for 'a political unit (*umma*) as distinct from all the people (of the world)'. [84] Significantly, the various Jewish tribes were declared 'one community (*umma*) with the believers', [85] and further: 'To the Jew who follows us belong help and equality', and 'the Jews have their religion and the Muslims have theirs'. [86] This made them equal before the law – a principle usually attributed to a secular state. As Prof. Sharif al Mujahid has remarked, 'the *Misaq* conceded to the Jewish tribes the same rights, the same privileges and the same obligations as were accorded to the believers.' [87]

Pakistan's first Constituent Assembly

As far as Jinnah was concerned, he was earnestly following the examples of the Quran and the Rasool in his politics. There is nothing in either the Quran or the Rasool's life to justify a religious basis for filling Pakistan's Constituent Assembly positions. Even if we were to entertain any notions of allowing only Muslims in the Constituent Assembly – i.e. appointing them based on their *faith*, they would have to conform to *Quranic* standards on faith, not *sectarian* standards invented by those

---

[82] Presidential address to the Constituent Assembly of Pakistan, Karachi, 11 August 1947 (CAP Debates Vol. I No. 2, p.20)

[83] We might add that on 14 August 1947 (just three days later) Jinnah explained that the tolerance and equal treatment accorded to non-Muslims in a Muslim state dated back 'thirteen centuries ago when our Prophet not only by words but by deeds treated the Jews and Christians handsomely after he had conquered them. He showed to them the utmost tolerance and regard and respect for their faith and beliefs.' (Address, Pakistan Constituent Assembly, 14 August 1947; CAP Debates Vol. I No. 4, p.52)

[84] Cited from S. Mujahid, 'Jinnah's Vision: An Indivisible Pakistani Nationhood' in *Journal of Management and Social Sciences* Vol. 5, No. 1, (Spring 2009), p.62

[85] Abd al-Malik Ibn Hisham, Muhammad Ibn Ishaq, Alfred Guillaume (1998 reprint) *The Life of Muhammad: a Translation of Isḥaq's Sirat Rasul Allah* London: Oxford University Press, p.232 (originally published 1955)

[86] Ibid. p.232, 233

[87] S. Mujahid 2009, p.62

whose conception of Islam is theocratic. Candidates would have to possess *eiman* (conviction) – that is, possess the character of a *momin*, who, as I have described in my earlier footnote, [88] demonstrates by action that he/she has the required credentials for a position of such responsibility. But in the newly acquired state of Pakistan, there were very few people, if any, with these credentials. Of course there were plenty of ulema who would gladly have taken the opportunity to join the Constituent Assembly, but since they were primarily religious and had no experience in dealing with political matters they were entirely unsuitable. History – as well as the Quran (9:19-20) – testifies to the fact that religious piety is not a valid qualification for administering the practical affairs of any state, let alone one professing to be Islamic. In any case, many (though not all) of these ulema were the same people who had opposed the idea of Pakistan from the outset. They were quislings of the type that the Quran has warned against 'allying' with, the ones that Jinnah described as 'traitors'. [89]

The vast majority of Muslims had simple beliefs and though they had been united based on their common faith, they were not sufficiently educated in Islamic principles.[90] Even many of the Leaguers didn't understand the essence of Islam. Iqbal had left behind his intellectual legacy in written form, in his literature, his poetry and his lectures. He had called for the next generation of thinkers to 'reconstruct' Muslim thought and revive the 'spiritual democracy which is the ultimate aim of Islam', [91] but his calls went largely unanswered. The early leaders of Pakistan declared that the Republic of Pakistan was also to be 'Islamic' but they had not learned from Iqbal or indeed from Jinnah about the real meaning of Muslim unity. They had become temporarily united only under Jinnah's awesome statesmanship, and within a few years of his death, petty rivalries soon re-emerged amongst them and they forgot about the original Pakistan idea. We have already seen that by 1954, attempts were being made to shirk the enormous responsibility of building a democratic, socialistic 'Islamic state'. [92]

---

[88] See footnote 79.

[89] Jinnah: 'What the League has done is to set you free from the reactionary elements of Muslims and to create the opinion that those who play their selfish game are traitors. It has certainly freed you from that undesirable element of Maulvis and Maulanas. I am not speaking of Maulvis as a whole class. There are some of them who are as patriotic and sincere as any other; but there is a section of them which is undesirable.' Speech delivered at the meeting of the Muslim University Union, Aligarh, 5 February 1938 (Yusufi Vol. II, p. 727)

[90] Though the principles of Islam are profoundly simple, a psychological assimilation of Islamic idealism can be difficult to achieve, especially in adulthood, as most people are exposed from birth to social and psychological paradigms that produce negative personality traits including for instance distrust, dishonesty, etc. as 'survival instincts', i.e. self-preservation. Personality reform thus takes time and effort. It is not without significance that the Quran was revealed piecemeal so that the Rasool could educate a small group of people over a number of years (see verses 25:32, 73:4). See also Myth no. 4 (Chapter 10).

[91] See *Reconstruction*, p.179-80

[92] See discussions on 1954 debates in Chapter 4, especially on the subject of fiscal matters.

In the absence of true *momineen*, (and in line with Quranic recommendation) Jinnah appointed people who were well educated, had demonstrated loyalty to Pakistan, and believed in the principles of 'justice and fairplay'. Many of the non-Muslims who joined the Muslim campaign for Pakistan had done so because they believed Jinnah when he told them that Pakistan would stand for justice and fairplay. They had all experienced religious and political discrimination, not least the downtrodden Scheduled Caste Hindus. This community had allied with the Muslim League rather than the Indian National Congress as Jinnah had assured them of their proper place in Pakistan. They had been promised that the state of Pakistan would uphold the universal principle of justice and fairplay and would thus guarantee the socio-economic uplift of all its citizens. The members of the first Constituent Assembly of Pakistan were appointed based solely on their competence and loyalty to the League, and Mandal was appointed for the same reasons.

Incidentally, for those who for some reason or other think that Mandal's job title (as Minister for Law and Labour) carries significance, it is worth remembering that Mr Mandal was not given the responsibility of authoring the constitution, but only to do his job as Minister of Law and Labour within the framework of the interim constitution that was already in place. The job of writing the proper constitution for Pakistan was one for the Constituent Assembly. No single individual was left alone to put together the document that set the rules for the entire country. Jinnah himself had asserted this when the press had asked him about the structure of the government. [93]

Whether or not some of the Constituent Assembly members were non-Muslim is irrelevant; all communities needed to voice their socio-political needs and concerns, and this is what their elected representatives were there to do. In the spirit of unity, faith and discipline, the entire Constituent Assembly was supposed to meet and mutually agree upon the constitution as per the Quran's instruction, the foundation of which was based on the Quranic principles of justice and fairplay.

It has yet to happen.

---

[93] See Jinnah's statement on protection for minorities in Pakistan, New Delhi, 13 July 1947 (NV Vol. VI, p.286) cited in Myth no. 3 (Chapter 10).

Chapter 13
The anecdotal myths

In Pakistan rumour passes for fact, gossip for history.
– *Prof. Akbar S. Ahmed*[1]

On Christmas day in 2008 - also Jinnah's birthday [2] - the well-known Pakistani political show *Capital Talk* hosted by Hamid Mir held a special programme asking a question that comes up periodically on such television shows: Was Jinnah the advocate of a secular state or an Islamic state? Of the three guests, [3] Dr Safdar Mahmood spoke as a pro 'Muslim Jinnah' historian, and Prof. Pervez Amirali Hoodbhoy spoke in favour of a 'secular Jinnah'.

Prof. Hoodbhoy's main point of reference in presenting Jinnah as a secularist was the speech of 11 August 1947. Dr Mahmood however made a number of references to Jinnah's speeches and political decisions that provided evidence to the contrary, and for this he appeared to come out on top. For some references to Jinnah's speeches he quoted from my first book *Secular Jinnah.* He also emphasised Jinnah's references to 'Islamic democracy' to show that the Quaid-i-Azam was not for a religious state, or theocracy, since he was also opposed to sectarianism.

Towards the end of the show the question came down to whether Jinnah was a religious man in his private life. Prof. Hoodbhoy had the final word on this particular subject when he mentioned that Jinnah was certainly not an 'orthodox' Muslim. In fact, so Hoodbhoy said, what Jinnah 'ate, what he drank, and how he dressed' proved that he was certainly not orthodox; but Hoodbhoy did 'not wish to discuss it' further on the show. (What follows is the fourteenth myth).

---

1 A.S. Ahmed 1997, p.190

2 Jinnah's official birthday is 25 December 1876 but the date is disputed by due to evidence from Jinnah's school records suggesting that his birthday was 20 October 1875. See Bolitho 1954, p.3-4

3 The three guests consisted of Dr Safdar Mahmood, historian and senior columnist of Urdu paper *Jang*, Senator S.M. Zafar representing a distinctly secular-Muslim Muslim position, and Prof. P.A. Hoodbhoy.

Myth no. 14: Jinnah was too Western in his dealings in politics and in his lifestyle. He knew nothing about Islam; he was irreligious in his private life.

When I was writing *Secular Jinnah* in 2004, I gave considerable thought as to whether or not to discuss the myths about Jinnah's personal life and the private statements he allegedly made off the record. At the time I preferred to present the Jinnah whose speeches are on record and leave it to the readers to judge for themselves how likely it was that he was not true to his faith in his private life. I stated that I was not prepared to 'waste ink' [4] on such frivolous myths. At any rate, I myself have always consciously avoided making references to anecdotal evidence to back my own views on Jinnah, even though there is plenty of such evidence available, and it can easily be shown to be more reliable than that which backs a 'secular Jinnah'. Therefore I did not feel compelled to deal with the corresponding anecdotal myths. But the rumours and stories circulating about Jinnah are so widespread and have been used by so many commentators, including scholars supposedly trained in the historical method, that I decided to include this chapter in this book.

Jinnah once said in response to some statements made by certain people [5] against him in 1945:

> It is not only painful and regrettable that they have stooped to such a low depth of meanness in as much as they are directed to show that I am not a Mussalman, but the allegations made by them in their speeches against me and my private life are tissues of falsehood.
>
> It seems that they had no other argument against the creed, policy and programme of the Muslim League and our stand for which we are carrying on the struggle but to resort to this mean practice in spreading this falsehood regarding me with a view to excite [*sic*] fanaticism and passions of some Mussalmans.
>
> I am sure that no Mussalman who has even a grain of common sense would believe in such vile, reckless and false allegations against me which are sought to be broadcast in the Hindu press. [6]

---

[4] S. Karim 2005, p.106

[5] The people in question were Mazhar Ali Azhar, leader of the Ahrar movement (he is most famous for having labelled Jinnah *Ka'fir-i-Azam* – the 'great unbeliever' – in verse), and Muhammad Inayatullah Khan Mashriqi, leader of the Khaksar movement. The Hindu press had published their defamatory speeches against Jinnah on 17 and 18 September 1945. The young man who tried to assassinate Jinnah in July 1943 was allegedly a member of the Khaksars.

[6] Statement repudiating charges made by Mazhar Ali and Mashriqi, Quetta, 24 September 1945 (Yusufi Vol. III, p.2060). *Eastern Times* articles covering the full story of the accusations (20-21 September 1945) appear in Saeed (ed.) 1983, p.233-236

Indeed, it is only people without a better argument against their rivals who tend to resort to attempts at character assassination. We will now review a number of anecdotal myths about Jinnah. The one outstanding feature that they all have in common is that they fail to stand up even to mild scrutiny.

Jinnah's marriage

Pro-secularists who write about Jinnah's personal life all invariably write that he 'married a non-Muslim'. The facts simply are that Ruttenbai ('Ruttie') Petit (1900-1929) was a Parsi by birth, and Jinnah's second wife. [7] At Jinnah's request she converted to Islam the day before she married him, even going through a formal ceremony in a mosque. [8] It could be argued that she did so for convenience, but then again she was known for her strong will and it is highly unlikely that she would have done anything that she did not wish to do. She was a supportive wife and accompanied Jinnah in his political activities. [9] Their only child Dina was raised as a Muslim. [10] Ruttie lived as a Muslim and when she died of colitis at the age of just 29, she was buried in accordance with Muslim rites.

Jinnah's diet

A great many commentators in and out of Pakistan make references to Jinnah's alleged diet, namely that he drank alcohol and ate pork. As we will see shortly, these claims are backed by no real evidence. What is surprising however is that so many trained academics are prone to repeating them. Unfortunately Prof. Hoodbhoy in particular is notorious

---

[7] When he was just sixteen, Jinnah's parents had arranged his marriage to Emi Bai, a distant relative, just before he departed to England for his apprenticeship. He never got to know her, for she died shortly after he reached England. (F. Jinnah 1987, p.61-2, 75)

[8] Q. Aziz 1997, p.37-8

[9] For details, see Q. Aziz 1997, p.40-45

[10] By a remarkable coincidence Dina was born in London at midnight, 14/15 August 1919, precisely 28 years to the day before Pakistan formally appeared on the map (midnight, 14/15 August 1947). When Jinnah moved to England in the early 1930s after his wife's death, his sister Fatima was responsible for teaching Dina about Islam. (Q. Aziz (2001) *Jinnah and Pakistan* Karachi: Islamic Media Corporation, p.85). Some biographers claim that Dina and her father were permanently estranged because she married a Parsi-born Christian, Neville Wadia, against her father's wishes (he had asked her to convert Neville to Islam). But evidence indeed exists that any estrangement was short-lived and they maintained a happy and healthy relationship (A.S. Ahmed 1997, p.16-17). Nevertheless Dina did not see her father often due to his absolute dedication to the Pakistan movement (She has expressed anger over Pakistanis' failure to recognise that her father sacrificed his life for Pakistan; see her interview to A.S. Ahmed in op. cit. 1997, p.173). Nor did she visit Pakistan at all after independence when her father was alive; she attended his funeral in 1948, and only visited Pakistan a few times thereafter. Dina spent her life in the UK and in New York at various times; and the latter is where she passed away on 2 November 2017, at the age of 98.

for making dietary references in innuendo whenever he speaks or writes on Jinnah, and Jinnah's best known and respected biographer, Prof. Stanley Wolpert, has flouted the rules of historical objectivity in mentioning them. The late Indian Muslim historian Dr Rafiq Zakaria, whose contempt for Jinnah is no secret, referred to them at every opportunity. M.J. Akbar and Dr Ajeet Jawed are further examples from India, Louis Fischer is the American example, and Collins and Lapierre[11] and Prof. Ian Talbot are examples from Britain. Incidentally, one of Talbot's old articles mentioning that Jinnah 'drank alcohol and ate pork' was recently reprinted in Dr M.R. Kazimi's book, *Jinnah: Views and Reviews* in Pakistan, but here the dietary reference was edited out. [12]

The main point of telling these stories is obviously to depict Jinnah as an 'irreligious' man, who could therefore never seriously advocate an 'Islamic state'. To find out the truth, we need to look at where the stories originally appear, and also to see if those who were closest to Jinnah – preferably those who lived with him day to day – have ever corroborated them.

If we begin with the alcohol references, we can see that they have existed from very early on. *Time* magazine, which had always painted a very negative image of Jinnah, [13] contained the following obituary printed just over a week after his death:

> Enemies among the Moslems whispered against him: "Jinnah does not wear a beard; Jinnah does not go to the mosque; Jinnah drinks whiskey." [14]

The obituary had opened with the following words:

> Out of the travail of 400 million in the Indian subcontinent have come two symbols – a man of love and a man of hate. Last winter the man of nonviolence, Gandhi, died violently at the hands of an assassin. Last week the man of hate, Mohamed Ali Jinnah, at 71, died a natural death in Karachi, capital of the state he had founded. His devoted and equally fanatic sister, Fatima,

---

[11] See R. Zakaria (2001) *The Man who Divided India: an Insight into Jinnah's Leadership and its Aftermath* Mumbai: Popular Prakashan, p.29-30, 164-5; M.J. Akbar (1985) *India: The Siege Within* New York: Penguin Books, p.32; A. Jawed (1998) *Secular and Nationalist Jinnah* New Delhi: Kitab Publishing House, p.129, 265; L. Collins and D. Lapierre (1975) *Freedom at Midnight* New York: Simon & Schuster, p.116, 152; L. Fischer (1954) *Gandhi; His Life and Message for the World* New York: New American Library/Mentor, p.150

[12] Compare Talbot's 'Jinnah and the Making of Pakistan' in *History Today*, Vol. 34 Issue 2, 1984 p.5-10, with the same article as it appears in M.R. Kazimi (ed.) 2005, p.80-90

[13] See Q. Aziz 1997, p.178-181 for a review of *Time* magazine's 'chronic' animosity towards Jinnah and the Pakistan demand before and long after partition.

[14] 'Pakistan: That Man', obituary article in *Time* magazine (US edition), 20 September 1948. http://www.time.com/time/magazine/article/0,9171,799165,00.html (Last accessed 4 Sept 2009). Spellings retained from original.

> was at his side; so was his daughter, Mrs Dinah Wadia, whom he had disowned because she married a Parsee (as he had done before her). [15]

Objective it is not. The founder/editor of *Time*, Henry Robinson Luce, continually depicted Jinnah as a 'man of hate', and a megalomaniac. [16]

Of course in Jinnah's time it was not uncommon – indeed it is the case even today [17] – for liberal Muslims in the subcontinent to drink alcohol, so it is probable that Jinnah drank at least in his earlier life. His daughter Dina maintained that he drank in moderation. [18] Of course, she left home when she was seventeen [19] and didn't see her father much after she married. [20] Jinnah's old friend Yahya Bakhtiar told Prof. Akbar S. Ahmed that Jinnah had given up alcohol towards the end of his life. [21] Ilahi Bakhsh, the doctor who treated Jinnah in his last days, has described the diet that he prescribed Jinnah in detail. He does not mention alcohol even medicinally. [22]

At any rate, the allegations that he ate pork are considered far more offensive to Muslims than the claims about his drinking. This may seem trivial to Westerners, but Prof. Akbar S. Ahmed has explained the issue:

> For Muslims the flesh of pig is *haram*, forbidden, because it is considered unclean. To eat it is also culturally symbolic of crossing a line. ... Even the most liberal of Muslims [including those who drink] would not touch pork. [23]

Muslims who drink are not unheard of. Pork consumption however, as Prof. Ahmed has explained, is the crossing of a line, i.e. indicative of *leaving* Islam. We can see the significance therefore of the accusations about Jinnah's diet. Only two detailed stories about Jinnah's supposed consumption of pork exist, and both originate from M.C. Chagla's *Roses*

---

15 Ibid.

16 See Q. Aziz 1997, 178-81.

17 The late Pakistani politician M.P. Bhandara, who also owned the largest brewery in Pakistan (Murree Brewery in Rawalpindi), told the well-known British comedian-turned-travel writer Michael Palin that it was foolish to assume that there was no demand for alcohol in Pakistan. Palin observed that the brewery most likely depended on Muslim customers as it couldn't survive if its only customers were non-Muslims. See Michael Palin's TV documentary series *Himalaya*, broadcast on the BBC in 2004 (summary of which is also available at Palin's website at http://palinstravels.co.uk/book-3665 (Last accessed 10 May 2010)

18 A.S. Ahmed 1997, p.200

19 See Dina Wadia's interview to Hector Bolitho on 2 October 1952 (S. Mujahid (ed.) (2007) *In Quest of Jinnah: Diary, Notes and Correspondence of Hector Bolitho* Karachi: Oxford University Press, p.88)

20 See footnote 10.

21 A.S. Ahmed 1997, p.200

22 See I. Bakhsh (1978 reprint) *With the Quaid-i-Azam in his Last Days* Karachi: Quaid-i-Azam Academy (originally published 1949, Lahore: Maktab-tul-Ma'arif)

23 A.S. Ahmed 1997, p.201

in December. The first is to the effect that Mrs Ruttie Jinnah once brought a tray of ham sandwiches to Jinnah – in front of his Muslim colleagues – during an election campaign. Embarrassed, her husband had them sent away. [24] The second story goes that Jinnah and Chagla were at a train station for lunch, and Jinnah ordered a plate of sausages. An 'old, bearded Muslim' and his young 'grandson' joined them at their table, and the child picked up a sausage out of curiosity and ate one. Afterwards, Jinnah scolded Chagla for not stopping the child. Chagla replied that he had not said anything in case this damaged Jinnah's election campaign (since Jinnah had ordered the meal and had subsequently invited them to the table). Chagla had, as he dramatically put it, sent the child to 'eternal damnation' for Jinnah. [25] The poisonous undertone is unmissable. Though many commentators acknowledge that Chagla is the originator of these stories, in fact it seems he may have been expanding upon a casual statement in Louis Fischer's well-known biography on Gandhi, first published in 1954: 'Jinnah was not a devout Moslem. He infringed the Islamic code by drinking alcohol, eating pork, and seldom going to a mosque.' [26]

We need not comment on any aspect of the stories themselves, but we will look at the sources. M.C. Chagla was Jinnah's honorary secretary in the 1920s. When the Bombay Provincial League formally rejected the Report in 1928, Chagla, who supported it, resigned. He also strongly opposed the Two-Nation Theory and Jinnah's call for partition. So disappointed was he that Jinnah had turned 'communal' that he even blamed Jinnah's sister Fatima for being 'partly responsible for the transformation brought about in Jinnah'. He went as far as to allege that she enjoyed her brother's 'diatribes against the Hindus, and if anything, injected an extra dose of venom into them'. [27] Like Muhammad Munir, Chagla later became a Chief Justice, but in this case of the Bombay High Court, as he remained in India after partition. [28] Louis Fischer was an American journalist who was famously sympathetic to Gandhi. In 1918, as a member of the Jewish Legion, Fischer fought the Turks to try and capture Palestine. [29] As a supporter of the Zionist cause, there can be no doubt that he despised Jinnah, especially since Jinnah frequently spoke out against Jewish settlements in Palestine, and the League issued

---

24 M.C. Chagla 1974, p118

25 Ibid. p.118-9

26 L. Fischer 1954, p.150

27 M.C. Chagla 1974, p.119

28 See A.G. Noorani (2005) for a brief overview of how Chagla denounced 'Pakistan ceaselessly' and simultaneously proved not to be a genuine Indian nationalist.

29 The Jewish Legion was a military unit of Jews from around the world aiding the British in their fight against the Ottoman Empire. David Ben-Gurion (later to become the founder and first Prime Minister of Israel) was amongst those who set it up in Canada in 1918.

resolutions condemning the British for supporting them. [30] Indeed, Fischer tried to malign Jinnah by suggesting that he had a 'personal' vendetta against Nehru and Gandhi, that he had a 'hatred of Hindus', that he was 'psychotic', and that he was comparable to Hitler. [31] It goes without saying that Fischer, like Chagla, seems to have plucked these claims out of thin air. Indeed Fischer has provided no source for his information. Thus it is easy to discount the claims as both authors are biased and there is no other supporting evidence.

The late veteran journalist Qutubuddin Aziz and anthropologist Prof. Akbar S. Ahmed have both offered evidence from credible sources to counter these claims. Prof. Ahmed interviewed Jinnah's daughter Dina Wadia in the 1990s and she confirmed that the story was baseless. [32] In the 1970s, she also countered the personal allegations against her father in writing as follows:

> Some of my father's critics say that he was arrogant. This is incorrect. He was not the hail-fellow-well-met type; he was, like me, a very private person. On matters of principle, he always stood firm. He was never false to himself or to others in private or public life. [*sic*]
>
> When others say things which are untrue about him I get angry, and angrier still when some writers who had no contact with him feel free to pretend an intimate knowledge and quote me as a source. They say fantastic things, such as that he ate pork, *which Muslims never do.* They cover with fiction their gaps in knowledge about the human side of my father. [33]

(Note by contrast, that Jinnah's grandson Nusli Wadia later claimed his grandfather ate pork, but the claim is unreliable, [34] not least because it disregards the firsthand testimony of his mother shown above.)

Qutubuddin Aziz interviewed Jinnah's chauffeur (Mr Bradbury) in England during Jinnah's period of self-imposed exile. Bradbury confirmed that pork produce was never on the menu at Jinnah's home in

---

[30] See for example Jinnah's presidential speeches as well as the resolutions passed at the ML Annual Sessions at Lucknow, October 1937, and Patna, December 1938; see also resolutions passed at ML Annual Sessions at Lahore, March 1940, and Delhi, April 1943

[31] L. Fischer op. cit., p.150-2

[32] A.S. Ahmed 1997, p.201

[33] 'Jinnah: the man Remembered' in H. Jalal, A. Merriam (eds.) et al. (1977) *Pakistan: Past & Present: A Comprehensive Study Published in Commemoration of the Centenary of the Birth of the Founder of Pakistan* London: Stacey International, p.54. Emphasis mine.

[34] See Nusli Wadia's interview in the television series *Face to Face* aired on 4 March 2000 (BBC World). At the start of the interview he acknowledges that he has only one complete memory of his grandfather (he was four years old when Jinnah died). When he remarks a couple of minutes later that Jinnah 'got into the habit of eating bacon and eggs when he lived in England', it is clear that he is not speaking as a witness. Since none of the credible witnesses have attested that Jinnah ate pork, we safely can assume that Nusli Wadia's statement draws from the speculative writings of the commentators we have reviewed above.

Hampstead; [35] and in a separate publication Aziz also refers to Jinnah's butler, who likewise never claimed that Jinnah ate pork. [36]

Though the pork anecdotes are undoubtedly inadmissible, academics have not hesitated to include them in their works. That commentators such as Dr Ajeet Jawed and Dr Rafiq Zakaria in India and Collins and Lapierre on the British side have made these claims – and then presented them in the most derogatory manner – is hardly surprising. But when even a supposedly neutral outsider such as American historian Prof. Stanley Wolpert makes them, we have to wonder what went wrong. Wolpert's celebrated biography, *Jinnah of Pakistan*, famously included Chagla's anecdotes and caused controversy. [37] When asked by Zia ul-Haq's Islamic advisor to remove the dietary references from the Pakistani edition, Wolpert refused on the ground that 'the truth about great men needs to be known and discussed'. [38] The *truth*? With respect, the evidence that he used to establish the 'truth' is woefully biased and unreliable. It is the norm in biographical literature to add a few anecdotes to reveal the human side and perhaps even personality flaws of historical figures. This is not in question. But even anecdotal evidence is subject to scrutiny for reliability, context and authenticity; and Wolpert has failed to follow these rudimentary and commonsensical rules of the historical method. It is a pity, because there is no doubt that Wolpert holds Jinnah in high esteem, as is evident both in his biography on Jinnah and his other works. He also writes in a style that is enjoyable and accessible to the general reader. But he has been criticised for some factual errors in *Jinnah of Pakistan*,[39] and his inclusion of these dietary anecdotes only serve to further undermine the credibility of his otherwise commendable book. On the other hand, this issue would perhaps never have arisen at all had the Pakistani authorities given Wolpert a better argument for omitting the dietary references than merely saying that they would offend Muslims.

Jinnah as a 'practising' Muslim

Did Jinnah pray? It is likely with his hectic lifestyle that he did not pray often. But did he never pray? No. Jinnah may not have been a 'pious' Muslim in the religious sense; indeed, he was the first to admit that he was not 'learned in theology', but he nevertheless claimed to be a

---

35 Q. Aziz 2001, p.86

36 Q. Aziz 1997, p.56

37 S. Wolpert (1984) *Jinnah of Pakistan* New York: Oxford University Press, p.78-9

38 See Stanley Wolpert's interview to *Rediff*, March 1997. http://inhome.rediff.com/news/mar/01nehru.htm (Last accessed 23 May 2010)

39 See A.S. Ahmed 1997, p.24-5, 177; also Francis Robinson (2000) *Islam and Muslim History in South Asia* New Delhi: Oxford University Press, p.268

'humble and proud' follower of his faith. [40] There is photographic and press evidence of him praying in congregation; he himself has made passing reference to praying alongside his chauffeur, whilst emphasising the fact that in congregation all Muslims stand 'side by side' regardless of social class. [41] His aforementioned chauffeur Bradbury has said that Jinnah attended a mosque in East London. [42] Most importantly, Jinnah understood the deeper sociological implications of congregational prayer. The following is from his Eid Day message in 1939:

> When our Prophet preached action he did not have in mind *only the solitary life of a single human being*, the deed he accomplishes only within himself, the prayer and all it involves spiritually.
>
> According to the Holy Quran a very real connection exists between prayer and life. You will remember how many and wonderful are the opportunities given to us to meet our fellow beings, to study them, to understand them, and through understanding serve them and you will notice that all these opportunities have been created by laying down the law for prayers.
>
> Five times during the day we have to collect in the mosque of our *mohalla*, [43] then every week on Friday we have to gather in the Juma mosque; then again twice a year we have to congregate in the biggest mosque or *maidan* outside the town on the Id [Eid] day, and lastly there is the Hajj to which Muslims from all parts of the world journey, once at least in their lifetime, to commune with God in the House of God. You will have noticed that this plan of our prayers must necessarily bring us into contact not only with other Muslims but also with the members of all communities whom we must encounter on our way. I don't think that these injunctions about our prayers could have been merely a happy accident. *I am convinced that they were designed thus to afford men opportunities of fulfilling their social instincts.* [44]

This speech has clear parallels to one of Iqbal's *Reconstruction* lectures:

> The real object of prayer, however, is better achieved when the act of prayer becomes congregational. *The spirit of all true prayer is social.* … A congregation is an association of men who, animated

[40] Presidential address at the Special Pakistan Session of the Punjab Muslim Students' Federation, Lahore, 2 March 1941 (Yusufi Vol. II, p.1334)

[41] Speech at Muslim League Branch in Britain, London, 13 December 1946. (Yusufi Vol. IV, p.2482)

[42] Q. Aziz 2001, p.85

[43] *Mohalla* – locale, neighbourhood

[44] Eid Day broadcast from All-India Radio, 13 November 1939 (Yusufi Vol. II, p.1060-1). Emphasis mine except on Urdu terms. Spellings retained from original.

by the same aspiration, concentrate themselves on a single object and open up their inner selves to the working of a single impulse. It is a psychological truth that association multiplies the normal man's power of perception, deepens his emotion, and dynamizes his will to a degree unknown to him in the privacy of his individuality. ... With Islam, however, this socialisation of spiritual illumination through associative prayer is a special point of interest. As we pass from the daily congregational prayer to the annual ceremony round the central mosque of Mecca, you can easily see how the Islamic institution of worship *gradually enlarges the sphere of human association.* [45]

Moving on, Prof. Hoodbhoy has outlined exactly what it is about Jinnah that (in his view) makes him 'irreligious':

> Truth was an immediate casualty when General Zia-ul-Haq brought his new Islamic vision of Pakistan in 1979. Immediately thereafter, Mr Jinnah had to be entirely resurrected and reconstructed as an Islamic – rather than Muslim – leader.
>
> This task challenged even the best of spin-masters. As perhaps the most Westernized political leader in Indian Muslim history, Jinnah was culturally and socially far more at ease with the high society of cosmopolitan Bombay and metropolitan London than with those who he led and represented. *His Urdu was barely understandable. Nor were his culinary tastes quite those of strict Muslims.* But the authorities of Pakistan Television took this, as so much else, in their stride. So, in the 1980s*, a steady stream of profound pieties emanated from a stern, sherwani-clad man* who filled television screens across the country. *Gone were his elegant suits from Seville Row, as was any reference to his marriage to a Parsi woman.* Mr Jinnah had miraculously morphed into a deep-thinking Islamic scholar. [46]

To Prof. Hoodbhoy, dressing a particular way and being able to speak Urdu are supposedly 'Islamic' traits. [47] But there is no teaching in Islam to the effect that the ability to speak any particular language is a prerequisite to being a Muslim (not even Arabic). No language is divine. Jinnah did not speak Urdu very fluently, but then his mother tongue was

---

45 *Reconstruction*, p.92

46 P.A. Hoodbhoy 2007, p.3300

47 In fairness, much is said even in intellectual circles about so-called 'Muslim culture', to which perhaps Hoodbhoy has alluded. But I am agreement with Anwar H. Syed who has written that 'the billing of this Muslim culture as a cohesive agent not only for Pakistan, but for the entire Muslim world, may be a misperception.' (A.H. Syed 1982, p.99) Culture varies from region to region (leave alone country to country); it is dictated by everything from ethnicity to language and religion, and is expressed in art, music and architecture. But whilst Islam might inspire the growth of cultures, it is in itself no more a 'culture' than it is a 'religion'.

Gujarati. The same can be said for Western versus Eastern clothes. It is true that Jinnah consciously changed his style of dress from 1937 onwards, just as the members Congress wore *khaddar* [48] clothing as a cultural symbol of Indian nationalism. The man famed for his sophisticated style and his love of Seville Row suits began appearing at public functions and at League meetings and Sessions in a *sherwani* [49] and the Karakul cap (now better known as the 'Jinnah cap'). Again, he pulled off that look as only he could. But other than being symbolic of Jinnah's pride in his Indian Muslim heritage, none of these things, whether language or dress or anything else, is proof of his being a 'good' Muslim. Image means nothing. As such, Hoodbhoy makes this point exactly – that the *sherwani* was an image. But even if Jinnah had never touched a *sherwani,* and had never spoken a word of Urdu, this would not have altered the fact of his being a bona fide Muslim leader. Hoodbhoy has made the same basic mistake as the ulema in British India in the 1940s, when they accused the Leaguers of being poor Muslims.

Jinnah's sect

By birth Jinnah was a Khoja Ismaili – a sub-sect of Shiism, but – depending on whom you ask – he either converted to another sub-sect of Shiism (the Asna Ashari or 'Twelver' sect) early in life, or he became a Sunni in his later life. The dispute over his sectarian affiliation is connected in this case to the debate over his politics. If he remained a Shia, then arguably he is more likely to have remained a secularist, or even a secular-Muslim, right up to the end of his life. If he was a Sunni, then it is easier to argue that in his last few years he transformed into a religious leader with some form of 'Islamic state' on the agenda. The dispute however is not centred on theological differences between Shia and Sunni, [50] but on statistics. The point is made clear in the following statement by Dr Kazimi: 'Religious majorities prefer an ideological state, religious minorities prefer a secular state'. [51] A Shia in today's Pakistan is a numerical minority. If Jinnah is shown to belong to a religious minority, then it is inconceivable that he would advocate an Islamic state which would inevitably put the brute majority (in this case, the Sunni) in power.

---

[48] *Khaddar* – plain Indian cotton.

[49] *Sherwani* – Indian knee-length coat.

[50] Most Shiites believe that the bona fide 'Islamic state' died with the Prophet of Islam, and opinion amongst them varies on how this affects the legitimacy of any subsequent Muslim state as 'Islamic' before the return of their messiah, the 'Hidden Imam'. For those who believe that only the Hidden Imam can establish an 'Islamic state', all Muslim-run states may conceivably have any political character, including one in which religion and state are separated. Of course this means that Shia Muslims can conceivably also create an Islamic (religious) state, present-day Iran being the obvious case in point.

[51] M.R. Kazimi 2008, p.46. (The same statement appears as the opening line of his review of *Secular Jinnah* in *Dawn*, 13 August 2006.)

But in Jinnah's case, establishing his 'sect' is not only futile but irrelevant. In fact, the High Court of Sind ruled in 1970 that certainly by the end of his life he was a Muslim of no sect. [52] He became the first person in Pakistan to be legally recognised as a Muslim of no sectarian affiliation, a fact made more remarkable by the fact that he was also the founder of the country. The second person to be recognised as a simple, non-sectarian Muslim was his own sister, Fatima. [53] Jinnah's speeches and behaviour [54] also provide ample proof that he was neither Shia nor Sunni, and that he thoroughly disapproved of sectarian division. At any rate, the change in Jinnah's 'ideological' orientation from secular-Muslim to simply Muslim was not even a matter of religion, as we have already seen in the course of this book.

Off the record

The following statements appear from time to time in pro-secularist literature. To save space, we need only cover them briefly. Again, they share the common trait of being coming from completely unreliable or even non-existent sources.

Pakistan was a blunder

Jinnah supposedly told an unnamed doctor on his deathbed that Pakistan was 'the biggest blunder' of his life.

The original source (later cited by M.J. Akbar [55] and also in *Time* magazine [56]) is an article in the Peshawar newspaper *Frontier Post.* The article was written by M. Yahya Jan, the son-in-law of Khan Abdul Ghaffar Khan of the NWFP (better known as Bacha Khan, or 'Frontier Gandhi'). [57] Late journalist Qutubuddin Aziz, who protested against *Time* magazine's article at the time, has remarked:

---

52 *All-Pakistan Legal Decisions* 1970, High Court of Sind, no. 450 (Miscellaneous Application No. 11/1968).

53 Fatima Jinnah was later also found to be neither Shia nor Sunni but a Muslim in 'accordance with the Quranic concepts'. (*All Pakistan Legal Decisions* 1985, High Court of Sind, Karachi, no. 365; ruled 23 December 1984) However her case is ongoing since some of her family are still continuing proceedings for estate-related reasons.

54 Dr Safdar Mahmood has made the interesting observation for example that a Sunni alim (singular for ulema) performed the ceremony of Ruttie Petit's conversion to Islam, yet a Shia alim performed the couple's wedding ceremony a few days later. Dr Mahmood concludes: 'It may be easily surmised that Jinnah was above sectarianism'. (S. Mahmood, 'Jinnah's Vision of Pakistan' in *Journal of South Asian and Middle Eastern Studies* Vol. XXVI, No. 3, Spring 2003, p.53)

55 M.J. Akbar (1988) *Nehru: The Making of India* New York: Viking, p.433

56 See Carl Posey, 'The Great Pleader for a Muslim State', in *Time*, 23 December 1996

57 Khan Abdul Ghaffar Khan (founder of the Red Shirts) was vehemently opposed to Pakistan to the end. In the provincial elections of 1945, the Red Shirts and the Congress were accused of adopting underhand tactics – including vote rigging – to try and secure the NWFP as a Congress province.

> Yahya Jan was in his 80s when he wrote the mendacious quote in the *Frontier Post* of what he claimed had been told to him 35 years earlier i.e. in 1952 by Jinnah's physician. Why did Yahya Jan wait for that long [*sic*] to make this dubious anti-Pakistan disclosure? The physician, Colonel Ilahi Baksh, who had treated Jinnah with other doctors in the last few weeks of his life, never mentioned such a statement or quote in his book about his medical treatment of Jinnah. [58]

In fact Yahya Jan merely wrote a new version of a statement originally invented by an Indian writer in 1951 and attributed to Jinnah:

> To a Hindu friend he [Jinnah] confided, "Look here, I never wanted this damned Partition! It was forced upon me by Sardar Patel. And now they want me to eat the humble pie and raise my hands in defeat." That Hindu, needless-to-say a youthful capitalist of Pakistan, was Mr Jinnah's most favourite friend in those earlier days of chaos; and confusion. [59]

As with Yahya Jan's story, the Hindu friend is not named, and the anecdote appears for the first time some years after Jinnah's death.

Jinnah's private pledge that Pakistan was to be a 'secular state'

> It is a fact that Jinnah never called for Pakistan to be a secular state – not publicly, at least. Jinnah's statements from the 1930s onwards do not contain a single occurrence of the word 'secular' … It is reputed that Jinnah privately pledged (to an American diplomat) that Pakistan would be a 'secular state' (using these words). But, as a statesman and politician, he had a different line.[60]

The above passage is from Prof. Hoodbhoy's 2007 lecture. Note that the 'American diplomat' to whom Jinnah supposedly makes this revelation is not named. Also, this is the first instance I have ever seen of this story. If an earlier source indeed exists, I have not yet found it; and until we know who the mysterious diplomat is, we cannot even begin to check truthfulness of the account. Prof. Hoodbhoy provides no information whatsoever as to his source. But taking into account all that we have presented in this book showing that Jinnah was neither a secularist nor a secular-Muslim, we can safely assume that the claim is pure fiction.

---

[58] Q. Aziz 1997, p.181. Spellings retained from original.

[59] H.K. Ramani (1951) *Pakistan X-Rayed* Delhi: New Age, p.11. Also cited (with slightly different words, substituting 'partition' for 'Pakistan') in A. Jawed 1998, p.281)

[60] P.A. Hoodbhoy 2007, p.3301

Raja of Mahmudabad's testimony

In 1970 an article by the Raja of Mahmudabad [61] appeared in a well-known compilation volume on partition. The following passage from this article has been reproduced by many pro-secularist commentators:

> My advocacy of an Islamic state brought me into conflict with Jinnah. He thoroughly disapproved of my ideas and dissuaded me from expressing them publicly from the League platform lest the people might be led to believe that Jinnah shared my view and that he was asking me to convey such ideas to the public. As I was convinced that I was right and did not want to compromise Jinnah's position, I decided to cut myself away and for nearly two years kept my distance from him, apart from seeing him during the working committee meetings and on other formal occasions. It was not easy to take this decision as my meetings with Jinnah had been very close in the past. Now that I look back I realise how wrong I had been. [62]

The Raja goes on to suggest that the League leadership was secular-minded (including Jinnah) and only used religion as a propaganda tool.[63] 0He was a well-intentioned and genuine Leaguer but there is no doubt that he had an institutionalised understanding of the Islamic state. Here is one example of his 'advocacy of an Islamic state' which makes the point clear. His speech is passionate and in places inspiring. He even cites Iqbal, but he also exposes the limits of his understanding of Islam:

> The State will conform to the laws as laid down in Islam. It will deal justly and fairly with every community and every section of its constituent members. The unchangeable laws of Islam will *ipso facto* be applied and enforced. *There will be no fresh legislation in regard to them because Islam has already legislated them for ever and ever.* [64]

This is the fatal flaw in the Raja's thought, which explains why Jinnah asked him not to repeat his ideas from the League platform (and at any rate we also know that Jinnah had explicitly instructed Leaguers many times to not begin discussing the constitution until after Pakistan was

---

61 The Raja of Mahmudabad (Mohammad Amir Ahmad Khan (1914-1973) was a treasurer of the League and also founder-president of both the All-India Muslim Students' Federation and the Muslim National Guards.

62 Raja of Mahmudabad, 'Some Memories', in Philips & Wainwright (ed.) (1970) *The Partition of India* Massachusetts: MIT Press, p.388-9

63 Ibid. p.389

64 Raja of Mahmudabad's address at Bombay Presidency ML Conference, Hubli, 24 May 1940. (*Indian Annual Register* Vol. I (1940), p.319)

won. The Raja had been disobeying a direct order).[65] It seems that an Islamic state and a religious state were the same thing to the Raja. [66] Jinnah's opposition to his particular conception of an Islamic state led the Raja to the erroneous conclusion that Jinnah was a secularist. By cutting himself off and keeping his distance from Jinnah (as he himself has testified), he failed to ever understand the actual point of Jinnah's admonition. Years after Jinnah's death the Raja reviewed his own position and, whilst he left behind his former rigid interpretation of Islam, he had still missed the point and so took on a secular-Muslim viewpoint. As the Raja's son has written about him in recent years:

> [The Raja] went into self-imposed exile to Iraq in 1947 and spent nearly ten years living in Karbala and Baghdad. He became a Pakistani citizen in 1957 … Raja Mohammad Amir Ahmad remained restless even after changing his citizenship and continued to question the politics of his past relentlessly and ruthlessly. From a person who had founded the Islami Jama'at [67] in the early forties *he changed to an ardent supporter of secularism* in matters of politics and government and *recalled with deep respect and affection the views of Jinnah in support of a secular approach* to the political programme of Pakistan and especially in regard to the *secular Constitution which Jinnah wanted for the republic.* [68]

Meanwhile, Dr M.R. Kazimi has in a journal article referred to another anecdotal story involving a conversation between the Raja and Jinnah, taken from an unpublished autobiography.

> The Raja started by saying that since the Lahore Resolution had been passed earlier that year, if and when Pakistan was formed, it was undoubtedly to be an Islamic State with the Sunna and Sharia as its bedrock. The Quaid's face went red and he turned to ask Raja whether he had taken leave of his senses? Mr Jinnah added: "Did you realize that there are over seventy sects and differences of opinion regarding the Islamic faith, and if what the Raja was suggesting was to be followed, the consequences would be a struggle of religious opinion from the very inception of the State leading to its very dissolution." Mr Jinnah banged his

65 See Myth no. 4 (Chapter 10) discussing Jinnah's views on the future constitution.

66 Hence in the same speech he referred to the future Pakistan as a 'democratic-theocratic' state. (Op. cit.)

67 The Raja had been a founder-member of the Islamic Jamaat, a body within the Muslim League which aimed to infuse Muslims with Islamic teachings. Its members consisted of Aligarh University professors including Prof. M. Afzal Husain Qadri.

68 Raja M.A.M. Khan Sulaiman, 'My Family and the Independence Movement' in *Dawn*, 30 December 2006

hands on the table and said: "we shall not be an Islamic State, but a liberal, democratic Muslim State." [69]

To Kazimi (who has also cited the Munir quote on the same page of the above article) this implies Jinnah's preference for secularism. However we can actually draw one of two possible conclusions about the anecdote. One is to reject it as entirely fabricated. The other is that the account is essentially true but Jinnah has been misinterpreted. His criticism of the religious state – that is, of the Raja's 'Islamic state' – is clearly based on his aversion to sectarianism. The statement about seventy sects fits the view of a non-sectarian Muslim.

Elsewhere Kazimi has also pointed out that whilst Jinnah objected to the Raja's Islamic (religious) state 'for historical' and 'not ideological' reasons, he and the Raja were in agreement on 'Islamic socialism'. [70] Noting that other prominent Leaguers including Iqbal and Liaquat Ali Khan also spoke along the lines of Islamic socialism, he makes an astute and principally correct observation:

> All these are Muslim League stalwarts, so the question which arises is how is it possible for people to disagree on an Islamic State but agree on Islamic Socialism? The Holy Quran 68:7-14 specifies the types of people who should not be obeyed, it does not proscribe any political system. On the other side, strictures against economic crimes are clear and manifest: Usury, hoarding, gambling, cheating in weights and measures. It is on avoidance of these ills that societies' pillars have to be raised. What structure is to be based on these pillars is again left to society. [71]

Iskander's question

> Before we all left Delhi, I said to the Quaid-i-Azam one day, 'Sir, we are all agreed to go to Pakistan; but what kind of polity are you going to have? Are you going to have an Islamic State?' 'Nonsense,' he replied, 'I am going to have a modern State.' [72]

An Indian commentator in repeating the same story has predictably remarked: 'And [a] *modern state* must be a *secular state*.' [73]

---

[69] Isha'at Habibullah's autobiography (undated / not published) p.108-9, as cited in M.R. Kazimi 2008, p.48

[70] See M.R. Kazimi, 'Raja Mahmudabad, a Pillar of Strength of the Muslim League' in *Dawn*, 30 December 2006; also M.R. Kazimi 2008, p.48

[71] Kazimi 2006, op. cit.

[72] Khan Abdul Wali Khan (1987) (translated by Syeda Saiyidain Hameed) *Facts are Facts: the Untold Story of India's Partition* New Delhi: Vikas Pub. House, p.158

[73] See Prakash Almeida (2001) *Jinnah: Man of Destiny* Delhi: Kalpaz Publications, p.243 (emphasis mine). The story also appears R. Zakaria 2001, p.161

Though we would expect to discover that the Pakistani military officer Iskander Mirza (himself an avowed secularist) was responsible for this anecdote, to the best of my research it is not on record (at least, not in English), though the author does claim that Mirza 'wrote' this story.[74] The author in this case is Khan Abdul Wali Khan, son of 'Frontier Gandhi'. Again he does not provide any source, and Iskander Mirza is not alive to corroborate or deny the story (in fact he had died long before this story appeared in Khan's book).

Jinnah's confession that he is still an Indian

Indian academic Prof. Ajeet Jawed summarises Jinnah's psychological condition after partition as follows:

> He became a pathetic creature. He couldn't undo his past. He wanted to come back to India. In fact, he considered himself to be an Indian. What a tragedy of a person like Jinnah. He is reported to have said in a meeting of the All India Muslim League at Karachi: *I tell you that I still consider myself to be an Indian.* For the moment I have accepted the Governor-Generalship of Pakistan. But I am looking forward to a time when I would return to India and take my place as a citizen of my country. In the interests of Pakistan I would appeal to Indian Muslims to be true to India, to be loyal to India even as I would tell Hindus here to be true to Pakistan and to be loyal to Pakistan. That is the only royal road to our mutual problems. [75]

This story also originates in India, this time in M.S. Mantreshwar Sharma's *Peeps into Pakistan*; [76] where yet again the author provides no source for Jinnah's 'reported' statement that he still considered himself to be an Indian (and that too after the announcement of partition). In fact it seems Sharma (himself a newspaper editor) has taken his claim from an article that appeared in *Morning News* in August 1947. It quotes Jinnah as having said:

> Replying to another question Mr Jinnah said: "I am going to Pakistan as a citizen of Hindustan. I am going because the people

74 Ibid.

75 A. Jawed 1998, p.295

76 See M.S.M. Sharma (1954) *Peeps into Pakistan* Patna: Pustak Bhandar, p.18. Sharma, best known as the editor of Karachi's *Daily Gazette*, had remained in Pakistan after partition but returned to India shortly after Jinnah's death. Though he expressed his high regard for Jinnah in his book, he took a dim view of Pakistan which he believed was developing as 'medieval State with an impossible, theocratic conception' (op. cit. p.199).

of Pakistan have given me the opportunity to serve them. But this does not imply I cease to be a citizen of Hindustan ..." [77]

This report was exposed as a fabrication just a couple of days later, when Jinnah released the following press statement:

> My attention has been drawn to a report appearing in certain sections of the press purporting to give summary of my address to the Muslim League Members of the Indian Constituent Assembly. I wish to say that the report is a piece of concoction and I regret that a report of this kind should have been given publicity which is purely misleading and mischievous. [78]

It goes without saying that there is nothing in the records of the League meetings in 1947 (or any time) to indicate that he said anything to the effect that he was still an Indian. To the contrary, he had actually said on record in 1946: '*I don't regard myself as an Indian*'. [79] After partition he continually insisted that Pakistan would not rejoin India. For one example, here is an excerpt from his interview to Reuters in October 1947:

> I want to make it quite clear that Pakistan will never surrender and never agree in any shape or form to any constitutional union between the two sovereign states with one common centre. ... We must try to stop any effort or attempt which is intended to bring about a forced union of the two Dominions. The methods advocated for the achievement of this end are:
>
> 1. Bring about a revolt by Muslims against the Muslim League and the Pakistan government.
>
> 2. Failing that making the leaders of Pakistan realise the folly of the two nation theory and change their ways and force them once again to agree to join the Union and thereby create a single India by war. [80]

It could be said that this statement is prophetic.[81]

---

[77] See news report, *Morning News*, 1 August 1947 and *Star of India*, 2 August 1947. (NV Vol. VI, p.339-40 fn)

[78] Press statement, New Delhi, 7 August 1947 (in *Dawn*, 8 August). (Op. cit. p.339-40).

[79] Interview to foreign editor, *News Chronicle* (London); Delhi, 12 April 1946. (NV Vol. IV, p.624)

[80] Interview with Duncan Hooper, Reuters' special correspondent, Karachi, 23 October 1947 (NV Vol. VII, p.73-5). For another example, see Jinnah's address at Karachi Chamber of Commerce, 27 April 1948 (NV Vol. VII, p.377)

[81] In validation of this statement, Dr Waheed Ahmad has reproduced a press report citing a speech of Sardar Patel in which he said that Congress accepted partition only to speed up the transfer of power from Britain to India, while still 'hoping that reunion was inevitable, sooner or later', and threatening armed aggression against any Princely State that delayed in acceding

An alternative anecdote

I stated earlier that there are plenty of anecdotes about Jinnah that fit his persona as described throughout this book. But here we will only include one by the late Dr Javid Iqbal, son of the Islamic philosopher. He has told the story of the day in June 1936 (he was twelve years old) when his father called him to his bedroom and told him to be present that afternoon with his autograph book, as a guest was visiting. Iqbal had never made this request of his son before. Javid Iqbal writes:

> While father knew I possessed an autograph book, this was the only time in my life he ordered me to bring it before his expected guest. It not only indicated the respect and admiration in which he held his guest, he wanted the next generation also to extend the same degree of respect and admiration to him. Curiously I asked 'Who is coming Abbajan?' The brief answer was 'The leader of the Muslims'. I did not quite understand what he said as I had never heard of any leader of the Muslims. In those days, Jinnah was not known as the Quaid-i-Azam. …
>
> … When I entered the drawing room of our house at 4 p.m. on that day, I saw a very smart, tall and thin gentleman sitting on the sofa along with my father. On the next sofa was seated also a tall and thin lady in an elegant white sari. The gentleman wore a flawless well-tailored cream-coloured silk suit. … I silently advanced the autograph book towards the gentleman. He took out a pen from the inner pocket of his jacket and while signing his name in the autograph book glanced at me with his sharp eyes. Then with a mischievous smile on his face, he asked: 'Do you also write poetry?' 'No sir!' I answered. But suddenly followed the next question: 'Then what are you going to do when you grow up?' I did not know what to say and therefore remained silent. The gentleman turned towards my father and laughing casually remarked: 'He doesn't answer?' 'He won't answer,' replied my father emphatically. 'He is waiting for you to tell him what to do.'[82]

---

to the Indian Union. While Patel accepted the independence of Pakistan, he also admitted his belief that having partitioned Bengal and the Punjab would eventually 'result in the seceding areas desiring to reunite with India.' (*Leader*, 13 August 1947, reporting Patel's public address on the Independence Week Celebrations, New Delhi, 11 August 1947; NV Vol. VII, p.71-2 fn; also original text in P.N. Chopra (ed.) (1998) *The Collected Works of Sardar Vallabhbhai Patel* Delhi: Konark Publishers, p.152-5). Dr Ahmad also includes the text of a letter dated 6 December 1947 from Sir Edward Penderel Moon to a British Major in which Moon wrote: 'My own feeling is that within 5 years Pakistan will have been reabsorbed into India by sheer force … or by a sort of consent induced by the compulsion of events.' (Ibid. p.75 fn)

[82] Javid Iqbal, 'Reminiscences' in L.H. Merchant & S. Mujahid (eds.) 2009, p.93, 95-6.

Javid Iqbal further writes that over the years he has been asked many times by Pakistani youth what type of leader Jinnah was. He writes that in answering their question, he always first explains that Jinnah conceived of Pakistan as a democratic welfare state, with no discrimination between citizens based on faith; that Jinnah respected human rights, civil liberties and the rule of law; and that he believed in the emancipation of women. Adding that these principles are 'not repugnant to Islam', he then gives his answer:

> I tell the boys and girls 'In the light of what I have stated, you are free to fix the portrait of Quaid-i-Azam in any frame you like – conventionalist, reconstructionist or secularist.' I also tell them that since my childhood, I have been conditioned to idealize him. Guess what I think he was![83]

---

[83] Ibid. p.97. For confirmation of the answer, see Chapter 5.

Chapter 14
The Quran and Jinnah's speeches

> We have become a completely independent sovereign nation not by bloodshed but by peaceful methods. It was not I alone who achieved it. I had millions with me and especially [the] masses. The intelligentsia came last; the masses came first.
>
> – *M.A. Jinnah, a few days before partition* [1]

During Jinnah's time Pakistan was in transition. It had an interim parliamentary government, and a constitution based on the Government of India Act 1935. Jinnah hoped that the Constituent Assembly would form a permanent Constitution within two years, [2] but he died long before the task was completed. [3] Since then Pakistan has remained in political limbo, having changed its constitution several times in its short history. It has been 'Islamic' only in name.

There has been much debate over the kind of Pakistan Jinnah would have set up had he lived longer. It could be argued that in principle there is not much difference between the view of the secularists and the 'ideologues': as such both agree that he sought a welfare state and equality before the law. The main contention is whether they view Jinnah's values as Islamic or secular. We have already shown why Jinnah was neither a 'secularist' nor a 'religionist', nor even a 'secular-Muslim'. Here we will show how this translates into his work in Pakistan after partition.

Jinnah's burden

Jinnah almost certainly knew that he was dying and would not live to see the constitution-making process completed. Though he had been appointed on 23 August 1947 as the Legal Guide [4] for the Constituent Assembly in drafting the constitution, he was first and foremost the

---

[1] Public address, Karachi Club, Karachi, 9 August 1947 (NV Vol. VI, p.348)

[2] Jinnah: 'it will take eighteen months to two years before the new Constitution of Pakistan is ready'. (Speech in reply to the address presented by a Deputation of members of the Quetta Parsi Community, Quetta, 13 June 1948; Yusufi Vol. IV, p.2778) It was also speculated in the press that Jinnah himself was working on a constitution (see report summarising the same speech, as reported in *Leader* 20 June 1948; NV Vol. VII p.435fn), though no draft has ever emerged from among Jinnah's papers.

[3] The first constitution was not completed until 1954, and even this was never implemented.

[4] Announced in *Dawn*, 25 August 1947; as cited in K. Sayeed 1960, p.275.

Governor-General [5] of the new state, and numerous crises diverted his attention. For one there was the issue of the Princely States. Most of them joined either India or Pakistan before formal partition; but Hyderabad, Junagadh, and Kashmir were either undecided or wanted to remain entirely independent. The Muslim ruler of Junagadh (ruling over a Hindu-majority population) opted to accede to Pakistan; and the Hindu ruler of Jammu and Kashmir (ruling over a Muslim-majority population) was more inclined towards joining India. The Indian Government annexed the Junagadh territory and the first Indo-Pak war was declared over Kashmir.[6] Hyderabad, the largest of the Princely States with a Hindu-majority population (and the Muslim ruler of which had hoped to remain entirely independent) was also annexed by invasion, just a day after Jinnah's death.

Another problem was India's refusal to abide by the terms of the transfer of power to give Pakistan its rightful share of assets. Gandhi however did everything to try and get the Indian Government to honour the terms. In January 1948 he went on a fast to this end as well as to protest against the war over Kashmir. Many of his fellow countrymen resented his action; they unjustly thought he was merely being sympathetic to Muslims. They failed to appreciate that he was also protesting in the name of peace. Three days later the Indian Government conceded and agreed to transfer the 550 million rupees that belonged to Pakistan. [7] Through the principle of *Satyagraha* to which he had been committed for so many years, Gandhi had emerged victorious; but tragically on this occasion, it cost him his life. On 30 January 1948, a Hindu extremist shot and killed him at a prayer meeting.

---

5 Jinnah relinquished his position as chairman of the Muslim League on 25 February 1948, when the League constitution and rules were changed to thereafter bar anyone in government office from simultaneously being an office-bearer in the Muslim League. Though a motion was tabled to exempt Jinnah from the rule, he refused on the grounds that as Governor-General his job was to safeguard the interests of all parties in Pakistan. (Address, Pakistan Muslim League Council, Karachi, 25 February 1948, as reported in *Star of India*, 26 February 1948. (NV Vol. VII, p.205-6)

6 At first the Maharajah of Kashmir did not wish to declare his real preference, aware that it could lead to civil uprising. In late August 1947 frustrated Muslims in Poonch (western Kashmir) took matters into their own hands; they revolted and set up their own government (Azad Kashmir). The Maharaja in turn ordered the expulsion of Muslims from Jammu district. Five thousand Pakistani guerrilla tribesmen from the NWFP took it upon themselves to cross the border to aid their co-religionists (though some in India thought this was a state-sponsored move on Pakistan's part). The Maharaja finally declared his intention to join India and asked for Indian military assistance. (Mountbatten and Nehru had put pressure on the Maharaja, and Mountbatten had sent Indian troops to Kashmir before the state had formally decided which country to join. See interview of Alastair Lamb in A.S. Ahmed 1997, p.138; and also Wolpert 2006, p.158, p.183-190 for details of Nehru's obsession with having Kashmir for India on both personal and political grounds, and his refusal to settle the issue either by diplomacy or by plebiscite). This was the start of the first Indo-Pak war in October 1947, which would not end until 1 January 1949, a few months after Jinnah's death.

7 At that time this was equivalent to £30 million. However the full amount was never paid back. (A.S. Ahmed 1997, p.141)

Then there were Pakistan's internal problems. The most immediate concerns included the influx of millions of refugees from India. To deal with this crisis, the Pakistan Government set up an Emergency Committee and Jinnah set up the Quaid-i-Azam Relief Fund soon afterwards (both in September 1947). Jinnah also had to contend with provincialism (which as we know, had always been a threat to Muslim solidarity even before partition). Some virulently anti-Pakistan Muslims (such as the Congressite Khan brothers who still lived in the NWFP) were deliberately causing problems. [8] Within Pakistan's first year, owing to political intrigues and the mishandling of the settlement of refugees in Sind, Jinnah also directed that its Chief Minister, Muhammad Ayub Khuhro, be dismissed over charges of 'maladministration', 'gross misconduct' and 'corruption'. [9]

As a separate issue, a federal 'Ministry of States and Frontier Regions' was formed in July 1948 to bring the tribal regions of the North-West

---

8 In August 1947 the NWFP the Congress ministry led by Dr Khan Sahib (Khan Abdul Jabbar Khan, brother of Bacha Khan) refused to willingly resign even though the province had by referendum voted for Pakistan and a League Government. Jinnah had expected the British to remove the ministry before 15 August i.e. independence, but when they did not, eventually he directed the Governor of the NWFP, George Cunningham to do so (see Cunningham's telegram to Jinnah, 22 August 1947 NV Vol. VII, xlvi fn). Khalid bin Sayeed has noted that Jinnah was reluctant to do so as he probably knew it might (and did) create a precedent. (K. Sayeed 1960, p.294-5) Bacha Khan meanwhile had tried to rouse provincialist feelings in the NWFP before and after partition by advocating a separate 'Pathanistan', a movement that eventually lost ground against Jinnah's repeated messages of Muslim unity and warnings against provincialism. (See various press reports in NV Vol. VII 360 fn, 363 fn) Conversely, as shown in this chapter, similar messages of Jinnah in East Bengal were insufficient to prevent the growing resentment of East Bengalis towards their compatriots in the Punjab.

9 Press communiqué issued from the Governor of Sind's Secretariat, Karachi, 26 April 1948, as printed in the *Star of India*, 28 April 1948 (NV Vol. VII, p. 370-2). The dismissal of Khuhro, while often and somewhat glibly criticised as an authoritarian precedent, was ultimately the outcome of problems involving the two ever-persisting evils of Pakistan – namely provincial power struggles and landlords – and their impact on the refugee crisis. Khuhro fell out first with the Governor of Sind over the latter's right to reallocate portfolios without consultation, and another controversy began between himself and two of his ministers. The Governor of Sind presented evidence of Khuhro's alleged corruption to Jinnah. Meanwhile, surplus refugees that could not be rehabilitated in West Punjab were allocated to other provinces including Sind, creating resentment by the local population and inciting provincial populism. Khuhro and other landlords tried to systematically drive out the refugees, who were a threat to their feudal interests. Furthermore, the move by the central government to make Karachi the capital of Pakistan, bringing in as it did administrators and other civilians who were non-Sindhi, and making Karachi a separate federal entity, was also viewed by Khuhro and others as an attempt to take control of Sind's provincial capital city. It was in view of all these events that Jinnah met with Khuhro in late April 1948 to hear his version of events, and later asked Khuhro to willingly resign. When Khuhro refused, Jinnah was left with no option but to ask the Governor of Sind to dismiss him and formally investigate the charges. Even after Jinnah's death, Khuhro and others in Sind continued to resist the Central Government's attempts to introduce land reforms (See K. Sayeed 1956, p.305-10). Khuhro was also frequently under the spotlight for corruption offences and was dismissed from office for a second time in 1951.

Frontier, Baluchistan, Baluch Tribals adjoining West Punjab, the excluded areas comprising the Northern Areas and Azad Jammu and Kashmir, and Princely States that acceded to Pakistan. The ministry was under Jinnah's direct control. Similarly the province of Baluchistan was placed essentially under his personal charge since it was a Chief Commissioner's Province (i.e. it did not have an elected legislature, [10] and the Chief Commissioner who administered the state was selected by the Governor-General).

In addition, Jinnah's own party members were already bickering over their petty personal interests, and in so doing undermining the Muslim League. The power struggle in the Punjab between Mian Mumtaz M.K. Daultana (along with his political ally Sardar Shaukat Hayat Khan) and Nawab Iftikhar Hussain Khan of Mamdot for example, had begun from the moment of Pakistan's founding in 1947. There are conflicting opinions as to whether this particular dispute was truly political or personal; [11] but at any rate Jinnah attempted, at their request, [12] to resolve the feud. Once it became clear that appeals to a higher sense of duty were falling on deaf ears, Jinnah decided to wash his hands of the affair and let the Punjab government, as headed by Governor of the Punjab (Sir Francis Mudie) to work out their problems for themselves. [13] In the end Mamdot received the backing of the Legislative Assembly to remain in his post as Chief Minister of the Punjab, and Daultana and Khan decided to resign. Whatever the real reasons for the fallout, one political scientist has remarked that these landlords ultimately placed their class interests above party loyalty, to the extent that even the direct intervention of Jinnah himself 'failed to compel one Punjabi landlord to act against another'. [14] For similar reasons it seems, Jinnah was unable to single-handedly prevent landlord elements from marginalising those who tried to introduce socialist welfare policies in

---

[10] The Chief Commissioner however consulted with the *Shahi Jirga*, the tribal leaders.

[11] For contrasting views presenting the personal and political rivalries respectively, see for example Lawrence Ziring (1997) *Pakistan in the Twentieth Century: A Political History* Oxford: Oxford University Press, p.84; versus Ali Usman Qasmi (2014) *The Ahmadis and the Politics of Religious Exclusion in Pakistan* London: Anthem Press, p.72.

[12] See press note, *Civil & Military Gazette*, 16 May 1948 (NV Vol. VII, p.398). Jinnah had also called them to see him the month before at Karachi, at the same time that he was also having to deal with the problem in Sind (as described in previous footnote). See report of *Leader*, 24 April 1948, the headline of which reads: 'Sind and W. Punjab tangles – Jinnah to help in solution', NV Vol. VII, p.359; also *Dawn* reports the same day, op.cit. p.397 fn).

[13] The press note reads: 'The West Punjab Governor will, therefore, proceed in the normal course to take the necessary steps towards choosing and summoning his Ministers'. Ibid. p.398-9. It is worth noting that while some scholarship claims that Jinnah asked Mudie to make the decision (see for example Ziring who describes this supposed deferring to Mudie as 'weakness' (op. cit.)), in fact Jinnah had merely asked Mudie to adhere to his position as 'constitutional Governor' (See Jinnah's letter to Mudie, 18 May 1948; NV Vol. VII, p.618), and likewise this is all that is meant in Jinnah's press note of 16 May 1948.

[14] Maya Tudor (2013) *The Promise of Power: The Origins of Democracy in India and Autocracy in Pakistan* Cambridge: Cambridge University Press, p.179

line with what he had anticipated for the state, [15] including the abolishment of the *zamindari* (landlord) system. [16]

Jinnah's insistence on Urdu as the *lingua franca* of Pakistan meanwhile was met with some resentment by people in East Bengal (later named East Pakistan) who felt that their distinct provincial culture was being undermined. Jinnah temporarily succeeded in assuring them that they could retain Bengali as the language of their half of Pakistan, but there could be only one central state language 'for inter-communication between the various provinces' so that the component parts of Pakistan could 'march forward in unison', and besides which he argued that Urdu 'is nearest to the language used in other Islamic countries'. [17] He also warned that the people 'who in the past have betrayed the Musalmans or fought against Pakistan' were now consciously trying to 'exploit the language controversy ... to create a split among the Muslims of this State'. [18] Although local leaders such as Fazlul Huq hotly accused him of being on a moral high horse, and of making 'unfounded statements' on the basis of 'wrong information', [19] Jinnah's warnings about the impact of the movement on Pakistan's political unity would later be proven correct.

Nevertheless many commentators have criticised Jinnah for his stance, [20] essentially placing him alongside those whose reasons for

---

15 See Jinnah's references to Islamic economic policy, cited in Myth nos. 2 and 3 (Chapter 10).

16 For a review of how 'class interests prevailed over party policy' and prevented the abolishment of landlordism, see M.G. Kabir (1980) *Minority Politics in Bangladesh* New Delhi: Vikas Publishing House, p.34-5.

17 Speech at Dacca University Convocation, Dacca, 24 March 1948 (Yusufi Vol. IV p.2725-6).

18 Ibid. p.2724-5.

19 See Fazlul Huq's criticisms as reported in *Civil & Military Gazette*, 24 March 1948 (NV Vol. VII, p.255). Fazlul Huq accused Jinnah of having descended from his 'high pedestal' to 'thunder' against 'quislings', on the basis of false information supplied to Jinnah by officials at Dacca. Haq said there were in fact no quislings, and the real reason for public restlessness at the time was 'maladministration' by the appointed ministry rather than 'political promptings'. Prof. Abul Kashem (1920-1991), the leading activist of the Bengali Language Movement and later co-founder of the *Khilafat-e-Rabbani* Party in 1952, showed more restraint in his response to events, due to his faith in Jinnah, coupled with a strong belief in the idea of Pakistan as an Islamic welfare state. He believed that a direct appeal to Jinnah could have resolved the issue, if only the activists had been given the chance to show him that in fact they comprised a loyal group from within the ranks of the Muslim League, and they were acting in the interests of Pakistan, not against it. (See Nurul Kabir, 'The Bangla Language Movement: Beginning of the beginning Part III' in *New Age*, 25 February 2016, citing Abul Kashem's words from A. Matin & A. Rafique (2005 edition) *Bhasha Andolan: Itihas O Tatparjya*, Dhaka: Sahitya Prakash)

20 Criticisms revolve about the fact that 1) as early as 1937 Jinnah had supported a resolution to make Urdu as the official language of the Muslim League at Lucknow (though it was retracted at his own suggestion after Bengali leaders had protested. Note this incident does not appear in the record of the proceedings; a resolution calling for efforts to 'make Urdu the universal language of India' was adopted instead (see *Foundations* Vol. I p.279); 2) that he selected Urdu-speaking and non-Bengali politicians (in particular K. Nazimuddin and M.A.H. Ispahani respectively) as central leaders in East Bengal over local Bengalis before and after partition (scholarship suggests that Jinnah distrusted Suhrawardy for example, but while there is no clear consensus as to why this was the case, it may be fairly assumed that Jinnah was not

supporting a single state language were motivated by self-interest. Others have acknowledged, either implicitly or explicitly, that Jinnah's statements on language were not made for these selfish reasons; but nevertheless agree that they 'lacked his customary shrewdness', suggesting that he must have been 'badly advised'. [21]

Others still have placed the issue in context of the bigger picture. G.W. Choudhury, himself from what was then East Bengal, and who later, as Minister of Communications in Pakistan (1969-71) advocated a confederation for the two wings of the country, has written that in 1948 Jinnah was motivated by a need to strengthen 'national unity'. Pakistan, he argues, was still dealing with the aftermath of partition, especially the influx of refugees, and the fact that constitution-making had scarcely started, not to mention that suddenly the 'Indian Press of West Bengal which had always opposed the demands of Bengali Muslims gave its full support to this movement, and the Hindu Congress readily gave its blessing'. This was 'a political movement in the guise of a linguistic issue'; it was 'encouraging provincial feelings', and so was a 'serious threat' to Pakistan. Under these circumstances, Jinnah's 'firmness in suppressing provincialism in 1948 was a right step' [*sic*]. [22]

Although Prof. Choudhury also maintains that even from an academic viewpoint, [23] 'Jinnah was right in advising the nation to adopt one language in 1948', he notes that by 1954 the political climate was changing (after Jinnah's death the Language Movement had only accelerated, and even resulted in the killing of pro-Bengali student activists in 1952 at the hands of police), and it was 'unrealistic and unwise to ignore the demands of the people of East Bengal' and to 'impose uniformity of language' to the detriment of the very national unity that Jinnah sought with a single state language. [24] That same year Pakistan's first Constituent Assembly unanimously voted in favour of having both Bengali and Urdu as state languages, following the campaign of the Bengali Language Movement; and this was enacted in the 1956 constitution, remaining in place up until the establishment of Bangladesh in 1971.

---

comfortable with the Suhrawardy-Hashim faction's vision of a separate Bengal); 3) that otherwise patriotic Pakistanis were unjustly labelled by Jinnah (though he never named them) as 'quislings', merely for their involvement in the Bengali Language Movement. (These arguments appear in Harun-or-Rashid's (1987, 2003 revised) *The Foreshadowing of Bangladesh*).

[21] See France Bhattacharya, 'East Bengal: Between Islam and a Regional Identity' in C. Jaffrelot (ed.) (2004) (translated by Gillian Beaumont) *A History of Pakistan and Its Origins* London: Anthem Press, p.45. Stanley Wolpert meanwhile, a known admirer of Jinnah, refers to this incident as his 'worst political blunder'. (S. Wolpert 2006, p.180)

[22] G.W. Choudhury 1959, p.127-8.

[23] Choudhury writes that from an 'abstract point of view, the multi-lingual state is not desirable' as it creates 'many problems'. (Op. cit. p.130) Note that more recent scholarship is reassessing this long-held view of multilingual states, though not disagreeing with it outright. For an interesting discussion of the political dimension, see Hamza Alshenqeeti & Naif

These developments notwithstanding, in the years after Jinnah's death, politicians in East Pakistan made increasing demands for regional autonomy, partly making use of the alleged social and racist discrimination [25] based on everything from language to ethnicity and even separate electorates to bolster public support in their half of Pakistan. Indeed, amongst the earliest threats for secession would be those made on the floor of Pakistan's first Constituent Assembly in 1954, long before East Pakistan would formally become independent as Bangladesh. [26]

Alsaedi, 'Is Multilingualism a Problem? The Effects of Multilingualism at the Societal Level' in *Annual Review of Education, Communication, and Language Sciences* 2012, Vol. 9, p.63-84.

24 Ibid.

25 This is not to say that there was no such discrimination. Indeed some politicians in Western Pakistan treated Bengalis as an inferior class of people, based largely on caste mentality still ingrained in these former Indian Muslims, and this no doubt contributed to the rise of East Bengali nationalism and the creation of present-day Bangladesh (see A.S. Ahmed 1997, p.238-42. For a detailed study see the well-known book Harun-or-Rashid (1987) *The Foreshadowing of Bangladesh: Bengal Muslim League and Muslim League and Muslim Politics, 1936-1947* Dhaka: Asiatic Society of Bangladesh). The resistance to having Bengali as a state language – notwithstanding Jinnah's own stance discussed above – also reflects this attitude; and its implications have been summed up by Bengali writer and politician Abul Mansur Ahmed, who famously warned just a few weeks after the birth of Pakistan that having Urdu as the sole state language would have disastrous consequences for educated Bengali-speaking Pakistanis, who would be rendered officially 'illiterate' and thus 'ineligible' for government jobs, in exactly the same way that the British had made the Muslims of India 'uneducated' by 'replacing Persian with English' in India. (See A.M. Ahmed, 'Bangla Bhashai Hoibe Amader Rashtra Bhasha' ('Bengali must be made our state language'), in Abul Kashem et al. (1947) *Pakistaner Rashtra Bhasha: Bangla Na Urdu?* ('State Language of Pakistan-Bengali or Urdu?') Dacca: Tamuddin Majli; as cited in Nurul Kabir, 'The Bangla Language Movement: Beginning of the beginning Part III' in *New Age*, 25 February 2016). Many people today believe that the secession of former East Pakistan has proven that the Two-Nation Theory (as a communalist concept) is a failure – i.e. that the religious bond was insufficient for maintaining national cohesion. However, as should be clear from our review of the Two-Nation Theory, it only affirms that Muslims themselves – or certainly, their leadership – were not adhering to the Quranic principle of civil unity. The failure of the East and West wings of Pakistan to remain united occurred because of mundane controversies such as state language and political and economical inequities (East Bengal suffered terrible economic problems once partition deprived it of vital resources that remained in West Bengal), exacerbated by bureaucratic incompetence and self-serving interests. Neither side was free from blame. As Prof. Sharif al Mujahid has pointed out, it is not without significance that the party that led Bangladesh to secede in 1971, and which declared its commitment to secularism, was itself overthrown a few years later. (Op. cit. 2001, p.100-101) In fact the masses have never given up on the idea of attaining justice and liberty through Islam, and so we find that in Bangladesh today the same ideological arguments continue unabated as they do in Pakistan. See for example the incident described in my letter titled 'Thank you Chaudhry Sahib!' appearing in *Daily Times*, 4 January 2007.

26 See Shri Bhupendra Kumar Dutta's speech, 21 September 1954; CAP Debates Vol. XVI No. 31, p.550. In this case the threat was made based on the issue of separate electorates. As an interesting aside, Chief Justice Munir claimed to have personally suggested to President Ayub Khan in 1962 that perhaps the option for 'secession' should be given to East Pakistan. (Munir 1980, p.92-3)

Jinnah's power

Much has been written about Jinnah's political and constitutional powers as Governor-General, and how he used those powers. The Indian Independence Act 1947, the Act of British Parliament that effected the partition of India to create India and Pakistan, also laid down that the two countries would be governed temporarily by the Government of India Act 1935 until they had framed their own constitutions, though in the meantime they were free to modify and adapt both the 1935 Act and the Independence Act itself. (Under Section 9 of the Independence Act the Governor-General would initially be empowered to modify the two Acts up until 31 March 1948; and thereafter, this power would belong solely to the Constituent Assembly).

Under the Government of India Act 1935 as adapted in Pakistan (properly called the Pakistan (Provisional Constitution) Order, 1947), the powers given to the Governor-General were similar to those exercised by the viceroys of former British India. But the Government of India Act 1935 had originally been written to serve the colonial masters of British India; and the powers they had possessed were deemed too substantial for the Governor-General of a Dominion to assume. It was in view of this that sections 9-17 of the original Government of India Act 1935, as well as the Ninth Schedule under which the viceroys had exercised their power, were edited or deleted in the adapted Act by the British in consultation with Pakistan's provisional government prior to independence, in order to remove the discretionary provisions which would give the Governor-General essentially dictatorial powers. [27] They also explicitly limited his powers via Section 8 of the adapted Act, in which it was stated that his (and a Provincial Governor's) discretionary powers would 'cease to have effect' in Pakistan. [28] In practice this meant that the Governor-General could only exercise his powers with the consent of the Constituent Assembly. [29]

Yet this did not prevent Governor-General Jinnah from becoming technically more powerful than even the viceroys of former British India. This was due in part to the fact that deletions notwithstanding, the potential ability to dismiss provincial governments remained 'inherent' [30] in the adapted Act under Section 51; under Section 9, as we have noted above, he could make modifications to the Act itself until at

27 Details of the changes are given in K. Sayeed 1956, p.15-20. We could say these were prerogative powers, since the powers of the Governor-General (i.e. Viceroy) under the Government of India Act 1935 shared clear parallels with the Royal Prerogative still in effect in the United Kingdom.

28 Section 8, subsection 2a.

29 Sayeed notes however that unlike the constitutions of other Dominions, there was 'no specific provision' in the adapted Act 'which laid down that the Governor-General was to act on advice' – which was a 'striking omission'. (K. Sayeed 1956, p.22)

30 Op. cit. p.70.

least 31 March 1948; [31] and Section 17 granted him discretionary powers relating to the building up of the federal government and the allocation of ministerial posts. [32] Hence Jinnah did not wilfully seek these powers for himself, as his critics allege; they were in fact already granted to the Governor-General in the temporary constitution.

This was not all. Jinnah was elected as the President of both the Constituent Assembly and the Legislature, and, as we have noted already, he was also appointed the Constituent Assembly's Legal Guide. Furthermore, he was not only the founder of the country, but also its very architect, and the supreme advocate of its ideological basis, the Two-Nation Theory. In short, Jinnah was the head of a new 'Islamic state'. As Khalid bin Sayeed remarks:

> Even though powers of the Governor-General exercisable "in his discretion" and "individual judgement" had disappeared, yet the all-powerful Quaid-i-Azam was still there, and if he wanted, he could exercise most of those powers which were now available to him in slightly different forms. The new forms of power were those of Quaid-i-Azam, the Governor-General, Quaid-i-Azam, the President of the Constituent Assembly, Quaid-i-Azam, the President of the Federal Legislature, Quaid-i-Azam, the Legal Guide to the Assembly, and Amirul-Milat Quaid-i-Azam Mohammad Ali Jinnah. [33]

These were the reasons why he was called the 'Quaid-i-Azam', and why the title was conferred legally upon him on 15 August 1947. [34] They also go a long way in justifying why he became the first Governor-General of Pakistan instead of Mountbatten, who was originally expected to be appointed as Governor-General of both India and Pakistan. [35]

The enormity of Jinnah's prestige and esteem in the eyes of his people can neither be overstated nor overlooked. In fact it could be described as

---

31 Ibid. (referring to Section 9, subsections 1 and 5 of the Independence Act.) On 2 March 1948 this was extended to 31 March 1949 (Ibid.)

32 K. Sayeed 1956, p.24, 42.

33 Op. cit. p.51. It might be noted that in Sayeed's 1960 book *The Formative Phase* (a reworking of his PhD thesis) where this same passage appears, the final line referring to 'Amirul-Milat Quaid-i-Azam Mohammad Ali Jinnah' has been deleted.

34 Resolution to address M.A. Jinnah as 'Quaid-i-Azam Mohammad Ali Jinnah' in all official documents from 15 August 1947, as adopted on 12 August 1947. (CAP Debates Vol. I No. 3, p.47)

35 Critics have levelled the accusation that Jinnah insisted on taking the position in breach of an agreement between the League and Congress that Mountbatten would simultaneously hold the same office in both countries (Jinnah denied that this agreement was even made; see press conference, New Delhi, 13 July 1947; NV Vol. VI, p.277). However Khalid bin Sayeed (1956, op. cit. p.6, 11) has shown that Jinnah put his name forward since his people wanted this; not to mention that the League could hardly have trusted Mountbatten, with his thinly-veiled pro-Congress bias, to be neutral in the role.

being a power in a class of its own. This merits some consideration. Indeed, as Prof. Sayeed has revealed in detail, the newly formed central government of Pakistan depended heavily on this prestige of the Quaid-i-Azam to try and take control in some difficult situations that it could not manage otherwise. [36] For example, in both the cases of Khuhro in Sind, and of the Daultana-Mamdot tussle in the Punjab outlined above, Jinnah was expressly brought in to intervene. [37] The Constituent Assembly even passed laws in order to give the Governor-General more power so they could legally call for his help whenever circumstances demanded it. [38] As Churchill once said, 'where there is great power there is great responsibility', except that in Jinnah's case, the constituent assembly entrusted him with greater powers in order to give him greater responsibility. Yet it should not surprise us to find that even all the attempts to empower this one capable man was not enough to root out the problems caused by provincialism and landlordism. It was not, after all, Jinnah's job to tackle these issues alone.

The question of dictatorship

Critics of Jinnah have pointed to the fact that before Jinnah no Governor-General had ever had a ministry under his direct control. They also highlight Jinnah's introduction of Section 92A in July 1948 – which empowered the Governor-General to dismiss a given province through its Governor – as evidence of his autocratic methods (while Jinnah himself never made use of this particular law, [39] it was used later by others in government.) Yet Section 92A was introduced purely as an emergency measure under the extremely difficult circumstances that had arisen with partition, [40] in the same way that the central government passed laws to deal with the refugee rehabilitation crisis, for example. [41] It laid down that the Governor-General could direct the provincial Governor to assume the powers normally exercised by the provincial government. Since the Governor-General no longer possessed discretionary powers, it meant in practice that the Central Government would take over. This power could only be utilised in the event of a 'grave emergency' threatening peace and security in Pakistan, and

---

36 For further details, for which unfortunately there is scant room for a review here, see Khalid bin Sayeed's PhD thesis *The Central Government of Pakistan 1947-1951*; full bibliographical reference given in Chapter 10, footnote 80. The thesis was the basis of Sayeed's *Pakistan: The Formative Phase* (1960), though the thesis contains some details not included in the better-known book, in particular those relating to the Sind controversy.

37 K. Sayeed 1956, p.65.

38 Op. cit. p.103-6. Such laws also served to strengthen the central government machinery to the same end.

39 In dismissing the NWFP ministry and Khuhro in Sind, Jinnah utilised Section 51, subsection 5, and not Section 92A as is sometimes erroneously stated by commentators.

40 Op. cit. p. 37-8.

41 Op. cit. p103-6.

hindering the provincial government from functioning properly. In any case Jinnah did not envision this as a permanent law, since the Constituent Assembly was expected to draw up a new constitution entirely in due course.[42] In fact he made remarks to this effect at a press conference held soon after the announcement that he was to become Pakistan's Governor General, at which he was asked some loaded questions about his powers:

> **Question:** 'Will the powers of the Governor-General of Pakistan be the conventional powers of a Dominion Governor-General?'
>
> **Mr Jinnah:** "It is all there in the wording of the Bill (India Independence Bill). You better study that Bill. There are going to be adaptations from the Government of India Act of 1935. At any rate, up to March 31, 1948, there are many powers which are vested in the Governor-General."
>
> **Question:** 'Does the adaptation you refer to pertain to the present powers of the Governor-General?'
>
> **Mr Jinnah:** "*To begin with, it does.* It will depend again upon the adaptation which is now in the process of being drafted which may be accepted by each state. The Bill itself says that *the present system of government – administrative, legislative and so on, cannot be snapped straightaway.* Therefore, *during the transitional period, certain adaptations have got to be made until the final constitution emerges* from the Constituent Assemblies of the two states. These adaptations are still being hammered out but it is all subject to the supreme power of the Constituent Assemblies to change anything they like after August 15." [43]

We might also note that Jinnah never attempted to introduce any law that would have empowered the Governor-General to dissolve the Constituent Assembly under any circumstances, probably because he fully believed in its sovereign status. [44]

Still the question remains. Certainly he was a centralist, a strong-willed politician and commanded much respect and authority. But was Jinnah a dictator?

Sayeed answers the question as follows:

---

42 Sayeed argues much the same in op.cit. p.41-2, 71-2.

43 Press conference, New Delhi, 13 July 1947; NV Vol. VI, p.284-5. This perhaps also explains why Jinnah later advised a 'study' of the adapted Act, which, he held, revealed that 'the executive authority flows from the Head of the Government of Pakistan, who is the Governor-General' – at least for the time being, even though ordinarily the Prime Minister is head of government. (See his address to the Pakistan Army Officers and Men, Quetta, 14 June 1948, as reported in *Civil & Military Gazette*, 15 June 1948; NV Vol. VII, p.412)

44 Note the remarks at the end of the same press conference. See also Jinnah's 11 August 1947 speech as cited in Chapter 4, footnote 105.

> But one must always keep in mind the role that Quaid-i-Azam played in Pakistan's politics and the sanctions on which his authority and leadership depended. It would not be correct to compare him even with a benevolent dictator like Kemal Pasha of Turkey or Bismarck of Germany because both these men had efficient military machines at their disposal to enforce their authority. Quaid-i-Azam had acquired his remarkable hold over the Muslims before Partition itself when he had hardly any offices to offer to his followers. [45]

So Jinnah did not have a military regime. But if we are to compare him to the dictators of his time – of which there were quite a few, benevolent and not – we might also look at how he treated those who opposed him. Commentators who sympathise with those who were disciplined or dismissed while Jinnah was in power might do well to remember that none of these individuals suffered a long-lasting setback in their careers as a result of his actions; many if not all of them came back to similar or better positions later. None became financially destitute; not one of them was forced by his order to leave their homes, or the country. And we find that under his Governor-Generalship no one was harassed, falsely imprisoned, tortured, executed, or mysteriously made to disappear. There was no secret police, no targeting of undesirable groups or individuals, – that is, no government-sponsored terrorism of any kind. In other words, Jinnah bore none of the hallmarks of a dictator.

Building a nation-state

We have only briefly reviewed some of the issues that Jinnah was faced with in the fledging state, and yet somehow – even as he was dying – he shouldered all of these responsibilities and even lived to see the first budget come through dispelling the myth that Pakistan was not economically viable. [46]

Though Jinnah did not live to contribute towards the constitution, he nevertheless dedicated the last few months of his life to set in place two major prerequisites for a future polity that would uphold liberty, justice and solidarity, and thus be Islamic.

---

[45] Op. cit. 133-4.

[46] Pakistan's first budget (presented 28 February 1948) showed an estimated revenue and expenditure of Rs. 897.3 million and Rs. 896.8 million respectively, showing a marginal surplus of Rs. 500,000. The following year, after Jinnah's death, revised estimates (28 February 1949) showed a revenue of Rs. 956.4 million and an expenditure of Rs. 952.1 million, raising the actual surplus from just Rs. 500,000 to Rs. 4.3 million. (See Central Budget for 1949-50, presented by Ghulam Mohammed, 28 February 1949 in Constituent Assembly (Legislature) of Pakistan Debates: Official Report Vol. I, p.219)

1) The first prerequisite – the foundations of which he had set in place before partition in order to achieve independence – was Muslim unity. In order to be true to the spirit of Islam Muslims are instructed not to divide into sects or parties. [47] Doing so is tantamount to polytheism (*shirk*) in Quranic terms:

> Allah forgives not that partners should be set up with Him … to set up partners with Allah is to devise a sin most heinous indeed. (4:48) [48]

> Verily, as for those who have broken the unity of their faith and have become sects – you have nothing to do with them. (6:159) [49]

In other words: Do not associate authorities with Him (do not engage in *shirk*), thereby destroying unity and becoming opposing religious sects or even political parties. [50]

Yet as everyone knows, contemporary Islam is rife with sects and to make matters worse too many Muslims divide themselves on tribe or caste, language and culture before they even look at their spiritual bonds (or lack thereof). Jinnah managed something of a miracle in the short-term when he succeeded in rallying the support of Muslims across the spectrum, as well as non-Muslims. He constantly reminded the Muslims of their Islamic duty to maintain unity:

> Give up the idea of Shia, Sunni, Wahabi. Unity should be our watchword. … Some say we are Punjabis and others say they are Bengalis or Delhiwallas. Such [sic – an] attitude is baneful to Muslims. We are but servants of Islam. [51]

> Pakistan is the embodiment of the unity of the Muslim nation and so it must remain. That unity we, as true Muslims, must

---

[47] See footnote 50 below on the Arabic word *hizb*.

[48] Ali.

[49] Asad modernised.

[50] That the Quran opposes both religious and political division is clear from other Quranic verses including 11:17, 38:11 and 40:4. All these verses refer to like-minded 'parties leagued together' (*ahzab*) against the teachings of Revelation and the Messengers; hence, in verse 5:56 (as cited in Chapter 12) 'the partisans of God' or 'party of God' (*hizballah*) as the essence of the Two-Nation Theory. The word *hizb* (plural *ahzab*) means literally both 'party' and 'sect' (Asad footnote at 13:36). The primary meaning however is 'party, portion division or class' in a general sense, in particular a party formed to tackle a common issue, or 'any party agreeing in hearts and actions, whether meeting together or not' (Lane Book I (Part 2), p.559, under entry: **حزب**). It goes without saying that this naturally fits with the Islamic worldview which does not differentiate between spirit and state.

[51] Address to a Meeting of Muslim girl students and ladies, New Delhi, 3 November 1946 (Yusufi Vol. IV, p.2444)

jealously guard and preserve. If we begin to think of ourselves as Bengalis, Punjabis, Sindhis etc., first and Muslims and Pakistanis only incidentally, then Pakistan is bound to disintegrate.[52]

Whatever I have done, I did as a servant of Islam, and only tried to perform my duty and made every possible contribution within my power to help our Nation. It has been my constant endeavour to try to bring about unity among Musalmans, and I hope that in the great task of reconstruction and building up Great and Glorious Pakistan, that is ahead of us, you realise that solidarity is now more essential than it ever was for achieving Pakistan, which by the grace of God we have already done. I am sure that I shall have your fullest support in this mission. I want every Musalman to do his utmost and help me and support me in creating complete solidarity among the Musalmans, and I am confident that you will not lag behind any other individual or part of Pakistan. We Musalmans believe in one God, one Book – the Holy Quran – and one Prophet. So we must stand united as one Nation.[53]

Once again Jinnah was echoing the sentiments of Iqbal:

[Islam] finds the foundation of world-unity in the principle of 'Tauhid'. Islam, as a polity, is only a practical means of making this principle a living factor in the intellectual and emotional life of mankind. It demands loyalty to God, not to thrones. And since God is the ultimate spiritual basis of all life, loyalty to God virtually amounts to man's loyalty to his own ideal nature.[54]

The essence of 'Tauhid' as a working idea is equality, solidarity, and freedom. The state, from the Islamic standpoint, is an endeavour to transform these ideal principles into space-time forces, an aspiration to realise them in a definite human organisation.[55]

The pure brow of the principle of Tauhid has received more or less an impress of heathenism, and the universal and impersonal character of the ethical ideals of Islam has been lost through a process of localisation. The only alternative open to us, then, is to tear off from Islam the hard crust which has immobilised an essentially dynamic outlook on life, and to

---

[52] Broadcast speech from Radio Pakistan, Dacca, 28 March 1948. (Yusufi Vol. IV, p.2739)

[53] Address to the Tribal Jirga at Government House, Peshawar, 17 April 1948. (Yusufi Vol. IV, p.2759)

[54] *Reconstruction*, p.147

[55] Ibid. p.154

> rediscover the original verities of freedom, equality, and solidarity with a view to rebuild our moral, social and political ideals out of their original simplicity and universality.[56]

As we have already observed, Jinnah made himself a role model for Muslim unity in belonging to no sect. That he and his sister were both recognised in a court of law as non-sectarian Muslims is a world first, not to mention a monumental proof of their dedication to the principle of *tauheed.* This has an enormous significance that has yet to be fully appreciated. Jinnah's example, if followed, could open up new avenues for evolving a polity that dismisses all distinctions of caste and creed based explicitly on a spiritual outlook.

Jinnah's sheer strength of personality and willpower held Muslims together before and after partition. Had unity prevailed, then Quranic principles would have taken priority and the Government would have focused on improving the lives of all Pakistani citizens, instead of splitting into various parties and entering into pointless power struggles based on nothing more than personal, religious and cultural differences.

2) The second prerequisite was to form a constitution containing core principles that would safeguard the civil rights of all, regardless of caste, creed, or sect. This would have prevented various parties – religious and political – from merely seeking power for themselves, since they would have been bound by the constitution to work with each other rather than against each other.[57] As Jinnah stated in that Reuters interview:

> The Government will run the administration and control the legislative measures by its Parliament and the collective conscience of the Parliament itself will be a guarantee that minorities need not have any apprehension of any injustice being done to them. Over and above that there will be provisions for the protection and safeguard of the minorities which in my opinion must be embodied in the constitution itself. And this will leave no doubt as to the fundamental rights of the citizens,

---

[56] Iqbal's discussion of the thoughts of Said Halim Pasha, the Grand Vizier of Turkey (Op. cit. p.156)

[57] The late Chief Justice A.R. Cornelius criticised modern democracy in his famous lecture *Islam and Hunan Rights* (delivered at the Pakistan Academy for Rural Development, Peshawar, 8 November 1977) as follows: 'The equation of the social contract between the surrender by the citizen of part of his natural liberty to his community in order to gain greater freedom and through participation in a form of representative government, seeming to obey none but himself has proved illusory. The price of democracy is partisan politics, and the citizen must needs develop immunity to that insidious poison.' (R. Braibanti (ed.) 1999, p.287-8). For further information on Cornelius, see Appendix II.

> protection of religion and faith of every section, freedom of thought and protection of their cultural and social life.[58]

Had Jinnah lived long enough to help form the core of the constitution of Pakistan using the Islamic principles of liberty, justice and solidarity, it may have been enough to instil a belief in the minds of the masses that a progressive welfare state and an Islamic state are not in conflict; rather the two are essentially the same.

We will end here with some highlights of Jinnah's speeches, and the Quranic principles that inspired his words. They reveal much about Jinnah's character, and the depth of his knowledge of Islamic idealism. His genius lay in presenting Quranic idealism in plain language.

Theocracy and despotism

Quran

> They[59] take their priests and their anchorites to be their lords in derogation of Allah ... yet they were commanded to worship [obey][60] but One Allah ... (9:31)[61]

> It is not (possible) for any human being to whom Allah had given the Scripture and wisdom and the prophethood that he should afterwards have said to mankind: Be slaves of me instead of Allah. (3:79)[62]

Jinnah

> ... Pakistan is not going to be a theocratic state – to be ruled by priests with a divine mission.[63]

> You may rest assured that you will be safer under our system of Government than you will be under a Government which is

---

[58] Interview with Doon Campbell, Reuters' Correspondent, New Delhi, 21 May 1947. (Yusufi Vol. IV p.2565)

[59] In this verse 'They' are Jews and Christians, but the principle applies to all human beings who follow the law. Anyone who forms a religious or a political party that vies for power is challenging the sole authority of the Constitution and hence is guilty of *shirk* in Quranic terms.

[60] 'Worship' (*ibadat*) meaning obey, abide by (the Law of God). See Myth no. 7 (Chapter 10).

[61] Ali.

[62] Pickthall modernised. Again, see also Myth no. 7 (Chapter 10) for a discussion of this verse.

[63] Broadcast talk on Pakistan to the people of United States of America, Karachi, 26 February, 1948. (NV Vol. VII, p.216)

based on one man rule. If it is good it is Islam and if it is bad it is not Islam. Islam is Justice. [64]

One God and the *equality of manhood* is one of the fundamental principles of Islam. [65]

Democracy and constitutionalism

Quran

[Those are the ones] who (conduct) their affairs by mutual Consultation (42:38) [66]

It is not (possible) for *any human being* to whom Allah had given the Scripture and wisdom and the prophethood that he should afterwards have said to mankind: Be slaves of me instead of Allah. (3:79) [67]

For they who do not judge in accordance with what God has bestowed from on high are, indeed, deniers of the truth! (5:44) [68]

In contemporary language the collective meaning of these verses is that although all affairs of the state are subject to 'mutual consultation', no one, not even the head of state, can make a decision that violates the core principles of the constitution, otherwise the whole system will be placed in jeopardy.

Jinnah

The constitution of Pakistan can only be framed by the *Millat* and the people. [69]

Remember that those Governments which are not based on popular trust cannot prosper. Democracy is in the blood of the Musalmans and we have stood for equality, fraternity, and liberty and there is no chance of one man acting on his whims. [70]

---

64 Speech at a reception given by the Memon Chamber of Commerce, Bombay, 27 March 1947 (Yusufi Vol. IV, p2538)

65 Address to the Bar Association, Karachi, on the occasion of the Holy Prophet's birthday, Karachi, 25 January 1948 (Yusufi Vol. IV, p.2670).

66 Ali.

67 Pickthall modernised. See also Myth no. 7 (Chapter 10) for a discussion of this verse.

68 Asad.

69 Presidential Address delivered at the ML Annual Session, Delhi, 24 April 1943. (Yusufi Vol. III, p.1720)

70 Speech at a reception given by the Memon Chamber of Commerce, Bombay, 27 March 1947 (Yusufi Vol. IV, p.2538)

> ... I am sure that it [Pakistan's constitution] will be of a democratic type, embodying the essential principles of Islam. ... Islam and its idealism have taught us democracy. It has taught equality of men, justice and fairplay to everybody.[71]

> ... I have had one underlying principle in mind, the principle of Muslim democracy. It is my belief that our salvation lies in following the golden rules of conduct set for us by our great law-giver, the Prophet of Islam. Let us lay the foundation of our democracy on the basis of truly Islamic ideals and principles. Our Almighty has taught us that "our decisions in the affairs of the State shall be guided by discussions and consultations".[72]

Socio-economic justice

Quran

The Quran contains a number of principles alluding to economy, including *adl, ihsan, sadaqaat* and *zakaat.* Economics and sociology are interdependent, and likewise these Quranic principles have both sociological and economic implications.

> Allah enjoins justice and kindness, and giving to kinsfolk ... (16:90)[73]

Adl ('justice') is a word for giving what is due to others, i.e. bringing all people to socio-economic equity. *Ihsan* ('giving') is better translated as 'indemnification', since (unlike *adl*) the word infers generosity beyond duty[74] in the sense of compensation for injustice or loss.

> O you who have attained to faith! Remain conscious of God, and give up all outstanding gains from usury, if you are (truly) believers (2:278)[75]

Note that the word *riba* is usually translated as usury but it is better translated simply as interest, since usury refers to excessive interest, whereas the Arabic word *riba* means simply 'increase', no matter how

---

71 Jinnah's broadcast talk on Pakistan to the people of United States of America, Karachi, 26 February 1948. (NV Vol. VII, p.216)
72 Speech at Sibi Durbar, Sibi, 14 February 1948 (Yusufi Vol. IV, p.2682)
73 Pickthall modernised.
74 See Lane Book I (Part 2), p.570
75 Asad.

small that increase may be; [76] hence the Quran does not allow any rate of interest.

> ...whatever you may give out in usury so that it might increase through (other) people's possessions will bring (you) no increase in the sight of God (30:39) [77] (Emphasis mine).

> O you who have attained to faith! Do not devour one another's possessions wrongfully – not even by way of trade based on mutual agreement. (4:29) [78]

The Quran not only outlaws illegal means of acquiring wealth (such as fraud and other forms of black marketing), but also outlaws all forms of interest, even when mutually agreed between two parties, because it hinders socio-economic equity. Bank and personal loans that accrue interest and also other institutes based on tenancy (such as landlordism) are included in this injunction, since they allow property owners to accumulate wealth from others' physical input, amounting to economic exploitation. Of course it goes without saying that putting the abolishment of *riba* would require some years of gradual reform and could not be brought about overnight; but it is certainly not impossible. If two of the three symbols of tyranny [79] are already being abandoned in history, surely it is only a matter of time before the third one is as well.

The other major Quranic economic principle – *zakaat* [80] – mentioned in numerous verses, is a form of obligatory contribution [81] in which the surpluses of economic production are returned to the revenue department for redistribution towards vital services and in particular (after ending poverty and raising living standards) for opening the potential of society. The Quran does not specify a particular rate of *zakaat* but recommends that any contribution to the state should be 'whatever you can spare' (2:219). [82]

---

76 This explanation of the Arabic word *riba* is given in Asad's commentary on verse 30:39. See also Lane Book I (Part 3), p.1023, where the following meaning is given: 'what ye give of *anything* for the sake of receiving more in return' (emphasis mine).

77 Asad.

78 Asad.

79 See reference to Quran 29:39 in Chapter 12. In today's language they can be understood as dictatorship (whether as kingdoms or authoritarian states), theocracy, and capitalism.

80 *Zakaat*: a word meaning development, growth, or nourishment, as well as purification. It implies a 'purification' of the economy. Asad hence translates the term as 'purifying dues'. See his commentary note on verse 2:42.

81 Neither the word 'tax' nor 'charity' accurately translates *zakaat* – see Glossary.

82 Asad.

Jinnah

In your Government you will be making the greatest contribution to what is known as social justice or in what I might call a Socialistic Government. Social justice is one of the fundamentals of Islam. That is the duty of any state and it must show to the world that it believes in economic and social justice.[83]

You are only voicing my sentiments and the sentiments of millions of Musalmans when you say that Pakistan should be based on [the] sure foundations of social justice and Islamic socialism – no other 'ism' – which emphasise equality and brotherhood of man. [84]

I shall watch with keenness the work of your Research Organisation in evolving banking practices compatible with Islamic ideals of social and economic life. The economic system of the West has created almost insoluble problems for humanity, and to many of us it appears that only a miracle can save it from [the] disaster that is now facing the world. It has failed to do justice between man and man and to eradicate friction from the international field. On the contrary, it was largely responsible for the two world wars in the last half century. … We must work our destiny in our own way, and present to the world [an] economic system based on [the] true Islamic concept of equality of manhood and social justice. [85]

It is not our purpose to make the rich richer and to accelerate the process of the accumulation of wealth in the hands of [a] few individuals. We should aim at levelling up the general standard of living amongst the masses … Our ideal should not be capitalistic but Islamic, and the interests and welfare of the people as a whole should be kept constantly in mind. [86]

Here I should like to give a warning to the landlord and capitalists who have flourished at our expense by a system which is so vicious, which is wicked and which makes them so selfish that it is difficult to reason with them. The exploitation of the masses has gone into their blood. They have forgotten the lesson

---

[83] Speech at a reception given by the Memon Chamber of Commerce, Bombay, 27 March 1947 (Yusufi Vol. IV p.2534)

[84] Public address, Chittagong, 26 March 1948 (NV Vol. VII, p.289)

[85] Speech on the occasion of the opening ceremony of the State Bank of Pakistan, Karachi, 1 July 1948. (NV Vol. VII, p.428-9)

[86] Address to the members of the League Planning Committee, New Delhi, 5 November 1944. (Yusufi Vol. III, p.1961)

of Islam. Greed and selfishness have made these people subordinate to the interests of others in order to fatten themselves. ... There are millions and millions of our people who hardly get one meal a day. Is this civilisation? Is this the aim of Pakistan? Do you visualise that millions have been exploited and cannot get one meal a day! [*sic*] If that is the idea of Pakistan, I would not have it. If they [the landlords] are wise they will have to adjust themselves to the new modern conditions of life. If they don't, God help them; we shall not help them. [87]

A citizen who does black marketing commits, I think, a greater crime than the biggest and most grievous of crimes. These black marketeers are really knowing, intelligent and ordinarily responsible people, and when they indulge in black marketing, I think they ought to be very severely punished, because they undermine the entire system of control and regulation of foodstuffs and essential commodities, and cause wholesale starvation and want and even death. [88]

Nepotism

Quran

O you who believe! take not for protectors your fathers and your brothers if they love infidelity above Faith: if any of you do so, they do wrong. (9:23) [89]

In other words, all positions of responsibility must be given based on personal merit. If a family member is more interested in acquiring power for him/herself than working for the benefit of society (hence 'infidelity above Faith'), then he/she is not fit for such a position. No one should be favoured as a family member or by having influential friends.

Jinnah

Here again it is a legacy which has been passed on to us. Along with many other things, good and bad, has arrived this great evil – the evil of nepotism and jobbery. This evil must be crushed relentlessly. I want to make it quite clear that I shall never tolerate any kind of jobbery, nepotism or any influence directly or indirectly brought to bear upon me. Wherever I will find that such

---

87 Presidential address delivered at the ML Annual Session, Delhi, 24 April 1943. (Yusufi Vol. III, p.1720)

88 Presidential address to the Constituent Assembly of Pakistan, Karachi, 11 August 1947. (CAP Debates Vol. I No. 2, p.19)

89 Ali modernised.

> a practice is in vogue, or is continuing anywhere, low or high, I shall certainly not countenance it. [90]

Jinnah lived up to his claims and led by example. He made Lady Haroon, Sir Abdullah Haroon's wife, head of the women's wing of the Muslim League rather than his sister Fatima. He declined to use his influence to help a young man find work, despite the fact that this young man was the great-grandson of Sir Syed Ahmad Khan. [91] When Iqbal's eldest son wrote to Jinnah and asked him for a League ticket, Jinnah informed him to go through the regular route. [92] Jinnah was averse to anyone dropping names to gain influence or advantage.

Treatment of minorities (non-Muslims)

Quran – Civil equity

> We have conferred dignity on the children of Adam ... (17:70)[93]

> ... any who believe in [the Laws of] Allah and the Last Day, and work righteousness, – on them shall be no fear, nor shall they grieve. (5:69) [94]

> ... so long as they [the non-Muslims] remain true to you, be true to them ... (9:7) [95]

Collective meaning: All human beings are equal by virtue of being human. As long as all citizens are true to the state, then they will be treated fairly and justly irrespective of faith.

Jinnah – Civil equity

> The creation of the new State has placed a tremendous responsibility on the citizens of Pakistan. It gives them an opportunity to demonstrate to the world how can a nation, [*sic*] containing many elements, live in peace and amity and work for the betterment of all its citizens, irrespective of caste or creed. [96]

---

[90] Reference same as footnote 88 above.

[91] A.S. Ahmed 1997, p.89-90

[92] See letters between Aftab Iqbal and Jinnah, 13 and 18 May 1946 respectively (W. Ahmad 2009, p.194-6)

[93] Asad. For a more detailed explanation of this verse see Myth no. 5 (Chapter 10).

[94] Ali.

[95] Asad.

[96] Message on the eve of the inauguration of the Pakistan Broadcasting Service, Karachi, 15 August 1947. (Yusufi Vol. IV, p.2610)

> [The minorities] will have their rights and privileges and no doubt, along with it goes the obligation of citizenship. Therefore, the minorities have their responsibilities also and they will play their part in the affairs of this State. As long as the minorities are loyal to the State and owe true allegiance and as long as I have any power, they need have no apprehension of any kind.
>
> ... You cannot have a minority which is disloyal and plays the role of sabotaging the State. That minority, of course, becomes intolerable in any State. I advise Hindus and Muslims, both of them; I advise every citizen to be loyal to his State. [97]

Quran – Freedom of conscience

> Let there be no compulsion in *deen* (2:256) [98]

This succinct but profound Quranic principle affords a non-Muslim community religious freedom in the state. Asad's translation for this verse is 'Let there be no coercion in matters of faith', which reveals more clearly that this Quranic principle relates to religious freedom. This injunction forbids the compulsory conversion of non-Muslim (or minority) communities to Islam, and in doing so upholds their right not to believe in the sanctity i.e. the divine origin of the Quran, although as citizens of the state they must be law-abiding and fulfil their responsibilities within the socio-political context.

Jinnah – Freedom of conscience

> Minorities to whichever community they belong, will be safeguarded. Their religion or faith or belief will be secure. There will be no interference of any kind with their freedom of worship. They will have their protection with regard to their religion, faith, their life, their culture. They will be, in all respects, the citizens of Pakistan without any distinction of caste or creed. [99]

Civil unity

Quran

> And hold fast, all together, by the rope which Allah (stretches out for you), and be not divided among yourselves. (3:103) [100]

---

[97] Statement on protection for minorities in Pakistan, New Delhi, 13 July 1947 (Yusufi Vol. IV, p.2587)

[98] Ali.

[99] Ibid. (Yusufi Vol. IV, p.2587)

[100] Ali.

> Be not like those who are divided amongst themselves and fall into disputations after receiving Clear Signs [101] (3.105) [102]

Collectively these verses mean 'remain loyal to the constitution as a united society and do not become divided'. Since Islam is a *deen*, this warning against division (*shirk*) refers both to political and sectarian division. Note that in the political context this includes provincialism (encompassing language and culture differences) and social class.

Jinnah

> I am sure you must realise that in a newly formed State like Pakistan, consisting moreover as it does of two widely separated parts, cohesion and solidarity amongst all its citizens, from whatever part they may come, is essential for its progress, nay for its very survival. Pakistan is the embodiment of the unity of the Muslim nation and so it must remain. That unity we, as true Muslims, must jealously guard and preserve. If we begin to think of ourselves as Bengalis, Punjabis, Sindhis etc., first and Muslims and Pakistanis only incidentally, then Pakistan is bound to disintegrate. [103]

> West Pakistan is separated from East Pakistan by about a thousand miles of the territory of India. The first question a student from abroad should ask himself is – how can this be? How can there be unity of government between areas so widely separated? I can answer this question in one word. It is "faith": faith in Almighty God, in ourselves and in our destiny. But I can see that people who do not know us well might have difficulty in grasping the implications of so short an answer. Let me, for a moment, build up the background for you.
>
> The great majority of us are Muslims. We follow the teachings of the Prophet Muhammad (peace be upon him). We are members of the brotherhood of Islam in which all are equal in rights, dignity and self-respect. Consequently, we have a special and a very deep sense of unity. [104]

> Give up the idea of Shia, Sunni, Wahabi. Unity should be our watchword. … Some say we are Punjabis and others say they are

---

101 'Clear Signs' means in this context 'evidence of the Truth'.

102 Ali.

103 Broadcast speech from Radio Pakistan, Dacca, 28 March 1948. (Yusufi Vol. IV, p.2739)

104 Broadcast talk to the people of Australia as Governor-General, 19 February 1948. (NV Vol. VII, p.189-90; quotation marks in original)

Bengalis or Delhiwallas. Such [an] attitude is baneful to Muslims. We are but servants of Islam. [105]

The Muslim League is not going to tolerate or allow anyone to create disruption among the Mussalmans by asking them to organise themselves separately into castes or tribes. We recognise no one as a Jat or a Pathan or even as a Shia or a Sunni. We can't tolerate any such caste being created and encouraged because it will not be possible to retain Pakistan if those distinctions [*sic*] were allowed. These castes are responsible for the slavery of India. [106]

You must learn to distinguish between your love for your Province and your love and duty to the State as a whole. Our duty to the State takes us a stage beyond provincialism. … Our duty to the State often demands that we must be ready to submerge our individual or provincial interests into the common cause for [the] common good. Our duty to the State comes first; our duty to our Province, to our district, to our town and to our village and ourselves comes next. Remember we are building up a State which is going to play its part in the destinies of the whole Islamic World. We therefore, need a wider outlook, an outlook which transcends the boundaries of provinces, limited nationalism and racialism. We must develop a sense of patriotism which should galvanise and weld us all into one united and strong nation. That is the only way we can achieve our goal, the goal of our struggle, the goal for which millions of Musalmans have lost their all and laid down their lives. [107]

Charity (Relief Aid)

Quran

Alms are for the poor and the needy, and those employed to administer the (funds); for those whose hearts have been (recently) reconciled (to Truth); [108] for those in bondage and in debt; in the cause of Allah; and

[105] Address at a meeting of Muslim girl students and ladies, New Delhi, 3 November 1946. (Yusufi Vol. IV, p.2444)

[106] Speech at the concluding Session of the Punjab Muslim Students' Federation Conference, Lahore, 19 March 1944. (Yusufi Vol. III, p.1863)

[107] Speech in reply to the address presented by the Students of Islamia College, Peshawar, 12 April 1948. (Yusufi Vol. IV p.2746-7)

[108] 'Those whose hearts have been (recently) reconciled (to Truth)' i.e. the poorest people and refugees who wish to become citizens of the State but cannot contribute to it financially (see S. Ahmed's translation for this verse).

> for the wayfarer: (thus is it) ordained by Allah, and Allah is full of knowledge and wisdom. (9:60) [109]

Sadaqaat ('alms') [110] are voluntary payments given by citizens to a body appointed by the government (hence, 'those employed to administer the funds') to bring about socio-economic stability in times of crisis, usually the very earliest stages of setting up the state. As the Quran's aim is to take the growth of humanity beyond just the material, and as shown in the above verse, *Sadaqaat* payments primarily focus on this material stage, namely ending poverty and raising living standards.

Jinnah

> The sufferings that have been inflicted on our people in the East Punjab, Delhi and various other parts of the Dominion of India have few parallels in their extent. … Since we assumed office, my Government and myself have been spending the best part of our time and energy in dealing with this grave crisis …
>
> We have now to think in terms of affording relief to those millions of our brethren who have been stricken by this calamity. The nation is aware that an Emergency Committee of the Cabinet has been constituted for the purpose … We are determined to mobilise the resources of the State to the fullest extent to cope with this colossal task and overcome all difficulties.
>
> But in a national crisis of such magnitude, the resources of the State must necessarily be supplemented by those of the people themselves and private charity and their support and co-operation can accomplish much which Government organisations and aid alone cannot.
>
> I have given the most anxious and careful thought as to how this can be done and have decided to institute forthwith … the 'Quaid-i-Azam's Relief Fund'. …
>
> I appeal to the nation to come forward with generous contributions to this fund and to stint no sacrifice or effort for this purpose. There are millions who are living in safety and security and enjoying the comforts of life, while countless

---

109 Ali.

110 *Sadaqaat* is a word ultimately meaning truth, or sincerity. More specifically, it is to deliver on a promise, i.e. to prove the sincerity of a pledge through action. *Sadaqaat* as a term could imply any such action, but insofar as it applies to economic practice, *sadaqaat* is payment either to a government body in excess of the compulsory 'tax', *zakaat*, or given as private 'charity'. *Sadaqaat* payments apply when there is little socio-economic balance (9:60), or in times of unexpected crisis at home or abroad (this is why the word *sadaqaat* is usually translated in English as 'alms-giving'). It is entirely voluntary. Naturally we would expect that people who claim to have *eiman* (conviction) in the sanctity of the law will actively substantiate their claim by paying *sadaqaat* most generously beyond their legal obligations.

numbers of their fellow human beings have suffered and are suffering grievously. …

Let every man and woman resolve from this day to live henceforth strictly on an austerity basis in respect of food, clothing and other amenities of life and let the money, foodstuffs and clothing thus saved be brought to this common pool for the relief of the stricken.[111]

Women

Quran

> O mankind! Be conscious of your Sustainer, who has created you out of one living entity, and out of it created its mate, and out of the two spread abroad a multitude of men and women. And remain conscious of God, in whose name you demand (your rights) from one another, and of these ties of kinship. Verily, God is ever watchful over you! (4:1) [112]

This is yet another reference to the equality of all humans, male or female, by virtue of having a common origin. They are equal companions of each other and are equally entitled to assert their rights.

> The Believers, men and women, are protectors one of another: they enjoin what is just, and forbid what is evil ... (9:71) [113]

In other words, men and women support one another mutually and are equally capable of upholding the law and maintaining society. This verse refers specifically to the characteristics of the 'believing' men and women, but as a principle it applies to humanity in general.

> Hence, do not covet the bounties which God has bestowed more abundantly on some of you than on others. Men shall have a benefit from what they earn, and women shall have a benefit from what they earn. Ask, therefore, God (to give you) out of His bounty: behold, God has indeed full knowledge of everything. (4:32) [114]

Both men and women have their strengths and weaknesses but everyone is entitled to receive the benefit from the effort they put into the work they do.

---

111 Appeal to the nation for contribution to the 'Quaid-i-Azam Relief Fund' for refugees, Karachi, 12 September 1947. (Yusufi Vol. IV, p.2618-9)

112 Asad.

113 Ali.

114 Asad.

Jinnah

> No nation can make any progress without the cooperation of its women. If Muslim women support their men, as they did in the days of the Prophet of Islam, we should soon realise our goal.[115]

> I have always maintained that no nation can ever be worthy of its existence that cannot take with them their women. No struggle can ever succeed without women ever participating side by side with men. …
>
> You young ladies are more fortunate than your mothers. You are being emancipated. I don't mean that you should copy the West. But I do mean that man must be made to understand and made to feel that woman is his equal and that woman is his friend and comrade and they together can build up homes, families and the nation.[116]

> We are the victims of evil customs. It is a crime against humanity that our women are shut up within the four walls of the houses as prisoners. … let us try to raise the status of our women according to our own Islamic ideas and standards. There is no sanction anywhere for the deplorable conditions in which our women have to live. … The woman has the power to bring up children on right lines. Let us not throw away this asset.[117]

> … if political consciousness is awakened amongst our women, remember your children will not have much to worry about …[118]

> There are certain things which can be done by men. There are others which can be done by women. But both together can do anything and everything.[119]

Again Jinnah led by example; his sister Fatima Jinnah supported him dedicatedly throughout the Pakistan movement. She attended every annual Muslim League session from 1940 onwards, and she played a

---

115 Speech at the Jinnah Islamia College for Girls, Lahore, 22 November 1942 (Yusufi Vol. III, p.1658)

116 Address to students of Jinnah Islamia College for Women, Lahore, 25 March 1940 (Yusufi Vol. II, p.1189-90)

117 Speech at the Meeting of the Muslim University Muslim League, Aligarh, 10 March 1944. (NV Vol. III, p.414)

118 Presidential address, ML Annual Session, Lahore, 22 March 1940 (NV Vol. I, p.486)

119 Address at a meeting of Muslim girl students and ladies, New Delhi, 3 November 1946. (Yusufi Vol. IV, p.2444)

central role in organising women to do their part in supporting the League, as a member of the AIML Women's Subcommittee.[120]

Conclusion

Hopefully these examples should suffice to demonstrate how staunchly Jinnah abided by Quranic principles both in letter and in spirit. He was especially dedicated to living by the most important Quranic principle, tauheed, or unity. He had fought all his life for universal civil rights and with the advent of the Pakistan movement he struggled to rally the Muslims to become a united people. But almost as soon as he passed away, the hitherto united Muslim leaders of Pakistan finally showed their true colours and unity fell apart, and the principle of tauheed was utterly violated. *Shirk*, the antonym of *tauheed*, is the only unpardonable offence in the Quran (4:48). Jinnah at least was not guilty of this crime.

By Quranic standards Mahomed Ali Jinnah was a true Muslim; his sense of ethics and integrity were unmatched by any of his contemporaries. His unwavering belief in human rights motivated virtually every decision he made during his political career. It was his political actions in the name of civil equity that earned him the honorary title of 'ambassador of Hindu-Muslim unity' when he still worked with Congress; it was his disillusion with the political attitude of the Congress that eventually compelled him to resign and lead the fight for independent Pakistan instead, having realised that civil equity would never happen in a united India. In short, he wanted a separate homeland to ensure civil equity for all of its citizens. Thus his beliefs were constant, and his actions were consistent with them.

I have always found it strange that writers of every camp make such an issue of the fact that Jinnah changed from being an Indian nationalist to leading the Pakistan movement instead. The advocates of a secular Jinnah try to play down his shift from Hindu-Muslim unity to an exclusively Muslim cause, since it goes against their argument that he was not truly motivated by Islam; hence they focus on the fact that he was disillusioned with Congress and make use of the three-piece argument to maintain that he was always a secularist. Some advocates of a 'communalist' Jinnah (mainly right-wing Hindus) claim that he was a religious fundamentalist and that his switch in political loyalty was motivated by a hunger for power. Some advocates of a 'Muslim Jinnah' (the so-called 'ideologues') meanwhile lament that he spent so long working with Congress that he acquired the 'ambassador' title in the first place, since it gradually led to his reputation as a secularist today. However, all of these writers forget that his struggle was always for universal civil rights and his honorary title had only ever reflected that. His increasingly 'religious' i.e. Islamic speeches towards the end of his

[120] See A.S. Ahmed 1997, p.12 and Q. Aziz 1997, p.62

life indicate not a political tactic to rally communal support, but rather the fact that he had acquired a deeper and more conscious understanding of Islam. The proof of this comes from the fact that Jinnah continued to refer to Islamic idealism in virtually every post-partition speech right up until his death in 1948, and the fact that he carried out his duties as head of state in an Islamic fashion, upholding the principle of Muslim unity first and foremost, as well as the principles of justice and fairplay, among others.

Thus Jinnah may have abandoned his honorary post, but not his principles. He never changed as a beacon of human rights. True to his convictions until his last day, the former ambassador of Hindu-Muslim unity simply became the ambassador of Pakistani unity instead.

> VERILY, for all men and women who have surrendered themselves unto God, and all believing men and believing women, and all truly devout men and truly devout women, and all men and women who are true to their word, and all men and women who are patient in adversity, and all men and women who humble themselves (before God), and all men and women who give in charity, and all self-denying men and self-denying women, and all men and women who are mindful of their chastity, and all men and women who remember God unceasingly: for (all of) them has God readied forgiveness of sins and a mighty reward. (33:35) [121]

[121] Asad.

Glossary

Adl: A word that appears in verse 16:90 alongside **ihsan**. It means justice, i.e. all people are entitled to have their needs met, including proper healthcare and education as well as food and shelter, and no individual should be privileged over another socio-economically.

Core principles: A reference in this book to the timeless immutable principles of the **Quran** that cannot be altered in any way by human intervention. These principles form the foundation of the constitution in an Islamic polity.

Deen: A holistic word meaning 'mode of existence'. The word makes no distinction between the temporal and the spiritual, in accordance with the Islamic worldview.

Dhimmi: A word with the meaning of 'protected ones', used to refer to non-Muslims living in a (traditionalist) Islamic state. Such minority communities are expected to pay an ongoing poll tax in return for security and religious freedom. As protected citizens they are not required to fight in war alongside Muslims and instead of paying *zakaat* they pay *jizya* (which is understood to be at a lower rate than *zakaat*). However the word does not appear in the Quran and is evidently an historical concept.

Economic principles of the Quran: The principles designed to bring people to socio-economic equity, based on the principles of **adl**, **ihsan**, **sadaqaat** and **zakaat**. Since economics and sociology are interdependent, and these principles have both sociological and economic implications, they are instrumental to Islamic social justice. See the definitions of the individual principles for further information.

Eiman: The Arabic word for conviction. As the word suggests, conviction is more than simple 'faith', which in religious philosophy usually refers to blind faith. A person of conviction (a **momin**) is someone who fully comprehends the Islamic legacy and becomes convinced of its divine origin, and thereafter actively attests to this through action (see also **sadaqaat**).

Haman: A religious leader of Moses' time symbolising religious tyranny in the **Quran**.

Haraam: In **sharia**, a word meaning 'prohibited' or outlawed.

Hizb: A word meaning both (political) 'party' and (religious) 'sect'.

Ihsan: A word that appears in verse 16:90 alongside **adl**. It means 'create balance', 'giving' (a favour without expecting a full return, or to ease another's burden) and 'perfection' (I have used the word 'indemnification' to encompass these meanings), and in the political context it is a reference to the state's responsibility to compensate all individuals in the event of injustice or loss. People who for various reasons (such as severe disability) cannot earn for themselves are also entitled to receive indemnification.

Islam: A verbal noun literally meaning, '(willing) submission'. It is the name of the 'way of life' (or System) decreed by God in the **Quran**, encompassing both socio-politics and spirituality.

Islamic state: A state in which Quranic **core principles** form the foundation of the constitution (at minimum) and are actively implemented. An 'Islamic state' as described in this book is not to be mixed up with the religious theocracy usually referred to by the same name. There are no Islamic states on earth today.

Jizya: A word with a root meaning of 'repay' or 'compensate'. While *jizya* has traditionally become associated with an ongoing tribute or poll tax to be paid by **dhimmis**, in the Quran it appears just once in the context of a one-time penalty for treaty violations.

Ka'fir: (Plural: ka'fireen) A Quranic word for a person who has learned about the Quranic teachings and has comprehended them, but still refuses to acknowledge their veracity and abide by them, invariably for selfish reasons. Ka'fireen therefore is not a word to describe non-Muslim citizens of the state in general, but only those who reject outright that its law has any practical value and hence are bent on violating it for their own interests.

Lahore Resolution: The resolution passed in March 1940 at the 27th Session of the All-India Muslim League, Lahore. It marked the formal call for Muslim independence from India.

Millat: An Urdu word for the **ummah**. See also **qaum.**

Misaq-i-Medina: Arguably the world's first written constitution, a compact made between the **Rasool**'s people and the local tribes of Medina in around 622 AD.

Momin: (Plural: *momineen*) A person who professes and actively proves that he/she possesses **eiman**.

Munafiq: (Plural: *munafiqeen*) A Quranic word for someone who claims to be loyal to the law of Islam but isn't loyal in practice. Rather than abide by the law sincerely and thus work for the public good, such a person prefers to follow his/her own selfish whims, and thus is a traitor to the state. The munafiqeen represent an internal source of rebellion against the constitution and are thus **ka'fireen** in disguise.

Muslim/civil unity: A term used in this book to describe solidarity on the basis of **tauheed**. Muslim unity is a precursor to universal human or civil unity since the ultimate aim of Muslim unity is to leave at peace with all other people.

Mutual consultation: The principle of the **Quran** that all affairs of the state must be settled through dialogue and discussion and must involve the whole of the **ummah**. 'Islamic democracy' is based upon this principle.

Pharaoh: The Egyptian ruler of Moses' time symbolising political tyranny in the **Quran**.

Pro-secularist theory: The argument that Jinnah sought a secular/materialist political system (modern democracy) for Pakistan.

Qaroon: The extremely wealthy and oppressive magnate of Moses' time who symbolises economic tyranny in the **Quran**.

Qaum: In traditional Islam, the *qaum* refers to community bound by ethnicity, culture and geography, in other words, much like the modern concept of a nation. Many Muslims differentiate between this word and *millat* which is understood as referring explicitly to the Muslim community.

Quaid-i-Azam: A title meaning 'Great Leader' that Jinnah acquired as his popularity grew amongst the Indian Muslims and he became acknowledged as their champion.

Quran: In Islam, the Scripture containing the final **Revelation**.

Rabb: A word in the **Quran** usually translated as 'Lord', but which actually refers to God's attribute of nourishing and nurturing everything in the universe via physical natural laws.

Rasool: A Quranic word meaning 'messenger', or disseminator of the Message. Although this word tends to be used by Muslims solely to refer to the final Messenger, as a term it applies to all the previous Messengers who also 'received the Message' (the word for such a 'recipient' is *Nabi*).

Riba: A word meaning 'increase' (of any size), and so is the term for interest (though it is usually mistranslated as 'usury').

Sadaqaat: A word ultimately meaning truth, or sincerity. More specifically, it is to deliver on a promise, i.e. to prove the sincerity of a pledge through action. Sadaqaat as a term could imply any such action, but insofar as it applies to economic practice, sadaqaat is payment either to a government body in excess of the compulsory contribution, **zakaat**, or given as private 'charity'. Sadaqaat applies when there is little socio-economic balance (9:60), or in times of unexpected crisis at home or abroad (which is why the word sadaqaat is usually translated in English as 'alms-giving', though the Quranic form of 'charity' does not come at the expense of human dignity – see verses 2:263-4, 2:271). It is entirely voluntary. People who claim to have **eiman** (conviction) in the sanctity of the law will naturally substantiate their claim by paying sadaqaat most generously beyond their legal obligations.

Secular Islam / Synthesis: A term for describing the beliefs of liberal Muslims who believe in a 'synthesis' between Muslim values and modern concepts of state.

Shariah: A word for Muslim law.

Shirk: The antonym of **tauheed**, and thus normally translated as 'polytheism'. It refers to obeying any authority – religious or political – on a par with that of God. *Shirk* is the only unpardonable offence according to the **Quran**.

Tauheed: A word referring to the unity of God; it is the basis of the Islamic worldview. In the political context, this also means united allegiance to one law and can be described as 'civil unity'.

Two-Nation Theory: A term commonly credited to Sir Syed Ahmad Khan; it is based on the Quranic teaching that God only recognises two types of people: those who adhere to universal principles, and those who do not. The term 'Two-Nation Theory' itself is generally used to describe the specific situation in India prior to partition, this being that there were two distinct nations – Hindu and Muslim – completely separate in their respective 'ways of life' and that hence they could not coexist peacefully in a united India. This was the principle upon which the Indian Muslims sought independent Pakistan. Many people today believe that the separation of former East Pakistan from Pakistan to form independent Bangladesh in 1971 has proven that the Two-Nation Theory as a 'communal' concept is a failure; in reality however, all it proves is that the Muslims themselves are divided and are no longer true to the Quranic principle of **tauheed**.

Ulema/ulama: (Singular: *alim*). A word literally meaning 'learned people'. Today's ulema are religious clerics.

Ummah: A word for the citizens of an Islamic society, including Muslims and non-Muslims. While the Urdu word *millat* has the same technical meaning, it is generally used to refer to Muslims alone.

Zakaat: A word meaning development, growth, or nourishment, as well as purification. In an Islamic state the surplus of all acquisition is returned to the government for distribution to those who need it (or individuals spend it on others as and where it is needed). Although people tend to assume that zakaat is a monetary tax (if not a form of charity, though only the word **sadaqaat** refers to charity of a kind), the **Quran** has not stated that it applies only to money; it can actually apply to all forms of acquisition and produce. Nor is it a 'tax' in the sense of being paid at a rate set by the state, whether variable or fixed. *Zakaat* as an economic principle applies to surplus only (2:219, 25:67) and therefore it cannot become an unaffordable burden on any citizen (6:152, 6:164, 35:18, 65:7). The long-term implications of this are obvious. However unfeasible this notion may seem, even to Muslims, economic practice (as we know it) can change completely, and money can potentially become redundant.

Appendix I
Core principles of the Quran

Below are the core principles of the Quran that are essential to the establishment of a bona fide (active) Islamic state. Rather than discuss these in length I have simply referred to the Quran verse number(s) where the principles appear.

Universal civil rights

All humans are equal by virtue of being human and having a common origin (4:1, 10:19, 17:70, 49:13). Hence people of all races (30:23), women (4:32), impoverished people (9:60), and disabled people (70:25) are to be treated as equals.

The principle of universal civil rights alone morally justifies social justice.

Social justice

All humans have a right to equal socio-economic treatment, irrespective of race, caste or creed (2:62, 5:69). All have a right to receive justice (*adl*) and to receive indemnification (*ihsan*) in the event of injustice or loss (16:90). It follows that no economic principles should be put into effect that would hinder the processes of socio-economic justice (30:39, 4:29).

Democracy and constitutionalism

Since all receive the same protection, rights and privileges by law, they must collectively abide by the same core principles of the constitution (3:103-5, 4:59) in order to retain socio-economic balance. They must settle their affairs by mutual consultation (42:38) without abrogating the core of the constitution (42:10). No human can act as ruler over another, whether as a politician, a monarch or a cleric (3:79, 9:31). The head of state is no exception to this rule (3:79). It follows that there can be no division into religious sects or political parties that vie for control and power, and who challenge the authority of the constitution (30:31-2). Violation of this principle threatens the balance of the system and thus amounts to high treason (4:48).

Freedom of conscience

No one can be forced to convert to Islam (none can be forced to believe in the sanctity of the law, nor can the Islamic state be established by force) (2:256, 10:99-100). Once the core principles are embodied as a permanent fixture in the constitution, all members of the state will be expected to be law-abiding citizens; all citizens will be treated equally regardless of faith (2:62, 2:112, 5:69). However, no other Quranic principles will ever become binding upon society in general (other than upon the 'believers' or *momineen* (33:36)) until the benefits of such laws are fully understood and accepted by all the people (5:48).

Appendix II
Non-Muslims on Jinnah and Pakistan

Following are some examples of writings and letters by non-Muslim minorities who either supported the Pakistan movement, or the Muslim League, or in some way confirmed that they had understood the Pakistan idea. This is to dispel the myth that the League was a 'communal' body concerned only with its own interests.

Jogendra Nath Mandal

First however we make a special mention of Jogendra Nath Mandal (1904-1968), the Scheduled Castes Federation leader who staunchly supported the Pakistan movement despite intense opposition from the Mahasabha and the Congress. [1] After partition he was appointed as Minister for Law and Labour in the Central Cabinet of Pakistan. In September 1950, he left for India in what the Pakistani government believed to be a personal trip to see his ill son. The government did not know Mandal had left Pakistan for good until after his resignation letter written to Liaquat Ali Khan was published in the Indian press in October 1950. In the letter Mandal wrote that he had left Pakistan, among other reasons, because Pakistan's leadership was not faithful to the promises of 'equal treatment' made to the minorities in the Lahore Resolution and in Jinnah's 11 August 1947 speech. [2] Speaking at the Constituent Assembly meeting a few days later, Liaquat Ali Khan poured scorn on the letter, which he maintained was a contradiction of Mandal's entire political position of loyalty to Pakistan up until that point. He attributed Mandal's exit in part to personal intrigues, but more significantly, he mentioned having received information that Mandal was working with 'militant Hindu organisations in West Bengal which are openly advocating aggression against East Pakistan'. [3] However, in light of the pressures Mandal had faced from such militants and others before partition, as well as his hitherto complete loyalty to Pakistan (by Khan's

---

[1] See Chapter 8, footnote 22.

[2] Letter is reproduced in full in M.G. Kabir 1980, p.131-52. Mandal's other stated reasons for leaving Pakistan included his fears over the development of Pakistan as a state that divided people on the basis of religion, and his horror at witnessing the aftermath of the Dacca riots of 1950.

[3] Speech of Liaquat Ali Khan, 14 October 1950. CAP Debates Vol. II No.11, p.652

own admission), Khan's information seems somewhat doubtful. [4] Furthermore, the fact that the resignation letter had reportedly been edited by the unnamed member of a prominent family in Calcutta before publication in the press [5] suggests that the exact causes of Mandal's sudden resignation are not as clear-cut as they may seem, and further investigation is needed.

Mrs K.L. Rallia Ram

Mrs Ram, a Christian based in Lahore, was a founding member and Secretary of the Indian Social Congress. She was a supporter of Jinnah and maintained correspondence with him, sending him cuttings and information about political affairs in the Punjab (she was also the widow of K.L. Rallia Ram who had been a member of the Punjab Provincial Legislative Council). [6] Jinnah wrote back regularly to thank her for her trouble and to express his appreciation of the 'instructive and useful' information she was sending him. [7] Her letters provide an insight into the views of non-Hindu communities other than Muslims who opposed a 'Hindu raj' for the same reasons.

> … I wondered whether we could organise a common front against this deadly foe, the Caste System, which threatens to engulf not only the Muslims but also other communities of India. Swami Dharma Theertha, the founder of the Indian Social Congress and I entirely agree with your stand for Pakistan ...
>
> Since the League Convention resolution [8] is an open challenge not only to the Hindus, but also to the whole world that they are determined to resist all efforts to be yoked under a people whose social and economic machinery threatens the very existence of Muslims and others who differ in their way of life from Hindus, it is up to all these elements to unite under a common banner to expose this poisonous social structure undemocratic in character. In order to strengthen the case of a separate homeland, the wicked implications of the caste system have to be thoroughly exposed.
>
> … The Muslims, the Christians and other communities of India have to be told how the Hindu castes are a standing insult to all of them and an obstacle to national unity and common

---

[4] Although Mandal was known to have been influenced by Subhas Chandra Bose (younger brother of Sarat Chandra Bose), the fierce nationalist whose legacy is tainted by his affiliations with Nazi Germany and Imperial Japan, there is no apparent evidence in scholarship that Mandal worked with extreme Hindu nationalist groups at any point in his career.

[5] Ibid. p.654 (Khan citing the Calcutta newspaper *The Nation*)

[6] Biographical information taken from W. Ahmad 2009, p.538

[7] See full correspondence in W. Ahmad 2009, p.431-92

[8] Meaning the Delhi Resolution of 9 April 1946 (see Appendix V for text)

citizenship. All freedom loving people have to raise their voice against the castes.[9]

What the Muslim nation needs at this time is a flood of publicity, the necessity of which I have been emphasising for the last six months. Hindus do think with greater rapidity than the Muslims who have been sleeping all these years ... For Mahatma Gandhi has again and again said in his speeches at various times that the majority of Muslims and Christians come from the low-caste Hindus and should revert to the old fold. The desire of capturing the central government of the land and steadily work for a united India is also a part of the plan to slowly and steadily work for the re-conversion of Muslims [and] Christians back into the Hindu fold ...[10]

I am sending you some more cuttings from the press. I particularly want to bring the fact of minority's [*sic*] leanings towards the Muslim League to your notice. Now that things are settling down and everybody has seen and is keenly watching the doings of the caste Hindu government at the Centre, it has set people to thinking [*sic*] and they are beginning to realise what the implication of such a step could mean to those who do not see eye to eye with the caste Hindus who are taking full advantages of bringing in a full *Ramraj* in the land of many nationalities.[11]

Miscellaneous public examples

A couple of other examples from non-Muslim members of the public offering support for the League appear in the Nation's Voice collection compiled by the late Dr Waheed Ahmad:

Letter from a member of the public (District Darjeeling), 17 August 1946

Sir,

Would you kindly let me know whether there is any bar to a non-Muslim being a member of the Muslim League. If not, I shall be glad to know how this can be arranged. If, however, this is not admissible, would you please instruct me as to how a non-Muslim, who has faith in your leadership and holds you as one of the greatest statesmen of the world at the present time, can best serve his country without conversion to Islam.

---

[9] Mrs Ram to Jinnah, 29 May 1946 (W. Ahmad 2009, p.431-2).

[10] Mrs Ram to Jinnah, 2 September 1946 (Op. cit. p.459)

[11] Mrs Ram to Jinnah, 22 September 1946 (Op. cit. p.468-9)

Apologising for the trouble and thanking you in anticipation,
Yours faithfully,
S.K. Ghosh [12]

In his reply, dated 10 September, Jinnah wrote: '... technically a non-Muslim cannot become a member of the Muslim League, but we welcome anyone who sympathises with us who can in his own way help us and support our cause.' He advised Mr Ghosh to get in touch and 'have a talk' with M.A.H Ispahani, who was then a member of the Working Committee of the Bengal Provincial Muslim League. [13]

Letter from a Hindu, Mrs Meenambal Siva Raj, President, Dr Ambedkar Students' Home (Trichnopoly), 6 November 1946

Mrs Raj wrote to Jinnah to thank him for nominating J.N. Mandal to the Interim Government by giving him a seat out of the five reserved for the League, as 'compensation to the wrong done to us by the British government and the Brahmin-dominated Congress'. She added: 'We look forward to a bright future and a respectable place in the national life of this subcontinent. This will be quite possible provided all the seven crores of the untouchables embrace Islam as Dr B.R. Ambedkar indicated in London and Mr Mandal at [the] New Delhi meeting.' [14]

Chief Justice Cornelius

Alvin Robert Cornelius (1903-1991) was born in the UP and had been serving in the Indian Civil Service (ICS) as a judge in Lahore up until partition. When the ICS officers were given the choice to either remain in India or move to Pakistan, Cornelius chose the latter. As a member of

---

12 NV Vol. V, p.267 fn

13 Ibid. p.267-8

14 Ibid. p.267 fn. In 1995 Rashid Salim Adil (a Dalit convert to Islam) released a booklet in Hindi titled *Baba Saheb Doctor Ambedkar Aur Islam* ('Dr Ambedkar and Islam') Delhi: Aman Publications), in which he argued that Ambedkar would have converted to Islam (taking the Untouchables community with him) but did not do so as he faced political pressure from Hindus. This intriguing argument notwithstanding, it is difficult to verify the accuracy of the claim by Mrs Raj that Ambedkar recommended the wholesale conversion of Untouchables to Islam. In 1935-6 Dr Ambedkar did consider whether his people should convert to Islam, Sikhism or Christianity, primarily for the political advantages such conversions would bring. However he took issue with aspects of conventional Islam (though not its fundamental teachings; see for instance Chapter X in Ambedkar 1946a), and seemed somewhat uncomfortable with the idea of bolstering Muslim numbers to the point where 'the danger of Muslim domination' would 'become real' in India. He also felt that a mass conversion to Christianity would 'strengthen the hold of the British' over India. At this time he chose to convert to Sikhism 'in the interest of the country', as converting to Islam or Christianity would 'denationalise' his people. (See his statement reproduced in *Indian Annual Register*, Vol. II (1936), p.277-8). However, in 1956 shortly before his death Ambedkar changed his religion again; he and several hundred thousand Dalits converted to Buddhism.

the judiciary, he famously dissented against the Federal Court's decision to uphold the right of Ghulam Mohammed to have dissolved the first Constituent Assembly in 1954. In 1960 he became the Chief Justice of Pakistan, following Chief Justice Munir's retirement.

A Roman Catholic his whole life, Cornelius not only held Islamic values in high esteem but 'sought to validate the Islamic legal system and blend it with British legal norms', sometimes even expressing his preference for Shariah over 'western legal canons'. [15] Indeed, he even referred to himself a 'Constitutional Muslim'. [16] He also was acutely aware that the dichotomy between the universalistic Muslim concept of unity (for which he used the term *wahdat*) and territorial nationalism with its majority-driven democracy had been the impetus behind the Indian Muslims' demand for partition, [17] and appreciated that 'there are basic imperatives, some of a non-material nature, which guide [Pakistan's] destiny.' [18]

Cornelius had a good grasp of the central principles of Islam and implicitly understood that these were at the heart of the Pakistan idea.

> If you have looked at the basic doctrine of Islam, its truth and strength-in-simplicity, the potencies for growth, spiritual integrity for the individual, outward and visible power through unity for the community, that are built into its rituals of *namaz* [prayer], the fast and the pilgrimage, which are still being extensively practised, the reason for the current of Islamicization [*sic*] in Muslim countries, that have re-sensed their identity and place in the World, will become apparent. [19]

> [In Muslim countries of Africa and Asia] education in the European mode and the adoption of European techniques in political, judicial and administrative activities have created a dichotomy, against the basic Muslim beliefs of the people, held also, under the veneer, by the educated classes, which can only be resolved in one way – return to WAHDAT, the principle of integral unity, based on surrender of the will to Allah, appearing clearly in the agencies and instrumentalities of the state. [20]

> Democracy, with its pretence of subsumation of the individual will to the formation of a General Will, through the starkly divisive process of elections, must fight a stern and losing battle against WAHDAT, that obliges obedience to Allah and his

---

15 Cornelius to Dr Ralph Braibanti, 14 November 1977 (Ralph Braibanti (ed.) 1999, p.194)

16 Op. cit. p.3

17 See Cornelius to Braibanti, 1 March 1978 (Op. cit. p.197)

18 Cornelius to Braibanti, 4 July 1966 (Op. cit. p.188)

19 Cornelius to Braibanti, 14 November 1977 (Op. cit. p.194). Spellings retained from original.

20 Cornelius to Braibanti, 1 March 1978 (Op. cit. p.196-7)

Prophet (PBUH), to the Quran and the Sunnah. In Pakistan, a considerable section among thinking citizens inclines to the view that all policies, administrative, economic, etc. should not only be in line with those master guide lines, but should also be seen to be so. Isms, per se, will not do. [21]

I am a neo-Thomist in attitude, and am slowly beginning to understand what is built into the Constitution of Pakistan, in the way of political obligation, and what I can see distinctly, I try to project, as a matter of constitutional duty. In so doing, I have learnt that a non-Muslim can only be a full citizen of Pakistan if, *on the secular side*, [22] he conforms to the requirements of the Objectives Resolution, read with the first 8 Articles, that is Parts I (the Republic of Pakistan) and II (Fundamental Rights and Principles of Policy). So far as I can see, at present, this is entirely possible, and would be easy, if there were some formulation of the basic principles contained in the Scriptures of Islam, in regard to equality, tolerance, social justice etc. [23]

---

[21] Ibid. p.197. Capitalisation of *wahdat* (a word for unity with an etymological link to *tauheed*) retained from original.

[22] Emphasis in original.

[23] Cornelius to Braibanti, 3 July 1965 (Op. cit. p.184)

Appendix III
Constitutional schemes and the Lahore Resolution

Here we will briefly overview the general features of the main schemes placed in front of the Muslim League in February 1940. The schemes run in order of 'secessionist' (partition) to 'separatist' (provincial autonomy but within an all-India frame).

The main outline of Rahmat Ali's scheme is included in Chapter 7 and so it is not covered here.

Overview of the problem

Muslim distribution across the subcontinent was the main issue with which constitutional thinkers had to grapple. There were 600 million people in the subcontinent (including both British India and the States). Of the 95 million or so Muslims in the subcontinent, more than 80 million were in British India. Three quarters of these (approx. 60 million) were concentrated between the northwest (Punjab, Sind, NWFP, Baluchistan) and northeast (Bengal, Assam). Any territorial demand for a totally separate state would obviously leave the other quarter in Hindustan, plus the 15 million in the States. The difficulty therefore was how to provide a territorial state for the greater proportion and simultaneously defend the rights of Muslims in the Hindu-majority zones. At the same time, the Muslims shared these territories with around 48 million non-Muslims putting the Muslims in a bare majority at 55%. It was for these reasons that even those with secessionist leanings tried to account for all Muslims throughout the subcontinent and prevent them from being subjected to a 'Hindu Raj'.

The Aligarh scheme (secession)

This scheme was authored by a team from Aligarh headed by Prof. Syed Zafar ul-Hasan and Dr M.A.H. Qadri. [1] It envisioned the creation of three wholly independent and sovereign states: 'Pakistan' in north-western India (Punjab, NWPF, Sind and Baluchistan; 'Bengal' in eastern India (Bengal, including Bihar and Sylhet division of Assam); and

[1] M. Afzal Husain Qadri, 'The Problem of Indian Muslims and its Solution', 2 February 1939 (Quaid-i-Azam Papers, File no. 135; as reproduced in M.L. Gwyer & A. Appadorai (eds.) (1957) *Speeches and Documents on the Indian Constitution, 1921-47* London: Oxford University Press, Vol. II, p.462-5

'Hindustan' (the rest of British India). [2] Pakistan and Bengal were to represent 'Muslim India' and Hindustan 'Hindu India'. [3] In addition the scheme called for the creation of two new autonomous provinces within Hindustan: Delhi Province (including Delhi, Meerut and Aligarh) and Malabar Province (Malabar and adjoining areas up to the coast). The two new provinces would contain 28 and 27 percent Muslim populations respectively. [4] Delhi of course was the former capital of a bygone Mughal India; and it along with Aligarh in Malabar was a symbol of Muslim culture. It was assumed that the two Muslim sovereign states in the northwest and east would ensure the safeguard of these Muslim-minority provinces.

The Aligarh professors were opposed to all talk of an all-India centre. [5] Their scheme called for the three respective states to have separate treaty relations with the British Crown, and proposed a 'joint Court of Arbitration' to settle disputes amongst themselves. [6] Muslims left out of the Pakistan and Bengal zones were to be treated as a 'nation in minority' [7] – that is, they would still be considered nationals of Bengal and Pakistan in principle. The same would be true of Hindu minorities inside Pakistan, who would remain nationals of Hindustan. The idea was to assure reciprocal safeguards, for which the unfortunate term 'hostage theory' was deployed by some politicians later on. [8] (Jinnah denounced this line of thought as held by such politicians. [9])

The Confederacy scheme (separation / open to secession)

Next in terms of secessionist leanings was the confederacy scheme [10] written by Major Kifait Ali under his penname 'A Punjabi'. His scheme envisioned a tripartite confederation: 'Indusstan Federation' (the north-west), 'Bengal Federation' (Bengal and contiguous Muslim-majority areas) and 'Hindu India Federation'. [11] In creating these Federations Major Ali proposed the partition of Punjab and Bengal. The Nawab of

---

2 Op. cit. p.463

3 Op. cit. p.462-3

4 Op. cit. p.464

5 See footnote 41.

6 Op. cit. p465

7 Ibid. Similarly, Jinnah later referred to Muslims in Muslim-minority provinces as belonging to 'sub-national groups'. (See address at the Muslim Students' Conference, Jullundur, 14 November 1942; NV Vol. III, p.98)

8 See for example Penderel Moon (1962) *Divide and Quit* Delhi: Oxford University Press, p.20; Choudhry Khaliquzzaman 1961, p.424-7; A.K. Azad 1959, p.144.

9 See press conference, New Delhi, 13 July 1947 (NV Vol. VI, p.281-2). Here Jinnah was asked about his thoughts on statements made by Congress leaders to the effect that if non-Muslim minorities were treated badly in Pakistan, Muslim minorities in India may also suffer. He replied: 'I hope they will get over this madness and follow the line I am suggesting.'

10 'A Punjabi' (1939)*Confederacy of India* Lahore: Nawab Sir Muhammad Shah Nawaz Khan of Mamdot, p.17

11 Op. cit. p.10-12

Mamdot (who published the scheme) also suggested that the Hindu India Federation could be split again into three federations to separate Rajasthan and the Deccan states. Ali envisioned a loose confederal centre with the central authority vested in the Viceroy. The centre would be financially maintained by contributions from the Federations.[12]

Major Ali, who had also written articles for the Majlis-i-Kabir Pakistan of Lahore, emphasised that Indian Muslims should act as 'separationists-cum-confederationists'. [13] He added that he had named the north-west federation 'Indussstan' and not 'Pakistan' because the word 'Pakistan' had acquired 'some unwholesome and alien associations which are far from our mind.' [14] He believed in view of the population distribution problem that a confederation was the preferred solution, but if the Hindus did not agree with it then he was all for being 'simply separationists, demanding secession of our regions from Hindu India without any link between them'. [15]

Cultural Zones scheme (separation)

The 'cultural zones' scheme [16] by Dr Sayyid Abdul Latif was in development from 1938, following the publication of his pamphlets *The Cultural Future of India* (1938) and *The Muslim Problem in India* (1939). [17] It proposed an all-India federation (including the Princely states) in which provinces would be created out of culturally homogeneous areas.[18] The centre would be loose, with the central list of subjects 'limited to the barest minimum', and residuary powers would vest with the federal units. [19] A third of seats would be assigned to whichever community was in the minority at the units and states level; and two-fifths of the seats would be assigned to Muslims at the all-India centre. [20] The units and states would have the right of secession. [21] The scheme also proposed the possibility of population transfer, with 'machinery to organise and regulate such migration'. [22] But he made it clear that a 'Union with a federal form of constitution peculiar to Indian conditions'

---

12 Op. cit. p.13

13 Op. cit. p.17

14 Op. cit. p.18

15 Op. cit. p.17

16 S.A. Latif (1943) *The Pakistan Issue* Lahore: Sh. Muhammad Ashraf, p.50-7 (developed from 1938 onwards. *The Muslim Problem in India* also appears in op. cit. p.2-12)

17 The first pamphlet suggested that though the Muslims and Hindus of India represented two 'cultures', they could 'form a nation of the type of Canada where two different races lived in separate zones of their own while working together for a common country' (Latif 1943, xxiiii, in preface note written by Dr Nazir-ud-din Hasan). The later *Muslim Problem in India* was more detailed.

18 S.A. Latif 1943, p.50-1

19 Op. cit. p.52

20 Op. cit. p.55

21 Op. cit. p.52-3

22 Op. cit. p.57

was in India's 'best interests'.[23] Latif hailed from Hyderabad, a Hindu-majority Princely state with a Muslim ruler, and so he too was naturally motivated by a desire to keep all Muslims within India, in the interests of Muslims in minority provinces.

Zonal scheme (separation – provincialist)

Sikandar Hayat Khan's British-backed[24] 'zonal scheme'[25] was devised on a cultural basis rather than in terms of the Hindu-Muslim divide. It created seven zones with 'regional' legislatures; these legislatures consisted of both British Indian provinces and Princely States merged together on a regional basis rather than as 'two distinct components', as this was considered 'conducive to the solidarity of the country and the stability of the Central Government'.[26] Representation in these regional legislatures would be apportioned according to the provisions of the 1935 Act.[27] The scheme gave Punjab dominating power in the northwest zone, and yet gave bare majority representation to Muslims in the northwest and Bengal zones. Other than a loose centre and advocating a third of seats at the centre to Muslims,[28] the scheme indicated a clear preference for Indian unity. Sikandar Hayat thus wrote: 'a Federation of some kind is not only desirable but indispensable for the ordered and peaceful progress of the country as a whole'.[29] This was hardly surprising, since Sikandar was premier of the Punjab and a provincialist who was also 'Punjabi first'.

Fate of the schemes

The features of all the schemes were taken into consideration when the Lahore Resolution was drafted. As such it seemed to simultaneously give its assent to both Major Ali's Confederacy scheme and the Aligarh scheme. All three documents – the Aligarh scheme, the Confederacy scheme and the Lahore Resolution – were secessionist in tone. The Aligarh and Confederacy schemes also shared a common ideological element. The Aligarh professors wrote: 'The Pakistan Federation will be a Muslim State. ... The realization of this federation will open a new and

---

23 Op. cit. p.50

24 That Sikandar Hayat's scheme was in development with British knowledge and approval as early as 1938 is evident from the correspondence between Viceroy Craik and Linlithgow dated 5 June 1938 and 20 March 1939. It wasn't until July 1939 that Hayat handed copies of his scheme on paper to Gandhi and Jinnah in confidence, and publicised it in the press within the same month. (See M. Arshad 2001, p.370-1)

25 Sikandar Hayat Khan (1939) *Outlines of a Scheme of Indian Federation* Lahore: Mufid-i-Am Press; as reproduced in M.L. Gwyer & A. Appadorai (eds.) 1957, p.455-62

26 M.L. Gwyer & A. Appadorai (eds.) 1957, p.456

27 Op. cit. p.458

28 Op. cit. p.459

29 Op. cit. p.456

living future for the Muslims of India and will have a far-reaching effect on the whole of the Islamic world.'[30] Major Ali meanwhile wrote that the purpose of his scheme was to make 'Islam a living force and a successful social, political and economic system'.[31] This element of the 'Pakistan idea' was, as we have already seen, the backbone of the Two-Nation Theory, and found its ultimate expression in the Delhi Resolution of 1946 (Appendix V).

Like Major Ali's Confederacy, the Lahore Resolution implied a federal relationship between the two Muslim states, and in addition it deferred the secessionist demand, but not indefinitely. Whereas Ali deemed it necessary to remain permanently in India for the sake of Muslims throughout the subcontinent, the Lahore Resolution implied that secession was 'finally' the ultimate object. In this it came closer to being in line with the thought of the Aligarh professors. Both the Lahore Resolution and the Aligarh scheme focused on British India, both created up to two states in the north-west and east, and both consciously did not refer to an all-India centre. But whilst the Lahore Resolution did leave the door open for the possible acquisition of extra zones (via its proposed 'territorial adjustments'), realistically it could not have justifiably included Delhi and Malabar. The two zones were the old and new symbols of Muslim culture respectively, but they were not contiguous to the two major Muslim zones, and at any rate they were technical Muslim minority areas.

The underlying spirit of Ali's Confederacy was that confederation was the better option for the sake of protecting Muslim interests across India, but secession was the final option if all else failed. This sentiment was practically a prophecy; it was fulfilled when the League temporarily agreed to the Cabinet Mission 'Union' of 1946 and subsequently dropped it in favour of immediate partition.

The Lahore Resolution did not support either Sikandar Hayat Khan's zonal scheme or Dr Latif's scheme, both of which sought a permanent united India. The only part of the Lahore Resolution that catered to Hayat's scheme (or rather, his provincialist sentiments) was the line promising that the constituent units of the 'states' would be 'autonomous and sovereign'. Nevertheless, both these latter all-India schemes were eventually to be written off by the League.

Sikandar Hayat Khan's Zonal scheme – Rejected

The League could not as a matter of policy support Sikandar Hayat's scheme, first because it contradicted their resolve to oppose any federal

30 M.L. Gwyer & A. Appadorai (eds.) 1957, p.463

31 'A Punjabi' 1939, p.227 (see also op. cit. p.95-8 for a surprisingly farsighted discussion of the likely implications of establishing what Major Ali describes as an 'Islamic economic system', in an otherwise capitalistic world.)

schemes resembling the Government of India Act 1935, and second because the scheme did not offer the substance of power to Muslims.

Choudhry Khaliquzzaman has recalled how Sikandar's scheme was formally rejected in the Working Committee on 4 February 1940:

> I also pointed out to the members that recently Sir Sikandar Hayat Khan had published a scheme ... [which] provided for a confederal structure. Personally, I said, I would suggest confining our demand to the separation of Muslim zones, viz. N.W.F.P, Sind, Baluchistan and Punjab in the north-west and Bengal and Assam in the east and would leave the rest to the Congress to deal with. At this stage Sir Sikandar who was sitting to the right of Mr Jinnah started pleading for his confederal scheme and Mr Jinnah opposing it. [*sic*] The discussion went on for about two hours when finally, with the concurrence of the members, Mr Jinnah rejected Sir Sikandar's scheme ... I do not know how many people realise when it was that for the first time the Muslim League Working Committee decided to claim the division of India. [32]

Sikandar Hayat himself also testified that the final Lahore Resolution was not in line with his original scheme. In 1941, he told the Punjab Legislative Assembly that he had authored the original draft of the Lahore Resolution but that the final version had been 'radically amended by the [League's] Working Committee'. [33] His version, he said, had accounted for a centre and co-ordination of the activities of the various units, but that this part of his scheme had been 'eliminated'. [34] He washed his hands of any responsibility for the Lahore Resolution, declaring that it was not of his making, but the League's. [35] He was eager to assure his non-Muslim colleagues that the Punjab did not endorse a 'Muslim Raj'. If that was what Pakistan meant, then he wanted 'nothing to do with it'. Besides, he did not support the 'Pakistan bogey', a 'catchphrase' that had been introduced not by the League but by 'our Hindu friends'. He did not seek an 'extra-territorial' Pakistan; his focus was 'just Punjab', and it would remain as 'Punjab whatever anybody may say'.[36] Of course he was enticed by the line in the Lahore Resolution promising 'autonomous and sovereign' units. Yet he made no comment whatsoever on the final paragraph of the Lahore Resolution.

---

32 C. Khaliquzzaman 1961, p.233-4

33 Sikandar Hayat Khan's speech, extracted from a Report of the Punjab Legislative Assembly Debates, 11 March 1941, as reproduced in V.P. Menon 1957, p.444

34 Ibid.

35 Sikandar Hayat: '[It is] a travesty of fact to describe the League resolution as it was finally passed as my resolution.' (Ibid.)

36 Ibid. p.444-5

His political conduct [37] shows that his views remained unchanged up until his death in December 1942.

S. A. Latif's Cultural Zones Scheme – Rejected

In 1940-2, Dr Latif tried to get his scheme formally sanctioned by the League, via a series of meetings with Abdullah Haroon's 'Constitution Committee' (actually just the League's Foreign Committee). [38] When Latif telegrammed Jinnah in October 1940 for permission to meet with Congress leaders in order to discuss his scheme with them, Jinnah telegrammed a refusal, adding: 'any Congress Hindu leader welcomed see me' [instead]. [39] Two days later he also warned Latif that his scheme was 'fundamentally different from the basic principle laid down in the Lahore Resolution'. [40] Yet in March 1941, Latif sent a copy of a letter to Jinnah in respect of a Report (based on his scheme) that had been drafted by Haroon's 'Constitution Sub-Committee'. [41] This had been done without Jinnah's knowledge. Jinnah curtly replied that the scheme

---

[37] The 'Sikandar-Jinnah Pact' was made between Jinnah and Sikandar Hayat Khan in October 1937 following the Lucknow Session. Hayat, as leader of the Unionist party that had won most of the Muslim seats in the 1936-7 provincial elections, would encourage his party members to join the Muslim League, while the Unionist party would continue its ministry without interference, and retain its own name. But in 1938 after Hayat had taken control of the Punjab Muslim League, he reorganised it to replace its original members with Unionist members. Iqbal had warned Jinnah beforehand that Hayat was attempting to 'kill' the League so he could retain provincial power for himself. (Iqbal to Jinnah, 10 November 1937; *Letters of Iqbal*, p.31). Jinnah apparently decided too much was at stake at the all-India level to risk alienating Hayat at this stage; and so the reorganised Punjab Muslim League was allowed to persist despite complaints from other loyal Muslim Leaguers. Later in 1941, when Jinnah instructed the League not to join the National Defence Council, Hayat disobeyed the order, but soon had to resign due to public pressure organised by the Punjab Muslim Students' Federation (S. Mujahid 1981, p.443-4 fn). In 1942, shortly before his death, he quit the League's Working Committee.

[38] Haroon was a keen supporter of Latif's scheme. He had circulated Dr Latif's original pamphlet in 1938. He also wrote the preface for Latif's book *The Muslim Problem in India* (1939) in which he described Latif's ideas as being 'the first stage in the fulfilment of the object in view'. (S.A. Latif 1943, xxv)

[39] S. A. Latif 1943, p.59

[40] Jinnah to Latif, 12 October 1940 (op. cit. p.62). Latif believed that the Lahore Resolution 'amounts to no more than a strong desire for the utmost freedom from an external Centre in the North-West and the North-East of India where the Muslims are in the majority'. (p.106)

[41] Op. cit. p.93-100. Dr Qadri meanwhile wrote to Abdullah Haroon a frank criticism of the Report: 'I strongly feel that nothing like "central machinery" or "centre" should creep into our demands either in *letter* or *spirit*. It savours of All-India Federation or Hindu Raj. It should be meant as well as named as a *pact* of sovereign Muslim states with the rest of India.' (Emphasis in original) He added: 'the transitional stage implicit in the Lahore Resolution does not in the least mean any Muslim status short of complete independence and full sovereignty at any stage either transitional, *vis a vis* the British Government or the Hindu India.' (Qadri to Haroon, 23 February 1941; S.A. Latif 1943, p.95) Dr Latif in turn attacked the Aligarh scheme's inclusion of Delhi and Malabar, accusing the Punjab and Aligarh members in the Foreign Committee of having 'imperialistic designs over essentially non-Muslim areas'. (Latif to Haroon, 8 March 1941; op. cit. p.98)

was certainly not officially connected with the League (nor was *any* scheme for that matter), and reprimanded both Latif and Haroon for repeatedly referring to the non-sanctioned sub-committee. [42] Dr Latif was not dissuaded; he sent a circular to 'select leaders' of the Congress and the League outlining his scheme in May 1941. No one on the League's side sent him a reply, [43] and so the Report was consequently put aside by default. Dr Latif, who had always felt that 'complete separation' was 'unthinkable', [44] and who evidently over-estimated his own importance, found himself frustrated by what he publicly called Jinnah's 'obstructionist tactics'. [45] Jinnah was not impressed when he learned that Dr Latif had also taken it upon himself to carry on discussions with the Congress leaders without the League's formal sanction. Following the publication of some correspondence between Dr Latif, the Congress President (A.K. Azad) and Nehru in 1942, [46] Jinnah remarked that it was a 'pre-arranged correspondence' and clearly a publicity stunt rather than 'a real earnest for a settlement'. This was a fair claim, as the Congress had not approached the League to discuss the matters contained in the correspondence, but instead had merely printed it in the press.

Jinnah made his feelings on the matter abundantly clear. The majority of Muslims could 'no longer be treated as children', and he had no time for those whose activities contradicted the aims of the League. Hence he expressed 'pity' for Congress President Azad because he represented 'neither the Hindus nor the Musalmans', and had 'no voice in the counsels of the Congress'. He also referred bluntly to Dr Latif (without taking his name) as 'a busy-body of a Muslim'. [47]

---

[42] Jinnah to Latif, 15 March 1941 (op. cit. p.100).

[43] On the Congress side, only Rajendra Prasad answered Latif's letters in detail, and even then the subsequent correspondence went nowhere. (See op. cit. p.101, 104-113)

[44] Op. cit. xxxiii

[45] Latif's interview with the Associated Press of India, Hyderabad, 3 August 1942 (op. cit. p.137)

[46] This correspondence is reproduced in Latif 1943, p.114-120. In this correspondence, Dr Latif attempted to gauge the Congress' official stance on granting units the right to secession of units in a future federal India. The Congress had passed two resolutions that year, one that had granted this right and the second which subsequently appeared to negate the first. Nehru's letter to Latif ambiguously stated that whilst the first resolution still stood, secession of any unit 'would not be welcomed by us, and it would *inevitably depend* on certain geographical and other factors'. (Letter dated 6 August 1942; op. cit. p.119; emphasis mine)

[47] Jinnah's press statement, 7 August 1942 (NV Vol. III, p.34)

Appendix IV
The Lahore Resolution (text)

While approving and endorsing the action taken by the Council and the Working Committee of the All-India Muslim League, as indicated in their resolutions dated the 27th of August, 17th and 18th of September and 22nd of October 1939 and 3rd of February 1940 on the constitutional issue, this Session of the All-India Muslim League emphatically reiterates that the scheme of federation embodied in the Government of India Act, 1935, is totally unsuited to, and unworkable in the peculiar conditions of this country and is altogether unacceptable to Muslim India.

It further records its emphatic view that while the declaration dated the 18th of October 1939 made by the Viceroy on behalf of His Majesty's Government is reassuring in so far as it declares that the policy and plan on which the Government of India Act, 1935, is based will be reconsidered in consultation with the various parties, interests and communities in India, Muslims in India will not be satisfied unless the whole constitutional plan is reconsidered *de novo* and that no revised plan would be acceptable to Muslims unless it is framed with their approval and consent.

Resolved that it is the considered view of this Session of the All-India Muslim League that no constitutional plan would be workable in this country or acceptable to the Muslims unless it is designed on the following basic principles, *viz.*, that geographically contiguous units are demarcated into regions which should be so constituted, with such territorial readjustments as may be necessary that the areas in which the Muslims are numerically in a majority as in the North-Western and Eastern zones of India should be grouped to constitute 'Independent States' in which the constituent units shall be autonomous and sovereign.

That adequate, effective and mandatory safeguards should be specifically provided in the constitution for minorities in these units and in the regions for the protection of their religious, cultural, economic, political, administrative and other rights and interests in consultation with them and in other parts of India where the Musalmans are in a minority adequate, effective and mandatory safeguards shall be specifically provided in the constitution for them and other minorities for the protection of their religious, cultural, economic, political, administrative and other rights and interests in consultation with them.

This Session further authorises the Working Committee to frame a scheme of constitution in accordance with these basic principles, providing for the assumption finally by the respective regions of all powers such as defence, external affairs, communications, customs and such other matters as may be necessary. [1]

[1] Lahore Resolution, 23 March 1940 (NV Vol. I, p.587)

Appendix V
The Delhi Resolution (text)

Whereas in this vast subcontinent of India a hundred millions are the adherents of a faith which regulates every department of their life (educational, social, economic and political), whose code is not confined merely to spiritual doctrines and tenets or rituals and ceremonies and which stand in sharp contrast to the exclusive nature of Hindu Dharma and philosophy and which has fostered and maintained for thousands of years a rigid caste system resulting in the degradation of 60 million human beings to the position of untouchables, creation of unnatural barriers between man and man and superimposition of social and economic inequalities on a large body of the people of this country, and which threatens to reduce Muslims, Christians and other minorities to the status of irredeemable helots, socially, and economically;

Whereas the Hindu caste system is a direct negation of nationalism, equality, democracy and all noble ideals that Islam stands for;

Whereas the different historical backgrounds, traditions, cultures and social and economic order of the Hindus and Muslims have made impossible the evolution of a single Indian nation inspired by common aspirations and ideals and whereas after centuries they still remain two distinct major nations;

Whereas soon after the introduction by the British of the policy of setting up political institutions in India on the lines of western democracies based on majority rule which meant that the majority of one nation or society could impose its will on the majority of the other nation or society in spite of their opposition as was amply demonstrated during the two and a half years regime of Congress government in the Hindu majority provinces under the Government of India Act 1935 when the Muslims were subjected to untold harassment and oppression as a result of which they were convinced of the futility and ineffectiveness of the so-called safeguards provided in the constitution and in the Instrument of Instructions to the Governors and were driven to the irresistible conclusion that in a united Indian federation, if established, the Muslims even in majority provinces would meet with no better fate and their rights and interests could never be adequately protected against the perpetual Hindu majority at the centre;

Whereas the Muslims are convinced that with a view to save Muslim India from the domination of the Hindus and in order to afford them full scope to develop themselves according to their genius, it is necessary to constitute a sovereign independent state comprising Bengal and Assam in the north-east zone and the Punjab, North-West Frontier Province, Sind and Baluchistan in the north-west zone;

This Convention of the Muslim League Legislatures of India, central and provincial, after careful consideration, hereby declares that the Muslim nation will never submit to any constitution for a united India and will never participate in any single constitution-making machinery set up for the purpose, and that any formula devised by the British government for transferring power from the British to the peoples of India which does not conform to the following just and equitable principles calculated to maintain internal peace and tranquillity in the country will not contribute to the solution of the Indian problem:

That the zones comprising Bengal and Assam in the north-east and the Punjab, North-West Frontier Province, Sind and Baluchistan in the north-west of India, namely Pakistan zones, where the Muslims are in a dominant majority, be constituted into a sovereign independent state and that an unequivocal undertaking be given to implement the establishment of Pakistan without delay;

that two separate constitution-making bodies be set up by the people of Pakistan and Hindustan for the purpose of framing their respective constitutions;

that the minorities in Pakistan and Hindustan be provided with safeguards on the lines of the All-India Muslim League Resolution passed on 23 March 1940 at Lahore;

that the acceptance of the Muslim League demand of Pakistan and its implementation without delay are the sine qua non for the Muslim League cooperation and participation in the formation of an interim government at the centre.

This Convention further emphatically declares that any attempt to impose a constitution an a united India basis or to force any interim arrangement at the centre contrary to the Muslim League demand will leave the Muslims no alternative but to resist such imposition by all possible means for their survival and national existence.[1]

---

1 Resolution moved at the AIML Legislators' Convention, Delhi, 9 April 1946 (NV Vol. IV, p.653-7)

Appendix VI
The Objectives Resolution (text)

In the name of *Allah*, the Beneficent, the Merciful;

WHEREAS sovereignty over the entire universe belongs to God Almighty alone and the authority which He has delegated to the State of Pakistan through its people for being exercised within the limits prescribed by Him is a sacred trust;

This Constituent Assembly representing the people of Pakistan resolves to frame a constitution for the sovereign independent State of Pakistan;

WHEREIN the State shall exercise its powers and authority through the chosen representatives of the people;

WHEREIN the principles of democracy, freedom, equality, tolerance and social justice, as enunciated by Islam, shall be fully observed;

WHEREIN the Muslims shall be enabled to order their lives in the individual and collective spheres in accord with the teachings and requirements of Islam as set out in the Holy Quran and the *Sunna*;

WHEREIN adequate provision shall be made for the minorities freely to profess and practise their religions and develop their cultures;

WHEREBY the territories now included in or in accession with Pakistan and such other territories as may hereafter be included in or accede to Pakistan shall form a Federation wherein the units will be autonomous with such boundaries and limitations on their powers and authority as may be prescribed;

WHEREIN shall be guaranteed fundamental rights including equality of status, of opportunity and before law, social, economic and political justice, and freedom of thought, expression, belief, faith, worship and association, subject to law and public morality;

WHEREIN adequate provision shall be made to safeguard the legitimate interests of minorities and backward and depressed classes;

WHEREIN the independence of the Judiciary shall be fully secured;

WHEREIN the integrity of the territories of the Federation, its independence and all its rights including its sovereign rights on land, sea and air shall be safeguarded;

So that the people of Pakistan may prosper and attain their rightful and honoured place amongst the nations of the World and make their full contribution towards international peace and progress and happiness of humanity. [1]

[1] Objectives Resolution (original wording) as presented by Liaquat Ali Khan in the Constituent Assembly on 7 March 1949 and passed on 12 March 1949 (CAP Debates Vol. V No. 5, p.100-1)

Appendix VII
Bhandara's bill

Minocher Pestonjee Bhandara (1938-2008), affectionately known as 'Minoo', was a long-serving member of Pakistan's PML-Q [1] party. Other than being a businessman, owning Pakistan's biggest brewery, he also served in the National Assembly in the 1980s and again from 2002 onwards until his death in 2008.

Mr Bhandara will be best remembered for his attempts to challenge the 'ideology of Pakistan', an ideology which, as far as he was concerned, has always remained 'undefined'. His ultimate aim was to secularise the country. He tried to effect this change via constitutional amendments.

In October 2004, he successfully moved a resolution to have Jinnah's 11 August 1947 speech included in the country's curricula at all levels. [2] He worked on the assumption that Jinnah was also a secularist and that his 11 August 1947 speech represents a departure from the Two-Nation Theory and so-called 'Islamic ideology'. This was seen as a victory by those educationists of Pakistan who have long alleged that the 11 August speech has been deliberately censored over the years. [3]

In September 2006, he tried to have articles 62 and 63 of the constitution containing the words 'ideology of Pakistan' deleted, on the grounds that 'the ideology of Pakistan is not a concept which is known to our law'. [4] Though the resolution was rejected in the Pakistan

---

[1] PML-Q – Pakistan Muslim League (Quaid)

[2] See resolution regarding Jinnah's speech of 11 August 1947, passed 19 October 2004 (*The National Assembly of Pakistan Debates Official Report* Vol. XXII (2004) Karachi: Manager of Publications, p.624-5).

[3] The claims about the censorship attempts immediately after 11 August 1947 are entirely anecdotal (see for instance the detailed accounts given Zamir Niazi (2010 revised) *The Press in Chains* Karachi: Oxford University Press, p.58-62) and so are impossible to verify. In any case the speech was reported by most press agencies and newspapers the next day, including *Dawn* (NV Vol. VI, p.355 fn). Nor have I been able to establish when these rumours first appear on record (the earliest date Niazi provides is 1976, citing a lecture incidentally given by Chief Justice Munir (op. cit. p.61)). Leaving aside later attempts to black out the speech in the press or in the education syllabus, we note that the censorship issue never came up at all during the Constituent Assembly debates of 1949 over the Objectives Resolution. It was not even mentioned during the no-holds-barred debates of August 1954, in which opposition ministers produced every piece of evidence they could find in favour of a secular Jinnah in order to discredit the government's 'Islamic' aims.

[4] See M.P. Bhandara's speech, 12 September 2006; *The National Assembly of Pakistan Debates Official Report* Vol. XXXVII (2006) Islamabad: National Book Foundation, p.3002

National Assembly, Ardeshir Cowasjee later quite rightly pointed out that 'the honourable representatives of the people of Pakistan were not in unanimity as to what exactly is the ideology [of Pakistan]', and thus Bhandara had succeeded in making a point. [5]

Mr Bhandara's most significant constitutional contribution came in 2007. Before we continue however we must provide a little background.

Objectives Resolution in the constitution

The Objectives Resolution of 1949 was made the preamble of the 1956 constitution, in edited form. [6] Secularist critics however felt that the 'sovereignty in Allah' clause contradicted the 'sovereignty of the people' in the Munir quote. In 1985, by Presidential Order No. 14, the Objectives Resolution was made a substantive part of the constitution and became Article 2A. This again raised controversy, and more so due to a typographical error in the Article. In the original Objectives Resolution, the clause in question reads: 'Wherein adequate provision shall be made for the minorities freely to profess and practise their religions and develop their cultures'. But the word 'freely' was omitted when rendered in Article 2A. Whether or not this was intentional remains unknown, though the error was formally rectified on 19 April 2010, when the 18th Amendment Bill was passed into law.

The 11 August Bill

On 13 February 2007, Mr Bhandara successfully moved the introduction of a private members' bill in the National Assembly – called the Constitution (Amendment) Bill, 2006. [7] Through the bill Bhandara sought to insert a new clause into the constitution – Article 2B, which in short would make Jinnah's 11 August 1947 speech a substantive part of the constitution alongside the Objectives Resolution.

The bill was not made law that day; it had not even passed the first stage. It had merely been introduced and was referred to a Standing Committee for review before it would be sent back to the National Assembly for a vote. In Pakistani legislative procedure, a bill to amend the constitution must be passed both in the National Assembly and the

---

[5] See A. Cowasjee's obituary to Bhandara, 'A Master Brewer' in *Dawn*, 22 June 2008

[6] In short, the line referring to 'the authority which He has delegated to the State of Pakistan through its people' was deleted so the first paragraph read: 'Whereas sovereignty over the entire universe belongs to Allah Almighty alone, and the authority to be exercised by the people of Pakistan within the limits prescribed by Him is a sacred trust'. A paragraph stating that Jinnah had 'declared that Pakistan would be a democratic State based on Islamic principles of social justice' was also added.

[7] See motion to introduce the Constitution (Amendment) Bill, 2006, passed 13 February 2007 (*The National Assembly of Pakistan Debates Official Report* Vol. XXXIX (2007) Islamabad: National Book Foundation, p.549-551)

Senate in turn; in both these Houses it must receive a total of no less than two-thirds of votes in its favour. Once passed in both Houses it must receive the President's assent to become law. [8]

The same day that the bill was introduced, the *Dawn* quoted Mr Bhandara as having said that the aim was for the bill to act as an 'ideological balance' to the Objectives Resolution enshrined in Article 2A. [9] A couple of days later, he told the press that he wanted the bill to be a part of the Constitution because 'it presents the secular thoughts of Muhammad Ali Jinnah and his dream to see Pakistan not as a *religious* state, but a *modern* one' (emphasis mine). He also said he would work on his bill and seek support for it. [10]

Correspondence with Mr Bhandara

On 21 April 2007 Mr Bhandara issued a notice in *Dawn* asking the public to show support for his bill via an online petition. [11] I learned about the petition from Ardeshir Cowasjee's column in *Dawn*, [12] and upon visiting Mr Bhandara's website, I found a contradiction with regards to the aims of the bill and the 11 August speech, and felt compelled to write to him about it. This initial email led to correspondence and also unexpectedly to my becoming personally involved with the draft bill. Mr Bhandara asked me to write a new draft to be placed before the Standing Committee for consideration. Eventually he also told me that he wanted to render the 11 August speech as Article 2A, in place of the Objectives Resolution, which in turn would become Article 2B. I am reproducing the correspondence in full here, beginning with my first email to Mr Bhandara. For the most part it is self-explanatory. Both Mr Bhandara's draft and mine are also included within the body of the correspondence.

Subject: August 11 1947 Speech
Delivery-Date: Friday, April 27, 2007

Dear Mr Bhandara

Having read Mr Ardeshir Cowasjee's column in this week's Dawn, I visited your website, only to find myself a little confused. On one hand, I absolutely agree that the Quaid-i-Azam's vision for Pakistan was meant

---

8 *National Assembly of Pakistan Procedural Manual* (online at the Pakistan Government website). http://www.na.gov.pk/publications/proceduralmanual.pdf (Last accessed 18 July 2007)

9 *Dawn* report, 14 February 2007.

10 See *AKI* (Italy) and *Deccan Chronicle* [online] reports, both 16 February 2007.

11 http://quaidsvision11august1947.info (Last accessed 29 April 2007; the site was online for only a short time). See also Bhandara, 'Quaid's Concept of Pakistan' in *Dawn*, 25 March 2007.

12 See A. Cowasjee 'I will not Remove the Uniform' in *Dawn*, 22 April 2007

to be, to quote from your homepage, a 'state imbued by the lofty ideals of Islam'. But on the other, your suggestion on a different page that his speech of 11th August 1947 advocates a 'rejection of religion in the business of the State' is quite misleading. For one thing, it contradicts the former statement regarding the Quaid's vision. This contradiction would require correction before anyone could safely sign your petition. What the speech of 11th August actually said was that an individual's faith should not be a factor when it comes to the business of the state, not that 'religion' (or rather, religious idealism) itself has no business in the state. Universal ideals – namely, equality before the law, fraternity and religious freedom, must necessarily be a part of the constitution; and whilst these ideals are generally termed 'humanistic', they are actually inspired from universal religious (and thus Islamic) ideals. This is why the Quaid-i-Azam stated that democracy was introduced by Islam 'over 1,300 years ago'. Yes, it is true that a church state produced by organised religion – or theocracy – was not on the Quaid-i-Azam's agenda, but only because theocracy is antithetical to bona fide Islam. (This is not modernist or reformist interpretation, but a fact. Only a few mullahs representing organised religion, who are actually motivated by their own self-serving interests, would ever suggest otherwise.). Iqbal said it best when he said that religion in its higher manifestations is neither dogma, nor priesthood, nor ritual. The text on your homepage referring to the 'lofty ideals of Islam' therefore could not be more accurate. But if your proposed amendment was introduced as it was, then there would always be a danger that someone might take it literally and thus wish to impose a nationalism that opposes all religion, including its 'lofty idealism'. This is why no Pakistani who truly believes in religious freedom ought to sign it.

Yours Sincerely,

Saleena Karim (United Kingdom)

Subject: (No subject)
Delivery-Date: Saturday, April 28, 2007

Dear Ms Saleena Karim

Thank you for your thoughtful email of April 27th.

In a constitutional interpretation of the 'lofty ideals of Islam', we can take inspiration from Allama Iqbal's declaration which you have very aptly quoted that religion in its higher manifestation is neither dogma nor priesthood, nor ritual. This formulation, I consider, is very close to

Quaid's vision, which is totally opposite to politics based on a literal interpretation of religion.

I shall be guided by your thoughtful remarks when the matter comes up in the Standing Committee which will examine my Bill.

I leave it to you to decide whether you wish to support the Bill.

Regards, M P Bhandara

Subject: Re: 11 August 1947 Speech
Delivery-Date: Saturday, April 28, 2007

Dear Mr Bhandara

Many thanks for your reply dated 28th April. I am heartened to know that you are taking my remarks into account. If your proposed Bill is truly faithful to those ideals that the Quaid-i-Azam advocated, and reflects the true context of his 11th August 1947 speech (meaning civil equality regardless of faith), and if this is made clear in your petition, then there is no reason why every sensible Pakistani should not support it.

Yours Sincerely

Saleena Karim

Subject: (No subject)
Delivery-Date: Monday, April 30, 2007

Dear Ms Saleena Karim

In reference to your last mail, I invite you to make a draft amendment which will incorporate the essence of Quaid's 11th August 1947 speech tempered by the 'lofty ideals of Islam' as interpreted by Allama Iqbal.

The Bill intends to insert in Article 2 of the Constitution the quintessence of our Quaid's declaration.

Regards, M P Bhandara

Subject: Re:
Delivery-Date: Monday, April 30, 2007

Dear Mr Bhandara

Thank you kindly for your invitation. I will consider it and get back to you as soon as possible.

Yours Sincerely

Saleena Karim

Subject: Re:
Delivery-Date: Tuesday, May 1, 2007

Dear Mr Bhandara

Further to our recent email correspondence, please find enclosed a copy of a draft amendment to be inserted as Article 2B. It incorporates the full essence of the Quaid-i-Azam's 11 August speech and it offers both a balance and a support to the Objectives Resolution which was incorporated as Article 2A of the constitution recently. Of course the speech need not be tempered by Islamic ideals, since the speech is in itself absolutely faithful to these ideals and not in conflict with them. I have tried to make this clear in the amendment.

I have just for the sake of information added a couple of notes at the end of the attached file which should explain it further. I hope this will be acceptable to the National Assembly.

Yours Sincerely

Saleena Karim

Text of the drafts

M.P. Bhandara's original draft for an Article 2B

[TO BE INTRODUCED IN THE NATIONAL ASSEMBLY]

A BILL further to amend the Constitution of the Islamic Republic of Pakistan.

WHEREAS it is expedient further to amend the Constitution of the Islamic Republic of Pakistan for the purpose hereinafter appearing.

It is hereby enacted as follows: -

1. **Short title and commencement:-**

(1) This Act may be called the Constitution (Amendment) Act, 2006.
(2) It shall come into force at once.

2. **Insertion of new Article 2B in the Constitution:-** In the Constitution of the Islamic Republic of Pakistan, after Article 2A the following new Article shall be inserted, namely: -

"**2B: Quaid-e-Azam's speech of August 11, 1947 to form part of substantive provisions:-** The speech of the Quaid-e-Azam Mohammad Ali Jinnah of 11th August, 1947 delivered in the first meeting of the Constituent Assembly of Pakistan reproduced in the Annexure is hereby made substantive part of the Constitution and shall have effect accordingly."

STATEMENT OF OBJECTS AND REASONS

It is generally recognized that the creation of the State of Pakistan, against all odds, imposed by the British, Hindu dominated political parties of British India, and fundamentalist Islamic groups, was the singular achievement of the Quaid-i-Azam Mohammad Ali Jinnah (Rehmat Ullah alaihai). Therefore the directions he gave in his speech on the day this country came into existence in the First Session of the Constituent Assembly of Pakistan be given the status of a 'grund-norm' and be deemed to be part of the Constitution.

Sd/-
M.P. Bhandara
Member, National Assembly

S. Karim's draft for an Article 2B

[TO BE INTRODUCED IN THE NATIONAL ASSEMBLY]

A BILL further to amend the Constitution of the Islamic Republic of Pakistan

WHEREAS it is expedient further to amend the Constitution of the Islamic Republic of Pakistan for the purpose hereinafter appearing:

AND WHEREAS the Objectives Resolution states that the principles of democracy, freedom, equality, tolerance and social justice as enunciated by Islam shall be fully observed;

WHEREIN adequate provision shall be made for the minorities to freely profess and practise their religions and develop their cultures;

It is hereby enacted as follows:-

1. **Short title and commencement:-**

(1) This Act may be called the Constitution (Amendment) Act, 2007.

(2) It shall come into force at once.

2. **Insertion of Article 2B in the Constitution:-** In the Constitution of the Islamic Republic of Pakistan, after Article 2A the following Article shall be inserted, namely:-

"2B: 1) **Quaid-i-Azam's speech of 11 August 1947 to form part of substantive provisions:-** The principles in Quaid-i-Azam Mohammad Ali Jinnah's speech of 11 August 1947 delivered in the first meeting of the Constituent Assembly of Pakistan (reproduced in the Annexure) are hereby made a substantive part of the Constitution and shall have effect accordingly.

"2) In application the Quaid-i-Azam's speech of 11 August 1947 shall act as a reiteration in more explicit terms of the lofty ideals of Islam outlined in the Objectives Resolution."

STATEMENT OF OBJECTS AND REASONS

Quaid-i-Azam Mohammad Ali Jinnah is on record as having said that he sought to create Pakistan in order to implement the universal ideals of equality, justice and fair play, which he frequently reminded Muslims are Islamic ideals. In upholding these ideals he was also opposed to theocracy, a conviction similar to that of the Islamic philosopher Allama Muhammad Iqbal, known as the 'spiritual founder' of Pakistan, who understood that a state ruled by clerics is antithetical to Quranic ideals. Quaid-i-Azam's speech of 11 August 1947 explicitly calls for the implementation of these ideals, which include the protection of life, property and religious beliefs of all citizens, civic unity and equal rights, privileges and obligations of all citizens regardless of colour, caste or creed, as well as the elimination of bribery and corruption, black marketeering, jobbery and nepotism. Since the Objectives Resolution is a statement outlining the lofty ideals of Islam in a constitutional context, undoubtedly it corroborates the aforementioned speech.

Accompanying note sent to Mr Bhandara [13]

This draft has similarities to your original, except for the headers referring to the Objectives Resolution and the insertion of part (2B: 2). The reason I included a second part is quite self-explanatory, but essentially the point being made is that the speech of 11 August does not conflict with the Objectives Resolution in any way (and of course nor should it, to avoid a discrepancy in the constitution). If people believe that the Quaid-i-Azam upheld Islamic principles and that he was an honest individual who didn't contradict himself, then why should they object to the inclusion of the speech of 11 August 1947, or any other, in the constitution?

I have revisited the Objectives Resolution debates and it seems that even at that time, despite Liaquat Ali Khan's reassurances that the Objectives Resolution was not a prelude to theocracy, some people felt there was still a danger, to quote Mr B.C. Mandal, that 'the posterity may misinterpret it'. This in itself justifies an amendment designed to add further elucidation of the Objectives Resolution.

Subject: (No subject)
Delivery-Date: Wednesday, May 2, 2007

Dear Ms Saleena Karim

Thank you for the prompt response.

I think your draft is brilliant and it will certainly be one of the best drafts placed for standing committee consideration.

I would like the Quaid-i-Azam's speech insertion to be Article 2A and the existing Article 2A to be numbered as Article 2B as this is the chronological order.

---

13 This explanatory note was sent to Mr Bhandara along with the draft document.

It appears that you are a good lawyer; tell me more about yourself. I will request you to garner support for my Bill from Pakistanis resident in UK on my website: www.quaidsvision11august1947.info Particulars of the Bill can be sent on the website.

Regards, M P Bhandara

Subject: Re:
Delivery-Date: Thursday, May 3, 2007

Dear Mr Bhandara

(My apologies for the delay.) Thank you kindly for your message and your feedback. Last night I sent a copy of the draft to a friend to look at. If he finds it acceptable it he will be able to rally much more mass support than I would personally. I was awaiting his response before I came back to you but as he hasn't yet [*sic*] I am writing again in the meantime to confirm receipt of your most recent message.

I must admit that whilst I personally I see no problem with the two amendments (2A and 2B) appearing in either order, I believe that swapping them around would probably be viewed with suspicion by some people and thus significantly reduce the chances of the new amendment being adopted. The main objection would be that whilst the speech of 11 August 1947 is chronologically older, the Objectives Resolution remains the oldest contribution to the constitution. If however the amendments are left in the same order, the new one will still have the desired effect, in that it will be an explicit reiteration of universal ideals as they appear in the Objectives Resolution, a kind of safety valve to prevent misuse of said Resolution. But of course this is only my opinion.

You have asked me about what I do. I am actually a researcher/writer with an interest in the way Quaid-i-Azam's speeches have been interpreted by various researchers. My book 'Secular Jinnah' has been positively received in academic circles as well as general readers. Its website can be found at:

http://www.cyberblurb.co.uk

If you have any further questions about my work please do not hesitate to ask.

With regards to the petition for support I can also help advertise it via my website and even collect petition signatures online if that would help.

Yours Sincerely

Saleena Karim

Subject: (No subject)
Delivery-Date: Saturday, May 5, 2007

Dear Ms Saleena Karim

Thank you for your effort in rallying support for my website. I am persuaded by your argument on the numbering sequence.

Is your book 'Secular Jinnah' available in Pakistan? If not, can you send me a copy provided you permit me to reimburse you for all costs including postage.

Are you by any chance related to the late Mr Masud Karim of Karachi?

With kind regards,

M P Bhandara

Subject: Re: 5th May 07
Delivery-Date: Sunday, May 6, 2007

Dear Mr Bhandara

Thank you kindly for your email dated 5th May. I have spoken to one or two other people and they are quite happy with the alternative draft as is; they have said they will be willing to support the petition for it once both your and my websites make a copy of it available to view on the Internet. So that there is no chance of misunderstanding by anyone, on my website I will make it clear that this amendment is in the best interests of Pakistan based on a matter of principle, because as a nonpartisan writer I have no affiliation with any political party or group. Whether or not you intend to use my name on the draft we must both agree that if any part of the draft is edited later without my knowledge or consent (including the 'statement of object and intent') I will not take any personal responsibility for the changes. Once you confirm this is acceptable, I will begin rallying support for the amendment. The easiest way to make everything clear to all interested persons is for both our websites to link to one another and for both to state that aside from agreeing on the proposed amendment (2007) itself the authors of each respective website (namely, you and I) are not responsible for or endorse the views and content produced by the authors of the other. I believe this would be a fair arrangement for both of us.

I will also post this email and your confirmation on my website.

I hope you will find this acceptable.

Yours Sincerely

Saleena Karim

Subject: Re: further to last email
Delivery-Date: Sunday, May 6, 2007

Dear Mr Bhandara

Further to your last email, I do not happen to be related to the late Mr Masud Karim. As regards 'Secular Jinnah', it is not readily available in Pakistan. Around fifty copies were sent for distribution by a non-profit organisation last year and as far as I know they are no longer available. However I insist on sending you a copy from here with my compliments. Please provide me with a postal address and I will arrange for a copy to be sent to you.

Yours Sincerely

Saleena Karim

Subject: (No subject)
Delivery-Date: Monday, May 7, 2007

Dear Ms Saleena Karim

Thank you for your note of 5th May.

It is not advisable at the moment to put the several drafts (including yours) that we have received on the website (I have received six so far). I don't wish a controversy to develop; this will weaken our case.

In the event that your draft is chosen with or without amendment we shall certainly keep you posted.

In view of the current situation the standing committee is not overly inclined to examine the Bill at an early date.

Thank you once again for all your efforts.

It is very kind of you to send me a complimentary copy of your 'Secular Jinnah'.

My postal address is as under: -

No.1, National Park Road

Murree Brewery Estate, Rawalpindi, Pakistan

Tel. +92-51-9273428

Why don't you get a publisher in Pakistan?

With kind regards,

M P Bhandara

Subject: Re:
Delivery-Date: Monday, May 7, 2007

Dear Mr Bhandara

Thank you kindly for your email of this morning. Yes, of course I understand the situation at your end – thank you in advance for keeping me posted. I wish you well whatever you decide.

Thank you also for your address. I will be sending out a copy of the book and will let you know once it has been posted. As for getting it printed in Pakistan, a number of people have made a similar suggestion over the past couple of years. I will give it some thought.

Yours Sincerely

Saleena Karim

[After this email I sent Mr Bhandara a copy of *Secular Jinnah* and he emailed to confirm receipt and promised to read it. I did not hear from him again, and as far as I know he did not get the chance to push for the bill's final ratification over the next year. Sadly, he died in June 2008 following an accident during a trip to China.]

Concluding remarks

Mr Bhandara's sincerity of purpose is not in doubt. In his mind either the 'ideology of Pakistan' needed clarification or the reference thereof had to be omitted. Individuals such as Chief Justice Cornelius and Mian Iftikhar-ud-Din would have understood this sentiment.[14] Nevertheless, it goes without saying that Mr Bhandara was a staunch secularist, so he preferred omission rather than clarification of the term 'ideology of Pakistan'. He believed that the 11 August speech was secular in content and spirit and so he sought to show that it contradicted the Islamic content of the constitution.[15] Once Article 2B had become law, no doubt the supposed contradiction would have been used to justify the eventual deletion of the Islamic content in the constitution. The next step would likely have been to make another attempt to remove the words 'ideology of Pakistan', and thus accelerate the development of a purely materialist state. Conversely, my aim was to prevent such a perceived contradiction by getting the 11 August speech recognised in its correct context.

---

[14] As we have shown in this book, both of these individuals had effectively pointed out that simply declaring the state would be 'Islamic' was not enough. Even Mr Bhandara's father, P.D. Bhandara, made similar statements. Quranic principles needed to be included and adhered to in order to give substance to this declaration. As such this remains true today.

[15] He admitted as much around a month before our correspondence began, when he wrote in *Dawn*: 'The tenor and content of the Quaid-e-Azam's speech, which includes the direction, "you may belong to any religion or caste or creed – that has nothing to do with the business of the State", runs counter to Article 2 of the 1973 Constitution, which says: "Islam shall be the state religion of Pakistan." … How do we resolve this contradiction?' At the end of his article, he added: 'It is proposed that the grundnorm of Pakistan is Quaid-i-Azam's speech of August 11, 1947, and it be incorporated as a substantive part of the Constitution in Article 2. … [the bill] aims at restoring the ideals of the Quaid … ' (See M.P. Bhandara, 'Quaid's Concept of Pakistan' in *Dawn*, 25 March 2007)

Appendix VIII
The Munir quote in literature

The following is a tiny selection of writings out of what probably number thousands, in which the Munir quote and the two-pronged argument (Munir quote plus 11 August 1947 speech) appear. The list has been updated in this revised edition to include more recent instances, which continue to appear in new literature to the present, along with commentary in footnotes where relevant.

Note that this list has been created solely to demonstrate how frequently the Munir quote and the two-pronged argument are used in literature, almost exclusively by pro-secularist commentators.

The first part of this list comprises examples of the standalone Munir quote, and the second half lists those writings containing the two-pronged argument.

Munir quote (standalone)

Nazir Ahmad (1997) *Qur'anic and non-Qur'anic Islam* Lahore: Vanguard Books, p.151 [1]

S.M. Shamsul Alam (2015) *Governmentality and Counter-Hegemony in Bangladesh* Hampshire: Palgrave Macmillan, p.34

James N. D. Anderson (1976) *Law Reform in the Muslim World* London: Athlone Press, p.175

Sailesh Kumar Bandopadhaya (1991) *Quaid-i-Azam Mohammad Ali Jinnah and the Creation of Pakistan* New Delhi: Sterling Publishers, p.203

Geoff Brown, 'Pakistan: Failing State or Neoliberalism in Crisis?', in *International Socialism* Issue 150, Spring 2016 (http://isj.org.uk/pakistan-failing-state-or-neoliberalism-in-crisis) Last accessed 16 May 2017

D.H. Butani (1984) *The Future of Pakistan* New Delhi: Promilla, p.144

Muhammad Kamran, 'Democratic Pakistan – Liberal or Islamic State', in *Tribal Post* (online), 13 March 2016

[1] In this particular case, the Munir quote has been wrongly dated 11 August 1947.

(http://tribalpost.pk/opinion/3627/pakistan-liberal-or-islamic-state) Last accessed 31 May 2016

Iqtidar Karamat Cheema (2006) *Quaid-i-Azam Mohammad Ali Jinnah as Governor-General of Pakistan* Lahore: University of the Punjab, p.222. (The chapter containing the quote also appears at Nazaria Pakistan Trust (http://nazariapak.info/Quaid-e-Azam/Legacy-Personality.php) Last accessed 29 Dec 2009)

G.W. Choudhury (1959) *Constitutional Development in Pakistan* Lahore: Longman, Green & Co. Ltd., p.63

Noor ul Haq (2013) *Challenge of Identity and Governance – Quaid's Vision: The Way Forward* (IPRI Paper 17) Islamabad: Islamabad Policy Research Institute, p.28-29

Abul Hasanat (1974) *Let Humanity Not Forget: The Ugliest Genocide in History, Being a Resume of Inhuman Atrocities in Inhuman Atrocities in East Pakistan, Now Bangladesh* Dacca: Muktadhara, p.30

Zafar Hilaly (2009) 'Heading Towards Victory', in *News International*, 11 June

Tahir Kamran 'Early Phase of Electoral Politics in Pakistan: 1950s', in *Research Journal of South Asian Studies* Vol. 24, No. 2, Jul-Dec 2009, p.261

Muhammad Reza Kazimi, 'Pakistan: The Founder's View', in *Journal of Management and Social Science* Vol. 4, No. 1, Spring 2008, p.48

Barkat Ali Khan, 'Education; as an Instrument, for Democratic System in Context of Fundamental Rights, in Pakistan', online article for PLJ Law Site (undated but 2009) (http://www.pljlawsite.com/2009art4.htm) Last accessed 4 June 2016

Yuvraj Krishan (2002) *Understanding Partition: India Sundered, Muslims Fragmented* Mumbai: Bharatiya Vidya Bhavan, p.261

V.B. Kulkarni (1988) *Pakistan, its Origin & Relations with India* New Delhi: Sterling Publishers, p.117

Rachel Fell McDermott et al (eds.) (2014) *Sources of Indian Traditions Vol. 2: Modern India, Pakistan and Bangladesh* (third edition) New York: Columbia University Press, p.765

Sharif al Mujahid (1981) *Quaid-i-Azam Jinnah: Studies in Interpretation* Karachi: Quaid-i-Azam Academy, p.254

Anthony O'Mahony, 'Muslim-Christian Relations in India', in Anthony O'Mahony, Ataullah Siddiqui (eds.) (2001) *Christians and Muslims in the Commonwealth: A Dynamic Role in the Future* London: Altajir World of Islam Trust, p.213 [2]

Farid Panjwani, 'Religious Education in Pakistan: Salvation or Subjugation?', in Jerome Satterthwaite et al (eds.) *Educational Counter-Cultures: Confrontations, Images, Vision* Staffordshire: Trentham Books, p.87

Nadeem F. Paracha, 'Smokers' Corner: Cherry-picking Iqbal, splitting Jinnah: the Pakistani nationalist conundrum', in *Dawn*, 25 September 2016

Avril Powell, 'Perceptions of the South Asian Past: Ideology, Nationalism and School History Textbooks', in Nigel Crook (ed.) (1996) *The Transmission of Knowledge in South Asia: Essays on Education, Religion, History, and Politics* Delhi: Oxford University Press, p.219 [3]

Abdur Rashid (2001) *From Makkah to Nuclear Pakistan* Lahore: Ferozsons, p.475

Arshad Javed Rizvi, *The Extremism in Pakistan: A Religio-Political Study.* Online research paper, posted 20 August 2015 at *Social Science Research Network*: (http://ssrn.com/abstract=2645637) Last accessed 4 June 2016

Mehboob Sada, 'Managing Christian-Muslim Relations', in *South Asian Composite Heritage* (New Delhi) Vol. 1 Issue 2, Sept-Nov 2005, p.6-7 (originally a paper presented at the University of Melbourne's International Colloguium, 11-13 Feb 2004)

Aoun Sahi, 'Sharia Bandwagon', in *The News on Sunday*, 16 February 2014

Guido Schmidt (2009) *Die verfassungsgeschichtliche Entwicklung Pakistans von der Unabhängigkeit 1947 bis zur Militärdiktatur 1958 Akademische Schriftenreihe* Verlag: GRIN Verlag, p.7

Sita Ram Sharma & S.R. Bakshi (eds.) (1994) *Encyclopaedia of Pakistan: Selective Documents of Pakistan Constitution* in 5 Volumes New Delhi: Rima Publishing House Vol. 5, p.125

---

[2] Again, the author cites the Munir quote but dates it 11 August speech 1947.

[3] Powell's source for the Munir quote in this instance is a 'privately published' education textbook: A. Qayum Sher (1990 second revised edition) *Pakistan Studies* Lahore: Book Trader, p.194

Prakash K. Singh (2009) *Encyclopaedia on Jinnah* in 5 volumes New Delhi: Anmol Publications Vol. 5, p.194

Marvi Sirmed, 'Pakistan ka matlab kya?', in *Daily Times* 25 Mar 2017

Tahir Wasti (2009) *The Application of Islamic Criminal Law in Pakistan: Sharia in Practice* Leiden/Boston: Brill, p.4. Also 'The Application of Qisas and Diyat Law in Pakistan', in Eugene Cotran & Martin Lau (eds.) (2009) Yearbook of Islamic and Middle Eastern Law, Volume 13 (2006-2007) Boston: Brill, p.98

Syed M. Zulqurnain Zaidi (2003) *The Emergence of Ulema in the Politics of India and Pakistan* 1918-1949: A Historical Perspective California: Writers Club Press, p.100

Two-pronged argument

Najmul Abedin (1973) *Local Administration and Politics in Modernising Societies: Bangladesh and Pakistan* Dacca: National Institute of Public Administration, p.92

Ishtiaq Ahmed, 'Pakistan, Islam, Secularism Democracy: A Phantasmagoria of Conflicting Muslim Aspirations', in *Oriente Moderno*, No. 1, 2004, Vol. XXIII, (LXXXIV), p.16. Also 'The Spectre of Islamic Fundamentalism over Pakistan (1947-2007)', in Rajshee Jetly (2009) Pakistan in Regional and Global Politics London/New Delhi: Routledge, p.156-8

Syed Jaffar Ahmed, 'Jinnah and the Notion of the Nation-State', in *The Counsel* Vol. 2, Autumn/Winter issue 2010, Karachi (http://www.counselpakistan.com/vol-2/featured-articles/jinnah-notion.php) Last accessed 31 May 2016

S. M. Shamsul Alam (1995) *The State, Class Formation, and Development in Bangladesh* Lanham: University Press of America, p.28-9. Also (2015) *Governmentality and Counter-Hegemony in Bangladesh* Hampshire: Palgrave Macmillan, p.34

Ausaf Ali (1998) *Broader Dimensions of the Ideology of Pakistan* Karachi: Royal Book Company, p.66

Salim Alvi (2003) *Pakistan: Illusion and Reality – Observations of a Journalist* Karachi: Ushba Publishing International, p.155

Rubina Anjum, 'Social Studies Curriculum in Elementary Public Schools of Pakistan', in *Journal of Research and Reflections in Education* Vol. 3, No.2, Dec 2009, p.105-6

Kalim Bahadur, 'Problems of Secularism in Pakistan', in Pandav Nayak (ed.) (1985) Pakistan, Dilemmas of a Developing State Jaipur: Aalekh Publishers, p.32. Also (1998) *Democracy in Pakistan: Crises and Conflicts* New Delhi: Har-Anand Publications, p.14.

B.P. Barua (1984) *Politics and Constitution-Making in India and Pakistan* New Delhi: Deep & Deep Publications, p.74

Mathew Joseph C., 'Islamisation: Ideology and Politics', in Ajay Behera and Mathew Joseph C. (eds.) (2004) *Pakistan in a Changing Strategic Context* New Delhi: University of Jammu, p.180

S.C. Chattopadhyaya (24 August 1954) *Constituent Assembly of Pakistan Debates Official Report (1947-1954),* Vol. XVI. Karachi: Government of Pakistan, p.288-9

Nazir Hussain Chaudhri (1973) *Chief Justice Muhammad Munir: His Life, Writings, and Judgements* Lahore: Research Society of Pakistan, p.201, 203

Muzaffar Ahmed Chaudhuri (1968) *Government and Politics in Pakistan* Dacca: Puthighar, p.10-11

Sheshrao Chavan (2007) *Mohammad Ali Jinnah: The Great Enigma* New Delhi: Authors Press, p.284-5

Shabir Choudhry (2017 ebook edition) *Kashmir Dispute, Pakistan and the UN Resolutions* Bloomington: Authorhouse, Chapter 2. Also (2004) *Kashmir Dispute, as I see it* London: Institute of Kashmir Affairs/Kashar

Ardeshir Cowasjee, 'Back to Jinnah', in *Dawn,* 3 February 2002. Also 'That Enduring Shame', in *Dawn,* 14 August 2011

Asghar Ali Engineer (1985) *Islam and Muslims: A Critical Reassessment* Jaipur: Printwell Publishers, p.122

Herbert Feldman (1955) *A Constitution for Pakistan* Karachi: Oxford University Press, p.20

Khalid Latif Gauba (1977) *Pakistan Today* Bombay: Thackers, p.106-7

Abdus Sattar Ghazali (1996) *Islamic Pakistan: Illusions & Reality* Islamabad: National Book Club, p.6-7

Srikanta Ghosh (1974) *Crisis in Administration* Calcutta: Eastern Law House, p.117

Anirudha Gupta, 'Cultural Dimensions', in Bimal Prasad (ed.) *Regional Cooperation in South Asia: Problems & Prospects* New Delhi: Vikas Publishing House, p.138

Sayyid Sibte Hasan (1986) *The Battle of Ideas in Pakistan* Karachi: Pakistan Publishing House, p.182-3

A.Z. Hilali (2005) *US-Pakistan Relationship: Soviet Invasion of Afghanistan* Hants: Ashgate Publishing Ltd., p.258

Hiz-u-Tahrir editorial, 'Mohammed Ali Jinnah Exposed', in *Khilafah* London: Hizb-u-Tahrir, December 1996

Pervez A. Hoodbhoy & Abdul H. Nayyar, 'Rewriting the History of Pakistan', in Mohammad Asghar Khan (ed.) (1985) *Islam, Politics and the State: The Pakistan Experience* London: Zed Books, p.170

A.K.A. Shamsul Huda (1997) *The Constitution of Bangladesh* Chittagong: Rita Court, Vol. 1, p.112

Arif Humayun (2010) *Connivance by Silence: How the Majority's Failure to Challenge Politically Motivated [Mis]interpretations of Qur'an Empowered Radicals to Propogate Extremism* Indiana: Xlibris, p.70

Syed Adnan Hussain (2015, unpublished PhD thesis) *Negotiating Pakistan: A Genealogy of a Post-colonial Islamic State* Toronto: University of Toronto, p.143 [4]

---

[4] This thesis on the Pakistan idea as 'Islamic state', in which Munir's work is reviewed prominently, is well researched and an interesting read. Unfortunately, its facile treatment of the Munir quote amounts to intellectual dishonesty. The author clearly knows about the issue with the quote (he references both my *Secular Jinnah* books) but fails to mention its exact words, and then dismisses it with the remark that it may have been 'incorrectly transcribed' (A.S. Hussain 2015, p.132 fn). Later when he cites the Munir quote in full, he takes care to ascribe the quote directly to Justices Munir and Kayani instead of Jinnah, yet he does not mention that it is a fabrication (ibid. p.143). Further, the thesis attempts to portray Munir as almost a victim of the increasingly authoritarian state at the helm of 'strongman' Ghulam Mohammed, a claim that is hardly convincing for obvious reasons. The author classifies Munir as a particular type of modernist-cum-secularist of a distinctly South Asian type, i.e. of the secular-Muslim or synthesis category (in which he also places Jinnah), and remarks: 'It may seem strange that Munir's secularism … is often mistakenly translated into Urdu as *la dini* (irreligious or without religion) … considering that he also authored two books and number

Afzal Iqbal (1984) *Islamisation of Pakistan* Delhi: Idarah-i Adabiyat-i Delli, p.33, 35. Also (1986) *Islamisation of Pakistan* Islamabad: Vanguard Books, p.33

Farahnaz Ispahani (2017 reprint) *Purifying The Land Of The Pure: Pakistan's Religious Minorities* New York: Oxford University Press, p.24. Also appears in original edition of the same title (2015) Uttar Pradesh: HarperCollins [5]

Asma Jahangir & Hina Jilani (2003) *The Hudood Ordinances: a Divine Sanction? A Research Study of the Hudood Ordinances and their Effect on the Disadvantaged Sections of Pakistan* Society Lahore: Sang-e-Meel Publications, p.174, 179

Arif Mohammed Khan 'Pakistan: Victim of Its Own Ideology', in *Eternal India* (New Delhi) Vol. 1, No. 9, Jun 2009, p.25

Hamid Khan (2001) *Constitutional and Political History of Pakistan* Oxford: Oxford University Press, p.76

Sayeed Hasan Khan, 'Secular Charter and Plural Society', in *The Island Online*, 4 May 2011. (http://island.lk/index.php?page_cat=article-details&page=article-details&code_title=24579) Last accessed 4 Jun 2016

Veena Kukreja, 'Islamic Fundamentalism in Pakistan', in Subrata Mukherjee & Sushila Ramaswamy (eds.) (2000) *Political Science Annual 1998-99* New Delhi: Deep & Deep Publications, p.397. Also (2003) *Contemporary Pakistan: Political Processes, Conflicts and Crises* New Delhi: Sage Publications, p.160-2

Jaferhusein I. Laliwala (2005) *Islamic Philosophy of Religion: Synthesis of Science Religion and Philosophy* New Delhi: Sarop & Sons, p.134-5

Abdul Wahab Liaquat (2012, unpublished Masters thesis) *Effect of Dogmatic Religiosity and Educational Environment on Moral Judgment Competence* Islamabad: International Islamic University, p.32

---

of widely read articles on Islam' (ibid. p.131-2). This essentially overlooks the position Munir takes as a secularist proper (i.e. of the Western conception) in *From Jinnah to Zia*, a book which, being his last, also represents his final testimony on the subject. (For our review of Munir's ideological position, see subsection 'A secular-Muslim approach' in Chapter 2.)

[5] Written by a politician who is also the granddaughter of M.A.H. Ispahani, the book produces the three-piece argument in toto. The author makes the far-fetched claim that Ghulam Mohammed was a Muslim fundamentalist who, in a public statement on 24 January 1948, declared his opposition to the separation of religion from the affairs of the state expressly as 'a direct swipe at Jinnah' and the speech of 11 August 1947. (F. Ispahani 2017, p.30). For our review of how committed Ghulam Mohammed really was to practising what he preached, see Chapter 3 (and in particular footnote 72 of that chapter).

Zulfikar Khalid Maluka (1995) *The Myth of Constitutionalism in Pakistan* Karachi: Oxford University Press, p.71 & 74

Sayyed Abul Ala Maudoodi (1956) *An Analysis of the Munir Report: A Critical Study of the Punjab Disturbances Inquiry Report* Translated from Urdu by Khurshid Ahmad Karachi: Jamaat-e-Islami Publications, p.131, 134 [6]

M. Munir & M.R. Kayani (1954) *Report of the Court of Inquiry Constituted under Punjab Act II of 1954 to Enquire into the Punjab Disturbances of 1953* Lahore: Government of Punjab, p.201-2

Muhammad Munir (1980) *From Jinnah to Zia* Lahore: Vanguard Books, p.29

Kuldip Nayar, 'Secularism 'door ast'', in *Dawn*, 23 February 2002

Farhad Nomani & Ali Rahnema (1994) *Islamic Economic Systems* London/New Jersey: Zed Books, p.113

Shah Mustafizur Rahman (2008) *Khilafat in Islam* Dhaka: S.A. Muhammad Talha M.Com., p.153. (http://laa-ilaha-illallah.info/Khilafat_in_Islam.pdf) Last accessed 20 Mar 2010

Muhammad Shoaib Pervez (2013) *Security Community in South Asia: India-Pakistan* London: Routledge p.59-60 [7]

Baljit Rai (1991) *Muslim Fundamentalism in the Indian Subcontinent* Baljit Chandigarh: B.S. Publishers, p.13

Abdur Rashid (2001) *From Makkah to Nuclear Pakistan* Lahore: Ferozsons, p.475

Subroto Roy (2011) *On the Alternative Theories of Pakistan and India about Jammu & Kashmir (And the One and Only Way These May Be*

---

[6] Dr Khurshid Ahmad's translation of Maududi's rebuttal to the Munir Report, though included on this list for information's sake, obviously does not truly count as a 'Munir quoter', since the quote only appeared as part of the review.

[7] This particular book – which won a National Outstanding Research Award from the Higher Education Commission of Pakistan in 2015 – only touched upon the ideological element briefly, as its main subject was the historical relationship between Pakistan and India. Its author argues that Jinnah was a 'fusionist Islamic secularist', though this is obviously just his term for what is better known as the synthesis category. The original dissertation, later published as the aforementioned monograph, was submitted to his university less than a week before *Secular Jinnah & Pakistan* was published. See (2010, PhD thesis) *The Socially Constructed Security Dilemma between India and Pakistan: an Exploration of norms for a Security Community* Leiden: Leiden University

Peacefully Reconciled): An Exercise in Economics, Politics, Moral Philosophy & Jurisprudence Undelivered lecture, posted at Roy's website on 22 Nov 2011 (https://independentindian.com/2011/11/22/pakistans-point-of-view-or-points-of-view-on-kashmir-my-as-yet-undelivered-lahore-lecture-part-i) Last accessed 4 Jun 2016

Mohammad Safdar, 'Religion & Politics in Pakistan', in Asghar Ali Engineer (ed.) (1985) *Islam in South and South-East Asia* , p.153-4

Rajendra Sareen (1984) *Pakistan, the India Factor* New Delhi: Allied Publishers, p.99. Also 'Pakistan', in Uma Shankar Bajpai (ed.) (1986) *India and its Neighbourhood* New Delhi: Lancer International/India National Centre, p.196

S.M.A. Sayeed (1995) *The Myth of Authenticity: A Study in Islamic Fundamentalism* Karachi: Royal Book Company, p.300

Niaz A. Shah (2006) *Women, The Koran and International Human Rights Law: The Experience of Pakistan* Leiden/Boston: Martinus Nijhoff Publishers, p.92

Saeed Shafqat (1989) *Political System of Pakistan and Public Policy: Essays in Interpretation* Lahore: Progressive Publishers, p.92. Also (1997) *Civil-Military Relations in Pakistan: From Zulfikar Ali Bhutto to Benazir Bhutto* Lahore: Westview Press, p.87

Jai Narain Sharma (ed.) (2008) *Encyclopaedia of Eminent Thinkers Vol. 13: The Political Thought of M.A. Jinnah* New Delhi: Concept Publishing Company, p.25

Stanko M. Vujica 'The Ahmadiyya Movement in Islam', in *Eastern World* Vol. 15, December 1961, p.16

Ibn Warraq, 'Secularism the only Answer to Pakistan's Sectarian Violence'. Free Press Society (online), 17 January 2011. (http://www.trykkefrihed.dk/secularism-the-only-answer-to-pakistans-sectarian-violence.htm) Last accessed 4 June 2016

Mohammad Waseem (1989) *Politics and the State in Pakistan* Lahore: Progressive Publishers, p.104

Shahla Zia, 'Discrimination in Pakistan Against Religious Minorities', in Rita Manchanda (ed.) (2010) *States in Conflict with their Minorities: Challenges to Minority Rights* in South Asia New Delhi: SAGE Publications, p.145

Bibliography

Books, journals, publications

'A Punjabi' (1939) *Confederacy of India* Lahore: Nawab Sir Muhammad Shah Nawaz Khan of Mamdot

Adil, R.S. (1995) *Baba Saheb Doctor Ambedkar Aur Islam* Delhi: Aman Publications

Afzal, M.R. (ed.) (1980) *Selected Speeches & Statements of Quaid-i-Azam Mohammad Ali Jinnah* Lahore: Research Society of Pakistan, Punjab University

Ahmad, A. (1967) *Islamic Modernism in India and Pakistan 1857-1964* Oxford: Oxford University Press

Ahmad, R. (1981) *Consitutional and Political Developments in Pakistan* 1951-54 Rawalpindi: Pak-American Commercial Ltd.

Ahmad, R. (1990) *Quaid-i-Azam's Perception of Islam and Pakistan* Rawalpindi: Alvi Publishers

Ahmad, R. (ed.) (1994) *Quaid-i-Azam Mohammad Ali Jinnah: Second Phase of his Freedom Struggle, 1924-1934* Islamabad: National Institute of Pakistan Studies, Quaid-i-Azam University

Ahmad, R. (ed.) (1996-2006) *The Works of Quaid-i-Azam Mohammad Ali Jinnah (1893-1924)* in 6 volumes Islamabad: National Institute of Pakistan Studies, Quaid-i-Azam University

Ahmad, W. 'Choudhary Rahmat Ali and the Concept of Pakistan', in *Journal of the Research Society of Pakistan*, January 1970

Ahmad, W. (1991) *Quaid-i-Azam Mohammad Ali Jinnah Speeches, Indian Legislative Assembly 1935-1947* Karachi: Quaid-i-Azam Academy

Ahmad, W. (ed.) (1992-2003) *Quaid-i-Azam Mohammad Ali Jinnah: The Nation's Voice* in 7 volumes Karachi: Quaid-i-Azam Academy

Ahmed, A.S. (1997) *Jinnah, Pakistan and Islamic Identity: the Search for Saladin* London: Routledge

Ahmed, I. (1987) *The Concept of an Islamic State: an Analysis of the Ideological Controversy in Pakistan* London: Frances Pinter

Ahmed, I. 'Pakistan Democracy, Islam and Secularism: A Phantasmagoria of Conflicting Muslim Aspirations', in *Oriente Moderno*, Vol. XXIII (LXXXIV). No.1. 2004, p.13-28

Ahmed, S. (2005) *The Quran as it Explains itself* (*QXP*) Florida: OurBeacon.com

Akbar, M.J. (1985) *India: The Siege Within* New York: Penguin Books

Akbar, M.J. (1988) *Nehru: the Making of India* New York: Viking

Alavi, H. (2001a) *The Rise of Religious Fundamentalism in Pakistan.* Paper given at South Asian Conference on Fundamentalism: Role of Civil Society. Dhaka, Bangladesh 1-2 June. (http://ourworld.compuserve.com/homepages/sangat/fundamen.htm) Last accessed 25 Aug 2006

Ali, A.Y., (1946) *The Holy Qur-an: Text, Translation and Commentary* in 2 volumes (third edition) New York: Hafner Publishing Company

Ali, C.R. (1933) *Now or Never: Are we to Live or Perish for Ever?* Cambridge: The Pakistan National Movement

Ali, C.R. (1947) *Pakistan: The Fatherland of the Pak Nation* (third edition) Cambridge: The Pakistan Liberation Movement

Almeida, P. (2001) *Jinnah: Man of Destiny* Delhi: Kalpaz Publications

Alshenqeeti, H. & Alsaedi, N. 'Is Multilingualism a Problem? The Effects of Multilingualism at the Societal Level' in *Annual Review of Education, Communication, and Language Sciences* 2012, Vol. 9

Ambedkar, B.R. (1946a) *Pakistan or Partition of India.* Bombay: Thacker & Co. Ltd

Ambedkar, B.R. (1946b) *What Congress and Gandhi have done to the Untouchables* Bombay: Thacker

Arshad, M. (2001, unpublished PhD thesis) *Muslim Politics and Political Movements in the Punjab 1932-1942* Bahawalpur: Islamia University

Asad, M. (2003) *The Message of the Qur'an* Bristol: The Book Foundation

Azad, A.K. (1959) *India Wins Freedom: an Autobiographical Narrative* Bombay: Orient Longman

Aziz, K.K. (1979) *Muslims Under Congress Rule, 1937-1939: a Documentary Record* Islamabad: National Commission on Historical and Cultural Research, Vol. II

Aziz, K.K. (1987) *Rahmat Ali: A Biography* Stuttgart: Steiner Verlag Wiesbaden

Aziz, Q. (1997) *Quaid-i-Azam Jinnah and the Battle for Pakistan* Karachi: Islamic Media Corporation

Aziz, Q. (2001) *Jinnah and Pakistan* Karachi: Islamic Media Corporation

Bakhsh, I. (1978 reprint) *With the Quaid-i-Azam in his Last Days* Karachi: Quaid-i-Azam Academy

Bakhtiar, L. (2009 revised edition) *The Sublime Quran* Chicago: Kazi Publications

Binder, L. (1961) *Religion and Politics in Pakistan* California: University of California Press

Bolitho, H. (1954) *Jinnah: Creator of Pakistan* London: John Murray

Bose, S. & Jalal, A. (eds.) (1997) *Nationalism, Democracy and Development: State and Politics in India* Delhi: Oxford University Press

Braibanti, R. (ed.) (1999) *Chief Justice Cornelius of Pakistan: An Analysis with Letters and Speeches* Karachi: Oxford University Press

Carter, L. (ed.) (2003) *Mountbatten's Report on the Last Viceroyalty, 22 March - 15 August 1947* New Delhi: Manohar

Carter, L. (ed.) (2006) *Punjab Politics: 1 January 1944 – 3 March 1947* New Delhi: Manohar

Chagla, M.C. (1973) *Roses in December* Bombay: Bharatiya Vidya Bhavan

Chakrabarty, B. (2004) *The Partition of Bengal and Assam, 1932-1947: Contour of Freedom* London: Routledge

Chattha, I. 'The impact of the redistribution of Pakistan's evacuee property on the patterns of land ownership and power in Pakistani Punjab in the 1950s', in Roger D. Long et al. (eds.) (2016) *State and Nation-Building in Pakistan: Beyond Islam and Security (Routledge Contemporary South Asia Series)* Abingdon: Routledge

Chaudhary, K.M. & Irshad, N. 'The Role of Ulema and Mashaikh in the Pakistan Movement' in *Pakistan Journal of Life and Social Sciences* (2005), Vol. 3 (Nos. 1-2)

Chavan, S. (2007) *Mohammad Ali Jinnah: The Great Enigma* New Delhi: Authors Press

Chopra, P.N. (ed.) (1998) *The Collected Works of Sardar Vallabhbhai Patel* Delhi: Konark Publishers

Choudhury, G.W. (1959) *Constitutional Development in Pakistan* Lahore: Longman, Green & Co Ltd.

Choudhury, G.W. (1967) *Documents and Speeches on the Constitution of Pakistan* Dacca: Green Book House

Collins, L. and Lapierre, D. (1975) *Freedom at Midnight* New York: Simon & Schuster

Constituent Assembly of Pakistan Debates: Official Report (1947-54) Karachi: Government of Pakistan in 21 volumes, Vols. I, II, V, XI, XII, XV, XVI

Dar, B.A. (ed.) (1967) *Letters and Writings of Iqbal* Karachi: Iqbal Academy

Durrani, F.K.K. (1944) *The Meaning of Pakistan* Lahore: Sh. Muhammad Ashraf

European Commission for Democracy through Law (1994), *The Modern Concept of Confederation* (Collection, Science & Technique of Democracy, No. 11) Strasbourg: Council of Europe

Fischer, L. (1954) *Gandhi; His Life and Message for the World* New York: New American Library/Mentor

Gandhi, M.K. (1999) *The Collected Works of Mahatma Gandhi* (Electronic Book) in 98 volumes New Delhi: Publications Division Government of India. Last accessed 12 Jun 2016 (http://www.gandhiserve.org/e/cwmg/cwmg.htm)

Ghazali, A.S. (1996) *Islamic Pakistan: Illusions and Reality* Islamabad: National Book Club

Guillaume, A. et al (1998 reprint) *The Life of Muhammad: a Translation of Isḥaq's Sirat Rasul Allah* London: Oxford University Press

Gwyer, M.L. & Appadorai, A. (eds.) (1957) *Speeches and Documents on the Indian Constitution, 1921-47* London: Oxford University Press, Vol. II

Hadley, A.T. (1972 reprint), *Economic Problems of Democracy* New York: Books for Libraries Press

Halliday, F. & Alavi, H. (eds.) (1988) *State and Ideology in the Middle East and Pakistan* London: Macmillan

Hamid, S.S. (1993 reprint) *Disastrous Twilight: A Personal Record of the Partition of India* London: Leo Cooper

Hamidullah, M. (2003 reprint) *Introduction to Islam* New Delhi: Kitab Bhavan

Harris, M.A. (ed.) (1976) *Quaid-i-Azam.* Karachi: Times Press

Hasan, K.S. (ed.) (1991) *Quaid-i-Azam's Unrealised Dream* Karachi: Royal Book Company

Hasan, K.S. (1992) *Sindh's Fight for Pakistan* Karachi: Royal Book Company

Hasan, S.S. (1976) *Plain Mr Jinnah* Karachi: Royal Book Company

Hashim, A. (1974) *In Retrospection* Dacca: Subarna Publishers

Hussain, A. et al. (2011) *Connecting the Dots: Education and Religious Discrimination in Pakistan. A Study of Public Schools and Madrassas* Washington: United States Commission on International Religious Freedom

Hoodbhoy, P.A. 'Jinnah and the Islamic State: Setting the Record Straight', in *Economic and Political Weekly*, (Mumbai) Vol. 42 No. 32, 11-17 August 2007, p.3300-3303

Hoodbhoy, P.A. & Nayyar, A.H. 'Rewriting the History of Pakistan', in Mohammad Asghar Khan (ed.) *Islam, Politics and the State: The Pakistan Experience* London: Zed Books

Iqbal, J. (1971 reprint) *Ideology of Pakistan* Lahore: Ferozsons

Iqbal, J. (2005 reprint) *Ideology of Pakistan* Lahore: Sang-e-Meel Publications

Iqbal, M. (1954) *Makatib-i Iqbal Banam Niaz-u-din Khan* Lahore: Bazm-i-Iqbal

Iqbal, M. (1971 reprint) *The Reconstruction of Religious Thought in Islam.* Lahore: Sh. Muhammad Ashraf

Iqbal, M. (1974 reprint) *Letters of Iqbal to Jinnah* Lahore: Sh. Muhammad Ashraf

Ispahani, M.A.H. (1966) *Qaid-e-Azam Jinnah as I Knew Him* Karachi: Forward Publications Trust

Ispahani, M.A.H. (1976) *M.A. Jinnah-Ispahani Correspondence, 1936-1948* Karachi: Forward Publications Trust

Jaffrelot, C. (ed.) (2004) (translated by Gillian Beaumont) *A History of Pakistan and Its Origins* London: Anthem Press

Jaffrelot, C. (2015) (translated by Cynthia Schoch) *The Pakistan Paradox: Instability and Resilience* New York: Oxford University Press

Jalal, A. (1994 reprint) *The Sole Spokesman: Jinnah, the Muslim League and the Demand for Pakisan* Cambridge: Cambridge University Press

Jalal, A. (1995) *Democracy and Authoritarianism in South Asia: A Comparative and Historical Perspective* Cambridge: Cambridge University Press

Jalal, A. 'Exploding Communalism: The Politics of Muslim Identity in South Asia' in S. Bose & A. Jalal (eds.) (1997) *Nationalism, Democracy and Development: State and Politics in India* Delhi: Oxford University Press

Jalal, A. (2000) *Self and Sovereignty: Individual and Community in South Asian Islam since 1850* London: Routledge

Jalal, A. (2013) *The Pity of Partition: Manto's Life, Times, and Work Across the India-Pakistan Divide* Princeton: Princeton University Press

Jalal, A. (2014) *The Struggle for Pakistan: A Muslim Homeland and Global Politics* Cambridge: Belknap Press/Harvard University Press

Jalal, H. (1977) *Pakistan: Past & Present: A Comprehensive Study Published in Commemoration of the Centenary of the Birth of the Founder of Pakistan* London: Stacey International

Jawed, A. (1998) *Secular and Nationalist Jinnah* New Delhi: Kitab Publishing House

Jinnah, F. & Mujahid, S. (ed.) (1987) *My Brother* Karachi: Quaid-i-Azam Academy

Jones, G.N. 'Pakistan: A Civil Service in an Obsolescing Imperial Tradition', in *Asian Journal of Public Administration*, December 1997, Vol. 19. No. 2

Jung, B.Y. (2000 reprint) *Manshoor-i-Pakistan: Quaid-i-Millat Nawab Bahadur Yar Jung ki Tareekhi Taqreer* Karachi: Bahadur Yar Jung Academy

Kabir, N. 'The Bangla Language Movement: Beginning of the beginning – III' in *New Age*, 25 February 2016

Karim, F. (2003) *Quran aur Pakistan.* Islamabad: Bazm-e-Ilmo-Fann International

Karim, S. (2005) *Secular Jinnah: Munir's Big Hoax Exposed* Cornwall: Exposure Publishing

Kazimi, M.R. (ed.) (2005) *M.A. Jinnah: Views and Reviews* Karachi: Oxford University Press

Kazimi, M.R. 'Pakistan: The Founder's View', in *Journal of Management and Social Sciences* Vol. 4, No. 1, (Spring 2008)

Khaliquzzaman, C. (1961) *Pathway to Pakistan* Lahore: Longmans

Khan, A.W.K. (1987) Facts are Facts: the Untold Story of India's Partition (translated by Syeda Saiyidain Hameed) New Delhi: Vikas Pub. House

Khan, M.A. (ed.) (1985) *Islam, Politics and the State: The Pakistan Experience* London: Zed Books

Khan, L.A. (1950) *Pakistan: The Heart of Asia (Speeches in the United States and Canada May and June 1950 by the Prime Minister of Pakistan)* Massachusetts: Harvard University Press

Khan, S. (ed.) (1976) *Speeches, Messages and Statements of Madr-i-Millat Mohtarama Fatima Jinnah (1948-1967)* Lahore: Research Society of Pakistan

Khan, Y. (2007) *The Great Partition: The Making of India and Pakistan* New Haven/London: Yale University Press

Kiljunen, K. (2004) *The European Constitution in the Making* Brussels: Centre for European Policy Studies

Krishan, Y. (2002) *Understanding Partition: India Sundered, Muslims Fragmented* Mumbai: Bharatiya Vidya Bhavan

Kumarasingham, H. (2017) 'A Transnational Actor on a Dramatic Stage – Sir Ivor Jennings and the Manipulation of Westminster Style Democracy: The Case of Pakistan', in *UC Irvine Journal of International, Transnational and Comparative Law* Vol. 2, p.33-56 (http://scholarship.law.uci.edu/ucijil/vol2/iss1/4) Last accessed 4 October 2017

Lane, E.W. (1968 reprint) *An Arabic-English Lexicon* in 8 parts Beirut: Librarie du Liban. (http://www.laneslexicon.co.uk) Last accessed 1 May 2010

Latif, S.A. (1943) *The Pakistan Issue* Lahore: Sh. Muhammad Ashraf

Mahmood, S. 'Jinnah's Vision of Pakistan', in *Journal of South Asian and Middle Eastern Studies* Vol. XXVI, No. 3, Spring 2003

Mansergh, N. et al. (eds.) (1970-1983) *Constitutional Relations Between Britain and India: The Transfer of Power* in 12 volumes London: Her Majesty's Stationery Office Vols. I, VI, VII, IX, X, XI, XII

Maududi, A.A. (1939) *Musalman aur Maujuda Siyasi Kashmakash* Pathankot: Tarujuman al-Quran, Vol. III

McDonough, S. (2002) *The Flame of Sinai: Hope and Vision in Iqbal* Lahore: Iqbal Academy

McGann, J.G. (2016) '2015 Global Go To Think Tank Index Report'. Philadelphia: TTCSP Global Go To Think Tank Index Reports, Paper 10

McGrath, A. (1996) *The Destruction of Pakistan's Democracy* Karachi: Oxford University Press

Menon, V.P. (1957) *The Transfer of Power in India* Princeton: Princeton University Press

Merchant, L.H. & Mujahid, S. (eds.) (2009) *The Jinnah Anthology* Karachi: Oxford University Press

Miller, J. (1984) *Rousseau: Dreamer of Democracy* Indianapolis: Hacket Publishing Co.

Ministry of Education (2006) *National Curriculum for Pakistan Studies IX-X, 2006.* Islamabad: Government of Pakistan

Ministry of the Interior/Education Division (1983 reprint) *Proceedings of the Pakistan Educational Conference, Held at Karachi, from 27th November to 1st December 1947.* Islamabad: Government of Pakistan

Mitra, N.N. (ed.) *The Indian Annual Register* Calcutta: Annual Register Office Vols. I (1940), II (1936), II (1945)

Moon, P. (1962) *Divide and Quit* Delhi: Oxford University Press, p.20

Morrow, J.A. (2013) *The Covenants of the Prophet Muhammad with the Christians of the World* Washington/NewYork: Angelico Press/Sophia Perennis

Mujahid, S. 'India - Pakistan Relations: An Analysis', in Dept. of International Relations/Karachi University (1964) *Foreign Policy of Pakistan: An Analysis* Karachi: The Allied Book Corporation

Mujahid, S. (1981) *Quaid-i-Azam Jinnah: Studies in Interpretation* Karachi: Quaid-i-Azam Academy

Mujahid, S. (2001) *Ideology of Pakistan* Islamabad: International University

Mujahid, S. (ed.) (2007) *In Quest of Jinnah: Diary, Notes and Correspondence of Hector Bolitho* Karachi: Oxford University Press

Mujahid, S. 'Jinnah's Vision: An Indivisible Pakistani Nationhood', in *Journal of Management and Social Sciences* Vol. 5, No. 1, Spring 2009

Munir, M. & Kayani, *Report of the Court of Inquiry Constituted under Punjab Act II of 1954 to Enquire into the Punjab Disturbances of 1953* Lahore: Superintendent, Government Printing

Munir, M. (1980 edition) *From Jinnah to Zia.* Lahore: Vanguard Books

Nasr, V.R. (2000) *International Relations of an Islamist Movement: The Case of the Jama'at-i Islami of Pakistan* New York: Council on Foreign Relations

National Assembly of Pakistan Debates Official Report Vol. XXII (2004) Karachi: Manager of Publications

National Assembly of Pakistan Debates Official Report Vols. XXXVII (2006), XXXIX (2007) Islamabad: National Book Foundation

Nayyar, A.H. & Salim, A. (eds.) (2003) *The Subtle Subversion: The State of Curricula and Textbooks in Pakistan* Islamabad: Sustainable Development Policy Institute (http://sdpi.org/publications/files/State%20of%20Curr&TextBooks.pdf) Last accessed 4 June 2016

Nayyar, A.H. (2013) *A Missed Opportunity: Continuing Flaws in the New Curriculum and Textbooks After Reforms* Islamabad: Jinnah Institute

Nehru, J. (1941) *Toward Freedom: The Autobiography of Jawaharlal Nehru* New York: The John Day Company

Niazi, Z. (2010 revised) *The Press in Chains* Karachi: Oxford University Press

Nichols, B. (1944) *Verdict on India* London: Jonathan Cape

Philips, C.H. & Cartwright, M.D. (eds.) 1970 *The Partition of India: Policies and Perspectives* Massachusetts: MIT Press

Pickthall, M.W. (1980 reprint) *The Meaning of the Glorious Qur'an.* London: Ta-Ha Publishers

Pirzada, S.S. (ed.) 1977, *Quaid-e-Azam Jinnah's Correspondence* Karachi: East and West Publishing Company

Pirzada, S.S. (ed.) (1980 reprint) *Foundations of Pakistan: All-India Muslim League Documents: 1906-1947* in 2 volumes. New Delhi: Metropolitan Book Co.

Pirzada, S.S. (ed.) (1984-6) *The Collected Works of Quaid-i-Azam Mohammad Ali Jinnah* in 3 volumes Karachi: East-West Publishing

Puckle, F. 'The Pakistan Doctrine: Its Origins and Power', in *Foreign Affairs* (New York) Vol. 24, No. 3, April 1946

Qureshi, M.N. (1999) *Pan-Islamism in British India: The Politics of the Khilafat Movement 1918-1924* Leiden: Brill

Qureshi, S. (ed.) (1998) *Jinnah: The Founder of Pakistan (in the eyes of his contemporaries and his documentary records at Lincoln's Inn)* Karachi: Oxford University Press

Rajagopalachari, C. (ed.) (1944) *Gandhi-Jinnah Talks* New Delhi: Hindustan Times

Ramani, H.K. (1951) *Pakistan X-Rayed* Delhi: New Age, p.11

Rashid, H. (2003 revised) *The Foreshadowing of Bangladesh: Bengal Muslim League and Muslim League and Muslim Politics, 1936-1947* Dhaka: The University Press

Report of the Basic Principles Committee (September 1954) Karachi: Government of Pakistan

Robinson, F. (2000) *Islam and Muslim History in South Asia* New Delhi: Oxford University Press

Saeed, A. (ed.) (1983), *The Eastern Times on Quaid-i-Azam.* Islamabad: National Institute of Historical and Cultural Research

Sayeed, K. (1956, PhD thesis) *The Central Government of Pakistan 1947-1951* Montreal: McGill University

Sayeed, K. (1960) *Pakistan: The Formative Phase,* Karachi: Pakistan Publishing House

Sayeed, K. (1968 revised) *Pakistan: The Formative Phase 1857-1948,* London: Oxford University Press

Sen, D. 'No matter how, Jogendranath had to be defeated': The Scheduled Castes Federation and the making of partition in Bengal, 1945–1947', in *Indian Economic & Social History Review,* 2012, Vol. 49 No.3, p.321–64

Sevea, I.S. (2012) *The Political Philosophy of Muhammad Iqbal: Islam and Nationalism in Late Colonial India* New York: Cambridge University

Schofield, V. (ed.) (1997) *Old Roads, New Highways: Fifty Years of Pakistan.* Karachi: Oxford University Press

Shahid, A.R. 'All-India Muslim League: Split and Reunification (1927-30)', in *Pakistan Journal of History & Culture*, 2007, Vol. XXVIII, No.1, p.155-168

Sharma, M.S.M. (1954) *Peeps into Pakistan* Patna: Pustak Bhandar

Sherwani, L.A. (ed.) (2008 reprint) *Speeches, Writings & Statements of Iqbal* New Delhi: Adam Publishers

Smith, D.E. (1963) *India as a Secular State* Princeton: Princeton University Press

Syed, A.H. (1982) *Pakistan: Islam, Politics and National Solidarity* New York: Praeger Publishers

Talbot, I. (1998) *Pakistan: A Modern History* London: C. Hurst & Co.

Toosy, M.S. (1976) *My Reminisces of Quaid-i-Azam: A Collection of Interviews and Talks with Quaid-i-Azam during November 1942 to May 1943* Islamabad: Ministry of Education, Government of Pakistan

Tudor, M. J. (2013) *The Promise of Power: The Origins of Democracy in India and Autocracy in Pakistan* Cambridge: Cambridge University Press

Umar, M. (ed.) (1973) *Quaid-i-Azam Mohammad Ali Jinnah: Rare Speeches 1910-1918* Karachi-Sukkur: Al-Mahfooz Research Academy

Wasti, S.M.J. (1982) *My Reminiscences of Choudhary Rahmat Ali* Karachi: Royal Book Company

Wavell, A.P. (Earl of) & Penderel Moon (ed.) (1973) *Wavell: The Viceroy's Journal* London: Oxford University Press

Weiss, A.M. (ed.) (1986) *Islamic Reassertion in Pakistan: The Application of Islamic Laws in an Islamic State* New York: Syracuse University Press

Wells, I.B. (2005) *Ambassador of Hindu-Muslim Unity: Jinnah's Early Politics* Delhi: Permanent Black

Wolpert, S. (1984) *Jinnah of Pakistan* New York: Oxford University Press

Wolpert, S. (2006) *Shameful Flight: The Last Years of the British Empire in India* New York: Oxford University Press

Yusufi, K.A.K. (ed.) (1988) *Quaid-i-Azam Muhammad Ali Jinnah – Some Rare Speeches and Statements* 1944-1947 Lahore: Punjab University

Yusufi, K.A.K (ed.) (1996) *Speeches, Statements & Messages of the Quaid-e-Azam* in 4 volumes Lahore: Bazm-i-Iqbal

Zaidi, Z.H. (ed.) (1993) *Jinnah Papers: Prelude to Pakistan*, Vol. I Part 1, 20 February – 2 June 1947. Lahore: Quaid-i-Azam Papers Project.

Zaidi, Z.H. 'Economic Vision of the Quaid-i-Azam', in The Pakistan Development Review Vol. 40 No. 4 Part II (Winter 2001)

Zakaria, R. (2001) *The Man who Divided India: an Insight into Jinnah's Leadership and its Aftermath* Mumbai: Popular Prakashan

Zimmerman, J.F. (2008 edition) *Contemporary American Federalism: the Growth of National Power* Albany: State University of New York

Zulfiqar, G.H. (ed.) (1997) *Pakistan as Visualised by Iqbal and Jinnah.* Lahore: Bazm-i-Iqbal

Newspapers, magazines, periodicals

AKI (Rome)
Daily Times (Lahore)
Dawn (Karachi)
Deccan Chronicle (Hyderabad)
Deccan Times (Madras)
The Express Tribune (Karachi)
The Friday Times (Lahore)
Frontline (Chennai)
History Today (London)
The Islamic Review (Woking)
New Age (Dhaka)
The New York Times (New York)
Rediff News (online, Mumbai)
Secular Perspective (Mumbai)
Time (New York)
Tehelka (New Delhi)
The Tribune (Chandigarh)

Websites

Pakistan Institute of International Affairs (Pakistan Horizon):
pakistanhorizon.wordpress.com

Marghdeen:
marghdeen.com

Patheos:
patheos.com

www.ingramcontent.com/pod-product-compliance
Lightning Source LLC
LaVergne TN
LVHW010530100826
845148LV00001B/147

* 9 7 8 0 9 5 7 1 4 1 6 8 1 *